For selected older vintages, ref...

D0070470

	0?									
ITALY										
Barolo, Barbaresco	9									
Chianti Classico Ris.	9									
Brunello	9	8	8	7	9	8	5	9	8	9
Amarone	9	6	8	5	9	8	5	7	9	7
SPAIN										
Ribera del Duero	5	5	6	9	8	8	5	8	7	8
Rioja (red)	7	6	6	9	9	7	6	8	8	7
PORTUGAL										
South	8	8	7	8	8	6	5	8	9	8
North	8	7	5	8	8	8	7	8	9	7
Port	9	8	7	8	8	9	6	7	9	7
USA										
California Cabernet	8	9	8	9	7	8	7	8	7	9
California Chardonnay	8	9	9	9	8	9	8	8	7	8
Oregon Pinot Noir	7	6	8	7	8	8	8	7	9	9
Wash. State Cabernet	8	7	8	9	8	8	7	8	9	9
AUSTRALIA										
Coonawarra Cabernet	8	6	9	10	8	8	9	9	6	8
Hunter Semillon	7	8	8	9	8	8	7	8	9	8
Barossa Shiraz	9	6	8	10	8	7	10	9	8	9
Marg. River Cabernet	9	9	6	10	9	8	7	10	8	10
NEW ZEALAND										
M'lborough Sauvignon	7	9	9	7	8	8	6	9	9	8
H'kes Bay Cab/Merlot	8	9	8	7	8	5	9	7	8	7
SOUTH AFRICA										
Stellenbosch Cabernet	9	9	9	7	8	9	5	9	8	7
S'bosch Chardonnay	9	9	8	8	9	8	6	7	7	8

Numerals (1–10) represent an overall rating for each year.
◗ Not ready ● Just ready ● At peak ◖ Past best ○ Not generally declared

OZ CLARKE

POCKET WINE BOOK 2010

TO SHARON

PLEASE ALWAYS
REMEMBER FOR
THE GOOD TIMES
& THE GREAT WINES!!!
    WITH LOVE,
        REKA xxx
BIRMINGHAM, JUNE 2010

PAVILION

This edition first published in 2009 by Pavilion Books

An imprint of
Anova Books Company Ltd
10 Southcombe Street
London W14 0RA

www.anovabooks.com
www.ozclarke.com

Editor Maggie Ramsay
Cartographer Andrew Thompson
Photography Michael Wicks
Desktop Publishing Jayne Clementson
Indexer Angie Hipkin

18th edition. First published in 1992.
Revised editions published annually.

A CIP catalogue for this book is available from the British
Library.

ISBN 978-1-862-05863-7

Printed and bound by Imago in China

Keep up to date with Oz on his website **www.ozclarke.com**. Here you can
find information about his books, wine recommendations, recipes, wine and
food matching, event details, competitions, special offers and lots more...

Thanks are due to the following people for their invaluable help with the
2010 edition and the generous spirit in which they have shared their knowl-
edge: Sarah Ahmed, Tony Aspler, Nicolas Belfrage MW, Dan Berger,
Stephen Brook, Bob Campbell MW, Giles Fallowfield, Peter Forrestal,
Elizabeth Gabay MW, Rosemary George MW, Natasha Hughes, James
Lawther MW, John Livingstone-Learmonth, Angela Lloyd, Wink Lorch,
Dan McCarthy, Dave McIntyre, Charles Metcalfe, Adam Montefiore,
Jasper Morris MW, Peter Richards, Victor de la Serna, Stephen Skelton
MW, Paul Strang, Stuart Walton.

CONTENTS

HOW TO USE THIS BOOK

The **World of Wine** section, starting on page 20, gives an overview of all the world's significant wine-producing countries. The most important countries are followed by a full list of the relevant entries in the A–Z section. Remember that regional A–Z entries guide you to further recommended producers in each region or appellation.

The A–Z section starts on page 58 and includes over 1600 entries on wines, producers, grapes and wine regions from all over the world. It is followed on page 316 by a **Glossary** of winemaking terms.

Detailed **Vintage Charts**, with information on which of the world's top wines are ready for drinking in 2010, can be found on the inside front and back covers; the front chart features vintages back to 1999; the back chart covers a selection of older vintages for premium wines.

Glass Symbols   These indicate the wines produced.

♥ Red wine   ♥ Rosé wine   ♀ White wine

The order of the glasses reflects the importance of the wines in terms of volume produced. For example:

♀♥   White followed by rosé wine

♥♥   Red followed by rosé, then white wine

Grape Symbols   These identify entries on grape varieties.

⁂ Red grape   ⁂ White grape

Star Symbols   These indicate wines and producers that are highly rated by the author.

★   A particularly good wine or producer in its category
★★   An excellent wine or producer in its category – one especially worth seeking out
★★★   An exceptional, world-class wine or producer

Best years   Recommended vintages are listed for many producer and appellation entries. Those listed in bold, e.g. **2007, 00**, indicate wines that are ready for drinking now, although they may not necessarily be at their best; those appearing in brackets, e.g. (2008), (06), are preliminary assessments of wines that are not released at the time of going to press.

Cross References   Wine names, producers and regions that have their own entries elsewhere in the A–Z are indicated by SMALL CAPITALS. **Grape varieties** are not cross-referred in this way, but more than 70 varieties, from Albariño to Zinfandel, are included.

Special Features   The A–Z section includes special 2-page features on the world's most important wine styles, regions and grape varieties. These features include recommended vintages and producers, as well as lists of related entries elsewhere in the A–Z.

Index   The Index contains over 4000 recommended producers. Some of the world's most famous brand names are also included.

INTRODUCTION

Can we change? Yes, we can. Can they change? Yes, they can. This is the simple question that we as consumers should be asking ourselves in the extremely taxing and nerve-racking year we've all been experiencing. And for producers who've ridden the fat cow bareback for a decade or more, they must ask the question too. The answer is the same. Yes, we can. Yes, they can. The detail is a bit less straightforward.

Let's look at it from our point of view as wine drinkers first. Our disposable income has been slashed, our sense of financial self-confidence has evaporated and our cosy belief that wine is good for us is under attack. Only a couple of years ago, newspapers were full of scientific studies showing that wine – and red wine in particular – is good for us. Now, alongside pictures of drunken yobs and sad-sack celebrities falling about the streets, we are also seeing a rising tide of scientific reporting saying wine is positively bad for us.

As I write this, I've got newspaper cuttings in front of me from the last few days. One says that drinking a glass of wine daily doubles your chances of developing a Parkinson's disease-like tremor. The other declares that the French government – yes, the *French* – has sent an advisory document to all doctors saying that 'the consumption of alcohol, and especially wine, is discouraged'. It also recommends that there is no amount of alcohol, however small, which is good for you. Whatever happened to those happy academics' reports begging us to drink a good two glasses of sturdy red a day – and live longer and healthier as a result?

So must we change into teetotallers? Absolutely not. Any more than we must stop drinking decent wine because of the economic downturn. Story angles in the media are cyclical, and a new generation of editors is probably bored with good news stories about wine. The pendulum will swing back, but in the meantime we must assert our rights as wine drinkers against sensationalist puritans. And if you are tempted to give up drinking good wine because of the shrinking amount of cash at your disposal, stand firm. There is an ocean of good wine from less fashionable places and less fashionable grape varieties that will see you saving money and quite possibly drinking better. But you may have to change.

In good times, you probably don't mind paying extra for prestigious labels from trendy, sought-after areas. But be honest with yourself. Are the wines worth it? Do the wines *taste* any better than the less well-known offerings? Or are they sometimes so smitten with the trendy afflictions of high alcohol, overripeness, overuse of new oak, that you could get a much more refreshing, satisfying drink from somewhere else for less? To say nothing of having to pay all the extra money to allow proprietors to buy unnecessarily long corks, unnecessarily fancy labels, ecologically unacceptable heavy designer bottles, glitzy, self-indulgent advertising and marketing promotions – do you want to pay for all that kind of baloney, or do you want to pay a fair price for a nice-tasting glass of wine?

Well, if we're prepared to change our drinking habits we can drink just as well during these tough times as in the easy times of a year or two ago. And if winemakers want to keep our business, they can help themselves by changing back to thinking of wine as a pure, healthy mealtime or recreational drink, rather than as an alcohol-fuelled body building contest. That might even remind newspaper editors to start publishing a few 'feel-good' stories about wine again.

There is, sadly, a new mood prevalent among winemakers, particularly at the higher end, with the better vineyards and the better finance, the better knowledge of the rest of the world's vinous efforts. Rather than try to explore and dig out the personality – the unique personality – that their vineyards

5

may contain, they prefer to purchase what is known as 'international' style in the all-too-often-realized hope that a coterie of internationally recognized wine critics will appreciate their efforts and mark them accordingly. Mark them well, sell them well. Smooth, suave, predictable – expensive. Well, while writing this, I've opened a variety of these well-regarded wines. I've made notes, and I've spat them away. But I do have a glass of wine to drink as I write. It's a humble 12% alcohol Vin de Pays de l'Aude from southern France. I taste the grapes, I taste the place, and it costs a tenth of what some of the others do. This is honest wine, refreshing, mouthwatering, appetizing. Everything I want a wine to be. If we need to downsize our wine requirements, let's change the language. Let's go back to what wine was supposed to be, what wine used to be. Refreshing, appetizing and, even at the top end, utterly, gorgeously drinkable. We'll be happier and we'll spend less.

In **France** I can get shed-loads of bright, refreshing wines, because 2007 and 2008 were cool, damp vintages and the wines were lighter, more fragrant, more refreshing. **Beaujolais**, the **Loire**, the **Rhône Valley** and **Languedoc-Roussillon** have produced lots of lovely reds, and **Bordeaux** 2001, 2002 and 2004 reds are still widely available and getting better by the gulp. France's 2007 whites are acidic, fragrant and delicious – and they're still on the shelves.

In **Italy** I'm going to be drinking more white than ever before – **Fiano**, **Falanghina**, **Verdicchio** – dry, tasty and *not* over-alcoholic. The reds from **Sicily** and the south are stronger, but very good. If I want lighter, fresher reds, I'll head for the **Veneto**. **Spain** still offers stunning reds – if you'll buy **Garnacha** and other varieties, rather than the ultra-fashionable Tempranillo. Its **rosés** are some of the world's best, and its **northern whites** get tastier every year. **Portugal**'s **Dão** region is at last showing why it used to be the country's most famous, while **Ribatejo** and **Alentejo** are pumping out serious amounts of lovely juicy reds.

Germany has had a series of good to excellent vintages and **Austria** manages to combine ripeness with mouthwatering cool-climate style. **Hungary**, as ever, provides fantastic value-for-money whites.

I love New World wines, but I *am* getting tired of too much alcohol and oak. So, I'll be drinking more **New York**, **Oregon** and **Washington** wines this year, and spending more time in **California**'s cooler regions like **Anderson Valley**, the **Sonoma Coast** and **Carneros**. If I want a budget drink, **Lodi** and **Paso Robles** do it best.

I used to drink so many **Australian** wines. Now I'm only going to get excited about **Western Australia** and bits of South Australia like **Clare** and **Eden** Valleys, **Adelaide Hills** and some of the lovely scented, balanced wines coming out of **Central Victoria**. It's the same with **New Zealand**. It used to be just about my favourite country. When they stop sugaring up and dumbing down their Sauvignons in particular, perhaps it will be again. I'll stick to the minority tastes of Gimblett Gravels reds and Awatere whites. In **South Africa** I'm keener on whites too. Lovely Sauvignons and balanced Chardonnays in an unbalanced Chardonnay world lead the way.

In **South America**, I still think **Chile** balances quite full alcohol with fruit and fragrance better than almost anywhere else. **Argentina** is a fundamentally warmer climate place, but wines from the high-altitude Uco Valley are tasty and ripe. Oh, and I've been tasting a lot of **Brazilian fizz** recently; sweet or dry, it's party-licious.

SOME OF MY FAVOURITES

The following are some of the wines I've enjoyed most this year. They're not definitive lists of 'best wines', but all the wines, regions and producers mentioned here are on an exciting roll in terms of quality. Some are easy to find; others are very rare or expensive, but if you get the chance to try them, grab it! You can find out more about them in the A–Z on pages 58 to 315: the cross-references in SMALL CAPITALS will guide you to the relevant entries.

WORLD-CLASS WINES THAT DON'T COST THE EARTH
- Tim ADAMS Shiraz, Australia
- ATA RANGI Célèbre, New Zealand
- BOEKENHOUTSKLOOF Syrah, South Africa
- CARMEN Nativa Cabernet Sauvignon, Chile
- Peter LEHMANN Margaret Semillon, Australia
- Viña Leyda, Cahuil Pinot Noir, SAN ANTONIO, Chile
- PLANETA, Santa Cecilia, Sicily, Italy
- ROC DE CAMBES, France
- Ch. SOCIANDO-MALLET, France
- Tokara White, STELLENBOSCH, South Africa
- VILLA MARIA Reserve Merlot, Hawkes Bay, New Zealand

BEST LOOKALIKES TO THE CLASSICS
Bordeaux-style red wines
- CULLEN Cabernet Sauvignon-Merlot, Australia
- Forest Hill Cabernet Sauvignon, GREAT SOUTHERN, Australia
- OPUS ONE, California
- VERGELEGEN, South Africa

Burgundy-style white wines
- CULLEN, Kevin John Chardonnay, Australia
- HAMILTON RUSSELL Chardonnay, South Africa
- LEEUWIN ESTATE Art Series Chardonnay, Australia
- Ramey, Chardonnay, RUSSIAN RIVER VALLEY, California

Champagne-style wines
- CAMEL VALLEY, Pinot Noir rosé, England
- Jansz (Vintage), YALUMBA, Australia
- ROEDERER ESTATE L'Ermitage, California

TOP-VALUE WINES
- Agustinos, Chile
- ALENTEJO and TERRAS DO SADO, Portugal
- Colomé, Torrontés, SALTA, Argentina
- CÔTES CATALANES reds and whites, France
- CÔTES DE GASCOGNE whites, France
- Doña Paula, MENDOZA, Argentina
- Old-vines Garnacha reds from Calatayud and Campo de Borja, ARAGÓN, Spain
- Hungarian whites
- Peter LEHMANN whites, Australia
- MAJELLA The Musician, Australia
- Marqués de Casa Concha range, CONCHA Y TORO, Chile
- Seigneurs d'Aiguilhe, CÔTES DE CASTILLON, France
- ZUCCARDI Serie A, Mendoza, Argentina

REGIONS TO WATCH
- AWATERE VALLEY, New Zealand
- Brazil, for sparkling wine
- CÔTES DE CASTILLON, France
- DÃO, Portugal
- ELQUI, Chile
- GREAT SOUTHERN, Australia
- Leyda, SAN ANTONIO, Chile
- PATAGONIA, Argentina
- RÍAS BAIXAS, Spain
- Santa Lucia Highlands, MONTEREY COUNTY, California
- SICILY, Italy
- Sussex, England
- UCO VALLEY, Mendoza, Argentina

PRODUCERS TO WATCH
- Antucura, UCO VALLEY, Argentina
- ASTROLABE, New Zealand
- Gérard Bertrand, Ch. l'HOSPITALET, Languedoc, France
- CASA MARÍN, San Antonio, Chile
- Viña Falernia, ELQUI, Chile
- O FOURNIER, Uco Valley, Argentina
- GIRARDIN, Burgundy, France
- Noemia, PATAGONIA, Argentina
- S C PANNELL, South Australia
- PONDALOWIE, Victoria, Australia
- Nicolas POTEL, Burgundy, France
- Philip Shaw, Orange, NEW SOUTH WALES, Australia

AUSTRALIA
- BROKENWOOD Semillon and Graveyard Shiraz
- CAPE MENTELLE Cabernet Sauvignon
- Henschke HILL OF GRACE Shiraz
- HOUGHTON Gladstones Shiraz

- LEEUWIN ESTATE Art Series Chardonnay
- MCWILLIAM'S Lovedale Semillon
- Charles MELTON Shiraz
- MOUNT HORROCKS Watervale Riesling
- PARKER COONAWARRA First Growth
- PRIMO ESTATE Moda Cabernet-Merlot
- ROCKFORD Basket Press Shiraz
- SKILLOGALEE Shiraz
- TYRRELL'S Vat 1 Semillon

RED BORDEAUX
- Ch. AUSONE
- Ch. CANON-LA-GAFFELIERE
- Ch. GRAND-PUY-LACOSTE
- Les Forts de LATOUR
- Ch. LÉOVILLE-BARTON
- Ch. LÉOVILLE-POYFERRÉ
- Ch. LYNCH-BAGES
- Ch. la MISSION-HAUT-BRION
- Ch. PICHON-LONGUEVILLE-LALANDE
- TERTRE-RÔTEBOEUF

BURGUNDY
- CARILLON, Bienvenues-Bâtard-Montrachet (white)
- COCHE-DURY, Corton-Charlemagne (white)
- B Dugat-Py, Charmes-CHAMBERTIN (red)
- J-N GAGNARD, Bâtard-Montrachet (white)
- Anne GROS, Clos de Vougeot (red)
- LAFON, Volnay Santenots (red)
- Paul Pillot, CHASSAGNE-MONTRACHET (white)
- M Rollin, CORTON-CHARLEMAGNE (white)
- A ROUSSEAU, Clos de la Roche (red)
- TOLLOT-BEAUT, Corton-Bressandes (red)

CALIFORNIA
- ALBAN
- Cline Cellars, Bridgehead ZINFANDEL, Contra Costa County
- DALLA VALLE
- LAUREL GLEN
- Long Meadow Ranch, NAPA VALLEY
- NEWTON The Puzzle
- Ramey, Hyde Vineyard Chardonnay, CARNEROS
- RIDGE Geyserville
- St Supéry, Dollarhide Cabernet Sauvignon, NAPA VALLEY
- SHAFER Hillside Select Cabernet Sauvignon
- Sean Thackrey, Orion Rossi Vineyard Syrah, NAPA VALLEY
- Viader, NAPA VALLEY

ITALIAN REDS
- ALLEGRINI Amarone and La Poja
- BOSCARELLI
- Giacomo CONTERNO, Barolo, Cascina Francia
- GAJA, Langhe, Sperss
- Illuminati Zanna, MONTEPULCIANO D'ABRUZZO
- ISOLE E OLENA Cepparello
- Mandrarossa Cartagho, Settesoli, SICILY
- Mormoreto, FRESCOBALDI
- PLANETA Santa Cecilia
- POLIZIANO Le Stanze
- SELVAPIANA Chianti Rufina, Riserva Bucerchiale

RHÔNE AND SOUTHERN FRANCE
- Ch. de BEAUCASTEL Roussanne Vieilles Vignes (white)
- Dom. du Colombier, HERMITAGE (white)
- CUILLERON, Condrieu les Chaillets
- Pierre Gaillard, CONDRIEU
- GRAILLOT, Crozes-Hermitage la Guiraude
- JAMET, Côte-Rôtie
- Dom. de la Janasse, CHÂTEAUNEUF-DU-PAPE Vieilles Vignes
- Dom. Santa Duc, GIGONDAS
- Vieux Donjon, CHÂTEAUNEUF-DU-PAPE

CABERNET SAUVIGNON
- BALNAVES, Australia
- HENSCHKE, Cyril Henschke, Australia
- Long Meadow Ranch, NAPA VALLEY, California
- PARKER COONAWARRA First Growth, Australia
- RIDGE Monte Bello, California
- SANTA RITA Floresta, Chile
- SASSICAIA, Tuscany, Italy
- STAG'S LEAP WINE CELLARS Fay, California
- TERRAZAS DE LOS ANDES Cheval des Andes, Argentina
- Miguel TORRES Manso de Velasco, Chile

CHARDONNAY
- CONCHA Y TORO Amelia, Chile
- Diamond Valley Vineyards, YARRA VALLEY, Australia
- GIACONDA, Australia
- HAMILTON RUSSELL, South Africa
- KUMEU RIVER, New Zealand
- Littorai, Mays Canyon RUSSIAN RIVER VALLEY, California

- Moreau-Naudet, CHABLIS Valmur, France
- NEWTON Unfiltered, California
- Ramey, Hudson Vineyard, CARNEROS, California
- RIDGE Monte Bello, California
- SAINTSBURY, Carneros, California
- SHAW & SMITH M3, Australia
- Tabalí/SAN PEDRO TARAPACÁ, Special Reserve, Limarí, Chile

MERLOT
- ANDREW WILL, Washington State
- Ch. ANGÉLUS, St-Émilion, France
- STEENBERG, South Africa
- CASABLANCA Nimbus Estate, Chile
- CONO SUR 20 Barrels, Chile
- LEONETTI CELLAR, Washington State
- ORNELLAIA Masseto, Tuscany, Italy
- Ch. PETRUS, Pomerol, France
- Ch. VALANDRAUD, St-Émilion, France
- WOODWARD CANYON, Washington State

PINOT NOIR
- ATA RANGI, New Zealand
- Borthwick Vineyard, Wairarapa, New Zealand
- R Chevillon, NUITS-ST-GEORGES les St-Georges, France
- DRY RIVER, New Zealand
- FELTON ROAD, New Zealand
- FLOWERS Camp Meeting Ridge, California
- Freycinet, TASMANIA, Australia
- Anne GROS, Clos de Vougeot, France
- LAFON, Volnay Santenots, France
- Viña Leyda, Lot 21, SAN ANTONIO, Chile
- SAINTSBURY Carneros, California
- E Rouget, ÉCHÉZEAUX, France
- VILLA MARIA Reserve, New Zealand

RIESLING
- Tim ADAMS, Clare Valley, Australia
- H DONNHOFF Oberhäuser Brücke, Nahe, Germany
- Eichinger, KAMPTAL, Austria
- GROSSET, Clare Valley, Australia
- Fritz Brauneberger Juffer Sonnenuhr, Mosel, Germany
- Dr LOOSEN, Mosel, Germany
- MOUNT HORROCKS, Australia
- Horst SAUER Escherndorfer Lump, Franken, Germany

SAUVIGNON BLANC
- Cape Campbell, MARLBOROUGH, New Zealand

- CASAS DEL BOSQUE, Chile
- Didier DAGUENEAU, Pouilly-Fumé, France
- Neil ELLIS Groenekloof, South Africa
- Ch. MALARTIC-LAGRAVIÈRE, Pessac-Léognan, France
- Ch. SMITH-HAUT-LAFITTE, Pessac-Léognan, France
- SAINT CLAIR Block 4 Sawcut, New Zealand
- STEENBERG, South Africa
- VAVASOUR, New Zealand
- VERGELEGEN, South Africa
- VILLA MARIA Reserve Clifford Bay, New Zealand

SYRAH/SHIRAZ
- Tim ADAMS Aberfeldy, Australia
- ALBAN, EdnaValley, California
- BROKENWOOD Graveyard Vineyard, Australia
- CAYUSE Cailloux Vineyard, Washington State
- Esk Valley Reserve, HAWKES BAY, New Zealand
- Falernia Reserve, ELQUI, Chile
- Peter LEHMANN Stonewell, Australia
- JAMET, Côte-Rôtie, France
- Penfolds GRANGE, Australia
- Two Hands, BAROSSA, Australia
- TRINITY HILL Homage, New Zealand
- The Willows, BAROSSA, Australia

FORTIFIED WINE
- Cossart Gordon Vintage Bual, MADEIRA WINE COMPANY
- CHAMBERS Rutherglen Muscat
- GONZALEZ BYASS Noé Pedro Ximénez
- GRAHAM Vintage Port
- HENRIQUES & HENRIQUES 15-year-old Madeira
- HIDALGO La Gitana Manzanilla
- NIEPOORT Vintage Port

SPARKLING WINE
- BILLECART-SALMON Cuvée N-F Billecart Champagne
- CAMEL VALLEY Pinot Noir, England
- CLOUDY BAY Pelorus, New Zealand
- DEUTZ Marlborough Cuvée, New Zealand
- Alfred GRATIEN Vintage Champagne
- Charles HEIDSIECK Mis en Caves Champagne
- Jansz, YALUMBA, Australia
- Charles MELTON Sparkling Red, Australia
- Le Mesnil Blanc de Blancs CHAMPAGNE

MODERN WINE STYLES

Not so long ago, if I were to have outlined the basic wine styles, the list would have been strongly biased towards the classics – Bordeaux, Burgundy, Sancerre, Mosel Riesling, Champagne. But the classics have, over time, become expensive and unreliable – giving other regions the chance to offer us wines that may or may not owe anything to the originals. *These* are the flavours to which ambitious winemakers the world over now aspire.

WHITE WINES

Ripe, up-front, spicy Chardonnay is the main grape and fruit is the key: apricot, peach, melon, pineapple and tropical fruits, spiced up with the vanilla and butterscotch richness of some new oak to make a delicious, approachable, fruit cocktail of taste. Australia, South Africa and Chile are best at this style, but all have begun to tone down the richness. Oak-aged Chenin from South Africa, Semillon from Australia and Semillon-Sauvignon from South-West France can have similar characteristics.

Green and tangy New Zealand Sauvignon was the originator of this style – zingy lime zest, nettles and asparagus and passionfruit – and South Africa now has its own tangy, super-fresh examples. Chile's San Antonio and Casablanca regions produce something similar, and there are good, less expensive versions from southern France and Hungary. Bordeaux and the Loire are the original sources of dry Sauvignon wines, and an expanding band of modern producers are matching clean fruit with zippy green tang. Spain's Rueda is zesty. Riesling in Australia is usually lean and limy.

Bone-dry, neutral The most famous, and most appetizing, examples are from Chablis. Producers of unoaked Chardonnay in cool parts of Australia, New Zealand and the USA are doing a good, but fruitier, impression. Many Italian and Greek whites from indigenous varieties fit this bill. Southern French wines are often like this, as are many basic wines from Bordeaux, South-West France, Muscadet and Anjou. Modern young Spanish whites and dry Portuguese Vinho Verdes are good examples. I don't like seeing too much neutrality in New World wines, but cheap South African and California whites are 'superneutral'. More interesting are Verdelhos and Chenins from Australia.

White Burgundy By this I mean the nutty, oatmealy-ripe but dry, subtly oaked styles of villages like Meursault at their best. Few people do it well, even in Burgundy itself, and it's a difficult style to emulate. California makes the most effort. Washington, Oregon, New York State and British Columbia each have occasional successes, as do top Australian, South African and New Zealand Chardonnays.

Perfumy, off-dry Gewurztraminer, Muscat and Pinot Gris from Alsace will give you this style and in southern Germany Gewürztraminer, Scheurebe, Kerner, Grauburgunder (Pinot Gris) and occasionally Riesling may also do it. In New Zealand, Riesling, Pinot Gris and Gewürztraminer can be excellent. Irsai Olivér from Hungary and Torrontés from Argentina are both heady and perfumed. Albariño in Spain is leaner but heady with citrus scent. Viognier is apricotty and scented in southern Europe, Australia, Chile, California, South Africa and New Zealand.

Mouthfuls of luscious gold Good sweet wines are difficult to make. Sauternes is the most famous, but the Loire, and sometimes Alsace, can also come up with rich, intensely sweet wines that can live for decades. Top sweeties from Germany and Austria are stunning. Hungarian Tokaji has a wonderful sweet-sour smoky flavour. Australia, California and New Zealand have some exciting examples and there are a few rare but excellent sweeties from South Africa and the USA.

RED WINES

Spicy, warm-hearted Australia is out in front at the moment through the ebullient brashness of her Shiraz reds – ripe, almost sweet, sinfully easy to enjoy. France's southern Rhône Valley is also motoring, and the traditional appellations in the far south of France are looking good. In Italy, Piedmont is producing delicious beefy Barbera and juicy exotic Dolcetto, Puglia has chocolaty Negroamaro and Sicily has Nero d'Avola. Spain's Ribera del Duero and Toro and Portugal's Alentejo also deliver the goods, as does Malbec in Argentina. California Zinfandel made in its most powerful style is spicy and rich; Lebanese reds have the succulent scent of the kasbah.

Juicy, fruity Beaujolais can be the perfect example, but leafy, raspberryish Loire reds, and Grenache and Syrah vins de pays are often better bets. Modern Spanish reds from Valdepeñas, Bierzo and La Mancha, and old-vine Garnachas from Campo de Borja and Calatayud, do the trick, as do unoaked Douros from Portugal and young Valpolicella and Teroldego in Italy. Young Chilean Merlots are juicy, and Argentina has some good examples from Bonarda, Tempranillo, Sangiovese and Barbera.

Deep and blackcurranty Chile has climbed back to the top of the Cabernet tree, though good producers in cooler parts of Australia produce Cabernets of thrilling blackcurranty intensity. New Zealand Merlot and Cabernet Franc are dense and rich yet dry. California too frequently overripens its Cabernet and Merlot, though restrained examples can be terrific. Top Bordeaux is on a rich blackcurranty roll since 2000: it's expensive but exciting – as is top Tuscan Cabernet.

Tough, tannic long-haul boys Bordeaux leads this field, and the best wines are really good after 10 years or so – but, except in years like 2005, minor properties won't age in the same way. It's the same in Tuscany and Piedmont – only the top wines last well – especially Brunello di Montalcino, Vino Nobile di Montepulciano, some IGT and DOCG wines from Chianti Classico, Barolo and Barbaresco. Portugal has some increasingly good Dão and Douro reds, and Spain's Toro and Ribera del Duero reds need aging.

Soft, strawberryish charmers Good Burgundy definitely tops this group. Rioja in Spain can sometimes get there, as can Navarra and Valdepeñas. Pinot Noir in California, Oregon, Chile and New Zealand is frequently delicious, and South Africa and Australia increasingly get it right too. Germany can hit the spot with Spätburgunder (Pinot Noir). Over in Bordeaux, of all places, St-Émilion, Pomerol and Blaye can do the business.

Rosé There's been a surge in rosé's popularity, probably led by California's blush Zinfandel and Grenache. But far better, drier rosés are also becoming popular, with Spain and France leading the way for drier styles and Chile, New Zealand and Australia the best for fuller pinks.

SPARKLING AND FORTIFIED WINES

Fizz This can be white, pink or red, dry or sweet, and I sometimes think it doesn't matter what it tastes like as long as it's cold enough and there's enough of it. Champagne can be best, but frequently isn't – and there are lots of new-wave winemakers making good-value lookalikes. Australia is tops for tasty bargains, followed by California, New Zealand and England. Spain pumps out oceans of good basic stuff.

Fortified wines There's nothing to beat the top ports and sherries in the deep, rich, sticky stakes – though Australia, California and South Africa have their own versions. The Portuguese island of Madeira produces fortifieds with rich, brown smoky flavours and a startling acid bite – and luscious Muscats are made all round the Mediterranean and in Rutherglen, Australia.

11

MATCHING FOOD AND WINE

Give me a rule, I'll break it – well, bend it anyway. So when I see the proliferation of publications laying down rules as to what wine to drink with what food, I get very uneasy and have to quell a burning desire to slosh back a Grand Cru Burgundy with my chilli con carne.

The pleasures of eating and drinking operate on so many levels that hard and fast rules make no sense. What about mood? If I'm in the mood for Champagne, Champagne it shall be, whatever I'm eating. What about company? An old friend, a lover, a bank manager – each of these companions would probably be best served by quite different wines. What about place? If I'm sitting gazing out across the shimmering Mediterranean, hand me anything, just as long as it's local – it'll be perfect.

Even so, there are some things that simply don't go well with wine: artichokes, asparagus, spinach, kippers and mackerel, chilli, salsas and vinegars, chocolate, all flatten the flavours of wines. The general rule here is avoid tannic red wines and go for juicy young reds, or whites with plenty of fruit and fresh acidity. And for chocolate, liqueur Muscats, raisiny Banyuls or Italy's grapy, frothy Asti all work, but some people like powerful Italian reds such as Barolo or Amarone. Don't be afraid to experiment. Who would guess that salty Roquefort cheese and rich, sweet Sauternes would go together? But they do, and it's a match made in heaven. So, with these factors in mind, the following pairings are not rules – just my recommendations.

FISH

Grilled or baked white fish White Burgundy or other fine Chardonnay, white Bordeaux, Viognier, Australian and New Zealand Riesling and Sauvignon.

Grilled or baked oily or 'meaty' fish (e.g. salmon, tuna, swordfish) Alsace or Austrian Riesling, Grüner Veltliner, fruity New World Chardonnay or Semillon; reds such as Chinon or Bourgueil, Grenache/Garnacha, or New World Pinot Noir.

Fried/battered fish Simple, fresh whites, e.g. Soave, Mâcon-Villages, Verdelho, Pinot Gris, white Bordeaux, or a Riesling Spätlese from the Pfalz.

Shellfish Chablis or unoaked Chardonnay, Sauvignon Blanc, Pinot Blanc; *clams and oysters* Albariño, Aligoté, Vinho Verde, Seyval Blanc; *crab* Riesling, Viognier; *lobster, scallops* fine Chardonnay, Champagne, Viognier; *mussels* Muscadet, Pinot Grigio.

Smoked fish Ice-cold basic fizz, manzanilla or fino sherry, Riesling, Sauvignon Blanc, Alsace Gewurztraminer or Pinot Gris.

MEAT

Beef and lamb are perfect with just about any red wine.

Beef/steak *Plain roasted or grilled* tannic reds, Bordeaux, New World Cabernet Sauvignon, Ribera del Duero, Chianti Classico, Pinotage.

Lamb *Plain roasted or grilled* red Burgundy, red Bordeaux, especially Pauillac or St-Julien, Rioja Reserva, New World Pinot Noir, Merlot or Malbec.

Pork *Plain roasted or grilled* full, spicy dry whites, e.g. Alsace Pinot Gris, lightly oaked Chardonnay; smooth reds, e.g. Rioja, Alentejo; *ham, bacon, sausages, salami* young, fruity reds, e.g. Beaujolais, Lambrusco, Teroldego, unoaked Tempranillo or Garnacha, New World Malbec, Merlot, Zinfandel/Primitivo, Pinotage.

Veal *Plain roasted or grilled* full-bodied whites, e.g. Pinot Gris, Grüner Veltliner, white Rioja; soft reds, e.g. mature Rioja or Pinot Noir; *with cream-based sauce* full, ripe whites, e.g. Alsace Pinot Blanc or Pinot Gris, Vouvray, oaked New World Chardonnay; *with rich red-wine sauce* (e.g. *osso buco*) young Italian reds, Zinfandel.

Venison *Plain roasted or grilled* Barolo, St-Estèphe, Pomerol, Côte de Nuits, Hermitage, big Zinfandel, Alsace or German Pinot Gris; *with red-wine sauce* Piedmont and Portuguese reds, Pomerol, St-Émilion, New World Syrah/Shiraz or Pinotage, Priorat.

Chicken and turkey Most red and white wines go with these meats – much depends on the sauce or accompaniments. Try red or white Burgundy, red Rioja Reserva, New World Chardonnay.

Duck Pomerol, St-Émilion, Côte de Nuits or Rhône reds, New World Syrah/Shiraz (including sparkling) or Merlot; also full, soft whites from Austria and southern Germany.

Game birds *Plain roasted or grilled* top reds from Burgundy, Rhône, Tuscany, Piedmont, Ribera del Duero, New World Cabernet or Merlot; also full whites such as oaked New World Semillon.

Casseroles and stews Generally uncomplicated, full-flavoured reds. The thicker the sauce, the fuller the wine. If wine is used in the preparation, match the colour. For strong tomato flavours see Pasta.

HIGHLY SPICED FOOD

Chinese Riesling, Sauvignon, Pinot Gris, Gewürztraminer, unoaked New World Chardonnay; fruity rosé; light Pinot Noir.
Indian Aromatic whites, e.g. Riesling, Sauvignon Blanc, Gewürztraminer, Viognier; non-tannic reds, e.g. Valpolicella, Rioja, Grenache.
Mexican Fruity reds, e.g. Merlot, Cabernet Franc, Grenache, Syrah/Shiraz, Zinfandel.
Thai/South-East Asian Spicy or tangy whites, e.g. Riesling, Gewürztraminer, New World Sauvignon Blanc, dry Alsace Muscat. Coconut is tricky: New World Chardonnay may work.

EGG DISHES
Champagne and traditional-method fizz; light, fresh reds such as Beaujolais or Chinon; full, dry unoaked whites; New World rosé.

PASTA, PIZZA
With tomato sauce Barbera, Valpolicella, Soave, Verdicchio, New World Sauvignon Blanc; *with meat-based sauce* north or central Italian reds, French or New World Syrah/Shiraz, Zinfandel; *with cream- or cheese-based sauce* gently oaked Chardonnay, though the Italians would drink unoaked whites from northern Italy; Valpolicella or soft Merlot; *with seafood/fish* dry, tangy whites, e.g. Verdicchio, Vermentino, Grüner Veltliner, Muscadet; *with pesto* New World Sauvignon Blanc, Dolcetto, Languedoc reds. *Basic pizza, with tomato, mozzarella and oregano* juicy young reds, e.g. Grenache/Garnacha, Valpolicella, Austrian reds, Languedoc reds.

SALADS
Sharp-edged whites, e.g. New World Sauvignon Blanc, Chenin Blanc, dry Riesling, Vinho Verde.

CHEESES
Hard Full reds from Italy, France or Spain, New World Merlot or Zinfandel, dry oloroso sherry, tawny port.
Soft LBV port, Zinfandel, Alsace Pinot Gris, Gewürztraminer.
Blue Botrytized sweet whites such as Sauternes, vintage port, old oloroso sherry, Malmsey Madeira.
Goats' Sancerre, Pouilly-Fumé, New World Sauvignon Blanc, Chinon, Saumur-Champigny.

DESSERTS
Chocolate Asti, Australian Liqueur Muscat, Banyuls, Canadian Cabernet Franc icewine.
Fruit-based Sauternes, Eiswein, fortified European Muscats.
Christmas pudding Asti, Australian Liqueur Muscat.

MATCHING WINE AND FOOD

With very special bottles, when you have found an irresistible bargain or when you are casting around for culinary inspiration, it can be a good idea to let the wine dictate the choice of food.

Although I said earlier that rules in this area are made to be bent, if not broken, there are certain points to remember when matching wine and food. Before you make specific choices, think about some basic characteristics and see how thinking in terms of grape varieties and wine styles can point you in the right direction.

In many cases, the local food and wine combinations that have evolved over the years simply cannot be bettered (think of ripe Burgundy with *coq au vin* or *boeuf bourguignon*; Chianti Riserva with *bistecca alla Fiorentina*; Musadet and Breton oysters). Yet the world of food and wine is moving so fast that it would be madness to be restricted by the old tenets. Californian cuisine, fusion food, and the infiltration of innumerable ethnic influences coupled with the re-invigoration of traditional wines, continuous experiment with new methods and blends and the opening up of completely new wine areas mean that the search for perfect food and wine partners is, and will remain, very much an on-going process.

Here are some of the characteristics you need to consider, plus a summary of the main grape varieties and their best food matches.

Body/weight As well as considering the taste of the wine you need to match the body or weight of the wine to the intensity of the food's flavour. A heavy alcoholic wine will not suit a delicate dish; and *vice versa*.

Acidity The acidity of a dish should balance the acidity of a wine. High-acid flavours, such as tomato, lemon or vinegar, should need matching acidity in their accompanying wines, but, almost by mistake, I've tried a few reds with salad dressing and the wine's fruit was enhanced, not wrecked. Was I lucky? More research needed, I think. Use acidity in wine to cut through the richness of a dish – but for this to work, make sure the wine is full in flavour.

Sweetness Sweet food makes dry wine taste unpleasantly lean and acidic. With desserts and puddings, find a wine that is at least as sweet as the food (sweeter than the food is fine). However, many savoury foods, such as carrots, onions and parsnips, taste slightly sweet and dishes in which they feature prominently will go best with ripe, fruity wines that have a touch of sweetness.

Salt Salty foods, such as blue cheese, and sweet wines match. Salty foods and tannin are definitely best avoided.

Age/maturity The bouquet of a wine is only acquired over time and should be savoured and appreciated: with age, many red wines acquire complex flavours and perfumes and a relative simplicity in the flavour of the food is often a good idea.

Tannin Red meat, when cooked rare, can have the effect of softening tannic wine. Mature hard cheeses can make rough wine seem gentle. Avoid eggs and fish with tannic wines.

Oak Oak flavours in wine vary from the satisfyingly subtle to positively strident. This latter end of the scale can conflict with food, although it may be suitable for smoked fish (white wines only) or full-flavoured meat or game.

Wine in the food If you want to use wine in cooking it is best to use the same style of wine as the one you are going to drink with the meal (it can be an inferior version though).

RED GRAPES

Barbera Wines made to be drunk young have high acidity that can hold their own with sausages, salami, ham, and tomato sauces. Complex, older or oak-aged wines from the top growers need to be matched with rich food such as beef casseroles and game dishes.

Cabernet Franc Best drunk with plain rather than sauced meat dishes, or, slightly chilled, with grilled or baked salmon or trout.

Cabernet Sauvignon All over the world the Cabernet Sauvignon makes full-flavoured reliable red wine: the ideal food wine. Cabernet Sauvignon seems to have a particular affinity with lamb, but it partners all plain roast or grilled meats and game well and would be an excellent choice for many sauced meat dishes such as beef casserole, steak and kidney pie or rabbit stew and substantial dishes made with mushrooms.

Dolcetto Dolcetto produces fruity purple wines that go beautifully with hearty meat dishes such as calves' liver and onions or casseroled pork, beef or game.

Gamay The grape of red Beaujolais, Gamay makes wine you can drink whenever, wherever, however and with whatever you want – although it's particularly good lightly chilled on hot summer days. It goes well with pâtés, bacon and sausages because its acidity provides a satisfying foil to their richness. It would be a good choice for many vegetarian dishes.

Grenache/Garnacha Frequently blended with other grapes, Grenache nonetheless dominates, with its high alcoholic strength and rich, spicy flavours. These are wines readily matched with food: barbecues and casseroles for heavier wines; almost anything for lighter reds and rosés – vegetarian dishes, charcuterie, picnics, grills, and even meaty fish such as tuna and salmon.

Merlot Merlot makes soft, rounded, fruity wines that are some of the easiest red wines to enjoy without food, yet are also a good choice with many kinds of food. Spicier game dishes, herby terrines and pâtés, pheasant, pigeon, duck or goose all team well with Merlot; substantial casseroles made with wine are excellent with Pomerols and St-Émilions; and the soft fruitiness of the wines is perfect for pork, liver, turkey, and savoury foods with a hint of sweetness such as Iberico, Parma or honey-roast ham.

Nebbiolo Lean but fragrant, early-drinking styles of Nebbiolo wine are best with Italian salami, pâtés, *bresaola* and lighter meat dishes. Top Barolos and Barbarescos need substantial food: *bollito misto*, rich hare or beef casseroles and *brasato al Barolo* (a large piece of beef marinated then braised slowly in Barolo) are just the job in Piedmont, or anywhere else for that matter.

Pinot Noir The great grape of Burgundy has taken its food-friendly complexity all over the wine world. However, nothing can beat the marriage of great wine with sublime local food that is Burgundy's heritage, and it is Burgundian dishes that spring to mind as perfect partners for the Pinot Noir: *coq au vin*, *boeuf bourguignon*, rabbit with mustard, braised ham, chicken with tarragon, *entrecôtes* from prized Charolais cattle with a rich red-wine sauce ... the list is endless.

Pinot Noir's subtle flavours make it a natural choice for complex meat dishes, but it is also excellent with plain grills and roasts. New World Pinots are often richer and fruitier – excellent with grills and roasts and a good match for salmon or tuna.

In spite of the prevalence of superb cheese in Burgundy, the best Pinot Noir red wines are wasted on cheese.

Sangiovese Tuscany is where Sangiovese best expresses the qualities that can lead it, in the right circumstances, to be numbered among the great grapes of the world. And Tuscany is very much 'food with wine' territory. Sangiovese wines such as Chianti, Rosso di Montalcino, Vino Nobile di Montepulciano and the biggest of them all, Brunello, positively demand to be drunk with food. Drink them with *bistecca alla Fiorentina*, roast meats and game, calves' liver, casseroles, hearty pasta sauces, *porcini* mushrooms and Pecorino cheese.

Syrah/Shiraz Whether from France (the Rhône Valley and Languedoc), Australia, California, South America or South Africa, this grape always makes powerful, rich, full-bodied wines that are superb with full-flavoured food. The classic barbecue wine when drunk young, Shiraz/Syrah also goes with roasts, game, hearty casseroles and charcuterie. It can be good with tangy cheeses such as Manchego or Cheshire.

Tempranillo Spain's best native red grape makes juicy wines for drinking young, and matures well in a rich (usually) oaky style. Tempranillo is good with game, cured hams and sausages, casseroles and meat grilled with herbs; it is particularly good with roast lamb. It can partner some Indian and Mexican dishes.

Zinfandel California's much-planted, most versatile grape is used for a bewildering variety of wine styles from bland, slightly sweet pinks to rich, succulent, fruity reds. And the good red Zinfandels themselves may vary greatly in style,

from relatively soft and light to big and beefy, but they're always ripe and ready for spicy, smoky, unsubtle food: barbecued meat, haunches of lamb, venison or beef, game casseroles, sausages, Tex-Mex, the Beach Boys, The Eagles – anything rowdy – Zin copes with them all. The pale blush style of Zinfandel goes well with tomato-based dishes, such as pizza and pasta, as well as with hamburgers.

WHITE GRAPES

Albariño Light, crisp, aromatic in a grapefruity way, this goes well with crab and prawn dishes as well as Chinese-style chicken dishes.

Aligoté This Burgundian grape can, at its best, make very versatile food wine. It goes well with many fish and seafood dishes, smoked fish, salads and snails in garlic and butter.

Chardonnay More than almost any other grape, Chardonnay responds to different climatic conditions and to the winemaker's art. This, plus the relative ease with which it can be grown, accounts for the marked gradation of flavours and styles: from steely, cool-climate austerity to almost tropical lusciousness. The relatively sharp end of the spectrum is one of the best choices for simple fish dishes; most Chardonnays are superb with roast chicken or other white meat; the really full, rich, New World blockbusters need rich fish and seafood dishes. Oaky Chardonnays are, surprisingly, a good choice for smoked fish.

Chenin Blanc One of the most versatile of grapes, Chenin Blanc makes wines ranging from averagely quaffable dry whites to the great sweet whites of the Loire. The lighter wines can be good as aperitifs or with light fish dishes or salads while the medium-sweet versions usually retain enough of their acidity to counteract the richness of creamy chicken and meat dishes. The sweet wines are superb with foie gras or blue cheese, and with fruit puddings – especially those made with slightly tart fruit.

Gewürztraminer Spicy and perfumed, Gewürztraminer has the weight and flavour to go with such hard-to-match dishes as *choucroute* and smoked fish. It is also a good choice for Chinese or any lightly spiced Oriental food, with its use of lemongrass, coriander and ginger, and pungent soft cheeses, such as Munster from Alsace.

Grüner Veltliner In its lightest form, this makes a peppery, refreshing aperitif. Riper, more structured versions keep the pepper but add peach and apple fruit, and are particularly good with grilled or baked fish.

Marsanne These rich, fat wines are a bit short of acidity, so match them with simply prepared chicken, pork, fish or vegetables.

Muscadet The dry, light Muscadet grape (best wines are *sur lie*) is perfect with seafood.

Muscat Fragrant, grapy wines coming in a multitude of styles, from delicate to downright syrupy. The drier ones are more difficult to pair with food, but can be delightful with Oriental cuisines; the sweeties really come into their own with most desserts. Sweet Moscato d'Asti, delicious by itself, goes well with rich Christmas pudding or mince pies.

Pinot Blanc Clean, bright and appley, Pinot Blanc is very food-friendly. Classic fish and chicken dishes, modern vegetarian food, pasta and pizza all match up well.

Pinot Gris In Alsace, this makes rich, fat wines that need rich, fat food: *choucroute*, *confit de canard*, rich pork and fish dishes. Italian Pinot Grigio wines are light quaffers. New World Pinot Gris is often delightfully fragrant and ideal with grilled fish.

Riesling Good dry Rieslings are excellent with spicy cuisine. Sweet Rieslings are best enjoyed for their own lusciousness but are suitable partners to fruit-based desserts. In between, those with a fresh acid bite and some residual sweetness can counteract the richness of, say, goose or duck, and the fuller examples can be good with Oriental food and otherwise hard-to-match salads.

Sauvignon Blanc Tangy green flavours and high acidity are the hallmarks of this grape. Led by New Zealand, New World Sauvignons are some of the snappiest, tastiest whites around and make good, thirst-quenching aperitifs. Brilliant with seafood and Oriental cuisine, they also go well with tomato dishes and goats' cheese.

Sémillon Dry Bordeaux Blancs are excellent with fish and shellfish; fuller, riper New World Semillons are equal to spicy food and rich sauces, often going even better with meat than with fish; sweet Sémillons can partner many puddings, especially rich, creamy ones. Sémillon also goes well with many cheeses, and Sauternes with Roquefort is a classic combination.

Viognier Fresh, young Viognier is at its best drunk as an aperitif. It can also go well with mildly spiced Indian dishes or chicken in a creamy sauce. The apricot aroma that typifies even inexpensive Viognier suggests another good pairing – pork or chicken dishes with apricot stuffing.

MAKING THE MOST OF WINE

,Most wine is pretty hardy stuff and can put up with a fair amount of rough handling. Young red wines can knock about in the back of a car for a day or two and be lugged from garage to kitchen to dinner table without coming to too much harm. Serving young white wines when well chilled can cover up all kinds of ill-treatment – a couple of hours in the fridge should do the trick. Even so, there are some conditions that are better than others for storing your wines, especially if they are on the mature side. And there are certain ways of serving wines which will emphasize any flavours or perfumes they have.

STORING

Most wines are sold ready for drinking, and it will be hard to ruin them if you store them for a few months before you pull the cork. Don't stand them next to the central heating or the cooker, though, nor on a sunny windowsill, as too much warmth will flatten the flavour and give a 'baked' taste.

Light and extremes of temperature are also the things to worry about if you are storing wine long-term. Some wines, Chardonnay for instance, are particularly sensitive to exposure to light over several months, and the damage will be worse if the bottle is made of pale-coloured glass. The warmer the wine, the quicker it will age, and really high temperatures can spoil wine quite quickly. Beware in the winter of garages and outhouses, too: a very cold snap – say –4°C (25°F) or below – will freeze your wine, push out the corks and crack the bottles. An underground cellar is ideal, with a fairly constant temperature of 10°–12°C (50°–53°F). And bottles really do need to lie on their sides, so that the cork stays damp and swollen, and keeps out the air.

TEMPERATURE

The person who thought up the rule that red wine should be served at room temperature certainly didn't live in a modern, centrally heated flat. It's no great sin to serve a big, beefy red at the temperature of your central heating, but I prefer most reds just a touch cooler. Over-heated wine tastes flabby, and may lose some of its more volatile aromas. In general, the lighter the red, the cooler it can be. Really light, refreshing reds, such as Beaujolais, are nice lightly chilled. Ideally, I'd serve Burgundy and other Pinot Noir wines at larder temperature (about 15°C/59°F), Bordeaux and Rioja a bit warmer (18°C/64°F), Rhône wines and New World Cabernet at a comfortable room temperature, but no more than 20°C/68°F.

Chilling white wines makes them taste fresher, emphasizing their acidity. White wines with low acidity especially benefit from chilling, and it's vital for sparkling wines if you want to avoid exploding corks and a tableful of froth. Drastic chilling also subdues flavours, however – a useful ruse if you're serving basic wine, but a shame if the wine is very good. A good guide for whites is to give the cheapest and lightest a spell in the fridge, but serve bigger and better wines – Australian Chardonnays or top white Burgundies – perhaps half-way between fridge and central-heating temperature. If you're undecided, err on the cooler side, for whites or reds. To chill wine quickly, and to keep it cool, an ice bucket is more efficient if filled with a mixture of ice and water, rather than ice alone.

OPENING THE BOTTLE

There's no corkscrew to beat the Screwpull, and the Spinhandle Screwpull is especially easy to use. Don't worry if bits of cork crumble into the wine – just fish them out of your glass. Tight corks that refuse to budge might be loosened if you run hot water over the bottle neck to expand the glass. If the cork is loose and falls in, push it right in and don't worry about it.

Opening sparkling wines is a serious business – point the cork away from people! Once you've started, never take your hand off the cork until it's safely out. Remove the foil, loosen the wire, hold the wire and cork firmly and twist the bottle. If the wine froths, hold the bottle at an angle of 45 degrees, and have a glass at hand.

AIRING AND DECANTING

Scientists have proved that opening young to middle-aged red wines an hour before serving makes no difference whatsoever. The surface area of wine in contact with air in the bottle neck is too tiny to be significant. Decanting is a different matter, because sloshing the wine from bottle to jug or decanter mixes it up quite thoroughly with the air. The only wines that really need to be decanted are those that have a sediment which would cloud the wine if they were poured directly – mature red Bordeaux, Burgundy and vintage port are the most common examples. Ideally, if you are able to plan that far in advance, you need to stand the bottle upright for a day or two to let the sediment settle in the bottom. Draw the cork extremely gently. As you tip the bottle, shine a bright light through from underneath as you pour in a single steady movement. Stop pouring when you see the sediment approaching the bottle neck.

Contrary to many wine buffs' practice, I would decant a mature wine only just before serving; elderly wines often fade rapidly once they meet with air, and an hour in the decanter could kill off what little fruit they had left. By contrast, a good-quality young white wine can benefit from decanting.

GLASSES

If you want to taste wine at its best, to enjoy all its flavours and aromas, to admire its colours and texture, choose glasses designed for the purpose and show the wine a bit of respect. The ideal wine glass is a fairly large tulip shape, made of fine, clear glass, with a slender stem. When you pour the wine, fill the glass no more than halfway to allow space for aromas. For sparkling wines choose a tall, slender glass, as it helps the bubbles to last longer.

KEEPING LEFTOVERS

Leftover white wine keeps better than red, since the tannin and colouring matter in red wine is easily attacked by the air. Any wine, red or white, keeps better in the fridge than in a warm kitchen. And most wines, if well made in the first place, will be perfectly acceptable, if not pristine, after 2 or 3 days re-corked in the fridge. But for better results it's best to use one of the gadgets sold for this purpose. The ones that work by blanketing the wine with heavier-than-air inert gas are much better than those that create a vacuum in the air space in the bottle.

FRANCE

I've visited most of the wine-producing countries of the world, but the one I come back to again and again, with my enthusiasm undimmed by time, is France. The sheer range of its wine flavours, the number of wine styles produced, and indeed the quality differences, from very best to very nearly worst, continue to enthral me, and as each year's vintage nears, I find myself itching to leap into the car and head for the vineyards of Champagne, of Burgundy, of Bordeaux and the Loire. France is currently going through a difficult period – aware that the New World is making tremendous strides and is the master of innovation and technology, yet unwilling to admit to the quality and character of this new breed of wines. But the best French producers learn from the newcomers while proudly defining their Frenchness.

CLIMATE AND SOIL
France lies between the 40th and 50th parallels north, and the climate runs from the distinctly chilly and almost too cool to ripen grapes in the far north near the English Channel, right through to the swelteringly hot and almost too torrid to avoid grapes overripening in the far south on the Mediterranean shores. In the north, the most refined and delicate sparkling wine is made in Champagne. In the south, rich, luscious dessert Muscats and fortified wines dominate. In between is just about every sort of wine you could wish for.

The factors that influence a wine's flavour are the grape variety, the soil and climate, and the winemaker's techniques. Most of the great wine grapes, like the red Cabernet Sauvignon, Merlot, Pinot Noir and Syrah, and the white Chardonnay, Sauvignon Blanc, Sémillon and Viognier, find conditions in France where they can ripen slowly but reliably – and slow, even ripening always gives the best flavours to a wine. Since grapes have been grown for over 2000 years in France, the most suitable varieties for the different soils and mesoclimates have naturally evolved. And since winemaking was brought to France by the Romans, generation upon generation of winemakers have refined their techniques to produce the best possible results from their different grape types. The great wines of areas like Bordeaux and Burgundy are the results of centuries of experience and of trial and error, which winemakers from other countries of the world now use as role models in their attempts to create good wine.

WINE REGIONS
White grapes generally ripen more easily than red grapes and they dominate the northern regions. Even so, the chilly Champagne region barely manages to ripen its red or white grapes on its chalky soil. But the resultant acid wine is the ideal base for sparkling wine: with good winemaking and a few years' maturing, the young still wine can transform into a golden honeyed sparkling wine of incomparable finesse.

Alsace, on the German border, is warmer and drier than Champagne (the vineyards sit in a rain shadow created by the Vosges mountains that rise above the Rhine Valley) but still produces mainly dry white wines, from grapes such as Riesling, Pinot Gris and Gewurztraminer that are seldom encountered elsewhere in France. With its clear blue skies, Alsace can provide ripeness, and therefore the higher alcoholic strength of the warm south, but also the perfume and fragrance of the cool north.

South-east of Paris, heading into limestone country, Chablis marks the northernmost tip of the Burgundy region, and the Chardonnay grape here produces very dry wines, usually with a streak of green acidity and minerality, but nowadays with a fuller softer texture to subdue any harshness.

It's a good 2 hours' drive further south to the heart of Burgundy – the Côte d'Or, which runs between Dijon and Chagny. World-famous villages such as Gevrey-Chambertin and Vosne-Romanée (where the red Pinot Noir dominates) and Meursault and Puligny-Montrachet (where Chardonnay reigns) here produce the great Burgundies that have given the region renown over the centuries. Lesser Burgundies – but they're still good – are produced further south in the Côte Chalonnaise, while between Mâcon and Lyon are the Mâconnais white wine villages (Pouilly-Fuissé and St-Véran are particularly tasty) and the villages of Beaujolais, famous for bright, easy-going red wine from the Gamay grape. The 10 Beaujolais Crus or 'growths' are the most important communes and should produce wine with more character and structure.

East of Burgundy, Jura makes unusual whites, good sparkling and light reds; Savoie, further south, has crisp whites and light, spicy reds.

South of Lyon, in the Rhône Valley, red wines begin to dominate. The Syrah grape makes great wine at Côte-Rôtie and Hermitage in the north, while in the south the Grenache and a host of supporting grapes (most southern Rhône reds will add at least Syrah, Cinsaut or Mourvèdre to their blends) make full, satisfying reds, of which Châteauneuf-du-Pape is the richest and most famous. The white Viognier makes lovely wine at Condrieu and Château-Grillet in the north.

The whole of the south of France has undergone considerable change over the last 20 years. Despite the financial woes of growers who over-extended themselves in the late 1990s, new ownership and a new generation are

producing exciting wines from previously unpromising lands. The traditional Provence, Languedoc and Roussillon vineyards make increasingly impressive reds from Grenache, Syrah, Mourvèdre and Carignan, as well as Cabernet Sauvignon (although it is declining in Provence) and some surprisingly fragrant whites. And with the new Languedoc appellation (covering the whole of Languedoc and Roussillon), the possibilities and freedom to improve by blending will be extended. Many of the tastiest and most affordable wines are vins de pays. Roussillon also makes fine sweet Muscats and Grenache-based fortifieds.

The south-west of France is dominated by the wines of Bordeaux, but has many other gems representing amazing value for money. Dry whites from Gascony and Bergerac can be exciting. Gaillac in the Tarn and Jurançon in the foothills of the Pyrenees produce some remarkable dry and sweet wines, while Madiran, Cahors, Fronton, Gaillac and Bergerac produce some of the best reds.

But Bordeaux is the king here. Cabernet Sauvignon and Merlot are the chief grapes, the Cabernet dominating the production of deep reds from the Médoc peninsula and its famous villages of Margaux, St-Julien, Pauillac and St-Estèphe on the left bank of the Gironde river. Round the city of Bordeaux are Pessac-Léognan and Graves, where Cabernet and Merlot blend to produce fragrant refined reds. On the right bank of the Gironde estuary, the Merlot is most important in the plump rich reds of St-Émilion and Pomerol. Sweet whites from Sémillon and Sauvignon Blanc are made in Sauternes, with increasingly good dry whites produced in the Entre-Deux-Mers, and especially in Graves and Pessac-Léognan.

The Loire Valley is the most northerly of France's Atlantic wine regions but, since the river rises in the heart of France not far from the Rhône, styles vary widely. Sancerre and Pouilly in the east produce tangy, *terroir*-influenced Sauvignon whites and some surprisingly good Pinot Noir reds. Along the river Cher, which joins the Loire at Tours, the best varieties are Sauvignon and Romorantin for whites, Gamay and Côt/Malbec for reds. In central Touraine, Saumur and Anjou the focus is squarely on Chenin Blanc in styles that range from bone dry to lusciously sweet, even sparkling and, for the reds, Cabernet Franc with a little Cabernet Sauvignon. Down at the mouth of the river, as it slips past Nantes into the Atlantic swell, the vineyards of Muscadet produce dry whites that take on the salty notes of the sea. At the vanguard of the natural wine movement, the Loire Valley is teeming with producers working as naturally as possible both in the vineyard and winery, the best of whom make highly characterful wines – look out for ambitious vins de table.

CLASSIFICATIONS

France has an intricate but eminently logical system for controlling the quality and authenticity of its wines. The system is divided into 4 broad classifications (in ascending order): **Vin de Table**, **Vin de Pays**, **VDQS** (Vin Délimité de Qualité Supérieure) and **AC** (Appellation Contrôlée). Within the laws there are numerous variations, with certain vineyards or producers singled out for special mention. The 1855 Classification in Bordeaux or the Grands Crus of Alsace or Burgundy are good examples. The intention is a system which rewards quality: Vin de Pays and VDQS wines can be promoted to AC, for example. The VDQS category will be removed after the 2010 vintage and local wine syndicates had to apply for either Vin de Pays or AC status by the end of 2008. The AC system is now under increasing attack from critics, both inside and outside France, who feel that it is outmoded and that too many poor wines are passed as of Appellation Contrôlée standard.

2008 VINTAGE REPORT

Déja vu in Bordeaux? Indifferent summer, the threat of mildew, then late-season sunshine to save the day – it sounds like 2007 all over again. There were a few subtle differences, though. Poor fruit set as well as mildew and frost and hail in certain areas (Entre-Deux-Mers, Graves, Pessac-Léognan, St-Émilion satellites) resulted in naturally tiny yields. July was marginally warmer and drier than in 2007 but the harvest was again late, especially as early September was cold and wet. Picking stretched from 25 September to at least 25 October, but I was in Margaux at the end of October and some Médoc growers said they wouldn't finish until early November. Looking at the wines, the dry whites are fresh and aromatic, but quantities are seriously low. After painstaking selection of botrytized grapes the Sauternes looks good, although perhaps not on a par with 2007. The reds are a little more concentrated and structured than in 2007, but variable according to producer and *terroir*. Could be some interesting buys, but all depends on the price.

The rest of the South-West got off to a poor and late start, with snow in January, a heatwave in February, and a cold, wet spring with plenty of localized hail and frost. Until August the summer was cool and grey, but then the sun came out and shone until the end of October, raising hopes of a good year after all, but with quantities sharply down. A cooler end to the autumn does not bode well for the late-picked sweet-wine grapes.

In Burgundy the second Sarkozy summer followed the miserable pattern of the first, but was once again saved by a fine September. The patchwork quilt of vineyards demonstrating the viticultural practices of different vignerons was even more apparent this year, as some had been ravaged by either oïdium or mildew if they messed up their treatments, whether chemical or organic. Quite a few producers will have a very short crop this year. What has been made is looking good, with a more succulent Pinot fruit than in 2007. The whites appear aromatic and opulent at this early stage. Bulk prices are showing signs of coming down, thank goodness.

2008 was a tricky vintage in Beaujolais, hail was a serious problem and July and August were damp. Luckily, an Indian summer helped the grapes to ripen in time for harvest, although it will pay to buy from the best producers.

A challenging year for the Rhône, with rain, cool weather, rot and a very small crop. Light reds, but the best have attractive fruit and will be charming; they may be underestimated by the gloom merchants, especially for old-vine wines and in later ripening places such as Gigondas. Expect interesting whites from both north and south.

In Provence, spring rains gave the vines a boost but also meant that mildew was a problem. A dry but not overly hot summer ended suddenly during the second half of the harvest when it turned cold and wet. A smaller harvest of healthy grapes has resulted in a more classic and refined vintage, with less alcohol, greater acidity, more fruit and fresher character, breaking the pattern set since 2000 of hot early vintages and big, alcoholic wines.

A wet spring and cool weather at flowering in the Languedoc. Some areas suffered from summer drought, so that yields are lower than usual. Hail struck the southern part of Faugères on the eve of the vintage. A good September has produced some fine wines throughout the region.

In the Loire Valley, quality not quantity sums up 2008. Frost-blighted Muscadet was down 50% on production; hail in Pouilly-Fumé and parts of Sancerre wreaked havoc. Elsewhere, poor flowering affected yields, as did rain and humidity that encouraged oïdium and mildew. Fortunately, glorious, dry, sunny conditions through September to late October compensated for the cool, humid spring and summer. With low yields across the region, dry whites and reds (especially Cabernet Francs) are beautifully aromatic and fresh, with better fruit concentration than 2007. The weather broke in late October and a month of rain dashed hopes for sweet wines; Chenin Blanc fans must content themselves with (superb) dry and demi-sec wines.

Owing to its more sheltered position, Alsace escaped the caning that many other regions of France took in 2008. Poor weather early in the season gave way to hot, humid summer conditions. Despite this, there is good acidity and pronounced fruit in the best wines, with Riesling showing up well, and there was a fair bit of noble rot around in October to make for some luscious sweet wines from Pinot Gris and Gewurztraminer. Growers who found themselves picking in the intermittent showers of early October can count themselves unlucky (especially if they were picking Pinot Noir).

After a cool and not very sunny summer, the 2008 harvest in Champagne began around the middle of September in near-perfect weather which miraculously – you'll hear the word 'miraculously' a lot when the French talk about their 2008 vintage – continued through two to three weeks of picking. Cool nights, bright days and almost no rain helped produce one of the healthiest crops for some time as well as keeping acid levels higher than in recent warmer years, which looks good for the aging potential of what is expected to be a widely declared vintage. Chardonnay and Pinot Noir fared better than Pinot Meunier, which had considerably lower yields.

French entries in the A–Z section (pages 58–315), by region.

Latour
Latour-Martillac
Latour-à-Pomerol
Laville-Haut-Brion
Léoville-Barton
Léoville-Las-Cases
Léoville-Poyferré
la Louvière
Lynch-Bages
Magdelaine
Malartic-Lagravière
Malescot St-
 Exupéry
Margaux
Maucaillou
Meyney
la Mission-Haut-
 Brion

Monbousquet
Montrose
Moueix, J P
Mouton-Cadet
Mouton-
 Rothschild
Nairac
Palmer
Pape-Clément
Pavie
Pavie-Macquin
Petit-Village
Pétrus
de Pez
Pichon-Longueville
Pichon-Longueville-
 Lalande
le Pin

Pontet-Canet
Potensac
Poujeaux
Prieuré-Lichine
Rauzan-Ségla
Reynon
Rieussec
Roc de Cambes
St-Pierre
Siran
Smith-Haut-Lafitte
Sociando-Mallet
Suduiraut
Talbot
Tertre-Rôteboeuf
la Tour Blanche
Troplong-Mondot
Trotanoy

Valandraud
Vieux-Château-
 Certan
d'Yquem

SEE ALSO
Bordeaux Red
 Wines
Bordeaux White
 Wines
St-Émilion Premier
 Grand Cru Classé

**BURGUNDY AND
 BEAUJOLAIS
ACS**
Aloxe-Corton
Auxey-Duresses
Bâtard-Montrachet
Beaujolais
Beaujolais-Villages
Beaune
Blagny
Bonnes-Mares
Bourgogne
Bourgogne-Côte
 Chalonnaise
Bourgogne-Hautes-
 Côtes de Beaune
Bourgogne-Hautes-
 Côtes de Nuits
Brouilly
Chablis
Chablis Grand Cru
Chambertin
Chambolle-Musigny
Chassagne-
 Montrachet
Chénas
Chiroubles
Chorey-lès-Beaune
Clos des Lambrays
Clos de la Roche
Clos St-Denis
Clos de Tart
Clos de Vougeot
Corton
Corton-Charlemagne
Côte de Beaune
Côte de Beaune-
 Villages
Côte de Brouilly
Côte de Nuits-
 Villages

Coteaux du
 Lyonnais
Crémant de
 Bourgogne
Échézeaux
Fixin
Fleurie
Gevrey-Chambertin
Givry
Irancy
Juliénas
Ladoix
Mâcon
Mâcon-Villages
Maranges
Marsannay
Mercurey
Meursault
Montagny
Monthelie
Montrachet
Morey-St-Denis
Morgon
Moulin-à-Vent
Musigny
Nuits-St-Georges
Pernand-Vergelesses
Pommard
Pouilly-Fuissé
Pouilly-Vinzelles
Puligny-Montrachet
Régnié
Richebourg
la Romanée
la Romanée-Conti
Romanée-St-Vivant
Rully
St-Amour
St-Aubin
St-Bris
St-Romain

St-Véran
Santenay
Savigny-lès-Beaune
la Tâche
Viré-Clessé
Volnay
Vosne-Romanée
Vougeot

PRODUCERS
d'Angerville,
 Marquis
Boisset
Bouchard Père et
 Fils
Bouzereau
Brocard, Jean-Marc
Buxynoise, La
Carillon & Fils, Louis
Cathiard, Sylvain
Chablisienne, La
Chandon de Briailles
Clair, Bruno
Coche-Dury, J-F
Dauvissat, René &
 Vincent
Drouhin, Joseph
Duboeuf, Georges
Dujac
Durup, Jean
Faiveley, Joseph
Gagnard, Jean-Noël
Girardin, Vincent
Gouges, Henri
Grivot, Jean
Gros
Hospices de Beaune
Jadot, Louis
Lafarge, Michel
Lafon
Laroche, Dom.

Latour, Louis
Leflaive, Dom.
Leflaive, Olivier
Leroy, Dom.
Liger-Belair
Méo-Camuzet
Montille, Dom. de
Mortet, Denis
Mugnier, J-F
Potel, Nicolas
Ramonet
Raveneau, Jean-
 Marie
Rion
Rodet, Antonin
Romanée-Conti,
 Dom. de la
Roumier, Georges
Rousseau, Armand
Sauzet
Tollot-Beaut
Verget
Vogüé, Comte
 Georges de
Vougeraie, Dom.
 de la

SEE ALSO
Aligoté
Beaujolais Nouveau
Burgundy Red
 Wines
Burgundy White
 Wines
Côte de Beaune
Côte de Nuits
Côte d'Or

CHAMPAGNE
Champagne AC
Champagne Rosé
Coteaux
  Champenois AC
Rosé des Riceys AC

PRODUCERS
Billecart-Salmon
Bollinger
Deutz
Gratien, Alfred
Heidsieck, Charles
Henriot
Jacquesson
Krug

Lanson
Laurent-Perrier
Moët & Chandon
Mumm, G H
Paillard, Bruno
Perrier, Joseph
Perrier-Jouët
Piper-Heidsieck
Pol Roger

Pommery
Roederer, Louis
Ruinart
Taittinger
Veuve Clicquot

**JURA AND
  SAVOIE**
Arbois AC
Château-Chalon AC

Côtes du Jura AC
Crémant du Jura
  AC
l'Étoile AC

Savoie

**LOIRE VALLEY
ACS**
Anjou Blanc
Anjou Rouge
Anjou-Villages
Bonnezeaux
Bourgueil
Cabernet d'Anjou
Cheverny
Chinon
Côte Roannaise
Coteaux de
  l'Aubance
Coteaux du Layon
Crémant de Loire
Gros Plant du Pays
  Nantais VDQS
Jasnières
Menetou-Salon

Montlouis-sur-Loire
Muscadet
Pouilly-Fumé
Pouilly-sur-Loire
Quarts de Chaume
Quincy
Reuilly
Rosé de Loire
St-Nicolas-de-
  Bourgueil
Sancerre
Saumur
Saumur-Champigny
Saumur Mousseux
Savennières
Touraine
Val de Loire, Vin de
  Pays du
Vouvray

PRODUCERS
Baudry, Bernard
Baumard, Dom. des
Blot, Jacky
Bourgeois, Dom.
  Henri
Clos de la Coulée-
  de-Serrant
Clos Naudin, Dom.
  du
Dagueneau, Didier
Druet, Pierre-
  Jacques
l'Ecu, Dom. de
Huet
Hureau, Ch. du
Mabileau, Frédéric
Mellot, Alphonse
Pierre-Bise, Ch.

Ragotière, Ch. de la
Richou, Dom.
Roches Neuves,
  Dom. des
Vacheron, Dom.
Villeneuve, Ch. de

**RHÔNE VALLEY
ACS**
Beaumes-de-Venise
Château-Grillet
Châteauneuf-du-
  Pape
Clairette de Die
Collines
  Rhodaniennes,
  Vin de Pays des
Condrieu
Cornas
Costières de Nîmes
Côte-Rôtie
Coteaux de
  l'Ardèche, Vin de
  Pays des
Coteaux du
  Tricastin
Côtes du Rhône
Côtes du Rhône-
  Villages

Côtes du Vivarais
Crémant de Die
Crozes-Hermitage
Gigondas
Hermitage
Lirac
Lubéron
Muscat de
  Beaumes-de-
  Venise
Rasteau
St-Joseph
St-Péray
Tavel
Vacqueyras
Ventoux
Vinsobres

PRODUCERS
Allemand, Thierry
Beaucastel,
  Ch. de

Chapoutier, M
Chave, Jean-Louis
Clape, A
Clos des Papes
Colombo, Jean-Luc
Coursodon, Pierre
Cuilleron, Yves
Delas Frères
Font de Michelle,
  Dom.
Graillot, Alain
Guigal
Jaboulet Aîné, Paul
Jamet
l'Oratoire St-Martin,
  Dom. de
Perret, André
Rayas, Ch.
Réméjeanne,
  Dom. la
Rostaing, Réné
St-Gayan, Dom.

Sang des Cailloux,
  Dom. le
Tain, Cave de
Vieux Télégraphe,
  Dom. du

SEE ALSO
Cairanne
Rhône Valley

SOUTHERN FRANCE

SOUTH-WEST
ACS
Béarn
Bergerac
Buzet
Cahors
Côtes de Duras
Côtes de Gascogne,
  Vin de Pays des
Côtes du
  Marmandais
Côtes de St-Mont
  VDQS
Fronton
Gaillac

Irouléguy
Jurançon
Madiran
Marcillac
Monbazillac
Montravel
Pacherenc du Vic-
  Bilh
Pécharmant
Tursan VDQS

PRODUCERS
l'Ancienne Cure,
  Dom. de
Arretxea, Dom.
Aydie, Ch. d'
Berthoumieu, Dom.
Cauhapé, Dom.
Cèdre, Ch. du
Chapelle Lenclos
Clos de Gamot
Clos Triguedina
Clos Uroulat
Cosse-Maisonneuve,
  Dom.
Elian da Ros, Dom.

Montus, Ch.
Plageoles, Robert
Plaimont,
  Producteurs
Ramaye, Dom. de la
Rotier, Dom.
Tariquet, Dom. du
Tour des Gendres,
  Ch.
Verdots, Vignoble
  des

LANGUEDOC-
ROUSSILLON
ACS
Banyuls
Blanquette de
  Limoux
Cabardès
Collioure
Corbières
Coteaux du
  Languedoc
Côtes Catalanes,
  Vin de Pays des
Côtes du Roussillon
Côtes du
  Roussillon-Villages
Côtes de Thongue,
  Vin de Pays des
Crémant de Limoux
Faugères
Fitou
Gard, Vin de Pays du

Hérault, Vin de Pays
  de l'
Limoux
Maury
Minervois
Muscat de
  Frontignan
Muscat de
  Rivesaltes
Muscat de St-Jean-
  de-Minervois
Oc, Vin de Pays d'
Rivesaltes
St-Chinian

PRODUCERS
Alquier, Dom. Jean-
  Michel
Antugnac, Dom. d'
Borie la Vitarèle
Canet-Valette,
  Dom.

Casenove, Ch. la
Cazes, Dom.
Clos de l'Anhel
Clos Bagatelle
Clos Centeilles
Clos Marie
Clot de l'Oum
Denois, J-L
Estanilles, Ch. des
Gauby, Dom.
Grange des Pères,
  Dom. de la
Hecht & Bannier
l'Hortus, Dom. de
l'Hospitalet, Ch.
Mas Blanc, Dom. du
Mas Bruguière
Mas la Chevalière
Mas de Daumas
  Gassac
Mont Tauch, les
  Producteurs du

Nizas, Dom. de
Peyre Rose, Dom.
Prieuré de St-Jean
  de Bébian
Sieur d'Arques, les
  Vignerons du
Skalli-Fortant de
  France
Tour Boisée, Ch.
Val d'Orbieu, les
  Vignerons du
Voulte-Gasparets,
  Ch. la

PROVENCE
ACS
Bandol
les Baux-de-
  Provence
Bellet
Bouches-du-Rhône,
  Vin de Pays des
Cassis
Coteaux d'Aix-en-
  Provence

Coteaux Varois
Côtes de Provence
Palette

PRODUCERS
d'Eole, Dom.
Esclans, Ch. d'
Pibarnon, Ch. de
Richeaume, Dom.
Romanin, Ch.
Sorin, Dom.
Trévallon, Dom. de
Vannières, Ch.

SEE ALSO
Clape, La
Languedoc-
  Roussillon
Pic St-Loup
Provence
Roussillon

CORSICA
Arena, Dom.
  Antoine
Corse AC, Vin de

27

ITALY

The cultivation of the vine was introduced to Italy 2500 to 3000 years ago, by the Greeks (to Sicily and the south) and by the Etruscans (to the north-east and central zones). Despite this great tradition, Italian wines as we know them today are relatively young. New attitudes have resulted, in the last 35 years or so, in a great change in Italian wine. The whole industry has been modernized, and areas like Tuscany, Piedmont, Veneto and Campania are now among the most dynamic of any in the world. With her unique characteristics, challenging wine styles and mass of grape varieties, Italy is now ready again to take on the role of leadership she has avoided for so long.

GRAPE VARIETIES AND WINE REGIONS

Vines are grown all over Italy, from the Austrian border in the north-east to the island of Pantelleria in the far south, nearer to North Africa than to Sicily. The north-west, especially Piedmont, is the home of many of the best Italian red grapes, like Nebbiolo (the grape of Barolo and Barbaresco), Dolcetto and Barbera, while the north-east (Friuli-Venezia Giulia, Alto Adige and the Veneto) is more noted for the success of native white varieties like Garganega and Prosecco, reds like Corvina and Corvinone, and imports like Pinot Grigio, Chardonnay and Sauvignon. The Po Valley is Lambrusco country west of Bologna, while Sangiovese rules in the hills to the east. Tuscany is best known for its Chianti, Brunello di Montalcino and other wines from the native Sangiovese grape as well as its famed Super-Tuscans. On the east coast,

Verdicchio and Montepulciano make wines ranging from popular to serious. South of Rome, where the Mediterranean climate holds sway, modern winemakers are revelling in the chance to make exciting wines from varieties of long tradition, such as Negroamaro and Primitivo (in Puglia), Aglianico, Fiano and Greco (in Campania and Basilicata) and Gaglioppo (in Calabria). The islands have their own varieties: red Nero d'Avola and white Inzolia in Sicily, red Cannonau and Carignano and white Vermentino in Sardinia.

CLASSIFICATIONS

Vino da Tavola, 'table wine', is used for wine that is produced either outside the existing laws, or in an area where no delimited zone exists. Both cheap, basic wines and inspired innovative creations like the so-called Super-Tuscans used to fall into this anonymous category. Now the fancy wines have become either DOC (particularly in Piedmont with its Langhe and Piemonte DOCs) or IGT. Remaining Vini da Tavola are labelled simply as bianco, rosso or rosato without vintages or varietal or geographical indications.

IGT (Indicazione Geografica Tipica) began taking effect with the 1995 vintage to identify wines from certain areas as an equivalent of the French Vin de Pays. A great swathe of both ordinary and premium wines traded their Vino da Tavola status for a regional IGT, of which there are now some 120.

DOC (Denominazione di Origine Controllata) is the main classification for wines from designated zones made following traditions that were historically valid but often outdated. Recently the laws have become more flexible, encouraging producers to reduce yields and modernize techniques, while bringing quality wines under new appellations that allow for recognition of communes, estates and single vineyards. If anything, the problem today is a surfeit of DOCs. There are now over 350, a good number of which are unnecessary or repetitive.

DOCG (Denominazione di Origine Controllata e Garantita) was conceived as a 'super-league' for DOCs that promised high class but didn't always provide it. Wines are made under stricter standards that have favoured improvements, but the best guarantee of quality remains the producer's name. Currently DOCGs number 35 and rising.

Thus with IGTs, DOCs and DOCGs there are in excess of 500, far too many for clarity in marketing terms. What Italy's denominations need is a good pruning, which is what they're going to get, or at least what the EU means to give them. Starting from August 2009, the plan is to reduce the total number of DOCGs, DOCs and IGTs to just 182 DOPs and IGPs: **DOP** and **IGP** (Denominazione di Origine Protetta and Indicazione Geografica Protetta; *protetta* = protected). So far the effect has mainly been confusion, with both the new denominations and the old allowed on labels. We hope to be able to present a clearer picture in next year's *Pocket Wine Book*.

2008 VINTAGE REPORT

From the centre of the country northward, torrential late-spring rains lasting the biblical 40 days and 40 nights (give or take) left many growers in despair over mildew and mud. It was especially nightmarish for organic growers. However, the weather cleared up for flowering and there followed a spectacularly dry summer with occasional violent storms which with the welcome rain also brought unwelcome hail in some places. Temperatures were highish but it was a dry heat on the whole, and continuing fine weather through the vintage, with warm days and cool nights, meant healthy ripe grapes of good balance, in pretty good numbers to boot. We can look forward to some cracking Barolo and Barbaresco, some excellent Valpolicella and

Amarone, delicious Chianti and Brunello and deep-coloured, rich Montepulciano. If anything, the deep south fared even better (less spring rainfall), so there'll be some classic Aglianico and Taurasi.

Italian entries in the A–Z section (pages 58–315).

GERMANY

Dull, semi-sweet wines with names like Liebfraumilch, Niersteiner Gutes Domtal and Piesporter Michelsberg used to dominate the export market, but they are rapidly vanishing off all but the most basic radar screens. Instead, we are seeing a better range of single-estate wines of fine quality, although the choice, except at special wine merchants, is very limited. Throughout Germany, both red and white wines are year by year, region by region, grower by grower, becoming fuller, better balanced and drier.

GRAPE VARIETIES

Riesling makes the best wines, at least in northerly regions such as the Mosel and Rheingau, in styles ranging from dry to intensely sweet. Other white wines come from Grauburgunder/Ruländer (Pinot Gris), Weissburgunder (Pinot Blanc), Gewürztraminer, Silvaner, Scheurebe and Rieslaner, although Müller-Thurgau produces much of the simpler wine. Plantings of red grape varieties now account for 37% of the nation's vineyard. Good reds are being made in the south of the country from Spätburgunder (Pinot Noir) and Lemberger.

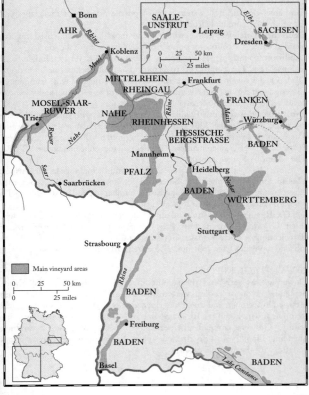

WINE REGIONS

Many of the most delectable Rieslings come from villages such as Bernkastel, Brauneberg, Ürzig and Wehlen on the Mosel, and Kiedrich, Johannisberg and Rüdesheim in the Rheingau. Characterful dry Mosel Rieslings are the speciality of villages such as Winningen near Koblenz. The Nahe makes superb Rieslings in Schlossböckelheim and Traisen, and Niederhausen has the region's best vineyards. Rheinhessen's top wines are the excellent racy Rieslings produced on steep riverside slopes in Nackenheim and Nierstein, but growers such as Keller are showing the real potential of some inland sites. Franken is the one place the Silvaner grape excels, often made in a powerful, dry, earthy style. The Pfalz is climatically similar to Alsace and has a similar potential for well-rounded, dry whites, plus rapidly improving reds. Baden also produces fully ripe wine styles, which should appeal to an international market accustomed to rich, dry wines. In Württemberg many red wines are thin and dull, but there are a few producers who understand the need for weight and flavour. The other smaller wine regions make little wine and little is exported, although the Ahr has a growing reputation for Pinot Noir.

CLASSIFICATIONS

Germany's classification system is based on the ripeness of the grapes and therefore their potential alcohol level.

Deutscher Tafelwein (table wine) is the most basic term, used for any blended wine; it accounts for only a tiny percentage of production.

Landwein (country wine) is a slightly more up-market version, linked to 19 regional areas. These must be Trocken (dry) or Halbtrocken (medium-dry).

QbA (Qualitätswein bestimmter Anbaugebiete) is 'quality' wine from one of 13 designated regions, but the grapes don't have to be very ripe, and sugar can be added to the juice to increase alcoholic content.

QmP (Qualitätswein mit Prädikat) or 'quality wine with distinction' is the top level; from August 2007 the term will be replaced by ' Prädikatswein'. There are 6 levels of QmP (in ascending order of ripeness): Kabinett, Spätlese, Auslese, Beerenauslese, Eiswein, Trockenbeerenauslese (TBA). The addition of sugar is forbidden.

Since 2000, there have been 2 designations for varietal dry wines: **Classic** for 'good' wines and **Selection** for 'top-quality' wines, but they haven't really caught on. And an increasing number of good estates use single-vineyard names only on their top selections.

The Rheingau has introduced an official classification – Erstes Gewächs (First Growth) – for its best sites. Other regions have evolved similar classifications – called Grosses Gewächs (or Erste Lage in the Mosel) – to indicate top wines from top sites. These are nearly always dry wines.

2008 VINTAGE REPORT

Flowering was early and the summer fine with sufficient rainfall. Mid-September brought cooler, wetter weather, and some rot. But the sun returned in October, and the grapes ripened fully, if slowly. This is not a year for opulent wines, and the Rieslings are mostly QbA and Kabinett, with fine acidity. Growers compare the vintage to 2004. Burgundian varieties, including Pinot Noir, also ripened slowly, but growers are happy, if not ecstatic, with the eventual quality.

German entries in the A–Z section (pages 58–315).

AUSTRIA

I can't think of a European nation where the wine culture has changed so dramatically over a generation as it has in Austria. Austria still makes great sweet wines, but a new order based on world-class medium- and full-bodied dry whites and increasingly fine reds has emerged.

WINE REGIONS AND GRAPE VARIETIES

The Danube runs through Niederösterreich, scene of much of Austria's viticulture. The Wachau produces great Riesling and excellent pepper-dry Grüner Veltliner. The Riesling is powerful and ripe, closer in style to Alsace than Germany. Next up the Danube are Kremstal and Kamptal, rapidly improving as fine dry white regions with a few good reds. The Weinviertel, in the north-east, produces large quantities of decent reds and Grüner Veltliner whites. Burgenland, south of Vienna, produces the best reds, mostly from local varieties Zweigelt, Blaufränkisch and St-Laurent. Also, around the shores of the Neusiedler See, especially near the towns of Rust and Illmitz, Burgenland produces some superb dessert wines. Further south, in Steiermark, Chardonnay and Sauvignon are increasingly oak-aged, though many drinkers still prefer the racy unoaked 'classic' wines from these varieties.

CLASSIFICATIONS

Wine categories are similar to those in Germany, beginning with **Tafelwein** (table wine) and **Landwein** (country wine). **Qualitätswein** must come from one of the 16 main wine-producing regions. Like German wines, quality wines may additionally have a special category: Kabinett, Spätlese, Auslese, Beerenauslese, Ausbruch, Trockenbeerenauslese. Since most Austrian wines are either dry or nobly sweet, these categories count for less than in Germany. The Wachau has a ripeness scale for dry whites: Steinfeder wines are made for early drinking, Federspiel wines can last three years or so and the most powerful wines are known as Smaragd. The first Austrian appellations, known as DAC, are starting to appear, but as yet they have had little impact.

2008 VINTAGE REPORT

The summer was essentially wet and miserable, with much disease and rot. The autumn was cool too, which further delayed ripening, but there was less rain and disease. Some organic and biodynamic growers had severe difficulties. Much of the harvest only began in late October, and grape sorting was essential. Quality seems good, especially in Steiermark (Styria). Some Wachau growers picked too early, so quality will vary. Burgenland reds have good fruit but are fairly light.

Austrian entries in the A–Z section (pages 58–315).

SPAIN

The technical make-over of Spain's long-dormant wine scene was largely complete by 2000. Since that date, we have witnessed a progressive refinement of the wines, as increasing numbers of producers eschewed the over-oaking and ultra-powerful style that had been a hallmark of this country's revolution. Not coincidentally, forgotten regions and forgotten native grape varieties have now come to the fore.

WINE REGIONS

Galicia in the green, hilly north-west grows Spain's most aromatic whites. The heartland of the great Spanish reds, Rioja, Navarra and Ribera del Duero, is situated between the central plateau and the northern coast. Further west along the Duero, Rueda produces fresh whites and Toro good ripe reds. Cataluña is principally white wine country (much of it sparkling Cava), though there are some great reds in Priorat and increasingly in Terra Alta and Montsant. Aragón's reds and whites are looking good too, with an impressive relaunch of Aragón's great (but neglected for too long) native grape Garnacha. The central plateau of La Mancha makes mainly cheap reds and whites, though smaller private estates are improving spectacularly. Valencia, known for inexpensive and unmemorable wines, is now producing, with neighbouring Murcia, increasingly ambitious and rich reds. Andalucía's specialities are the fortified wines – sherry, Montilla and Málaga. There has been a notable rebirth of viticulture and winemaking in both the Balearics and the Canary Islands.

CLASSIFICATIONS

Vino de Mesa, the equivalent of France's Vin de Table, is the lowest level. For a while, it was used for some non-DO 'Super-Spanish'.

Vino de la Tierra is Spain's equivalent of France's Vin de Pays.

DO (Denominación de Origen) is the equivalent of France's AC, regulating grape varieties and region of origin. In Castilla-La Mancha, this category now

encompasses single-estate DOs (Denominación de Origen – Vino de Pago). **DOCa** (Denominación de Origen Calificada) is a super-category. Only two regions (Rioja and Priorat) have been promoted.

Vino de Pago (single-estate wine) is a new appellation used only, for the time being, in two regions, Castilla-La Mancha and Navarra.

2008 VINTAGE REPORT

Again, as in 2007, this was an uneven vintage, marked by humidity and uncommonly mild temperatures in most regions in early summer, which led to high occurrences of mildew and oïdium (downy mildew) and cut overall production levels by some 20%. There was a window of warm weather in September that salvaged the harvest; surprisingly, Rioja and Navarra had a much drier harvesting season than regions closer to the Mediterranean, even though the harvest stretched to the end of October. Rueda was one of the rare regions with an increased harvest.

Spanish entries in the A–Z section (pages 58–315).

REGIONS	Priorat	Domecq	Raïmat
Andalucía	Rías Baixas	Enate	Remelluri
Aragón	Ribera del Duero	Faustino	Rioja Alta, La
Balearic Islands	Rioja	Freixenet	Riojanas, Bodegas
Canary Islands	Rueda	González Byass	Rodríguez, Telmo
Castilla-La Mancha	Somontano	Guelbenzu	Romeo, Benjamín
Castilla y León	Toro	Hidalgo	Sandeman
Cataluña	Utiel-Requena	López de Heredia	Torres
Galicia	Valdepeñas	Lustau, Emilio	Valdespino
Valencia		Marqués de	Vall-Llach
	PRODUCERS	Cáceres	Vega Sicilia
DO/DOCA	Aalto	Marqués de Griñón	Viñas del Vero
Bierzo	Allende	Marqués de	
Cariñena	Artadi	Murrieta	**SEE ALSO**
Cava	Barbadillo	Marqués de Riscal	Airén
Costers del Segre	Campillo	Martínez Bujanda	Albariño
Jerez y Manzanilla	Campo Viejo	Mas Doix	Graciano
Jumilla	Chivite	Mauro	Grenache Noir
Málaga	Clos Erasmus	Muga	Mourvèdre
Mancha, La	Clos Mogador	Osborne	Parellada
Montilla-Moriles	Codorníu	Palacios, Álvaro	Tempranillo
Navarra	Contino	Pesquera	
Penedès	CVNE	Pingus, Dominio de	

PORTUGAL

Investment and imagination are paying off in this attractive country, with climates that vary from the mild, damp Minho region in the north-west to the subtropical island of Madeira. Use of native grapes, occasionally blended with international varieties, means that Portugal is now a rich source of characterful wines of ever-increasing quality.

WINE REGIONS

The lush Vinho Verde country in the north-west gives very different wine from the parched valleys of the neighbouring Douro, with its drier, more continental climate. The Douro, home of port, is also the source of some of Portugal's best unfortified red wines. In Beiras, which includes Bairrada and

Dão, soil types are crucial in determining the character of the wines. Estremadura and Ribatejo use native and international varieties in regions influenced either by the maritime climate or by the river Tagus. South of Lisbon, the Terras do Sado and Alentejo produce some exciting table wines – and the Algarve is waking up. Madeira is unique, a volcanic island 850km (530 miles) out in the Atlantic Ocean.

CLASSIFICATIONS

Vinho de Mesa is the lowest level, but commercially important as so much off-dry to medium-dry rosé is exported in this category.

Vinho Regional (11 in number) is equivalent to French Vin de Pays, with laws and permitted varieties much freer than for IPR and DOC.

IPR (Indicação de Proveniência Regulamentada) is the intermediate step for wine regions hoping to move up to DOC status. Many have been promoted in the past few years, leaving just 4 IPRs, not all of which will definitely become DOCs.

DOC (Denominação de Origem Controlada) Equivalent to France's AC; there are now 27 DOC regions.

2008 VINTAGE REPORT

After a dry winter, welcome rain fell in April to replenish water reserves in the soils. It was less welcome when the rains continued into May in parts of the country, flowering was less successful, and final quantities of grapes were reduced. Taking Portugal as a whole, quantity was only down about 8% on the 2007 harvest; the south was affected more than the north. Although the summer was cool it was mainly dry, and the grapes had enough sun to ripen well. Good weather continued throughout the harvest. Yields were up to 40% down with the good winemakers, but everyone talks of good wines. The jury's still out on port, but good wines have been made in Vinho Verde and the Douro. Bairrada had a great year for its Baga reds, and both red and white Dão are good. Estremadura and Ribatejo have excellent wines, and quality is up in the Terras do Sado and Alentejo, too, though quantities are down. Overall, whites are good and reds are looking excellent.

Portuguese entries in the A–Z section (pages 58–315).

USA

The United States has more varied growing conditions for grapes than any other country in the world, which isn't so surprising when you consider that the 50 states of the Union cover an area that is larger than Western Europe; and although Alaska doesn't grow grapes in the icy far north, Washington State does in the north-west, as does Texas in the south and New York State in the north-east, and even Hawaii, lost in the pounding surf of the Pacific Ocean, manages to grow grapes and make wine. Every state, including Alaska (thanks to salmonberry and fireweed), now produces wine of some sort or another; it ranges from some pretty dire offerings, which would have been far better distilled into brandy, to some of the greatest and most original wines to be found in the world today.

GRAPE VARIETIES AND WINE REGIONS

California is far and away the most important state for wine production. In its determination to match the best red Bordeaux and white Burgundy, California proved that it was possible to successfully re-interpret the classic European role models in an area thousands of miles away from their home. However, there is more to California than this. The Central Valley produces the majority of the simple beverage wines that still dominate the American market. Napa and Sonoma Counties north of San Francisco Bay do produce great Cabernet and Chardonnay, but grapes like Zinfandel and Merlot also make their mark and the Carneros, Russian River Valley and Sonoma Coast areas are highly successful for Pinot Noir, Chardonnay and sparkling wines. In the north, Mendocino and Lake Counties produce good grapes. South of San Francisco, in the cool, foggy valleys between Santa Cruz and Santa Barbara, and the Santa Lucia Highlands in Monterey County, Chardonnay, Pinot Noir and Syrah are producing exciting cool-climate but ripe-flavoured wines.

Oregon, with a cooler and more capricious climate than most of California, perseveres with Pinot Noir, Chardonnay, Pinot Gris, Pinot Blanc and Riesling with patchy success. Washington, so chilly and misty on the coast, becomes virtual desert east of the Cascade Mountains and it is here, in irrigated vineyards, that superb reds and whites can be made, with thrillingly focused fruit.

Main vineyard areas

Seattle
WASHINGTON STATE
Portland
OREGON
MENDOCINO
NORTH COAST
LAKE
SONOMA NAPA
San Francisco
Santa Cruz
CENTRAL COAST
CALIFORNIA
CENTRAL VALLEY
San Luis Obispo
Santa Barbara
Los Angeles
SOUTH COAST

0   150 km
0   100 miles

In New York, winemakers in the Finger Lakes are creating a regional style and national reputation for dry Riesling. Long Island continues to impress with classically styled Merlot, Cabernet Sauvignon and Cabernet Franc, as well as Chardonnay to pair with the local lobster. Improved vineyard practices have enabled growers to cope with the vagaries of the region's inconsistent weather, resulting in an overall increase in quality from year to year.

Other states have seen dramatic growth in the wine industry over the past decade. Established industries in Virginia, Maryland, Pennsylvania, Texas and Missouri have led the way, but look also for new growth in North Carolina, Georgia and Michigan.

CLASSIFICATIONS

The AVA (American Viticultural Area) system was introduced in the 1980s. It does not guarantee a quality standard, but merely requires that at least 85% of grapes in a wine come from the specified AVA. There are over 190 AVAs, more than 100 of which are in California. AVAs come in all shapes and sizes, varying from the largest, Ohio River Valley, which spans an area of 67,340 sq km (26,000 sq miles) to the smallest, Cole Ranch, which covers a little less than a quarter of a square mile.

2008 VINTAGE REPORT

In California, 2008 was one of the oddest vintages in memory. It started with a bizarre wave of icy-cold weather in the spring that actually froze some vineyards in the North Coast and wrecked tonnage totals. Spring was cooler than normal, but warm summer temperatures rose to such heights by late July that picking came earlier than usual, with many varieties all seeming to ripen at once. By early September, every winery was in fast-forward mode. Rapid sugar development was seen until late September, when a cooling trend slowed everything down.

In Washington, the word to describe the season was 'delayed'. A cold, wet spring resulted in delayed flowering. By mid-summer, the vintage was clearly going to be late. The summer was cooler than preceding vintages, similar to the summer of 1999. Many growers decided to reduce crop levels, in anticipation of a difficult season. White varieties were harvested in mid-September in good, cool conditions. Red grapes were left to hang in an attempt to get higher sugars, but the weather remained cold and wet; Cabernet Sauvignon seems worst affected. By early November, the vines stopped producing sugar. A predictably variable vintage for reds – Merlot seems to be the most successful variety. Whites will have lower alcohol than usual, with great flavour concentration.

In Oregon, poor weather at flowering produced small, uneven bunches. Berry size was smaller than usual, resulting in more tannic wines. The summer was cold in comparison to recent vintages and the harvest was late – very late. Predictions in early September were dire. But the rains stayed away, and by early October shy optimism had turned to pronounced enthusiasm. Many winemakers believe that the quality of their 2008s is exceptional. Cool conditions for ripening ultimately resulted in lower alcohol levels and excellent purity of flavour. Some growers harvested too early, trying to avoid rains that never came, but experienced producers waited until the danger passed, allowing them to craft ageworthy wines.

The growing season along the East Coast was more typically rainy than the previous two years, requiring vintners to employ all the tricks of their trade. Reds fared better than whites, especially in the mid-Atlantic region, where a series of tropical storms disrupted early harvest.

USA entries in the A–Z section (pages 58–315) by state.

AUSTRALIA

Australian wine today enjoys a reputation still well out of proportion to the quantity of wine produced (total output is about a quarter that of France), though volumes are mushrooming. The New World wine revolution – emphasizing ripe, rich fruit, seductive use of oak, labelling by grape variety and consumer-friendly marketing – has been led by wine warriors from the southern seas. There's more than enough sunshine and not nearly enough rain to grow the grapes, so most growers are guaranteed ripeness but rely heavily on irrigation for their vines to survive. Dynamic and innovative winemakers ensure a steady supply of new wines, wineries and even regions, but consolidation and internationalization of larger operators seem to be causing an unwarranted and unwelcome dumbing down of flavour. Nonetheless, there are many distinctive wines from quality producers that show regional or single site character.

GRAPE VARIETIES

Varietal wines remain more prized than blends. Shiraz has long been a key varietal and is more fashionable than Cabernet Sauvignon. Renewed respect for old-vine Grenache and Mourvèdre has seen these former workhorse varieties transformed into premium wines. Merlot and – in cooler-climate regions – Pinot Noir lead the pack of alternative red varieties and Australia's endless appetite for experiment has found prospective new stars in Petit Verdot, Tempranillo, Nebbiolo and Sangiovese. Among white grapes the position of Chardonnay remains unchallenged, although Semillon and Riesling both have a longer track record. Sauvignon Blanc is enjoying a massive boost to its popularity both as a varietal and as part of a blend with Semillon, especially as an easy-drinking white. Rhône varieties Marsanne and

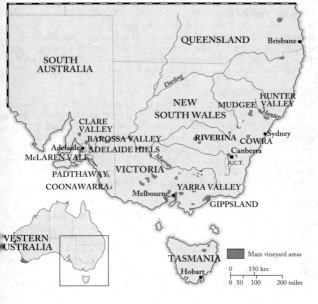

Viognier (now fashionably included in blends with Shiraz) are both impressive and Verdelho and Pinot Gris are making a strong case for themselves as alternatives to Chardonnay. Sweet whites are produced from Semillon and Muscat – both the top-class Brown Muscat (a sub-variety of Muscat Blanc à Petits Grains) and the more workaday Muscat Gordo Blanco.

WINE REGIONS

Western Australia is a vast state, virtually desert except for its south-western coastal strip. The sun-baked region near Perth is best suited to throaty reds and fortified wines, yet winery and vineyard expertise has become more sophisticated and decent aromatic dry whites are now being made. The most exciting wines, both red and white, come from Margaret River and Great Southern down toward the coast.

South Australia dominates the wine scene – it grows the most grapes, makes the most wine and is home to most of the nation's biggest wine companies. There is more to it, however, than attractive, undemanding, gluggable wine. The Clare Valley produces outstanding cool-climate Riesling, as well as excellent Shiraz and Cabernet. The Barossa is home to some of the planet's oldest vines, particularly Shiraz and Grenache. Eden Valley, in the hills to the east of the Barossa Valley, excels at crisp, steely Rieslings and scented Shiraz. McLaren Vale, Coonawarra and other parts of the Limestone Coast also make many thrilling reds

Victoria was Australia's major producer for most of the 19th century until her vineyards were devastated by phylloxera. It's only recently that Victoria has regained her position as provider of some of the most startling wine styles in the country: stunning liqueur Muscats; thrilling dark reds from Central Victoria; urbane Yarra Valley and Mornington Peninsula reds and whites.

New South Wales was home to the revolution that propelled Australia to the front of the world wine stage (in the Hunter Valley, an area that remains a dominant force). However, the state is a major bulk producer in Riverina, and a clutch of new regions in the Central Ranges are grabbing headlines.

Tasmania, with its cooler climate, is attracting attention for top-quality Pinot Noirs and Champagne-method sparkling wines – and there is excellent potential for Riesling and Gewürztraminer.

CLASSIFICATIONS

Formal appellation control, restricting certain grapes to certain regions, is virtually unknown; regulations are more of a guarantee of authenticity than a guide to quality. In a country so keen on inter-regional blending for its commercial brands, a system resembling France's AC could be problematic. However, the Label Integrity Program (LIP) guarantees all claims made on labels and the Geographical Indications (GI) committee is busy clarifying zones, regions and sub-regions – albeit with plenty of lively, at times acrimonious, debate about where some regional borders should go.

2009 VINTAGE REPORT

The catastrophic bushfires that ravaged the Yarra Valley and threatened Beechworth, Bendigo, Gippsland and Heathcote have etched themselves indelibly into the hearts and minds of Australians – and the 2009 vintage will always be overshadowed by their memory. In terms of the grape harvest, less than 5% of the Yarra's vineyard land was damaged or destroyed by the fires, although yields were already well below usual. What is not known at this stage is the impact of smoke taint on grapes in several parts of Victoria. What is clear is that there will be many very fine wines from the Yarra Valley.

Early estimates indicated a reduction of about 10% on the 2008 crop – after the low of 2007 and high of 2005. Winter was drier and warmer than usual, although rain in November–December, especially in the cooler regions, benefited the vines. Temperatures leading up to vintage were exceptionally mild apart from a period of extreme heat in late January–early February in the eastern states. McLaren Vale and Langhorne Creek were the worst affected, although warm-climate varieties such as Tempranillo and late-ripening Cabernet should be very good indeed. In any case, the spells of extreme heat came earlier than in 2008, so the impact on most red varieties was minimal.

Quantity may be down slightly but the Hunter Valley and other New South Wales regions, Canberra, Queensland and Tasmania all report good to outstanding quality. Winemakers in South Australia are very happy with the harvest: those in Clare are delighted by the quality of Riesling and producers in the Barossa were raving about the Grenache and Mourvèdre. Western Australia has had arguably its best-ever white wine vintage, and its reds are likely to be spectacular.

In summary, this will be a much better vintage than initial reports suggest. The key to its success will be the long, mild ripening period and rainfall at helpful times. Expect substantial variation within regions as clever viticulturists and thoughtful winemakers overcome tricky weather events.

Australian entries in the A–Z section (pages 58–315).

NEW ZEALAND

New Zealand's wines, though diverse in style, are characterized by intense fruit flavours, zesty acidity and pungent aromas – the product of cool growing conditions and high-tech winemaking.

GRAPE VARIETIES

Until recently, New Zealand's fame has rested on one grape variety: Sauvignon Blanc. The bracing, tangy style of New Zealand's first Sauvignons redefined the world's expectations of the grape. But this rapidly maturing wine industry has many more tricks up its sleeve. The other major white grapes are Chardonnay in a melony, peachy style, succulent Pinot Gris and fragrant Riesling, with Gewürztraminer on the rise and Viognier now making an appearance. Among reds, Cabernet Sauvignon and Merlot have been around for some time, either fruity and berryish or in a more serious Bordeaux style, sometimes blended with Cabernet Franc and/or Malbec; Syrah is fashionable, spicy and scented; and Pinot Noir, now the country's number one red, is bidding to be taken seriously in the Premier League of world wine.

WINE REGIONS

Nearly 1600km (1000 miles) separate New Zealand's northernmost wine region from the country's (and the world's) most southerly wine region, Central Otago. In terms of wine styles it is useful to divide the country into two parts. The warmer climate of Hawkes Bay and one or two pockets around Auckland produce the best Cabernet Sauvignon, Merlot and Cabernet Franc as well as increasingly good Syrah. Waiheke Island and Hawkes Bay's Gimblett Gravels have some of the most exciting red wine vineyards. Martinborough and Wairarapa are noted for Pinot Noir. In the South Island, Nelson is good for Pinot Noir and aromatic whites, while Marlborough is the hub of the industry, famous for Sauvignon Blanc, but also excellent for fizz, Chardonnay, Riesling and Pinot Noir. Waipara is small but produces very characterful reds and whites, while Central Otago produces fabulous Pinot Noir, vibrant Riesling and an increasing amount of flavoursome Pinot Gris.

CLASSIFICATIONS

Labels guarantee geographic origin. The broadest designation is New Zealand, followed by North or South Island. Next come the 10 or so regions. Labels may also name specific localities and individual vineyards.

2009 VINTAGE REPORT

Favourable flowering set the scene for a large vintage, although many growers reacted by shoot thinning and removing bunches to reduce crop levels. La Niña weather patterns brought warm conditions at the beginning of the ripening period in most wine regions. A wet, cool February slowed ripening and sparked a botrytis outbreak in susceptible varieties. By early March, many growers feared the worst, but a long dry spell lasting nearly two months revived hopes that it would be a very good vintage, particularly for later-ripening varieties such as Cabernet Sauvignon and Syrah. In terms of quantity the harvest is expected to be similar to 2008's large vintage, although vineyard area has increased significantly. Hawkes Bay produced many outstanding red wines; its white wines are variable thanks to unseasonal rain. Gisborne and Wairarapa/Martinborough were less affected by rain than other North Island regions and made generally excellent white and red wines. Marlborough Sauvignon Blanc enjoyed a good vintage thanks, in part, to growers reducing cropping levels. Central Otago suffered from a cooler than average vintage but was saved by the long, dry autumn weather and is expected to make good, if not great, Pinot Noir.

New Zealand entries in the A–Z section (pages 58–315).

REGIONS	PRODUCERS		
Auckland	Astrolabe	Hunter's	Pegasus Bay
Awatere Valley	Ata Rangi	Jackson Estate	Saint Clair
Canterbury	Babich	Kumeu River	Seifried
Central Otago	Church Road	Martinborough	Seresin
Gisborne	Cloudy Bay	Vineyard	Sileni
Hawkes Bay	Coopers Creek	Matua Valley	Stonyridge
Kumeu/Huapai	Craggy Range	Millton	Te Mata
Marlborough	Delegat's	Montana	Trinity Hill
Martinborough	Dry River	Neudorf	Vavasour
Nelson	Felton Road	Ngatarawa	Villa Maria
Waiheke Island	Fromm	Nobilo	Wither Hills
	Goldwater Estate	Palliser Estate	
		Pask, C J	

SOUTH AMERICA

ARGENTINA

We have been talking about the Argentine renaissance for several years. Now it's a reality. After various economic crises and political instability, Argentina and its wines are emerging from the ashes. The Upper Mendoza River region and the high Uco Valley, both located in Mendoza, are the main sources of great Malbec (Argentina's flagship red wine grape), but there are also exciting, aromatic examples in cooler areas like Río Negro and Neuquén, down in Patagonia, and ripe and dense versions in Salta, to the north of the country. That region is also the best area for the perfumed and heady white Torrontés (the other Argentine speciality). Foreign investment is focussed on Mendoza, where around 80% of the country's wine is made. New luxury hotels and spas in the wine country add glamour to this Argentine wine boom.

CHILE

We're seeing the name Carmenère more and more frequently on wine labels. Previously this grape's brilliance was hidden under the better-known title of 'Merlot' (Chilean Merlot is still some of the world's best thanks to its blending with Carmenère). Now the dark, rich, savoury flavours of Carmenère are proudly presented, especially from numerous established vineyard sites in the Rapel Valley. Cabernet Sauvignon and Merlot, from Maipo and elsewhere, are still Chile's best-known wines, but superb, fragrant Pinot Noir is appearing from coastal areas such as San Antonio, and excellent Syrah is being made in cool coastal areas like Limarí as well as the warmer Central Valley. Chile's fruity Chardonnay is some of the New World's best balanced, while exciting Sauvignon Blanc, Riesling and Gewürztraminer are becoming common from the coastal and southerly regions such as Bío Bío. Maule is experiencing a revival helped by old-vine Carignan and new investment from Spain and Italy.

46

URUGUAY

Most of the vines are on clay soils in the Canelones region around Montevideo, which has high rainfall in a relatively cool climate: the thick-skinned, rot-resistant black Tannat grape from South-West France is the leading variety. A clutch of modern wineries are working hard to soften the tannic Tannat; they are also producing snappy Sauvignon Blanc and fresh Cabernet Franc and Merlot. Best producers: Bouza, Carrau, Castillo Viejo, Los Cerros de San Juan, Filgueira, Juanicó, PISANO, Stagnari, Toscanini, Viñedo de los Vientos.

BRAZIL

Look at Brazil, how vast it is. Yet in all this expanse, running from 33° South to 5° North, there's nowhere ideal to site a vineyard. Aridity is the problem in the north, humidity in the south. Even so, they do manage to make some very attractive wines, often with less than 13% alcohol, and vineyards on the Uruguayan border and the far south-east are promising. The Vale de São Francisco in the far north is an ambitious tropical undertaking, producing two harvests a year. Sparkling wine is the most consistent Brazilian style.

OTHER COUNTRIES

Peru has seemingly good vineyard sites in the Ica Valley south of Lima, but apart from Tacama it produces little of any interest winewise. Bolivia has few vineyards, but they're incredibly high. Venezuela's chief claim to fame is that some of her subtropical vines give three crops a year!

2009 VINTAGE REPORT

A hot and dry vintage on both sides of the Andes meant a challenging year for producers in 2009. Those who got their irrigation and canopy management right will make ripe, concentrated reds; those who didn't will make baked, insipid wines. As ever, choose your producer with care. Chile enjoyed its hottest March in 95 years; expect higher alcohols and lower acidity than both 2008 and 2007. Only those whites from cooler areas with scrupulous vineyard management will be good – Casablanca in general saw notably high yields. In Argentina, production was down, with early figures showing the lowest yield in a decade. The harvest was up to 2 weeks early as sugar levels rose fast, which will mean wines with plenty of alcohol. Good vineyards, especially those in the cooler areas of the Uco Valley, will make fruit-forward, round, dense reds.

South American entries in the A–Z section (pages 58–315).

SOUTH AFRICA

As South Africa's wine industry celebrates its 350th birthday, the country's wines continue to perform well on the international competition circuit as well as in the export field; over 350 million litres were exported during the 12 months to July 2008, well ahead of projected figures. Markets too are spreading, with the US becoming an important destination for South African wine; Africa and the East also show encouraging interest. For the first time in 10 years, there's been an increase, albeit tiny, in per capita consumption locally; about time, as new wine producers continue to open at the rate of one a week, mainly, but not exclusively, in the heart of the Western Cape winelands. There has also been a victory for Riesling enthusiasts; from the 2010 vintage, Riesling sold on the South African market will be permitted to be labelled without the descriptor Rhine or Weisser; this was previously required to avoid confusion with the locally named Cape Riesling (a little known variety from South-West France called Crouchen Blanc).

Quality across both whites and reds continues to improve; a problem described as burnt rubber in some red wines is being researched by Stellenbosch University. The new generation of winemakers are playing a major role in raising standards and broadening the range of styles.

GRAPE VARIETIES AND WINE REGIONS
The Cape's winelands run roughly 400km (250 miles) north and east of Cape Town, although small pockets of new vineyards are taking the winelands way outside their traditional territory. Wine, albeit in tiny quantities, is now being produced from grapes grown in the mountains above the Eastern Cape town of Plettenberg Bay, better known for its holidaymakers than its vines, and from vineyards in the Drakensberg region of KwaZulu-Natal. Plantings generally continue to decrease. New white grape vineyards – mainly Chenin

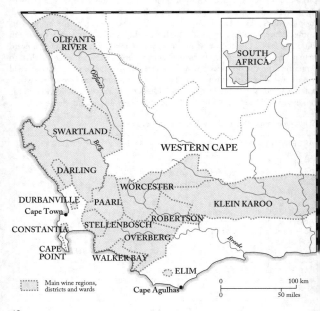

Blanc, Chardonnay, Sauvignon Blanc and Colombard – outstrip reds by nearly 5 to 1, and Chenin remains the most planted variety. Red varieties, led by Cabernet Sauvignon and Shiraz, cover just under 45% of the vineyards, with all major varieties either static or decreasing in area. The emphasis remains on classic, international varieties such as Cabernet Sauvignon, Merlot, Chardonnay and Sauvignon Blanc, with small quantities of Verdelho, Malbec, Nebbiolo, Sangiovese, Tannat and Tempranillo in the mix. But Rhône varieties still generate most excitement: as well as Syrah/Shiraz, there's Grenache, Cinsaut and Mourvèdre for reds, and Viognier, Grenache Blanc and Roussanne for whites.

With the major grape varieties being planted over the entire Western Cape winelands, there is little typicity of origin, although some areas are historically associated with specific varieties or styles. Stellenbosch lays claim to some of the best red wines; maritime-influenced Constantia, and Cape Point on the other side of the Peninsula mountain chain, produce exhilarating Sauvignon Blanc, a variety also showing great promise in other coastal areas, right from Upper Langkloof, a ward in the eastern part of Klein Karoo, to Durbanville and Darling on the west coast and even further north to Doring Bay near Vredendal in the Olifants River region, as well as upland Elgin in the Overberg district. Many of these areas are also producing distinctive blends of Semillon and Sauvignon Blanc. Other cool areas include Walker Bay, where the focus is Pinot Noir. Chardonnay, long associated with inland Robertson, is now making its mark with Cap Classique sparkling wines as well as citrous, nutty still wines. As a warmer area, Robertson is also recognized for fortifieds, both Muscadel (Muscat) and port styles. Inland areas such as Swartland along the west coast have good affinity with Shiraz and other Rhône varieties; white blends including Chenin, Chardonnay and Viognier are also starting to create waves.

CLASSIFICATIONS

The Wine of Origin (WO) system divides wine-producing areas into regions, districts, wards, estates and single vineyards. Varietal, vintaged wines must be made from at least 85% of the named grape and vintage.

2009 VINTAGE REPORT

A dream vintage for many: a very cold, wet winter was followed by mild weather in spring and early summer, the traditional heat arriving nearly a month late. The crop is generally extremely healthy – a really good vintage with some standout wines. The one caveat: those affected by smoke from the fires will have to make severe selections.

South African entries in the A–Z section (pages 58–315).

WINE REGIONS	Boekenhoutskloof	Hamilton Russell	Saxenburg
Constantia WO	Bouchard Finlayson	Hartenberg Estate	Simonsig
Durbanville WO	Buitenverwachting	Jordan	Spice Route
Elgin WO	Cape Chamonix	Kanonkop	Springfield Estate
Franschhoek WO	Cape Point	Klein Constantia	Steenberg
Paarl WO	Cluver, Paul	KWV	Thelema
Robertson WO	De Trafford	L'Avenir	Veenwouden
Stellenbosch WO	Distell	Meerlust	Vergelegen
Walker Bay WO	Ellis, Neil	Morgenhof	Villiera
	Els, Ernie	Mulderbosch	Warwick
PRODUCERS	Fairview	Rust en Vrede	
Beck, Graham	Glen Carlou	Rustenberg	SEE ALSO
Beyerskloof	Grangehurst	Sadie Family	Pinotage

OTHER WINE COUNTRIES

ALGERIA With many vines over 40 years old, there should be great potential here, but political uncertainty hinders progress despite government support. The western coastal province of Oran produces three-quarters of Algeria's wine, including the soft but muscular Coteaux de Tlemcen wines and dark, beefy reds of the Coteaux de Mascara. Average production is around 75 million bottles a year.

BELGIUM Belgium's vineyards were established by the Romans, but it is only within the past 20 years that climate change has once again allowed vines to thrive, and the country now has a budding wine industry, admittedly on a very small scale. There are about 20 commercial producers, many of whom are based in an area known as Hageland, east of Brussels. They are proud of their appellation system – not too surprising this close to the global capital of rules and regulations. Pitting itself against one of the strongest, most varied beer and food cultures in the world, Belgian wine is rising to the challenge and finding a place on restaurant lists. Pinot Noir and Chardonnay are grown for sparkling and still wines, most notably some Chablis-like Chardonnay.

BULGARIA After success in the 1980s and disarray in the 90s, some progress followed the introduction of new wine legislation in 2001, and investment in new vineyards is beginning to gather pace. Entry into the EU in 2007 has encouraged a more positive attitude in the vineyards, and there are signs of single-estate wines emerging, although in some regions there is shortage of vineyard workers as they seek employment in wealthier EU states. New World influences are having some effect, although few wines shine. Cabernet Sauvignon and Merlot dominate, but local grapes – plummy Mavrud, meaty Gamza, deep Melnik, fruity white Dimiat and Misket – can be good. Established wineries such as BOYAR ESTATES, Khan Krum and Suhindo are being joined by new operations every year, some financed by local businesses, others with international backing. Stork Nest and Bessa Valley are two of the largest, and anyone doubting Bulgaria's potential should taste the eminently affordable and excellent Enira wines from Bessa Valley (owned by Stephan von Neipperg of Ch. CANON-LA-GAFFELIÈRE in St-Emilion in France).

CANADA The strict VQA (Vintners Quality Alliance) maintains high standards in British Columbia and Ontario, and there is continuing progress in the 2 most important regions – OKANAGAN VALLEY in British Columbia and the NIAGARA PENINSULA in Ontario. Sweet icewine, made primarily from white Vidal and Riesling, but occasionally from Cabernet Franc, is still Canada's trump card. Pinot Gris, Chardonnay, Riesling and Gewürztraminer lead the way in non-sweet whites; Merlot, Cabernet Franc, Cabernet Sauvignon, even Syrah in British Columbia and Pinot Noir in Ontario, are producing the tastiest red wines. The best producers include Cave Spring, Chateau des Charmes, le CLOS JORDANNE, HENRY OF PELHAM, Hidden Bench, INNISKILLIN, Southbrook, Stratus, Tawse and THIRTY BENCH in the Niagara Peninsula and Black Hills Estate, Blue Mountain, Burrowing Owl, CedarCreek, JACKSON TRIGGS, INNISKILLIN, MISSION HILL, Quails' Gate, Road 13 and SUMAC RIDGE in the Okanagan Valley.

CHINA Though China officially promotes wine (especially red), its potential remains unfulfilled as the majority of Chinese are reluctant to drink it. This isn't surprising when you consider the relative incompatibility of much Chinese cuisine with the dry, slightly bitter flavours of much red wine

Aromatic and zesty whites suit the food much better, but red is the lucky colour in China and it's red that every producer wants to push. However, as the Chinese economy expands, demand for its wines is increasing, particularly in the cities. Home-grown premium wines are emerging and foreign investment proceeds apace with continual improvements in viticulture and winemaking. Exactly what effect Ch. LAFITE-ROTHSCHILD's decision to create a wine estate there will have isn't clear. But one thing is clear: Lafite-Rothschild is the most clamoured-for of the top French reds. Anything local with the Lafite imprimatur *will* sell and *won't* be cheap. China now ranks as the sixth-biggest wine producer in the world, with massive new plantings every year – mainly international grapes such as Chardonnay and Cabernet Sauvignon, with some traditional Chinese, German and Russian varieties. There are now over well over 400 wineries. Major producers include Changyu, Dynasty, Great Wall, HUADONG and Xintian. One of China's biggest problems is where to plant grapes with the potential for top quality. The most popular region is Shandong on the eastern coast, but persistent summer rains and wet autumns mean it's difficult to achieve top-quality reds. Ningsha, 2000km (1240 miles) inland from Shandong, with a continental climate and long dry autumns, is the latest hot tip for reds. The south-west province of Yunnan has become popular with growers and several new wineries have been established here, despite pretty extreme conditions.

CROATIA Croatia has a strong viticultural heritage and an undercurrent of rising potential: bulk whites dominate but small private producers are emerging. What the country needs now is more investment, more technology in the vineyard and winery and a fair price for the grapes; planned membership of the EU will undoubtedly help. Tourism is flourishing and this should help popularize the wines – so long as foreigners can pronounce them. The best vineyards are on the Dalmatian coast, where international varieties are being planted alongside gutsy indigenous grapes: deep, tannic Plavac Mali – related to Zinfandel – has long produced the top red wines. The original site for Zinfandel (locally known as Crljenak, and down to just half a dozen vines) has been replanted and should become a shrine for Zinheads. The most popular white grapes are Malvazija (Malvasia) and Grasevina (Welschriesling), which vary widely in style and quality. GRGICH of California has a winery on the Peljesac peninsula. Frano Milos (also on the Peljesac peninsula) and Kozlovic and Matosevic in Istria are other names to look for.

CYPRUS There is potential, but modernization in the vineyards is slow, as they are divided up into so many small holdings. Large wineries like Sodap and Keo have moved to the hills, nearer to cooler vineyards in the Troodos Mountains. Smaller wineries like Vlassides and Kyperounda show promise. Good reds from the indigenous Maratheftiko grape. Lefkada is useful in blends and Xynisteri is capable of fresh whites if grown at altitude. COMMANDARIA has been famous since the Crusades.

THE CZECH REPUBLIC The vineyards of Bohemia in the north-west and Moravia in the south-east are mainly planted with white varieties – Grüner Veltliner, Müller-Thurgau, Riesling, Pinot Blanc, Pinot Gris – with pockets of red such as St-Laurent and Lemberger (Blaufränkisch). Beer is far more important than wine in the Czech culture, but in a world where too many wines are becoming excessively oaky and alcoholic, the fragile, scented, low-alcoholic charms of Czech wine become more and more attractive.

DENMARK Grapes shouldn't grow this far north: Copenhagen, like Edinburgh in Scotland, is just below the 56th parallel. But as global warming pushes the threshold for viticulture ever northward and new grape varieties are developed to thrive here, the EU permitted commercial wine production in 2000, with a list of approved varieties. The industry is still tiny, with about 40 growers taking advantage of the long hours of sunshine to ripen their grapes. Neighbouring southern Sweden, with very similar conditions, is also getting in on the act.

ENGLAND The UK's winegrowing industry has celebrated more than 50 vintages since the 'revival' of commercial vineyards in the early 1950s. However, with around 1250ha (3088 acres) of vines, 350 vineyards (many very small), 120 wineries and an average annual output of around 2.2 million bottles, it is still minute. Nevertheless, producers have learnt which varieties are successful (Bacchus, Schönburger and Seyval Blanc for whites; Rondo, Regent, Dornfelder and Pinot Noir for reds; and, increasingly, Chardonnay, Pinot Noir and Pinot Meunier for quality sparklers), how to train and trellis them to cope with the (usually) cool summers and – most importantly – how to make sound, sometimes excellent, wines. In particular, sparkling wines have shown they can equal CHAMPAGNE in quality and the area planted to the classic Champagne varieties is now approximately 50% of the UK total. Growers from Champagne are taking notice and several famous houses have been looking for sites; a producer of very good Champagne from Avize has planted 4ha (10 acres) in Hampshire and more are sure to follow. Regulations now require growers to submit their wines for testing before they can label them 'English'; wines labelled 'UK table wine' should be avoided. The most popular winemaking counties are: West Sussex (NYETIMBER, RIDGEVIEW), Kent (Balfour, Biddenden, CHAPEL DOWN, Sandhurst), Surrey (DENBIES), Essex (New Hall), Hampshire, (Wickham and Somborne Valley), East Sussex (BREAKY BOTTOM, Davenport), Devon (SHARPHAM), Gloucestershire (THREE CHOIRS), Berkshire (STANLAKE PARK) and Cornwall (CAMEL VALLEY). 2007 and 2008 were both difficult years for growers, with poor flowering conditions leading to small harvests. What was picked should be good, though.

GEORGIA Georgia faces many challenges – lack of regulation, resistance to change, counterfeiting, and a recent ban on exports to Russia, its biggest market – but its diverse climates (from subtropical to moderate continental) and soils could produce every style imaginable. The tourist industry is vibrant and helping introduce Georgian wines to a wider audience. International and indigenous varieties abound; the peppery, powerful red Saperavi could be a world-beater. Most wine is still pretty rustic, but investment is beginning to have an effect, with GWS (Georgian Wines & Spirits Company, 75% owned by Pernod Ricard) leading the way.

GREECE Sadly, the Athens Olympics in 2004 didn't make quite the impact for the country's wines as had been hoped, although their reputation, their distribution and their sales continue to improve. The new generation of winemakers and grape growers, many of them trained in France, Australia or California, have a clear vision of the flavours they want to achieve and their wines are modern but marvellously original too. Polarization between cheap bulk and expensive boutique wines continues, but large companies such as Boutari, Kourtakis and Tsantalis are upping the quality stakes and flavours improve every vintage. More vineyard and marketing work – many labels are still difficult to understand – is needed. International plantings have led to surprising and successful blends with indigenous varieties such as the red Agiorgitiko, Limnio and Xynomavro, and white Assyrtiko (often blended with Sémillon), Moschofilero and Roditis. Quality areas: Naousa and Nemea for reds, SAMOS for sweet Muscats, Patras for dessert Mavrodaphne. Wineries to watch include: Aidarinis, Argyros, ANTONOPOULOS, Gentilini, GEROVASSILIOU, Hatzimichali, Kyr Yanni, Domaine Costa LAZARIDI, Mercouri, Papaïoannou, Strofilia and Tselepos.

HUNGARY Hungary makes remarkably good whites, improving reds and outstanding sweet wines, and has joined the EU, yet few of us have much idea about her as a wine country. Stringent regulations and investment/advice from Australian and western European companies and consultants – for example at the BALATONBOGLÁR winery – have put Hungary back on the international wine map. There is renewed interest in native varieties such as Furmint and Irsai Olivér for whites, Kékfrankos (Blaufränkisch) and Kadarka (the traditional grape used in BULL'S BLOOD) for reds, and top Hungarian winemakers – Akos Kamocsay (at HILLTOP), Vilmos Thummerer and others – are now a solid force. But price and reputation remain low and many vineyards are being abandoned out of desperation. TOKAJI in particular has yet to develop the world-class reputation its wines deserve.

INDIA India's climate is generally unsuitable for wine production: only a small percentage of the 50,000ha (123,500 acres) of vines is used for wine; both international varieties and ancient Indian ones, such as Arkesham and Arkavati, are planted. Wine consumption is increasing rapidly and with punitive import duties on foreign bottles the potential for growth is evident. CHATEAU INDAGE, with vineyards in the Maharashtra hills east of Mumbai (Bombay), dominates the market and produces still and sparkling wines. Sula Vineyards is leading the way with screwcaps on all its wines – bright, fresh, positively cool-climate flavours are the result – and is planning to bring its area under vines up to 650ha (1600 acres). Advice from international wine guru Michel Rolland put Grover Vineyards in Bangalore on the map. There'll be a lot more in the future.

ISRAEL Fine wine is being made in cooler regions – Upper Galilee, Golan Heights and Judean Hills. Bordeaux blends based on Cabernet Sauvignon and delicious dessert wines can be top class. The future may lie in Mediterranean varieties. Shiraz is successful wherever planted, and there are some good-quality old-vine Carignan and Petite Sirah. Viticulture is technologically advanced and wineries tend to be up-to-date. The best wines are produced by Dom. du CASTEL, YATIR, and Yarden, the top label of the Golan Heights Winery. Carmel's Upper Galilee wines represent quality and value. All these wineries are kosher, which shows this designation need not affect quality. Israel's best non-kosher wineries are Clos de Gat and Margalit.

Kosher wine, necessary for observant Jews and usually suitable for vegans and vegetarians, can be genuinely good. Regular winemaking methods are used, but there has to be a religious Jewish workforce and yeasts, cleaning and fining materials have to be certified as kosher. There are kosher wineries in many other parts of the world besides Israel: for example Covenant, Hagafen and Herzog in California. Several top French wineries – such as LAURENT-PERRIER, Ch. LÉOVILLE-POYFERRÉ, Ch. PONTET-CANET and Ch. VALANDRAUD – and some big brands such as SKALLI-FORTANT DE FRANCE and MOUTON-CADET make a kosher cuvée.

JAPAN As long as there is confusion between which wines are 100% locally grown and which are multi-country blends (which most are), Japanese wines, especially those made from indigenous varieties such as Koshu, will never really be appreciated by an international audience. One has to assume that the present situation suits most producers, who sell almost all their wines locally. However, the Japanese are increasingly interested in wine, and their national wine show now attracts entries from around the world. Despite humid conditions, wine is produced in almost every province. SUNTORY is in the best region, Yamanashi, and is expanding its vineyards. Other main players are Mercian, Sapporo, Manns and the unpromising-sounding Domaine Sogga.

LEBANON Very good reds with the full fruit of the Lebanese sun and spiciness of the eastern Mediterranean/Middle East. Most wineries lie in the Bekaa Valley. CHATEAU MUSAR, for years unchallenged, now has some quality rivals: Ch. Kefraya and Ch. Ksara have made good wine for a while; they are joined by Massaya, Clos St Thomas, Dom. Wardy and Dom. des Tourelles. Promising new boutique wineries include Karam and Ch. Belle-Vue.

LUXEMBOURG With one of the world's highest levels of wine consumption per capita, very little wine is exported. Co-operatives dominate here and quality is about what you would expect. Plantings of Elbling and Rivaner (Müller-Thurgau) are in decline, and are being replaced with quality varietals such as Riesling, Pinot Noir, Chardonnay and Gewürztraminer. *Crémant* (sparkling) wines continue to increase in quality and popularity.

MALTA The first impression of Malta is of an arid rocky island squeezed full of people and with barely enough soil to grow basic food crops. And it *never* seems to rain. Well, it does rain, and its limestone rock is able to absorb and hold a significant amount of water in reserve. Even so, water is scarce, but the vine doesn't need much – often the morning and evening dews from the sea breezes is enough to keep it going. Most wines used to be made from imported Italian grapes, and they weren't bad. But, especially on the small island of Gozo – famous locally for being green, but green is a relative term in Malta – serious vineyards are being developed and attractive wines are now available from 100% Maltese grapes. They're good, but you can taste the sun.

MEXICO In the far north-west of Mexico, in Baja California, some good reds are made by L A CETTO as well as by smaller companies such as Monte Xanic and Casa de Piedra. In the rest of the country, only high-altitude areas such as the Parras Valley and Zacatecas have the potential for quality wines. Casa Madero, in the Parras Valley, has some success with Cabernet Sauvignon. Other promising grape varieties include Nebbiolo, Petite Sirah, Tempranillo, Zinfandel and Barbera, with Viognier and Chardonnay also planted.

MOLDOVA Moldovan winegrowers suffered a major setback in 2006 when their main export market, Russia, banned imports of their wines. Standards of winemaking and equipment leave much to be desired, but fruit quality is good, and international players, including PENFOLDS and winemakers Jacques Lurton, Hugh Ryman and Alain Thiénot, have worked with local wineries. However, chaotic social conditions have led to many attempts being abandoned.

MONTENEGRO This red-wine-dominated part of the former Yugoslavia shows some potential in the beefy Vranac grape with its bitter cherry flavours – but the worst wines are really poor.

MOROCCO Known for big, sweet-fruited reds that once found a ready blending market in France. France is still the biggest export market, but the wines have improved dramatically since the 1990s and domestic consumption is increasing, especially among young urban professionals. Massive investment by Castel Frères kickstarted the renaissance, and quality is on the rise at Morocco's leading producer, Celliers de Meknès. Domaine el Baraka and Domaine Larroque are promising, and French producers Bernard Magrez, Gerard Depardieu and Alain GRAILLOT are making some good wines here, specially from Syrah.

NETHERLANDS The vineyard area is expanding rapidly: it is estimated that by 2010 there will be around 200ha (500 acres), in the hands of more than 100 commercial growers, most of whom sell all their wines locally. There are vineyards in most provinces, but the best are in the southern part of the country, in the rolling hills of Limburg. Chardonnay is the most promising grape variety. Growers have set themselves the additional challenge of living up to Holland's 'green' image, and are looking into what can be achieved organically.

ROMANIA The huge vineyard area has declined somewhat in recent years as hybrid grape varieties are pulled up, to be replanted with *Vitis vinifera* grapes such as Pinot Noir, Cabernet Sauvignon, Merlot and the native Feteasca Negra for reds, Pinot Gris and Chardonnay for whites. International-backed ventures such as Cramele Recas, Halewood (Prahova Valley) and Carl Reh are a sign of the mini-revolution, but challenges remain. The appellation system is of limited value, although Dealul Mare, Murfatlar and Cotnari all have ancient reputations. Accession to the EU in 2007 has done little to help the fortunes of Romanian growers as there is now a shortage of labour to work the vineyards and there has been an increase in the amount of wine being imported into Romania from Spain and Italy.

SLOVAKIA The eastern part of the old Czechoslovakia, with its cool-climate vineyards, is dominated by white varieties – Pinot Blanc, Riesling, Grüner Veltliner, Irsai Olivér – with the occasional fruity Frankovka (Blaufränkisch) red. Western investment at the state winery at Nitra and smaller wineries such as Gbelce and Hurbanovo near the Hungarian border at Komárno, is rapidly improving the quality.

SLOVENIA Many of the old Yugoslav Federation's best vineyards are here. Potential is considerable, and some interesting wines are emerging, with whites generally better than reds. A simplified appellation system and the increasing popularity of Slovenia as a holiday and second-home region should increase availability. On the Italian border, Brda and Vipava have go-ahead co-operatives, and Kraski Teran is a red wine of repute. The Movia range, from the Kristancic family, looks promising.

SWITZERLAND Fendant (Chasselas) is the main grape for spritzy but neutral whites from the VALAIS and VAUD. Like the fruity DÔLE reds, they are best drunk very young. German-speaking cantons produce whites from Müller-Thurgau and mostly light reds and rosés from Pinot Noir (Blauburgunder); top producers, such as Daniel GANTENBEIN, make more powerful versions. Italian-speaking TICINO concentrates on Merlots, which have been increasingly impressive since 2000. Serious wines, especially in Valais, use Syrah, Chardonnay, Marsanne and traditional varieties like

Amigne and Petite Arvine. Indeed, the traditional varieties, of which there are many, are undergoing a revival. Pinot Noir from the Valais is greatly improved. See also NEUCHÂTEL.

THAILAND I first tasted Thai wine a few years ago: it was a light and fruity red and impressive for what I thought of as subtropical conditions. Since then, serious Shiraz and Chenin Blanc wines have shown that Thailand's high-altitude vineyards are capable of some tasty offerings. The Thai Wine Association is attempting to regulate the composition and quality of Thai wines and the once-common practice of blending local and imported wines (without declaring it on the label) is lessening.

TUNISIA Ancient wine traditions have had an injection of new life from international investment, and results so far are encouraging. Tourism soaks up most of the production and little is exported.

TURKEY The world's fourth-largest grape producer, but only 2–4% ends up as wine. Wine growers have a difficult time in Turkey because of a traditional antipathy to wine; the local market prefers to drink the anise-flavoured spirit raki, and the Muslim anti-alcohol influence is growing. Local varieties are Bogazkere and Okugozu (for reds) and Narince (white). Kavaklidere is the best producer using local varieties, while Doluca is more modern in style; Kayra has the resources to match them. There's an encouraging number of new boutique wineries: the most promising are Buyulubag and Corvus.

UKRAINE The Crimea's vineyards are the most important, producing hearty reds, sweet and sparkling wines; there's a surprisingly good sweet red sparkler, and sweet Muscatels are considered to be a cause for national pride, especially the Massandra brand. The Odessa region is successful with its sparkling wines, the three best-known facilities being the Inkerman winery, Novyi Svet and Zolota Balka. Future European investment is said to be in the pipeline, so let's see.

A–Z

OF WINES, PRODUCERS, GRAPES & WINE REGIONS

In the following pages there are over
1600 entries covering the world's top wines, as well as leading
producers, main wine regions and grape
varieties, followed on page 316 by a glossary of wine terms
and classifications.

On page 4 you will find a full explanation of
How to Use the A–Z. On page 325 there is an index
of all wine producers in the book, to help you find the
world's best wines.

AALTO *Ribera del Duero DO, Castilla y León, Spain* Former VEGA SICILIA winemaker Mariano García and ex-RIBERA DEL DUERO boss Javier Zaccagnini created this winery in 1999. From the outset, they have challenged top Spanish producers with their dense but elegant reds, Aalto★★ and old vines cuvée Aalto PS★★. Best years: (2006) 05 04 **03 01 00 99**.

ABRUZZO-MOLISE *Italy* Abruzzo, which winewise embraces the small region to the south called Molise, stretches from the Adriatic coast to the mountainous Apennine interior. White Trebbiano d'Abruzzo DOC is usually dry and neutral; the MONTEPULCIANO D'ABRUZZO DOC is generally a strapping, peppery red of real character, but increasingly a rosé called Cerasuolo. Overproduction has been a problem, but quality is on the increase with new vineyard training techniques and the establishment of new DOCs. My favourites are the ripe but balanced flavours of Illuminati's reds.

ACACIA *Carneros AVA, California, USA* Leading producer of Chardonnay and Pinot Noir from CARNEROS. The regular Carneros Chardonnay★ is restrained but attractive. Pinot Noirs include Carneros★ and the superb Beckstoffer Vineyard★★ – the wines have moved to a riper, meatier style of late. Best years: (Pinot Noir) 2007 06 05 **03 02 01 00 99 97 96 95**.

ACHAVAL-FERRER *Mendoza, Argentina* A former garage winery created in 1998, and now one of Argentina's most sought-after labels. 80-year-old vines in the La Consulta area of UCO VALLEY produce Finca Altamira★★★, a Malbec bursting with personality. Also superb single-vineyard Malbecs Bella Vista★★★ and Mirador★★★ and more approachable red blend Quimera★. Best years: 2006 **05 04 03 02 01**.

JEAN-BAPTISTE ADAM *Alsace AC, Alsace, France* Long-established family vineyard in Ammerschwihr with a reputation for luscious, classically perfumed Gewurztraminer★★ from the newly created Kaefferkopf Grand Cru, as well as concentrated Riesling★★, herbaceous Pinot Gris★ and an exciting Pinot Noir★★ given 18 months in oak. Best years: (Kaefferkopf Gewurztraminer) (2008) 07 **05 04 02 01 00 99 98 97 95**.

TIM ADAMS *Clare Valley, South Australia* Important maker of fine, traditional wine from his own and bought-in local grapes. Classic dry Riesling★★, oaky Semillon★★, and rich, opulent Shiraz★★ (sometimes ★★★) and Cabernet★★. The botrytis Semillon★ can be super, The Fergus★★ is a glorious Grenache-based blend, and minty, peppery Aberfeldy Shiraz★★★ is a remarkable, at times unnerving, mouthful of brilliance from 100-year-old vines. Best years: (Aberfeldy Shiraz) (2008) 06 05 04 03 02 01 **00 99 98 96 94**.

Tim Adams

2003
RIESLING
CLARE VALLEY
WINE OF AUSTRALIA FROM CLARE VALLEY
750mL 12.0%Vol

ADELAIDE HILLS *South Australia* Small, exciting region 30 minutes' drive from Adelaide. High altitude affords a cool, moist climate ideal for fine table wines and superb sparkling wine. Consistently good Sauvignon Blanc and Chardonnay, promising Pinot Noir and increasingly exciting fleshy Shiraz. Best producers: Ashton Hills★, Bird in Hand★, HENSCHKE★★ Longview, Nepenthe★★, PETALUMA★★, RIPOSTE★, SHAW & SMITH★★, Geoff WEAVER★★.

ADELSHEIM VINEYARD *Willamette Valley AVA, Oregon, USA* Over the past 3 decades, Adelsheim has established a reputation for excellent, generally unfiltered, Pinot Noir – especially cherry-scented Elizabeth's Reserve★

and Bryan Creek Vineyard★ – and for rich Chardonnay Caitlin's Reserve★. Also a bright, minerally Pinot Gris★. Best years: (Elizabeth's Reserve) (2007) 06 05 **04 03 02**.

AGLIANICO DEL VULTURE DOC *Basilicata, Italy* Red wine from the Aglianico grape grown on the steep slopes of Mt Vulture. Despite the zone's location almost on the same latitude as Naples, the harvest here is sometimes later than in BAROLO, 750km (470 miles) to the north-west, because the Aglianico grape ripens very late at altitude. The best wines are structured, complex and long-lived. Best producers: Basilium★, Bisceglia★, D'Angelo★★, Elena Fucci★, Cantine del Notaio★★, Paternoster★★, Tenuta del Portale, Le Querce★, Consorzio Viticoltori Associati del Vulture (Carpe Diem★). Best years: (2008) (07) (06) 05 **04 03 01 00 98 97**.

AHR *Germany* The Ahr Valley is a small (545ha/1345-acre) mainly red wine region south of Bonn. Chief grape varieties are the Spätburgunder (Pinot Noir) and (Blauer) Portugieser. Adeneuer, Deutzerhof★, Meyer-Näkel★★ and Stodden★ are the best of a growing band of serious producers.

AIRÉN Spain's – and indeed the world's – most planted white grape can make fresh, modern, but generally neutral-flavoured wines, with some eye-opening exceptions, such as Ercavio's stunning old-vines white from Toledo. Airén is grown all over the centre and south of Spain, especially in La MANCHA, VALDEPEÑAS and ANDALUCIA (where it's called Lairén).

ALBAN *San Luis Obispo County, California, USA* Based in the cool Arroyo Grande district of Edna Valley, RHONE specialist John Alban first produced Viognier in 1991. Today he offers 2 bottlings: Estate★★ and Central Coast★. Roussanne★★ is laden with honey notes. Syrah is represented by 3 bottlings: Reva★★★, Lorraine★★ and Seymour's Vineyard★★. Intense Grenache★★ and Pandora★★, a blend of about 60% Grenache, 40% Syrah, round out the line-up. These are some of America's purest expressions of Rhône varietals, despite some extremely high alcohol levels. Best years: (Syrah) 2006 **05 04 03 02 01 00 99**.

ALBARIÑO Possibly Spain's most characterful white grape. It is a speciality of RIAS BAIXAS in Galicia in Spain's rainy north-west and, as Alvarinho, in Portugal's VINHO VERDE region. When well made, Albariño wines have fascinating flavours of apricot, peach, grapefruit and Muscat grapes, refreshingly high acidity, highish alcohol – and unrefreshingly high prices. The ever-present danger to quality is excessive yields.

ALENQUER DOC *Estremadura, Portugal* Maritime-influenced hills north of Lisbon, producing wines from (mostly) local grape varieties such as Castelão (Periquita) and Trincadeira, but also from Cabernet, Syrah and Chardonnay. Many wines are simply labelled ESTREMADURA. Best producers: Quinta do Carneiro, Quinta de Chocapalha★, Quinta da Cortezia, Quinta do Monte d'Oiro★★, Quinta de Pancas, Casa SANTOS LIMA★. Best years: (reds) 2007 **05 04 03 01 00**.

ALENTEJO *Portugal* A large chunk of southern Portugal south and east of Lisbon and, along with the DOURO, one of Portugal's fastest improving red wine regions. Potential is far from realized, but already some of Portugal's finest reds come from here. Vinho Regional wines are labelled Alentejano.

59

Best producers: (reds) Azamor (Petit Verdot★), BACALHOA★ (Tinto da Ânfora Grande Escolha★★), Borba co-op★, CORTES DE CIMA★, Dona Maria★, ESPORAO★★, Fita Preta J M da FONSECA★, Fundação Eugénio de Almeida (Cartuxa★, Pera-Manca★★), Paulo Laureano Vinus★, MALHADINHA NOVA★★, Monte da Penha, Mouchão★★, Quinta do Mouro★, Francisco Nunes Garcia, João Portugal RAMOS★★, SOGRAPE★, Quinta da Terrugem★★/ALIANCA. Best years: (reds) (2008) **05 04 01 00**.

ALEXANDER VALLEY AVA *Sonoma County, California, USA* Important AVA, centred on the northern Russian River, which is fairly warm, with only patchy summer fog. Cabernet Sauvignon is highly successful here with lovely, juicy fruit not marred by an excess of tannin. Chardonnay may also be good but is often overproduced and lacking in ripe, round flavours. Merlot and old-vine Zinfandel can be outstanding from hillside vineyards. Best producers: Alexander Valley Vineyards★, CLOS DU BOIS★, De Lorimier★, GEYSER PEAK★, JORDAN★, Murphy-Goode★★, SEGHESIO★★, SILVER OAK★★, SIMI★, Trentadue★★. See also RUSSIAN RIVER VALLEY AVA, SONOMA COUNTY. Best years: (reds) 2005 04 03 **02 01 99 97 95 91 90**.

ALGARVE *Portugal* Holiday region with mostly red wines in 4 DOCs: Lagoa, Lagos, Portimão and Tavira. Look out for reds and rosés from Sir Cliff Richard's Vida Nova, Quinta do Barranco Longo and Morgado da Torre.

CAVES ALIANÇA *Beira Litoral, Portugal* Aliança makes crisp, fresh white and soft, approachable red BAIRRADAS★. Also made, either from its own vineyards or bought-in grapes or wines, are reds from the DAO (Quinta da Garrida★) and ALENTEJO (Quinta da Terrugem★★). Quinta dos Quatro Ventos★★ from the DOURO is the top red, a blend of Tinta Roriz Touriga Franca and Touriga Nacional.

ALIGOTÉ French grape, found mainly in Burgundy, whose basic characteristic is a lemony tartness. It can make extremely refreshing wine especially from old vines, but is generally rather dull and lean. The best comes from the village of Bouzeron in the COTE CHALONNAISE, where Aligoté has its own appellation. Occasionally also found in Moldova and Bulgaria. Drink young. Best producers: (Burgundy) M BOUZEREAU, COCHE-DURY★, A Ente★, J-H Goisot★, D MORTET★, TOLLOT-BEAUT, Villaine★.

ALLEGRINI *Valpolicella DOC, Veneto, Italy* High-profile producer in VALPOLICELLA Classico, making single-vineyard La Grola★★ and Palazzo della Torre★★. These are now under the regional Veronese IGT – originally to distance them from the low regard in which much of Valpolicella was held until recently. These, and the barrique-aged La Poja★★★ (made solely with the Corvina grape), show the great potential that exists for Valpolicella as a table wine. Outstanding AMARONE★★★ and RECIOTO Giovanni Allegrini★★. Best years: (Amarone) (2008) (07) 06 **04 03 01 00 97 95**.

THIERRY ALLEMAND *Cornas AC, Rhône Valley, France* Thierry Allemand has 5ha (12 acres) of high-quality hillside vines. He keeps yields low, use little sulphur and seeks to make wines with clear fruit and precise tannins. He produces 2 unfiltered expressions of CORNAS at its intense and powerful best: Chaillot★★ is marginally the lighter; Reynard★★ is from a parcel of very old Syrah. Also makes St-Péray. Best years: (Reynard) 2007 06 05 04 03 **01 00 99 98 96 95 94 91 90**.

ALLENDE *Rioja DOCa, Rioja, Spain* One of the most admired new names in RIOJA making a mix of single-vineyard (*pago*) and high-quality blends. Scented, uncompromisingly concentrated reds include Aurus★★, Calvario★★ and fresh, vibrant Allende★★. There is also a marvellous, scented white★★. Best years: (reds) (2006) 05 04 **03 02 01 00 99 98**.

ALMAVIVA★★★ *Maipo, Chile* State-of-the-art joint venture between CONCHA Y TORO and the Baron Philippe de Rothschild company (see MOUTON-ROTHSCHILD), located in MAIPO Valley's Tocornal vineyard at the foot of the Andes. A memorably powerful red from old Cabernet Sauvignon vines planted in alluvial, stony soils; it can be drunk at 5 years but should age for 10. Best years: 2005 **04 03 02 01**.

ALOXE-CORTON AC *Côte de Beaune, Burgundy, France* An important village at the northern end of the CÔTE DE BEAUNE producing mostly red wines from Pinot Noir. Its reputation is based on the 2 Grands Crus, CORTON (mainly red) and CORTON-CHARLEMAGNE (white only). Other vineyards in Aloxe-Corton used to be a source of tasty, good-value Burgundy, but nowadays the reds rarely exhibit their former characteristic blend of ripe fruit and appetizing savoury dryness. Almost all the white wine is classified as Grand Cru. Best producers: d'Ardhuy★, CHANDON DE BRIAILLES★, M Chapuis★, Marius Delarche★, Dubreuil-Fontaine★, Follin-Arbelet★, Camille Giroud★, Antonin Guyon★, JADOT★, Mallard, Rapet★, Comte Senard★, TOLLOT-BEAUT★★. Best years: (reds) (2008) 07 06 05 **03 02 99 97 96 95**.

DOM. JEAN-MICHEL ALQUIER *Faugères AC, Languedoc, France* This estate shows how good FAUGERES can be. Barrel aging of all wines, and low yields for the special cuvées, Les Bastides★★ and La Maison Jaune★. Also a good white Roussanne-Marsanne blend. Best years: (Bastides) 2007 06 05 **04 03 01 00**.

ALSACE AC *Alsace, France* Tucked away on France's eastern border with Germany, Alsace produces some of the most individual white wines of all, rich in aroma and full of ripe, distinctive flavours. Alsace is almost as far north as CHAMPAGNE, but its climate is considerably warmer and drier. Wines from the 51 best vineyard sites can call themselves Alsace Grand Cru AC and account for 4% of production; quality regulations are more stringent and many individual crus have further tightened the rules. Riesling, Muscat, Gewurztraminer and Pinot Gris are generally considered the finest varieties in Alsace and were originally the only ones permitted for Grand Cru wines, although Sylvaner is now legal in Zotzenberg and further changes will follow. Pinot Blanc can produce good wines too. Reds from Pinot Noir are improving fitfully. Alsace labels its wines by grape variety and, apart from the Edelzwicker blends and CREMANT D'ALSACE fizz, nearly all Alsace wines are made from a single variety, although blends from certain Grand Cru sites, such as Altenberg de Bergheim and Kaefferkopf, are now recognized. Medium-dry or sweeter wines are now, as of the 2004 vintage, labelled *moelleux*. Vendange Tardive means 'late-harvest'; the grapes (Riesling, Muscat, Pinot Gris or Gewurztraminer) are picked late and almost overripe, giving higher sugar levels and potentially more intense flavours. The resulting wines are usually rich and mouthfilling and often need 5 years or more to show their personality. Sélection de Grains Nobles – late-harvest wines made from superripe grapes of the same varieties – are invariably sweet and usually affected by noble rot; they are among Alsace's finest, but are very expensive to produce (and to buy). Best producers: J-B ADAM★★, Lucien Albrecht★, Barmès-Buecher★, J Becker, Léon

Beyer★, P BLANCK★★, Bott-Geyl★★, A Boxler★, Ernest Burn★★, DEISS★★★
Dirler-Cadé★★, Pierre Frick★, Rémy Gresser★, HUGEL★, Josmeyer★★
Kientzler★, Klur, Kreydenweiss★★, Seppi Landmann★, A MANN★★, Meyer
Fonné, Mittnacht Frères, MURE★★, Ostertag★★, Pfaffenheim co-op, Ribeauvill
co-op, Rieflé★, Rolly Gassmann★, Martin Schaetzel, Charles Schléret
Schlumberger★, SCHOFFIT★★, Louis Sipp, Bruno Sorg★, Marc Tempe
TRIMBACH★★, TURCKHEIM co-op★, WEINBACH★★, Paul Zinck★, ZIND
HUMBRECHT★★★. Best years: 2007 **05 04 02 01 00 98 97 96 95**.

ALTARE Barolo DOCG, Piedmont, Italy Elio Altare crafts some of the mos
stunning of Alba's wines: BARBERA D'ALBA★, Dolcetto d'Alba★★ and eve
finer BAROLO Vigneto Arborina★★★ and Barolo Brunate★★★. Thoug
he is a professed modernist, his wines are intense, full and structure
while young, but with clearly discernible fruit flavours, thanks largely t
tiny yields. He also makes 3 barrique-aged wines under the LANGHE DOC
Arborina★★★ (Nebbiolo), Larigi★★★ (Barbera) and La Villa★★
(Nebbiolo-Barbera). Altare is one of several producers that mak
L'Insieme★★ (a Nebbiolo-Cabernet-Barbera blend). Best years: (Barolc
(2008) (07) (06) 04 **03 01 00 99 98 96 95**.

ALTO ADIGE Trentino-Alto Adige, Italy A largely German-speaking province
originally called Südtirol. The region-wide DOC covers 25 types of wine
Reds range from light and perfumed when made from the ubiquitous (bu
diminishing in importance) Schiava grape, to fruity and more structured fror
the Cabernets or Merlot, to dark and velvety if Lagrein is used. Excess oak ca
mar their delightful fruit. Whites include Chardonnay, Gewürztraminer
Pinot Bianco, Pinot Grigio, Riesling and Sauvignon, and are usually fresh an
fragrant. There is also some good sparkling wine. Much of the wine come
from well-run co-ops, although there are some excellent individual producer
Sub-zones include the previously independent DOCs of Santa Maddalena an
Terlano. Best producers: (individual) Abbazia di Novacella★, Casòn Hirschprunn★
Peter Dipoli★★, Egger-Ramer★, Franz Gojer★, Franz Haas★★, Haderburg★★
Hofstätter★★, Kränzl★, LAGEDER★★, Laimburg★, Loacker★, Josephus Mayr★, Mur
Gries★★, Josef Niedermayr★, Ignaz Niedriest★, Plattner Waldgries★, Peter Pligε
Kuenhof★★, Hans Rottensteiner★, Heinrich Rottensteiner★, TIEFENBRUNNER★★
Elena Walch★, Baron Widmann★; (co-ops) Caldaro★, Colterenzio★, Girlar
Cornaiano★, Gries★★, Nals-Margreid★★, Prima & Nuova/Erste & Neue★, San Michel
Appiano★★, Santa Maddalena★, Terlano★★, Termeno★★. See also TRENTINO.

ALTOS LAS HORMIGAS Mendoza, Argentina A rising star in Argentina
founded in 1995. Altos Las Hormigas Malbec is an opulent example c
the grape, while Reserva Viña Hormigas★ is packed with pure, dens
blackberry and cherry flavours. Colonia Las Liebres is a delightful, juic
Bonarda. Best years: (Viña Hormigas) 2006 **05 04 03 02**.

ALVARINHO See ALBARINO.

CASTELLO DI AMA Chianti Classico DOCG, Tuscany, Italy Model estate c
CHIANTI CLASSICO, with outstanding Chianti Classico★★, plus single
vineyard Riservas★★★ (Bellavista and La Casuccia). L'Apparita★★★ i
one of Italy's best Merlots. Also good Chardonnay Al Poggio★
Best years: (Chianti Classico) (2008) (07) 06 **04 03 01 00 99 97 95**.

AMARONE DELLA VALPOLICELLA DOC Veneto, Italy A brilliantl
individual, bitter-sweet style of VALPOLICELLA made from grapes shrivelle
on mats for months after harvest. The wine, which can reach 16% c
alcohol and more, differs from the sweet RECIOTO DELLA VALPOLICELLA i

that it is fermented to near-dryness, the grapes having been left on the mats a month or two less. Wines from the Classico zone are generally the best, with exceptions from DAL FORNO, Corte Sant'Alda and Roccolo Grassi. **Best producers:** Accordini★★, ALLEGRINI★★★, Bertani★★, Brigaldara★, Brunelli★, BUSSOLA★★★, Michele Castellani★★, Corte Sant'Alda★★, Valentina Cubi★★, DAL FORNO★★★, Guerrieri-Rizzardi★★, MASI★★, QUINTARELLI★★★, Le Ragose★★, Roccolo Grassi★, Le Salette★★, Serègo Alighieri★, Speri★★, Tedeschi★★, Tommasi★, Villa Monteleone★★, VIVIANI★★, Zenato★★. **Best years:** (2008) 06 **04 03 01 00 97**.

AMIGNE Ancient Swiss grape variety that is virtually limited to 40ha (100 acres) around Vétroz in the VALAIS. The wine has an earthy, nutty intensity and benefits from a few years' aging. **Best producers:** Bonvin, A Fontannaz, Jean-René Germanier, Vieux Moulin.

DOM. DE L'ANCIENNE CURE *Bergerac AC and Monbazillac AC, South-West France* Christian Roche exemplifies the best of BERGERAC, with textured elegant reds★, crisp dry whites★ and balanced, luscious sweet MONBAZILLAC★★. Top cuvées L'Abbaye★ and L'Extase★★ for both reds and whites. **Best years:** (reds) (2008) 06 **05** 04.

ANDALUCÍA *Spain* Fortified wines, or wines naturally so strong in alcohol that they don't need fortifying, are the speciality of this southern stretch of Spain. Apart from sherry (JEREZ Y MANZANILLA DO), there are the lesser, sherry-like wines of Condado de Huelva DO and MONTILLA-MORILES DO, and the rich, sweet wines of MÁLAGA DO. These regions also make some modern but bland dry whites; the best are from Condado de Huelva. Red wine is now appearing from producers in Málaga, Cádiz, Seville, Granada and Almería provinces.

ANDERSON VALLEY AVA *California, USA* Small appellation (less than 245ha/600 acres) in western MENDOCINO COUNTY that produces brilliant wines. Most vineyards are within 15 miles of the Pacific Ocean, making this one of the coldest AVAs in California. Delicate Pinot Noirs and Chardonnays, and one of the few places in the state for first-rate Gewürztraminer and Riesling. Superb sparkling wines with healthy acidity and creamy yeast are highlights as well. **Best producers:** Brutocao★, Greenwood Ridge★, HANDLEY★★, Lazy Creek★, NAVARRO★★★, ROEDERER ESTATE★★, SCHARFFENBERGER CELLARS★★.

ANDREW WILL WINERY *Washington State, USA* Winemaker Chris Camarda makes delicious blends of BORDEAUX varietals from a range of older WASHINGTON vineyards. At the top are the complex Champoux Vineyard★★★ and the opulent Ciel du Cheval★★★. Wine from the estate vineyard, Two Blondes Vineyard★, shows young vine character. Sorella★★, a blend of the best barrels each vintage, can be outstanding with age. **Best years:** (reds) (2007) 06 05 **04 03 01 00**.

CH. ANGÉLUS★★★ *St-Émilion Grand Cru AC, 1er Grand Cru Classé, Bordeaux, France* One of the best-known ST-EMILION Grands Crus, with an energetic owner and talented winemaker. Rich, dark, spicy, modern St-Émilion. Promoted to Premier Grand Classé in 1996 and on top form. **Best years:** 2007 06 05 04 **03 02 01 00 99 98 96 95 92 90 89 88 85**.

MARQUIS D'ANGERVILLE *Volnay, Côte de Beaune, Burgundy, France* The late Jacques d'Angerville for half a century produced an exemplary range o elegant Premiers Crus from VOLNAY, the subtlest of the COTE DE BEAUNE' red wine appellations. Quality is, clearly, improving further. Clos de Ducs and Taillepieds are ★★★. All should be kept for at least 5 years Best years: (top reds) (2008) 07 06 05 03 02 99 **98 97 96 95 91 90.**

CH. D'ANGLUDET★ *Margaux AC, Haut-Médoc, Bordeaux, France* This English-owned château makes a gentle, unobtrusive but generally attractive red that is never overpriced and has been gaining weight in recent vintages. It ages well for at least a decade. Best years: 2006 05 04 0: **02 00 98 96 95 94 90 89 88.**

ANJOU BLANC AC *Loire Valley, France* Ill-defined AC; ranges from bone dry to sweet, from excellent to dreadful; the best are dry. Up to 20% Chardonnay or Sauvignon can be added, but many of the leading producers – some preferring the Vin de Pays du VAL DE LOIRE label – use 100% Chenin from top sites once dedicated to sweet COTEAUX DU LAYON Best producers: M Angeli/Sansonnière★★, S Bernaudeau, des Chesnaies★ P Delesvaux★, Fesles★, L Herbel, Richard Leroy★, Montgilet/V Lebreton Mosse★, Ogereau★, PIERRE-BISE★, Pithon-Paillé★, RICHOU★, Roulerie★ Soucherie★. Best years: (top wines) 2008 **07 06 05 04 03 02.**

ANJOU ROUGE AC *Loire Valley, France* Anjou reds (from Cabernet Sauvignon and Franc or Pineau d'Aunis) are increasingly successful Usually fruity, easy-drinking wine, with less tannin than ANJOU-VILLAGES Wines made from Gamay are sold as Anjou Gamay. Best producers Brizé★, B Courault, Dom. F L★, PIERRE-BISE (Anjou Gamay), Putille, RICHOU★ Roulerie. Best years: (top wines) (2008) **06 05 04 03 02 01.**

ANJOU-VILLAGES AC *Loire Valley, France* Superior Anjou red from 46 villages, and made from Cabernet Franc and Cabernet Sauvignon Anjou-Villages Brissac's schist soils produce particularly firmly structured wines which reward aging. Best producers: Bablut/Daviau★ P Baudouin, Brizé★, de Conquessac, P Delesvaux★, Deux Arcs, Montgilet V Lebreton★, de la Motte, Ogereau★, PIERRE-BISE★★, Putille★, RICHOU★★ Rochelles★, la Varière/Beaujeau. Best years: 2006 **05 04 03 02 01 97 96.**

ANSELMI *Veneto, Italy* Roberto Anselmi (with PIEROPAN) has shown that once much-maligned SOAVE can have personality when carefully made Using ultra-modern methods he has honed the fruit flavours of his San Vincenzo★★ and Capitel Foscarino★★ and introduced small-barrel aging for single-vineyard Capitel Croce★★ and luscious, SAUTERNES-like I Capitelli★★ (sometimes ★★★), as well as the Cabernet Sauvignon Realdà. All sold under the regional IGT rather than Soave DOC. Best years: (I Capitelli) (2008) (07) **05 04 03 01 00.**

ANTINORI *Tuscany, Italy* World-famous Florentine family firm that has been involved in wine since 1385, but it is Piero Antinori, the current head, who has made the Antinori name synonymous with quality and innovation CHIANTI CLASSICO wines like Badia a Passignano★ (Riserva★★), Pèppoli★ and Tenute Marchese Antinori Riserva★★ are consistently good, but i was Antinori's development of the SUPER-TUSCAN concept of superior wine outside the DOC that launched a quality revolution during the 1970s TIGNANELLO★★ and, especially, SOLAIA★★★ can be great wines. Othe Tuscan wines include VINO NOBILE La Braccesca★★, Bramasole Syrah from Cortona DOC, BRUNELLO DI MONTALCINO Pian delle Vigne★★ and BOLGHERI Guado al Tasso★★ (a Cabernet-Merlot blend; also a Vermentino white) Interests further afield include PRUNOTTO in Piedmont, Tormaresca in

PUGLIA, FRANCIACORTA's Montenisa, Bátaapáti in Hungary and Albis in Chile. A joint venture with CHATEAU STE MICHELLE in the USA acquired STAG'S LEAP WINE CELLARS in 2007. Best years: (reds) (2008) (07) 06 **04 03 01 00** 99 97. See also Castello della SALA.

ANTONOPOULOS *Patras AO, Peloponnese, Greece* Boutique winery producing barrel-fermented Chardonnay★★, Cabernet Nea Dris (New Oak)★, a blend of Cabernets Sauvignon and Franc, and Private Collection★, a promising Agiorgitiko-Cabernet blend.

DOM. D'ANTUGNAC *Limoux AC, Languedoc, France* Two young Burgundians, Jean-Luc Terrier and Christian Collovray, are producing impressive Pinot Noir and Chardonnay in the cool LIMOUX region. Côté Pierre Lys is the Pinot Noir, with finesse and complexity. Chardonnay Les Gravas★ is barrel-fermented and aged, balancing richness with apples and cream freshness. Best years: (Les Gravas) (2008) 07 06 05 **04 01**.

ARAGÓN *Spain* Aragón stretches south from the Pyrenees to Spain's central plateau. Winemaking has improved markedly, first of all in the cooler, hilly, northern SOMONTANO DO, and now also further south, in Campo de Borja DO, Calatayud DO and CARIÑENA DO; these 3 areas have the potential to be a major budget-price force in a world mad for beefy but fruity reds.

ARAUJO *Napa Valley AVA, California, USA* Boutique winery whose great coup was to buy the Eisele vineyard, traditionally a source of superb Cabernet. Araujo Cabernet Sauvignon★★★ is now one of California's most sought-after reds, combining great fruit intensity with powerful but digestible tannins. Altagracia is a red BORDEAUX blend; Syrah★★ is impressive. Also Viognier and an attractively zesty Sauvignon Blanc★★.

ARBOIS AC *Jura, France* The largest of the ACs in the Jura region, with the sub-appellation Pupillin. All the Jura styles are made here, including sparkling CRÉMANT DU JURA and the region's best reds, from Trousseau and Poulsard. Most widely seen outside the region are the whites, from Chardonnay or the local Savagnin. Some have a sherry-like flavour that is most concentrated in *vin jaune*; others are fruity or more 'Burgundian' and mineral. There is also a rare, sweet *vin de paille*. Best producers: Fruitière Vinicole d'Arbois★, L Aviet★, Dugois★, Ligier, F Lornet★, H Maire, P Overnoy/Houillon★, D Petit, la Pinte★, J Puffeney★★, Renardière, Rijckaert★, Rolet, A & M Tissot★★, J Tissot★, Tournelle★. Best years: (2007) 06 **05 04 02 00**.

DOM. ANTOINE ARENA *Patrimonio AC, Corsica, France* Family-owned vineyard in Patrimonio, which specializes in white wines based on Vermentino, white Bianco Gentile (a local grape which had fallen into disuse) and stunning reds under the Carco, Grotte di Sole★ and Morta Maio labels. Best years: (Grotte di Sole) 2005 04 03 **01 00**.

ARGIOLAS *Sardinia, Italy* Sardinian star making DOC wines Cannonau (Costera★), Monica (Perdera) and Vermentino (Costamolino★) di Sardegna and IGT Isola dei Nuraghi blends: Turriga★★ and Korem★ are powerful, spicy reds; Angialis★★ is a golden, sweet white.

ARGYLE *Willamette Valley AVA, Oregon, USA* In 1987, Brian Croser and Rollin Soles planned a world-class New World sparkling wine firm; the cool WILLAMETTE VALLEY was ideal for late-ripened Pinot Noir and Chardonnay. Argyle sparkling wine★ was soon followed by barrel-fermented Chardonnay★ and Pinot Noir★. The Reserve★★, Nuthouse★★ and Spirithouse★★ bottlings show just how much potential this large winery possesses. Best years: (Pinot Noir) (2007) 06 05 **04 03 02**.

ARNEIS Italian grape grown in the ROERO hills in PIEDMONT. Arneis is DOC(
in Roero, producing dry white wines which, at best, have an attracti
(appley, herbal) perfume. Good ones can be expensive, but cheap
versions rarely work. COOPERS CREEK makes a good one in New Zealan.
Best producers: Brovia★, Cascina Chicco★, Correggia★, Deltetto★, GIACOSA★
Malvirà★, Angelo Negro★, PRUNOTTO★, Sorilaria★, Vietti★, Gianni Voerzio★

DOM. ARRETXEA Irouléguy AC, South-West France   Michel and Thérès
Riouspeyrous are the growers to look out for in Irouléguy. Whites are cris
full and dry; the rosé is directly pressed rather than drawn off the red juic.
Good reds★, with top Cuvée Haitza★★ rather like a refined MADIRAN
style, but still gutsy and macho. Best years: (2008) 06 **05 04 02 01**.

CH. L'ARROSÉE★ St-Émilion Grand Cru AC, Grand Cru Classé, Bordeaux, Fran.
This small property, just south-west of the historic town of ST-EMILIO!
makes really exciting wine: rich, chewy and wonderfully luscious, with
comparatively high proportion (40%) of Cabernet. New investment fro!
2002. Drink after 5 years, but may be cellared for 10 or more. Best year
2007 06 05 04 **03 02 01 00 98 96 95 90**.

ARROWOOD Sonoma Valley AVA, California, USA   Richard Arrowood started h
winery in 1986. The wines have mostly been tip-top – beautifully balance.
Cabernet★★, superb Merlot★★, deeply fruity Syrah (Saralee's★★
Kuljian★★, Le Beau Mélange★), lovely, velvety Chardonnay★ (Ala!
Vineyards★★) and fragrant Viognier★★. In 2006 the winery was acquire.
by Jackson Family Wines. Founder Arrowood now divides his tim
between this property and a new brand, Amapola Creek. Best year
(Cabernet Sauvignon) 2004 03 **02 01 00 99 97 96 95 94 91 90**.

ARTADI Rioja DOCa, País Vasco, Spain   This former co-op is now producir.
some of RIOJA's deepest, most ambitious reds, but they in no wa
overshadow the delightful, floral Joven★ and the excellent, scented an.
fairly priced Viñas de Gain★★. Blockbusters include Grande
Añadas★★★, superlative Viña El Pisón★★★ and fascinating, richly rip
Pagos Viejos★★★. Best years: (2006) 05 04 03 **01 00 98 96 95 94**.

ASCHERI Piedmont, Italy   Winemakers in PIEDMONT for at least 5 centurie
The Ascheri style is forward and appealingly drinkable, whether it b
BAROLO (Vigna dei Pola★, Sorano★), Dolcetto d'Alba (Vigna Nirane★
or NEBBIOLO D'ALBA. Montalupa Rosso and Bianco are made from Syra
and Viognier. The Cristina Ascheri MOSCATO D'ASTI is delightful.

ASTI DOCG Piedmont, Italy   Asti Spumante, the world's best-selling swe.
sparkling wine, was long derided as light and cheap, though promotic
to DOCG signalled an upturn in quality. Made in the province of Ast
under a denomination which includes the rarer MOSCATO D'ASTI, the wir
is now called simply Asti. Its light sweetness and refreshing sparkle mak
it ideal with fruit and a wide range of sweet dishes. Drink young. Be
producers: Araldica, Bera★, Cinzano★, Contero, Giuseppe Contratto★, Casci.
Fonda★, FONTANAFREDDA, Gancia★, Martini & Rossi★, Cascina Pian d'Or★.

ASTROLABE Marlborough, South Island, New Zealand   High-flying MARLBOROU(
wine producer launched by winemaker Simon Waghorn in 2001. Th
Voyage range includes a consistently good, powerful Sauvignc
Blanc★★, taut dry Riesling and subtly oaked Chardonnay. Th
Discovery range showcases Marlborough sub-regions and includes tw
excellent Sauvignon Blancs, from AWATERE★★ and Kekerengu★★. Th
Experience range is restricted to tiny parcels of experimental wines. Be
years: (Sauvignon Blanc) **2007 06 05**.

ATA RANGI *Martinborough, North Island, New Zealand* Small, high-quality
winery. Stylish, concentrated reds include seductively perfumed cherry/
plum Pinot Noir★★★, a rare, herb-scented Syrah and an impressive
Cabernet-Merlot-Syrah blend called Célèbre★★. Whites include big,
rich Craighall Chardonnay★, delicately luscious Lismore Pinot Gris★★
and a concentrated, mouthwatering Sauvignon Blanc★. A succulent
Kahu botrytis Riesling is made when vintage conditions allow. Best years:
(Pinot Noir) (2008) 07 **06** 03 01 00 99.

ATLAS PEAK *Atlas Peak AVA, Napa, California, USA* Established in 1987 by
ANTINORI of Italy, this mountaintop winery in the south-east corner of the
NAPA VALLEY was a leader in Californian Sangiovese without ever achieving
a consistent style. The brand is now focused entirely on Cabernet
Sauvignon from 4 specific mountain vineyards. Best years: 2003 **02** 01 99.

AU BON CLIMAT *Santa Maria Valley AVA, California, USA* Pace-setting winery
in this cool region, run by talented, ebullient Jim Clendenen, whose
early inspiration was BURGUNDY. The result is a range of lush
Chardonnays★★ and intense Pinot Noirs★★ (Isabelle Morgan and
Knox Alexander bottlings can be ★★★). He also makes BORDEAUX-style
reds, Italian varietals (both red and white) and some exotic sweeties.
Cold Heaven Viognier is made by Clendenen's wife, Morgan. Best years:
(Pinot Noir) 2006 05 04 **03** 02 01 00 99 98 97 96 95; (Chardonnay) 2007 06
05 04 03 02 01.

AUCKLAND *North Island, New Zealand* Vineyards in this region are
concentrated in the districts of Henderson, KUMEU/HUAPAI, Matakana and
WAIHEKE ISLAND. Clevedon, south of Auckland, is a fledgling area that shows
promise. Best years: (Cabernet Sauvignon) 2007 **05** 04 02 00 99 98.

CH. AUSONE★★★ *St-Émilion Grand Cru AC, 1er Grand Cru Classé, Bordeaux, France*
This beautiful property is situated on what are perhaps the best slopes in
ST-EMILION. Owner Alain Vauthier has taken it to new heights since 1996
and the wines now display stunning texture and depth and the promise of
memorable maturity. A high proportion (50%) of Cabernet Franc beefs
up the Merlot. Second wine: La Chapelle d'Ausone. Best years: 2007 06 05
04 03 **02** 01 00 99 98 97 96 95 94 90 89 88 86 85.

AUXEY-DURESSES AC *Côte de Beaune, Burgundy, France* Auxey-Duresses is
a backwater village up a valley behind MEURSAULT. The reds should be light
and fresh but can often lack ripeness. At its best, and at 3–5 years, the
white is dry, soft, nutty and hinting at the creaminess of a good
Meursault, but at much lower prices. Of the Premiers Crus, Les
Duresses is the most consistent. Best producers: (reds) Comte Armand★★,
J-P Diconne★, Maison Leroy, M Prunier★, P Prunier★; (whites) R Ampeau★,
d'Auvenay (Dom. LEROY)★★, J-P Diconne★, DROUHIN★, J-P Fichet★, Gras,
Olivier LEFLAIVE★, Maison Leroy★, M Prunier★. Best years: (reds) (2008) 07 06
05 **03** 02 99; (whites) (2008) 07 **06** 05 04 02.

AVIGNONESI *Vino Nobile di Montepulciano DOCG, Tuscany, Italy* Ex-proprietors
the Falvo brothers led Montepulciano's revival as one of TUSCANY's best
zones. At one time, wines like Il Marzocco★ (Chardonnay) and
Desiderio★★ (Merlot-Cabernet) received more attention, but today the
focus is back on top-quality classics, VINO NOBILE★ and its superior version,
made only in top years, Grandi Annate★★. The VIN SANTO★★★ is highly
sought-after; there's also a rare red version from Sangiovese, Occhio di
Pernice★★★. Best years: (Vino Nobile) (2008) (07) 06 **04** 03 01 00 99.

AWATERE VALLEY *Marlborough, South Island, New Zealand* Sub-region of MARLBOROUGH that's cooler and windier than the better-known Wairau Valley. In terms of vineyard area Awatere is larger than HAWKES BAY. Awatere Sauvignon offers a concentrated Marlborough style with typical nettle, tomato leaf and green capsicum characters, while Chardonnay is taut and mineral. Pinot Noir can be very good but may lack ripeness in cool vintages. Best producers: Clifford Bay★, Clos Marguerite★, Tohu★, VAVASOUR★★, VILLA MARIA★★, Yealands★. Best years: (Sauvignon Blanc) 2007 06 05.

CH. D'AYDIE *Madiran AC, South-West France* The Laplace family owns this important MADIRAN château, whose top wine is a full-blown Tannat-based Madiran★★; softer Madiran cuvées called Ode d'Aydie★ and Autour du Fruit blend Tannat with a little Cabernet. Also simple, fruity Aramis Vin de Pays du Comté Tolosan. Oak-aged white PACHERENCS★ are excellent. Best years: (reds) (2008) 06 05 04 02 01; (sweet whites) (2008) 07 05 04 03.

BABICH *Henderson, North Island, New Zealand* Family-run winery with prime vineyard land in MARLBOROUGH and HAWKES BAY. Irongate Chardonnay★ is an intense, steely wine that needs plenty of cellaring, while full-flavoured reds under the Winemakers' Reserve label show even greater potential for development. Flagship wine The Patriarch★★ is a red BORDEAUX blend from Hawkes Bay. Marlborough whites include stylish Sauvignon Blanc★, tangy Riesling and light, fruity Pinot Gris. Best years: (premium Hawkes Bay reds) 2007 06 04 02 00.

BACALHÔA VINHOS DE PORTUGAL *Terras do Sado, Portugal* Forward-looking operation, using Portuguese and foreign grapes with equal ease. Quinta da Bacalhôa★ is an oaky, meaty Cabernet-Merlot blend, Palácio da Bacalhôa★★ even better; Tinto da Ânfora★ a rich and figgy ALENTEJO red (Grande Escolha★★ version is powerful and cedary); and Cova da Ursa★ a toasty, rich Chardonnay. Portugal's finest sparkling wine, vintage-dated Loridos Extra Bruto★, is a decent CHAMPAGNE lookalike. Só Syrah ('só' means 'only' in Portuguese, as in 'only Syrah') is characterful if atypical. Also excellent 20-year-old Moscatel de SETUBAL★★.

BAD DÜRKHEIM *Pfalz, Germany* This spa town has some good vineyards and is the headquarters of the dependable Vier Jahreszeiten co-op. Best producers: Darting, Fitz-Ritter, Hensel, Karl Schaefer★, Egon Schmitt. Best years: (2008) 07 05 04 03 02 01 99 98.

BADEN *Germany* Very large, 16,000ha (39,520-acre), wine region stretching from FRANKEN to the Bodensee (Lake Constance). Its dry whites and reds show off the fuller, softer flavours Germany can produce in the warmer climate of its southerly regions. Many of the best non-Riesling German wines come from here, as well as many good barrel-fermented and barrel-aged wines. Germany's best co-operatives are located here, but the number of quality-oriented private estates is growing. See also KAISERSTUHL, ORTENAU.

BAGA Important red grape in BAIRRADA, which has been one of the few regions in Portugal to rely mainly on one variety. Also planted in smaller quantities in DÃO and the RIBATEJO. It can give deep, complex, blackberryish wine, but aggressive tannin is a continuing problem.

BAIRRADA DOC *Beira Litoral, Portugal* Bairrada, along with the DOURO, DÃO and ALENTEJO, can be the source of many of Portugal's best red wines. These can brim over with intense raspberry and blackberry fruit, with austere tannins that take quite a few years to soften. Traditionally made from a minimum of 50% of the tannic Baga grape; rules changed in 2003 to admit a load of 'international' grapes into the Bairrada fold. The whites are coming on fast with modern vinification methods. With an Atlantic climate, vintages can be very variable. **Best producers: (reds)** Caves ALIANCA★, Quinta das Bágeiras★, Quinta de Baixo★, Campolargo★, Cantanhede co-op, Quinta do Encontro, Caves do Freixo, Caves Messias (Quinta do Valdeiro Reserva★), Casa de Saima★★, Caves SAO JOAO★★, SOGRAPE, Sidónio de Sousa★★; **(whites)** Caves SAO JOAO★★, SOGRAPE (Reserva★). **Best years: (reds) (2008) 05 04 03 01 00 97.**

BALATONBOGLÁR WINERY *Transdanubia, Hungary* Premium winery in the Lake Balaton region, which has benefited from heavy investment and the expertise of viticulturist Dr Richard Smart and wine consultant Kym Milne, but still needs to work to improve quality, particularly in the inexpensive but dumbed-down range sold under the Chapel Hill label.

BALEARIC ISLANDS *Spain* Medium-bodied reds and soft rosés were the mainstays of Mallorca's 2 DO areas, Binissalem and Plà i Llevant, until Anima Negra began making impressive, deep reds from the native Callet grape. **Best producers: 4 Kilos Vinícola★★, Anima Negra★★, Hereus de Ribas, Miquel Gelabert★, Toni Gelabert★, Miquel Oliver, Son Bordils★.**

BALNAVES *Coonawarra, South Australia* Long-term residents of COONAWARRA, the grape-growing Balnaves family decided to become involved in making wine in the mid-1990s. With the talented Pete Bissell as winemaker, Balnaves is now among the best producers in the region. Reserve Cabernet The Tally★★★ is complex, wonderfully structured and deeply flavoured; the regular Cabernet★ is well priced and an excellent example of Coonawarra style.

BANDOL AC *Provence, France* A lovely fishing port with vineyards high above the Mediterranean, producing some of the best reds and rosés in Provence. The Mourvèdre grape gives Bandol its character – dense colour, warm, smoky black fruit and a herby fragrance. The reds happily age for 10 years, sometimes more, but can be very good at 3–4. The rosés, delicious and spicy but often too pricey, should be drunk young. Also a small amount of neutral, overpriced white. **Best producers: la Bastide** Blanche★, la Bégude★, Bunan★, Frégate★, le Galantin★, J P Gaussen★★, Gros' Noré★, l'Hermitage★, Lafran-Veyrolles★, la Laidière★, Mas Redorne★, la Noblesse★, PIBARNON★★, Pradeaux★★, Ray-Jane★, Roche Redonne★, Ste-Anne★, Salettes★, SORIN, la Suffrène, Tempier★, Terrebrune★, la Tour du Bon★, VANNIERES★★. **Best years: 2007 06 05 03 01 00 99 98 97 96.**

BANFI *Brunello di Montalcino DOCG, Tuscany, Italy* High-tech American-owned firm which is now a force in Italy. Chardonnay (Fontanelle★), Cabernet (Tavernelle★) and Merlot (Mandrielle★) are successful, but even better are BRUNELLO Riserva Poggio all'Oro★★ and Brunello Poggio alle Mura★★. SUPER-TUSCANS Summus★★ (a blend of Sangiovese, Cabernet and Syrah) and Excelsus★★ (Cabernet-Merlot) are also very good. Also has cellars (Vigne Regali) in PIEDMONT for GAVI and fizz. **Best years: (top reds) (2008) (07) (06) 04 03 01 99 98 97.**

BANNOCKBURN *Geelong, Victoria, Australia* The Hooper family has 27ha (67 acres) of mature vines, from which all the estate's wines are sourced. Most notable are Sauvignon Blanc★★, Chardonnay★★, Pinot Noir★★ and Shiraz★, and 4 limited-release wines: my favourite, the complex and classy Alain GRAILLOT-influenced Range Shiraz★★; MEURSAULT-like SRH Chardonnay★★; powerful, gamy Serre Pinot Noir★★; and dense, tightly coiled yet elegant Stuart Pinot★★. Michael Glover, winemaker since 2005, has made his mark, ensuring that Bannockburn remains one of the country's pre-eminent boutique wineries. **Best years:** (Shiraz) (2008) 06 05 04 03 **02 01 00 99 98 97 96 94 92 91**.

BANYULS AC *Roussillon, France* One of the best *vins doux naturels*, made mainly from Grenache, with a strong plum and raisin flavour. *Rimage* – vintaged early bottlings – and tawny styles are the best. Best drunk after dinner, though often served as an apéritif in France. **Best producers:** Cellier des Templiers★, CHAPOUTIER, Clos de Paulilles★, l'Étoile★, MAS BLANC★★, la Rectorie★★, la Tour Vieille★, Vial Magnères★.

BARBADILLO *Jerez y Manzanilla DO, Andalucía, Spain* The largest sherry company in the coastal town of Sanlúcar de Barrameda makes a wide range of good to excellent wines, in particular salty, dry manzanilla styles (Solear★★, En Rama unfiltered★★★) and intense, nutty, but dry amontillados and olorosos (Amontillado Príncipe★★, Oloroso Cuco★★). Neutral dry white Castillo de San Diego is a bestseller in Spain.

BARBARESCO DOCG *Piedmont, Italy* This prestigious red wine, grown in the LANGHE hills south-east of Turin, is often twinned with its neighbour BAROLO to demonstrate the nobility of the Nebbiolo grape. Barbaresco can be a shade softer and less powerful, and is not required by law to age as long (2 years minimum compared with 3), but at the top level is often indistinguishable from Barolo. As in Barolo, traditionalists excel, led by Bruno GIACOSA. Even though the area is relatively compact (575ha/1420 acres), styles can differ significantly between vineyards and producers. Best vineyards: Asili, Bricco di Neive, Crichet Pajè, Gallina, Marcorino, Martinenga, Messoirano, Moccagatta, Montestefano, Ovello, Pora, Rabajà, Rio Sordo, Santo Stefano, Serraboella, Sorì Paitin. **Best producers:** Barbaresco co-op★★, CERETTO★★, Cigliuti★★, Stefano Farina★★, Fontanabianca★★, GAJA★★, GIACOSA★★★, Lano★, Marchesi di Gresy★★, Moccagatta★★, Fiorenzo Nada★★, Castello di Neive★★, Oddero★, Paitin★★, Pelissero★★, Pio Cesare★★, PRUNOTTO★★, Albino Rocca★★, Bruno Rocca★★, Sottimano★★, La Spinetta★★, Castello di Verduno★★, Vietti★★. **Best years:** (2008) (07) 06 **04 03 01 00 99 98 97 96 95**.

BARBERA A native of north-west Italy, Barbera vies with Sangiovese as the most widely planted red grape in the country. When grown for high yields its natural acidity shows through, producing vibrant quaffers. Low yields from the top PIEDMONT estates create intensely rich and complex wines. Oaked versions can be stunning. Significant plantings in California, Argentina and Australia.

BARBERA D'ALBA DOC *Piedmont, Italy* Some outstanding Barbera comes from this appellation. The most modern examples are supple and generous and can be drunk almost at once. More intense, dark-fruited versions require at least 3 years' age, but might improve for as much as 8. **Best producers:** G Alessandria★★, ALTARE★, Azelia★★, Boglietti★★, Brovia★, Burlotto★★, CERETTO★, Cascina Chicco★, Cigliuti★, CLERICO★, Elvio Cogno★★, Aldo CONTERNO★★, Giacomo CONTERNO★★, Conterno-Fantino★, Corino★, Correggia★, Elio Grasso★, Giuseppe MASCARELLO★, Moccagatta★, M Molino★★, Monfalletto-Cordero di Montezemolo★★, Oberto★, Parusso★★, Pelissero★, F Principiano★★, PRUNOTTO★★, RATTI★,

Albino Rocca★★, Bruno Rocca★, SANDRONE★★, P Scavino★★, La Spinetta★★, Vajra★★, Mauro Veglio★★, Vietti★★, Gianni Voerzio★★, Roberto VOERZIO★★★. Best years: (2008) 07 **06 04 03 01**.

ARBERA D'ASTI DOC *Piedmont, Italy* While Dolcetto d'Asti is usually light and simple, Barbera wines show a greater range of quality. Unoaked and barrique-aged examples can compete with the best BARBERA D'ALBA and rival some of the better Nebbiolo-based reds. Best examples can be kept for 5–6 years, occasionally longer. Best producers: Araldica/Alasia★, La Barbatella★★, Pietro Barbero★★, Bava★, Bertelli★★, Braida★★, Cascina Castlèt★, Coppo★★, Hastae (Quorum★), Martinetti★★, Il Mongetto★★, PRUNOTTO★★, La Spinetta★★, Vietti★★, Vinchio-Vaglio Serra co-op★. Best years: (2008) 07 **06 04 03 01**.

ARBOURSVILLE VINEYARDS *Virginia, USA* Founded by Italy's Zonin winemaking family in 1976, on property that features the ruins of a mansion designed by Thomas Jefferson for his friend, James Barbour. Under winemaker Luca Paschina since 1990, the wines have shown consistent improvement. An enticing range of French and Italian styles: Octagon★, a flagship BORDEAUX blend based on Merlot, and Cabernet Franc Reserve★ are standouts.

ARDOLINO DOC *Veneto, Italy* Zone centred on Lake Garda, giving, at best, light, scented red and rosé (*chiaretto*) wines to be drunk young, from the same grape mix as neighbouring VALPOLICELLA. Bardolino Superiore is DOCG. Best producers: Cavalchina★, Corte Gardoni★, Guerrieri-Rizzardi★, Le Fraghe, MASI, Le Vigne di San Pietro★, Zeni.

AROLO DOCG *Piedmont, Italy* Renowned red wine, named after a village south-west of Alba, from the Nebbiolo grape grown in around 1500ha (3700 acres) of vineyards in the steep LANGHE hills, the best coming from near the top (*bricco*) of those hills. Having in the post-WWII period gone to excesses of austerity, Barolo in the 1990s almost threatened to go too far in the other direction, its subtle floral/wild fruit aromas being drowned all too often under expensive but irrelevant oak smells of vanilla and toast. Thankfully 21st-century producers are finding their way back to the 'tar and roses' of the grape while managing to keep Nebbiolo's fierce tannins and biting acidity under control. Distinct styles of wine are said to be made in the zone's villages, though individual producers may make wines not conforming to the mould: Barolo and La Morra make the most perfumed wines; Monforte and Serralunga the most structured. Barolo is frequently labelled by vineyard, though the producer's reputation often carries more weight. Best vineyards: Arione, Bricco delle Viole, Brunate, Bussia Soprana, Cannubi, Cerequio, Conca dell'Annunziata, Fiasco, Francia, Gavarini, Ginestra, Monfalletto, Monprivato, Rocche dell'Annunziata, Rocche di Castiglione, Santo Stefano di Perno, La Serra, Vigna Rionda, Villero. Best producers: C Alario★★, G Alessandria★★, ALTARE★★, Azelia★★, Boglietti★★, Bongiovanni★★, Brovia★★, Burlotto★★, Cappellano★★, CERETTO★★, CHIARLO★, CLERICO★★★, Aldo CONTERNO★★, Giacomo CONTERNO★★★, Conterno-Fantino★★, Corino★★, Luigi Einaudi★★, GIACOSA★★★, Elio Grasso★★, M Marengo★★, Bartolo MASCARELLO★★★, Giuseppe MASCARELLO★★★, Monfalletto-Cordero di Montezemolo★★, Oberto★★, Oddero★★, Parusso★★, Pio Cesare★★, Pira★★, E Pira & Figli★★, F Principiano★★, PRUNOTTO★★, Renato RATTI★, Revello★★, Giuseppe Rinaldi★★, Rocche dei Manzoni★★, SANDRONE★★★, P Scavino★★, M Sebaste★★, Vajra★★, Mauro Veglio★★, Castello di Verduno★★, Vietti★★, Vigna Rionda★★, Gianni Voerzio★★, Roberto VOERZIO★★★. Best years: (2008) (07) (06) 04 03 01 00 99 98 97 96 95 90 89 88.

BAROSSA

South Australia

The Barossa Valley, an hour or so's drive north o Adelaide in South Australia, is the heart of th Australian wine industry. The giants of the industr have their major wineries here – Jacob's Creek, Wol Blass, Penfolds and Yalumba – alongside around 50 o so smaller wineries, producing or processing up to 60% of the nation's wine. However, this percentage is based mostly on grape trucked in from other regions, because the Barossa's vineyard themselves grow less than 10% of Australia's grapes. Yet Barossa-grow grapes, once rejected as uneconomical for their low yields, are nov increasingly prized for those same low yields.

Why? Well, it's highly likely that the world's oldest wine vines are ir the Barossa. The valley was settled in the 1840s by Lutheran immigrant from Silesia, who brought with them vines from Europe, mos importantly, as it turned out, cuttings from the Syrah (or Shiraz) variet of France's Rhône Valley. And because Barossa has never been affecte by the phylloxera louse, which destroyed most of the world's vineyards ir the late 19th century, today you can still see gnarled, twisted old vine sporting just a few tiny bunches of priceless fruit that were planted b refugees from Europe all of a century and a half ago, and are still tende by their descendants. A new wave of winemakers has taken up the caus of the Barossa vines with much zeal and no small amount of nationa pride, and they now produce from them some of the deepest, mos fascinating wines, not just in Australia, but in the world.

GRAPE VARIETIES

Shiraz is prized above all other Barossa grapes, able to conjur headswirling, palate-dousing flavours. Barossa is the main source o Shiraz grapes for Penfolds Grange, the wine that began the revolution ir Australian red wine in the 1950s. Cabernet Sauvignon can be very goo in the best years and similarly potent, as are the Rhône varieties of head Grenache and deliciously earthy Mourvèdre; some of the most excitin examples are from the original vines planted in the 19th century. Al these varieties are largely grown on the hot, dry, valley floor, but just t the east lie the Barossa Ranges, and in these higher, cooler vineyards especially in those of the neighbouring Eden Valley, some of Australia' best and most fashionable Rieslings are grown, prized for their steel attack and lime fragrance. But even here you can't get away from Shiraz and some thrilling examples come from the hills, not least Henschke' Hill of Grace and Mount Edelstone.

CLASSIFICATIONS

The Barossa was among the first zones to be ratified within th Australian system of Geographical Indications and comprises the region of Barossa Valley and Eden Valley. The Barossa lies within Sout Australia's collective 'super zone' of Adelaide.

See also GRANGE, SOUTH AUSTRALIA; and individual producers.

BEST YEARS

(Barossa Valley Shiraz) (2008) 06
05 **04 03 02 01 00 99 98 97 96
94 91 90** 86;
(Eden Valley Riesling) **2008 07
06 05 04 03 02 01 00 99 98 97
96 95**

BEST PRODUCERS

Shiraz-based reds
BAROSSA VALLEY ESTATE, Bethany,
Rolf BINDER, Grant BURGE, Burge
Family, Dutschke, John DUVAL,
Elderton (Command), GLAETZER,
Greenock Creek (Block Shiraz,
Seven Acre), HENSCHKE, Hewitson,
JACOB'S CREEK (Centenary Hill),
Jenke, Trevor Jones, Kalleske,
Langmeil, Peter LEHMANN, Charles
MELTON, PENFOLDS (RWT,
GRANGE), Chris Ringland,
ROCKFORD, ST HALLETT, Tim Smith,
Spinifex, Teusner, Thorn Clarke,
TORBRECK, Torzi Matthews,
TURKEY FLAT, Two Hands,
The Willows, YALUMBA (Octavius).

Riesling
Bethany, Wolf BLASS (Gold Label),
Grant BURGE, Leo Buring
(Leonay), HENSCHKE, Hewitson,
JACOB'S CREEK (Steingarten),
Peter LEHMANN, Mesh, Radford
Dale, ROCKFORD, Ross Estate,
ST HALLETT, Torzi Matthews,
YALUMBA (Heggies, Pewsey Vale).

**Cabernet Sauvignon-based
reds**
Rolf BINDER, Grant BURGE,
Greenock Creek, HENSCHKE,
Peter LEHMANN, ST HALLETT,
The Willows.

**Other reds (Grenache,
Mourvèdre, Shiraz)**
Rolf BINDER, Grant BURGE, Burge
Family (Olive Hill), Charles
Cimicky, Elderton (Ode to
Lorraine), HENSCHKE, Jenke
(Mourvèdre), Kalleske, Langmeil,
Peter LEHMANN, Charles MELTON,
PENFOLDS (Bin 138), Teusner,
TORBRECK, TURKEY FLAT,
Two Hands.

Semillon
Grant BURGE, HENSCHKE, Heritage,
Jenke, Peter LEHMANN, ROCKFORD,
TURKEY FLAT, The Willows.

BAROSSA VALLEY See pages 72–3.

BAROSSA VALLEY ESTATE *Barossa, South Australia* Half owned by local
growers, with some of the best-sited vineyards in BAROSSA, and half by
industry giant Constellation. Flagship reds are huge, gutsy Barossa
beauties E&E Black Pepper Shiraz★★, Ebenezer Shiraz★★ and E&E
Sparkling Shiraz★★, all of them bursting with ripe plum fruit, spice and
plenty of vanilla oak. Excellent value in the E Bass Shiraz and budget-
priced E Minor range. Best years: (E&E Black Pepper Shiraz) (2008) (06) 05
04 **02 01 99 98 96 94**.

JIM BARRY *Clare Valley, South Australia* After buying Australia's most famous
Riesling vineyard in 1986, they had to wait until 2005 for the trademark
to expire. Now Jim Barry has a flagship white, The Florita★, to head a
quartet of classy, perfumed Rieslings (Watervale★★, Lodge Hill★★).
Medium-priced Lodge Hill Shiraz★ is impressive, but the winery is best
known for its rich, fruity McRae Wood Shiraz★★ and heady, palate-
busting Armagh Shiraz★★. Best years: (Armagh Shiraz) (2006) 05 04 02 **01
99 98 96 95 92 89**.

BARSAC AC *Bordeaux, France* Barsac, lying close to the river Garonne and
with the little river Ciron running along its eastern boundary, is the largest
of the 5 communes in the SAUTERNES AC, and also has its own AC, which is
used by most, but by no means all, of the top properties. In general, the
wines are a little less luscious than other Sauternes, but from good estates
they can be marvellous. Best producers: CLIMENS★★★, COUTET★★, DOISY-
DAËNE★★, Doisy-Dubroca★, DOISY-VEDRINES★★, Myrat★, NAIRAC★, Piada,
Suau★. Best years: 2007 05 **03 02 01 99 98 97 96 95 90 89 88 86 83**.

BASILICATA *Italy* Southern Italian region best known for one wine, the
potentially excellent, gutsy red called AGLIANICO DEL VULTURE.

BASSERMANN-JORDAN *Deidesheim, Pfalz, Germany* Since 1996, this famous
estate has been making rich yet elegant Rieslings★★ from Deidesheim
and FORST. Best years: (2008) 07 06 05 **04 03 02 01 99 98 97 96**.

CH. BATAILLEY★ *Pauillac AC, 5ème Cru Classé, Haut-Médoc, Bordeaux, France*
A byword for reliability and value for money among the PAUILLAC Classed
Growth estates. Marked by a full, obvious blackcurrant fruit, not too
much tannin and a luscious overlay of creamy vanilla. Lovely to drink at
only 5 years old, the wine continues to age well for at least 15 years. Best
years: 2006 05 **04 03 02 00 98 96 95 94 90 89 88**.

BÂTARD-MONTRACHET AC *Grand Cru, Côte de Beaune, Burgundy, France*
This Grand Cru produces some of the world's greatest whites – full, rich
and balanced, with a powerful mineral intensity of fruit and fresh acidity.
There are 2 associated Grands Crus: Bienvenues-Bâtard-Montrachet and
the minuscule Criots-Bâtard-Montrachet. All can age for a decade –
indeed, they ought to. Best producers: Blain-Gagnard★★, CARILLON★★★,
DROUHIN★★★, Fontaine-Gagnard★★, J-N GAGNARD★★★, JADOT★★★, Louis
LATOUR★★, Dom. LEFLAIVE★★★, Olivier LEFLAIVE★★, Marc Morey★★★, Pierre
Morey★★★, Michel Niellon★★★, RAMONET★★★, SAUZET★★★, VERGET★★.
Best years: (2008) 07 06 05 04 **03 02 01 00 99 97 92 89**.

BERNARD BAUDRY *Chinon, Loire Valley, France* Baudry, recently joined by
his son Matthieu, crafts supple, elegant Cabernet Franc. Aspect and soil
type differentiate four site-specific CHINON cuvées: Les Granges
(sand/gravel) and Les Grézeaux★ (gravel/clay) are for earlier drinking
while Le Clos Guillot★★ (limestone/clay/tuffeau) and La Croix

Boissée★★ (clay/limestone) reward patience. Good dry white and rosé too. Best years: (top reds) (2008) **06 05 04 03 02 01 00**.

DOM. DES BAUMARD *Coteaux du Layon, Loire Valley, France* Well-sited vineyards produce sensational QUARTS DE CHAUME★★★ that requires aging, as well as rich, honeyed, impeccably balanced COTEAUX DU LAYON Clos de Ste-Catherine★★. Also fine steely, mineral-scented SAVÈNNIERES Clos du Papillon★★ and Clos St-Yves★★, with a late-harvest Trie Spéciale★★ in top years. Idiosyncratic Vert de l'Or Verdelho varies in sweetness according to vintage. Good CREMANT DE LOIRE★ and sound ANJOU reds. Best years: (Quarts de Chaume) 2007 06 05 **03** 02 **01 99 97 96 95 90 89**.

LES BAUX-DE-PROVENCE AC *Provence, France* This AC has proved that organic and biodynamic farming can produce spectacular results, mainly due to the warm dry climate. Good fruit and intelligent winemaking produce some of the more easily enjoyable reds in Provence. Best producers: Hauvette★, Lauzières, Mas de la Dame★, Mas de Gourgonnier★, Mas Ste-Berthe★, ROMANIN★, Terres Blanches★. Best years: (2007) 06 05 04 **03 02 01 00 99 98 97**.

BAY OF FIRES *Tasmania, Australia* The Tasmanian arm of Constellation has become more important in the past decade as HARDYS' chief sparkling winemaker, Ed Carr, has increasingly focused on the region's ultra-cool climate. HARDYS' best bubbly has been rebranded Bay of Fires Arras★★. There are also excellent sparkling wines under the Tigress★ label, as well as a brilliant range of cool-climate table wines (Pinot Noir★).

BÉARN AC *South-West France* Since 2000, there seems to have been an improvement in quality of wines of all three colours. Best producers: CAUHAPÉ, Guilhemas, Lapeyre★, Nigri.

CH. DE BEAUCASTEL *Châteauneuf-du-Pape AC, Rhône Valley, France* The Perrin family makes some of the richest, most profound reds (often ★★★) in CHATEAUNEUF-DU-PAPE, with an unusually high percentage of Mourvèdre and Syrah, which can take at least a decade to show at their best. The white Roussanne Vieilles Vignes★★★ is classy, exquisite and long-lived. They also produce COTES DU RHÔNE Coudoulet de Beaucastel red★★ and white★ and GIGONDAS Dom. des Tourelles★★. Under the Domaines Perrin label is a range of increasingly good southern reds, including RASTEAU★ and VINSOBRES★. Best years: (reds) 2007 06 05 04 **03 01 00 99 98 97 96 95 94 90 89 88 86 85**; (whites) (2008) 07 06 05 **04 03 01 00 99 98 97 96 95 94 90 89**.

BEAUJOLAIS AC *Beaujolais, Burgundy, France* Wine region in the beautiful hills that stretch down from Mâcon to Lyon, producing predominantly red wine from the Gamay grape. Beaujolais is best known for BEAUJOLAIS NOUVEAU, which accounts for nearly 40% of the production, although the popularity of nouveau has faded since its heyday in the 1970s and 80s. The better-quality reds, each having their own appellation, come from the north of the region and are BEAUJOLAIS-VILLAGES and the 10 single Cru villages; from north to south these are ST-AMOUR, JULIENAS, MOULIN-A-VENT, CHENAS, FLEURIE, CHIROUBLES, MORGON, REGNIE, BROUILLY and COTE DE BROUILLY. There is a growing buzz about the area: standards of production have improved dramatically in recent years as a new wave of producers (a younger generation of locals, and winemakers from both Burgundy in the north and the Rhône in the south) have begun investing in the area. Furthermore, growing consumer demand for food-friendly wines with lower alcohol levels may help to spark renewed interest in the area. In good vintages simple Beaujolais is light, fresh, aromatic and delicious to drink, but in poorer vintages the wine can be drab and acidic. A little rosé is also made from Gamay, and a small quantity of Beaujolais Blanc is made from Chardonnay. Best producers: (reds) J-P Brun/Terres Dorées★, A Chatoux★, Coquard (Clochemerle), J-F Garlon★, G Subrin/Jarentes.

BEAUJOLAIS NOUVEAU *Beaujolais AC, Burgundy, France* Also known as Beaujolais Primeur, this is the first release of bouncy, fruity Beaujolais on the third Thursday of November after the harvest. Once a simple celebration of the new vintage, nouveau was badly over-hyped and, as a result, is nowhere near as popular as it once was. Quality is generally reasonable and the wine can be delicious until Christmas and the New Year, but thereafter is likely to throw a slight sediment and soon loses the vivacious fresh fruit that made it so appealing in its youth.

BEAUJOLAIS-VILLAGES AC *Beaujolais, Burgundy, France* Beaujolais-Villages can come from one of 38 villages in the north of the region. Top examples rival the BEAUJOLAIS Crus, having more body, character, complexity and elegance than simple Beaujolais and representing all the pleasure of the Gamay grape at its best. Best villages are Lancié, Quincié and Perréon. Best producers: Ch. de Belleverne★, Ch. Cambon★, Côtes de la Molière, DUBOEUF, Ch. du Pavé★, Gilles Roux/de la Plaigne★.

BEAULIEU VINEYARD *Napa Valley AVA, California, USA* The late André Tchelistcheff, winemaker from the 1930s to the late 60s, had a major role in creating this icon for NAPA Cabernet. After he left, Beaulieu lived on its reputation for too long. However, Private Reserve Cabernet Sauvignon★ seems to have returned to form. Tapestry★ (meritage red) is good, as are Chardonnay★ and Pinot Noir★ from CARNEROS, and Syrah★. Best years (Private Reserve) 2005 04 03 **01 00 99** 98 97 96 95 94 92 91 90 87.

BEAUMES-DE-VENISE AC *Rhône Valley, France* Area famous for its scented, honeyed sweet wine, MUSCAT DE BEAUMES-DE-VENISE. The local red wine is also good, and received its own appellation from the 2004 vintage. It is full of dark fruit and crisp tannins and can age well for 8–10 years. Best producers: (reds) Balma Venitia (Beaumes-de-Venise) co-op, Beaumalric, Bernardins, Cassan★, Durban★, Fenouillet, les Goubert, Redortier.

BEAUNE AC *Côte de Beaune, Burgundy, France* Most of the wines are red, with delicious, soft red-fruits ripeness. There are no Grands Crus but some excellent Premiers Crus, especially Boucherottes, Bressandes, Clos des Mouches, Fèves, Grèves, Marconnets, Teurons, Vignes Franches. White-wine production is increasing – DROUHIN makes outstanding, creamy, nutty Clos des Mouches★★★. Best producers: (growers) Croix-Germain/Ch. de Chorey★★, LAFARGE★★, de MONTILLE★, Albert Morot-Rateau, TOLLOT-BEAUT★★; (merchants) BOUCHARD PERE ET FILS★★, Champy★, Chanson★, DROUHIN★★, Camille Giroud★★, JADOT★★, Labouré-Roi★. Best years: (reds) (2008) 07 06 05 **03 02 99**; (whites) (2008) 07 06 **05 04 02.**

CH. BEAU-SÉJOUR BÉCOT★★ *St-Émilion Grand Cru AC, 1er Grand Cru Classé, Bordeaux, France* Demoted from Premier Grand Cru Classé in 1986 and promoted again in 1996, this estate is on top form. Brothers Gérard and Dominique Bécot produce firm, ripe, richly textured wines that need at least 8–10 years to develop. Best years: 2007 06 05 04 **03 02 01** 00 99 98 96 95 90 89 88 86.

BEAUX FRÈRES *Willamette Valley AVA, Oregon, USA* The goal here is to make ripe, unfiltered Pinot Noir★ that expresses the essence of their 10ha (24-acre) vineyard atop Ribbon Ridge in the Chehalem Valley. A parcel known as the Upper Terrace★★★ yields exceptional fruit from Dijon clones. Best years: (2007) 06 05 04 **03 02.**

GRAHAM BECK WINES *Robertson WO, South Africa* A 2-cellar operation, overseen by Pieter Ferreira. ROBERTSON's potential for Cap Classique sparkling is realized in an elegant, rich NV Brut★, a toastily fragrant, creamy, barrel-fermented and ageworthy Blanc de Blancs★ and an occasional quirky sparkling Pinotage★. Single-vineyard duo The Ridge Syrah★ and flavoursome, succulent Lonehill

Chardonnay★ lead the Robertson table wines. Viognier is good too. Top wines from FRANSCHHOEK include Old Road Pinotage★, The Joshua Shiraz-Viognier★★, DURBANVILLE-sourced Pheasants' Run Sauvignon Blanc★ and single-vineyard Coffestone Cabernet★. The William★, a Cabernet Sauvignon-Pinotage blend, shows promise and aging potential.

BEDELL CELLARS *Long Island, New York State, USA* Winemaker Kip Bedell helped establish LONG ISLAND's reputation with his Bordeaux-styled Merlot★ (Reserve★★) and red blends. The wines have continued to improve under new ownership, with Bedell still chief winemaker. Sister winery Corey Creek produces a noteworthy Gewürztraminer.

BEECHWORTH *Victoria, Australia* Beechworth was best known as Ned Kelly country before Rick Kinzbrunner planted the hilly slopes of sub-Alpine north-east Victoria and started making wines at GIACONDA. Now boutique wineries produce tiny volumes at high prices and are on a steep learning curve. BROKENWOOD has a major new vineyard here, called Indigo. **Best producers:** Amulet (Shiraz★★), BROKENWOOD, Castanga★ (Shiraz★★), Cow Hill★, GIACONDA★★★, Savaterre (Chardonnay★★), Sorrenberg★.

BEIRAS *Portugal* This large Portuguese province includes the DOCs of DÃO, BAIRRADA, Távora-Varosa and Beira Interior. Vinho Regional wines use Portuguese red and white varieties along with international grapes such as Cabernet Sauvignon and Chardonnay. **Best producers:** Caves ALIANÇA, Quinta do Cardo★, Quinta dos Cozinheiros, Quinta dos Currais, Figueira de Castelo Rodrigo co-op, Quinta de Foz de Arouce★, Filipa Pato★, Luís PATO★★, Rogenda, Caves SÃO DÃO (Quinta do Poço do Lobo), Quinta dos Termos. **Best years:** 2005 **04 03 01 00**.

CH. BELAIR★★ *St-Émilion Grand Cru AC, 1er Grand Cru Classé, Bordeaux, France* Belair is next to AUSONE on ST-EMILION's limestone plateau. Now owned by *négociant* J-P MOUEIX. The soft, supremely stylish wines are drinkable at 5–6 years, but also capable of long aging. **Best years:** 2006 05 04 03 02 01 00 99 98 95 90 89 88 86 85.

BELLAVISTA *Franciacorta DOCG, Lombardy, Italy* Specialist in FRANCIACORTA sparkling wines, with a very good Cuvée Brut★★ and 4 distinctive Gran Cuvées★★ (including an excellent rosé). Vittorio Moretti★★ is made in exceptional years. Also produces lovely still wines, including white blend Convento dell'Annunciata★★★, Chardonnay Uccellanda★★ and red Casotte★ (Pinot Nero) and Solesine★★ (Cabernet-Merlot).

BELLET AC *Provence, France* Tiny AC in the hills behind Nice; the wine is nearly equally divided between red, white and rosé, and is usually overpriced, although domaines such as Toasc are now producing cheaper vin de pays from young vines. **Best producers:** Ch. de Bellet★, Ch. de Crémat★, Dom. de Toasc. **Best years:** (2008) **07 06 05 04**.

BENDIGO *Central Victoria, Australia* Warm, dry, former gold-mining region which is now home to about 40 small-scale, high-quality wineries. Th best wines are rich, ripe, distinctively minty Shiraz and Cabernet. Bes producers: Balgownie, Blackjack★, Bress, Chateau Leamon, Passing Cloud PONDALOWIE★, Turner's Crossing★, Water Wheel. Best years: (Shiraz) (2008 06 05 04 03 02 01 00 99 98 97 95 94 93 91 90.

BERCHER *Burkheim, Baden, Germany* A top KAISERSTUHL estate. High point are the powerful oak-aged Spätburgunder★★ (Pinot Noir) reds, Grau burgunder★★ (Pinot Gris) and Chardonnay★ dry whites, which marr richness with perfect balance, and dry Muskateller★, which is firn elegant and tangy. Best years: (whites) (2008) 07 05 **04** 03 02; (reds) (200 07 06 05 04 **03** 02.

BERGERAC AC *South-West France* The Bergerac vineyards are an easter extension of Bordeaux, using the same grape varieties as those used in th BORDEAUX ACS. The underrated reds are generally like a light, fresh clare a bit grassy but with a good, raw blackcurrant fruit and hint of eartl Côtes de Bergerac AC is one step up, and its wines are usually aged i wood. The better reds can age for at least 3–5 years. The fresh dry white are for early drinking. Sweet whites are more ambitious and general' produced under their own more specific appellations: MONBAZILLA Saussignac, MONTRAVEL and Rosette. Best producers: l'ANCIENNE CURE★ Bélingard, la Colline★, Eyssards, Fontenelles, la Jaubertie, Marnières, le Miaudoux, Monestier-la-Tour, TOUR DES GENDRES★★, VERDOTS★. Best year (reds) (2008) 06 **05** 04 02 01 00.

BERGSTRÖM *Willamette Valley AVA, Oregon, USA* The Bergström family uses biodynamic farming to bring out the best character from the *terroir* of their 9ha (23-acre) estate vineyard. The primary focus is on Pinot Noir, with Bergström Vineyard★★ and de Lancellotti Vineyard★★ forming the greater part of the production. Cumberland Reserve★★★ is a multi-

Bergström
WINERY
2006
BERGSTRÖM VINEYARD
PINOT NOIR
DUNDEE HILLS AVA

vineyard blend that can rival many fine Burgundies in its complexit Also small amounts of Chardonnay★ and Riesling★★. Best years: (red 2007 06 **05** 04.

BERINGER *Napa Valley AVA, California, USA* Beringer, part of the Foster Wine Group, mass-produces some fairly average varietal labels, but al offers a serious range of top-class Cabernet Sauvignons. The Priva Reserve Cabernet can be ★★★ and is one of NAPA VALLEY's finest yet mo approachable; the Chabot Vineyard★★ can be equally impressive. Th Knight's Valley Cabernet Sauvignon★ is made in a lighter style and good value. Beringer also makes red★★ and white★ Alluvium (merita wines) from Knight's Valley. The powerful Private Reser Chardonnay★★ is ripe and toasty. Bancroft Ranch Merlot★★ fro HOWELL MOUNTAIN is also very good. Best years: (Cabernet Sauvignon) 20 03 02 01 00 99 98 97 96 95 94 93 91 90 87 86.

BERNKASTEL *Mosel, Germany* Both a historic wine town in the Midd MOSEL and a large Bereich. Top wines, however, come only from vineya sites around the town – the most famous of these is the overpric Doctor vineyard. Many wines from the Graben and Lay sites are often good and cost a fraction of the price. Best producers: Dr LOOSEN★

MOLITOR★, Pauly-Bergweiler★, J J PRUM★★, S A PRUM★, SELBACH-OSTER★★, Studert-Prüm★, Dr H Thanisch★, WEGELER★★. Best years: (2008) 07 06 05 **04 02 01 99 98 97**.

DOM. BERTHOUMIEU *Madiran AC and Pacherenc du Vic-Bilh AC, South-West France*
Didier Barré's wines dead-heat with a handful of others for top place in these appellations. The top red Cuvée Charles de Batz★★ (the real name of d'Artagnan, fictionalized in *The Three Musketeers*) is outstanding. His best PACHERENCS★ are just as good. Best years: (reds) (2008) 05 **04** 02 01 00; (Pacherenc) 2007 **05 04 03 00**.

BEST'S *Grampians, Victoria, Australia* Viv and Chris Thomson run this historic winery, with vineyards dating back to 1868. There have been more recent plantings in the GRAMPIANS and at Lake Boga in the Murray Darling region. The premium range is called Great Western, with superb Bin No. 0 Shiraz★★, good Cabernet★, and a Riesling★ that shows flashes of brilliance. The Thomson Family Shiraz★★ is an outstanding cool-climate Shiraz. Best years: (Thomson Family Shiraz) (2008) 06 05 04 **01 99 98 97 95 94 93 91 90**.

BETZ FAMILY WINERY *Columbia Valley AVA, Washington State, USA* Bob Betz MW spent decades travelling the wine world promoting Washington wines before staking a claim in the goldrush of this young industry. Since 1997, he has crafted wines of uniquely stylish character. Two BORDEAUX-style red blends: Clos de Betz★ and ageworthy, powerful Cabernet Sauvignon-based Père de Famille★★. The Syrah La Côte Rousse★, named for its Red Mountain origin, is opulent; Syrah La Serenne★★ shows more polish and finesse. Best years: (2007) 06 **05** 04.

CH. BEYCHEVELLE★ *St-Julien AC, 4ème Cru Classé, Haut-Médoc, Bordeaux, France* This beautiful château can make wine of Second Growth quality. It has a charming softness even when young, but takes at least a decade to mature into ST-JULIEN's famous cedarwood and blackcurrant flavour. In the best years it is worth its high price and, after a period of inconsistency, quality has become more regular since the late 1990s. Second wine: Amiral de Beychevelle. Best years: 2007 06 05 **04 03 00** 99 **98 96 95 90 89**.

BEYERSKLOOF *Stellenbosch WO, South Africa* Pinotage (Reserve★★) rules at maestro Beyers Truter's property: it contributes to every style from good fizz to a traditional vintage port style, including a flavoursome dry Pinotage rosé and two versions of a succulent Cabernet-Pinotage-Merlot blend called Synergy (Reserve★). There's also the striking Cabernet Sauvignon-based Field Blend★★ (previously named Beyerskloof). Best years: (Field Blend/Beyerskloof) **2004 03 02 01 00 99 98 97 96 95**.

BIANCO DI CUSTOZA DOC *Veneto, Italy* Dry white wine from the shores of Lake Garda, made from a blend of grapes including SOAVE's Garganega. Drink young. Best producers: Cavalchina★, Gorgo★, Montresor★, Le Vigne di San Pietro★, Zeni★.

BIENVENUES-BÂTARD-MONTRACHET AC See BÂTARD-MONTRACHET.

BIERZO DO *Castilla y León, Spain* Sandwiched between the rainy mountains of GALICIA and the arid plains of CASTILLA Y LEON. The arrival of Alvaro PALACIOS, of PRIORAT fame, and his nephew Ricardo Pérez Palacios, with their inspired Corullón★★ red, shed an entirely new and exciting light on the potential of the Mencía grape. Best producers: Bodega del Abad★, Casar de Burbia★, Pérez Caramés, Castro Ventosa★, Estefanía, Luna Beberide★, Paixar★★, Descendientes de José Palacios★★, Peique★, Pittacum★, Prada a Tope, Dominio de Tares★, Valtuille★★.

JOSEF BIFFAR *Deidesheim, Pfalz, Germany* Frequent changes in winemaker have led to somewhat inconsistent dry and sweet Rieslings (often ★, sometimes ★★) from Deidesheim, Ruppertsberg and WACHENHEIM. Best years: (2008) 07 06 05 **04 03 02 01 99**.

BILLECART-SALMON *Champagne AC, Champagne, France* High-quality family-controlled CHAMPAGNE house which makes extremely elegant wines that become irresistible with age. Greatly increased volumes have sadly dumbed down the non-vintage Brut★, but non-vintage Brut Rosé★★, Blanc de Blancs★★★, vintage Cuvée N-F Billecart★★★ and Cuvée Elisabeth Salmon Rosé★★ are all excellent. Clos Saint-Hilaire★★★ is a single-vineyard vintage Blanc de Noirs. Best years: (2002) 00 **98 97 96 95 90 89 88 86 85 82**.

ROLF BINDER *Barossa, South Australia* Rolf and Christa Binder's family winery was known as Veritas until 2004, when the name was changed to avoid confusion with a Veritas winery in the US. The motto *In vino veritas* – In wine there is truth – still holds true. There's certainly truth in the bottom of a bottle of Hanisch Shiraz★★★ or Heysen Shiraz★★★. The Shiraz-Mataro Pressings★★ (known locally as Bull's Blood) and 'Heinrich' Shiraz-Grenache-Mataro★★ blends are lovely big reds; Cabernet-Merlot★★ also impresses. Under the Christa Rolf label, Shiraz-Grenache★ is good and spicy with attractive, forward black fruit.

BINGEN *Rheinhessen, Germany* A small town and also a Bereich, the vineyards of which fall in both the NAHE and RHEINHESSEN. The best vineyard is the Scharlachberg, which produces some exciting wines stinging with racy acidity and the whiff of minerals. Best producers: Kruger-Rumpf, Villa Sachsen. Best years: (2008) 07 06 05 **04 02 01**.

BIONDI-SANTI *Brunello di Montalcino DOCG, Tuscany, Italy* Franco Biondi-Santi's Greppo estate has created both a legend and an international standing for BRUNELLO DI MONTALCINO. The Biondi-Santi style has remained deeply traditional, while that of other producers has moved on. The very expensive Riserva★★, with formidable levels of tannin and acidity, deserves a minimum 10 years' further aging after release before serious judgement is passed on it. Franco's son, Jacopo, has created his own range of wines at Castello di Montepò, including Sassoalloro★★, a barrique-aged Sangiovese, and Sangiovese-Cabernet-Merlot blend Schidione★★. Best years: (Riserva) (2008) (07) (06) (04) (03) (01) (99) 97 95 **90 88 85 83 82 75 64 55 45**.

BLAGNY AC *Côte de Beaune, Burgundy, France* The red wine from this tiny hamlet above MEURSAULT and PULIGNY-MONTRACHET can be fair value, if you like a rustic Burgundy. Actually much more Chardonnay than Pinot Noir is grown here, but this is sold as Puligny-Montrachet, Meursault Premier Cru or Meursault-Blagny. Best producers: R Ampeau★, Lamy-Pillot★, Martelet de Cherisey, Matrot★. Best years: (2008) 07 06 05 **04 03 02 99**.

DOM. PAUL BLANCK *Alsace AC, Alsace, France* One of ALSACE's most interesting and reliable domaines, although real character only shows in the Grand Cru wines. Riesling★★ and Vieilles Vignes Gewurztraminer★★ from the Furstentum Grand Cru (also the source of super-rich Pinot Gris SGN★★★) stand out. Riesling Schlossberg★★ and Pinot Gris Altenbourg★★ offer depth and finesse. Best years: (Grand Cru Riesling) 2007 05 **04 02 01 00 98 97 96 95**.

BLANQUETTE DE LIMOUX AC *Languedoc-Roussillon, France* Refreshing fizz from the Mauzac grape, which makes up a minimum 90% of the wine and gives it its striking 'green apple skin' flavour – the balance is made up of Chardonnay and Chenin Blanc. The traditional (CHAMPAGNE) method is used. The more rustic *méthode rurale*, finishing off the original fermentation inside the bottle, is used under a separate appellation, Blanquette Méthode Ancestrale. **Best producers: Collin, Fourn★, Guinot, Martinolles★, Rives-Blanques★, SIEUR D'ARQUES★.** See also CREMANT DE LIMOUX AC and pages 282–3.

WOLF BLASS *Barossa Valley, South Australia* Wolf Blass, with its huge range, remains a cornerstone (with PENFOLDS) of Australia's largest wine company, the Foster's Wine Group. The wines do still faintly reflect the founder's dictum that they must be easy to enjoy, though I long for them to do better. The reds show overt oak, sometimes clumsy, and occasionally capture the traditional Blass mint and blackcurrant charm. Whites are on the oaky side, except for the Rieslings, which are good, though sweeter and less vibrant than they used to be, including Gold Label Riesling★. Black Label★, a red blend released at 4 years old, is expensive but good. Ultra-expensive Platinum Label Shiraz★ is quite impressive. Regional varietals under the Blass label reflect the winemaking style rather than regional taste, whatever the label says. The Eaglehawk range is reliable quaffing wine. **Best years: (Black Label) (2008) 06 03 02 01 99 98 97 96 95 91 90 88 86; (Platinum Shiraz) (2008) 06 05 04 03 02 01 99 98.**

BLAUBURGUNDER See PINOT NOIR.

BLAUER LEMBERGER See BLAUFRANKISCH.

BLAUFRÄNKISCH Good, ripe Blaufränkisch has a taste similar to raspberries and white pepper or even beetroot. Hungarian in origin, it does well in Austria, where it is the principal red grape of BURGENLAND. The Hungarian vineyards (where it is called Kékfrankos) are mostly just across the border on the other side of the Neusiedlersee. Called Lemberger in Germany, where almost all of it is grown in WURTTEMBERG. Also successful in NEW YORK STATE and (as Lemberger) in WASHINGTON STATE (getting better with global warming!).

BLAYE See PREMIÈRES CÔTES DE BLAYE AC.

JACKY BLOT *Loire Valley, France* When he created Domaine de la Taille aux Loups in MONTLOUIS-SUR-LOIRE and VOUVRAY in 1988, Jacky Blot's use of barrel fermentation and new oak caused controversy. However, rigorous selection of pristine, ripe grapes produces sparkling, dry and sweet whites with tremendous fruit purity. Top Montlouis-sur-Loire cuvées Rémus (sec)★★ and Romulus (liquoreux)★★ are groundbreaking – with staggeringly good 'Plus' versions in exceptional vintages: Romulus Plus 2003★★, Rémus Plus 2006★★. Since 2002 Blot makes three powerful, well-structured reds at Domaine de la Butte★★ in BOURGUEIL AC from separate parcels of south-facing vineyards. **Best years: (whites) (sec) 2008 07 06; (moelleux) 2005 03 02 97 96 95 90.**

BOEKENHOUTSKLOOF *Franschhoek WO, South Africa* Perched high in the FRANSCHHOEK mountains, this small winery is named after the surrounding Cape beech trees. The flagship trio comprises punchy, savoury Syrah★★; deep, long-lived Cabernet Sauvignon★★; and sophisticated Semillon★★ from 100-year-old vines. Placed between these and the fruit-focused, good-value Porcupine Ridge★ range is the burly, expressive Chocolate Block★★, a Cabernet Sauvignon-Shiraz blend with Grenache and Cinsaut. **Best years: (premium reds) 2006 05 04 03 02 01 00 99 98 97.**

BORDEAUX RED WINES

Bordeaux, France

 This large area of South-West France, centred on the historic city of Bordeaux, produces a larger volume of fine red wine than any other French region. Wonderful Bordeaux-style wines are produced in California, Australia, South Africa and South America, but the home team's top performers still just about keep the upstarts at bay. Around 800 million bottles of red wine a year are produced here. The best wines, known as the Classed Growths, account for a tiny percentage of this figure, but some of their lustre rubs off on the lesser names, making this one of the most popular wine styles.

GRAPE VARIETIES

Bordeaux's reds are commonly divided into 'right' and 'left' bank wines. On the left bank of the Gironde estuary, the red wines are dominated by the Cabernet Sauvignon grape, with varying proportions of Cabernet Franc, Merlot and Petit Verdot. At best they are austere but perfumed with blackcurrant and cedarwood. The most important left bank areas are the Haut-Médoc (especially the communes of Margaux, St-Julien, Pauillac and St-Estèphe) and, south of the city of Bordeaux, the ACs of Pessac-Léognan and Graves. On the right bank, Merlot is the predominant grape, which generally makes the resulting wines more supple and fleshy than those of the left bank. The key areas for Merlot-based wines are St-Émilion and Pomerol, Fronsac and Côtes de Castillon.

CLASSIFICATIONS

Red Bordeaux is made all over the region. At its most basic, the wine is simply labelled Bordeaux or Bordeaux Supérieur. Above this are the more specific ACs covering sub-areas (such as the Haut-Médoc) and individual communes (such as Pomerol, St-Émilion or Margaux). Single-estate Crus Bourgeois (a qualification applied for and judged on a yearly basis from the 2007 vintage) are the next rung up on the quality ladder, followed by the Crus Classés (Classed Growths) of the Médoc, Graves and St-Émilion. The famous classification of 1855 ranked the top red wines of the Médoc (plus one from Graves) into 5 tiers, from First to Fifth Growths (Crus); there has been only one change, in 1973 promoting Château Mouton-Rothschild to First Growth status. Since the 1950s the Graves/Pessac-Léognan region has had its own classification, for red and white wines. St-Émilion's classification (for red wines only) has been revised several times, the last modification being in 2006; the possibility of re-grading can help to maintain quality. Curiously, Pomerol, home of Château Pétrus, arguably the most famous red wine in the world, has no official pecking order. Many top Bordeaux châteaux also make 'second wines', which are cheaper versions of their Grands Vins.

See also BORDEAUX, BORDEAUX-CÔTES DE FRANCS, BORDEAUX SUPERIEUR, CANON-FRONSAC, CÔTES DE BOURG, CÔTES DE CASTILLON, FRONSAC, GRAVES, HAUT-MEDOC, LALANDE-DE-POMEROL, LISTRAC-MEDOC, LUSSAC-ST-EMILION, MARGAUX, MEDOC, MONTAGNE-ST-EMILION, MOULIS, PAUILLAC, PESSAC-LEOGNAN, POMEROL, PREMIÈRES CÔTES DE BLAYE, PREMIÈRES CÔTES DE BORDEAUX, PUISSEGUIN-ST-EMILION, ST-EMILION, ST-ESTÈPHE, ST-GEORGES-ST-EMILION, ST-JULIEN; and individual châteaux.

BEST YEARS

2006 05 04 03 **01 00 98 96 95 90 89 88 86 85 83 82 78 75 70 66 64 61**

BEST PRODUCERS

Graves, Pessac-Léognan
Dom. de CHEVALIER, HAUT-BAILLY, HAUT-BRION, la LOUVIERE, MALARTIC-LAGRAVIERE, la MISSION-HAUT-BRION, PAPE-CLEMENT, SMITH-HAUT-LAFITTE.

Margaux BRANE-CANTENAC, FERRIÈRE, MALESCOT ST-EXUPERY, MARGAUX, PALMER, RAUZAN-SEGLA, SIRAN, du Tertre.

Pauillac GRAND-PUY-LACOSTE, HAUT-BAGES-LIBERAL, LAFITE-ROTHSCHILD, LATOUR, LYNCH-BAGES, MOUTON-ROTHSCHILD, PICHON-LONGUEVILLE, PICHON-LONGUEVILLE-LALANDE, PONTET-CANET.

Pomerol le BON PASTEUR, Certan-de-May, Clinet, la CONSEILLANTE, l'EGLISE-CLINET, l'EVANGILE, la FLEUR-PETRUS, GAZIN, LAFLEUR, LATOUR-A-POMEROL, PETIT-VILLAGE, PETRUS, le PIN, TROTANOY, VIEUX-CHATEAU-CERTAN.

St-Émilion ANGELUS, AUSONE, BEAU-SEJOUR BECOT, BELAIR, CANON, CANON-LA-GAFFELIERE, CHEVAL BLANC, Clos Fourtet, la Dominique, FIGEAC, Grand Mayne, MAGDELAINE, MONBOUSQUET, La Mondotte, PAVIE, PAVIE-MACQUIN, Rol Valentin, TERTRE-ROTEBOEUF, TROPLONG-MONDOT, VALANDRAUD.

St-Estèphe CALON-SEGUR, COS D'ESTOURNEL, HAUT-MARBUZET, LAFON-ROCHET, MONTROSE, les Ormes de Pez.

St-Julien BRANAIRE-DUCRU, DUCRU-BEAUCAILLOU, GRUAUD-LAROSE, LAGRANGE, LANGOA-BARTON, LEOVILLE-BARTON, LEOVILLE-LAS-CASES, LEOVILLE-POYFERRE, ST-PIERRE, TALBOT.

BORDEAUX WHITE WINES

Bordeaux, France

This is France's largest fine wine region but, except for the sweet wines of Sauternes and Barsac, Bordeaux's international reputation is based solely on its reds. From 52% of the vineyard area in 1970, white wines now represent only 12% of the present 120,000ha (296,500 acres) of vines. Given the size of the region, the diversity of Bordeaux's white wines should come as no surprise. There are dry, medium and sweet styles, ranging from dreary to some of the most sublime white wines of all. Bordeaux's temperate southern climate – moderated by the influence of the Atlantic and of two rivers, the Dordogne and the Garonne – is ideal for white wine production, particularly south of the city along the banks of the Garonne.

GRAPE VARIETIES
Sauvignon Blanc and Sémillon, the most important white grapes, are both varieties of considerable character and are usually blended together. They are backed up by smaller quantities of other grapes, the most notable of which is Muscadelle (unrelated to Muscat), which lends perfume to sweet wines and spiciness to dry.

DRY WINES
With the introduction of new technology and new ideas, many of them influenced by the New World, Bordeaux has become one of France's most exciting white wine areas. There are both oaked and unoaked styles. The unoaked are leafy, tangy and stony-dry. The barrel-fermented styles are delightfully rich yet dry, custard-cream softness mellowing leafy acidity and peach and nectarine fruit.

SWEET WINES
Bordeaux's most famous whites are its sweet wines made from grapes affected by noble rot, particularly those from Sauternes and Barsac. The noble rot concentrates the flavours, producing rich, honeyed wines replete with pineapple and peach flavours, and which develop a lanolin and beeswax depth and a barley sugar and honey richness with age. On the other side of the Garonne river, Cadillac, Loupiac and Ste-Croix-du-Mont also make sweet wines; these rarely attain the richness or complexity of a top Sauternes, but they are considerably less expensive.

CLASSIFICATIONS
The two largest dry white wine ACs in Bordeaux are Bordeaux Blanc and Entre-Deux-Mers. There are plenty of good dry wines in the Graves and Pessac-Léognan regions; the Pessac-Léognan AC, created in 1987, contains all the dry white Classed Growths. The great sweet wines of Sauternes and Barsac were classified as First or Second Growths in 1855.

See also BARSAC, BORDEAUX, BORDEAUX-CÔTES DE FRANCS, BORDEAUX SUPERIEUR, CADILLAC, CERONS, CÔTES DE BOURG, ENTRE-DEUX-MERS, GRAVES, LOUPIAC, PESSAC-LEOGNAN, PREMIÈRES CÔTES DE BLAYE, PREMIÈRES CÔTES DE BORDEAUX, STE-CROIX-DU-MONT, SAUTERNES; and individual châteaux.

(dry) **2007 06 05 04 02 01 00 99 98 96 95**; (sweet) 2007 05 **03 02 01 99 98 97 96 95 90 89 88 86 83**

BEST PRODUCERS

Dry wines

Pessac-Léognan Dom. de CHEVALIER, Couhins-Lurton, FIEUZAL, HAUT-BRION, LATOUR-MARTILLAC, LAVILLE-HAUT-BRION, la LOUVIERE, MALARTIC-LAGRAVIERE, SMITH-HAUT-LAFITTE;
Graves Archambeau, Ardennes, Brondelle, Chantegrive, Clos Floridène, Magneau, Rahoul, Respide-Médeville, St-Robert (Cuvée Poncet-Deville), Vieux-Ch.-Gaubert, Villa Bel Air.

Entre-Deux-Mers BONNET, de Fontenille, Nardique-la-Gravière, Ste-Marie, Toutigeac, Turcaud.

Bordeaux AC l'Abbaye de Ste-Ferme, Bauduc, DOISY-DAENE (Sec), LYNCH-BAGES, Ch. MARGAUX (Pavillon Blanc), REYNON, Roquefort, TALBOT, Thieuley, Tour de Mirambeau.

Premières Côtes de Blaye Charron (Acacia), Haut-Bertinerie, Cave des Hauts de Gironde co-op (Chapelle de Tutiac), Tourtes (Prestige).

Sweet wines

Sauternes and Barsac CLIMENS, Clos Haut-Peyraguey, COUTET, DOISY-DAENE, DOISY-VEDRINES, FARGUES, GILETTE, GUIRAUD, LAFAURIE-PEYRAGUEY, NAIRAC, Raymond-Lafon, RIEUSSEC, Sigalas-Rabaud, SUDUIRAUT, la TOUR BLANCHE, YQUEM.

Cadillac Fayau, Manos, Mémoires.

Cérons Ch. de Cérons, Grand Enclos du Ch. de Cérons.

Loupiac Clos Jean, Cros, Mémoires, Noble.

Ste-Croix-du-Mont Loubens, Pavillon, la Rame.

BOIREANN *Queensland, Australia* Peter and Therese Stark established Boireann in 1995 as a retirement project to specialize in red wines, with 400 Cabernet vines. It's now QUEENSLAND's most impressive winery, with a 1.5ha (3.5-acre) vineyard planted to 10 red varieties plus Viognier for the flagship fragrant, plush Shiraz-Viognier★★. Other stunning reds include: Merlot★★, Cabernet Sauvignon★ and, from 2008, the seductive Lurnea blend (Merlot, Cabernets Sauvignon and Franc and Petit Verdot). A frost wiped out the 2007 vintage; a replacement range of very good reds was made from growers' fruit.

BOISSET *Burgundy, France* Jean-Claude Boisset bought his first vineyards in 1964 and began a *négociant* company whose extraordinary success has enabled him to swallow up many other long-established names such as Jaffelin, Ponelle, Ropiteau and Héritier Guyot in the CÔTE D'OR, Moreau in CHABLIS, Cellier des Samsons and Mommessin in BEAUJOLAIS and others elsewhere in France. Most of these companies are designed to produce commercially successful rather than fine wine, excepting Domaine de la VOUGERAIE and, recently, Boisset itself. Also projects in California, Canada, Chile and Uruguay.

BOLGHERI DOC *Tuscany, Italy* Zone named after an arty village in the northern MAREMMA with, originally, simple white and rosé wines, later major reds based on Cabernet, Merlot and/or Syrah. There is a special sub-zone for SASSICAIA. Best producers: Ca' Marcanda★ (GAJA), Guado a Tasso★★ (ANTINORI), Grattamacco★★, Le MACCHIOLE★★, ORNELLAIA★★, Poggio al Tesoro★, Michele Satta★★. Best years: (reds) (2008) (07) (06) **05** 0 03 01 00 99 98 97.

BOLLINGER *Champagne AC, Champagne, France* One of the great CHAMPAGN houses, with good non-vintage (Special Cuvée★) and vintage wine (Grande Année★★★), made in a full, rich, rather old-fashioned style (Bollinger is one of the few houses to ferment its base wine in barrels.) I also produces a range of rarer vintages, including Vintage RD★★★, and Vieilles Vignes Françaises Blanc de Noirs★★ from ancient, ungrafte Pinot Noir vines. New delightfully soft, creamy non-vintage Brut Rosé Bollinger bought Champagne Ayala, a neighbour in Ay, in 2005. Bes years: (Grande Année) 2000 **99** 97 96 **95** 92 90 89 88 85 82 79.

CH. LE BON PASTEUR★★ *Pomerol AC, Bordeaux, France* Owned by Miche Rolland, Bordeaux's most famous winemaker. The wines are expensive but they are always deliciously soft and full of lush fruit. Best years: 200 05 04 03 01 00 99 98 96 95 94 90 89 88 85.

BONNES-MARES AC *Grand Cru, Côte de Nuits, Burgundy, France* A large Gran Cru straddling the communes of CHAMBOLLE-MUSIGNY and MOREY-ST-DENIS commendably consistent over the last few decades. Bonnes-Mare generally has a deep, ripe, smoky plum fruit, which starts rich and chew and matures over 10–20 years. Best producers: d'Auvenay (Dom LEROY)★★★, BOUCHARD PÈRE ET FILS★★, DROUHIN★★, Drouhin-Laroze★ DUJAC★★★, Robert Groffier★★★, JADOT★★★, D Laurent★★, J-MUGNIER★★, ROUMIER★★, de VOGÜE★★, VOUGERAIE★★★. Best year (2008) 07 06 05 03 02 **01** 99 **98** 96 **95** 93 90.

CH. BONNET *Entre-Deux-Mers AC, Bordeaux, France* This region's pioneerin estate for quality and consistency. Large volumes of good, fruit affordable ENTRE-DEUX-MERS★ and BORDEAUX AC rosé and red, particular the barrel-aged Réserve★. Drink this at 3–4 years and the others youn Also a special cuvée, Divinus★. Owner André Lurton is also th proprietor of Ch. La LOUVIERE and other properties in PESSAC-LEOGNAN.

BONNEZEAUX AC *Loire Valley, France* One of France's great sweet wines, Bonnezeaux is a zone within the COTEAUX DU LAYON AC. Quality is variable, but top wines are world class. It can age very well in good vintages. Best producers: M Angeli/Sansonnière★★★, Fesles★★★, Godineau★★, des Grandes Vignes★★, Petit Val★★, Petits Quarts★★, Terrebrune★★, la Varière★★. Best years: 2007 06 05 **04 03 02 01 99 97 96 95 90 89**.

BONNY DOON *Santa Cruz Mountains AVA, California, USA* Randall Grahm has a particular love for Rhône and Italian varietals: Le Cigare Volant★★ is a blend of Grenache and Syrah and is Grahm's homage to CHÂTEAUNEUF-DU-PAPE. His Ca' del Solo Italianate wines are delightful. Grahm's new PACIFIC RIM winery in Washington focuses entirely on Riesling.

BORDEAUX AC *Bordeaux, France* One of the most important ACs in France, covering reds, rosés and the dry, medium and sweet white wines of the entire Gironde region. Most of the best wines are allowed specific district or commune ACs (such as MARGAUX or SAUTERNES) but a vast amount of Bordeaux's wine – delicious, atrocious and everything in between – is sold as Bordeaux AC. At its best, straight red Bordeaux is marked by bone-dry leafy fruit and an attractive earthy edge, but far more frequently the wines are tannic and raw – and often overpriced. Good examples usually benefit from a year or so of aging. Bordeaux Blanc has joined the modern world with an increasing number of refreshing, pleasant wines. These may be labelled as Bordeaux Sauvignon. Drink young. Bordeaux Clairet is a pale red wine, virtually rosé but with a little more substance. Best producers: (reds) BONNET★, d:vin★, Dourthe (Numéro 1), Ducla, Fontenille★, Gadras, Sirius, Thieuley★, Tour de Mirambeau; (whites) l'Abbaye de Ste-Ferme★, Bauduc★, DOISY-DAËNE★, Dourthe (Numéro 1★), LYNCH-BAGES★, MARGAUX (Pavillon Blanc★★), REYNON★, Roquefort★, TALBOT★, Thieuley★, Tour de Mirambeau★. See also pages 82–5.

BORDEAUX-CÔTES DE FRANCS AC *Bordeaux, France* Tiny area east of ST-EMILION; part of new Côtes de Bordeaux AC from 2008; the top wines are good value. The Thienpont family (Ch. Puygueraud) is the driving force. Best producers: les Charmes-Godard★, Franc-Cardinal, Francs (Les Cerisiers★★), Laclaverie★, Marsau★, Nardou, Pelan★, la Prade★, Puygueraud★★, Vieux Saule. Best years: **2005 04 03 01 00 98**.

BORDEAUX SUPÉRIEUR AC *Bordeaux, France* Covers the same area as the BORDEAUX AC but the wines must have an extra 0.5% of alcohol, a lower yield and a longer period of maturation. Many of the best petits châteaux are labelled Bordeaux Supérieur. Best producers: (reds) Barreyre★, Beaulieu Comtes des Tastes★, de Bouillerot★, des Chapelains, de Courteillac★, Grand Village★, Parenchère★, Penin★, Pey la Tour★, le Pin Beausoleil★, Reignac★, Thieuley (Réserve Francis Courselle★), Tire-Pé★.

BORIE LA VITARÈLE *St-Chinian AC, Languedoc, France* The Izarn family produces two ST-CHINIANs, which express the different soils of their organic vineyard: Les Crès★, dominated by Syrah, is spicy and warm; Les Schistes is cooler, more elegant. Best years: (2008) 06 05 **04 03 01 00**.

LUIGI BOSCA *Mendoza, Argentina* Founded by the Arizú family in 1901 and still family-owned, this winery has 400ha (1000 acres) in LUJÁN DE CUYO and Maipú. Try the mineral Finca Los Nobles Chardonnay★, the dense, chocolaty Finca Los Nobles Malbec-Verdot★ and the more complex and sophisticated Malbec-based blend Gala 1★★ and Cabernet-based Gala 2★. Icono★ (from 2005 vintage) is a Malbec-Cabernet blend. Best years: (reds) 2006 **05 04 03 02 01**.

BOSCARELLI *Vino Nobile di Montepulciano DOCG, Tuscany, Italy* Arguably
Montepulciano's best producer, crafting rich and stylish reds with
guidance from star enologist Maurizio Castelli. VINO NOBILE★★, Riserva
del Nocio★★ and the barrique-aged SUPER-TUSCAN Boscarelli★★ are all
brilliant. Best years: (2008) (07) (06) **04 03 01 00 99 97**.

BOUCHARD FINLAYSON *Walker Bay WO, South Africa* Pinotphile Peter
Finlayson produces classy Pinot Noir (Galpin Peak★ and occasional Tête
de Cuvée★★). His love of Italian varieties is reflected in Hannibal★★, a
multi-cultural mix led by Sangiovese with Pinot Noir, Nebbiolo, Barbera
and Shiraz. Chardonnays (Kaimansgaat/Crocodile's Lair★ – now
fresher, more citrusy and less obviously oaky – and full, nutty home
grown Missionvale★) are plausibly Burgundian. Sauvignon Blanc★ is
tangy and fresh. Best years: (Pinot Noir) 2007 06 **05 04 03 02 01 00 99**.

BOUCHARD PÈRE ET FILS *Beaune, Burgundy, France* Important merchant
and vineyard owner, with vines in some of Burgundy's most spectacular
sites, including CORTON★★, CORTON-CHARLEMAGNE★★, Chevalier-
Montrachet★★ and le MONTRACHET★★★. The firm is owned by
Champenois Joseph HENRIOT, who is now realizing the full potential here.
Wines from the company's own vineyards are sold under the Dom. du
Château de Beaune label. Best years: (top reds) (2008) 07 06 05 03 **02 00 99**

BOUCHES-DU-RHÔNE, VIN DE PAYS DES *Provence, France* Wines from
3 areas: the coast, a zone around Aix-en-Provence and the Camargue.
Mainly full-bodied, spicy reds, with estates like Trevallon making use of
the vin de pays status to use a high percentage of Cabernet Sauvignon.
Unusual varieties include Caladoc (Grenache x Malbec) at la Michelle
and Arinaroa (Merlot x Petit Verdot) at St-Pierre. Rosé can be good too.
Best producers: Ch. Bas, l'Île St-Pierre, Mas de Rey, la Michelle, TREVALLON★★
Best years: (reds) **2007 06 05**.

DOM. HENRI BOURGEOIS *Sancerre AC, Loire Valley, France* Large-scale outfit
in SANCERRE with 67ha (166 acres) of domaine vineyards and a substantial
négociant business extending into other Loire appellations, plus Clos
Henri label in New Zealand. Consistently high quality from the vin de
pays Petit Bourgeois up. The Monts Damnés cuvées★ from
precipitously steep slope have bags of mineral character. Old-vine, soil-
specific bottlings Jadis★★ (Sauvignon Gris on Kimmeridgian clay)
d'Antan★★ (silex) and the rare barrel-fermented Étienne Henri★★ are
among the finest in Sancerre. Good red Sancerre too. Best years: (top
wines) 2008 07 **06 05 04 02**.

BOURGOGNE AC *Burgundy, France* Bourgogne is the French name
anglicized as 'Burgundy'. This generic AC mops up all the Burgundian
wine with no AC of its own, resulting in massive differences in style and
quality. The best wines will usually come from a single grower's vineyard
just outside the main village ACs of the COTE D'OR; such wines may be the
only way we can afford the joys of fine Burgundy. If the wine is from a
grower, the flavours should follow a regional or local style. However, if the
address on the label is that of a négociant, the wine could be from
anywhere in Burgundy. Pinot Noir is the main red grape, but Gamay
from a declassified BEAUJOLAIS cru is, absurdly, allowed. Red Bourgogne
usually light, fruity in an upfront strawberry and cherry way, and should be
drunk within 2–3 years. The rosé (Pinot Noir) can be pleasant, but little is
produced. Bourgogne Blanc is a usually bone-dry Chardonnay wine and
most should be drunk within 2 years. Bourgogne Passe-tout-Grains is
made from Gamay with a minimum 33% of Pinot Noir, while Bourgogne

Grand Ordinaire is rarely more than a quaffing wine, drunk in local bars. Best producers: (reds/growers) G Barthod★★, COCHE-DURY★, Dugat-Py★★, Germain/Ch. de Chorey★, LAFARGE★, MEO-CAMUZET★★, P RION★★, ROUMIER★, VOUGERAIE★; (reds/merchants) DROUHIN★, GIRARDIN★, JADOT★, Labouré-Roi, Maison Leroy★★, N POTEL★★; (reds/co-ops) BUXYNOISE★, Caves des Hautes-Côtes★; (whites/growers) M BOUZEREAU★, Boyer-Martenot★, J-M BROCARD★, COCHE-DURY★★, J-P Fichet★, P Javillier★★, Ch. de Meursault★, Pierre Morey★, Guy Roulot★; (whites/merchants) DROUHIN★, FAIVELEY, JADOT★, Olivier LEFLAIVE, RODET★; (whites/co-ops) BUXYNOISE, Caves des Hautes-Côtes. Best years: (reds) (2008) **07 05**; (whites) 2008 **07 06**. See also pages 90–3.

BOURGOGNE ALIGOTÉ AC See ALIGOTE.

BOURGOGNE-CÔTE CHALONNAISE AC *Côte Chalonnaise, Burgundy, France* The AC covers vineyards to the west of Chalon-sur-Saône around the villages of Bouzeron, RULLY, MERCUREY, GIVRY and MONTAGNY. Best producers: X Besson, BUXYNOISE co-op★, Villaine★. Best years: (reds) (2008) **07 05**; (whites) (2008) **07 06**.

BOURGOGNE-HAUTES-CÔTES DE BEAUNE AC *Burgundy, France* The hills behind the great CÔTE DE BEAUNE are a good source of affordable Burgundy. The red wines are lean but drinkable, as is the slightly sharp Chardonnay. Best producers: Caves des Hautes-Côtes★, J-Y Devevey★, L Jacob★, J-L Joillot★, Ch. de Mercey★/RODET★, Naudin-Ferrand★, C Nouveau★. Best years: (reds) (2008) **07 06 05**; (whites) **2008 07 06 05**.

BOURGOGNE-HAUTES-CÔTES DE NUITS AC *Burgundy, France* Attractive, lightweight wines from the hills behind the CÔTE DE NUITS. The reds are best, with an attractive cherry and plum flavour. The whites tend to be rather dry and flinty. Best producers: (reds) D Duband★, FAIVELEY★, A-F GROS★, M GROS★, A Guyon★, Caves des Hautes-Côtes★, Jayer-Gilles★★, T LIGER-BELAIR★, A Verdet★; (whites) Caves des Hautes-Côtes★, Champy★, Jayer-Gilles★, Thévenot-le-Brun★. Best years: (reds) (2008) **07 06 05**; (whites) **2008 07 06 05**.

BOURGUEIL AC *Loire Valley, France* Fine red wine from between Tours and Angers, made with Cabernet Franc, sometimes with a little Cabernet Sauvignon. A concerted quality drive, together with a good run of vintages, is shedding its reputation for rusticity; expect plump raspberry and plum fruit. Best producers: Y Amirault★★, Audebert (estate wines★), BLOT/la Butte★★, T Boucard★, P Breton★, la Chevalerie, Clos de l'Abbaye★, Max Cognard, DRUET★★, Forges, Lamé-Delisle-Boucard, la Lande/Delaunay, F MABILEAU★, Nau Frères★, Ouches★, Les Pins, Raguenières★. Best years: (2008) **06 05 04 03 02 01 97 96**. See also ST-NICOLAS-DE-BOURGUEIL.

BOUZEREAU *Meursault, Côte de Beaune, Burgundy, France* An extended family of vignerons, all making a range of whites from MEURSAULT and neighbouring villages, plus some less interesting CÔTE DE BEAUNE reds. Best at the moment are Dom. Michel Bouzereau & Fils★ and Vincent Bouzereau★. Best years: (whites) (2008) **07 06 05 04 02**.

BOYAR ESTATES *Bulgaria* The leading distributor of Bulgarian wines, selling more than 65 million bottles worldwide each year. Quality is erratic: many reds are raw and tannic, whites are merely decent.

BRACHETTO An unusual Italian grape native to Piedmont, Brachetto makes every style from dry and still to rich, sweet passito and sweet, frothy light red wines with a Muscat-like perfume, as exemplified by Brachetto d'Acqui DOCG. Best producers: (dry) Contero, Correggia★, Scarpa★; (Brachetto d'Acqui) BANFI★, Braida★, G Marenco★.

BURGUNDY RED WINES

Burgundy, France

 Rich in history and gastronomic tradition, the region of Burgundy (Bourgogne in French) covers a vast tract of eastern France, running from Auxerre, south-east of Paris, down to the city of Mâcon. As with its white wines, Burgundy's red wines are extremely diverse. The explanation for this lies partly in the fickle nature of Pinot Noir, the area's principal red grape, and partly in the historical imbalance of supply and demand between growers – who grow the grapes and make and bottle much of the best wine – and merchants, whose efforts originally established the reputation of the wines internationally.

WINE STYLES

Pinot Noir shows many different flavour profiles according to climate, soil and winemaking. The reds from around Auxerre (Épineuil, Irancy) in the north will be light, chalky and strawberry-flavoured. Also light, though more rustic and earthy, are the reds of the Mâconnais in the south, while the Côte Chalonnaise offers solid reds from Givry and Mercurey.

The top reds come from the Côte d'Or, the heartland of Burgundy. Flavours sweep through strawberry, raspberry, damson and cherry – in young wines – to a wild, magnificent maturity of Oriental spices, chocolate, mushrooms and truffles. The greatest of all – the world-famous Grand Cru vineyards such as Chambertin, Musigny, Richebourg and Clos de Vougeot – are in the Côte de Nuits, the northern part of the Côte d'Or from Nuits-St-Georges up towards Dijon. Other fine reds, especially Volnay, Pommard and Corton, come from the Côte de Beaune. Some villages tend towards a fine and elegant style (Chambolle-Musigny, Volnay), others towards a firmer, more tannic structure (Gevrey-Chambertin, Pommard).

The Beaujolais should really be considered as a separate region, growing Gamay on granitic soils rather than Pinot Noir on limestone, though a small amount of Gamay has also crept north to be included in the lesser wines of Burgundy.

CLASSIFICATIONS

Most of Burgundy has 5 increasingly specific levels of classification: regional ACs (e.g. Bourgogne), specified ACs covering groups of villages (e.g. Côte de Nuits-Villages), village wines taking the village name (Pommard, Vosne-Romanée), Premiers Crus (good village vineyard sites) and Grands Crus (the best individual vineyard sites). At village level, vineyard names in small letters are called *lieux-dits*.

See also ALOXE-CORTON, AUXEY-DURESSES, BEAUJOLAIS, BEAUNE, BLAGNY, BONNES-MARES, BOURGOGNE, BOURGOGNE-COTE CHALONNAISE, BOURGOGNE-HAUTES-COTES DE BEAUNE/NUITS, CHAMBERTIN, CHAMBOLLE-MUSIGNY, CHASSAGNE-MONTRACHET, CHOREY-LÈS-BEAUNE, CLOS DE LA ROCHE, CLOS ST-DENIS, CLOS DE VOUGEOT, CORTON, CÔTE DE BEAUNE, CÔTE DE NUITS, CÔTE D'OR, CREMANT DE BOURGOGNE, ECHEZEAUX, FIXIN, GEVREY-CHAMBERTIN, GIVRY, IRANCY, LADOIX, MÂCON, MARANGES, MARSANNAY, MERCUREY, MONTHELIE, MOREY-ST-DENIS, MUSIGNY, NUITS-ST-GEORGES, PERNAND-VERGELESSES, POMMARD, RICHEBOURG, la ROMANEE-CONTI, ROMANEE-ST-VIVANT, RULLY, ST-AUBIN, ST-ROMAIN, SANTENAY, SAVIGNY-LÈS-BEAUNE, la TÂCHE, VOLNAY, VOSNE-ROMANEE, VOUGEOT; and individual producers.

(2008) 07 06 05 **03 02 01 99 98 96 95 90**

BEST PRODUCERS

Côte de Nuits B Ambroise, Arlaud, l'Arlot, Robert Arnoux, Denis Bachelet, G Barthod, A Burguet, Cacheux-Sirugue, S CATHIARD, Charlopin, J Chauvenet, R Chevillon, Chopin-Groffier, B CLAIR, CLOS DES LAMBRAYS, CLOS DE TART, J-J Confuron, P Damoy, Drouhin-Laroze, C Dugat, B Dugat-Py, DUJAC, Sylvie Esmonin, Fourrier, Geantet-Pansiot, H GOUGES, GRIVOT, R Groffier, GROS, Hudelot-Noëllat, Jayer-Gilles, F Lamarche, Lechenaut, Philippe Leclerc, Dom. LEROY, LIGER-BELAIR, H Lignier, MEO-CAMUZET, Denis MORTET, Mugneret, Mugneret-Gibourg, J-F MUGNIER, Perrot-Minot, Ponsot, RION, Dom. de la ROMANEE-CONTI, Rossignol-Trapet, Roty, E Rouget, ROUMIER, ROUSSEAU, Sérafin, Taupenot-Merme, J & J-L Trapet, de VOGUE, VOUGERAIE.

Côte de Beaune R Ampeau, d'ANGERVILLE, Comte Armand, Bize, H Boillot, J-M Boillot, CHANDON DE BRIAILLES, COCHE-DURY, Courcel, Germain/Ch. de Chorey, Michel LAFARGE, LAFON, de MONTILLE, J Prieur, TOLLOT-BEAUT.

Côte Chalonnaise Joblot, M Juillot, Lorenzon, Raquillet, de Suremain, Villaine.

Merchants BOUCHARD PERE ET FILS, Champy, DROUHIN, FAIVELEY, V GIRARDIN, Camille Giroud, JADOT, Labouré-Roi, D Laurent, Maison Leroy, Nicolas POTEL, RODET.

Co-ops BUXYNOISE, Caves des Hautes-Côtes.

BURGUNDY WHITE WINES

Burgundy, France

White Burgundy has for generations been thought of a the world's leading dry white wine. The top wines have remarkable succulent richness of honey and hazelnut melted butter and sprinkled spice, yet are totally dry. Such wines are all from the Chardonnay grape and the finest are generally produced in the Côte de Beaune, the southern part of th Côte d'Or, in the communes of Aloxe-Corton, Meursault, Puligny Montrachet, Chassagne-Montrachet and St-Aubin, where limeston soils and the aspect of the vineyard provide perfect conditions for even ripening of grapes. However, Burgundy encompasses many more win styles than this, even if no single one quite attains the peaks of quality o those 5 villages on the Côte de Beaune.

WINE STYLES

Chablis in the north traditionally produces very good steely wines aggressive and lean when young, but nutty and rounded – though sti very dry – after a few years. Modern Chablis is frequently a softer, milde wine, easy to drink young, and sometimes enriched (or denatured) b aging in new oak barrels.

There is no doubt that Meursault and the other Côte de Beaun villages can produce stupendous wine, but it is in such demand tha unscrupulous producers are often tempted to maximize yields and cu corners on quality. Consequently white Burgundy from these famou villages must be approached with caution. Lesser-known villages such a Pernand-Vergelesses and St-Aubin often provide good wine at lowe prices. There are also good wines from some villages in the Côte d Nuits, such as Morey-St-Denis, Nuits-St-Georges and Vougeot, thoug amounts are tiny compared with the Côte de Beaune.

South of the Côte d'Or the Côte Chalonnaise is becoming mor interesting for quality white wine now that better equipment fo temperature control is becoming more widespread and oak barrels ar being used more often for aging. Rully and Montagny are the mos important villages, though Givry and Mercurey can produce nice white too. The minor Aligoté grape makes some attractive, if acidic, wine especially in Bouzeron.

Further south, the Mâconnais is a large region, two-thirds plante with Chardonnay. There is some fair sparkling Crémant de Bourgogne and some very good vineyard sites, in particular in St-Véran and i Pouilly-Fuissé. Increasingly stunning wines can now be found, thoug there's still a lot of dross.

See also ALOXE-CORTON, AUXEY-DURESSES, BÂTARD-MONTRACHET, BEAUJOLAIS, BEAUNE, BOURGOGNE, BOURGOGNE-COTE CHALONNAISE, BOURGOGNE-HAUTES-COTES DE BEAUNE/NUITS, CHABLIS, CHASSAGNE-MONTRACHET, CORTON, CORTON-CHARLEMAGNE, CÔTE DE BEAUNE, CÔTE DE NUITS, CÔTE D'OR, CREMANT DE BOURGOGNE, FIXIN, GIVRY, LADOIX, MÂCON, MACON-VILLAGES, MARANGES, MARSANNAY, MERCUREY, MEURSAULT, MONTAGNY, MONTHELIE, MONTRACHET, MOREY-ST-DENIS, MUSIGNY, NUITS-ST-GEORGES, PERNAND-VERGELESSES, POUILLY-FUISSE, POUILLY-VINZELLES, PULIGNY-MONTRACHET, RULLY, ST-AUBIN, ST-ROMAIN, ST-VERAN, SANTENAY, SAVIGNY-LÈS-BEAUNE, VIRE-CLESSE, VOUGEOT; and individual producers.

BEST PRODUCERS

Chablis Barat, J-C Bessin, Billaud-Simon, P Bouchard, A & F Boudin, J-M BROCARD, D Dampt, R & V DAUVISSAT, D-E Defaix, Droin, DURUP, W Fèvre, J-H Goisot, J-P Grossot, LAROCHE, Long-Depaquit, Malandes, Louis Michel, C Moreau, Moreau Naudet★, Picq, Pinson, RAVENEAU, Vocoret.

Côte d'Or (Côte de Beaune) R Ampeau, d'Auvenay (LEROY), Blain-Gagnard, H Boillot, J-M Boillot, Bonneau du Martray, M BOUZEREAU, Boyer-Martenot, CARILLON, CHANDON DE BRIAILLES, Coche-Debord, COCHE-DURY, Marc Colin, Dancer, Arnaud Ente, J-P Fichet, Fontaine-Gagnard, J-N GAGNARD, A Gras, P Javillier, F Jobard, R Jobard, LAFON, H Lamy, Dom. LEFLAIVE, Matrot, Bernard Morey, Marc Morey, Pierre Morey, M Niellon, P Pernot, J & J-M Pillot, RAMONET, M Rollin, G Roulot, SAUZET, VERGET, VOUGERAIE.

Côte Chalonnaise S Aladame, H & P Jacqueson.

Mâconnais D & M Barraud, A Bonhomme, Bret Brothers, Cordier, Corsin, Deux Roches, J-A Ferret, Ch. Fuissé, Guffens-Heynen/VERGET, Guillot-Broux, O Merlin, Robert-Denogent, Ch. des Rontets, Saumaize-Michelin, la Soufrandière, J Thévenet.

Merchants BOUCHARD PERE ET FILS, Champy, DROUHIN, FAIVELEY, V GIRARDIN, JADOT, Labouré-Roi, Louis LATOUR, Olivier LEFLAIVE, Maison Leroy, Rijckaert, RODET, VERGET.

Co-ops la BUXYNOISE, la CHABLISIENNE, Lugny, Viré.

CH. BRANAIRE-DUCRU★★ *St-Julien AC, 4ème Cru Classé, Haut-Médoc, Bordeaux,*
France After a long period of mediocrity, 1994 and subsequent vintages
have confirmed a welcome return to full, soft, chocolaty form, with some
added muscle in recent vintages. Best years: 2006 05 **04 03 02 01 00 99 98**
96 95 94.

BRAND'S *Coonawarra, South Australia* COONAWARRA firm, owned by MCWILLIAM'S
with 100ha (250 acres) of new vineyards as well as some ancient vines
planted in 1893. Ripe Laira Cabernet★ is increasingly attractive; Patron's
Reserve★★ (Cabernet with Shiraz and Merlot) is excellent. New life has
been breathed into Shiraz★, and the opulent Stentiford's Reserve★
(from 100-year-old vines) shows how good Coonawarra Shiraz can be.
Merlot★★ is among Australia's best examples of the variety. Best years
(reds) (2008) 06 05 **04 03 02 01 00 99 98 97 96 94 90**.

CH. BRANE-CANTENAC★★ *Margaux AC, 2ème Cru Classé, Haut-Médoc,*
Bordeaux, France After a drab period, Brane-Cantenac returned to form
during the late 1990s. Henri Lurton has taken over the family property
and is making some superb wines, particularly the 2000, although don't
expect flavours to be mainstream – years like 2002 and 2003 are tasty but
wild. Best years: 2007 06 05 **04 03 02 01 00 99 98 96 95 89**.

BRAUNEBERG *Mosel, Germany* Small village with 2 famous vineyard sites:
Juffer and (especially) Juffer Sonnenuhr, whose wines have a honeyed
richness and creaminess rare in the Mosel. Best producers: Bastgen★, Fritz
HAAG★★★, Willi Haag★, Paulinshof★, M F RICHTER★★, SCHLOSS LIESER★★. Best
years: (2008) 07 06 05 **04 03 02 01 99 97**.

BREAKY BOTTOM *Sussex, England* Small vineyard in the South Downs
near Lewes. Peter Hall is a quirky, passionate grower, now only making
delicious sparkling wines, principally from Seyval Blanc★, which
continue to improve. Newer plantings include Chardonnay and Pinot
Noir, which will soon be in sparkling wine blends.

GEORG BREUER *Rüdesheim, Rheingau, Germany* Intense dry Riesling from
RUDESHEIM Berg Schlossberg★★★, Berg Rottland★★ and RAUENTHAL
Nonnenberg★★. Also a remarkable Sekt★. Quality remains very high
despite Bernhard Breuer's untimely death in 2004. Best years: (Berg
Schlossberg) (2008) 07 06 05 04 **03 02 01 00 99 98 97**.

BRIGHT BROTHERS *Ribatejo, Portugal* The Fiúza-Bright operation is
located in the town of Almeirim; Fiúza-labelled wines are from local
vineyards planted to both Portuguese and French varieties. Australian
Peter Bright also makes Brightpink, Brightwhite and Brightred table
wines, in aluminium bottles, and red and white Fado ALENTEJO wines.

JEAN-MARC BROCARD *Chablis, Burgundy, France* Dynamic winemaker who
has built up this 80ha (200-acre) domaine almost from scratch, and is
now one of Chablis' most reliable and satisfying producers. The Premier
Crus (including Montée de Tonnerre★★, Montmains★★) and slow-
evolving Grands Crus (les Clos★★★ stands out) are tremendous, while
the basic Chablis, especially Vieilles Vignes★★, are some of the best on
the market. Brocard also produces a range of BOURGOGNE Blancs★ from
different soil types. Now adopting an increasingly organic – and in some
cases biodynamic – approach to his vineyards. Best years: (2008) 07 **06**
04.

BROKENWOOD *Hunter Valley, New South Wales, Australia* High-profile
winery with delicious traditional unoaked HUNTER Semillon★★
(sometimes ★★★). Best wine is classic Hunter Graveyard Vineyard
Shiraz★★★. Cricket Pitch reds and whites are cheerful, fruity reads

drinkers. New Indigo vineyard at BEECHWORTH is making very promising Chardonnay, Viognier, Pinot Noir and Nebbiolo. Best years: (Graveyard Vineyard Shiraz) (2007) 05 04 03 02 **00 99 98 96 95 94 93 91 90 89 88 86**.

RONCO WINE CO. *California, USA* Maker of the Charles Shaw range of wines – known as 'Two-Buck Chuck' because of their $2 price tag. There's now a $5 Napa Cabernet Sauvignon. The company is run by maverick Fred Franzia, who famously said 'wine's too damned expensive'. He is grand-nephew of the late Ernest GALLO, and he owns 14,000ha (35,000 acres) of California vineyard land, marketing 10 million cases of wine under more than a dozen brands.

ROUILLY AC *Beaujolais, Burgundy, France* Largest of the 10 BEAUJOLAIS Crus; at its best, the wine is soft, fruity, rich and brightly coloured. Best producers: Ch. de la Chaize, DUBOEUF (Ch. de Nervers), J-C Lapalu★★, A Michaud★, Point du Jour (Les Bruyères★), Ch. Thivin★★. Best years: **2008 07**.

ROWN BROTHERS *North-East Victoria, Australia* Highly successful family winery, producing a huge range of varietal wines, which have improved significantly in recent years. Good fizz and fine stickies★★. Top-of-the-range Patricia wines (Cabernet★★, sparkling Pinot-Chardonnay★★) are Brown's best yet. Premium grapes are from cool King Valley, mountain-top Whitlands and new vineyard at HEATHCOTE.

RÜNDLMAYER *Kamptal, Niederösterreich, Austria* Willi Bründlmayer makes wine in a variety of Austrian and international styles, but his outstanding dry Riesling (Alte Reben★★★) from the great Heiligenstein vineyard and Grüner Veltliner (Ried Lamm★★★) are the best; high alcohol is matched by superlative fruit and mineral flavours. Also excellent Chardonnay★★ and good Sekt★. Best years: (Zöbinger Heiligenstein Riesling) (2008) 07 06 **05 04 03 02 01 00 99**.

RUNELLO DI MONTALCINO DOCG *Tuscany, Italy* Powerful red wine produced from Sangiovese (known locally as Brunello). Traditionally needed over 10 years to soften, but modern practices result in more fruit-rich wines, yet still tannic enough to age very well, if not as spectacularly as sometimes claimed. Best producers: Agostina Pieri★★, Altesino★ (Montosoli★★), BANFI★ (Riserva★★), Barbi★, BIONDI-SANTI★★, Gianni Brunelli★★, Camigliano★★, La Campana★, Caparzo★ (La Casa★★), Casanova di Neri★★★, Casanuova delle Cerbaie★★, CASE BASSE★★★, Castelgiocondo/FRESCOBALDI (Riserva★), Centolani★ (Pietranera★★), Cerbaiona★★, Ciacci Piccolomini d'Aragona★★, Donatella Cinelli Colombini★, Col d'Orcia★★, COSTANTI★, La Gerla★★, Le Gode★★, Gorelli-Due Portine★, Greppone Mazzi★, Maurizio Lambardi★★, Lisini★★, Mastrojanni★★ (Schiena d'Asino★★★), Siro Pacenti★★★, Pian dell'Orino★★, Pian delle Vigne★★/ANTINORI, Piancornello★★, Pieve Santa Restituta★★, La Poderina★, Poggio Antico★★, Poggio San Polo★★, il POGGIONE★★ (Riserva★★★), Le Potazzine★★, Salvioni★★, Livio Sassetti-Pertimali★★, Talenti★★, La Togata★★, Valdicava★★, Villa Le Prata★★. Best years: (2008) (07) (06) 04 **03 01 00 99 98 97 95 90 88 85**.

RUNELLOGATE Anglicized joke-name for a no-joke scandalette which in spring 2008 saw many Brunello producers investigated and the 2003-vintage wines of 4 of the biggest sequestrated for the alleged blending of grapes other than Sangiovese into what is supposed to be a 100% varietal wine. Montalcino has bounced back partially, but it remains to be seen what will happen regarding the 2004s, 05s, 06s and 07s, all of which were made, and in cask or bottle, by spring 2008.

BUCELAS DOC *Estremadura, Portugal* A tiny but historic DOC. The wine
♀ are whites based on the Arinto grape (noted for its high acidity). Fo
attractive, modern examples try Quinta da Murta or Quinta da Romeira
(Morgado de Santa Catherina★).

VON BUHL *Deidesheim, Pfalz, Germany* Large estate, sold in 2005 to Achin
♟ Niederberger, the new owner of BASSERMANN-JORDAN. Top Rieslings nov
invariably ★★. Best years: (Grosses Gewächs Rieslings) (2008) 07 06 05 04 0
02 01 99.

BUITENVERWACHTING *Constantia WO, South Africa* Beautiful old property
♟ part of the Cape's original CONSTANTIA wine farm. Sauvignon Blanc★ i
penetrating and zesty; Husseys Vlei Sauvignon Blanc★ is bigger an
more pungent. Ripe, fruit-laden Chardonnay★ and elegant, subtl
Husseys Vlei★★ version. These and a light racy Riesling can improv
with a little aging. The aristocratic Christine★★, with deep flavours an
firm, dry structure, remains one of the Cape's most accurate BORDEAU
lookalikes. Best years: (Christine) (2005) 04 03 02 01 00 99 98 97 96 95

BULL'S BLOOD *Hungary* Kékfrankos (Blaufränkisch) grapes sometime
♟ replace robust Kadarka in the blend, thinning the blood; some produce
blend with Cabernet Sauvignon, Kékoporto or Merlot. New regulation
should improve the quality of Bikavér ('bull's blood') in the 2 permitte
regions, Eger and Szekszárd. Winemakers such as Vilmos Thummere
are working hard on this front, putting some balls back into the win

GRANT BURGE *Barossa Valley, South Australia* A leading producer in th
♟ BAROSSA, with extensive vineyard holdings and a wide range, includir
chocolaty Filsell Shiraz★ and rich Meshach Shiraz★★, Cameron Va
Cabernet★ and Shadrach Cabernet★ (now sourced entirely from Baross
fruit), RHONE-style Grenache-Shiraz-Mourvèdre blend Holy Trinity★
fresh Thorn Riesling★, oaky Zerk Semillon-Viognier, and the excellen
value Barossa Vines range. Recent vintages have shown a welcom
reduction in oak. Best years: (Meshach) (2008) (06) (05) 04 02 99 98 96 9
94 91.

BURGENLAND *Austria* 4 regions: Neusiedlersee, including Seewinkel f
sweet wines; Neusiedlersee-Hügelland, famous for sweet wines, now also b
reds and fruity dry whites; Mittelburgenland, for robust Blaufränkisch rec
and Südburgenland, for good reds. Best producers: Paul Achs★, FEILE
ARTINGER★★, Gesellmann★, Gernot Heinrich★★, Juris★, Kerschbaum
Kollwentz★★, KRACHER★★★, KRUTZLER★★, Helmut Lang★★, A & H Nittnaus★
OPITZ★, Pöckl★★, Prieler★, Schröck★, Ernst Triebaumer★★, UMATHUM★
VELICH★★.

BURGUNDY See BOURGOGNE AC and pages 90–3.

BÜRKLIN-WOLF *Wachenheim, Pfalz, Germany* One of Germany's large
♟ privately owned estates, with nearly 86ha (212 acres) of vineyards. Sin
the mid-1990s it has been in the first rank of the PFALZ's produce
Biodynamic since 2005. The powerful, spicy dry Rieslings are now ★★
★★★. Best years: (Grosses Gewächs Rieslings) (2008) 07 06 05 04 03 02 0

BURMESTER *Port DOC, Douro, Portugal* Shipper established in 1730, a
♟ now owned by the Galician firm Sogevinus, which also owns Cále
Barros and Kopke. Vintage PORT has improved, as has the Burmes
Vintage. As well as refined 10- and 20-year-old tawnies★, there a
some outstanding old colheitas★★ which extend back over 100 yea
Also decent Late Bottled Vintage and oak-aged DOURO red, C.

Burmester. Gilbert is a range aimed at younger drinkers. **Best years:** (Vintage) **2003 00 97 95 94**.

TOMMASO BUSSOLA *Valpolicella DOC, Veneto, Italy* Tommaso Bussola's AMARONE Vigneto Alto★★★ combines elegance with stunning power. Amarone Classico TB★★ is similar with slightly less finesse, and even the basic Amarone★ is a challenge to the palate. The Ripasso VALPOLICELLA Classico Superiore TB★★ is one of the best of its genre, and the RECIOTO TB★★★ is consistently excellent. **Best years:** (2008) (07) (06) **04 03 01 00 99 97 95**.

LA BUXYNOISE *Côte Chalonnaise, Burgundy, France* One of Burgundy's top co-operatives, producing affordable, well-made Chardonnay and Pinot Noir. The light, oak-aged BOURGOGNE Pinot Noir★ and the red and white Clos de Chenôves★, as well as the nutty white MONTAGNY★, are all good, reasonably priced, and best with 2–3 years' age.

BUZET AC *South-West France* Good BORDEAUX-style red wines from the same mix of grapes, at a lower price. There is very little rosé and the whites are rarely exciting. **Best producers:** Buzet co-op, Dom. du Pech★.

CA' DEL BOSCO *Franciacorta DOCG, Lombardy, Italy* Model estate, headed by Maurizio Zanella, making some of Italy's finest and most expensive international-style wines: outstanding sparklers in FRANCIACORTA Brut★★, Dosage Zero★, Satén★★ and Cuvée Annamaria Clementi★★★. Still wines include good Terre di Franciacorta Rosso★, remarkably good Chardonnay★★★, Pinero★ (Pinot Noir) and BORDEAUX blend, Maurizio Zanella★★★. Also varietal Carmenère, Carmenero★.

CABARDÈS AC *Languedoc, France* Next door to MINERVOIS. Cabernet Sauvignon and Merlot are allowed, as well as the usual French Mediterranean grape varieties. At best, full-bodied, chewy and rustically attractive – and attractively priced. **Best producers:** Cabrol★, Jouclary, Pennautier★, Salitis. **Best years:** (2008) 06 **05 04 03**.

CABERNET D'ANJOU AC *Loire Valley, France* Rosé made from both Cabernets; generally medium dry or semi-sweet; Rosé d'Un Jour is a very good rosé vin de table, picked overripe and not chapitalized, made by 8 rebellious growers, led by Mark Angeli. Drink young. **Best producers:** M Angeli/Sansonnière, Hautes-Ouches, Ogereau, Petites Grouas, Terrebrune.

CABERNET FRANC Often unfairly dismissed as an inferior Cabernet Sauvignon, Cabernet Franc comes into its own in cool zones or areas where the soil is damp and heavy. It can have a leafy freshness linked to raw but tasty blackcurrant-raspberry fruit; lighter wines drink well slightly chilled. In France it thrives as a single varietal in the LOIRE VALLEY and is blended with Cabernet Sauvignon and Merlot in BORDEAUX, especially ST-EMILION (AUSONE, CHEVAL BLANC) and POMEROL (LAFLEUR). Moderately successful where not overproduced in northern Italy, especially ALTO ADIGE and FRIULI, although some plantings here have turned out to be Carmenère, and increasingly preferred to Cabernet Sauvignon in Tuscany (Le MACCHIOLE's Paleo Rosso is an outstanding example of pure Cabernet Franc). It is the red of choice for many winemakers in the eastern United States, performing especially well in the FINGER LAKES and VIRGINIA. Experiments with Cabernet Franc on CALIFORNIA's North Coast and in WASHINGTON STATE show promise. There are also some good South African, Chilean and Australian examples.

CABERNET SAUVIGNON See pages 98–9.

CABERNET SAUVIGNON

Wine made from Cabernet Sauvignon in places like Australia, California, Chile, Bulgaria, even in parts of southern France has become so popular that many people may not realize where it all started – and how Cabernet became the great, omnipresent red wine grape of the world.

WINE STYLES

Bordeaux Cabernet It all began in Bordeaux. With the exception of lively bunch of Merlot-based beauties in St-Émilion and Pomerol, the greatest red Bordeaux wines are based on Cabernet Sauvignon, with varying amounts of Merlot, Cabernet Franc and possibly Petit Verdot blended in. The blending is necessary because by itself Cabernet makes such a strong, powerful, aggressive and assertive wine. Dark and tannic when young, the great Bordeaux wines need 10–20 years for the aggression to fade, the fruit becoming sweet and perfumed as fresh blackcurrants, with a fragrance of cedarwood, of cigar boxes, mingling magically among the fruit. It is this character that has made red Bordeaux famous for at least two centuries.

Cabernet worldwide When winemakers in other parts of the world sought role models to try to improve their wines, most of them automatically thought of Bordeaux and chose Cabernet Sauvignon. It was lucky that they did, because not only is this variety easy to grow in almost all conditions – cool or warm, dry or damp – but that unstoppable personality always powers through. The cheaper wines are generally made to accentuate the blackcurrant fruit and the slightly earthy tannins. They are drinkable young, but able to age surprisingly well. The more ambitious wines are aged in oak barrels, often new ones, to enhance the tannin yet also to add spice and richness capable of developing over a decade or more. Sometimes the Cabernet is blended – usually with Merlot, sometimes with Cabernet Franc, and occasionally with other grapes: Shiraz in Australia, Sangiovese in Italy, Tempranillo in Spain.

Europe Many vineyards in southern France now produce good affordable Cabernet Sauvignon. Spain has produced some good Cabernet blends, as has Portugal. Italy's red wine quality revolution was sparked off by the success of Cabernet in Tuscany, and all the leading regions now grow it. Eastern Europe grows lots of Cabernet, but of widely varying quality, while the Eastern Mediterranean and North Africa are beginning to produce tasty examples. Austria has had some success but is returning to Blaufränkisch and Zweigelt.

New World There is a general move toward darker, denser, more serious Cabernets, even in countries like Chile and Australia, whose Cabernet triumphs have until now been based on gorgeous blackcurrant fruit. I hope they don't ditch too much of the fruit, but I have to say that a lot of these new contenders are excellent. Argentina is also pitching in with some powerful stuff. California's reputation was created by its strong, weighty Cabernets; it's at a bit of a crossroads right now, with some producers going to superhuman lengths to concentrate and overripen their wines, while others show increasing restraint. My view is that most Napa Cabernets reached a peak of expression quite a few vintages ago and too many now exhibit thudding tannins and too much high alcohol and low acid fruit. Restraint isn't Napa's strong point, nor need it be, but some of its gaudy, ferocious beauty is being lost through over indulgence. Sometimes less is more.

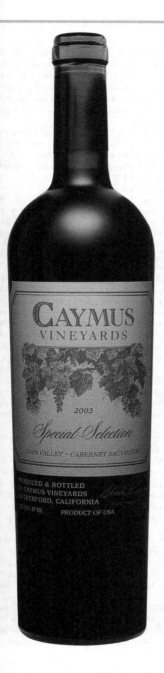

BEST PRODUCERS

France

Bordeaux Dom. de CHEVALIER, COS D'ESTOURNEL, GRAND-PUY-LACOSTE, GRUAUD-LAROSE, LAFITE-ROTHSCHILD, LATOUR, LEOVILLE-BARTON, LEOVILLE-LAS-CASES, LEOVILLE-POYFERRE, LYNCH-BAGES, Ch. MARGAUX, MOUTON-ROTHSCHILD, PICHON-LONGUEVILLE, RAUZAN-SEGLA; *Provence* TREVALLON.

Other European Cabernets

Italy BANFI, CA' DEL BOSCO, Col d'Orcia (Olmaia), GAJA, ISOLE E OLENA, LAGEDER, MACULAN, ORNELLAIA, Castello dei RAMPOLLA, SAN LEONARDO, SASSICAIA, SOLAIA, TASCA D'ALMERITA, Castello del TERRICCIO, TUA RITA.
Spain Blecua, Enate, Jané Ventura, MARQUES DE GRINON, TORRES.

New World Cabernets

Australia BALNAVES, CAPE MENTELLE, CULLEN, HARDYS (Thomas Hardy), HENSCHKE, HOUGHTON (Jack Mann, Gladstones), HOWARD PARK, LEEUWIN, MAJELLA, MOSS WOOD, PARKER COONAWARRA ESTATE, PENFOLDS (Bin 707), PENLEY ESTATE, PETALUMA, SANDALFORD, WENDOUREE, The Willows, WIRRA WIRRA, Woodlands, WYNNS, Zema.

New Zealand BABICH, CRAGGY RANGE, Esk Valley, GOLDWATER, Matariki, STONYRIDGE, TE MATA, Vidal, VILLA MARIA.

USA (California) ARAUJO, BERINGER, Bryant Family, CAYMUS, CHIMNEY ROCK, DALLA VALLE, DIAMOND CREEK, DOMINUS, DUNN, Grace Family, HARLAN, HARTWELL, LAUREL GLEN, Long Meadow Ranch, Peter MICHAEL, MINER, MONDAVI, NEWTON, PHELPS, RIDGE, St Supéry, SCREAMING EAGLE, SHAFER, SILVER OAK, SPOTTSWOODE, STAG'S LEAP, Viader; *(Washington)* ANDREW WILL, DELILLE CELLARS, DUNHAM CELLARS, Fidelitas, LEONETTI, QUILCEDA CREEK, Three Rivers, WOODWARD CANYON.

Chile ALMAVIVA, Altaïr, CARMEN, CASABLANCA, CONCHA Y TORO, HARAS DE PIRQUE, QUEBRADA DE MACUL, SANTA RITA, Miguel TORRES.

Argentina CATENA, COBOS, TERRAZAS DE LOS ANDES, Pascual Tosa (Magdalena).

South Africa BEYERSKLOOF, BOEKENHOUTSKLOOF, BUITEN-VERWACHTING, DE TRAFFORD, Neil ELLIS, GRANGEHURST, KANONKOP, Le Riche, RUSTENBERG, SAXENBURG, THELEMA, VEENWOUDEN, VERGELEGEN.

99

CADENCE *Red Mountain AVA, Washington State, USA* A range of vineyard specific reds. Tapteil Vineyard★★★, a powerful Cabernet Sauvignon dominated blend, is the flagship; Ciel du Cheval Vineyard★★★ is more forward and juicy. Two reserve wines are produced from the estate vineyard, Cara Mia Vineyard. Bel Canto★★ is a Cabernet Franc-Merlot dominant blend, and Camerata★★ is a Cabernet Sauvignon-dominant red. Best years: (2007) 06 05 **04 03 02 01**.

CADILLAC AC *Bordeaux, France* Sweet wine from the southern half of the PREMIERES CÔTES DE BORDEAUX. Styles vary from fresh, semi-sweet to richly botrytized. The wines have greatly improved in recent vintages. Drink young. Best producers: Fayau (Cuvée Grains Nobles★), Ch. du Juge, Manos★, Mémoires★, REYNON★. Best years: 2007 **05 03 02 01** 99 98.

CAHORS AC *South-West France* Important South-West red wine region. This dark, traditionally tannic wine is made from at least 70% Auxerrois (Malbec or Côt) and has an unforgettable, rich plummy flavour when ripe and well made – which is less often than I'd wish. Ages well. Best producers: la Caminade★, Cayrou, du CÈDRE★, Clos la Coutale★, CLOS DE GAMOT★★, CLOS TRIGUEDINA★, COSSE-MAISONNEUVE (les Laquets★★), Gaudou, Haut-Monplaisir, Haute-Serre, Lagrezette, Lamartine★, Latuc, la Reyne, le Rigalets★. Best years: (2008) 06 05 **04 02 01** 98 90.

CAIRANNE *Rhône Valley, France* One of the top two villages entitled to the COTES DU RHÔNE-VILLAGES appellation, offering full, herb-scented reds and solid whites. Best producers: D & D Alary★★, Ameillaud★, Brusset★, Cave de Cairanne★, les Hautes Cances★, ORATOIRE ST-MARTIN★★, Présidente★, Rabasse-Charavin★, M Richaud★★. Best years: (reds) **2007 06 05 04 03 01** 99.

CALABRIA *Italy* Italy's poorest, most backward and most corrupt region. CIRÒ, Donnici, Savuto and Scavigna DOC reds from the native Gaglioppo grape, and whites from Greco, are much improved thanks to great winemaking expertise. In a very restricted field the two leading producers remain Librandi – who have added the red Magno Megonio★★, from the obscure Magliocco variety, and the white Efeso★★, from the Mantonico grape, to an already fine range – and Odoardi, with their excellent Scavigna Vigna Garrone★.

CALERA *San Benito, California, USA* A pace-setter for California Pinot Noir with 5 estate wines: Reed★★, Selleck★★, Jensen★★, Mills★★ and Ryan★. They are complex, fascinating wines with power and originality and capable of aging. Mt Harlan Chardonnay★★ is excitingly original too. CENTRAL COAST Chardonnay★ and Pinot Noir★ are good value. Small amounts of Viognier★★ are succulent with sensuous fruit. Best years: (Pinot Noir) (2007) 06 05 04 **03 02 01** 00 99 97 96 95; (Chardonnay) 2007 **05 04 03 02 01** 00 99.

CALIFORNIA *USA* California's importance is not simply in being the fourth largest wine producer in the world (behind France, Italy and Spain). Most of the revolutions in technology and style that have transformed the expectations and achievements of winemakers in every country of the world – including France – were born in the ambitions of a band of California winemakers during the 1960s and 70s. They challenged the old order, with its regulated, self-serving elitism, and democratized the world of fine wine to the benefit of every wine drinker. This revolutionary fervour is less evident now. And there are times when Californians seem too intent establishing their own particular New World old order. A few figures: there are around 194,000ha (480,000 acres) of wine grape vineyards, producing around 20 million hectolitres (500 million gallons) of wine annually, about 90% of all wine made in the USA. A large proportion comes from the hot, inland CENTRAL VALLEY. See also CENTRAL COAST, MENDOCINO COUNTY, MONTEREY COUNTY, NAPA VALLEY, SAN LUIS OBISPO COUNTY, SANTA BARBARA COUNTY, SONOMA COUNTY.

CH. CALON-SÉGUR★★ *St-Estèphe AC, 3ème Cru Classé, Haut-Médoc, Bordeaux, France* Long considered one of ST-ESTÈPHE's leading châteaux, but in the mid-1980s the wines were not as good as they should have been. Vintages from the mid-1990s have been more impressive, with better fruit and a suppler texture. Second wine: Marquis de Calon. Best years: 2007 06 05 04 03 **02 01 00 98 96 95 90 89 86.**

CAMEL VALLEY *Cornwall, England* The enterprising Lindos, Bob and Sam, are sparkling wine specialists who favour Seyval Blanc and Reichensteiner over classic CHAMPAGNE varieties; the result is the quintessentially English Camel Valley Brut★. Sparkling Pinot Noir★★ (white and rosé) is also excellent, and still wines (dry white Bacchus★, Rosé★) are good, too.

CAMPANIA *Italy* Three regions – PUGLIA, SICILY and Campania – lead the evolution in Italy's south. Campania has made excellent progress in the white department, with varietals from Greco di Tufo, Fiano, Falanghina and several other native grapes; Feudi di San Gregorio★★ have a particularly good range of whites. On the red side, other producers besides the venerable MASTROBERARDINO have begun to realize the potential of Campania's soil, climate and grapes, especially with the red Aglianico. The leading red wines are Montevetrano★★★ (Cabernet-Merlot-Aglianico) and Galardi's Terra di Lavoro★★★ (Aglianico-Piedirosso), but also look for top Aglianicos from Antonio Caggiano★★, De Conciliis★, Feudi di San Gregorio★★, Luigi Maffini★, Michele Moio★, Salvatore Molettieri★, Orazio Rillo★, San Paolo, Cantina del Taburno★ and others that fall outside the main DOCs. DOC(G)s of note are FALERNO DEL MASSICO, Fiano di Avellino, Greco di Tufo, Ischia, TAURASI and Vesuvio.

CAMPILLO *Rioja DOCa, País Vasco, Spain* An upmarket subsidiary of Bodegas FAUSTINO, producing some exciting new red RIOJAS★. The wines are often Tempranillo-Cabernet Sauvignon blends, with masses of ripe, velvety fruit. Best years: (Reserva) 2004 **03 01 99 98 96 95 94.**

CAMPO DI SASSO *Tuscany, Italy* Brothers Piero and Lodovico ANTINORI's venture in the commune of Bibbona, near BOLGHERI, with plantings of Cabernet Franc, Petit Verdot and Merlot. Wines include Insoglio del Cinghiale, Il Pino di Biserno and Biserno (from 2010).

CAMPO VIEJO *Rioja DOCa, Rioja, Spain* The largest producer of RIOJA is owned by Pernod Ricard. Reservas★ and Gran Reservas★ are reliably good, as are the elegant, all-Tempranillo Reserva Viña Alcorta and the barrel-fermented white Viña Alcorta. Albor Tempranillo is a good modern young Rioja, packed with fresh, pastilley fruit. Best years: (Reserva) 2005 04 **03 01 98 96 95 94.**

CANARY ISLANDS *Spain* The Canaries have a treasure trove of pre-phylloxera vines, and a total of 9 DOs. The sweet Malvasia from Lanzarote

DO and La Palma DO is worth a try, and there are a couple of remarkable fresh dry whites; otherwise stick with the young reds. Best producers: El Grifo Monje, Viña Norte, Tacande★, Tanajara★, Teneguía, Viñátigo★.

CANBERRA DISTRICT New South Wales, Australia Cool, high altitude (800m/2600ft) may sound good, but excessive cold and frost can be problematic. Lark Hill and Helm make exciting Riesling, Lark Hill and Brindabella Hills some smart Cabernet blends, and CLONAKILLA sublime Shiraz. The Hunter's First Creek is sourcing stunning Sauvignon Blanc from here. Best producers: Brindabella Hills★, CLONAKILLA★★★, Doonkuna★ Helm★, Lake George★, Lark Hill★, Madew★, Mount Majura.

DOM. CANET-VALETTE St-Chinian AC, Languedoc, France Marc Valette i uncompromising in his quest to make great wine: organic cultivation low yields and traditional *pigeage* (foot-stomping) are just some of hi methods. The wines offer an enticingly rich expression of ST-CHINIAN grape varieties and clay-limestone soils. Cuvées include Une et Mill Nuits (1001 Nights)★ and the powerful, complex Syrah-Mourvèdre L Vin Maghani★★. Best years: (Le Vin Maghani) (2008) 07 06 05 04 **03** 01 0C

CANNONAU Sardinian name of Spain's Garnacha and France's Grenach Noir. In SARDINIA it produces deep, tannic reds, but lighter, modern, dr red wines are gaining in popularity, although traditional sweet an fortified styles can still be found. Best producers: (modern reds) ARGIOLAS SELLA & MOSCA; Dolianova, Dorgali, Jerzu, Alberto Loi, Ogliastra, Oliena, Sant Maria La Palma and Trexenta co-ops.

CH. CANON★ St-Émilion Grand Cru AC, 1er Grand Cru Classé, Bordeaux, Franc Canon can make some of the richest, most concentrated ST-EMILIONS, bu it went into steep decline before being purchased in 1996 by Chane (who also own RAUZAN-SEGLA). Signs are that things have returned t form. In good vintages the wine is tannic and rich at first but is wort aging 10–15 years. Second wine: Clos Canon. Best years: 2007 06 05 **04 0**º **02** 01 00 98 89 88 85.

CANON-FRONSAC AC Bordeaux, France This AC is the heart of th FRONSAC region. The wines are quite sturdy when young but can age fc 10 years or more. Best producers: Barrabaque (Prestige★), Cassagne Hau Canon (La Truffière★), la Fleur Cailleau, Gaby★, Grand-Renouil★, Hau Mazeris, Moulin Pey-Labrie★★, Pavillon, Vrai Canon Bouché. Best years: 200 05 03 01 00 98 96 95 90.

CH. CANON-LA-GAFFELIÈRE★★ St-Émilion Grand Cru AC, Grand Cru Class Bordeaux, France Owner Stephan von Neipperg has put this property a the top of the list of ST-EMILION GRAND CRU CLASSES. The wines are firm, ric and concentrated. He also owns Clos de l'Oratoire★★, Ch. l'Aiguilhe★ in the CÔTES DE CASTILLON, and the remarkable micro-cuvée L Mondotte★★. Best years: 2007 06 05 **04 03 02** 01 00 99 98 96 95.

CH. CANTEMERLE★ Haut-Médoc AC, 5ème Cru Classé, Bordeaux, France Wit La LAGUNE, the most southerly of the Crus Classés. The wines are delica in style and delightful in ripe vintages. Second wine: Les Allées c Cantemerle. Best years: 2007 06 05 **04** 03 01 00 98 96 95.

CANTERBURY South Island, New Zealand The long, cool ripening season the arid central coast of South Island favours white varieties, particular Chardonnay, Pinot Gris, Sauvignon Blanc and Riesling, as well as Pino

Noir. The northerly Waipara district produces Canterbury's most exciting wines, especially from Riesling and Pinot Noir. Best producers: Mountford★, PEGASUS BAY★★, Daniel Schuster★, Waipara West★. Best years: (Pinot Noir) (2008) 07 06 03 02 01 00; (Riesling) 2008 07 06 04 02.

CAPE CHAMONIX *Franschhoek WO, South Africa* Talented winemaker, Gottfried Mocke, has firmly established himself as one of the leading young turks after seven vintages at this high-lying FRANSCHHOEK property. Best known for his seamlessly oaked, naturally fermented Chardonnays; citrus/creamy standard★, refined, distinctive Reserve★★ with lengthy maturation track record. Barrel-fermented Sauvignon Blanc★ is also individual and ageworthy, showing both richness and cool minerals. Pure-fruited, silky-textured Pinot Noir★ gains in complexity with every vintage. Best years: (Chardonnay) 2007 06 05 04 03 02 01.

CAPE MENTELLE *Margaret River, Western Australia* Leading MARGARET RIVER winery, owned by LVMH. Chief winemaker Rob Mann continues to impress as Cape Mentelle produce superb, cedary gamy Cabernet★★, impressive Shiraz★★ and Chardonnay★★, tangy Semillon-Sauvignon Blanc★★ and wonderfully chewy Zinfandel★★. Wallcliffe wines are very good: densely concentrated Shiraz★★, taut Sauvignon Blanc-Semillon★. All wines benefit from cellaring – whites up to 5 years, reds 8–15. Best years: (Cabernet Sauvignon) (2008) (07) 05 04 03 02 01 94.

CAPE POINT VINEYARDS *Cape Point WO, South Africa* Pioneering property influenced by bracing Atlantic breezes. Whites respond with vigour and purity. Sauvignon Blanc★★ is astonishing, ocean-fresh, new and original. Partially barrel-fermented Semillon★★ tantalizes with tangerine and lemongrass intensity, while Isliedh★★, a barrel-fermented blend of both varieties, combines power with subtlety. Early reds, from a warmer site, also show promise. Best years: (whites) 2008 07 06 05 04 03 02 01.

CAPEL VALE *Geographe, Western Australia* The Pratten family's winery sources fruit from its own vineyards in Geographe, Mount Barker, PEMBERTON and MARGARET RIVER. After an erratic history, this is now a winery very much on the up, using only the best varieties from each region. Cheap and cheerful Debut range includes velvety Merlot★ and easy-drinking Pinot Noir. There's an impressive Regional Series, and two single-vineyard wines: intense yet fine Whispering Hill Riesling★★ and elegant, beautifully structured Whispering Hill Shiraz★★. Best years: (Whispering Hill Riesling) 2008 07 06 04 03 02 01 00 98 97.

CARIGNAN The dominant red grape in the south of France is responsible for much boring, cheap, harsh wine. But when made by carbonic maceration, the wine can have delicious spicy fruit. Old vines are capable of dense, rich, impressive reds, as shown by the odd success in France, California, Chile, Lebanon and Israel. In South Africa it is mainly used in Rhône-style blends. Although initially a Spanish grape (as Cariñena or Mazuelo), it is not that widespread there, but is useful for adding colour and acidity in RIOJA and CATALUNA, and has gained unexpected respect in PRIORAT.

CARIGNANO DEL SULCIS DOC *Sardinia, Italy* Carignano is now
producing wines of quite startling quality. Rocca Rubia★, a barrique-
aged Riserva from the Santadi co-op, with rich, fleshy and chocolaty
fruit, is one of SARDINIA's best reds. Baie Rosse★★ is a step up; even better
is the more structured and concentrated Terre Brune★★. Best producer:
Santadi co-op. Best years: (2008) (07) 06 **05 04 03 01 00**.

LOUIS CARILLON & FILS *Puligny-Montrachet, Côte de Beaune, Burgundy, France*
Excellent family-owned estate in PULIGNY-MONTRACHET. The emphasis is
on traditional, finely balanced whites of great concentration, rather than
new oak. Look out for Premiers Crus les Referts★★, Champs Canet★★
and les Perrières★★★, and the tiny but exquisite production of
Bienvenues-BÂTARD-MONTRACHET★★★. Reds from CHASSAGNE-
MONTRACHET★, ST-AUBIN★ and MERCUREY★ are good, too. Best years: (whites)
(2008) 07 06 05 **04 03 02**.

CARIÑENA DO *Aragón, Spain* The largest DO of ARAGON, baking under the
mercilessly hot sun in inland eastern Spain, Cariñena has traditionally
been a land of cheap, deep red, alcoholic wines from the Garnacha grape.
(Confusingly the Carignan grape is called Cariñena in Spain, but is
practically absent from the Cariñena region.) Since the late 1990s,
however, temperature-controlled fermentation has been working
wonders with this unfairly despised grape, and Tempranillo and
international grape varieties like Cabernet Sauvignon are being planted
widely. Best producers: Añadas★, San Valero (Monte Ducay, Don Mendo),
Solar de Urbezo, Victoria★.

CARLEI *Victoria, Australia* Outstanding biodynamic producer, with
Chardonnay★★ and Pinot Noir★ from YARRA VALLEY and Shiraz★★ from
HEATHCOTE. Sergio Carlei's signature blends are Tre Rossi★ (Shiraz-
Barbera-Nebbiolo), Tre Amici (Sangiovese-Cabernet-Merlot) and Tre
Bianchi (Sauvignon with small amounts of Semillon and Chardonnay).
The modestly priced Green Vineyards range offers very good regional
varietals: Chardonnay and Pinot Noir from the Yarra, Heathcote Shiraz,
Central Victorian Cabernet and Cardinia Ranges Pinot Gris.

CARMEN *Maipo, Chile* Some of the best reds in MAIPO, including Gold
Reserve★★, a limited release made with Carmen's oldest Cabernet
Sauvignon vines, Reserve Carmenère-Cabernet★★, balanced, complex
Wine Maker's Reserve★★ and organic Nativa Cabernet Sauvignon★★.
Best years: (reds) (2007) **05 04 03 02 01 00 99**.

CARMENÈRE An important but forgotten constituent of BORDEAUX blends in
the 19th century, historically known as Grande Vidure. Planted in Chile,
it was generally labelled as Merlot until 1994 (and often still is). When
ripe and made with care, it has rich blackberry, plum and spice flavour
with an unexpected but delicious bunch of savoury characters – grilled
meat, soy sauce, celery, coffee – thrown in. A true original. Also found in
northern Italy, where it has been confused with Cabernet Franc.
Argentina and China. Being replanted experimentally in Bordeaux.

CARMIGNANO DOCG *Tuscany, Italy* Red wine from the west of Florence,
renowned since the 16th century and revived in the 1970s by Capezzana.
The blend (Sangiovese, plus 10–20% Cabernet) is one of Tuscany's most
refined wines and can be quite long-lived. Although Carmignano is
DOCG, DOC applies to a lighter red Barco Reale, rosé Vin Ruspo and
fine VIN SANTO. Best producers: Ambra★ (Vigne Alte★★), Artimino,

Capezzana★★, Le Farnete/E Pierazzuoli★ (Riserva★★), Piaggia★★, Pratesi★, Villa di Trefiano★. Best years: (2008) (07) 06 **04 03 02 01 00 99 98 97**.

CARNEROS AVA *California, USA* Hugging the northern edge of San Francisco Bay, Carneros includes parts of NAPA and SONOMA Counties. Windswept and chilly with morning fog off the Bay, it is a top cool-climate area, suitable for Chardonnay and Pinot Noir as table wine and as a base for sparkling wine. Merlot and Syrah are also coming on well. Best producers: ACACIA★★, Buena Vista★, Carneros Creek★, DOMAINE CARNEROS★★, Gloria Ferrer, HdV★★, Ramey★★, RASMUSSEN★★, SAINTSBURY★★, Truchard★★. Best years: (Pinot Noir) 2007 06 05 **04 03 02 01 99 98**.

CARNUNTUM *Niederösterreich, Austria* 890ha (2200-acre) wine region south of the Danube and east of Vienna, with a strong red wine tradition. Best producers: Artner★, Glatzer, G Markowitsch★, Pitnauer★.

CASA LAPOSTOLLE *Rapel, Chile* Owned by Marnier-Lapostolle of France, with consultancy from leading BORDEAUX winemaker Michel Rolland. Cuvée Alexandre Merlot★★, from the acclaimed Apalta area in COLCHAGUA, was its first hit back in 1994, now eclipsed by red blend Clos Apalta★★★. Also rich, creamy Cuvée Alexandre Chardonnay★ from the CASABLANCA Valley and Borobo, a peculiar blend of Pinot Noir, Carmenère, Cabernet Sauvignon, Syrah and Merlot.

CASA MARÍN *San Antonio, Chile* Impressive whites, led by single-vineyard Sauvignon Blancs: Laurel★★ is powerful, full of mineral and intense chilli and fruit flavours, while Cipreses★★★ shows the influence of the Pacific Ocean in its citrus and stony aromas. Casona Vineyard Gewürztraminer★, Miramar Riesling★ and Estero Sauvignon Gris★ are good, too – and there's juicy, cool-climate Pinot Noir★ as well as the outstanding new Miramar Syrah★.

CASABLANCA *Chile* Coastal valley with a cool-climate personality that is powerful proof of Chile's ability to do regional style. Whites dominate, with best results from Sauvignon Blanc, Chardonnay and Gewürztraminer. That said, the Pinot Noir is some of Chile's best, and some producers (Casas del Bosque, Kingston, Loma Larga) make top-quality cool-climate Syrah. Best producers: CASABLANCA★, CASAS DEL BOSQUE★, CONCHA Y TORO★, CONO SUR★, EMILIANA ORGÁNICO★, ERRÁZURIZ★, Kingston★★, Loma Larga★★, MONTES★, Quintay★. Best years: **2007 06 05 04**.

CASABLANCA, VIÑA *Casablanca, Chile* The cool Santa Isabel vineyard in CASABLANCA is the source of top wines under the Nimbus Estate label: quince-edged Chardonnay★, rose- and lychee-filled Gewürztraminer★, excellent, tangy, intense Sauvignon Blanc★, inky-black Cabernet Sauvignon★ and low-yield Merlot★★. Flagship red blend Neblus★ is made only in the best years.

CASAS DEL BOSQUE *Casablanca, Chile* This winery, located in the cool westerly part of CASABLANCA, has a special focus on Sauvignon Blanc (Reserve★). The reds are good too, especially the red blend Estate Selection★ and Reserve Syrah★, all from Casablanca's western slopes. Best years: **2007 06 05 04**.

CASE BASSE *Brunello di Montalcino DOCG, Tuscany, Italy* Gianfranco Soldera unblushingly proclaims his BRUNELLO DI MONTALCINO★★★ and Brunello di Montalcino Riserva★★★ wines (the latter usually under the Intistieti label) to be the best of their genre and, maddeningly, he's pretty much right. A fanatical biodynamist, Soldera believes perfect grapes are all you need to make great wine. He ages his wines for a minimum of 5 years in large old (and hence neutral) oak barrels; the result is a wine of brilliant colour and an amazing intensity and complexity of perfumes. Best years (2008) (07) (06) (04) (03) 01 99 **98 97 95 93 90 88 85**.

CH. LA CASENOVE *Côtes du Roussillon AC, Roussillon, France* Former photojournalist Étienne Montès, with consultant enologist Jean-Luc COLOMBO, has developed an impressive range, including a perfumed white Vin de Pays Catalan made from Macabeu and Torbat, MUSCAT DE RIVESALTES★, RIVESALTES★ and 2 predominantly Syrah reds: Pla del Rei★★ and Commandant François Jaubert★★. Drink this with at least 5 years bottle age. Best years: (François Jaubert) 2005 04 **00**.

CASSIS AC *Provence, France* A picturesque fishing port near Marseille. The white wine, based on Ugni Blanc and Clairette, is overpriced but can be good if fresh. The red wine is light, but the rosé can be pleasant. Best producers: Bagnol★, Caillol, Clos Ste-Magdelaine★, la Ferme Blanche★ Fontblanche, Ch. de Fontcreuse, Mas de Boudard. Best years: (white) (2008) **07 06 05 04 02**.

DOM. DU CASTEL *Judean Hills, Israel* Israel's leading quality winery Complex Grand Vin★★ is made from 5 BORDEAUX varieties. Delicately balanced Blanc du Castel is a barrel-fermented Chardonnay★ with good acidity from the Jerusalem Hills. Best years: (reds) 2006 05 04 **03 02 00 97**

CASTEL DEL MONTE DOC *Puglia, Italy* An arid, hilly zone, and an ideal habitat for the Uva di Troia grape, producing long-lived red wine of astonishing character. There is also varietal Aglianico, some good rosé and the whites produced from international varieties are improving. Best producers: RIVERA★, Santa Lucia, Tormaresca★/ANTINORI, Torrevento★ Best years: (2008) 07 **06 04 03 01**.

CASTELLARE *Chianti Classico DOCG, Tuscany, Italy* Fine estate with excellent CHIANTI CLASSICO★ and deeper, richer Riserva★★. Coniale★★ (Caberne Sauvignon), Canonico★ (Chardonnay) and Spartito★ (Sauvignon Blanc are all ripe and fruity. Top wine I Sodi di San Niccolò★★ is an unusual Sangiovese-Malvasia Nera blend, intense but finely perfumed.

CASTILLA-LA MANCHA *Spain* The DOs of the central plateau, LA MANCHA and VALDEPEÑAS, make white wines from the Airén grape, and some good reds from the Cencibel (Tempranillo). Méntrida DO, Manchuela DO Ribera del Júcar DO, Almansa DO and the new Uclés DO make fast improving reds. The most ambitious wines made here are those from MARQUÉ DE GRIÑON's Dominio de Valdepusa★ estate near the Tagus river and the Dehesa del Carrizal★ and Pago de Vallegarcía★ estates, both in the Toledo mountains. Uribes Madero's Calzadilla★ in Cuenca province, Finca Sandoval★★, Ponce★, Alto Landón and Monegrillo from Manchuela Ercavio★ from Toledo, Adaras from Almansa, Arrayan★ and Jiménez Landi★ from Méntrida and Manuel Manzaneque's Cabernet-based reds★ and Chardonnay★ from Sierra de Alcaraz in Albacete province are full of promise. Manzaneque now has his own DO, Finca Élez, as do the Dominio de Valdepusa and Dehesa del Carrizal.

CASTILLA Y LEÓN *Spain* This is Spain's harsh, high plateau, with long cold winters and hot summers (but always cool nights). A few rivers, notably the Duero, temper this climate and afford fine conditions for viticulture. After many decades of winemaking ignorance, with a few exceptions like VEGA SICILIA, the situation has changed radically for the better in all of the region's DOs: RIBERA DEL DUERO, RUEDA, BIERZO, Cigales and TORO. Dynamic winemaker uch as Telmo RODRIGUEZ and Mariano García (AALTO and MAURO) have won huge critical acclaim for the region.

CATALUÑA *Spain* Standards vary among the region's DOs. PENEDES, between Barcelona and Tarragona, has the greatest number of technically equipped wineries in Spain, but doesn't make a commensurate number of superior wines. In the south, mountainous PRIORAT has become a new icon for its heady, raging reds, and the neighbouring DOs of Montsant and Terra Alta are following in its footsteps, albeit more affordably, with top wines from Acùstic, Joan d'Anguera★, Celler de Capçanes★, Europvin Falset★, Venus La Universal★ (Montsant) and Bàrbara Forés and Celler Piñol★★ (Terra Alta). Inland COSTERS DEL SEGRE and Conca de Barberá make potentially excellent reds and whites. Up the coast, Alella makes attractive whites and Empordá-Costa Brava, by the French border, is showing signs of life. Cataluña also makes most of Spain's CAVA sparkling wines. The Catalunya DO allows (generally) inexpensive blends from anywhere in the region.

CATENA ZAPATA *Mendoza, Argentina* Argentinian pioneer Nicolás Catena's admiration for California is evident in the ripe, gentle, oaky Alamos range. However, Catena has vines in some of the best *terroirs* in MENDOZA and the wines in the Alta range – Chardonnay★, Cabernet Sauvignon★★ and Malbec★★ – are now developing a recognizable sense of place. Cabernet-based Nicolás Catena Zapata★★ and Malbec Argentino★★ are top-flight. Caro★, a joint venture with LAFITE-ROTHSCHILD, successfully combines French restraint with Argentinian panache.

SYLVAIN CATHIARD *Vosne-Romanée, Côte de Nuits, Burgundy, France* Sylvain Cathiard first achieved international recognition in the late 1990s and has made brilliant wines even in difficult vintages since then. The stars are VOSNE-ROMANEE Les Malconsorts★★★ and ROMANÉE-ST-VIVANT★★★ but his village Vosne-Romanée★★ and NUITS-ST-GEORGES Aux Murgers★★ are excellent too. Best years: (2008) 07 06 05 **03 02 00 99**.

DOM. CAUHAPÉ *Jurançon AC, South-West France* Henri Ramonteu has been a major influence in JURANCON, proving that the area can make complex dry whites as well as more traditional sweet wines. Chant des Vignes★ is a dry, unoaked Jurançon Sec; the oaked version is Sève d'Automne★. Top wines are dry La Canopée★★, sweet Noblesse du Temps★★ and barrel-fermented Quintessence★★★. Best years: (sweet) 2007 05 **04 03 00 97 95**.

CAVA DO *Spain* Cava, the Catalan name for CHAMPAGNE-method fizz, is made throughout Spain, but most comes from CATALUÑA. Grapes are the local trio of Parellada, Macabeo and Xarel-lo, although some good Cavas in Cataluña as well as VALENCIA are made with Chardonnay and Pinot Noir. The best-value, fruitiest Cavas are generally the youngest, with no more than the minimum 9 months' aging. A number of top-quality wines are now produced but are seldom seen abroad, since their prices are too close to those of Champagne to attract international customers. **Best producers:** Can Feixes, Can Ràfols dels Caus★, Castell de Vilarnau, Castellblanch, CODORNÍU★, Colet★, FREIXENET, Gramona★, Juve y Camps, Marqués de Monistrol, Parxet★, RAÏMAT, Raventós i Blanc, Rovellats, Signat★, Agustí Torelló★, Dominio de la Vega★, Jané Ventura.

CAYMUS VINEYARDS *Napa Valley AVA, California, USA* Caymus Caberne Sauvignon★ is ripe, intense and generally tannic; it can be outstanding a a Special Selection★★★. Conundrum★ is an exotic, full-flavoured whit blend. Also successful MONTEREY Chardonnay under the Mer Soleil★★ label. Best years: (Special Selection) (2006) 05 04 03 **02 01 00 99 98 97 95 9 91 90 87 86 84**.

CAYUSE VINEYARDS *Walla Walla Valley AVA, Washington State, USA* Winemaker Christophe Baron has created a cult label here. His super Viognier★★★ is crisp, floral and spicy, yet he is best known for hi Syrahs. Using French clones, he farms a vineyard reminiscent of some i CHATEAUNEUF-DU-PAPE for its large stones. Vineyard-designated Syrah include Cailloux★★, with a distinctive mineral flavour and chocolat depth, and En Cerise★★, with more cherry and raspberry flavour bu equal richness. The Bionic Frog★★ sports a cartoon-ish label but is serious Syrah, reminding me of a northern RHÔNE version. Cabernet based Camaspelo★ is a fascinating redcurrant and jalapeño-scente wine. Best years: (Syrah) (2007) 06 05 **04 03 02**.

DOM. CAZES *Rivesaltes, Roussillon, France* The Cazes brothers make outstandin MUSCAT DE RIVESALTES★★, RIVESALTES Tuilé★★ and the superb RIVESALTE Aimé Cazes★★, and also produce a range of table wines. Soft red, whit and rosé Le Canon du Maréchal★ are good, as are the CÔTES D ROUSSILLON-VILLAGES Ego★, the Syrah-Grenache-Mourvèdre blend Alter and Cabernet-based Vin de Pays des Côtes Catalanes Le Credo★.

CH. DU CÈDRE *Cahors AC, South-West France* Pascal Verhaeghe leads th new generation of CAHORS winemakers. His wines are dark, richl textured, with a generous coating of chocolaty oak. There are 3 cuvées Le Prestige★★; the 100% Auxerrois (Malbec) Le Cèdre★, which is age in new oak barrels for 20 months; and Cuvée GC★, which is fermente and aged in oak. All benefit from at least 5–6 years' bottle age. Best year (Le Cèdre) (2008) 05 **04 01 00**.

CENCIBEL See TEMPRANILLO.

CENTRAL COAST AVA *California, USA* Huge AVA covering virtuall every vineyard between San Francisco and Los Angeles, with a numbe of sub-AVAs, such as SANTA CRUZ MOUNTAINS, Santa Ynez Valley, SANT MARIA VALLEY and Monterey. There is superb potential for Pinot Noir an Syrah in Santa Lucia Highlands in MONTEREY COUNTY. See also SAN LU OBISPO COUNTY, SANTA BARBARA COUNTY.

CENTRAL OTAGO *South Island, New Zealand* The only wine region in Ne Zealand with a continental rather than maritime climate. Technically th ripening season is long and cool, suiting Pinot Noir, Gewürztramine Chardonnay and Pinot Gris, but there are usually periods of considerable hea during the summer to intensify flavour. Long autumns have produced som excellent Rieslings. There are already nearly 100 wineries and an explosion o plantings, both in good areas like Bannockburn and Lowburn, and i marginal zones. Latest expansion is to the Waitaki Valley in northern Otago

Best producers: Akarua★, Carrick★★, Char Farm★, FELTON ROAD★★, Gibbston Valley Kawarau Estate★, Mt Difficulty★★, Mou Edward★, Mount Maude, Nevis Bluff Peregrine★★, Pisa Range★, Quartz Reef★ Rippon★★, Two Paddocks★, Wild Earth Best years: (Pinot Noir) (2008) 07 06 05 03 0

CENTRAL VALLEY *California, USA* This vast area grows 70% of California's wine grapes, used mostly for cheaper styles of wine, along with brandies and grape concentrate. It is a hot area, where irrigated vineyards tend to produce excess tonnages of grapes. It is often said that it is virtually impossible to produce exciting wine in the Central Valley, but in fact the climatic conditions in the northern half are not unlike those in many parts of Spain and southern France and, viewed overall, quality has improved in recent years. Vineyards in the Lodi AVA have expanded to around 40,000ha (over 90,000 acres), making Lodi the volume and quality leader for Chardonnay, Merlot, Zinfandel and Cabernet; Lodi Zinfandel shows most potential. Other sub-regions with claims to quality are the Sacramento Valley and the Delta area. Best producers: (Lodi) Ironstone★, Jessie's Grove★, McManis★, Mettler Family★, Michael-David★, RAVENSWOOD (Lodi★), Woodbridge/MONDAVI.

CENTRAL VALLEY *Chile* The heart of Chile's wine industry, encompassing the valleys of MAIPO, RAPEL, CURICÓ and MAULE; most major producers are located here. The key factor determining mesoclimate differences is the distance relative to the Coastal Ranges and the Andean Cordillera.

CENTRAL VICTORIA *Victoria, Australia* This zone comprises the regions of BENDIGO, HEATHCOTE, Goulburn Valley and the cooler Strathbogie Ranges and Upper Goulburn. Central Victoria, with its mostly warm conditions, produces powerful and individual wines. The few wineries on the banks of the Goulburn River feature fine Shiraz and Marsanne; reds from the high country are rich but scented and dry; whites are delicate and scented. Best producers: Jasper Hill★★★, Mitchelton★, Paul Osicka★, PONDALOWIE★, TAHBILK★, Wild Duck Creek★.

CERETTO *Piedmont, Italy* This merchant house was one of the chief modern producers in BAROLO in the 1970s and 80s. Today, Barolo (Bricco Rocche★★, Brunate★ and Prapò★), BARBARESCO (Bricco Asili★), BARBERA D'ALBA Piana★ and white Arneis Blangè, while still good, are being overtaken by smaller, more specialist, growers. Ceretto also produces an oak-aged LANGHE red, Monsordo★, from Cabernet, Merlot, Pinot Nero and Nebbiolo. An unusual white counterpart, Arbarei, is 100% Riesling. A good fizz, La Bernardina, is made from Chardonnay and Pinot Noir.

CÉRONS AC *Bordeaux, France* An AC for sweet, soft, mildly honeyed wine in the GRAVES region of Bordeaux. The wine is not quite as sweet as SAUTERNES and not so well known, nor so highly priced. Most producers now make dry wine under the Graves AC. Best producers: Ch. de Cérons★, Chantegrive★, Grand Enclos du Château de Cérons★, Haura, Seuil. Best years: 2007 05 03 02 01 99 98 97 96 95 90 89.

L A CETTO *Baja California, Mexico* Mexico's most successful winery relies on mists and cooling Pacific breezes to temper the heat of the Valle de Guadalupe in the northern part of Baja California. Italian Camillo Magoni makes ripe, fleshy Petite Sirah★, oak-aged Cabernet Sauvignon, Zinfandel and Nebbiolo. Whites, led by Chardonnay and Chenin, are greatly improved. Also good fizz.

CHABLAIS *Vaud, Switzerland* A sub-region of the VAUD, south-east of Lake Geneva along the right bank of the Rhône. Most of the vineyards lie on the alluvial plains but 2 villages, Yvorne and Aigle, benefit from much steeper slopes. Most of the thirst-quenchingly dry whites are made from Chasselas. The reds are from Pinot Noir, as is a rosé speciality, Oeil de Perdrix. Drink whites and rosés young. Best producers: Badoux, la Baudelière, Conne, J & P Testuz★.

CHAMPAGNE AC

Champagne, France

The Champagne region produces the most celebrated sparkling wines in the world. It is the most northerly AC in France – a place where grapes struggle to ripen fully but provide the perfect base wine to make fizz. Champagne is divided into 5 distinct areas – the best are the Montagne de Reims, where the Pinot Noir grape performs brilliantly, and the Chardonnay-dominated Côte des Blancs south of Épernay. In addition to Chardonnay and Pinot Noir, the other main grape permitted for the production of Champagne is Pinot Meunier.

The wines undergo a second fermentation in the bottle, producing carbon dioxide which dissolves in the wine under pressure. Through this method Champagne acquires its crisp, long-lasting bubbles and a distinctive yeasty, toasty dimension to its flavour. If you buy a bottle of Coteaux Champenois, a still wine from the area, you can see why they decided to make bubbly instead; it usually tastes mean and tart, but is transformed by the Champagne method into one of the most delightfully exhilarating wines of all.

That's the theory anyway, and for 150 years or so the Champenois have persuaded us that their product is second to none. It can be, too, except when it is released too young or sweetened to cover up a sour unripeness. When that periodically happens you know that, once again, the powers of marketing have triumphed over the wisdom and skills of the winemaker. But as Champagne expertise begins to turn out exciting sparklers in California, Australia and New Zealand, the Champagne producers must re-focus on quality or lose much of their market for good.

The Champagne trade is dominated by large companies or houses called négociants-manipulants, recognized by the letters NM on the label. The récoltants-manipulants (RM) are growers who make their own wine, and they are becoming increasingly important for drinkers seeking characterful Champagne.

STYLES OF CHAMPAGNE

Non-vintage Most Champagne is a blend of 2 or more vintages. Quality varies enormously, depending on who has made the wine and how long it has been aged. Most Champagne is sold as Brut, which is a dry, but rarely bone-dry style, but more extremely dry styles – called Extra Brut, Ultra Brut, Brut Zero and the like – are appearing. Strangely, Extra Dry denotes a style less dry than Brut.

Vintage Denotes Champagne made with grapes from a single vintage. As a rule, it is made only in the best years, but far too many mediocre years were declared in the 1990s.

Blanc de Blancs A lighter, and at best highly elegant, style of Champagne made solely from the Chardonnay grape.

Blanc de Noirs White Champagne made entirely from black grapes, either Pinot Noir, Pinot Meunier, or a combination of the two.

Rosé Pink Champagne, made either from black grapes or (more usually) by mixing a little still red wine into white Champagne.

De luxe cuvée In theory the finest Champagne and certainly always the most expensive, residing in the fanciest bottles.

See also CHAMPAGNE ROSE; and individual producers.

2002 **99 98 96 95 90 89 88 85 82**

BEST PRODUCERS

Houses BILLECART-SALMON, BOLLINGER, Cattier, Delamotte, DEUTZ, Drappier, Duval-Leroy, Gosset, Alfred GRATIEN, Charles HEIDSIECK, HENRIOT, JACQUESSON, KRUG, LANSON, LAURENT-PERRIER, Bruno PAILLARD, Joseph PERRIER, PERRIER-JOUET, Philipponnat, PIPER-HEIDSIECK, POL ROGER, POMMERY, Louis ROEDERER, RUINART, Salon, TAITTINGER, VEUVE CLICQUOT.

Growers Michel Arnould, Paul Bara, Barnaut, Beaufort, Beerens, Roger le Brun, Chartogne-Taillet, Paul Déthune, Diebolt Vallois, Daniel Dumont, Egly-Ouriet, René Geoffroy, Gimonnet, H Goutorbe, André Jacquart, Lamiable, Larmandier, Larmandier-Bernier, Launois, Margaine, Serge Mathieu, J Michel, Moncuit, Jérôme Prévost, Alain Robert, Secondé, Selosse, de Sousa, Tarlant, Vilmart.

Co-ops Beaumont des Crayères, H Blin, Nicolas Feuillatte, Jacquart, Mailly, Le Mesnil, Union Champagne.

De luxe cuvées Belle Époque (PERRIER-JOUET), N-F Billecart (BILLECART-SALMON), Blanc de Millénaires (Charles HEIDSIECK), Clos des Goisses (Philipponnat), Clos de Mesnil (KRUG), Comtes de Champagne (TAITTINGER), Cristal (Louis ROEDERER), Cuvée Josephine (Joseph PERRIER), Cuvée Sir Winston Churchill (POL ROGER), Cuvée William Deutz (DEUTZ), Dom Pérignon (MOET & CHANDON), Dom Ruinart (RUINART), Grand Siècle (LAURENT-PERRIER), Grande Dame (VEUVE CLICQUOT), Noble Cuvée (LANSON), Vintage RD (BOLLINGER).

CHABLIS AC *Burgundy, France* Chablis, lying closer to CHAMPAGNE than to the COTE D'OR, is Burgundy's northernmost outpost. When not destroyed by frost or hail, the Chardonnay grape makes a crisp, dry white wine with a steely mineral fruit which can be delicious. Several producers have taken to barrel-aging for their better wines, resulting in some full, toasty positively rich dry whites. Others are intentionally producing a soft creamy, early-drinking style, which is nice but not really typical Chablis Outlying vineyards come under the Petit Chablis AC and these wines should be drunk young. The better straight Chablis AC should be drunk at 2–4 years, while a good vintage of a leading Chablis Premier Cru may take 5 years to show its full potential. About a quarter of Chablis is designated as Premier Cru, the best vineyards on the rolling limestone slopes being Fourchaume, Mont de Milieu, Montmains, Montée de Tonnerre and Vaillons. Best producers: Barat★, J-C Bessin (Fourchaume★★), Billaud-Simon★ (Mont de Milieu★★), Pascal Bouchard★, A & F Boudin★★ BROCARD★★, la CHABLISIENNE★, Collet★, D Dampt★, R & V DAUVISSAT★★ D-E Defaix★, Droin★, DROUHIN★, DURUP★ (Montée de Tonnerre★★) W Fèvre★★, J-P Grossot (Côte de Troesme★★), LAROCHE★, Long-Depaquit Malandes (Côte de Léchêt★★), Louis Michel★★, de Moor★, Christian Moreau★★, Moreau-Naudet★, Picq (Vaucoupin★★), Pinson★, RAVENEAU★★ Vocoret★★. Best years: (Chablis Premier Cru) (2008) 07 **06 05 02 00**.

CHABLIS GRAND CRU AC *Burgundy, France* The 7 Grands Crus (Bougros, les Preuses, Vaudésir, Grenouilles, Valmur, les Clos and les Blanchots) facing south-west across the town of Chablis are the heart of the Chablis vineyards. Oak barrel-aging takes the edge off taut flavours adding a rich warmth to these fine wines. Droin and Fèvre are the most enthusiastic users of new oak, but use it less than they used to. Never drink young: 5–10 years are needed before you can see why you spent your money. Best producers: J-C Bessin★★, Billaud-Simon★★, Pascal Bouchard★ BROCARD★★, la CHABLISIENNE★★, R & V DAUVISSAT★★★, D-E Defaix★★ Droin★★, W Fèvre★★★, LAROCHE★★, Long-Depaquit★★, L Michel★★ Christian Moreau★★★, Moreau-Naudet★★, Pinson★★, RAVENEAU★★★ Servin★, Vocoret★★. Best years: (2008) 07 06 05 **02 00 99 98 96 90**.

LA CHABLISIENNE *Chablis, Burgundy, France* Substantial co-op producing nearly a third of all CHABLIS. The wines are reliable and can aspire to something much better. The best are the oaky Grands Crus – especially les Preuses★★ and Grenouilles (sold as Ch. Grenouille★★) – but the basic unoaked Chablis★, the Vieilles Vignes★★ and the numerous Premiers Crus★ are good, as is the red BOURGOGNE Épineuil. Best years (whites) (2008) 07 **06 05 03 02**.

CHAMBERS *Rutherglen, Victoria, Australia* Legendary family winery making sheer nectar in the form of Muscat and Muscadelle (Tokay). The secret is Bill Chambers' ability to draw on ancient stocks put down in wood by earlier generations. His Grand★★ and Rare★★★ blends are national treasures. The Cabernet and Shiraz table wines are good, the whites pedestrian.

CHAMBERTIN AC *Grand Cru, Côte de Nuits, Burgundy, France* The village of GEVREY-CHAMBERTIN, the largest COTE DE NUITS commune, has no fewer than 9 Grands Crus (Chambertin, Chambertin-Clos-de-Bèze, Chapelle-Chambertin, Charmes-Chambertin, Griotte-Chambertin, Latricières-Chambertin, Mazis-Chambertin, Ruchottes-Chambertin and the rarely seen Mazoyères-Chambertin), which can produce some of Burgundy's greatest and most intense red wine. Its rough-hewn fruit, seeming to win with fragrant perfumes for its first few years, creates remarkable flavours as the wine ages. Chambertin and Chambertin-Clos-de-Bèze are neighbours on the slope above the village and the two greatest sites, but overproduction is a recurrent problem with some producers. Best producers: Denis Bachelet★★ (Charmes), BOUCHARD PÈRE ET FILS★★, Charlopin★, B CLAIR★★, P Damoy★★, DROUHIN★★, Drouhin-Laroze★★, C Dugat★★★, B Dugat-Py★★★, FAIVELEY★★ (★★★ since 2005), JADOT★★, D Laurent★★, Dom. LEROY★★★, Denis MORTET★★★, H Perrot-Minot★★, Ponsot★★, Rossignol-Trapet★★, J Roty★★ (Charmes), ROUMIER★★ (Ruchottes), ROUSSEAU★★★, J & J-L Trapet★★, VOUGERAIE★★. Best years: (2008) 07 06 05 03 02 **01 00** 99 **98 97 96** 95 93 90.

HAMBOLLE-MUSIGNY AC *Côte de Nuits, Burgundy, France* AC with the potential to produce the most fragrant, perfumed red Burgundy, when not over-cropped. Encouragingly, more young producers are now bottling their own wines. Best producers: Amiot-Servelle★, G Barthod★★, J-J Confuron★, DROUHIN★★, DUJAC★★, R Groffier★★, Hudelot-Baillet★, Hudelot-Noëllat★, JADOT★★, Dom. LEROY★★, F Magnien★, Marchand-Grillot★, D MORTET★, J-F MUGNIER★★, RION★★, ROUMIER★★, VOGUE★★. Best years: (2008) 07 06 05 03 **02 01** 99 98 96 95 93 90.

HAMPAGNE See pages 110–11.

HAMPAGNE ROSÉ *Champagne AC, France* Good pink CHAMPAGNE – usually a little weightier than white – has a delicious fragrance of cherries and raspberries. The top wines can age well, but most rosé Champagne should be drunk on release, as young as possible. Best producers: (vintage) BILLECART-SALMON★★, BOLLINGER★★, Gosset★★, Charles HEIDSIECK★★, JACQUESSON★★, LAURENT-PERRIER (Grand Siècle Alexandra★★★), MOËT & CHANDON★★ (Dom Pérignon★★★), PERRIER-JOUET (Belle Époque★), POL ROGER★★, POMMERY (Louise★★), Louis ROEDERER★★ (Cristal★★★), RUINART (Dom Ruinart★★★), TAITTINGER (Comtes de Champagne★★), VEUVE CLICQUOT★★ (Grande Dame★★★); (non-vintage) Paul Bara★, E Barnaut★★, Beaumont des Crayères★, BILLECART-SALMON★★, Egly-Ouriet★★, Henri Giraud★, Jacquart★, KRUG★★, LANSON★, LAURENT-PERRIER★, MOËT & CHANDON, RUINART★, TAITTINGER, Vilmart★. Best years: 2002 00 99 98 96 **95 90** 89 88 85 82. See also pages 110–11.

HANDON DE BRIAILLES *Savigny-lès-Beaune, Côte de Beaune, Burgundy, France* The de Nicolays – François and his sister Claude – combine modern sophistication with traditional values to produce refined, savoury reds, notably PERNAND-VERGELESSES★ (including Premier Cru Île de Vergelesses★★) and CORTON★★, and an equally good range of whites from Pernand-Vergelesses★, Corton★ and CORTON-CHARLEMAGNE★★. Best years: (reds) 2007 06 05 **03 02** 99 98 96.

HANNING DAUGHTERS *Long Island, New York State, USA* A boutique winery in LONG ISLAND's Hamptons AVA that produces exciting but hard-to-find wines, including a racy Sauvignon Blanc★, a Muscat-based blend called Sylvanus★ and a juicy Blaufrankisch★.

HAPEL DOWN *Kent, England* The UK's largest winery, producing around 500,000 bottles a year. Most grapes are grown under contract by growers in the south and east of England, although 30ha (74 acres) of Chardonnay and Pinot Noir were planted in 2008 on a recently purchased site in Kent. Wines of good to very good quality, especially non-vintage Chapel Down Brut, Pinot Reserve Sparkling★ and still Bacchus★ and Rosé. Tullens Pinot Noir★ is a remarkable new scented English red.

CHARDONNAY

I never thought I'd see myself write this. Yes, we are getting bored with Chardonnay. Not all Chardonnay: there's probably more top Chardonnay being produced right now than ever before. And for millions of wine drinkers the Chardonnay revolution (easy to pronounce, easy to swallow) has only just begun. But in the heart of the wine world – the middle market, where people care about flavour but also care about price – we're getting fed up. Far too much sugary, over-oaked, unrefreshing junk has been dumped into our laps recently, from countries and producers who should know better. Add to this the increasingly desperate dirt-cheap offerings at the rump end of the market, and you'll see why I think the great golden goose of Chardonnay has the carving knife of cynicism and greed firmly held against its neck. The next few years will show whether it wishes to be the supremely versatile all-rounder or the sloppy jack of all trades and master of none.

WINE STYLES

France Although a relatively neutral variety if left alone (this is what makes it so suitable as a base wine for top-quality Champagne-method sparkling wine), the grape can ripen in a surprising range of conditions, developing a subtle gradation of flavours going from the sharp apple-core greenness of Chardonnay grown in Champagne or the Loire Valley through the exciting, bone-dry yet succulent flavours of white Burgundy to a round, tropical flavour in Languedoc-Roussillon.

Other regions Italy produces Chardonnay that can be bone dry and lean or fat, spicy and lush. Spain does much the same. California and Australia virtually created their reputations on great, viscous, almost syrupy, tropical fruits and spice-flavoured Chardonnays; the best producers have moved away from this style. Some of the best New World Chardonnays, dry but ripe, fresh and subtly oaked, are coming from South Africa. Unoaked versions from more mature vines offer increasingly characterful, food-friendly drinking. New Zealand is producing beautifully balanced Chardonnays, their fragrant fruit only subtly oaked, while Chile and Argentina are rapidly learning how to make fine wine from it too. Add Germany, Austria, Canada, New York State, Greece, Portugal, Slovenia, Moldova, Romania, England, Belgium, even China, and you'll see it can perform almost anywhere.

Using oak The reason for all these different flavours lies in Chardonnay's wonderful susceptibility to the winemaker's aspirations and skills. The most important manipulation is the use of the oak barrel for fermenting and aging the wine. Chardonnay is the grape of the great white Burgundies and these are fermented and matured in oak (not necessarily new oak); the effect is to give a marvellous round, nutty richness to a wine that is yet savoury and dry. This is enriched still further by aging the wine on its lees.

The New World winemakers sought to emulate the great Burgundies, planting Chardonnay and employing thousands of oak barrels (mostly new), and their success has caused winemakers everywhere else to see Chardonnay as the perfect variety – easy to grow, easy to turn into wine and easy to sell to an adoring public. But as in all things, familiarity can breed contempt.

BEST PRODUCERS

France *Chablis* Billaud-Simon, DAUVISSAT, Droin, Fèvre, LAROCHE, C Moreau, RAVENEAU; *Côte d'Or* R Ampeau, H Boillot, J-M Boillot, Bonneau du Martray, BOUCHARD, CARILLON, COCHE-DURY, M Colin, DROUHIN, A Ente, J-P Fichet, J-N GAGNARD, V GIRARDIN, JADOT, F Jobard, LAFON, H Lamy, Dom. LEFLAIVE, B Morey, M Niellon, RAMONET, G Roulot, SAUZET, VERGET; *Mâconnais* D & M Barraud, Bret, Guffens-Heynen/VERGET, O Merlin, J Thévenet.

Other European Chardonnays
Austria BRUNDLMAYER, Kollwentz, TEMENT, VELICH; *Germany* JOHNER, REBHOLZ, WITTMANN; *Italy* Castello di AMA, BELLAVISTA, CA' DEL BOSCO, GAJA, ISOLE E OLENA, LAGEDER, Lis Neris, Pomino Benefizio/ FRESCOBALDI, Castello della SALA, TIEFENBRUNNER (Linticlarus), Vie di Romans; *Spain* CHIVITE, ENATE, Manzaneque, Muñoz, Nekeas, Señorío de Otazu, TORRES.

New World Chardonnays
Australia BANNOCKBURN, Bindi (Quartz), Brookland Valley, CAPE MENTELLE, Chapman Grove (Atticus), CULLEN, By FARR, GIACONDA, GROSSET, HOWARD PARK, LEEUWIN, OAKRIDGE (864), PENFOLDS (Yattarna), PETALUMA, PIERRO, Savaterre, SHAW & SMITH, TAPANAPPA, TARRAWARRA, TYRRELL'S, VOYAGER, Yering Station (Reserve).

New Zealand BABICH, CHURCH ROAD, CLOUDY BAY, CRAGGY RANGE, DRY RIVER, FELTON ROAD, FROMM, GOLDWATER, KUMEU RIVER, MATUA VALLEY, MILLTON, MONTANA, MORTON ESTATE, NEUDORF, PALLISER, PEGASUS BAY, SAINT CLAIR, SERESIN, TRINITY HILL, VAVASOUR, Vidal, VILLA MARIA, WITHER HILLS.

USA ARROWOOD, AU BON CLIMAT, CALERA, CHATEAU ST JEAN, DOMAINE DROUHIN OREGON, DUTTON GOLDFIELD, FLOWERS, HdV, IRON HORSE, KISTLER, MARCASSIN, MATANZAS CREEK, MERRYVALE, Peter MICHAEL, NEWTON, Ramey, RIDGE, ROCHIOLI, SAINTSBURY, SANFORD, SHAFER, SILVERADO, STEELE, STONY HILL, TALBOTT.

South Africa Ataraxia, BUITEN-VERWACHTING, CAPE CHAMONIX, ELLIS, HAMILTON RUSSELL, JORDAN, MULDERBOSCH, THELEMA, VERGELEGEN, Waterford.

South America CATENA, CONCHA Y TORO, CONO SUR, DE MARTINO, ERRAZURIZ, MONTES, Sol de Sol/ Aquitania, Tabalí/SAN PEDRO, Viña Leyda/SAN PEDRO.

CHAPEL HILL *McLaren Vale, South Australia* Chief winemaker Michael Fragos's efforts and some exceptional vintages have added a further dimension to the powerful, classy reds of Chapel Hill. The Cabernet Sauvignon★★ is a blend of mature MCLAREN VALE and COONAWARRA fruit, while the Shiraz★★ is all McLaren Vale. Good Unwooded Chardonnay★ and fascinating, bone-dry, honey-scented Verdelho★★. Best years: (Shiraz) (2008) 06 05 04 02 **01 98 97 96 95 94 93 91**.

CHAPELLE-CHAMBERTIN AC See CHAMBERTIN AC.

CHAPELLE LENCLOS *Madiran AC, South-West France* A leading name in MADIRAN, Patrick Ducournau is the inventor of microoxygenation, or *microbullage* – bubbling tiny amounts of oxygen into the wine, either during fermentation or during barrel aging. More recently he has switched his interest to the marketing of oak chips and has delegated to his Laplace cousins at Ch. d'AYDIE the making of his Chapelle Lenclos★★ and Dom. Mouréou★, legendary, ripe, concentrated reds, which need at least 5 years to mature. Best years: (2008) 06 05 **04 01 00 99 98**.

M CHAPOUTIER *Rhône Valley, France* The biodynamic house of Chapoutier is in the vanguard of progress in viticulture, and is producing serious, exciting wines. The HERMITAGE la Sizeranne★★ and special plot-specific Ermitages (les Greffieux★★, l'Ermite★★, le Méal★★ and le Pavillon★★★), rich white Hermitage de l'Orée★★ and l'Ermite★★★, CROZES-HERMITAGE les Varonniers★★, ST-JOSEPH les Granits★★ (red and white), and CHATEAUNEUF-DU-PAPE Barbe Rac★ and Croix de Bois★ are all good, but some reds show excess oak. Large-volume Crozes-Hermitage les Meysonniers and COTES DU RHONE Belleruche are good value. Also BANYULS, COTEAUX DU TRICASTIN and Australian joint ventures. Best years (la Sizeranne) 2007 06 05 04 **03 01 00 99 98 95 94 91 90 89 88**.

CHARDONNAY See pages 114–15.

CHARMES-CHAMBERTIN AC See CHAMBERTIN AC.

CHASSAGNE-MONTRACHET AC *Côte de Beaune, Burgundy, France* Some of Burgundy's greatest white wine vineyards (part of le MONTRACHET and BÂTARD-MONTRACHET, all of Criots-Bâtard-Montrachet) are within the village boundary. The white Chassagne Premiers Crus are not as well known, but can offer nutty, toasty wines, especially if aged for 4–8 years Blanchots Dessus, Caillerets, Romanée, Ruchottes and Morgeots are among the best. Ordinary white Chassagne-Montrachet is usually enjoyable; the red is a little earthy, peppery and plummy and can be an acquired taste. Look out for reds from the following Premiers Crus: Clos de la Boudriotte, Clos St-Jean and Clos de la Chapelle. Best producers (whites) Blain-Gagnard★★, B Colin, M Colin★★, P Colin★, J-N GAGNARD★★ V GIRARDIN★★, V & F Jouard★, H Lamy★, B Morey★★, M Morey★★ M Niellon★★, J & J-M Pillot★★, P Pillot★, RAMONET★★, VERGET★★; (reds CARILLON★, R Clerget★, V GIRARDIN★★, B Morey★★, RAMONET★★ Best years: (whites) (2008) 07 06 05 **02 00 99**; (reds) (2008) 07 05 03 **02 99**

CHASSELAS Chasselas is considered a table grape worldwide. Only in BADEN (where it is called Gutedel) and Switzerland (called FENDANT) is i thought to make decent light, dry wines with a slight prickle. A few Swiss examples, notably from CHABLAIS and DEZALEY, rise above this.

CH. CHASSE-SPLEEN★ *Moulis AC, Haut-Médoc, Bordeaux, France* Chasse Spleen is not a Classed Growth – but during the 1980s it built tremendous reputation for ripe, concentrated and powerful wines unde the late proprietor, Bernadette Villars. The château is now run by Villars' daughter Céline, and recent vintages are approaching the form of the old days. Second wine: l'Ermitage de Chasse-Spleen. Best years: 2007 06 05 **04 03 02 01 00 99 96 95 90 89.**

CHÂTEAU-CHALON AC *Jura, France* The most prized – and pricey – *vin jaune*, it is bottled exclusively in the 62cl *clavelin*. If you find a bottle, beware – the awesome flavour will shock your tastebuds like no other French wine. Made from the Savagnin grape and aged like sherry under a yeast flor, but in old barrels, it is not released until 6 years after the vintage and can be kept for decades. Best producers: Baud★, Berthet-Bondet★★, Bourdy★★, Butin★, Crédoz★, Durand-Perron★, J Macle★★, H Maire, F Mossu★. Best years: (2002) 00 **99 98 97 96 95 93 92 90 89 88.**

CHÂTEAU-GRILLET AC★★ *Rhône Valley, France* This rare and very expensive RHONE white from a 3ha (7-acre) vineyard, made from Viognier and aged in used oak, has a magic reek of orchard fruit and harvest bloom when young but is best drunk after 5 years, and decanted. More reserved, more refined than CONDRIEU. Best years: 2007 06 05 **04 03 01 00 98 95.**

CHATEAU INDAGE *Maharashtra, India* India's first traditional-method sparkling wine appeared in the 1980s, with technical assistance from Champagne's PIPER-HEIDSIECK. Dry sparklers are firm, fresh and chunky – though quality is somewhat erratic. Omar Khayyám is produced from a blend of Chardonnay, Ugni Blanc, Pinot Noir and Pinot Meunier. A demi-sec and a good pink fizz are also produced. Red and white table wines use both international and indigenous Indian grape varieties such as Bangalore Purple and Arkavati.

CHATEAU MONTELENA *Napa Valley AVA, California, USA* NAPA winery producing classic California Chardonnay★★ and an estate Cabernet★★ that are impressive, if slow to develop. The Napa Valley Cabernet★ is an elegant wine for younger consumption. Best years: (Chardonnay) 2007 06 **05 04 03 02 01**; (Cabernet) 2005 03 **02 01 00 99 98 91 90.**

CHATEAU MUSAR *Ghazir, Lebanon* Founded by Gaston Hochar in the 1930s, managed for many years by his Bordeaux-trained son Serge; now the winery is gradually being passed to the next generation. From an unlikely blend of primarily Cabernet Sauvignon, old-vine Carignan and Cinsaut comes a wine of real, if wildly exotic, character, with sweet dried fruits and good aging potential: Hochar says that red Ch. Musar★★ 'should be drunk at 15 years'. Style oscillates between classic Bordeaux and spicy Rhône. Hochar Père & Fils and Cuvée Musar are less complex, more fruit-forward alternatives. White★ is made from indigenous Obaideh (like Chardonnay) and Merwah (similar to Semillon). Best years: (red) 2001 00 **97 95 94 91 88.**

CHATEAU ST JEAN *Sonoma Valley AVA, California, USA* Once known almost entirely for its range of Chardonnays (Belle Terre★★, Robert Young★★), St Jean has emerged as a producer of delicious reds, including a BORDEAUX-style blend called Cinq Cépages★★ and a Reserve Merlot★★. Now owned by the Foster's Group. Best years: (Chardonnay) 2006 **05 04 03 02 01 00 99**; (reds) 2005 04 03 **02 01 99 97 95 94.**

CHATEAU STE MICHELLE *Washington State, USA* Pioneering winery with an enormous range of wines, including several attractive vineyard-designated Chardonnays★ (some ★★), Cabernet Sauvignons★ and Merlots★, especially Cold Creek Vineyard★★ and Indian Wells★★ wines. Good Riesling, both dry and sweet, and increasingly interesting red Meritage★ and spicy Orphelin★★ Rhône-style blend. Partnership with Italy's ANTINORI and Germany's Ernst LOOSEN has produced dark, powerful Tuscan-style red Col Solare★★, attractive Riesling Eroica★ and a thrilling sweet version, Single Berry Select★★★, made in tiny quantities. Quality generally seems to be moving upwards. **Best years:** (premium reds) (2007) 06 05 **04** 03 02.

CHÂTEAUNEUF-DU-PAPE AC *Rhône Valley, France* A large (3350ha/ 8275-acre) vineyard area between Orange and Avignon. The sweetly fruited red wine is based on Grenache, plus Syrah and Mourvèdre (10 other varieties are also allowed). Always choose Châteauneuf from a single estate, distinguished by the papal coat of arms or mitre embossed on the neck of the bottle. Only 5% of Châteauneuf is white; made mainly from Grenache Blanc, Bourboulenc, Clairette and Roussanne, these wines can be surprisingly good. Top reds, particularly old-vine cuvées, will age for 10 years or more; many whites are best young. **Best producers:** (reds) P Autard★, L Barrot★, BEAUCASTEL★★★, Beaurenard★★, Bois de Boursan★★, H Bonneau★★, Bosquet des Papes★★, du Caillou★, les Cailloux★★, Chante-Perdrix★, CHAPOUTIER★, la Charbonnière★★, L Charvin★, Clos du Mont Olivet★★, CLOS DES PAPES★★★, Clos St-Jean, Cristia★, Font du Loup★, FONT DE MICHELLE★, Fortia★★, la Gardine★★, Giraud★, Grand Tinel★, Grand Veneur★, la Janasse★★, Marcoux★★, Mathieu★, Monpertuis★★, Mont-Redon★★, la Nerthe★★, Pégaü★★, RAYAS★★★, Roquette★, Roger Sabon★★, St-Siffrein, Solitude★★, Tardieu-Laurent★, P Usseglio★★, la Vieille-Julienne★★, Le Vieux Donjon★★, VIEUX TELEGRAPHE★★★; (whites) BEAUCASTEL★★★, CLOS DES PAPES★★, FONT DE MICHELLE★★, Grand Veneur★★, Marcoux★★, RAYAS★★, St-Cosme★, VIEUX TELEGRAPHE★★★. **Best years:** (reds) 2007 06 05 04 03 01 00 99 98 96 95 90 89 88.

JEAN-LOUIS CHAVE *Rhône Valley, France* Jean-Louis Chave's red HERMITAGE★★★ is one of the world's great wines, surpassed only by the Cathelin★★★, produced in exceptional years. His wonderful, richly flavoured white Hermitage★★★ (from Marsanne with some Roussanne) sometimes even outlasts the reds, as it quietly moves towards its honeyed, nutty zenith. Also a small amount of excellent red ST-JOSEPH★★ and an occasional stunning traditional sweet Vin de Paille★★. Expensive, but worth the money. *Négociant* business makes sound CÔTES DU RHÔNE Mon Coeur and St-Joseph Offerus. **Best years:** (reds) 2007 06 05 04 03 01 00 99 98 97 96 95 94 92 91 90 89 88 86 85 83 82 79 78; (whites) (2008) 07 06 05 04 03 01 00 99 98 97 96 95 94 93 92 91 90 89 88 85 83.

CHÉNAS AC *Beaujolais, Burgundy, France* The smallest of the BEAUJOLAIS Crus, Chénas offers a range of styles from light and elegant to austere and needing time to develop Burgundian tones. **Best producers:** Champagnon★, DUBOEUF, H Lapierre★, Piron et Lafon (Quartz★★), B Santé★. **Best years:** 2008 07 06.

CHENIN BLANC One of the most underrated and versatile white wine grapes in the world. In the LOIRE VALLEY, where it is also called Pineau de la Loire, it is responsible for sweet, medium, dry and sparkling wines. The great sweet wines of COTEAUX DU LAYON, QUARTS DE CHAUME, BONNEZEAUX and VOUVRAY are some of the longest-lived of all wines. There is an increasing emphasis on barrel-fermented and aged dry wines, especially in ANJOU, the best of which are a revelation. In South Africa, Chenin Blanc remains both the most planted and most uprooted variety but total plantings are now fairly stable: the best sites producing the best wines are lusher than their Loire counterparts, but just as good. Styles range from sparkling through easy-drinking, dryish wines and modern barrel-fermented versions to botrytized dessert wines. Chenin is also influential in quality white blends. New Zealand and Australia have produced good varietal examples, and it is also grown in California (DRY CREEK VINEYARD★★) and Argentina.

CH. CHEVAL BLANC★★★ *St-Émilion Grand Cru AC, 1er Grand Cru Classé, Bordeaux, France* Along with AUSONE, the leading ST-EMILION estate. Right on the border with POMEROL, it seems to share some of its sturdy richness, but with an extra spice and purity of fruit that is impressively, recognizably unique. An unusually high percentage (60%) of

Cabernet Franc is often used in the blend. Appealing when young, yet with a remarkable ability to age for many decades. Best years: 2007 06 05 04 03 02 01 00 99 98 97 96 95 94 90 89 88 86 85 83.

CHEVALIER-MONTRACHET AC See MONTRACHET AC.

DOM. DE CHEVALIER *Pessac-Léognan AC, Cru Classé de Graves, Bordeaux, France* Some of Bordeaux's finest wines. The red★★ starts out firm and reserved but over 10–20 years gains heavenly cedar, tobacco and blackcurrant flavour. Recent vintages have greater purity of fruit. The brilliant white★★★ is both fermented and aged in oak barrels; in the best vintages it will still be improving at 15–20 years. Best years: (reds) 2007 06 05 04 03 02 01 00 99 98 96 90 89 88; (whites) 2007 06 05 04 03 02 01 00 99 98 96 95 94 90 89 88.

CHEVERNY AC *Loire Valley, France* A little-known area south of Blois. The local speciality is the white Romorantin grape, which makes a bone-dry wine under the AC Cour-Cheverny, but the best whites are from Chardonnay. Also pleasant Sauvignon, Pinot Noir, Gamay and bracing CHAMPAGNE-method fizz. Drink young. Best producers: Cazin, Cheverny co-op, Gendrier/Huards★, Gueritte, H Marionnet, du Moulin, Salvard, Sauger, C Tessier/la Desoucherie, Tue-Boeuf★, de Veilloux.

CHIANTI DOCG *Tuscany, Italy* The most famous of all Italian wines, but there are many styles, depending on what grapes are used, where they are grown, and by which producer. It can be a light, fresh, easy-drinking red wine with a characteristic hint of bitterness, or it can be an intense, structured yet sleek wine in the same league as the best BORDEAUX. The vineyards are scattered over central Tuscany, either simply as 'Chianti' or Chianti plus the name of one of the 7 sub-zones: Colli Aretini, Colli Fiorentini, Colli Senesi, Colline Pisane, Montalbano, Montespertoli and Rufina. (There is some danger of the Chianti sub-zones losing their identity under new EU DOP rules.) Sangiovese is the main grape; traditionally it was blended with the red Canaiolo and white Malvasia and Trebbiano. Modern winemakers often make Chianti from Sangiovese alone or blended with 20% of Cabernet, Merlot, Syrah or, increasingly, with native grapes like Colorino. See also CHIANTI RUFINA, SUPER-TUSCANS. Best producers: (Chianti Colli Fiorentini) Baggiolino★, Le Calvane, Il Corno, Corzano e Paterno★, Lanciola★, Malenchini★, Pasolini dall'Onda★, Poppiano★, La Querce, Sammontana, San Vito in Fior di Selva; (Chianti Colli Senesi) Campriano, Carpineta Fontalpino★, Casabianca, Casale-Falchini★, Farnetella★, Ficomontanino★, Pacina★, Paradiso★, Pietrasarena.

CHIANTI CLASSICO DOCG *Tuscany, Italy* The original (if slightly enlarged) CHIANTI zone in the hills between Florence and Siena. Classico has led the trend in making richer, more structured and better-balanced wines. Nonetheless, until recently many producers used their best grapes for high-profile SUPER-TUSCANS. Since the 1996 vintage, Classico can be made from 100% Sangiovese, though winemakers all too often accept the option of including 20% 'international' grapes (see CHIANTI). Riserva must be aged at least 27 months (usually in barrel) and, like Chianti Classico *normale*, must use only red grapes. The finest Riserva wines can improve for a decade or more. Many of the estates also offer regular bottlings of red wine, round and fruity, for drinking about 2–5 years after the harvest. Best producers (Riserva or top cru): Castello di AMA★★★, ANTINORI★ (Riserva★★), Badia a Coltibuono★, Brancaia★, Cacchiano★★, Capaccia★★ Carpineto★, Casaloste★★, CASTELLARE★, Castell'in Villa★, Collelungo★★ Colombaio di Cencio★★, Dievole★, Casa Emma★★, FELSINA★★, Le Filigare★ FONTERUTOLI★★, FONTODI★★, ISOLE E OLENA★★, Il Mandorlo★★, La Massa★★ Melini★, MONSANTO★★★, Monte Bernardi★★, Il Palazzino★★, Paneretta★★ Panzanello★★, Poggerino★, Poggiopiano★★, Poggio al Sole (Casasilia★★★) Querceto★, QUERCIABELLA★★, Castello dei RAMPOLLA★★, RICASOLI (Castello di Brolio★★), RIECINE★★, Rignana★★, Rocca di Castagnoli★★, San Felice★★ San Giusto a Rentennano★★, San Polo in Rosso★, Casa Sola★★, Terrabianca★ Vecchie Terre di Montefili★★, Verrazzano★, Vignamaggio★, Villa Cafaggio★★ VOLPAIA★★. Best years: (2008) (07) 06 **04 03 01 99 97 95 90**.

CHIANTI RUFINA DOCG *Tuscany, Italy* Smallest of the CHIANTI sub-zones an enclave of the Apennine foothills to the east of Florence, where wines were noted for exceptional structure and longevity long before they joined the ranks of Chianti. Today the wines, particularly the long-lived Riserva Bucerchiale from SELVAPIANA and FRESCOBALDI's Montesodi, match the best of CHIANTI CLASSICO. Pomino DOC is a small (100ha/250-acre) high-altitude zone almost entirely surrounded by Chianti Rufina dominated by Frescobaldi, it makes greater use of French varieties such as Merlot, Cabernet and Chardonnay. Best producers: (Rufina Riservas) Basciano★★, Tenuta di Bossi★, Colognole★★, FRESCOBALDI★★, Grati/Villa di Vetrice★, Grignano★, Lavacchio★, SELVAPIANA★★★, Castello del Trebbio★ Best years: (2008) (07) 06 **04 03 01 99 97 95**.

MICHELE CHIARLO *Piedmont, Italy* From his winery base south of Asti Michele Chiarlo produces stylish wines from several PIEDMONT zones Single-vineyard BAROLOS★★ and BARBARESCOS★ top the list, but BARBERA D'ASTI★ and GAVI★ are reliable, too. The Monferrato DOC embraces Montemareto Countacc!★, a Barbera-Cabernet Sauvignon blend.

CHIMNEY ROCK *Stags Leap District AVA, California, USA* Powerful yet elegantly sculpted Cabernet Sauvignon★★ (Reserve★★) and a meritage blend called Elevage★★. There's also an ageworthy Elevage Blanc★ (a blend of Sauvignons Blanc and Gris), a tangy Fumé Blanc★ and a small amount of Cabernet Franc rosé. Best years: (Elevage) 2005 04 03 **02 01 00** 99 98 97 96 95.

CHINON AC *Loire Valley, France* Best red wine of the LOIRE VALLEY, made mainly from Cabernet Franc with an occasional dash of Cabernet Sauvignon. Lovely light reds full of raspberry fruit and fresh summer earth to drink young, and heavyweights for keeping; always worth buying a single-estate wine. Best producers: P Alliet★★, B BAUDRY★★, Baudry Dutour★, Dom. de Beauséjour, Logis de la Bouchardière, P Breton★ Coulaine★, Couly-Dutheil★, DRUET★, la Grille★, C Joguet★, la Noblaie★

Rouet, Wilfrid Rousse, P Sourdais★. Best years: (2008) **06** 05 **04 03 02 01** 97 **96 95**.

CHIROUBLES AC *Beaujolais, Burgundy, France* The highest in altitude of the BEAUJOLAIS Crus, producing a light, fragrant, delicious Gamay wine exhibiting all the attractions of a youthful Cru. Best producers: Cheysson★, la Combe au Loup★, D Desvignes★, la Grosse Pierre★, Ch. de Javernand. Best years: **2008 07**.

CHIVITE *Navarra DO, Navarra, Spain* Longtime leader in exports from NAVARRA. The Gran Feudo★ red and rosé are very good easy drinkers and unoaked Chardonnay★★ is excellent. The more upmarket reds have improved steadily in a restrained, claret-like style. The top range, called Colección 125, includes a red Reserva★, classy white Blanco★★ (barrel-fermented Chardonnay) and a characterful sweet Vendimia Tardía★★ from Moscatel de Grano Menudo (Muscat Blanc à Petits Grains). Chivite's northerly estate, Señorío de Arínzano★★, received a separate Vino de Pago appellation in 2008.

CHOREY-LÈS-BEAUNE AC *Côte de Beaune, Burgundy, France* One of those tiny, forgotten villages that make good, if not great, Burgundy at prices most of us can afford, with some committed producers too. Can age for 5–8 years. Best producers: Arnoux★, DROUHIN★, Germain/Ch. de Chorey★, Maillard★, TOLLOT-BEAUT★★. Best years: (2008) 07 **05 03 02 99**.

CHURCH ROAD *Hawkes Bay, North Island, New Zealand* A premium-wine project owned by Pernod Ricard. The reds seem a bit Bordeaux-obsessed, although Reserve wines, made in the best years, can be very good. Reserve Chardonnay★★ leapt in quality in recent years to become one of the country's best. Best years: (reds) 2007 **06 04 02 00**.

CHURCHILL *Port DOC, Douro, Portugal* Established in 1981, it was the first new PORT shipper for 50 years. The wines can be good, notably Vintage★, LBV★, Crusted★, single-quinta Gricha★ and a well-aged, nutty dry white port★, and are much more consistent since Quinta da Gricha was bought in 1999. Since 2003, Churchill Estates, an unfortified DOURO red, has also improved. Best years: (Vintage) **2003 00 97 94 91 85**; (Quinta da Gricha) **2003 01 99**.

CINSAUT Also spelt Cinsault. Found mainly in France's southern RHÔNE VALLEY, PROVENCE and LANGUEDOC-ROUSSILLON. Ideal for rosé wine. In blends, Cinsaut's low alcohol can help calm high-degree Grenache. Rare as a single varietal but CLOS CENTEILLES is a fine example. Mainstay of the blend for Lebanon's CHATEAU MUSAR. Popular as a bulk blender in South Africa, it is being rediscovered by enthusiasts of the Rhône style.

CIRÒ DOC *Calabria, Italy* The legend that this was the wine offered to champions in the ancient Olympics has often seemed a more potent reason to buy it than for its quality. Yet Cirò Rosso, a full-bodied red from the Gaglioppo grape, has improved remarkably of late. Non-DOC Gaglioppo-based IGTs, like Librandi's Gravello★★ (an oak-aged blend with Cabernet), are genuinely exciting. The DOC also covers a dry white from Greco and a rare dry rosé. Best producers: Caparra & Siciliani★, Librandi★ (Riserva★★), San Francesco★. Best years: (reds) (2008) (07) 06 **05 04 03 01 00**.

BRUNO CLAIR *Marsannay, Côte de Nuits, Burgundy, France* Top producer from MARSANNAY with several single-vineyard cuvées there and an impressive range from other top vineyards including CHAMBERTIN Clos de Bèze★★

121

and Gevrey-Chambertin Clos St-Jacques★★. Also good-value SAVIGNY La Dominade★★ and a delicious Marsannay rosé★. Best years: (top reds) (2008) 07 06 05 03 **02 01 99 98 96 90**.

CLAIRETTE DE DIE AC *Rhône Valley, France* Sparkling wine made from a minimum of 75% Muscat, off-dry, with a creamy bubble and a honeyed orchard-fresh fragrance. The *méthode Dioise* is used, which preserves the Muscat scent. An ideal light aperitif. Drink young. Best producers: Achard-Vincent★, Clairette de Die co-op, D Cornillon, Jacques Faure, J-C Raspail★. See also CREMANT DE DIE.

A CLAPE *Cornas, Rhône Valley, France* Leading estate in CORNAS – dense, reserved, tannic, consistently excellent wines, full of rich, roasted fruit and often ★★★. Second wine Renaissance is good lower-key Cornas. Clape also makes fine red and white CÔTES DU RHÔNE★ and decent ST-PERAY★. Best years: (Cornas) 2007 06 05 04 03 **02 01 00 99 98 97 96 95 9 91 90 89 88 86 85 83.**

LA CLAPE *Coteaux du Languedoc AC, Languedoc, France* The mountain of La Clape rises above the flat coastal fields south-east of Narbonne; its vineyards produce some excellent whites from Bourboulenc and Clairette, plus fine, herb-scented reds and rosés, mainly from Grenache, Syrah and Mourvèdre. Whites and reds can age. Best producers: Camplazens★★, Capitoul, l'HOSPITALET★, Mire l'Étang, Moyau★, Négly, Pech Céleyran★, Pech Redon★, Ricardelle★, Vires. Best years: (reds) (2008) 07 0 05 **04 03 01 00.**

CLARE VALLEY *South Australia* Historic upland region north of Adelaide with a deceptively moderate climate, able to grow both hot-climate and cool-climate grapes successfully, including fine, aromatic Riesling, marvellously textured Semillon, scented Viognier, rich, robust Shiraz and Cabernet blends and peppery but voluptuous Grenache. Best producers: (whites) Tim ADAMS★★, Jim BARRY★, Wolf BLASS (Gold Label★), Leo Burin (Leonay★★), Crabtree, GROSSET★★★, Kilikanoon★, KNAPPSTEIN★★ (Acklan Vineyard★★★), LEASINGHAM★, MITCHELL★, MOUNT HORROCKS★★, O'Lear Walker★★, PETALUMA★★★, Pikes★, SKILLOGALEE★, Taylors/Wakefield★; (red Tim ADAMS★★★, Jim BARRY★★, GROSSET★★, Kilikanoon★, KNAPPSTEIN★ LEASINGHAM★, MITCHELL★, O'Leary Walker★, Pikes★, SKILLOGALEE★, Taylor Wakefield, WENDOUREE★★★. Best years: (Shiraz) 2008 06 05 **04 03 02 01 99 9 97 96 94 92 91 90**; (Riesling) **2008** 06 05 04 03 **02 01 99 98 97 96 95.**

CLARENDON HILLS *McLaren Vale, South Australia* Winery with a name fo high-priced, highly extracted, unfined, unfiltered and unobtainable red Single-vineyard Astralis★★ is a hugely concentrated Syrah from ol vines, aged in 100% French new oak. Other Syrah ★★ labels off slightly better value, while Merlot★ and Cabernet Sauvignon★ aim 1 rub shoulders with great red BORDEAUX – although I'm not sure whic ones. Several cuvées of Old Vines Grenache★★ are marked by saturate black cherry fruit and high alcohol. Best years: (Astralis) (2008) (06) (05) 03 02 01 00 **98 96 95 94.**

CH. CLARKE★ *Listrac-Médoc AC, Bordeaux, France* This property had millio spent on it by the late Baron Edmond de Rothschild during the la 1970s, and from the 98 vintage leading Bordeaux winemaker Mich Rolland has been consultant enologist. The wines can have an attracti blackcurrant fruit and now a little more ripeness and polish. With a nam like Clarke, how could they possibly fail to seduce? There is also a sma production of dry white wine, le Merle Blanc★. Best years: 2007 06 05 (**03 01 00 99 98 96.**

OMENICO CLERICO *Barolo DOCG, Piedmont, Italy* Domenico Clerico produces consistently superlative BAROLO (Ciabot Mentin Ginestra★★★, Pajana★★★, Per Cristina★★★) and excellent BARBERA D'ALBA★ (Trevigne★★), all wonderfully balanced. His range also includes LANGHE Arte★★, a barrique-aged blend of Nebbiolo and Barbera. Best years: (Barolo) (2008) (07) (06) 04 **03** 01 **00** 99 98 97 96 95 93 90 89 88.

H. CLIMENS★★★ *Barsac AC, 1er Cru Classé, Bordeaux, France* The leading estate in BARSAC, with a deserved reputation for fabulous, sensuous wines, rich and succulent yet streaked with lively lemon acidity. Easy to drink at 5 years, but a good vintage will be richer and more satisfying after 10–15 years. Second wine: les Cyprès (also delicious). Best years: 2007 06 05 **04** 03 02 01 **00** 99 98 97 96 95 90 89 88.

LONAKILLA *Canberra, Australia* Small family winery, whose flagship Shiraz-Viognier★★★ is the benchmark for the style in Australia: elegant, lavender-scented, fleshily textured and complex, with the structure to age beautifully. Tim Kirk also produces very good Riesling★, Viognier★ and new Semillon-Sauvignon Blanc. More modestly priced O'Riada Shiraz★ (from local growers) and HILLTOPS Shiraz (from the nearby region).

LOS DE L'ANHEL *Corbières AC, Languedoc, France* In just a few years, Sophie Guiraudon and Philippe Mathias have started to produce remarkable wines with a power unusual even for the CORBIÈRES. Top wine is smooth, rich Les Dimanches★★; also Les Terrassettes★ and Les Autres. Best years: (Les Dimanches) (2008) 07 06 05 **04** 03 01 **00**.

LOS BAGATELLE *St-Chinian AC, Languedoc-Roussillon, France* Siblings Luc and Christine Simon produce various ST-CHINIANS: top wine La Gloire de Mon Père★ is made from Syrah, Mourvèdre and Grenache, and aged in 100% new oak barrels. Unoaked Mathieu et Marie★ is fruit-driven; Cuvée Camille et Juliette has spicy, herbal aromas. Also a MUSCAT DE ST-JEAN-DE-MINERVOIS.

LOS DU BOIS *Alexander Valley AVA, Sonoma County, California, USA* I've always been partial to the house style here: gentle, fruit-dominated SONOMA Chardonnay, Merlot and Cabernet. Top vineyard selections can be exciting: Calcaire Chardonnay★★, rich, strong Briarcrest Cabernet Sauvignon★★ and Marlstone★★, a red BORDEAUX-style blend. Riesling is the latest project. Now owned by Constellation. Best years: (reds) 2003 **02** 01 **00** 99 97 96 95 94 91 90 88 86.

LOS CENTEILLES *Minervois AC, Languedoc-Roussillon, France* Excellent MINERVOIS La Livinière and innovative vins de pays. Impressive Clos Centeilles★★ is the top wine; Capitelle de Centeilles★ and Carignanissime★ are 100% Cinsaut and 100% Carignan respectively. Best years: (2008) 07 06 05 **04** 03 02 **01** 00.

LOS DE LA COULÉE-DE-SERRANT *Savennières AC, Loire Valley, France* Nicolas Joly is biodynamics' most vocal proponent and now, with his winemaker daughter Virginie, produces the most powerfully concentrated, distinctive and ageworthy wines in SAVENNIÈRES. Eponymous top cuvée hails from monopole Clos de la Coulée de Serrant★★, a steep, walled 7ha (17-acre) vineyard with its own sub-appellation. Savennières Roche aux Moines★★ and Les Vieux Clos★ also impressive. Best years: (2007) 06 05 04 **03** 02 01 **00** 97 96 95 90 89.

CLOS ERASMUS★★★ *Priorat DOCa, Cataluña, Spain* Daphne Glorian's tir
estate turns out one of the most profound and personal reds in th
fashionable region of PRIORAT. Her small winery (formerly that of Alva
PALACIOS) also makes a convincing second wine, Laurel★. Best yea
(2007) 06 05 04 03 **02 01 00** 99 98 97 96 94.

CLOS DE GAMOT *Cahors AC, South-West France* In the same family for 40
years, this is benchmark CAHORS★★, which increases in subtlety an
complexity with aging. In exceptional years a special cuvée is made fro
centenarian vines★★. A cuvée called Clos Saint-Jean is al
outstanding★★. Best years: (2008) 05 **04 02 01** 98 90 85.

LE CLOS JORDANNE *Niagara Peninsula VQA, Ontario Canada* A joint ventu
between Canadian giant Vincor and Burgundy's BOISSET, producii
convincing Burgundy-style Pinot Noir★★ and Chardonnay★★ und
BURGUNDY-style designations. At the top end Le Grand Clos echo
Burgundy's Grand Cru; the single-vineyard wines show distinctive *terre*
differences; and the Village Reserve wines are from vineyards in t
village of Jordan. All organic.

CLOS DES LAMBRAYS AC★★★ *Grand Cru, Côte de Nuits, Burgundy, Frar*
This 8.8ha (22-acre) Grand Cru vineyard in MOREY-ST-DENIS is almo
entirely owned by the domaine of the same name, though Taupenc
Merme also has a few rows, not quite enough to make a barrel a ye
Thierry Brouin, manager at the Dom. des Lambrays, has raised his gai
in recent years by a more severe selection of fruit for the Grand Cru, ne
using only old vines. Best years: (2008) 07 06 05 **03 02 00** 99.

CLOS MARIE *Pic Saint-Loup, Coteaux du Languedoc AC, Languedoc, France* Sir
1995, Christophe Peyrus has been making 4 powerful red wines, blen
dominated by Syrah, that regularly wow tasters: Glorieuses
L'Olivette★, Simon★ and Métairies du Clos★. Also white cuvée Manc
Best years: (2008) 07 06 05 03 **01** 00.

CLOS MOGADOR★★★ *Priorat DOCa, Cataluña, Spain* René Barbier Fer
was one of the pioneers who relaunched the reputation of PRIORAT in t
1980s. The wine is a ripe, intense, brooding monster built to age. B
years: (2007) 06 05 04 03 01 **00 99** 98 97 96 95 94.

DOM. DU CLOS NAUDIN *Vouvray AC, Loire Valley, France* Philippe Fore
runs this first-rate VOUVRAY domaine. Depending on the vintage,
produces a range of styles: dry★★, medium-dry★★ and sweet★★ (r
Réserve★★★), as well as Vouvray Mousseux★★ and Pétillant★★. T
wines are supremely ageworthy. Best years: (Moelleux Réserve) 2005 03
96 95 90 89.

CLOS DES PAPES *Châteauneuf-du-Pape AC, Rhône Valley, France* This v
classy red CHATEAUNEUF-DU-PAPE★★★ has a high 20% of Mourvèdre, wh
gives structure, complexity and potential longevity. Nevertheless, ther
enough Grenache to ensure the wine's approachability in its youth a
provide an initial blast of fruit. The white★★ takes on the nu
character of aged Burgundy after 5 or 6 years. Best years: (red) 2007 06
04 **03 01 00** 99 98 97 96 95 94 90 89 88 83 81.

CLOS DE LA ROCHE AC *Grand Cru, Côte de Nuits, Burgundy, France* The b
and biggest of the 5 MOREY-ST-DENIS Grands Crus. The wine has a love
bright, red-fruits flavour when young, and should become ric
chocolaty or gamy with age. Best producers: DROUHIN★★★, DUJAC★★
Léchenaut★★, Dom. LEROY★★★, H Lignier★★★, Perrot-Minot★
Ponsot★★★, ROUSSEAU★★. Best years: (2008) 07 06 05 03 02 **01** 99 98 96
93 90.

LOS ST-DENIS AC *Grand Cru, Côte de Nuits, Burgundy, France* This small (6.5ha/16-acre) Grand Cru, which gave its name to the village of MOREY-ST-DENIS, produces wines which are sometimes light, but should be wonderfully silky, with the texture that only great Burgundy can regularly achieve. Best after 10 years or more. Best producers: Bertagna★★, Charlopin★★, DUJAC★★★, JADOT★★, Ponsot★★★. Best years: (2008) 07 06 05 03 02 **01 99 98 96 95 93 90**.

LOS DE TART AC★★★ *Grand Cru, Côte de Nuits, Burgundy, France* 7.5ha (18-acre) Grand Cru, a monopoly of the Mommessin family, run by Sylvain Pitiot. Intense, concentrated wines made by traditional methods with a modern result. Now exceptional quality – and price! Best years: (2008) 07 05 03 02 **01 00 99 96 95 90**.

LOS TRIGUEDINA★ *Cahors AC, South-West France* Jean-Luc Baldès makes some of the best-known and admired CAHORS. In top cuvée Prince Probus★★ he unites the strength of Cahors with elegance. Best years: (2008) 05 **04 02 01 98**.

OS UROULAT *Jurançon AC, South-West France* Charles Hours makes tiny quantities of stunningly good JURANÇON. Dry Cuvée Marie★★ has ripe fruit yet a deliciously refreshing finish. It ages just as well as the rich sweet Jurançon★★, which pulls together lemon, lime, honey and apricot: enjoyable young, but ages magnificently. Best years: 2007 **05 04 03 00**.

OS DU VAL *Napa Valley AVA, California, USA* Elegant Cabernet Sauvignon★ (STAGS LEAP DISTRICT★★), Chardonnay★, Merlot★, Pinot Noir★ and Zinfandel★. The Reserve Cabernet★ can age well. Best years: (Reserve Cabernet) 2004 03 **02 01 00 99 97 96 95 94 91 90 87 86 84**.

OS DE VOUGEOT AC *Grand Cru, Côte de Nuits, Burgundy, France* Enclosed by Cistercian monks in the 14th century, and today a considerable tourist attraction, this large (50ha/125-acre) vineyard is now divided among 80+ owners. As a result of this division, Clos de Vougeot has become one of the most unreliable Grand Cru Burgundies; the better wine tends to come from the upper and middle parts. When it is good it is wonderfully fleshy, turning deep and exotic after 10 years or more. Best producers: B Ambroise★★, Amiot-Servelle★★, Chopin★★, J-J Confuron★★★, R Engel★★★ (to 2004), FAIVELEY★★, GRIVOT★★★, Anne GROS★★★, JADOT★★, Dom. LEROY★★★, T LIGER-BELAIR★★, MEO-CAMUZET★★★, Denis MORTET★★★, Mugneret-Gibourg★★★, Ch. de la Tour★★, VOUGERAIE★★. Best years: (2008) 07 06 05 03 02 **01 00 99 98 96 95 93 90**.

OT DE L'OUM *Cotes du Roussillon-Villages AC, Roussillon, France* Eric Monné has been making powerful, dense wines since 2001, from 18ha (45 acres) of vines north of Perpignan, which he works organically. Wines include La Compagnie des Papillons★, Saint Bart Vieilles Vignes★ and top wine Numéro Uno★★, from Syrah grown on granite.

OUDY BAY *Marlborough, South Island, New Zealand* New Zealand's most successful winery, Cloudy Bay achieved cult status with the first release of its zesty, herbaceous Sauvignon Blanc in 1985. After a dip in the early 00s, the winery is getting back on form despite high production levels. Sauvignon Blanc★★ has regained a lot of its leafy zest. Sauvignon Blanc Te Koko★★ is very different: rich, creamy, oak-matured and bottle-aged. Cloudy Bay also makes Chardonnay★★, a late-harvest Riesling★★, superb ALSACE-style Gewürztraminer★★ and Riesling★★, and good Pinot Noir★. Vintage Pelorus★★ is a high-quality old-style CHAMPAGNE-method fizz and non-vintage Pelorus★★ is excellent too. Best years: (Sauvignon Blanc) **2007 06 04 03**.

PAUL CLUVER *Elgin WO, South Africa* Cool-loving varieties respond well
this high-lying area: Sauvignon Blanc shows mineral refinemen
Chardonnay★ is compact and layered. Also an often vibrant, dry
Riesling★ and thrilling Noble Late Harvest botrytis dessert★★ versi
and a subtle Gewürztraminer★★. A silky Pinot Noir and flavoursom
savoury Cabernet Sauvignon show reds have promise too.

COBOS *Mendoza, Argentina* Small operation owned
by Andrea Marchiori, Luis
Barraud and American Paul
Hobbs. Cobos offers voluptuous
single-vineyard Malbec★★ from
old vines in the Marchiori
vineyard in the Perdriel district of
MENDOZA. Its Bramare Cabernet
Sauvignon★ and Malbec★★ are

similarly ripe and succulent, while El Felino
Malbec★ offers simple, fresher flavours and great quality for its price.

J-F COCHE-DURY *Meursault, Côte de Beaune, Burgundy, France* Jean-Franço
Coche-Dury, now joined by his son Raphaël, is a modest superst
quietly turning out some of the finest wines on the COTE DE BEAUNE. F
best wines are his CORTON-CHARLEMAGNE★★★ and MEURSA
Perrières★★★, but even his BOURGOGNE Blanc★★ is excellent. His r
wines, from VOLNAY★★ and MONTHELIE★, tend to be cheaper than t
whites and are delicious to drink even when young. **Best years:** (whit
(2008) 07 06 05 04 **03 02 01 00 99 95**.

COCKBURN *Port DOC, Douro, Portugal* Best known for its Special Reser
ruby port, Cockburn also has stylish Vintage★ and Quinta dos Canai
Cockburn ports are now made by Symington Family Estates. **Best yea**
(Vintage) **2003** 00 97 94 91 70 63 60 55; (dos Canais) **2003** 01 00 95 9

CODORNÍU *Cava DO, Cataluña, Spain* The biggest CHAMPAGNE-meth
sparkling wine company in the world. Anna de Codorníu★ and Jau
Codorníu★ are especially good, but all the sparklers are better than t
CAVA average. Drink young for freshness. Codorníu also owns RAÏMAT
COSTERS DEL SEGRE, Masía Bach in the PENEDES and Bodegas Bilbaínas
RIOJA, and has a stake in Scala Dei in PRIORAT. They also own Artesa
NAPA, California.

COLCHAGUA *Rapel, Chile* RAPEL sub-region and home to several excit
estates, such as the acclaimed Apalta hillside vineyard, where C
LAPOSTOLLE, MONTES and others have plantings. Syrah and Carmenère
very well here. Chimbarongo and Los Lingues to the east are cooler d
to the influence of the Andes, while the Nancagua and Santa Cruz
much warmer. New vineyards toward the coast in Lolol and Marchíh
are delivering exciting reds and whites, especially Syrah and Viogni
Best producers: Araucano/Lurton★, CASA LAPOSTOLLE★★, Casa Silva★, CO
SUR★★, L F Edwards, EMILIANA ORGÁNICO (Coyam★★), MONTES★★, MontGr
Neyen★★, Ventisquero★, Viu Manent★.

COLDSTREAM HILLS *Yarra Valley, Victoria, Australia* Founded by Australi
wine guru James Halliday; owned by Foster's since 2005. Pinot Noi
(Reserve★★) is usually good: sappy and smoky with cherry fruit a
clever use of all-French oak. Chardonnay★ (Reserve★★) has subtlety a
delicacy but real depth as well. Reserve Cabernet★ can be very go
though not always ripe; Merlot★★ ripens more successfully. **Best yea**
(Reserve Pinot Noir) (2008) 06 **05 04 02 00 98 97 96**.

COLLI ORIENTALI DEL FRIULI DOC *Friuli-Venezia Giulia, Italy* This DOC covers 20 types of wine. Best known are the sweet whites from Verduzzo in the Ramandolo sub-zone and the delicate Picolit, but it is the reds – from the indigenous Refosco and Schioppettino, as well as imports like Cabernet – and dry whites, from Tocai Friulano (now Friulano), Ribolla, Pinot Bianco, Pinot Grigio and Malvasia Istriana, that show how exciting the wines can be. Prices are high. **Best producers:** Ca' Ronesca★, Dario Coos★, Dorigo★, Dri★, Le Due Terre★★, Livio FELLUGA★, Walter Filiputti★, Adriano Gigante★, Livon★, Meroi★, Miani★★, Davide Moschioni★★, Rocca Bernarda★, Rodaro★, Ronchi di Cialla★, Ronchi di Manzano★★, Ronco del Gnemiz★★, Scubla★, Sirch★, Specogna★, Le Vigne di Zamò★★, Zof★. Best years: (whites) (2008) 07 **06 04 02 01 00 99 98 97.**

COLLI PIACENTINI DOC *Emilia-Romagna, Italy* Home to some of EMILIA-ROMAGNA's best wines, this DOC covers 11 different types, the best of which are Cabernet Sauvignon and the red Gutturnio (a blend of Barbera and Bonarda) as well as the medium-sweet white and bubbly Malvasia. **Best producers:** Luretta★, Lusenti, Castello di Luzzano/Fugazza★, Il Poggiarello★, La Stoppa★, Torre Fornello★, La Tosa (Cabernet Sauvignon★). Best years: (reds) (2008) 07 **06 04 03 01 00.**

COLLINES RHODANIENNES, VIN DE PAYS DES *Rhône Valley, France* Exciting region between Vienne and Valence. The best wines are Syrah, although there are some good juicy Merlots and Gamays, too. **Best producers:** P & C Bonnefond★, COLOMBO★, CUILLERON (Viognier★), P Gaillard★, J-M Gérin (Viognier), JAMET★★, P Jasmin, Monteillet, M Ogier★, A PERRET (Syrah, Marsanne★), St-Desirat co-op, TAIN co-op, G Vernay★, Vins de Vienne (Sotanum★★). Best years: (reds) **2007 06 05 04 03 01.**

COLLIO DOC *Friuli-Venezia Giulia, Italy* Some of Italy's best and most expensive dry white wines are from these hills on the Slovenian border. There are 19 types of wine, from local (Tocai) Friulano and Malvasia Istriana to international varieties. The best are ageworthy. **Best producers:** Borgo Conventi★, Borgo del Tiglio★★, La Castellada★, Damijan★, Livio FELLUGA★★, Marco Felluga★, Fiegl★, GRAVNER★★, JERMANN★★, Edi Keber★, Renato Keber★, Livon★, Primosic★, Princic★, Puiatti★, Roncùs★★, Russiz Superiore★, SCHIOPETTO★★, Matijaz Tercic★★, Venica & Venica★★, Villa Russiz★★, Villanova★, Zuani★★. Best years: (whites) (2008) 07 **06 04 02 01 00.**

COLLIOURE AC *Roussillon, France* This tiny fishing port tucked away in the Pyrenean foothills makes a throat-warming red wine that is capable of aging for a decade but is marvellously rip-roaring when young. **Best producers:** (reds) Abbé Rous, Baillaury★, Clos de Paulilles★, MAS BLANC★★, la Rectorie★★, la Tour Vieille★, Vial Magnères★. Best years: 2004 03 **01 00 99 98.**

COLOMBARD In France, Colombard traditionally has been distilled to make Armagnac and Cognac, but has now emerged as a table wine grape in its own right, notably as a Vin de Pays des CÔTES DE GASCOGNE. At its best, it has a lovely, crisp acidity and fresh, aromatic fruit. The largest plantings of the grape are in California, where it generally produces rather less distinguished wines. South Africa can produce attractive refreshing wines, though much is used in brandy production. Australia also has some bright-eyed examples.

JEAN-LUC COLOMBO *Cornas AC, Rhône Valley, France* Colombo has long criticized traditional methods. His powerful, rich CORNAS is more opulent and has far less tannic grip than some. Top cuvées are les Ruchets★★ and the lush old-vines la Louvée★★, made in tiny quantities. Among hi *négociant* wines, CONDRIEU★★, CHÂTEAUNEUF-DU-PAPE★ an red and white HERMITAGE le Rouet★ stand out, although some labels don' always seem fully ripe. Also produces full, fragrant ST-PERAY la Belle de Mai★, good CÔTES DU RHÔNE★ and vins de pays from the RHÔNE, PROVENC and ROUSSILLON. Best years: (Cornas) 2007 **06 05 04 03 01 00 99 98 95**.

COLUMBIA CREST *Washington State, USA* An offshoot of CHATEAU ST MICHELLE, and now the largest winery in Washington State, producing top-calibre wines at everyday prices. Two Vines budget label is good Grand Estates Shiraz★ and Grand Estates Chardonnay★ are strong suits, as is the new H3★ label for Horse Heaven Hills fruit; these are good young but will age for several years. Reserve Syrah★ can be heavil oaked but has impressive style. Best years: (reds) 2007 **06 05 04 03 02**

COLUMBIA VALLEY AVA *Washington State, USA* The largest of WASHINGTON viticultural regions, covering a third of the state's landmass an encompassing both the YAKIMA VALLEY and WALLA WALLA VALLEY, as well a the newer AVAs of Red Mountain, Wahluke Slope, Rattlesnake Hill and Horse Heaven Hills. It produces 98% of the state's wine grapes Merlot, Cabernet Sauvignon and Chardonnay are the most widel planted varieties. Best producers: ANDREW WILL★★, BETZ★, CADENCE★★ CHATEAU STE MICHELLE★, COLUMBIA CREST★, DELILLE CELLARS★★, DUNHAN CELLARS★, Goose Ridge, HEDGES★, JANUIK★, L'ECOLE NO 41★★, LONG SHADOW VINTNERS★★, Matthews Cellars★★, QUILCEDA CREEK★★★, WOODWARI CANYON★★. Best years: (reds) (2007) 06 05 04 03 02.

COMMANDARIA *Cyprus* Amber, treacly wine made from red Mavro an white Xynisteri grapes, sun-dried before vinification and solera aging Potentially one of the world's great rich wines, but currently an historic footnote rather than a world beater. Keo's St John is the best.

CONCHA Y TORO *Maipo, Chile* Chile's biggest winery, Concha y Toro ha around 6000ha (15,000 acres) of vineyards and a talented group o winemakers. Casillero del Diablo★ is the excellent budget label an Marqués de Casa Concha is the next step up (reds ★★). Higher up Trio★ and Terrunyo★ are good labels for reds and whites. CASABLANC sourced Amelia★★ is the top Chardonnay and small amounts of variou excellent reds come out under the Winemaker's Lot label (usually ★★ The classic Cabernet Sauvignon-based Don Melchor★★★ impressively velvety and complex in recent releases. The Maycas rang from LIMARÍ offers crisp Sauvignon Blanc, ripe and dense Syrah and tang mineral Chardonnay★★. Trivento is an important Argentinian projec See also ALMAVIVA, CONO SUR, EMILIANA ORGÁNICO.

CONDRIEU AC *Rhône Valley, France* The home of Viognier. Wonderful fragrant but expensive wine. Ranges from scented, full and opulent t sweet, late-harvested. Condrieu is a sensation everyone should try, but is important to choose a good producer. Best drunk young Best producers: G Barge★, P & C Bonnefond★★, CHAPOUTIER★★, du Chêne★ L Chèze★, COLOMBO★★, CUILLERON★★★, DELAS★★, C Facchin★, Faury★ P Gaillard★★, Y Gangloff★★, J-M Gérin, GUIGAL★★ (Doriane★★ F Merlin★★, Monteillet★★, Mouton★★, R Niéro★, A Paret★★, A PERRET★★ C Pichon★★, ROSTAING★★, St-Cosme★★, G Vernay★★★, F Villard★★★.

CONERO DOCG See ROSSO CÒNERO DOC.

CONO SUR *Rapel, Chile* Dynamic sister winery to CONCHA Y TORO, whos Pinot Noir put the grape on the Chilean map. Basic releases are reliab attractive. The CASABLANCA-sourced 20 Barrels Pinot Noir★★ is rich an perfumed; top-of-the-range Ocio★★ is positively unctuous, yet refreshing, especially in the 2006 vintage. Minerally, crunchy 20 Barrels Sauvignon Blanc★★ is from one of Casablanca's coolest sites. Chardonnay★★, Merlot★★ and Cabernet Sauvignon★★, under 20 Barrels and Visión labels, are excellent, as are the Visión Riesling★★ and Gewürztraminer. Isla Negra offers drier, more 'European' flavours.

CH. LA CONSEILLANTE★★ *Pomerol AC, Bordeaux, France* Elegant, exotic, velvety wine that blossoms beautifully after 5–6 years but can age much longer. Second wine: Duo de Conseillante (from 2007). **Best years:** 2007 06 05 **04 03 02 01 00 99 98 96 95 94 90 89**.

CONSTANTIA WO *South Africa* The historic heart of South African wine, covering much of Simon van der Stel's original 1685 land grant. Today there are nine properties, stretching along the Constantiaberg from STEENBERG in the south to Constantia Glen in the north. Sauvignon Blanc thrust this cool-climate area into the limelight, but Chardonnays and Semillons are also good. Constantia Uitsig's elegant, flavoursome Constantia White★ reflects an increasing trend for the Semillon-Sauvignon blend. Cap Classique sparkling wines are also gaining in popularity. Many elegant reds are showing this is no one-horse area. **Best producers:** BUITENVERWACHTING★, Constantia Glen, Constantia Uitsig★, Eagles' Nest★, Groot Constantia (since 2004), High Constantia, KLEIN CONSTANTIA★, STEENBERG★. **Best years:** (whites) 2008 **07 06 05 04 03 02 01**.

ALDO CONTERNO *Barolo DOCG, Piedmont, Italy* One of BAROLO's finest traditionalist producers. He makes good Dolcetto d'Alba★, excellent BARBERA D'ALBA Conca Tre Pile★★, a barrique-aged LANGHE Nebbiolo Il Favot★★, red blend Quartetto★★ and 2 Langhe Chardonnays: unoaked Printaniè and Bussiador★, fermented and aged in new wood. Pride of the range, though, are his Barolos from the hill of Bussia. In top vintages he produces Vigna Colonnello★★★, Vigna Cicala★★★ and excellent Granbussia★★★, as well as a regular Barolo called Bussia Soprana★★. All these Barolos, though accessible when young, need several years to show their true majesty, but retain a remarkable freshness. **Best years:** (Barolo) (2008) (07) (06) **04 03 01 00 99 98 97 96 95 90 89 88**.

GIACOMO CONTERNO *Barolo DOCG, Piedmont, Italy* Aldo's late elder brother Giovanni, now followed by his son Roberto, took an even more traditional approach to winemaking. The flagship wine is BAROLO Monfortino★★★ (only released after some 5 or 6 years in large oak barrels) but Barolo Cascina Francia★★★ is also superb. Also excellent traditional BARBERA D'ALBA★★. **Best years:** (Monfortino) (2008) (07) (06) (04) (02) 01 00 99 **98 97 96 95 90 89 88 85 82 71**.

CONTINO *Rioja DOCa, Rioja, Spain* An estate on some of the finest RIOJA land, half-owned by CVNE but run with passion and skill as a boutique operation. The wines include a beautifully balanced Reserva★★, a scented single-vineyard Viña del Olivo★★ (sometimes ★★★) and a remarkable piercing innovative Graciano★★. These wines all age beautifully. The 2007 vintage saw a first experimental white★. **Best years:** (Reserva) (2005) (04) 03 02 **01 00 99 98 96 95 94 86 85**.

COONAWARRA *South Australia* On a flat limestone belt thinly veneered with terra rossa soil, Coonawarra can produce sublime Cabernet with blackcurrant leafy flavours and spicy Shiraz that age for years. Merlot can be good, too. An export-led boom fuelled significant new plantings, much of it outside the legendary terra rossa strip, and saw the production of disappointing light reds. An awareness of the risk to the region's

reputation has seen substantial changes to viticultural practice over th
past decade, accompanied by huge investment in revitalizing th
vineyards. Best producers: BALNAVES★★, Bowen, BRAND'S★★, HOLLICK★
JACOB'S CREEK/Orlando★★, KATNOOK★★, Ladbroke Grove, Leconfield
LINDEMANS, MAJELLA★★★, Murdock, PARKER★★, PENFOLDS★★, PENLEY★★
PETALUMA★★, WYNNS★★, Zema★. Best years: (Cabernet Sauvignon) (200
06 05 **04 03 02 01** 99 98 97 96 94 91 90 86.

COOPERS CREEK *Auckland, North Island, New Zealand*　Successful HAWKES BA
Chardonnay★ and tangy MARLBOROUGH Sauvignon Blanc★. GISBORI
Arneis★, Marlborough Riesling★ and Late Harvest Riesling★ are als
good. A smart range of Reserve reds from Hawkes Bay includes powerf
Syrah★ and complex Merlot★ and Cabernet Sauvignon blends★. Be
years: (Chardonnay) (2008) **07 06 04**.

FRANCIS FORD COPPOLA *Rutherford AVA, California, USA*　Movie directe
Francis Ford Coppola, now a serious wine producer, with volume
approaching 1 million cases, has split his winemaking activities betwee
luxury and lifestyle brands. The historic Inglenook Niebaum winery, a
elaborate NAPA tourist destination, has been renamed Rubicon Estat
Rubicon★, a BORDEAUX blend, lacked grace in early vintages but has no
taken on a more exciting personality. It still needs 5–6 years of agin
Coppola also offers Cask Cabernet★★, Edizione Pennino★ (Zinfande)
RC Reserve Syrah★ and tiny amounts of Merlot★★ and Cabern
Franc★★, as well as super-premium white blend Blancaneaux
Coppola has also acquired the former Chateau Souverain winery
SONOMA COUNTY, which has been renamed Rosso & Bianco. Bran
include Sofia bubblies and good-value Coppola Diamond Collectic
varietals. Best years: (Rubicon) 2005 04 03 **02 01** 00 99 97 96 95 94 91 8

CORBIÈRES AC *Languedoc, France*　This huge region, with it special cru
Boutenac, now produces some of the best reds in the LANGUEDOC, wi
juicy fruit and more than a hint of wild hillside herbs. Excellent youn
but wines from the best estates can age for years. White Corbières can
tasty – drink as young as possible. Best producers: (reds) Baillat
Caraguilhes★, Cascadais★, CLOS DE L'ANHEL★★, Embres-et-Castelmaure
Étang des Colombes★, Fontsainte★, Grand Crès★, Grand Moulin★, Ha
Gléon★, Hélène★, l'Ille★, Lastours★, Mansenoble★, Ollieux★, les Palais★, S
Auriol★, VOULTE-GASPARETS★★. Best years: (reds) (2008) 07 06 05 **04 03 01 0**

CORNAS AC *Rhône Valley, France*　Pure Syrah wines; attractive alternatives
pricey neighbours HERMITAGE and CÔTE-RÔTIE. When young, the wines a
a bold, dark red, almost black in the ripest years. The fruit comes with
mineral tang. Best producers: ALLEMAND★★, F Balthazar★, CLAPE★★
COLOMBO★★, Courbis★★, DELAS★, E & J Durand★★, JABOULET
J Lemencier★, J Michel★, V Paris★★, TAIN co-op★, Tardieu-Laurent★
Tunnel★, A Voge★★. Best years: 2007 06 05 **04 03 01** 00 99 98 97 96 95
91 90 89 88 85 83.

CORSE AC, VIN DE *Corsica, France*　Overall AC for CORSICA with 5 super
sub-regions: Calvi, Cap Corse, Figari, Porto Vecchio and Sartèr
Ajaccio and Patrimonio are entitled to their own ACs. The me
distinctive wines, mainly red, come from local grapes (Nielluccio a
Sciacarello for reds, Vermentino for whites). There are some rich swe
Muscats – especially from Muscat du Cap Corse. Best producers: ARENA
Canarelli★, Clos d'Alzeto★, Clos Capitoro, Clos Culombu★, Clos Landr
Clos Nicrosi★, Gentile, Leccia, Maestracci★, Comte Peraldi★, Renucc
Saparale, Signadore, Torraccia★.

CORSICA *France* This Mediterranean island has made some pretty dull and undistinguished wines in the past. The last decade has seen a welcome trend toward quality, with co-ops and local growers investing in better equipment and planting noble grape varieties – such as Syrah, Merlot, Cabernet Sauvignon and Mourvèdre for reds, and Chardonnay and Sauvignon Blanc for whites – to complement the local Nielluccio, Sciacarello and Vermentino. Whites and rosés are pleasant for drinking young; reds are more exciting and can age for 3–4 years. See also CORSE AC.

CORTES DE CIMA *Alentejo, Portugal* Excellent modern Portuguese reds. Blends of Aragonez (Tempranillo) and Syrah with Portuguese grapes such as Trincadeira and Touriga Nacional are used for spicy, fruity Chaminé★, oaked red Cortes de Cima★ and a splendid dark, smoky Reserva★★. Touriga★★ makes an aromatic varietal red and Incógnito★★ is a gutsy, black-fruited blockbuster Syrah. Best years: (2007) **05 04 03 01 00.**

CORTESE White grape variety planted primarily in south-eastern PIEDMONT in Italy; it can produce good, fairly acidic, dry whites. Sometimes labelled simply as Cortese Piemonte DOC, its main purpose in life is as the principal grape in GAVI.

CORTON AC *Grand Cru, Côte de Beaune, Burgundy, France* The only red Grand Cru in the CÔTE DE BEAUNE; ideally the wines should have the burliness and savoury power of the top CÔTE DE NUITS wines, combined with the seductively perfumed fruit of Côte de Beaune. Red Corton should take 10 years to mature, but many modern examples never get there. Very little white Corton is made. Best producers: B Ambroise★★, d'Ardhuy★★, Bonneau du Martray★★, CHANDON DE BRIAILLES★★, Dubreuil-Fontaine★★, FAIVELEY★★★, Camille Giroud★★★, Guyon★★, JADOT★★★, Dom. LEROY★★★, MEO-CAMUZET★★★, Prince de Merode★★, Senard★, TOLLOT-BEAUT★★★. Best years: (reds) (2008) 07 06 05 03 02 **01** 99 **98 96 95 90.**

CORTON-CHARLEMAGNE AC *Grand Cru, Côte de Beaune, Burgundy, France* Corton-Charlemagne, on the west and south-west flanks and at the top of the famous Corton hill, is the largest of Burgundy's white Grands Crus. It can produce some of the most impressive white Burgundies – rich, buttery and nutty with a fine mineral quality. The best should show their real worth only at 10 years or more. Best producers: Bonneau du Martray★★★, BOUCHARD PERE ET FILS★★, Champy★★, CHANDON DE BRIAILLES★★, COCHE-DURY★★★, DROUHIN★★, FAIVELEY★★, V GIRARDIN★★★, JADOT★★★, P Javillier★★, Louis LATOUR★★, Rapet★★, M Rollin★★, ROUMIER★★, TOLLOT-BEAUT★★★, VOUGERAIE★★. Best years: (2008) 07 06 05 04 03 **02 00** 99 97 95.

CH. COS D'ESTOURNEL★★★ *St-Estèphe AC, 2ème Cru Classé, Haut-Médoc, Bordeaux, France* One of the leading châteaux of Bordeaux. Despite a high proportion of Merlot (just under 40%), the wine is classically made for aging and usually needs 10 years to show really well. Recent vintages have been dark, brooding, powerful and, but for a wobble in 1998 and 99, of the highest order. Small production of white from 2005 and new state-of-the-art winery in

2009. Second wine: les Pagodes de Cos. Best years: 2007 06 05 04 03 02 0
00 96 95 94 90 89 88 86 85.

DOM. COSSE-MAISONNEUVE *Cahors AC, South-West France* Mathie
Cosse and Catherine Maisonneuve have become the cult growers
CAHORS, combining the best of the traditional and modern styles into ve
personal interpretations. From the fruity Le Combal★, move up throug
Le Petit Sid★★ to Les Laquets★★ and finally Le Sid★★, which refle
the iron that underlies the soil. Best years: (2008) 05 **04 02 01**.

COSTANTI *Brunello di Montalcino DOCG, Tuscany, Italy* One of the origina
highly respected Montalcino estates making fine BRUNELLO★★ a
Rosso★★, as well as Vermiglio★, a tasty partially barrique-ag
Sangiovese. Costanti's Brunello style went a bit oaky-modern in the 9
but is returning to its original elegant, restrained self. Calbello win
from the hill of Montosoli, include excellent Rosso★★ and Merlo
Cabernet blend Ardingo★★. Best years: (Brunello) (2008) (07) (06) 04 03
99 97 95 93 90 88 85 82.

COSTERS DEL SEGRE DO *Cataluña, Spain* DO on the 'banks of the Seg
in western CATALUNA, with a great array of grape varieties, generally go
quality and moderate prices. Best producers: Castell del Remei★, Celler
Cérvoles★, Tomás Cusiné★, RAIMAT★. Best years: (reds) 2006 05 **04 03 01 0**

COSTIÈRES DE NÎMES AC *Rhône Valley, France* Reds are generally bright a
perfumed, the best are substantial; rosés are good young gluggers; whi
are tasty versions of Marsanne and Roussanne. Best producers: l'Amarine
Grande Cassagne★, Lamargue, Mas des Bressades★, Mas Neuf, Mourgues
Grès★, Nages★, d'Or et de Gueules, la Patience, Roubaud, Tardieu-Laure
la Tour de Beraud★, la Tuilerie, Vieux-Relais★. Best years: **2007 06 05.**

CÔTE DE BEAUNE *Côte d'Or, Burgundy, France* Southern part of the C
D'OR; beginning at the hill of CORTON, north of the town of BEAUNE, t
Côte de Beaune progresses south as far as MARANGES, with white wir
gradually taking over from red.

CÔTE DE BEAUNE AC *Côte de Beaune, Burgundy, France* Small AC, high
the hill above the town of Beaune, named to ensure maximum confusi
with the title for the whole region. Best producers: Allexant, DROUHIN
VOUGERAIE★. Best years: (2008) 07 **05 03 02.**

CÔTE DE BEAUNE-VILLAGES AC *Côte de Beaune, Burgundy, France* R
wine AC covering 16 villages, such as AUXEY-DURESSES, LADOIX, MARANGES
the wine is a blend from several villages it is sold as Côte de Beaur
Villages. It can also cover the red wine production of mainly white wi
villages such as MEURSAULT. Best producers: DROUHIN★, JADOT★. Best yea
(2008) 07 **05 03 02.**

CÔTE DE BROUILLY AC *Beaujolais, Burgundy, France* Wine from the high
slopes of Mont Brouilly, a small but abrupt volcanic mountain in
south of the BEAUJOLAIS Crus area. The wine is deeper in colour and fr
and has more intensity than that of BROUILLY. Best produce
O Ravier★, Roches Bleues/Lacondemine★, Ch. Thivin★ (La Chapelle★
Zaccharie★★), Viornery★. Best years: **2008 07.**

CÔTE CHALONNAISE See BOURGOGNE-CÔTE CHALONNAISE.

CÔTE DE NUITS *Côte d'Or, Burgundy, France* This is the northern part of
great COTE D'OR and is *not* an AC. Almost entirely red wine country,
vineyards start in the southern suburbs of Dijon and continue south i
narrow swathe to below the town of NUITS-ST-GEORGES. The villages
some of the greatest wine names in the world – GEVREY-CHAMBER
VOUGEOT and VOSNE-ROMANEE etc.

ÔTE DE NUITS-VILLAGES AC *Côte de Nuits, Burgundy, France* Although not much seen, the wines (mostly red) are often good, not very deep in colour but with a nice cherry fruit. Best producers: (reds) D Bachelet★, Chopin-Groffier★, J-J Confuron, Gille, JADOT, Jourdan★, Loichet, Sérol★. Best years: (reds) (2008) 07 **06 05 03 02**.

ÔTE D'OR *Burgundy, France* Europe's most northern great red wine area and also the home of some of the world's best dry white wines. The name, meaning 'golden slope', refers to a 48km (30-mile) stretch between Dijon and Chagny which divides into the CÔTE DE NUITS in the north and the CÔTE DE BEAUNE in the south.

ÔTE ROANNAISE AC *Loire Valley, France* Small, improving AC in the upper LOIRE producing mostly light reds and rosés from Gamay. Non-appellation whites can be good. Best producers: Fontenay★, R Sérol★★.

ÔTE-RÔTIE AC *Rhône Valley, France* The Côte-Rôtie, or 'roasted slope', produces one of France's greatest and finest red wines. On its vertiginous slopes, the Syrah balances super ripeness with freshness, and the small amount of white Viognier sometimes included in the blend gives an unexpected exotic fragrance. Lovely young, it is better aged for 6–8 years. Best producers: G Barge★★, Bernard★, P & C Bonnefond★★, Bonserine★, B Burgaud★, Clusel-Roch★★, CUILLERON★★, DELAS★★, Duclaux★★, Gallet★, Garon★, J-M Gérin★★, GUIGAL★★, JAMET★★★, P Jasmin★★, S Ogier★★, Rosiers★, ROSTAING★★, J-M Stéphan★, Tardieu-Laurent★★, Vidal-Fleury★, F Villard★, Vins de Vienne★★. Best years: 2007 06 05 **04 03 01 00 99 98 95 94 91 90 89 88 85**.

OTEAUX D'AIX-EN-PROVENCE AC *Provence, France* The first AC in the south to acknowledge that Cabernet Sauvignon can enormously enhance the traditional local grape varieties such as Grenache, Cinsaut, Mourvèdre, Syrah and Carignan. The reds can age. Some quite good fresh rosé is made, while the whites, mostly still traditionally made, are pleasant but hardly riveting. Best producers: Ch. Bas★, les Bastides★, les Béates★★, Beaupré★, Calissanne★, J-L COLOMBO (Côte Bleue★★), d'EOLE★, Fonscolombe, Revelette★, Valdition, Vignelaure★. Best years: (reds) 2007 06 05 **04 03 01 00**.

OTEAUX DE L'ARDÈCHE, VIN DE PAYS DES *Rhône Valley, France* Increasingly good, lively red wines made from Cabernet Sauvignon, Syrah, Merlot or Gamay and dry, fresh whites from Chardonnay, Viognier or Sauvignon Blanc. Best producers: Vignerons Ardechois, Colombier, DUBOEUF, G Flacher, Louis LATOUR★, Pradel, St-Désirat, Vigier.

OTEAUX DE L'AUBANCE AC *Loire Valley, France* Smallish AC north of COTEAUX DU LAYON AC for sweet or semi-sweet white wines made from Chenin Blanc. Top sweet wines are now labelled Sélection de Grains Nobles, as in ALSACE. Best producers: Bablut/Daviau★★, Giraudières, Haute Perche★, Montgilet/V Lebreton★★, Princé, RICHOU★★, Rochelles★. Best years: 2007 06 05 **04 03 02 01 99 97 96 90**.

OTEAUX CHAMPENOIS AC *Champagne, France* Still wines from Champagne. Fairly acid with a few exceptions, notably from Bouzy and Ay. The best age for 5 years or more. Best producers: Paul Bara★, BOLLINGER★, Egly-Ouriet★, Geoffroy★, H Goutorbe, LAURENT-PERRIER, Joseph PERRIER, Ch. de Saran★/MOET & CHANDON. Best years: (2008) **00**4 03 02 **00 99 98 96**.

OTEAUX DU LANGUEDOC AC *Languedoc, France* Large and increasingly successful region situated between Nîmes and Narbonne, producing around 50 million bottles of beefy red, tasty rosé and surprisingly characterful whites. Twelve 'crus', including Montpeyroux, Quatourze and Cabrières, have historically been allowed to append their names to the AC – these are in the process of being delineated by climate and soil type. La CLAPE, Picpoul de Pinet, Terrasses du Larzac, Pézenas, Grès de Montpellier and PIC ST-LOUP have

already been officially recognized. This appellation will gradually be replaced by the larger Languedoc AC (see LANGUEDOC-ROUSSILLON). Best producers: l'Aiguelière★, Aupilhac★, Calage★, Clavel★, CLOS MARIE★, Coste★, Grès St-Paul★, Lacroix-Vanel★, Mas Cal Demoura★, Mas de Chimères★, Mas Jullien★, Mas de Martin, PEYRE ROSE★★, Poujol★, PRIEURE D[e] ST-JEAN DE BEBIAN★★, Puech-Haut★, St-Martin de la Garrigue★, Terr[e] Megère★. Best years: (2008) 07 06 05 **04 03 01 00**.

COTEAUX DU LAYON AC *Loire Valley, France* Sweet wine from the Layo[n] Valley, south of Angers. The wine is made from Chenin Blanc grape[s] that, ideally, are attacked by noble rot or, for intense but fresher style[s] dried by warm, autumnal breezes that concentrate grape sugars. In grea[t] years like 1996, and from a talented grower, this can be one of the world[s] exceptional sweet wines. Top wines are now labelled Sélection de Grain[s] Nobles, as in ALSACE. Six villages are entitled to use the Coteaux d[u] Layon-Villages AC and put their own name on the label; these wines a[re] definitely underpriced for the quality. Three sub-areas, BONNEZEAUX, Chaume and QUARTS DE CHAUME, have their own ACs. Best producer[s]: P Aguilas★★, P Baudouin★★, BAUMARD★★, Bergerie★★, Bidet★, Breuil★, Cady★★, P Delesvaux★★★, Duloquet, Dom. F L, Forges★★, Ogereau★[★], Passavant★, PIERRE-BISE★★★, Pithon-Paillé★, Quarres★, J Renou★[★], Roulerie★★, Sablonnettes★★, Sauveroy★, Soucherie★★. Best years: 2007 0[6] 05 **04 03 02 01 99 97 96 95 90 89**.

COTEAUX DU LOIR AC See JASNIERES AC.

COTEAUX DU LYONNAIS AC *Beaujolais, Burgundy, France* Good, ligh[t] BEAUJOLAIS-style reds and a few whites and rosés from scattered vineyar[ds] between Villefranche and Lyon. Drink young.

COTEAUX DU TRICASTIN AC *Rhône Valley, France* Direct, sometimes fu[ll] reds and rosés with juicy fruit. The nutty dry white is worth looking o[ut] for. Drink it young. Best producers: Décelle, Grangeneuve★, Lônes, St-Luc[y], la Tour d'Elyssas, Vieux Micocoulier. Best years: **2007 06 05**.

COTEAUX VAROIS AC *Provence, France* North of Toulon and stretchin[g] inland where it is notably cooler than the coast, this is an area to watc[h] with new plantings of classic grapes to improve quality. Best producer[s]: Alysses★, Calisse★, Chaberts★, Deffends★, Garbelle, Margüi★, Miraval★, Routas★, St-Estève, St-Jean-le-Vieux, Triennes★. Best years: 2007 **06 05 04 0[3]**

CÔTES DE BERGERAC AC See BERGERAC AC.

CÔTES DE BOURG AC *Bordeaux, France* The best red wines are earthy b[ut] blackcurranty and can age for 6–10 years. Very little white is made; mo[st] of it is dry and dull. Best producers: Brulesécaille★, Bujan★, FALFAS★, Foug[as] (Maldoror★), Garreau, Haut-Guiraud, Haut-Macô★, Haut-Mondésir★, Mac[ay] Mercier, Nodoz★, ROC DE CAMBES★★, Tayac, Tour de Guiet★. Best year[s]: **2005 03 02 01 00 99 98**.

CÔTES DE CASTILLON AC *Bordeaux, France*   Area east of ST-EMILION that has surged in quality recently. Good value, but prices are beginning to climb. The wines are full and firm, yet endowed with the lushness of St-Émilion. Can use new Côtes de Bordeaux AC label from 2008. Best producers: Dom. de l'A★★, Aiguilhe★★, Belcier, Cap-de-Faugères★, la Clarière Laithwaite, Clos l'Eglise★, Clos Les Lunelles★ (from 2001), Clos Puy Arnaud★★, Côte-Montpezat, Joanin Bécot★, Poupille★, Robin★, Veyry★, Vieux-Ch.-Champs-de-Mars★. Best years: 2006 **05 04 03 02 01 00 99 98**.

CÔTES CATALANES, VIN DE PAYS DES *Roussillon, France*   Covering much the same area as the CÔTES DU ROUSSILLON AC; co-ops dominate production but there is a growing number of talented individual producers, especially in the Fenouillèdes hills, benefiting from outside investment. Warm, rich, spicy reds, often from old-vines Grenache Noir and Carignan, plus Syrah; full-bodied minerally whites from Grenache Blanc and Gris and Macabeo. Best producers: CASENOVE, CAZES, GAUBY/le Soula, Matassa, Pertuisane, O Pithon, Preceptorie de Centenach, Soulanes.

CÔTES DE DURAS AC *South-West France*   AC between ENTRE-DEUX-MERS and BERGERAC, with good, fresh, leafy reds and whites from traditional BORDEAUX grapes. Drink young. Best producers: Chater★, Condom-Perceval (sweet white★★), Grand Mayne, Lafon, Laulan, Mouthes le Bihan★, Petit Malromé★. Best years: (reds) (2008) 06 **05** 04.

CÔTES DE FRANCS See BORDEAUX-CÔTES DE FRANCS.

CÔTES DE GASCOGNE, VIN DE PAYS DES *South-West France*   This is Armagnac country, but the tangy-fresh, fruity white table wines outsell everything else from the South-West put together. Best producers: Arton, Brumont★, Cassagnoles, de Joy, Lauroux, Millet★, Pellehaut, Producteurs PLAIMONT★, San de Guilhem, Sédouprat, TARIQUET★.

CÔTES DU JURA AC *Jura, France*   This AC includes a variety of ageworthy wines, including specialities *vin jaune* and *vin de paille*. Savagnin makes strong-tasting whites, often sherry-like; some Chardonnay is made in this style, others are dry and mineral, reminiscent of good MÂCON. Distinctive reds and rosés from local Poulsard and Trousseau and also from Pinot Noir. See also CRÉMANT DU JURA AC. Best producers: Ch. d'Arlay★, Baud★, Berthet-Bondet★, Boilley, Bourdy★, Chalandard★, Ganevat★★, Grand, A Labet★, J Macle★, Pignier★, Reverchon★, Rijckaert★★, Rolet, A & M Tissot★. Best years: (2007) 06 **05** 04 02.

CÔTES DU MARMANDAIS AC *South-West France*   The addition of grapes such as Abouriou, Cot, Fer Servadou, Gamay and Syrah to Merlot and Cabernet blends distinguishes these wines from those of downstream BORDEAUX. Best producers: Beaulieu★, Cocumont co-op, ELIAN DA ROS★★.

CÔTES DE PROVENCE AC *Provence, France*   Large AC mainly for fruity reds and rosés to drink young. Whites have improved. Best producers: Barbanau★, la Bernarde★, Clos d'Alari, Clos de la Procure, Commanderie de Peyrassol★, la Courtade★★, Coussin Ste-Victoire★, Cressonnière★, d'ESCLANS, Féraud★, Galoupet, Gavoty★, Jale, Mauvanne★, Minuty★, Ott★, Réal Martin★, RICHEAUME★, Rimauresq★★, Roquefort★, St-André de Figuière, Sarrins★, SORIN★, Élie Sumeire★, Les Valentines.

CÔTES DU RHÔNE AC *Rhône Valley, France*   AC for the whole RHÔNE VALLEY. Over 90% is red and rosé, mainly from Grenache, with some Cinsaut, Syrah, Carignan and Mourvèdre to add warm southern personality. Modern winemaking has revolutionized the style; today's wines are generally juicy, spicy and easy to drink, ideally within 5 years. Most wine is made by co-ops. Best producers: (reds) Amouriers★, d'Andézon★, les Aphillanthes★, A Brunel★, L Charvin★★, CLAPE★, COLOMBO★, Coudoulet de BEAUCASTEL★★, Cros de la Mûre★★, Espiers★, Estézargues co-op★, Fonsalette★★, FONT DE MICHELLE★, Gramenon★★, Grand Moulas★, Grand Prébois★, GUIGAL★, Haut Musiel, Hugues★, JABOULET★, la Janasse★, J-M Lombard★, Mas de Libian★, Mont-Redon, la Mordorée★, REMEJEANNE★, M Richaud★, Romarins, Rouge Garance, St-Estève d'Uchaux, ST-GAYAN, Ste Anne★, Santa Duc★, Tardieu-Laurent★, Tours★, Vieille Julienne★, Vieux Chêne★; (whites) Cassan, CLAPE★, Coudoulet de BEAUCASTEL★, P Gaillard★, REMEJEANNE★, Ste-Anne★. Best years: (reds) **2007 06 05**.

CÔTES DU RHÔNE-VILLAGES AC *Rhône Valley, France* AC covering 18 villages in the southern CÔTES DU RHÔNE that have traditionally made superior wine (especially CAIRANNE, RASTEAU, Laudun, Massif d'Uchaux, Séguret, Valréas, Sablet, Visan). Best are spicy reds that can age well. Best producers: Achiary★, Amouriers★, Beaurenard★, Boissan★, Bramadou, Bressy Masson★, de Cabasse★, Cabotte★, Chapoton★, D Charavin★, la Charbonnière★, Chaume-Arnaud★, Combe★, Coriançon★, Cros de la Mûre★, Durieu Espigouette★, Estézargues co-op★, Les Goubert, Gourt de Mautens★★, Gramenon★, Grand Moulas★, Grand Veneur★, Gravennes★, la Janasse★, Jérôme★, Lucena, Mourchon★, Pélaquié★, Piaugier★, Rasteau co-op★, REMEJEANNE★, Roche-Audran, ST-GAYAN★, St-Siffrein, Ste-Anne★, Saladin, la Soumade★, Tours★, Trapadis★, Valériane. Best years: (reds) **2007 06 05 04 03 01**.

CÔTES DU ROUSSILLON AC *Roussillon, France* ROUSSILLON's catch-all AC dominated by co-ops. It's a hot area, and much of the wine is baked and dull. But there's a lively bunch of estates making exciting reds and doing surprisingly good things with whites. Best producers: (reds) la CASENOVE★★, Vignerons Catalans, CAZES★, Chênes★, J-L COLOMBO★, Ferrer-Ribière★, Força Réal, Joliette, Laporte★, Mas Crémat★, Mossé, Olivier Pithon★, Rivesaltes co-op, Sarda-Malet★. Best years: (reds) 2005 **04 03 01 00 99**.

CÔTES DU ROUSSILLON-VILLAGES AC *Roussillon, France* Wines from the best sites in the northern CÔTES DU ROUSSILLON. Villages Caramany, Latour-de-France, Lesquerde and Tautavel may add their own name. Best producers: Vignerons Catalans, Calvet-Thunevin, CAZES★, Chênes★, Clos des Fées★, CLOT DE L'OUM★★, Fontanel★, Força Réal, Gardiés★, GAUBY★★, Jau, Mas Amiel★, Mas Crémat★, Roc des Anges, Schistes★. Best years: (reds) 2005 **04 03 01 00 99**.

CÔTES DE ST-MONT VDQS *South-West France* A good VDQS principally for a good range of whites, though there are red and rosé wines too. Best producer: Producteurs PLAIMONT★.

CÔTES DE THONGUE, VIN DE PAYS DES *Languedoc, France* Zone north-east of Béziers. More character than most vins de pays, and some dynamic estates are producing excellent results. Best producers: l'Arjolle★, les Chemins de Bassac, La Croix Belle, Magellan, Monplézy.

CÔTES DU VIVARAIS AC *Rhône Valley, France* Southern Rhône grapes (Grenache, Syrah, Cinsaut, Carignan) produce light, fresh reds and rosé for drinking young. Best producers: Vignerons Ardechois, Gallety★, Vigier

QUINTA DO CÔTTO *Douro DOC and Port DOC, Douro, Portugal* Unfortified DOURO wine expert. Quinta do Côtto red and creamy Paço de Teixer VINHO VERDE are good, and Grande Escolha★★ can be excellent, oaky and powerful when young, rich and cedary when mature. Best years: (Grand Escolha) 2001 **00 97 95 94 90 87 85**.

PIERRE COURSODON *St-Joseph AC, Rhône Valley, France* Family-owned 17ha (42-acre) domaine producing rich, oaked ST-JOSEPH★ from very old vines. The red wines need up to 4 years before they show a their magnificent cassis and truffle and violet richness, especially the top wine, La Sensonne★★, aged in new oak. Whites, from mature Marsanne vines, are good, too. Best years: (reds) **2007 06 05 04 03 01 00 99 98 95**.

CH. COUTET★★ *Barsac AC, 1er Cru Classé, Bordeaux, France* BARSAC's largest Classed Growth property has been in great form in recent years, and with its finesse and balance is once again a classic Barsac. Extraordinarily intense Cuvée Madame★★★ is made in exceptional years. Best years: 2007 05 **04 03 02 01 00 99 98 97 96 95 90 89 88**.

CRAGGY RANGE *Hawkes Bay and Martinborough, North Island, New Zealand* Premium HAWKES BAY wines include stylish Les Beaux Cailloux Chardonnay★★, a bold Cabernet blend called The Quarry★★, a rich Merlot blend known as Sophia★★ and the flagship Le Sol Syrah★★. Also elegant Seven Poplars Chardonnay★ and Gimblett Gravels Merlot★★★ from Hawkes Bay; fine Te Muna Road Pinot Noir★★ and Riesling★ from MARTINBOROUGH; restrained yet intense Avery Sauvignon Blanc★ and tangy Rapaura Road Riesling★ from MARLBOROUGH. Best years: (Syrah) (2008) **07 06 04 02 01**.

QUINTA DO CRASTO *Douro DOC and Port DOC, Douro, Portugal* Well-situated property with very good traditional LBV★★ and Vintage★★ port and massively enjoyable juicy red DOURO★★ and oaky but excellent Touriga Nacional★★. Flagship reds Vinha da Ponte★★ and Maria Teresa★★ can reach ★★★. Austere new Douro red Xisto★ is a joint venture with Jean-Michel Cazes of Ch. LYNCH-BAGES of Bordeaux. Best years: (Vintage port) 2004 **03 00 99 97 95 94**; (Touriga Nacional) 2005 **04 03 01**; (Ponte) **2004 03 00**; (Maria Teresa) 2005 **03 01 98**.

CRÉMANT D'ALSACE AC *Alsace, France* Good CHAMPAGNE-method sparkling wine from ALSACE, usually made from Pinot Blanc and/or Pinot Gris. Reasonable quality, if not great value for money. Best producers: J-B ADAM★, BLANCK★, Cave de Cleebourg, Dopff & Irion, Dopff au Moulin★, J Gross★, Kuentz-Bas, MURE★, Ostertag★, Pfaffenheim co-op, P Sparr★, A Stoffel★, TURCKHEIM co-op★.

CRÉMANT DE BOURGOGNE AC *Burgundy, France* Most Burgundian Crémant is white and is made either from Chardonnay alone or blended with Pinot Noir. The result, especially in ripe years, can be full, soft, almost honey-flavoured – if you give the wine the 2–3 years' aging needed for mellowness to develop. Best producers: A Delorme, Simonnet-Febvre, A Sounit, Veuve Ambal; and the co-ops at Bailly (the best for rosé★), Lugny★, St-Gengoux-de-Scissé and Viré.

CRÉMANT DE DIE AC *Rhône Valley, France* AC for traditional-method fizz made entirely from the Clairette Blanche grape. Less aromatic than CLAIRETTE DE DIE. Best producers: Jacques Faure, J-C Raspail.

CRÉMANT DU JURA AC *Jura, France* AC for fizz from all over Jura, which accounts for nearly a quarter of the region's production. Largely Chardonnay-based, with Poulsard, an interesting pale red grape, for the pinks. Best producers: Fruitière Vinicole d'Arbois, Ch. de l'Étoile★, Grand★, La Maison des Vignerons (Marcel Cabelier), Montbourgeau★, Rolet★, A & M Tissot★.

CRÉMANT DE LIMOUX AC *Languedoc, France* Sparkling wine made from a blend of Chardonnay, Chenin Blanc and Pinot Noir; the wines generally have more complexity than BLANQUETTE DE LIMOUX. Drink young. Best producers: l'Aigle★, Antech, Fourn, Guinot, Laurens★, Martinolles★, SIEUR D'ARQUES★.

CRÉMANT DE LOIRE AC *Loire Valley, France* CHAMPAGNE-method sparkling wine in Anjou and Touraine, with more fruit and yeast character than those of VOUVRAY and SAUMUR; increasingly Chardonnay is added to Loire stalwarts Chenin Blanc and Cabernet Franc, giving fresh, elegant fruit. Good to drink as soon as it is released. Can be excellent value. Best producers: l'Aulée, BAUMARD★, Berger Frères★, Bouvet-Ladubay★, Brizé★, Fardeau★, Girault, Gratien & Meyer★, Lambert★, Langlois-Château★, Michaud★, Nerleux/Regis Neau, Passavant★, Varinelles★.

CRIOTS-BÂTARD-MONTRACHET AC See BÂTARD-MONTRACHET AC.

CRISTOM *Willamette Valley AVA, Oregon, USA* Nestled in the Eola Hills, this winery specializes in Pinot Noir (Marjorie Vineyard★, Sommers Reserve★). White wines include barrel-fermented Chardonnay, Pinot Gris and Viognier. Best years: (Pinot Noir) (2007) 06 **05 04 03 02**.

CROFT *Port DOC, Douro, Portugal* Owned by the Fladgate Partnership (along with TAYLOR and FONSECA) since 2001, these wines are showing distinct improvements, especially at basic level. Vintage ports★★ have traditionally been elegant, rather than thunderous. Single-quinta Quinta da Roêda★ is pretty good in recent vintages. Best years: (Vintage) 2004 03 **00 94 91 77 70 66 63 55 45**; (Roêda) 2005 04 **97 95**.

CROZES-HERMITAGE AC *Rhône Valley, France* The largest of the northern Rhône ACs. Ideally, the pure Syrah reds should have a full colour and a strong, clear, black fruit flavour. You can drink them young, but in ripe years from a hillside site the wine improves greatly for 2–5 years. Too much clumsy oak can obscure the fruit. The best whites are fresh and clean, and should be drunk young, before the floral perfume disappears. Best producers: (reds) A Belle★★, Bruyères★★, CHAPOUTIER★ (Varonniers★★), Y Chave★ (Rouvre★★), Colombier★ (Cuvée Gaby★★) Combier★ (Clos des Grives★★), E Darnaud★★, DELAS★ (Le Clos★★, Dom des Grands Chemins★★, Tour d'Albon★★), O Dumaine★, Entrefaux★ L Fayolle★★, Ferraton★, GRAILLOT★★, Hauts Chassis, JABOULET, Murinais★ Pavillon-Mercurol★, Pochon★ (Ch. Curson★★), Remizières★★, G Robin★ Rousset (Picaudières★★), M Sorrel★, TAIN co-op (Les Hauts du Fief★) Tardieu-Laurent★, Vins de Vienne★; (whites) Y Chave★, Colombier★ Combier★, Dard & Ribo★, DELAS★, O Dumaine★, Entrefaux★ (Cuvée de Pends★★), Fayolle Fils & Fille★★, Ferraton★, GRAILLOT★, Martinelles, Mucyr Pochon (Ch. Curson★), Remizières★, M Sorrel★★. Best years: (reds) 2007 0 **05 04 03 01 00 99 98 95**.

YVES CUILLERON *Condrieu AC, Rhône Valley, France* With wines like Cuilleron's you can understand CONDRIEU's fame and high prices. Le Chaillets Vieilles Vignes★★★ is everything wine made from Viognic should be: rich and sensual, with perfumed honey and apricot aromas. L Petite Côte★★ and 18-month-aged Vertige★★ are also exceptional, an the late-harvest Ayguets★★★ is an extraordinary sweet whirl of drie apricots, honey and barley sugar. Cuilleron also makes ST-JOSEPH reds★★ and whites★★ and tiny quantities of ripe, dark, spicy CÔTE-RÔTIE★★. A joint venture, les Vins de Vienne, with Pierre Gaillard, François Villar and Pierre-Jean Villa, produces Vin de Pays des COLLINES RHODANIENNE Sotanum★★ (100% Syrah) and Taburnum★ (100% Viognier) fron ancient terraces just north of Vienne. Best years: (Condrieu) (2008) 07 0 **05 04 03 01**.

CULLEN *Margaret River, Western Australia* One of the original and bes MARGARET RIVER vineyards, established by Diana and Kevin Cullen an now run by their talented winemaker daughter Vanya. Superb Kevi

John Chardonnay★★★ is complex and satisfying; Sauvignon-Semillon★★ marries nectarines with melon and nuts. Diana Madeline Cabernet Sauvignon-Merlot★★★ is gloriously soft, deep and scented – and one of Australia's greats. Mangan Malbec-Petit Verdot-Merlot★★ is delicious. Best years: (Cabernet Sauvignon-Merlot) (2008) 07 05 04 **03 02** 01 **00** 99 98 97 96 95 94 92 91 90.

CURICÓ *Central Valley, Chile* Most of the big producers here have planted Cabernet Sauvignon, Merlot, Carmenère, Chardonnay and Sauvignon Blanc. It's a bit warm for whites, but the long growing season provides good fruit concentration for reds. Best producers: Echeverría★★, SAN PEDRO★, Miguel TORRES★★, VALDIVIESO★.

CUVAISON *Napa Valley AVA, California, USA* Red wines include tasty, focused Merlot★★, sound Cabernet Sauvignon★ and delicate Pinot Noir★. Decent Chardonnay; silky Reserve Chardonnay★ is worth seeking out. Best years: (Merlot) 2005 04 **03 02** 01 99 98 97 96 94.

CVNE *Rioja DOCa, Rioja, Spain* Compañía Vinícola del Norte de España is the full name of this firm, usually known as 'coonay'. Viña Real★ is one of RIOJA's few remaining well-oaked whites. Viña Real Reserva★ and Gran Reserva★ reds can be rich and meaty, and easily surpass the rather commercial Crianzas. Imperial Reserva★ is balanced and delightful; Gran Reserva★ is long-lived and impressive. Premium red Real de Asúa★. Best years: (reds) (2006) 05 04 **03 02** 01 98 96 95 94 91 90 89 87 86 85.

DIDIER DAGUENEAU *Pouilly-Fumé AC, Loire Valley, France* This much-needed innovator and quality fanatic in a complacent region died in 2008 and is succeeded by his son, Benjamin. Wines benefit from 4–5 years' aging and, although at times unpredictable, are generally intense and complex. The range starts with En Chailloux★★ and moves up through flinty Buisson Renard★★ to barrel-fermented Silex★★ and Pur Sang★★. Since 2004, also making a sweet JURANCON. Best years: (2008) 07 06 **05** 04 **03 02** 01.

ROMANO DAL FORNO *Valpolicella DOC, Veneto, Italy* VALPOLICELLA Superiore★★ from Monte Lodoletta vineyard, outside the Valpolicella Classico area, is a model of power and grace; AMARONE★★★ and RECIOTO DELLA VALPOLICELLA★★★, from the same source, are even more voluptuous. Best years: (Amarone) (2008) (07) (06) 04 **03** 01 00 97 96 95.

TENIMENTI LUIGI D'ALESSANDRO *Cortona DOC, Tuscany, Italy* The vineyards have benefited from massive investment. Il Bosco★★ and the 'second' wine, Cortona Syrah★, are both 100% Syrah. The white Fontarca★ blends Chardonnay with varying amounts of Viognier. Best years: (Il Bosco) (2008) (07) 06 **04 03** 01 00 99 97 95.

DALLA VALLE *Napa Valley AVA, California, USA* Stunning hillside winery, producing some of NAPA's most esteemed Cabernets. Maya★★★ is a magnificent blend of Cabernet Sauvignon and Cabernet Franc; the straight Cabernet Sauvignon★★★ is almost as rich. The wines drink well at 10 years, but will keep for 20 or more. Best years: (Maya) 2005 02 01 00 99 98 97 96 95 94 91 90.

DÃO DOC *Beira Alta, Portugal* Dão has steep slopes ideal for vineyards, and a great climate for growing local grape varieties, yet it's only just beginning to realize its potential for characterful, scented, austerely satisfying red and white wines. Best producers: (reds) Caves ALIANCA (Quinta da Garrida★), Boas Quintas (Quinta Fonte do Ouro★), Quinta de Cabriz★, Quinta das Maias★, Pape★★, Quinta da Pellada★★, Quinta do Perdigão, Quinta da Ponte Pedrinha, Quinta dos ROQUES★★, Quinta de Sães★, Caves SAO JOAO★, SOGRAPE★ (Quinta dos Carvalhais★), Quinta da Vegia★★; (whites) Quinta de Cabriz, Quinta das Maias★, Quinta dos ROQUES★★, Quinta de Sães★, SOGRAPE★. Best years: (reds) (2008) **05 04 03 01 00 99 97 96 95**.

D'ARENBERG *McLaren Vale, South Australia* Chester Osborn makes blockbuster Dead Arm Shiraz★★, Custodian Grenache★, Coppermine Road Cabernet Sauvignon★ and other blends from low-yielding old vines. These are big, brash, character-filled wines, and are continually being joined by more new ideas. Whites are increasingly sourced from the ADELAIDE HILLS, and deserve attention. Best years: (Dead Arm Shiraz) (2008) 06 05 04 **03 02 01 00 97 96 95**.

RENÉ & VINCENT DAUVISSAT *Chablis, Burgundy, France* CHABLIS at its most complex – refreshing, seductive and beautifully structured, with the fruit balancing the subtle influence of mostly older oak. Look for la Forest★★, the more aromatic Vaillons★★★ and the powerful les Clos★★★. Best years: (2008) 07 06 **05 03 02 00 99 95**.

MARCO DE BARTOLI *Sicily, Italy* Marco De Bartoli is most noted for a dry unfortified MARSALA-style wine called Vecchio Samperi – his idea of what Marsala was before the English merchant, John Woodhouse, first fortified it for export. Particularly fine is the 20-year-old Ventennale★★ – dry, intense and redolent of candied citrus peel, dates and old, old raisins. Also excellent MOSCATO PASSITO DI PANTELLERIA Bukkuram★★.

DE BORTOLI *Riverina, New South Wales/Yarra, Victoria, Australia* Large, family-owned company currently producing some of Australia's most interesting wines. Some top stuff from the YARRA VALLEY: Sauvignon★, Chardonnay★★, Shiraz★★, Cabernet★ and Pinot Noir★★. The RIVERINA winery first gained prominence by producing a sublime, world-class botrytized Semillon (Noble One★★★) but in recent times has had consumers smiling because of the quality of its budget-priced labels - Sacred Hill, Deen and Montage. VICTORIA-based quaffers in the Sero Windy Peak and Gulf Station ranges have their admirers too. Best years: (Noble One) (2008) (07) 06 04 03 02 **00 98 96 95 94 93 90**.

DE LOACH VINEYARDS *Russian River Valley AVA, California, USA* Revitalize under new owner BOISSET of France and run by Jean-Charles Boisset, this property makes an array of stylish Pinot Noirs★ from estate fruit, with brilliant consultant Greg LaFollette guiding the advances. Best years: 2006 **05 04 03 01**.

DE MARTINO/SANTA INÉS *Maipo, Chile* Old-established winery enjoying a renaissance, producing robust, concentrated red wines in the hands of talented Marcelo Retamal. Single Vineyard Carmenère★★ is one of Chile's best examples of this grape; Gran Familia Cabernet Sauvignon★★ is dense and complex. Single Vineyard Chardonnay★★ from LIMARÍ bids to be Chile's best Chardonnay.

DE TRAFFORD *Stellenbosch WO, South Africa* David Trafford is a leading exponent of new-wave Chenin Blanc, both dry and sweet. His rich ageworthy dry Chenin Blanc★ from venerable Helderberg vines is barrel fermented on its own yeast; the Straw Wine★★ is honey-tinged and succulent. Among the reds, both Cabernet Sauvignon★ and Merlot★ alone and with Shiraz in Elevation 393★, are classically styled and built to age. Shiraz★★, brimming with spicy richness, remains remarkably elegant for its size. Best years: (reds) 2007 06 **05 04 03 02 01 00 99 98**.

DEHLINGER *Russian River Valley AVA, California, USA* Outstanding Pinot Noir★★★ from vineyards in the cool RUSSIAN RIVER region a few miles from the Pacific, best at 5–10 years old. Also mouthfilling Chardonnay★★ and bold, peppery Syrah★★. Recent vintages of Cabernet Sauvignon★★ and (Cabernet-based) Claret★★ reflect a surge in quality. Best years: (Pinot Noir) (2007) 06 05 **04 03 02 01 00 99 98 97**.

MARCEL DEISS *Alsace AC, Alsace, France* Jean-Michel Deiss is fanatical about distinctions of *terroir* and, controversially for ALSACE, his top wines are now blends, named according to the vineyard – Grands Crus Altenberg, Mambourg and Schoenenbourg are all ★★★. These are outstanding wines of huge character, often with some residual sugar. Pinot Noir Burlenberg★★ is vibrant and delicious. Even basic Riesling St-Hippolyte★ and Pinot Blanc Bergheim are delightful. Best years: (Grand Cru blends) (2008) 07 **05 04 03 02 01 00 99**.

DELAS FRÈRES *Rhône Valley, France* Merchant (owned by ROEDERER) selling wines from the entire RHÔNE VALLEY, but with its own vineyards in the northern Rhône. Single-vineyard wines include dense, powerful red HERMITAGE★★ (les Bessards★★★), which needs a decade or more to reach its peak, perfumed CÔTE-RÔTIE la Landonne★★ and complex ST-JOSEPH Ste-Épine★★. The CROZES-HERMITAGE Dom. des Grands Chemins★★ and Tour d'Albon★★ are lovely, and CÔTES DU RHÔNE St-Esprit is good. Look out for the aromatic CONDRIEU Clos Boucher★★. Best years: (premium reds) 2007 06 05 04 **03 01 00 99 98 97 96 95 94 91 90 89 88 78**.

DELEGAT'S *Henderson, Auckland, North Island, New Zealand* One of New Zealand's largest family-run wineries and getting larger by the second as Oyster Bay becomes a major brand and its MARLBOROUGH fruit style becomes less evident. Delegat's Chardonnay (Reserve★), Cabernet and Merlot (Reserve★) are from HAWKES BAY. Best years: (Oyster Bay Sauvignon Blanc) **2007 06 04**.

DELILLE CELLARS *Columbia Valley AVA, Washington State, USA* DeLille Cellars produces BORDEAUX-style wines from some of the better vineyards in YAKIMA VALLEY. The flagship is Chaleur Estate Red★★, a powerful, ageworthy blend of Cabernet and Merlot. Chaleur Estate Blanc★★ (Semillon and Sauvignon Blanc) has a GRAVES-like character, albeit with a tad more alcohol. The second wine, D2★★, short for Deuxième, is an early-drinking red. Doyenne Syrah★★ shows outstanding potential. Best years: (Chaleur Estate Red) (2007) 06 05 **04 03 02 01**.

DENBIES *Surrey, England* UK's largest vineyard with 107ha (265 acres) of vines, planted on chalky slopes outside Dorking. Wines have been erratic over the years but have now reached a new plateau of quality with remarkably attractive whites, lively, refreshing rosé and decent fizz (Greenfields★). Pinot Noir-based Redlands can be good too.

JEAN-LOUIS DENOIS *Vin de Pays d'Oc, Languedoc, France* Maverick producer based in LIMOUX, who can't see a rule without breaking it. His Chloé★ red wine is made from Merlot and Cabernet, without any of the 'Mediterranean' varieties obligatory in Limoux; this wine mixes the flavours of BORDEAUX with just an extra bit of Mediterranean warmth. Also red and white Grande Cuvée★ and good fizz★.

DEUTZ *Champagne AC, Champagne, France* This small company has been owned by ROEDERER since 1993 and considerable effort and investment have turned a good producer into an excellent one. The non-vintage Brut★★ is now regularly one of the best in CHAMPAGNE, often boasting a cedary scent, while the top wines are the classic Blanc de Blancs★★, the weightier Cuvée William Deutz★★ and the de luxe vintage blanc de blancs Amour de Deutz★★. Deutz has licensed Pernod Ricard in New Zealand to use its brand on their sparkling wine. Best years: 2004 02 00 9 98 96 **95 90 89 88**.

DÉZALEY *Lavaux, Vaud, Switzerland* The top wine commune in the VAUD making powerfully powerful, mineral wines from the Chasselas grape. Best producers: Louis Bovard★, La Chenalettaz, Dubois★, E & L Fonjallaz★ Pinget★, J & P Testuz★.

D F J VINHOS *Portugal* In the early 1990s, UK wine shippers D & F began working with one of Portugal's most innovative winemakers, José Neiva in 1999 this relationship evolved into D F J Vinhos. Neiva is now sole owner. The Bela Fonte brand includes varietal reds Baga, Jaen★ and Touriga Franca★, all from BEIRAS. Other labels include Segada from the RIBATEJO, Manta Preta★ from ESTREMADURA, Pedras do Monte from TERRA DO SADO and Monte Alentejano from the ALENTEJO. At the top end are the Grand'Arte reds, including fruity, peppery Trincadeira★ and beefy Alicante Bouschet★, and prestige wines from the DOURO (Escada★, ALENQUER (Francos Reserva) and Estremadura (Consensus★).

DIAMOND CREEK *Napa Valley AVA, California, USA* Small Diamond Mountain estate specializing in Cabernet: Volcanic Hill★★★, Red Rock Terrace★★, Gravelly Meadow★★. Traditionally huge, tannic wines that when tasted young, I swear won't ever come round. Yet there's usually a sweet inner core of fruit that envelops the tannin over 10–15 years; recent releases show wonderful perfume and balance even in their youth. Best years: 2005 04 03 02 01 **00 99 98 97 96 95 94 92 91 90 87 86 84**.

SCHLOSSGUT DIEL *Burg Layen, Nahe, Germany* Armin Diel is now one of the leading producers of classic-style Rieslings. Spätlese and Auslese from Dorsheim's top sites (Burgberg, Goldloch, Pittermännchen) are regularly ★★. Good Sekt too. Best years: (2008) 07 06 05 **04 03 02 01 00 98**.

DISTELL *Stellenbosch, South Africa* South Africa's largest wine company; some of the allied wineries – such as Neethlingshof★, Stellenzicht★ and Durbanville Hills★ – are performing well. The Fleur du Cap range showing exciting improvement across the board. Two wineries in PAARL Nederburg and Plaisir de Merle★, are run separately. Nederburg starting to create a buzz with some unconventional blends as well a trademark botrytized Edelkeur★, sold only through an annual auction

CH. DOISY-DAËNE★★ *Sauternes AC, 2ème Cru Classé, Bordeaux, France* consistently good property in BARSAC (although it uses the SAUTERNES AC for its wines) and unusual in that the sweet wine is made exclusively from Sémillon. It ages well for 10 years or more. The extra-rich Extravagant★★★ is produced in exceptional years. Doisy-Daëne Sec★ a good, perfumed, dry white. Drink young. Best years: (sweet) 2007 06 0 **04 03 02 01 99 98 97 96 95 90 89**.

CH. DOISY-VÉDRINES★★ *Sauternes AC, 2ème Cru Classé, Bordeaux, France* Next door to DOISY-DAËNE (and also selling its wines under the SAUTERNES AC), Doisy-Védrines is a richly botrytized wine, fatter and more syrupy than most BARSAC. Best years: (sweet) 2007 05 **04 03 02 01 99 98 97 96 9 90 89 88 86**.

DOLCETTO One of Italy's most charming grapes, producing, for the most part, purple wines bursting with fruit. Virtually exclusive to PIEDMONT and LIGURIA, it boasts 11 DOCs and 1 DOCG (Dogliani) in Piemonte, with styles ranging from intense and rich in Alba, Ovada and Diano d'Alba, to lighter and more perfumed in Acqui and Asti. The most serious, longest-lasting wines are from Dogliani and Alba. Usually best drunk within 1–2 years, traditionally vinified wines can last 10 years or more. **Best producers:** (Alba) Alario★★, ALTARE★★, Boglietti★★, Bongiovanni★★, Bricco Maiolica★, Brovia★★, Elvio Cogno★★, Aldo CONTERNO★, Conterno-Fantino★★, B Marcarini★, Bartolo MASCARELLO★, Giuseppe MASCARELLO★★, Paitin★, Pelissero★★, PRUNOTTO★, RATTI★, Albino Rocca★★, SANDRONE★★, Vajra★★, Vietti★, Gianni Voerzio★, Roberto VOERZIO★; (Dogliani) M & E Abbona★, Chionetti★★, Luigi Einaudi★★, Pecchenino★★, San Fereolo★★, San Romano★.

DÔLE *Valais, Switzerland* Red wine from the VALAIS that must be made from at least 51% Pinot Noir, the rest being Gamay. Dôle is generally a light wine – the deeper, richer (100% Pinot Noir) styles may call themselves Pinot Noir. Most should be drunk young and lightly chilled. **Best producers:** M Clavien, Faye, Jean-René Germanier, A Mathier, Provins.

DOMAINE CARNEROS *Carneros AVA, California, USA* Very successful TAITTINGER-owned sparkling wine house. The vintage Brut could be called Taittinger's fizz from CHAMPAGNE, if made a little drier. Far classier are vintage Le Rêve★★★ (100% Chardonnay) and attractive Pinot Noirs★★.

DOMAINE CHANDON *Yarra Valley, Victoria, Australia* MOET & CHANDON's Aussie offshoot makes fine Pinot Noir-Chardonnay fizz: non-vintage Brut and Cuvée Riche, vintage Brut★★, Rosé★★, Blanc de Blancs★, Blanc de Noirs★, ZD★★ (Zero Dosage), YARRA VALLEY Brut★★ and a Tasmanian Cuvée★★; plus sparkling red Pinot-Shiraz★. Table wines, often of ★★ quality, under the Green Point label with Reserve Shiraz★★ standing out and Chardonnay increasingly impressive. The Green Point name is also used on fizz for export markets.

DOMAINE CHANDON *Napa Valley AVA, California, USA* California's first French-owned (MOËT & CHANDON) sparkling wine producer majors on reasonable price, but doesn't match the quality of Moët's subsidiaries in Australia or Argentina. Reserve bottlings can be rich and creamy. Étoile★ is an aged de luxe wine, also made as a flavourful Rosé★.

DOMAINE DROUHIN OREGON *Willamette Valley AVA, Oregon, USA* Burgundy wine merchant Robert DROUHIN bought 40ha (100 acres) in OREGON in 1987, with plans to make fine Pinot Noir on New World land, with an Old World philosophy. The regular Pinot Noir★ is lean but attractive, and the de luxe Pinot Noir Laurène★★ is supple and voluptuous. Pinot Noir Louise★★ is a selection of the finest barrels in the winery. Also very good Chardonnay Arthur★★. **Best years:** (Pinot Noir) (2008) (07) 06 05 **04 03 02 01 00 99 98 96**.

DOMAINE SERENE *Willamette Valley AVA, Oregon, USA* Ken and Grace Evenstad purchased 17ha (42 acres) of land in the WILLAMETTE VALLEY in 1989, naming the property after their daughter, Serene. Devoted to Pinot Noir and Chardonnay, they have established a fine reputation. The full-bodied Pinot Noir Evenstad Reserve★★ is aged in French oak and has striking black cherry and currant flavours. The Chardonnay Clos du Soleil★★, made from Dijon clones, has a rich apple and hazelnut character. **Best years:** (Pinot Noir) (2007) 06 05 **04 03 02 01 00 99**.

DOMECQ *Jerez y Manzanilla DO and Rioja DOCa, Spain* Formerly the largest of the sherry companies, it is now in a state of flux after acquisition by Pernod Ricard. Former Domecq brands Fino La Ina, Oloroso Río Viejo, Viña 25 and Botaina, and the soleras from which these wines come, have been sold to the Caballero group, the owners of rival bodega LUSTAU, while the Domecq brand itself is owned by Pernod Ricard. The old Domecq winery is now the property of Beam Global.

DOMINUS★★ *Napa Valley AVA, California, USA* Owned by Christian MOUEIX, director of Bordeaux superstar PETRUS. Wines are based on Cabernet Sauvignon, with leavenings of Merlot and Cabernet Franc. Early releases were excessively tannic, but recent wines are mellow and delicious. Best years: (2007) 06 05 04 03 **02 01 00** 99 97 96 95 94 91 90.

DONAULAND See WAGRAM.

DÖNNHOFF *Oberhausen, Nahe, Germany* Helmut Dönnhoff is the quiet winemaking genius of the NAHE, conjuring from a string of top sites some of the most mineral dry and naturally sweet Rieslings in the world. The very best are the subtle, long-lived wines from the Niederhäuser Hermannshöhle★★★ and Oberhäuser Brücke★★★ vineyards; Eiswein★★★ is equally exciting. Best years: (Hermannshöhle Riesling Spätlese) (2008) 07 06 05 **04 03 02 01 00** 99 98 97.

DOURO DOC *Douro, Portugal* As prices soar for the best wines, deciding whether to use top grapes for unfortified DOURO wine or PORT has become much harder for Douro producers. Quality can be superb when the lush, scented fruit is not smothered by new oak. Reds may improve for 10 years or more. Whites from higher-altitude vineyards have improved, but best drunk young. Best producers: (reds) ALIANCA (Quinta dos Quatro Ventos★★), Maria Doroteia Serôdio Borges (Fojo★★), Casal de Loivos★★, Chryseia★★, Quinta do CÔTTO★★, Quinta do CRASTO★★, FERREIRA★ (Barca Velha★★, Quinta da Leda★★), Quinta da Gaivosa★★, Quinta de Macedos★, Quinta do Maritávora★, Muxagat, NIEPOORT★★★, Quinta do NOVAL★★, Quinta do Passadouro (Reserva★★), Pintas★★, Poeira★★, Quinta do Portal★, RAMOS PINTO★ (Duas Quintas Reserva Especial★★), Quinta de Roriz★, Quinta de ROSA★, Quinta de San Jose, SOGRAPE, Quinta do Vale Dona Maria★★, Quinta do Vale Meao★★★, Quinta do Vale da Raposa★, Quinta do Vallado★ (Sousão★), Xisto★. Best years: (reds) (2008) (07) **05 04** 03 01 00 97 95.

DOW *Port DOC, Douro, Portugal* The grapes for Dow's Vintage PORT★★ come mostly from the Quinta do Bomfim, also the name of the excellent single quinta★★★. Dow ports are relatively dry compared with those of GRAHAM and WARRE (the 2 other major brands belonging to the Symington family). There are also good Crusted★ and some excellent aged tawnies★★. Quinta Senhora da Ribeira★ has made impressive ports since 1998, released 'en primeur'. Best years: (Vintage) **2003 00 97 94 91 83 80 77 70 66 63 60 55 45**; (Bomfim) **1999** 98 95 92 87 86 84; (Senhora Ribeira) 2005 04 **98**.

JOSEPH DROUHIN *Beaune, Burgundy, France* Burgundian merchant with substantial vineyard holdings in CHABLIS and the CÔTE D'OR, and DOMAINE DROUHIN OREGON. Consistently good, if expensive, wines from all over Burgundy. Look for BONNES-MARES★★, ROMANEE-ST-VIVANT★★★, BEAUNE Clos des Mouches (red★★ and white★★), le MUSIGNY★★★ and MONTRACHET★★★ from the Marquis de Laguiche. Drouhin offers fine value in Chablis★ and less glamorous Burgundian ACs, such as RULLY and ST-AUBIN★. The whites are impressively consistent; the reds are less powerful than some as the policy is to pursue elegance and style. Top reds and whites should be aged for at least 5 years; often better nearer 10. **Best years:** (top reds) (2008) 07 06 05 03 **02 00 99 96 95.**

PIERRE-JACQUES DRUET *Bourgueil AC, Loire Valley, France* A passionate producer with an esoteric approach. Druet's spicy, gravelly BOURGUEILS les Cent Boisselées★, Grand Mont★★ and Vaumoreau★★ are subtly different expressions of Cabernet Franc that attain wonderful purity with age – keep for at least 3–5 years. Also small quantities of CHINON★★. **Best years:** (top cuvées) (2007) 06 05 **04 03 02 01 00 99 97 96 90 89.**

DRY CREEK VALLEY AVA *Sonoma, California, USA* Best known for Sauvignon Blanc, Zinfandel and Cabernet Sauvignon, this valley runs west of ALEXANDER VALLEY AVA, and similarly becomes hotter moving northwards. **Best producers:** DRY CREEK VINEYARD★, Duxoup★, FERRARI-CARANO★, GALLO (Zinfandel★, Cabernet Sauvignon★), Lambert Bridge★, Michel-Schlumberger★, Nalle★, Pezzi King★, Preston★, Quivira★, Rafanelli (Zinfandel★★). **Best years:** (reds) 2006 05 03 **02 01 00 99 98 97 96 95.**

DRY CREEK VINEYARD *Dry Creek Valley AVA, California, USA* An early advocate of Fumé Blanc★, Dry Creek remains faithful to the brisk racy style and also makes a serious Reserve★ which improves with aging. DCV3★ (sometimes ★★) is from original plantings and displays subtle notes of fig and herb. A drink-young Chardonnay (Reserve★) is attractive, but the stars here are red Meritage★, Merlot★, Old Vine Zinfandel★★ and a superb Dry Chenin Blanc★★. **Best years:** (Old Vine Zin) 2006 05 **03 02 01 00 99 97 96 95.**

DRY RIVER *Martinborough, North Island, New Zealand* Low yields and an uncompromising attitude to quality at this tiny winery have created some of the country's top Gewürztraminer★★★, Pinot Gris★★★, powerful, long-lived Craighall Riesling★★★, sleek Chardonnay★★ and intense, succulent yet mineral Pinot Noir★★★. Excellent Syrah★★ is made in tiny quantities. Now owned by a wealthy American, but founder Neil McCallum continues as chief winemaker. Fingers crossed. **Best years:** (Craighall Riesling) 2008 **06 03 01 00 99;** (Pinot Noir) (2008) 07 **06 03 01 00.**

GEORGES DUBOEUF *Beaujolais, Burgundy, France* Known as the King of Beaujolais, Duboeuf is responsible for more than 10% of the wine produced in the region, although he is no longer considered by many to be among the region's most exciting producers. Given the size of his operation, the quality of the wines is reasonable. Duboeuf also makes and blends wine from the MÂCONNAIS, the southern RHÔNE VALLEY and the LANGUEDOC. His BEAUJOLAIS NOUVEAU is usually reliable, but his top wines are those he bottles for independent growers, particularly Jean Descombes★ in MORGON, Dom. des Quatre Vents★ and la Madone★ in FLEURIE and Dom. de la Tour du Bief★ in MOULIN-A-VENT.

DUCKHORN *Napa Valley AVA, California, USA* Best known for its very chunky, tannic Merlot★ – now, thankfully, softer and riper. The Cabernet Sauvignon★ and Sauvignon Blanc provide easier drinking. Paraduxx is a Zinfandel-Cabernet blend; Decoy is the budget line. The company's Pinot Noir★ project is Goldeneye in ANDERSON VALLEY. **Best years:** (Merlot) 2006 05 **03 02 01 99 98 97 96 95 94 91 90.**

CH. DUCRU-BEAUCAILLOU★★★ *St-Julien AC, 2ème Cru Classé, Haut-Médoc, Bordeaux, France* Traditionally the epitome of ST-JULIEN, mixing charm and austerity, fruit and firm tannins. Vintages from the mid-1980s to 1990 were flawed; back on form since 94, more luscious since 03. Second wine: la Croix de Beaucaillou. **Best years:** 2007 06 05 **04 03 02 01 00 99 98 96 95 94.**

145

DUJAC *Morey-St-Denis, Côte de Nuits, Burgundy, France* Owner Jacques Seysse estate is based in MOREY-ST-DENIS, with some choice vineyards elsewhere i the CÔTE DE NUITS. The wines are all perfumed and elegant, including small quantity of white Morey-St-Denis★, but the outstanding bottling are the Grands Cru – ÉCHÉZEAUX★★★, CLOS DE LA ROCHE★★★, BONNES MARES★★★ and CLOS ST-DENIS★★★, to which CHAMBERTIN and ROMANEE-ST VIVANT have been added since 2005. All need to age for a decade or more Son Jeremy makes *négociant* cuvées under the label Dujac Fils et Père Best years: (Grands Crus) (2008) 07 06 05 03 02 **01 00** 99 98 96 **95 90 89**

DUNHAM CELLARS *Columbia Valley AVA, Washington State, USA* Family owned winery in a rustic, remodelled airplane hangar near the Wal Walla airport. The wines here are powerful and extracted, includin Cabernet Sauvignon★★, Syrah★, a limited-release Lewis Vineyar Syrah Reserve★★, Trutina★ (a BORDEAUX-style blend), Three Legge Red (named after one of the winery dogs) and 'Shirley May Chardonnay. Best years: (reds) (2007) 06 05 **04 03 02 01**.

DUNN VINEYARDS *Howell Mountain AVA, California, USA* Massive, concer trated, hauntingly perfumed, long-lived Cabernet Sauvignon★★★ fro HOWELL MOUNTAIN; NAPA VALLEY Cabernets★★ are less powerful but sti scented. Thankfully Randy Dunn has resisted the move toward hig alcohol, and his wines' ability to age beautifully is evidence of this. Be years: 2005 03 01 **00 99** 97 96 95 94 93 92 91 90 88 87 86 85 84 82.

DURBANVILLE WO *South Africa* Tucked into the folds of the Tygerbe Hills, Durbanville borders Cape Town's northern suburbs. Cool breeze from both the Atlantic Ocean and False Bay suit Sauvignon Blanc: win are vivid, often with an invigorating minerality. Semillon also does we Merlot shows promise both as a varietal wine and blended with Cabern Sauvignon, though the latter sometimes struggles to ripen. Be producers: Diemersdal, Durbanville Hills★, Meerendal, Nitida★.

DURIF See PETITE SIRAH.

JEAN DURUP *Chablis, Burgundy, France* The largest vineyard owner CHABLIS, Jean Durup is a great believer in unoaked Chablis, which ten to be clean without any great complexity. Best are the Premiers Cr Fourchaume★ and Montée de Tonnerre★★. Wines appear under variety of labels, including l'Eglantière, Ch. de Maligny and Valéry. Be years: (2008) 07 **06 05**.

DUTTON GOLDFIELD *Russian River Valley AVA, California, USA* Racy, elega and deeply flavoured Chardonnays★, Pinot Noirs★★, Zinfandels★ and a superb cool-climate Syrah★★ from long-time cool-clima winemaker Dan Goldfield. Most of the fruit, grown by Steve Dutton, from RUSSIAN RIVER. The superb Freestone Hill Pinot Noir★★★ is fro one of the coldest parts of SONOMA COUNTY. Goldfield also makes wi from fruit grown in even-cooler Marin County. Most wines take years develop. Best years: (2007) 06 **05 04 01 99**.

JOHN DUVAL *Barossa Valley, South Australia* John Duval was the winemak for Penfolds GRANGE from 1986 to 2002. He started his family label 2003, specializing in Shiraz and Shiraz blends sourced from old-vi BAROSSA fruit. Plexus★★ is a plush, vibrant, deeply flavoured a approachable Shiraz-Grenache-Mourvèdre blend; Entity Shiraz★★★ seamless varietal that combines elegance, finesse and approachabili with concentration of flavour and power; ultra-concentrated Eli Shiraz★★ is made from the best parcels from the vintage. He al consults in WASHINGTON STATE, Chile and elsewhere in Australia.

ÉCHÉZEAUX AC *Grand Cru, Côte de Nuits, Burgundy, France* The Grands Crus of Échézeaux and the smaller and more prestigious Grands-Échézeaux are sandwiched between the world-famous CLOS DE VOUGEOT and VOSNE-ROMANÉE. Look for subtlety, intricacy, delicacy from Échézeaux and a little more weight, deepening over the years to a gamy, chocolaty richness from the 'Grands' version. **Best producers:** R Arnoux★★, BOUCHARD PERE ET FILS★★, Cacheux-Sirugue★★★, DROUHIN★★, DUJAC★★★, R Engel★★★ (to 2004), GRIVOT★★★, A-F GROS★★★, Jayer-Gilles★★★, Mugneret-Gibourg★★★, Perdrix★, Dom. de la ROMANÉE-CONTI★★★, E Rouget★★★. **Best years:** (2008) 07 06 05 03 02 **01** 99 **98** 97 96 95 93 90.

DOM. DE L'ÉCU *Muscadet Sèvre-et-Maine, Loire Valley, France* One of the finest producers in MUSCADET, especially the top cuvées from different soil types: Gneiss, Orthogneiss★ and fuller-bodied, minerally Granite★★. Pathetic yields for 2007 and 2008 owing to mildew and frost. Guy Bossard's biodynamically run estate also produces GROS PLANT DU PAYS NANTAIS white, a velvety red vin de pays Cabernet blend and a refreshing sparkler, Ludwig Hahn. **Best years:** (Granite) 2008 07 **06 05 04 03 02 01 00**.

EDEN VALLEY See BAROSSA, pages 72–3.

CH. L'ÉGLISE-CLINET★★★ *Pomerol AC, Bordeaux, France* A tiny 5.5ha (13-acre) domaine in the heart of POMEROL, with a very old vineyard – one of the reasons for the depth and elegance of the wines. The other is the winemaking ability of owner Denis Durantou. The wine is expensive and in limited supply. It can be enjoyed young, though the best vintages should be cellared for 10 years or more. Second wine: La Petite Église. **Best years:** 2007 06 05 **04 03 02 01 00** 99 98 96 95 94 93 90 89.

ELGIN WO *South Africa* This high-lying ward within the Overberg district is being targeted by some of the Cape's leading winemakers. Summer cloud helps to keep temperatures reasonable, creating good conditions for pure-fruited Sauvignon Blanc, Chardonnay, Riesling and Pinot Noir. **Best producers:** Paul CLUVER★, Neil ELLIS★★, Iona★, Oak Valley★, THELEMA★.

DOM. ELIAN DA ROS *Côtes du Marmandais AC, South-West France* Elian is making waves throughout France with his eclectic wines. His models are in ALSACE and BURGUNDY, and his love of the LOIRE shows in his use of Cabernet Franc. Top wines are Chante Coucou★ and Clos Baquey★★; these wines need aging. **Best years:** (2008) 05 **04 02 01 00**.

ELK COVE *Willamette Valley AVA, Oregon, USA* Back in 1974, Elk Cove was one of the pioneers of the WILLAMETTE VALLEY. Today the Campbell family produces Pinot Gris★, Riesling and a Riesling-based dessert wine called Ultima. Basic Pinot Noir★★ frequently matches the more expensive single-vineyard Pinot Noirs – Roosevelt, Windhill★ and La Bohème★. **Best years:** (Pinot Noir) (2007) 05 **04 03 02 01**.

NEIL ELLIS *Stellenbosch WO, South Africa* Winemaker and *négociant*, renowned for powerful, invigorating Groenekloof Sauvignon Blanc★★ and striking STELLENBOSCH reds (blackcurranty Cabernet Sauvignon★★, supple Cabernet-Merlot★). An ageworthy single-vineyard Syrah★ and Cabernet★ (both from Jonkershoek Valley fruit) and a subtly delicious Chardonnay★★ from cool ELGIN, confirm his versatility. **Best years:** (Cabernet) 2006 **05 04 03 01 00**; (whites) 2008 **07 06 05 04 03 02 01**.

ELQUI *Chile* Chile's northernmost wine region, with high-altitude vineyards, mainly planted to Cabernet Sauvignon. However, it is Syrah, in an elegant, fragrant style, that excels in this cool, sunny climate, along with crisp Sauvignon Blanc and fresh Chardonnay. **Best producers:** Falernia★ (Syrah★★), Mayu★, SAN PEDRO★.

ERNIE ELS *Stellenbosch WO, South Africa* Jean Engelbrecht's joint ventur
with his golfing friend Ernie Els has resulted in a dark, serious BORDEAU
blend under the Ernie Els★★ label. Engelbrecht Els★ forges Shiraz wit
Bordeaux varieties (Cabernets Sauvignon and Franc, Merlot, Malbe
and Petit Verdot), in a dense, rich, international style. The Guardia
Peak range offers quality blends and good-value varietal wine
Engelbrecht also makes outstanding Cirrus Syrah★★ in partnership wit
SILVER OAK of California. Best years: (Ernie Els) 2006 **05 04 03 02 01 00**.

ELTVILLE *Rheingau, Germany* Large town, making some of the RHEINGAU
most racy Rieslings. Best producers: Hessische Staatsweingüter (Kloste
Eberbach), Langwerth von Simmern★. Best years: (2008) 07 06 05 04 **02 01 99**

EMILIA-ROMAGNA *Italy* This region is divided into the western zone c
Emilia, best known for fizzy wines like LAMBRUSCO, and the eastern zone c
ROMAGNA, where Sangiovese is dominant. See also COLLI PIACENTINI.

EMILIANA ORGÁNICO *Colchagua, Chile* Venture from the Guilisas
family, main shareholders at CONCHA Y TORO, with leading winemake
Alvaro Espinoza contributing his biodynamic and organic approach t
viticulture. Adobe is good entry-level range; Novas★★ range
significantly better; and red five-variety blend Coyam★★ (sometime
★★★) is one of Chile's most fascinating wines. 'Super Coyam', calle
'G'★★, is a dense, powerful long-distance runner. Best years: (2007) 06 C
04 03 02 01.

EMRICH-SCHÖNLEBER *Monzingen, Nahe, Germany* Although Monzinge
is not the most prestigious of NAHE villages, Werner Schönleber h
steadily brought his 14ha (35-acre) property into the front ranks. H
vigorous, spicy Rieslings are consistently ★ to ★★ and his Eisweins a
★★★. Best years: (2008) 07 06 05 04 **03 02 01 99**.

ENATE *Somontano DO, Aragón, Spain* Barrel-fermented Chardonnay★ is ric
buttery and toasty, Gewürztraminer★ is exotic and convincin
International grape varieties also feature in the red Crianza, Reserva
(100% Cabernet Sauvignon), Reserva Especial★★ (Cabernet-Merlo
and blockbuster Merlot-Merlot and Syrah-Shiraz. Best years: (reds) 20
05 **04 03 01 00 99 98**.

ENTRE-DEUX-MERS AC *Bordeaux, France* This large AC between th
rivers Garonne and Dordogne increasingly represents some of th
freshest, snappiest dry white wine in France. In general, drink the late
vintage, though better wines will last a year or two. Most of Bordeaux
basic red wine under the Bordeaux AC comes from here too. Swe
wines are sold as PREMIÈRES CÔTES DE BORDEAUX, St-Macaire, LOUPIAC an
STE-CROIX-DU-MONT. Best producers: BONNET★, Castenet Greffier,
Fontenille★, Landereau★, Marjosse★, Nardique la Gravière★, Ste-Marie
Tour de Mirambeau★, Toutigeac★, Turcaud★.

DOM. D'EOLE *Coteaux d'Aix-en-Provence AC, Provence, France* Top wines fro
this organic estate are rosé Cuvée Caprice★ and Cuvée Léa★★, a 50:5
blend of Syrah and Grenache. Best years: 2007 06 05 **03 01 00**.

ERBACH *Rheingau, Germany* Erbach's famous Marcobrunn vineyard is on
of the top spots for Riesling along the Rhine. The village wines a
elegant while those from Marcobrunn more powerful and imposing. Be
producers: Jakob Jung★, Knyphausen★, Langwerth von Simmern★★, SCHLO
REINHARTSHAUSEN★★, Schloss Schönborn★. Best years: (2008) 07 06 05 04
02 01 99.

RBALUCE DI CALUSO DOC *Piedmont, Italy* Usually a dry or sparkling white from the Erbaluce grape, but Caluso Passito, where the grapes are semi-dried before fermenting, can be a fine sweet wine. Best producers: (Caluso Passito) Cieck★, Ferrando★, Orsolani★.

RDEN *Mosel, Germany* Middle MOSEL village with the superb Prälat and Treppchen vineyards. Wines are rich and succulent with a strong mineral character. Best producers: Christoffel★★, Erbes, Dr LOOSEN★★★, Mönchhof★★, Peter Nicolay★, Dr Weins-Prüm★. Best years: (2008) 07 06 05 04 03 02 01 99.

RRÁZURIZ *Aconcagua, Chile* Traditional but rapidly modernizing winery run by dynamic Eduardo Chadwick. Its portfolio includes SEÑA and Arboleda – originally joint ventures with MONDAVI, now 100% Errázuriz, and much improved as a result. The classic label is Don Maximiano Founder's Reserve★ (sometimes ★★), a Cabernet Sauvignon-based red from Aconcagua, also the source of La Cumbre Shiraz★, rich, perfumed Kai Carmenère★ and dense red The Blend★. Single-vineyard Cabernet Sauvignon Viñedo Chadwick★★ comes from Tocornal, a classic area of MAIPO. Also very good 'Wild Ferment' Chardonnay★★ and Pinot Noir★★ from CASABLANCA. Best years: (reds) (2007) 06 05 04 03 02 01.

H. D'ESCLANS *Côtes de Provence AC, Provence, France* Sacha Lichine has created what is claimed to be the 'most expensive rosé in the world', Garrus★, an explosive, wood-aged blend of old-vine Grenache and Rolle. For lesser mortals, there are Les Clans★, the château wine and the sweeter Whispering Angel★. First vintage was 2006.

SPORÃO *Reguengos DOC, Alentejo, Portugal* Huge estate in the heart of the ALENTEJO, where Australian David Baverstock makes a broad range of wines. Principal labels are Esporão (red★★ and white★ Reservas), Vinha da Defesa★, Monte Velho and Alandra. Also some delightful varietals: Trincadeira★, Aragonês★, Touriga Nacional★, Syrah★, Alicante Bouschet★ and Verdelho★. Best years: (reds) (2008) 07 05 04 01 00.

ST! EST!! EST!!! DI MONTEFIASCONE DOC *Lazio, Italy* Trebbiano-based white whose quality is distinctly inferior to the renown it has earned in myth. Best producers: Bigi (Graffiti), FALESCO (Poggio dei Gelsi★), Mazziotti (Canuleio★).

H. DES ESTANILLES *Faugères AC, Languedoc, France* The Louisons know that quality begins in the vineyard. Their best site is the Clos du Fou★★, with its very steep schistous slope planted with Syrah; the grape 'dominates' the wine (i.e. 100% – but AC regulations do not allow them to say so). Cuvée Prestige★★ includes a little Mourvèdre and Grenache. Also a wood-fermented and aged rosé, plus characterful white★. Best years: (reds) 2007 06 05 04 02 01.

TREMADURA *Portugal* Portugal's most productive region, occupying : western coastal strip and with an increasing number of clean, characterful nes. The leading area is ALENQUER DOC and there are eight other DOC ;ions; however, much of the wine, including some of the region's best, is ⸱ply labelled as Vinho Regional Estremadura, soon to change to Vinho gional Lisboa. Spicy, perfumed reds are often based on Castelão, but

Aragonez (Tempranillo), Cabernet Sauvignon, Syrah and Touriga Naciona contribute to top examples, which can benefit from 4 or 5 years' aging. To producers also make fresh, aromatic whites. Best producers: Agrovitis (Fonte da Moças★), Quinta de Chocapalha★, Quinta da Cortezia★, D F J VINHOS (Franco Reserva★), Grand'Arte Touriga Nacional★), Quinta dos Loridos (Merlot★), Quint do Monte d'Oiro★★, Quinta de Pancas, Companhia Agricola do Sanguinhal, Cas SANTOS LIMA★. See also BUCELAS. Best years: (reds) (2008) 07 **05 04** 03 01 00.

L'ÉTOILE AC *Jura, France*   A tiny area within the CÔTES DU JURA that has i own AC for whites, mainly Chardonnay and Savagnin, and for *vin jaun* and *vin de paille*. Best producers: Ch. de l'Étoile★, Genelet Montbourgeau★★, P Vandelle★. Best years: (2007) 06 **05** 04 02.

CH. L'ÉVANGILE★★ *Pomerol AC, Bordeaux, France*   A neighbour to PETRU and CHEVAL BLANC, this estate has been wholly owned and managed by th Rothschilds of LAFITE-ROTHSCHILD since 1999. The wine is quintessenti POMEROL – rich, fat and exotic. Recent vintages have been very goo (sometimes ★★★), but expect further improvement as the Rothschi effect intensifies. Second wine: Blason de l'Évangile. Best years: 2007 ● 05 **04** 03 02 01 00 99 98 96 95 94 93 90 89 88.

FABRE MONTMAYOU *Argentina*   French-owned company whose LUJÁN ● CUYO winery produces impressive Malbec★. The almost black, chocolat and-damsons Grand Vin★★ is a Malbec-based blend with Cabern Sauvignon and Merlot. Phebus Malbec is seductively mineral and flora Exciting recent releases from the winery in PATAGONIA (labelled Infinit in Argentina).

FAIRVIEW *Paarl WO, South Africa*   Owner Charles Back believes Sou Africa's strength, especially in warmer areas, lies with Rhône varietie These are expressed in the Goats range: the spicy Goat-Roti★ combin Shiraz with Viognier; Goats do Roam and Goats do Roam in Villag reds and rosé feature Pinotage with Shiraz, Grenache, Cinsau Mourvèdre and Viognier, while the whites★ blend Grenache Blar Clairette and Viognier. Complementing these is Bored Doe, a Merlc led, classic BORDEAUX-style blend. The French authorities are not amus but fans on both sides of the Atlantic can't get enough. Fine Shiraz★ (Eenzaamheid★★, The Beacon★★, Jakkalsfontein★★), Pinotage (Primo★★), Pegleg Carignan★, Merlot★ and Cabernet Sauvignon Good whites include Oom Pagel Semillon★★, Viognier★ a outstanding sweet wine La Beryl★★★. Back also owns SPICE ROUTE. Be years: (Shiraz) 2007 **06 05** 04 03 02 01 00.

JOSEPH FAIVELEY *Nuits-St-Georges, Côte de Nuits, Burgundy, France*   Ther been a revolution in this famous house since Erwan Faiveley took t helm in 2005. Gone are the dry-as-dust tannic reds, replaced by vibra fruit and a great sense of *terroir* from such famous vineyards CORTON★★★, CHAMBERTIN-Clos-de-Bèze★★★ and Mazis-Chambertin★ as well as a significant range of less expensive wines from MERCUREY among others. Recent vineyard acquisitions are expanding the off especially in PULIGNY★★ and MEURSAULT★. Best years: (top reds) (2008) 07 05 **99** 90; (whites) (2008) 07 **06** 05.

FALERNO DEL MASSICO DOC *Campania, Italy*   Falernian was one of ● ancient Romans' star wines. Today's DOC, with white Falanghina and re from either Aglianico and Piedirosso or from Primitivo, has so far promis more than it has delivered. Best producers: Michele Moio★, Villa Matild (Vigna Camarato★★). Best years: (reds) (2008) (07) 06 **05 04** 03 01 00.

FALESCO *Lazio, Italy* Property of the ubiquitous Cotarella brothers: Renzo is ANTINORI's technical director (responsible for SOLAIA, TIGNANELLO, etc.); Riccardo is a high-profile consultant enologist, working all over Italy from Piedmont to Sicily. Located at Montefiascone, the town of EST! EST!! EST!!!, their Poggio dei Gelsi★ is considered best of the genre, but they are better known for their Merlot Montiano★, the essence of smooth if somewhat soulless modernity. Best years: (Montiano) (2008) (07) 06 **04 03 01 00 99**.

CH. FALFAS★ *Côtes de Bourg AC, Bordeaux, France* Biodynamic estate making concentrated, structured wine that needs 4–5 years to soften. Le Chevalier★ is an old-vines cuvée. Best years: 2006 **05 04 03** 02 01 00.

CH. DE FARGUES★★ *Sauternes AC, Bordeaux, France* Property run by the Lur-Saluces family, who until 1999 also owned Ch. d'YQUEM. The quality of this fine, rich wine is more a tribute to their commitment than to the inherent quality of the vineyard. Best years: 2007 06 05 **04 03 02 01 99 98 97 96 95** 90 89 88 86.

GARY FARR *Geelong, Victoria, Australia* Having established BANNOCKBURN as one of Australia's best boutique wineries, Gary Farr is now making wine with his son, Nick, from his 4.8ha (12-acre) family vineyard. Farr is a traditionalist at heart who is relishing his new beginning and making wines of rare quality. The Viognier★ is heady, complex and alluring; the Chardonnay★ austere yet tangy and elegant; the Pinot Noir★★★ ethereal, fine and deliciously varietal; the Shiraz★★ meaty, savoury and minerally, dry and firm. Nick Farr makes more moderately priced wines under the Farr Rising label: classy, textural Chardonnay; delicate, silky smooth, dry Saignée (a rosé made from Pinot); and two silky yet weighty Pinot Noirs from GEELONG★ and MORNINGTON.

FAUGÈRES AC *Languedoc, France* The schistous hills north of Béziers in the Hérault produce red wines whose ripe, soft, rather plummy flavour marks them out from other LANGUEDOC reds. Best producers: Abbaye Sylva Plana★, Alézon, Jean-Michel ALQUIER★, Léon Barral★, Chenaie★, ESTANILLES★, Faugères co-op, Haut Lignières, HECHT & BANNIER★, la Liquière★, Moulin de Ciffre, Ollier-Taillefer (Castel Fossibus★), Saint-Antonin. Best years: 2007 06 05 **04 03 01**.

FAUSTINO *Rioja DOCa, País Vasco and Rioja, and Cava DO, Spain* Family-owned and technically very well equipped, this RIOJA company makes fair Reserva V and Gran Reserva I red Riojas, as well as a more modern, oak-aged red, Faustino de Autor, and fruit-driven Faustino de Crianza. But they could try harder – and they should. Best years: (reds) (2005) **04 03 01 99 98 96 95 94 92 91 90.**

FEILER-ARTINGER *Rust, Neusiedlersee, Burgenland, Austria* Kurt Feiler makes sumptuous Ausbruch dessert wines★★, the finest being labelled Essenz★★★. His dry whites are ★. Solitaire★★ is a suave red blend of Merlot with Blaufränkisch and Zweigelt. Best years: (sweet whites) (2008) 07 06 05 **04 02 01 00 99 98**; (Solitaire) (2007) 06 **05 04 03 02 01 00**.

LIVIO FELLUGA *Colli Orientali del Friuli DOC, Friuli-Venezia Giulia, Italy* A younger generation has continued the great work of Livio Felluga at this large Friuli estate. Merlot-Cabernet blend Vertigo★★, raspberryish straight Merlot Riserva Sossò★★, Pinot Grigio★, Picolit Riserva★★ and (Tocai) Friulano★ are all class acts. Shàrjs★ combines Chardonnay with Ribolla and oak, but there's more to stimulate the palate in Terre Alte★★, an aromatic blend of Friulano, Pinot Bianco and Sauvignon. Best years: (whites) (2008) 07 06 **04 02 01 00**.

FATTORIA DI FELSINA *Chianti Classico DOCG, Tuscany, Italy* Full, chunky CHIANTI CLASSICO★★ wines which improve with several years' bottle age. Quality is good to outstanding; most notable are the single-vineyard Riserva Rancia★★★ and (under the regional IGT Toscana) Sangiovese Fontalloro★★★. Also good Cabernet Maestro Raro★★ and Chardonnay I Sistri★★ . Best years: (Fontalloro) (2008) (07) 06 **04 03 01 00** 99 98 97 95.

FELTON ROAD *Central Otago, South Island, New Zealand* Runaway success with vineyards in the old goldfields of Bannockburn. Intensely fruity, seductive Pinot Noir★★ is surpassed by very limited quantities of concentrated, complex Block 3 Pinot Noir★★★ and Block 5★★★. Intense and spicy Calvert★★ and fleshy, scented Cornish Point Pinot Noir★★, from separate vineyards. Three classy Rieslings (all ★★) range from dry to sweet. Mineral, citrus unoaked Chardonnay★ can be one of New Zealand's best; barrel-fermented Chardonnay★★ is funky and delicious. Best years: (Pinot Noir) **2007** 06 05 03 02 01.

FENDANT *Valais, Switzerland* Chasselas wine from the steep slopes of the VALAIS. Good Fendant should be slightly *spritzig*, with a nutty character, but many are overcropped, thin and virtually characterless. Drink very young. Best producers: Chappaz, Jean-René Germanier, A Mathier, Fils Maye, Taillefer.

FERNGROVE *Great Southern, Western Australia* Ambitious winery founded in 1998, based in Frankland River. The quality potential in Frankland River is unquestioned, being sunny yet cool. Lack of water is a limiting factor, but that also means yields are naturally limited and flavours intensified – although I've noticed a slight coarsening of flavours recently. Cossack Riesling★ and Diamond Chardonnay★ are good but used to have more verve. Dragon Shiraz★ and King Malbec★ seem to improve and Majestic Cabernet Sauvignon★ is pretty serious. The flagship Stirlings Shiraz–Cabernet blend★ is beginning to realize its potential.

FERRARI *Trento DOC, Trentino, Italy* Founded in 1902, the firm is a leader for sparkling wine. Consistent, classy wines include Ferrari Brut★, Maximum Brut★, Perlé★, Rosé★ and vintage Giulio Ferrari Riserva del Fondatore★, aged 8 years on its lees and an Italian classic. Any relation? No, apparently Ferrari is one of the commonest names in Italy.

FERRARI-CARANO *Dry Creek Valley AVA, California, USA* Full-bodied Chardonnay: the regular bottling★ has apple-spice fruit, while the Reserve★★ is deeply flavoured with more than a touch of oak. Fumé Blanc★ is also good. Red wines include Trésor★★ (a BORDEAUX blend), Siena★★ (based on Sangiovese), Syrah★, Merlot★ and Zinfandel, with a new line of premium reds called PreVail. I'm a bit concerned about alcohol levels, which have been creeping upward recently. Best years: (reds) 2006 05 **03 02 01 00** 99 97 96 95.

FERREIRA *Port DOC and Douro DOC, Douro, Portugal* Old PORT house owned by SOGRAPE. Ferreira is best known for excellent tawny ports: creamy, nutty Quinta do Porto 10-year-old★ and Duque de Braganza 20-year-old★★. The Vintage★★ is increasingly good. Ferreira's unfortified wine operation, known as Casa Ferreirinha, produces Portugal's most sought-after red, Barca Velha★★★ (sometimes); made from DOURO grape varieties (mainly Tinta Roriz), it is produced only in the finest years – just 15 vintages since 1953. Marginally less good years are now sold as Casa Ferreirinha Reserva★ (previously Reserva Especial). Quinta da Leda reds★★ are also fine. Best years: (Vintage) **2003 00 97 95 94 91 85 83 82 7**7 77 70 66 63; (Barca Velha) **2000 99 95 91 85 83 82 81 78.**

CH. FERRIÈRE★★ *Margaux AC, 3ème Cru Classé, Haut-Médoc, Bordeaux, France*
Ferrière was bought by the Merlaut family, owners of Ch. CHASSE-SPLEEN, in 1992. It is now managed by Claire Villars, and the ripe, rich and perfumed wines are among the best in MARGAUX AC. Best years: 2006 05 **04 03** 02 01 00 99 98 96.

FETZER VINEYARDS *Mendocino County, California, USA* Important winery that I feel could push the quality level higher. Locals swear by the quality of the special cellar door releases, but we never see these in the outside world. Basic wines are good, with tasty Gewürztraminer, Riesling and Syrah★. Bargain-priced Valley Oaks line is decent value. Also a leader in organic viticulture with slowly improving Bonterra range: Chardonnay, Viognier★, Merlot, Roussanne★, Zinfandel★, Cabernet Sauvignon and Sangiovese. Best years: (reds) 2007 06 05 **03 02 01** 99 98 97 96.

FIANO Exciting, distinctive, low-yielding southern Italian white grape variety. Best producers: (Molise) Di Majo Norante; (Fiano di Avellino DOC in CAMPANIA) Colli di Lapio★, Feudi di San Gregorio★★, MASTROBERARDINO★, Terredora di Paolo★, Vadiaperti★; (non-DOC) L Maffini (Kràtos★★); (Sicily) PLANETA (Cometa★★), Settesoli (Inycon★); (Australia) Fox Gordon.

CH. DE FIEUZAL *Pessac-Léognan AC, Cru Classé de Graves, Bordeaux, France*
Under new ownership since 2001; efforts are being made to recapture the form of the 1980s, with help from the owner of ANGELUS. The red★ is drinkable almost immediately, but can age. The white★, a gorgeous, perfumed (and ageworthy) wine, is the star performer. Second wine (red and white): l'Abeille de Fieuzal. Best years: (reds) 2007 06 **01 00 98 96 95** 90 89 88; (whites) 2007 06 05 03 02 **01 00 99 98 96.**

CH. FIGEAC★★ *St-Émilion Grand Cru AC, 1er Grand Cru Classé, Bordeaux, France*
Leading property whose wine traditionally has a delightful fragrance and gentleness of texture. It has an unusually high percentage (70%) of Cabernets Franc and Sauvignon, making it more structured than other ST-EMILIONS. Somewhat erratic in the late 1980s, but since 1996 far more like the lovely Figeac of old. Second wine: la Grange Neuve de Figeac. Best years: 2007 06 05 **04** 03 02 01 00 99 98 96 95 90 89.

FINGER LAKES AVA *New York State, USA* Cool region in central NEW YORK STATE, where some winemakers are establishing a regional style for dry (and sweet) Riesling. Chardonnay and sparkling wines also star, with Pinot Noir and Cabernet Franc the best reds. Best producers: Anthony Road, Chateau Lafayette Reneau★, FOX RUN★, Dr Konstantin FRANK★, Heron Hill, LAMOREAUX LANDING★, Red Newt, Swedish Hill, Wagner, Hermann J WIEMER★.

Est. 1979

Hermann J. Wiemer
Riesling
Late Harvest
2007
Estate Bottled and Grown
FINGER LAKES   RESIDUAL SUGAR 4.9%
ALC. 9.0% BY VOL.   NATURAL SUG. HARVEST 23.1%

FITOU AC *Languedoc, France* One of the success stories of the 1980s. Quality subsequently slumped, but with the innovative MONT TAUCH co-op taking the lead, Fitou is once again an excellent place to seek out dark, herb-scented reds. Best producers: Abelanet, Bertrand-Bergé★★, Lerys★, Milles Vignes, MONT TAUCH co-op★, Nouvelles★, Rochelierre, Rolland, Roudène★. Best years: (2008) 07 06 05 **04 03 01** 00.

FIXIN AC *Côte de Nuits, Burgundy, France* Although it's next door to GEVREY-CHAMBERTIN, Fixin rarely produces anything really magical. The wines are often sold as CÔTE DE NUITS-VILLAGES. Increased quality from Joliet's Clos de la Perrière estate. Best producers: Charlopin★, Coillot, Galeyrand★, Pierre Gelin★, Alain Guyard★, Joliet/Clos de la Perrière★★. Best years: (reds) (2008) 07 **06** 05 **03** 02 **99**.

FLEURIE AC *Beaujolais, Burgundy, France* The best-known BEAUJOLAIS Cru Fleurie reveals the happy, carefree flavours of the Gamay grape at its best, plus heady perfumes and a delightful juicy fruit. But demand has meant that many wines are overpriced and dull. Best producers: de Beauregard★ Berrod★, P-M Chermette★/Vissoux, M Chignard★, Clos de la Roilette★ DUBOEUF (la Madone★, Quatre Vents★), la Madone/Despres★, Y Métras★ Métrat★, A & M Morel★, Point du Jour★, Verpoix★. Best years: **2008 07 06**.

CH. LA FLEUR-PÉTRUS★★ *Pomerol AC, Bordeaux, France* Like the better known PETRUS and TROTANOY, this is owned by the dynamic MOUEIX family. Unlike its stablemates, it is situated entirely on gravel soil and tends to produce tighter wines with less immediate fruit but considerable elegance and cellar potential. Among POMEROL's top dozen properties. Best years: 2006 05 **04 03** 02 01 **00** 99 98 96 95 94 90 89.

FLORA SPRINGS *Napa Valley AVA, California, USA* Best known for red wines such as Merlot★★, Cabernet Sauvignon★★ and a BORDEAUX blend called Trilogy★★. Barrel-fermented Chardonnay★★ tops the whites, and Soliloquy★, a barrel-fermented Sauvignon Blanc, has attractive melon fruit. The winery also works with Italian varietals; a weighty Pinot Grigio★ and a lightly spiced Sangiovese★ are consistent successes. Best years: (Trilogy) 2006 05 04 03 **02** 01 00 99 97 96 95 94 91.

FLOWERS *Sonoma Coast AVA, California, USA* Small producer whose estate vineyard, Camp Meeting Ridge, a few miles from the Pacific, yields wines of great intensity. Camp Meeting Ridge Pinot Noir★★★ and Chardonnay★★★ are usually made with native yeasts and offer wonderful exotic aromas and flavours. Wines from purchased fruit with SONOMA COAST designation are ★★. Best years: (Chardonnay) 2007 06 **05 0**· 03 01 00 99; (Pinot Noir) 2007 06 **05** 04 03 01 00 99 98 97 96.

TENUTE AMBROGIO & GIOVANNI FOLONARI *Tuscany, Italy* A few years ago the Folonari family, owners of the giant RUFFINO, split asunder and this father and son team went their own way. The properties/brands include Cabreo (Sangiovese-Cabernet Il Borgo★ Chardonnay La Pietra★) and Nozzole (powerful, long-lived Cabernet Il Pareto★★) in CHIANTI CLASSICO, plus VINO NOBILE estate Gracciano Svetoni, Campo del Mare in BOLGHERI and BRUNELLO producer La Fuga.

FONSECA *Port DOC, Douro, Portugal* Owned by the same group as TAYLOR (Fladgate Partnership), Fonseca makes ports in a rich, densely plummy style. Vintage★★★ is magnificent, the aged tawnies★★ uniformly superb. Guimaraens★★ is the 'off-vintage' wine, Crusted★ and Late Bottled Vintage★ are among the best examples of their styles, as is Bin No. 27★ of a premium ruby port. Quinta do Panascal★ is the single-quinta vintage. Best years: (Vintage) 2003 **00** 97 94 92 85 83 77 7· 70 66 63 55.

JOSÉ MARIA DA FONSECA *Terras do Sado, Portugal* Go-ahead company making a huge range of wines, from fizzy Lancers Rosé to serious reds. Best include Vinya★ (Syrah-Aragonez), Domingos Soares Franco Private Collection★, and Garrafeiras with codenames like CO★★ RA★★ and TE★★. Optimum★★ is top of the range. Periquita is the mainstay, with Clássico★ made only in the best years. Also SETUBAL made mainly from the Moscatel grape: 5-year-old★ and 20-year-old★★. Older vintage-dated Setúbals are rare but superb.

DOM. FONT DE MICHELLE *Châteauneuf-du-Pape AC, Rhône Valley, France* CHATEAUNEUF-DU-PAPE reds★★, in particular Cuvée Étienne Gonnet★★, that are stylish but still heady, with richness and southern herb fragrance – and good value for money. Fresh, accomplished whites★★. Best years: (Étienne Gonnet red) 2007 06 05 **04 03 01 00** 99 98 97 95 94 90 89.

FONTANAFREDDA *Barolo DOCG, Piedmont, Italy* Large property, formerly the hunting lodge of the King of Italy. As well as BAROLO Serralunga d'Alba★, it produces several single-vineyard Barolos★ (La Delizia★★), a range of PIEDMONT varietals, 4 million bottles of ASTI and a good dry sparkler, Contessa Rosa. Best years: (Barolo) (2008) (07) (06) **04 03 01 00** 99 97.

CASTELLO DI FONTERUTOLI *Chianti Classico DOCG, Tuscany, Italy* This estate has belonged to the Mazzei family since the 15th century. The focus is on CHIANTI CLASSICO Riserva★★, along with excellent SUPER-TUSCAN Siepi★★★ (Sangiovese-Merlot). Belguardo★ is a more recent venture in the MAREMMA, with IGT and MORELLINO DI SCANSANO wines.

FONTODI *Chianti Classico DOCG, Tuscany, Italy* The Manetti family has built this superbly sited estate into one of the most admired in CHIANTI CLASSICO, with fine *normale*★★ and Riserva Vigna del Sorbo★★. SUPER-TUSCAN Flaccianello della Pieve★★★, from a single vineyard of old vines, has served as a shining example of an excellent 100% Sangiovese. Pinot Nero and Syrah★ are made under the Case Via label. Best years: (Flaccianello) (2008) (07) (06) **04 03 01 00** 99 97 95 93 90 88 85.

FORADORI *Teroldego Rotaliano DOC, Trentino, Italy* Producer of dark, spicy, berry-fruited wines, including a regular TEROLDEGO ROTALIANO★ and barrique-aged Granato★★. Elisabetta Foradori's interest in Syrah is producing excellent results, both in the varietal Ailanpa★★ and the smoky, black-cherry lushness of Cabernet-Syrah blend Karanar★. Best years: (Granato) (2008) (07) 06 **04 03 01 00** 99 97.

FORST *Pfalz, Germany* Village with outstanding vineyard sites, including the Ungeheuer or 'Monster'; wines from the Monster can indeed be quite savage, with a marvellous mineral intensity and richness. Equally good are the Kirchenstück, Jesuitengarten, Freundstück and Pechstein. Best producers: BASSERMANN-JORDAN★★, von BUHL★★, BÜRKLIN-WOLF★★, MOSBACHER★, E Müller, WEGELER★, WOLF★★. Best years: (2008) 07 06 05 **04 03 02 01** 99 98.

O FOURNIER *Uco Valley, Mendoza, Argentina* Exciting Tempranillo and Malbec from old vines in the La Consulta area of the UCO VALLEY. Alfa Crux★★ (a Tempranillo-Malbec-Merlot blend) is top of the line, while Alfa Crux Malbec★★ is an excellent, juicy expression of Argentina's flagship red grape. Also top Syrah★★. B Crux★ is the lighter, but delicious, second label. O Fournier also has a venture in RIBERA DEL DUERO, Spain, with Fournier★★ and Alfa Spiga★ cuvées. A new venture in Chile is based in MAULE and SAN ANTONIO; the first release is Centauri Sauvignon Blanc★ from San Antonio. Best years: (reds) 2005 **04 03 02.**

FOX CREEK *McLaren Vale, South Australia* Impressive, opulent, superripe MCLAREN VALE reds. Reserve Shiraz★★ and Reserve Cabernet Sauvignon★★ have wowed the critics; JSM (Shiraz-Cabernets)★★ is rich and succulent; Merlot★★ is a little lighter but still concentrated and powerful. Vixen sparkling Shiraz★ is also lip-smacking stuff. Whites are comparatively ordinary, albeit fair value for money.

FOX RUN *Finger Lakes AVA, New York State, USA* A leading champion of Dry Riesling★, Fox Run teamed up in 2004 with Red Newt and Anthony Road wineries to produce Tierce, a co-operative effort to define a regional style for Riesling. Fox Run also features complex, ALSACE-style Gewürztraminer★ and an elegant Reserve Chardonnay★. Spicy attractive reds from Pinot Noir and Cabernet Franc, and a complex fruit-forward red Meritage.

FRANCIACORTA DOCG *Lombardy, Italy* CHAMPAGNE-method fizz made from Pinot and Chardonnay grapes. Still whites from Pinot Bianco and Chardonnay and reds from Cabernet, Barbera, Nebbiolo and Merlot are all DOC with the appellation Terre di Franciacorta. Best producers BELLAVISTA★★, Fratelli Berlucchi★, Guido Berlucchi★, CA' DEL BOSCO★★ Castellino★, Cavalleri★, La Ferghettina★, Enrico Gatti★, Monte Rossa★, Mosnel★, Ricci Curbastro★, San Cristoforo★, Uberti★, Villa★.

FRANCISCAN *Napa Valley AVA, California, USA* Consistently good wines at fair prices: the Cuvée Sauvage Chardonnay★★ is a blockbusting, savoury mouthful, and the Cabernet Sauvignon-based meritage Magnificat★ is very attractive. Part of huge Constellation, which also owns Moun Veeder Winery, where lean but intense Cabernet Sauvignon★★ of grea mineral depth and complexity is made, and Estancia, with remarkably good-value Chardonnay★ and Pinot Noir★ from CENTRAL COAST and Cabernet Sauvignon★ from ALEXANDER VALLEY, as well as its own Meritage★.

DR KONSTANTIN FRANK *Finger Lakes AVA, New York State, USA* The good doctor was a pioneer of *vinifera* grapes in the FINGER LAKES region in the 1960s. Now under the direction of his grandson Fred, the winery continues to spotlight the area's talent with Riesling★ and Rkatsiteli, an obscure Georgian grape. There's also some nice Chateau Frank fizz.

FRANKEN *Germany* 6000ha (14,820-acre) wine region specializing in dry wines – recognizable by their squat Bocksbeutel bottles (familiar because of the Portuguese wine Mateus Rosé). Silvaner is the traditional variety although Müller-Thurgau now predominates. The most famous vineyards are on slopes around WURZBURG, RANDERSACKER, IPHOFEN and Escherndorf.

FRANSCHHOEK WO *South Africa* Huguenot refugees settled in this picturesque valley, encircled by breathtaking mountain peaks, in the 17th century. Many wineries and other landmarks still bear French names The valley is recognized for its whites – Semillon is a local speciality (a few vines are over 100 years old) – though reds are establishing a reputation: La Motte Pierneef Shiraz-Viognier★ and Stony Brook Cabernet Sauvignon Reserve★ are among the most promising. Best producers: Graham BECK★, BOEKENHOUTSKLOOF★★, Cabrière Estate, CAPE CHAMONIX★, La Motte★, La Petite Ferme, L'Ormarins, Solms-Delta★, Stony Brook. Best years: (reds) 2006 **05 04 03 02 01 00**.

FRASCATI DOC *Lazio, Italy* One of Italy's most famous whites, frequently referred to as Rome's quaffing wine. The wine may be made from Trebbiano or Malvasia or any blend thereof; the better examples have a higher proportion of Malvasia. There's much mediocre stuff, but good Frascati is worth seeking out for its gentle, dry creaminess, most notably Vigna Adriana★★ (though it's now an IGT) from Castel de Paolis Other light, dry Frascati-like wines come from neighbouring DOCs in the hills of the Castelli Romani and Colli Albani, including Marino Montecompatri, Velletri and Zagarolo. Best producers: Casale Marchese★ Castel de Paolis★★, Colli di Catone★, Piero Costantini/Villa Simone★, Fontana Candida★, Zandotti★.

FREESTONE *Sonoma Coast AVA, California, USA* The Napa Valley's Joseph PHELPS wanted better sources of Chardonnay fruit so he planted 26ha (65 acres) in two parcels in the coldest region of SONOMA COUNTY. Luckily he also planted some Pinot Noir, because it is this variety which has best demonstrated the brilliance of the Freestone region. After declassifying four vintages, the 2006 Chardonnay★ and Pinot Noir★ were released to acclaim. Phelps surely will seek AVA status for Freestone.

FREIXENET *Cava DO, Cataluña, Spain* The second-biggest Spanish sparkling wine company (after CODORNÍU) makes the famous Cordon Negro Brut CAVA in a vast network of cellars in Sant Sadurní d'Anoia. Freixenet also owns a number of other Cava brands (including Castellblanch and Segura Viudas) as well as PENEDÈS winery René Barbier and a stake in PRIORAT's Viticultors del Priorat (Morlanda). Its international expansion has gathered pace in recent years with interests in Champagne, California, Australia, Argentina and Bordeaux.

FRESCOBALDI *Tuscany, Italy* Ancient Florentine company selling large quantities of inexpensive blended CHIANTI, but from its own vineyards (some 1000ha/2470 acres in Tuscany) it produces good to very good wines at Castello di Nipozzano (CHIANTI RUFINA Nipozzano Riserva★★, Montesodi★★ and my favourite, the BORDEAUX-blend Mormoreto★★), Castello di Pomino★ (Benefizio Chardonnay★) and Castelgiocondo★ (BRUNELLO DI MONTALCINO★★), where Sangiovese for Brunello and Merlot for

the SUPER-TUSCAN (and super-expensive) Luce are grown. Frescobaldi owns several other estates in Tuscany including, since 2005, a majority stake in the famous Bolgheri estate, ORNELLAIA. It also owns the historic Attems estate in COLLIO. Best years: (premium reds) (2008) (07) 06 **04 03 01 00 99 97 95**.

FRIULANO See TOCAI FRIULANO.

FRIULI GRAVE DOC *Friuli-Venezia Giulia, Italy* DOC in western Friuli covering 19 wine types. Good affordable Merlot, Refosco, Chardonnay, Pinot Grigio, Traminer and Tocai. Best producers: Borgo Magredo★, Di Lenardo★, Le Fredis★, Orgnani★, Pighin★, Pittaro★, Plozner★, Pradio★, Russolo★, Vigneti Le Monde★, Villa Chiopris★, Vistorta★. Best years: (whites) (2008) 07 **06 04 02**.

FRIULI ISONZO DOC *Friuli-Venezia Giulia, Italy* Classy southern neighbour of COLLIO with wines of outstanding value. The DOC covers 20 styles, including Merlot, Chardonnay, Pinot Grigio and Sauvignon. The best from neighbouring Carso DOC are also good. Best producers: (Isonzo) Borgo San Daniele★, Colmello di Grotta★, Sergio & Mauro Drius★★, Lis Neris★★, Masùt da Rive★, Pierpaolo Pecorari★★, Giovanni Puiatti★, Ronco del Gelso★★, Vie di Romans★★, Tenuta Villanova★; (Carso) Castelvecchio, Edi Kante★★. Best years: (whites) (2008) 07 **06 04 03 02 01 00 99 98 97**.

FRIULI-VENEZIA GIULIA *Italy* North-east Italian region bordering Austria and Slovenia. The hilly DOC zones of COLLIO and COLLI ORIENTALI produce some of Italy's finest whites from Chardonnay, Pinot Bianco, Pinot Grigio, Sauvignon and Friulano (Tocai), and excellent reds mainly from Cabernet, Merlot and Refosco. Good-value wines from the DOCs of Friuli Aquileia, FRIULI ISONZO, Friuli Latisana and FRIULI GRAVE, in the rolling hills and plains.

FROMM *Marlborough, South Island, New Zealand* Small winery where low
yielding vines and intensively managed vineyards are the secret behind
string of winning white wines, including fine Burgundian-style Clayvi
Vineyard Chardonnay★★, German-style Riesling★★ and Rieslin
Auslese★. Despite its success with whites, Fromm is perhaps best know
for intense, long-lived reds, including Clayvin Vineyard Pinot Noir★★★
Fromm Vineyard Pinot Noir★★ and a powerful, peppery Syrah★★. Bes
years: (Pinot Noir) 2007 06 **05 04 03 02 01 00.**

FRONSAC AC *Bordeaux, France* Small area west of POMEROL making good
value Merlot-based wines. The top producers have taken note of th
feeding frenzy in neighbouring Pomerol and sharpened up their ac
accordingly, with finely structured wines, occasionally perfumed, an
better with at least 5 years' age. Best producers: Carles (Haut-Carles★
Dalem★, la Dauphine★, Fontenil★, la Grave, Magondeau Beau-Site, Mayne
Vieil (Cuvée Aliénor★), Moulin Haut-Laroque★, Richelieu★, la Rivière
(Aria★), la Rousselle★, Tour du Moulin, les Trois Croix★, la Vieille Cure
Villars★. Best years: 2006 **05 03 01 00 98 96 95 90.**

FRONTON AC *South-West France* From north of Toulouse, some of th
most distinctive reds – silky, with hints of violets and licorice – of South
West France. Négrette is the chief grape, but certain producers add bit
at the cost of character by blending in Cabernet, which rather defeats th
object. Best producers: Baudare★, Bellevue-la-Forêt, Boujac, Cahuzac
Callory, Caze, Joliet, Laurou, Plaisance★, le Roc★. Best years: (2008) **06** 05 0

FUMÉ BLANC See SAUVIGNON BLANC, pages 274–5.

RUDOLF FÜRST *Bürgstadt, Franken, Germany* Paul Fürst's dry Rieslings★
are unusually elegant for a region renowned for its earthy white wine
while his Burgundian-style Spätburgunder (Pinot Noir) reds★★ an
barrel-fermented Weissburgunder (Pinot Blanc) whites★★ are some c
the best in Germany. Sensual, intellectual wines with excellent agin
potential. Best years: (dry Riesling) (2008) 07 06 05 **04 03 02 01**; (reds) (200
07 06 05 04 **03 02 01**.

JEAN-NOËL GAGNARD *Chassagne-Montrachet, Côte de Beaune, Burgundy, Franc*
Now run by Gagnard's daughter Caroline Lestimé, who consistent
makes some of the best wines of CHASSAGNE-MONTRACHET, particularl
Premiers Crus Caillerets★★★ and Morgeot★★. Top wine is rich, toas
BÂTARD-MONTRACHET★★★. All whites are capable of extended cellarin
Reds★ are good, but not in the same class. Best years: (whites) (2008) 07 0
05 **04 02 01 00** 99.

GAILLAC AC *South-West France* The whites, mainly from Mauzac and Le
de l'El, range from dry to ultra-sweet. Some more serious reds are mad
which require some aging. Reds and rosés are from other local grapes
Braucol, Duras – and sometimes Syrah. Some reds are matured in woc
and need some aging. Sparkling Gaillac undergoes only on
fermentation and has no added yeasts or sugar; less alcohol, too. Be
producers: Causses-Marines★★, Escausses★, Labarthe★, Mas Pignou, Palvié
Pialentou, PLAGEOLES★★, la RAMAYE★, ROTIER★.

GAJA *Barbaresco DOCG, Piedmont, Italy* Angelo Gaja was instrumental i
bringing about the transformation of PIEDMONT from an old-fashione
region that Italians swore made the finest red wine in the world yet th
rest of the world disdained, to an area buzzing with excitement. H
introduced international standards and charged staggeringly high price
thus giving other Piedmont growers the chance to get a decent retu
for their labours. Into this fiercely conservative area, full of fascinati

grape varieties but proudest of the native Nebbiolo, he introduced French grapes like Cabernet Sauvignon (Darmagi★★), Sauvignon Blanc (Alteni di Brassica★) and Chardonnay (Gaia & Rey★★). He has also renounced the Barbaresco and Barolo DOCGs for his best wines! Gaja's traditional strength has been in single-vineyard wines from the BARBARESCO region: his Sorì San Lorenzo★★★, Sorì Tildìn★★★ and Costa Russi★★★, now sold under the LANGHE Nebbiolo DOC, which permits 15% of other grapes in the blend, are often cited as Barbaresco's best of the modern style, although they tend to be more 'Gaja' than 'Barbaresco'. Only one 100% Nebbiolo bottling, of Barbaresco DOCG★★★, is now made. Sperss★★★ and Conteisa★★★ – from BAROLO, but sold as Langhe Nebbiolo wines – are also outstanding. Barbera Sitorey★ and Nebbiolo-Merlot-Cabernet-based Langhe Sito Moresco★ are less exciting. Gaja has also invested in BRUNELLO DI MONTALCINO (Pieve Santa Restituta) and BOLGHERI (Ca' Marcanda). Best years: (Barbaresco) (2008) (07) (06) 04 03 01 00 99 98 97 96 95 93 90 89 88 85 82 79 78 71 64 61.

GALICIA *Spain* Up in Spain's hilly, verdant north-west, Galicia is renowned for its Albariño whites. There are 5 DOs: RIAS BAIXAS can make excellent, fragrant Albariño, with modern equipment and serious winemaking; Ribeiro DO has also invested heavily in new equipment, and better local white grapes such as Treixadura are now being used; it's a similar story with the Godello grape in the mountainous Valdeorras DO, where producers such as the young Rafael Palacios, from the ubiquitous Rioja-based family, are reaching new heights for ageworthy, individual whites. Some increasingly ambitious reds from the Mencía grape are also made there and in the Ribeira Sacra DO. Monterrei DO is technically backward but shows some potential with its native white grape, Doña Blanca. Most wines are best drunk young.

GALLO *Central Valley, California, USA* Gallo, the world's second-largest wine company – and for generations a byword for cheap, drab wines – has made a massive effort to change its reputation since the mid-1990s. This began with the release of (expensive) Sonoma Estate Chardonnay and Cabernet Sauvignon. The Gallo of Sonoma label has been discontinued and replaced by the umbrella Gallo Family label, with emphasis on Sonoma Chardonnay and Cabernet Sauvignon, Zinfandel and Cabernet Sauvignon from DRY CREEK VALLEY and ALEXANDER VALLEY and other Chardonnay from several vineyards. New vineyards in RUSSIAN RIVER VALLEY and the SONOMA COAST have been planted to Pinot Noir and Pinot Gris (some of it to make the premium MacMurray wines). Even so, Gallo continues to produce oceans of ordinary wine. Turning Leaf and Sierra Valley aren't going to turn heads, but the company has taken Rancho Zabaco upscale and added a parallel brand, Dancing Bull, in which Sauvignon Blanc★ and Zinfandel★ are budding stars. In 2002, Gallo acquired historic Louis M Martini in NAPA VALLEY, adding the famed Monte Rosso vineyard to its holdings (Martini's Monte Rosso Cabernet Sauvignon★★ remains a top Cab) and then bought Mirassou, Barefoot Cellars, William Hill and CENTRAL COAST's Bridlewood.

GAMAY The only grape allowed for red BEAUJOLAIS. In general Gamay wine is rather rough-edged and quite high in raspy acidity, but in Beaujolais, so long as the yield is not too high, it can achieve a wonderful, juicy-fruit gluggability, almost unmatched in the world of wine. Elsewhere i France, it is successful in the Ardèche and the Loire and less so in th Mâconnais. In Switzerland it is blended with Pinot Noir to create DOL and Goron. There are occasional plantings in Canada, Brazil, New Zealand, Australia, South Africa, Italy and even England.

GANTENBEIN *Fläsch, Graubunden, Switzerland* Since 1982 Daniel Gantenbei has focused on producing intense and powerful versions of th Burgundian varieties, and has won a fine reputation above all for h Pinot Noir★★, as well as Chardonnay and Riesling. **Best years:** (Pinc Noir) (2008) (07) 06 05 **04 03 02 99**.

GARD, VIN DE PAYS DU *Languedoc, France* Mainly reds and rosés from th western side of the RHÔNE delta. Most red is light, spicy and attractive Some fresh young rosés and whites have been improved by mode: winemaking. **Best producers:** des Aveylans★, Baruel★, Cantarelles, Cost Plane, Grande Cassagne★, Guiot★, Mas des Bressades★.

GARNACHA BLANCA See GRENACHE BLANC.

GARNACHA TINTA See GRENACHE NOIR.

GATTINARA DOCG *Piedmont, Italy* One of the most capricious of Italy top red wine areas. The Nebbiolo wines should be softer and lighter tha BAROLO, with a delicious, black plums, tar and roses flavour if you're luck Drink within 10 years. Vintages follow those for Barolo. **Best producer** Antoniolo★, S Gattinara, Nervi★, Travaglini★.

DOM. GAUBY *Côtes du Roussillon-Villages AC, Roussillon, France* Gérard Gaub used to make burly but very tannic wines; now his wines are softer b marvellously concentrated and balanced. Highlights include powerf COTES DU ROUSSILLON-VILLAGES Vieilles Vignes★★, white and red l Calcinaires★★ and Muntada★★ as well as a gorgeously seductive whi vin de pays Coume Gineste★. **Best years:** (reds) 2005 04 **03 02 01** 00 9

GAVI DOCG *Piedmont, Italy* This fashionable and rapidly improving Cortese-based, steely, lemony white can age up to 5 years, providing it starts life with sufficient fruit. La Scolca's Spumante Brut Soldati★ is an admirable sparkling wine. **Best producers:** Battistina★, Bergaglio★,

Broglia★, La Chiara★, CHIARLO★, FONTANAFREDDA, La Giustiniana★★, P Cesare, San Pietro★, La Scolca★, Tassarolo★, Villa Sparina★.

CH. GAZIN★★ *Pomerol AC, Bordeaux, France* One of the largest châteaux : POMEROL, situated next to the legendary PETRUS. The wine, traditionally succulent, sweet-textured Pomerol, seemed to lose its way in the 198 but has now got much of its richness and character back under th management of owner Nicolas de Bailliencourt. **Best years:** 2007 06 05 0 03 02 01 00 99 98 96 95 94 90 89.

GEELONG *Victoria, Australia* Cool-climate, maritime-influenced regic revived in the 1960s after destruction by phylloxera in the 19th centur Can be brilliant; potentially a match for the YARRA VALLEY. Impressiv Pinot Noir, Chardonnay, Riesling, Sauvignon and Shiraz. **Best produce** Austin's, BANNOCKBURN★, By FARR★★, Farr Rising★, Scotchmans Hill★.

GEISENHEIM *Rheingau, Germany* Village famous for its wine school, whe the Müller-Thurgau grape was bred in 1882. Geisenheim's best-know vineyard is the Rothenberg, which produces strong, earthy wine

Best producers: Johannishof★, WEGELER★. Best years: (2008) 07 06 05 **04 03 02 01 99**.

GEROVASSILIOU *Macedonia AO, Greece* Bordeaux-trained Evángelos Gerovassiliou has 40ha (100 acres) of vineyards and a modern winery in Epanomi in northern Greece. High-quality fruit results in Syrah-dominated Gerovassiliou red★ and some fresh, modern whites, including a fine Viognier★ that lacks a little perfume but has fantastic fruit, barrel-fermented Chardonnay and Fumé, and the Gerovassiliou★ white, a most original Assyrtiko-Malagousia blend.

GEVREY-CHAMBERTIN AC *Côte de Nuits, Burgundy, France* A new generation of growers has restored the reputation of Gevrey as a source of well-coloured, firmly structured, powerful, perfumed wines that become rich and gamy with age. Village wines should be kept for at least 5 years, Premiers Crus and the 9 Grands Crus for 10 years or more, especially CHAMBERTIN and Clos-de-Bèze. The Premier Cru Clos St-Jacques is worthy of promotion to Grand Cru. Best producers: D Bachelet★★, Louis Boillot★, A Burguet★★, B CLAIR★★, P Damoy★★, DROUHIN★, C Dugat★★★, B Dugat-Py★★, DUJAC★★, S Esmonin★★, FAIVELEY★★, Fourrier★★, Geantet-Pansiot★★, JADOT★★, Denis MORTET★★★, Rossignol-Trapet★★, J Roty★★, ROUSSEAU★★★, Sérafin★★, J & J-L Trapet★★. Best years: (2008) 07 06 05 03 **02 01 99 98 96 95 93 90**.

GEWÜRZTRAMINER *Gewürz* means spice, and the wine certainly can be spicy and exotically perfumed, as well as being typically low in acidity. It is thought to have originated in the village of Tramin, in Italy's ALTO ADIGE, and the name Traminer is used by many producers. It makes an appearance in many wine-producing countries; quality is mixed and styles vary enormously, from the fresh, light, florally perfumed wines produced in Alto Adige to the rich, luscious, late-harvest ALSACE Vendange Tardive. Best in France's Alsace and also good in Austria's Styria (STEIERMARK), southern Germany, Chile and New Zealand. Improving in South Africa.

GEYSER PEAK *Alexander Valley AVA, Sonoma County, California, USA* Australian winemaker Daryl Groom set the tone for wines that tend to be accessible and fruit-driven. Typical are the fruity SONOMA COUNTY Cabernet★ and Merlot★ – ripe, juicy and delicious upon release. The Reserve Alexandre Meritage★★, a BORDEAUX-style blend, is made for aging, and the Reserve Shiraz★★ has a cult following. Block Collection features limited production, single-vineyard wines. There's also a highly popular Sauvignon Blanc★ (Block Collection★★). The winery was sold in December 2007 to Constellation (and has since been sold on) and Groom left to pursue other wine ventures, so we can only wait to see if quality holds up. Best years: (Alexandre) 2005 **02 01 00 99 98 97 94 91**.

GHEMME DOCG *Piedmont, Italy* Near neighbour and similar to GATTINARA. Best producers: Antichi Vigneti di Cantalupo★, Ioppa★.

GIACONDA *Beechworth, Victoria, Australia* In spite of (or perhaps because of) Giaconda's tiny production, Rick Kinzbrunner is one of Australia's most influential winemakers. Following on from his success, BEECHWORTH has become one of the country's most exciting viticultural regions. His tightly structured, minerally, savoury Chardonnay★★★ is one of Australia's best – as are both the serious and beautiful Pinot Noir★★★ and the deep, gamy, HERMITAGE-style Warner Vineyard Shiraz★★★. The

Cabernet★ is ripe, deep and complex. The Aeolia Roussanne an‹
Nantua Les Deux Chardonnay-Roussanne are complex and textural. Bes‹
years: (Chardonnay) (2008) (07) 06 05 04 **02 01 00 99 98 96 93 92**.

BRUNO GIACOSA Barbaresco DOCG, Piedmont, Italy One of the grea‹
🍷 winemakers of the LANGHE hills, indeed of Italy, still basically
traditionalist, though he has reduced maturation time for his BARBARESCO‹
and BAROLOS to a maximum of 4 years. Superb Barbarescos Asili★★★
Santo Stefano★★★ and Rabaja★★★, and Barolos including Rocche d‹
Falletto★★★ and Falletto★★. Excellent Barbera d'Alba★, Dolcett‹
d'Alba★, ROERO Arneis★, MOSCATO D'ASTI★★ and sparkling Extra Brut★★

GIGONDAS AC Rhône Valley, France Gigondas wines, mostly red and mad‹
🍷 mainly from Grenache, have fistfuls of chunky personality. Most drin‹
well with 5 years' age; some need a little more. Best producer‹
P Amadieu★★, la Bouïssière★★, Brusset★★, Cassan★★, Cayron★★, Clos d‹
Cazaux★★, Clos du Joncuas★, Cros de la Mûre★★, DELAS★, Espiers★★, Fon‹
Sane★, la Fourmone★, les Goubert★, Gour de Chaulé★, Grapillon d'Or★★
GUIGAL★, JABOULET, Longue-Toque★, Montvac★★, Moulin de la Gardette★★
les Pallières★★, Perrin et Fils★, Piaugier★, Raspail-Ay★★, Redortier★, Roubir‹
St-Cosme★, ST-GAYAN★, Santa Duc★★, Tardieu-Laurent★★, la Tourade‹
Tourelles★★, Trignon★. Best years: 2007 06 05 04 03 01 00 99 98 95 9‹

CH. GILETTE★★ Sauternes AC, Bordeaux, France These astonishing wines a‹
♀ stored in concrete vats as opposed to the more normal wooden barre‹
This virtually precludes any oxygen contact, and it is oxygen that age‹
wine. Consequently, when released at up to 30 years old, they a‹
bursting with life and lusciousness. Best years: 1988 86 85 83 82 81 79 7‹
76 75 70 67 61 59 55 53 49.

GIPPSLAND Victoria, Australia Diverse wineries along the southe‹
🍷 VICTORIA coast, all tiny but with massive potential. Results are errat‹
occasionally brilliant. Nicholson River's BURGUNDY-style Chardonnay c‹
sometimes hit ★★. Bass Phillip Reserve★★ and Premium★★ Pin‹
Noirs are among the best in Australia, with a cult following. McAlister‹
a red BORDEAUX blend, has also produced some tasty flavours. Be‹
producers: Bass Phillip★★, McAlister★, Nicholson River★.

VINCENT GIRARDIN Santenay, Côte de Beaune, Burgundy, France A leadi‹
🍷 grower in SANTENAY developed into a thriving négociant, with ‹
establishment in MEURSAULT. Bright, glossy reds from Santenay★
MARANGES★ and CHASSAGNE-MONTRACHET★★ are surpassed by excelle‹
VOLNAY★★ and POMMARD Grands Épenots★★★. Chassagne-Montrach‹
whites (Morgeot★★, Caillerets★★★) are perfectly balanced with go‹
fruit depth. CORTON-CHARLEMAGNE★★★ is exceptional. Girardin has al‹
revived the moribund Henri Clerc estate in PULIGNY-MONTRACHET. Be‹
years: (reds) (2008) 07 06 05 03 02 99; (whites) (2008) 07 06 05 04 02.

GISBORNE North Island, New Zealand Gisborne, with its hot, humid clima‹
and fertile soils, delivers both quality and quantity. Christened (by lo‹
growers) 'The Chardonnay Capital of New Zealand', although the focus‹
rapidly shifting to Pinot Gris, while Gewürztraminer and Chenin Blanc ‹
also a success. Good reds, however, are hard to find. Best produce‹
MILLTON★★, MONTANA, Vinoptima★★. Best years: (Chardonnay) 2007 05 04.

GIVRY AC Côte Chalonnaise, Burgundy, France Important CÔTE CHALONNA‹
🍷 village. The reds have an intensity of fruit and ability to age that ‹
unusual in the region. There are some attractive, fairly full, nutty whit‹

too. Best producers: Bourgeon★, Chofflet-Valdenaire★, B CLAIR★, Clos Salomon★, Joblot★★, F Lumpp★★, Ragot★, Sarrazin★. Best years: (reds) (2008) 07 **05** 03 02 99; (whites) (2008) 07 **06 05**.

GLAETZER *Barossa Valley, South Australia* Colin Glaetzer has been one of the BAROSSA VALLEY's most enthusiastic and successful winemakers for decades. He made his reputation working for other people, and now he and his son Ben make 4 tip-top Barossa wines for the family label. There is fleshy Wallace Shiraz-Grenache★, rich, superripe Bishop Shiraz★ (from 30–60-year-old vines), the amazingly opulent, succulent and velvety Amon-Ra Shiraz★★ and Anaperenna★★ (formerly Godolphin), a deep, dense Shiraz-Cabernet blend. Ben also makes reds and whites for the Heartland label using fruit from vineyards in Langhorne Creek and LIMESTONE COAST, but recent releases have lost their initial zip. Best years: (Bishop Shiraz) (2008) 06 **05** 04 02 01 99 98 96.

GLEN CARLOU *Paarl WO, South Africa* Started by the Finlaysons in the 1980s and now owned by Donald HESS. David Finlayson remains as winemaker. Elegant standard Chardonnay★ and restrained single-vineyard Quartz Stone Chardonnay★★, from organically grown grapes, lead the whites. Reds feature sweet-textured Pinot Noir★; deep, dry Syrah★; Grand Classique★, a red BORDEAUX blend with excellent aging potential; and concentrated Gravel Quarry Cabernet★, also organically grown. Best years: (Chardonnay) 2008 07 **06** 05 04 03 02.

CH. GLORIA★ *St-Julien AC, Haut-Médoc, Bordeaux, France* An interesting property, created out of tiny plots of Classed Growth land scattered all round ST-JULIEN. Generally very soft and sweet-centred, the wine nonetheless ages well. Same owner as Ch. ST-PIERRE. Second wine: Peymartin. Best years: 2007 06 05 **04** 03 02 01 00 99 98 96 95 90 89.

GOLDWATER ESTATE *Waiheke Island, Auckland, New Zealand* The first vineyard on WAIHEKE ISLAND. Top wines are intense, long-lived 'Goldie' Cabernet-Merlot★★ and elegant, cedary Esslin Merlot★★, with considerable depth and structure. Zell Chardonnay★★ from Waiheke looks exciting. Attractive New Dog Sauvignon Blanc★ and Roseland Chardonnay★ from MARLBOROUGH fruit. In 2006 Goldwater merged with Marlborough's VAVASOUR. Best years: (Waiheke reds) (2007) 05 **04** 02 00.

GONZÁLEZ BYASS *Jerez y Manzanilla DO, Andalucía, Spain* Tio Pepe★ fino is the world's biggest-selling sherry. The old sherries are superb: intense, dry Amontillado del Duque★★★; 2 rich, complex olorosos, sweet Matusalem★★ and medium Apóstoles★★; treacly Noé Pedro Ximénez★★★. One step down is the Alfonso Dry Oloroso★. The firm pioneered the rediscovery of single-vintage (non-solera) dry olorosos★★ and palos cortados★★.

HENRI GOUGES *Nuits-St-Georges, Côte de Nuits, Burgundy, France* The original Henri Gouges was mayor of NUITS-ST-GEORGES in the 1930s and was instrumental in classifying the large number of Premiers Crus in his appellation. Today, the domaine is back on form, producing impressive, meaty, long-lived reds (Les St Georges★★★, Clos des Porrets★★, Les Vaucrains★★) as well as excellent white Nuits-St-Georges Premier Cru La Perrière★★. Best years: (2008) 07 06 05 02 **01** 99 98 96 90.

GRAACH *Mosel, Germany* Important Middle MOSEL wine village with 4 vineyard sites, the most famous being Domprobst (also the best) and Himmelreich. A third, the Josephshöfer, is wholly owned by the von KESSELSTATT estate. The wines have an attractive fullness to balance their steely acidity, and great aging potential. Best producers: von KESSELSTATT★,

Dr LOOSEN★★, Markus MOLITOR★★, J J PRUM★★, S A PRUM★, Max Fer
RICHTER★, Willi SCHAEFER★★★, SELBACH-OSTER★★, Dr Weins-Prüm★. Bes
years: (2008) 07 06 **05 04 03 02 01 00 99 98 97**.

GRACIANO Rare, low-yielding but excellent Spanish grape, traditional i
RIOJA, NAVARRA and Extremadura. It makes dense, highly structured
fragrant reds, and its high acidity adds life when blended with low-aci
Tempranillo. In Portugal it is called Tinta Miúda. Also grown by BROW
BROTHERS and others in Australia.

GRAHAM *Port DOC, Douro, Portugal* Part of the Symington empire, makin
rich, florally scented Vintage Port★★★, sweeter than DOW's and WARRE'
but with the backbone to age. In non-declared years makes a fine vintag
wine called Malvedos★★. Six Grapes★ is one of the best premiur
rubies, and Crusted★★ and 10-year-old★ and 20-year-old★★ tawnie
are consistently good. Best years: (Vintage) **2003 00 97 94 91 85 83 80 7
75 70 66 63 60**; (Malvedos) 2001 **99 98 95 92 90**.

ALAIN GRAILLOT *Crozes-Hermitage AC, Rhône Valley, France* Excellent fami
estate producing powerfully concentrated, rich, fruity reds. The top win
is CROZES-HERMITAGE la Guiraude★★, but the regular Crozes
Hermitage★★ is wonderful too, and great for early drinking, as are th
ST-JOSEPH★★ and a lovely fragrant white Crozes-Hermitage★. Keep to
reds for at least 5 years. Son Max has promising Dom. des Lises estate
Best years: (la Guiraude) 2007 **06 05 04 03** 01 00 99 95 89.

GRAMPIANS AND PYRENEES *Victoria, Australia* Two adjacent cool-climat
regions in central western VICTORIA, producing some of Australia's mo
characterful Shiraz, distinguished Riesling, subtle Pinot Gris and savou
Chardonnay. Best producers: BEST'S★, Blue Pyrenees, Dalwhinnie★★, MOUN
LANGI GHIRAN★★, Redbank★, SEPPELT★★, Summerfield★, Taltarni. Best year
(Shiraz) 2007 06 05 04 03 **02 01 99 98 97 96 94 91 90**.

CH. GRAND-PUY-DUCASSE★ *Pauillac AC, 5ème Cru Classé, Haut-Médo
Bordeaux, France* After great improvement in the 1980s, form dipped i
the early 90s but recovered again after 95. Approachable after 5 years, b
the best vintages can improve for considerably longer. Second win
Artigues-Arnaud. Best years: 2007 06 05 **04 03 02 00 96 95 90** 89.

CH. GRAND-PUY-LACOSTE★★ *Pauillac AC, 5ème
Cru Classé, Haut-Médoc, Bordeaux, France* Classic
PAUILLAC, with lots of blackcurrant and cigar-box
perfume. It begins fairly dense, but as the wine
develops, the flavours mingle with the sweetness
of new oak to become one of Pauillac's most
memorable taste sensations. Second wine:
Lacoste-Borie. Best years: 2007 06 05 **04 03 02 00
99 98 96 95 94 90** 89 88 86 85 83.

GRANDS-ÉCHÉZEAUX AC See ÉCHÉZEAUX AC.

GRANGE★★★ *Barossa Valley, South Australia* In 1950, Max Schubert, chi
winemaker at PENFOLDS, visited Europe and came back determined
make a wine that could match the great BORDEAUX reds. Undeterred by
lack of Cabernet Sauvignon grapes and French oak barrels, he set
work with BAROSSA Shiraz and barrels made from the more punge
American oak. Initially ignored and misunderstood, Schubert eventual
achieved global recognition for his wine, a stupendously comple
thrillingly rich red that only begins to reveal its magnificence after

years in bottle – but is better after 20. Best years: (2006) (05) 04 02 01 99 98 96 **94 92 91 90 88 86 84 83 76 71 66 62 53**.

DOM. DE LA GRANGE DES PÈRES *Vin de Pays de l'Hérault, Languedoc, France* With only 500 cases produced each year, demand is high for the meticulously crafted unfiltered red, a blend of Syrah, Mourvèdre and Cabernet Sauvignon. The white★★, based on Roussanne, with Marsanne and Chardonnay, is produced in even smaller quantities. Best years: (red) 2006 05 04 03 02 01 **00 99 98 97**.

GRANGEHURST *Stellenbosch WO, South Africa* Boutique winery known for modern Pinotage★, Cabernet-Merlot★★ with Bordeaux-ish appeal and Nikela★, a blend of all three varieties with Shiraz and owner/winemaker Jeremy Walker's answer to the Cape blend. Recent additions to the range include two Cabernets (Reserve★) and Shiraz-Cabernet Reserve★. Best years: (Cabernet-Merlot) 2003 02 01 **00 99 98 97 95**.

GRANS-FASSIAN *Leiwen, Mosel, Germany* LEIWEN owes its reputation largely to Gerhard Grans. Both sweet and dry Rieslings have gained in sophistication over the years: Spätlese★★ and Auslese★★ from TRITTENHEIMER Apotheke are particularly impressive. Eiswein is ★★★ in good vintages. Best years: (2008) 07 06 05 **04 03 02 01 99 98**.

ALFRED GRATIEN *Champagne AC, Champagne, France* This small company makes some of my favourite CHAMPAGNE. Its wines are made in wooden casks, which is very rare nowadays. The non-vintage★★ blend is usually 4 years old when sold, rather than the normal 3 years, and can age further. The vintage★★★ is deliciously ripe and toasty when released but can age for another 10 years. The prestige cuvée, Cuvée Paradis★★, is non-vintage. Best years: 1998 **97 96 95 91 90 89 88 85 83**.

GRAVES AC *Bordeaux, France* The Graves region covers the area south of the city of Bordeaux to Langon, but the generally superior villages in the northern half broke away in 1987 to form the PESSAC-LEOGNAN AC. In the southern Graves, a new wave of winemaking has produced plenty of clean, bone-dry white wines with lots of snappy freshness, as well as more complex soft, nutty barrel-aged whites, and some juicy, quick-drinking reds. Sweet white wines take the Graves Supérieures AC; the best make a decent substitute for the more expensive SAUTERNES. Best producers: Archambeau★, Ardennes★, Brondelle★, Chantegrive★, Clos Floridène★★, Crabitey★, l'Hospital, Léhoul★, Magence, Magneau★, Rahoul, Respide-Médeville★, St-Robert (cuvée Poncet Deville★), Seuil, Venus, Vieux-Ch.-Gaubert★, Villa Bel-Air★; (sweet) Brondelle, Léhoul. Best years: (reds) 2005 04 01 00 98 96 95 90; (dry whites) 2007 **06 05 04 02 01 00 98 96**.

GRAVNER *Friuli-Venezia Giulia, Italy* Josko Gravner, FRIULI's most zealous winemaker, sets styles with his wood-aged, oxidative whites which people either love or hate. Along with high-priced Chardonnay★★, Sauvignon★★ and Ribolla Gialla★, he combines 6 white varieties in Breg★★. Reds are Rosso Gravner★ (predominantly Merlot) and Rujno★★ (Merlot-Cabernet Sauvignon).

GREAT SOUTHERN *Western Australia* A vast, cool-climate region encompassing the sub-regions of Frankland River, Denmark, Mount Barker, Albany and Porongurup. Frankland River is particularly successful with Riesling, Shiraz and Cabernet; Denmark with Chardonnay and Pinot Noir; Mount Barker with Riesling and Shiraz; Albany with Pinot Noir; Porongurup with Riesling. Plantings have boomed in recent years, especially in Frankland River. Best producers:

Alkoomi, Castle Rock★, FERNGROVE★, Forest Hill★, Frankland Estate★
Gilberts★, Goundrey★★, HAREWOOD★★, HOUGHTON★★, HOWARD PARK★★
PLANTAGENET★★, West Cape Howe★★.

GRECHETTO Italian grape centred on UMBRIA, the main component c
ORVIETO DOC, also making tasty, anise-tinged dry white varietal·
Occasionally used in VIN SANTO in TUSCANY. Best producers: Antonel·
Barberani-Vallesanta★, Caprai★, FALESCO★, Palazzone, Castello della SALA.

GRENACHE BLANC A common white grape in the south of France, bu
without many admirers. Except me, that is, because I love the pea·
scented wine flecked with anise that a good producer can achieve. Low
yield examples take surprisingly well to oak. Generally best within a yea
of the vintage, although the odd old-vine example can age attractivel·
Grown as Garnacha Blanca in Spain, where it's now producing som
stunning examples in PRIORAT. A few old vines are contributing to som
interesting wines in South Africa.

GRENACHE NOIR Among the world's most widely planted red grapes
the bulk of it in Spain, where it is called Garnacha Tinta. It is a ho·
climate grape and in France it reaches its peak in the southern RHON
especially in CHÂTEAUNEUF-DU-PAPE, where it combines great alcoho·
strength with rich, refined raspberry fruit and a perfume hot from th
herb-strewn hills. It is generally given more tannin, acid and structure b
blending with Syrah, Mourvèdre, Cinsaut or other southern Frenc
grapes. It can make wonderful rosé in TAVEL, LIRAC and CÔTES DE PROVENC
as well as in NAVARRA in Spain. It makes lovely juicy reds and pinks
ARAGON's Calatayud, Campo de Borja and CARIÑENA, and forms th
backbone of the impressive reds of PRIORAT; in RIOJA it adds weight to th
Tempranillo. It is also the basis for the *vins doux naturels* of BANYULS an
MAURY in southern France. Also grown in CALIFORNIA and SOUTH AUSTRAL·
where it is finally being accorded considerable respect as imaginati·
winemakers realize there is a great resource of century-old vines capab·
of making wild and massively enjoyable reds, either alone or wi·
Syrah and/or Mourvèdre in Rhône blends. More is being planted
South Africa, where it is a popular component in Rhône-style wines. S
also CANNONAU.

GRGICH HILLS ESTATE *Rutherford AVA, California, USA* Mike Grgich w·
winemaker at CHATEAU MONTELENA when its 1973 Chardonnay shock·
Paris judges by finishing ahead of French versions in the famous 19·
tasting. At his own winery he makes classic California Chardonnay★
which ages for at least a decade, ripe, tannic Cabernet★, plum·
Merlot★ and a huge, old-style Zinfandel★. Best years: (Chardonnay) 20·
05 **04 03 02 01 00 99 98 97 95**.

GRIOTTE-CHAMBERTIN AC See CHAMBERTIN AC.

JEAN GRIVOT *Vosne-Romanée, Côte de Nuits, Burgundy, France* Étienne Griv·
settled into a successful stride from 1995 and has raised his game fro·
2004 with increasingly ripe yet always fine and complex wines from·
host of VOSNE-ROMANÉE Premiers Crus (Beaumonts★★★) as well·
brilliant CLOS DE VOUGEOT★★★ and RICHEBOURG★★★. Expensive, but·
VOSNE-ROMANÉE★★ for value. Best years: (2008) 07 **06** 05 04 03 02 **01** 99
96 95.

GROS *Côte de Nuits, Burgundy, France* Brilliant CÔTE DE NUITS wines from various members of the family, especially Anne Gros, Michel Gros, Gros Frère et Soeur and Anne-Françoise Gros. Look out for CLOS DE VOUGEOT★★★, ECHEZEAUX★★★ and RICHEBOURG★★★ as well as good-value HAUTES-COTES DE NUITS★. Best years: (2008) 07 06 05 03 02 **01 99 98 96 95 90**.

GROS PLANT DU PAYS NANTAIS VDQS *Loire Valley, France* Gros Plant can be searing stuff, but this acidic wine is well suited to the seafood guzzled in the region. Look for a *sur lie* bottling and drink the youngest available. Best producers: Brochet, les Coins, l'ECU, la Grange, Saupin.

GROSSET *Clare Valley, South Australia* Jeffrey Grosset is a perfectionist, crafting tiny quantities of hand-made wines. A Riesling specialist, he sources single-vineyard Watervale★★★ and Polish Hill★★★ from his own properties; both are supremely good and age well. Cabernet blend Gaia★★ is smooth and seamless. Also three outstanding ADELAIDE HILLS wines: Piccadilly Chardonnay★★★, very fine Pinot Noir★★ and arguably Australia's finest, tautest Semillon-Sauvignon★★. Best years: (Riesling) 2008 06 05 **04 03 02 01 00 99 98 97 96 94 93 92 90**.

CH. GRUAUD-LAROSE★★ *St-Julien AC, 2ème Cru Classé, Haut-Médoc, Bordeaux, France* One of the largest ST-JULIEN estates. Until the 1970s these wines were classic, cedary St-Juliens; since the early 80s, the wines have been darker, richer and coated with new oak, yet inclined to exhibit an unnerving feral quality. Recent vintages have mostly combined considerable power with finesse, despite disappointments in 02 and 03. Second wine: Sarget de Gruaud-Larose. Best years: 2007 06 05 **04 01 00 99 98 96 95 90 89 88**.

GRÜNER VELTLINER Austrian grape, also grown in the Czech Republic, Slovakia and Hungary. It is at its best in Austria's KAMPTAL, KREMSTAL and the WACHAU, where the soil and cool climate bring out all the lentilly, white-peppery aromas. Styles vary from light and tart to savoury, mouthfilling yet appetizing wines equalling the best in Europe.

GUELBENZU *Spain* Family-owned bodega making good Azul★, from Tempranillo, Cabernet and Merlot, and rich, concentrated Cabernet Sauvignon-based Evo★. Lautus★★, from old vines, incorporates Garnacha in the blend. Guelbenzu has estates in both NAVARRA and ARAGON; the wines are non-DO and are labelled as Vinos de la Tierra Ribera del Queiles. Best years: (Evo) (2006) 05 **04 03 01 00 99 98**.

GUIGAL *Côte-Rôtie AC, Rhône Valley, France* Marcel Guigal is the most internationally famous name in the RHÔNE, producing wines from his own vineyards in COTE-ROTIE under the Ch. d'Ampuis★★★ label as well as Dom. de Bonserine★ (La Garde★★) and the Guigal range from purchased grapes (Côte-Rôtie Brune et Blonde is ★★ since 1998). La Mouline, La Turque and La Landonne all rate ★★★ in most critics' opinions. Well, I have definitely had profound wines from La Landonne and La Mouline, and to my surprise and delight the considerable new oak aging had not dimmed the Côte-Rôtie beauty and fragrance. However, Guigal is uniquely talented; lesser producers using this amount of new oak rarely manage to save the balance of the wine. CONDRIEU★★ (la Doriane★★★) is wonderfully fragrant. Red and white HERMITAGE★★ are also good, ST-JOSEPH★★ improving, as are the good-value red and white COTES DU RHÔNE★, chunky GIGONDAS★ and bright, full TAVEL rosé. Best years: (top reds) 2007 06 05 04 03 **01 00 99 98 97 95 94 91 90 89 88 85 83 82 78**.

CH. GUIRAUD★★ *Sauternes AC, 1er Cru Classé, Bordeaux, France* Since th
♀ 1980s this SAUTERNES estate has returned to the top-quality field. High
price reflects the fact that only the best grapes are selected and 50% new
oak used each year. New ownership from 2006. Keep best vintages fo
10 years or more. Second wine (dry): G de Guiraud. **Best years: 2007 06 0**
04 03 02 01 99 98 97 96 95 90 89 88.

GUNDERLOCH *Nackenheim, Rheinhessen, Germany*
♀ Fritz and Agnes Hasselbach's estate has become
one of Germany's best. Sensationally concentrated
and luscious Beerenauslese★★ and Trocken-
beerenauslese★★★ dessert Rieslings are expensive
for RHEINHESSEN, but worth it. Dry and off-dry
Rieslings, at least ★, however, are good value.
Late-harvest Spätlese and Auslese are ★★ year in,
year out. **Best years: (2008)** 07 06 **05 04 03 02 01 00**
99 98 97 95.

GUNDERLOCH

2004

Nackenheim
ROTHENBERG
Riesling Auslese

GUNDLACH-BUNDSCHU *Sonoma Valley AVA, California, USA* Family-owne
♒ winery, founded in 1858. From the Rhinefarm estate vineyards com
outstanding juicy, fruity Cabernet Sauvignon★★, rich and tightl
structured Merlot★★, Zinfandel★ and Pinot Noir★. Whites includ
Chardonnay★, attractive Riesling and dramatic dry Gewürztraminer★★
The Bundschu family also operates the boutique winery Bartholome
Park, which specializes in Cabernet blends.

FRITZ HAAG *Braneberg, Mosel, Germany* MOSEL grower with vineyards in th
♀ BRAUNEBERGer Juffer and Juffer Sonnenuhr. Pure, elegant Rieslings at leas
★★ quality, Auslese and above often reaching ★★★. **Best years: (2008) 0**
06 05 **04 03 02 01 99 98 97 96.**

REINHOLD HAART *Piesport, Mosel, Germany* Theo Haart produces sensa
♀ tional Rieslings – with blackcurrant, peach and citrus aromas – from th
great Piesporter Goldtröpfchen vineyard. Ausleses are often ★★★
Wines from his vineyards in Wintrich can be bargains. **Best years: (2008**
07 06 05 **04 02 01 99 98 97 96.**

HAMILTON RUSSELL VINEYARDS *Hemel en Aarde Valley WO, South Afric*
♒ Well-established WALKER BAY property focusing on Pinot Noir an
Chardonnay. Pinot Noir★★ is broad-shouldered and delicately scentec
while Chardonnay★★ is minerally and exciting, though 2007 i
unusually showy. Two separate operations, Southern Right an
Ashbourne, focus on Pinotage (Ashbourne★), while Southern Righ
Sauvignon Blanc★ is zingy and easy-drinking. **Best years: (Pinot Noi**
(2008) 07 **06 05 04 03 02 01 00 99**; (Chardonnay) 2008 07 **06 05 04 03 0**
01 00 99.

HANDLEY *Mendocino County, California, USA* Outstanding producer c
♒ sparkling wines, including one of California's best Brut Rosés★
Aromatic Gewürztraminer★★ and Riesling★★ are among the state
finest. Two bottlings of Chardonnay, from the DRY CREEK VALLEY★ an
ANDERSON VALLEY★, are worth seeking out. The Anderson Valley esta
Pinot Noirs (regular★, Reserve★★) are in a lighter, more subtle style.
new Syrah★ is excellent and Brightlighter White is a terrifi
Gewürztraminer-based blend. **Best years: (Pinot Noir Reserve) (2005) 04 0**
01 00 99.

HANGING ROCK *Macedon Ranges, Victoria, Australia* Highly individual, guts
♒ sparkling wine Macedon Cuvée★★ (stunning late-disgorge
Cuvée★★★) stands out at John and Ann (née TYRRELL) Ellis's ultra-cool

climate vineyard high in the Macedon Ranges. Tangy estate-grown 'The Jim Jim' Sauvignon Blanc★★ is mouthwatering stuff, while HEATHCOTE Shiraz★★ is the best red.

HARAS DE PIRQUE *Maipo, Chile* Located in Pirque, a sub-region of MAIPO in the foothills of the Andes, this winery has steadily grown in stature since production started in 2000. Elegance★★, a dense and spicy Cabernet Sauvignon, leads the portfolio. Character★★, another Cabernet, is equally impressive, though more approachable. A great discovery for Chilean Cabernet lovers. Savoury Albis is a joint venture with Italy's ANTINORI.

HARDYS *McLaren Vale, South Australia* Despite the takeover of BRL Hardy by American giant Constellation, wines under the Hardys flagship label so far still taste reassuringly Australian. Varietals (especially Shiraz and Grenache) under the Nottage Hill label are among Australia's most reliably good gluggers. Top of the tree are the Eileen Hardy Shiraz★★★ and Thomas Hardy Cabernet★★★, both dense reds for hedonists. Eileen Hardy Chardonnay★★ is more elegant, tightly structured and focused than it used to be. Best years: (Eileen Hardy Shiraz) (2008) (06) 05 04 03 02 01 00 **98 97 96 95 93**.

HAREWOOD *Great Southern, Western Australia* James Kellie made a name for himself as white winemaker for HOWARD PARK before his family purchased one of Denmark's finest vineyards, Harewood Estate. His portfolio now shows evidence of Kellie's knowledge of the GREAT SOUTHERN and his winemaking skill, especially with opulent Cabernet Sauvignon★★, gutsy yet silky smooth Frankland River Shiraz★★, intense, zesty Riesling★ and elegant single-vineyard Denmark Chardonnay★.

HARLAN ESTATE *Oakville AVA, California, USA* Estate in the western hills of OAKVILLE, whose BORDEAUX blend has become one of California's most sought-after reds. Full-bodied and robustly tannic, Harlan Estate★★★ offers layers of ripe black fruits and heaps of new French oak. Dense but thrilling upon release, the wine is built to develop for 10 years.

HARTENBERG ESTATE *Stellenbosch WO, South Africa* Shiraz is the prime performer at this Bottelary Hills winery. Regular Shiraz★ is fleshy and accessible, while two flagships, The Stork★ and single-vineyard Gravel Hill★★, reflect the soils they grow in. Merlot★ and Cabernet also perform well, but The Mackenzie Cabernet-Merlot blend★ tops both. Whites include a pair of Chardonnays (standard, and refined, complex The Eleanor★) and an off-dry, limy Riesling★. Best years: (premium reds) 2006 **05 04 03 02 01 00 98**.

HARTFORD FAMILY *Russian River Valley AVA, California, USA* Owned by Jess Jackson (of KENDALL-JACKSON). Very limited production wines from RUSSIAN RIVER, Green Valley and SONOMA COAST fruit bear the Hartford Court label. Pinot Noirs include the massive Arrendell Vineyard★★★. Seascape Vineyard Chardonnay★★ has textbook cool-climate intensity and acidity. Hartford label wines are blended from various sources. Sonoma Coast bottlings of Chardonnay★ and Pinot Noir★ are deeply flavoured and good value. Old-vine Zinfandels include Fanucchi-Wood Road★★, Highwire★, Dina's★, Jolene's★ and Russian River Valley★.

ARTWELL *Stags Leap District AVA, Napa Valley, California, USA* Wine collector Bob Hartwell has been producing a gloriously fruity and elegant Cabernet Sauvignon★★ from his small vineyard in the STAGS LEAP DISTRICT since 1993. Equally supple Merlot★★ and lower-priced Misté Hill★ Cabernet. Best years: (Cabernet Sauvignon) 2005 03 02 **01 00 99 98 97 96 94**.

HATTENHEIM *Rheingau, Germany* RHEINGAU village with 13 vineyard sites
including a share of the famous Marcobrunn vineyard. Best producers:
Barth★, Lang, Langwerth von Simmern★, SCHLOSS REINHARTSHAUSEN★★
Schloss Schönborn★. Best years: (2008) 07 06 05 **04 03 02 01 99**.

CH. HAUT-BAGES-LIBÉRAL★ *Pauillac AC, 5ème Cru Classé, Haut-Médoc*
Bordeaux, France Little-known PAUILLAC property that has quietly been
gathering plaudits for some years now: loads of unbridled delicious fruit
a positively hedonistic style – and its lack of renown keeps the price just
about reasonable. The wines will age well, especially the latest vintages.
Best years: 2006 05 **04 03 02 01 00 99 98 96 95 94 90 89**.

CH. HAUT-BAILLY★ *Pessac-Léognan AC, Cru Classé de Graves, Bordeaux, France*
Traditionally one of the softest and most charming of the PESSAC-LEOGNAN
Classed Growths, and on good form during the 1990s. New ownership
from 1998 has produced erratic returns so far, some wines being too
tough, some being almost milky soft, some being delicious (2000
onward). Drinkable early, but ages well. Second wine: la Parde-de-Haut
Bailly. Best years: 2007 06 05 **04 03 02 01 00 99 98 95 90 89 88 86**.

CH. HAUT-BATAILLEY★ *Pauillac AC, 5ème Cru Classé, Haut-Médoc, Bordeaux*
France This estate has produced too many wines that are light
attractively spicy, but rarely memorable. Owner François-Xavier Borie o
GRAND-PUY-LACOSTE is changing this and from 2004 the wines have shown
improvement, becoming distinctly more substantial. Best years: 2007 06 0
04 03 02 01 00 98 96 95 90 89.

CH. HAUT-BRION *Pessac-Léognan AC, 1er Cru Classé, Graves, Bordeaux, France*
This property's excellent gravel-based vineyard is now part of Bordeaux
suburbs. The red wine★★★ almost always deserves its status. There
also a small amount of white★★★ which, at its best, is magically rich ye
marvellously dry, blossoming out over 5–10 years. Second wine: (red) L
Clarence de Haut-Brion (Bahans-Haut-Brion until 2007). Best year
(red) 2007 06 05 04 **03 02 01 00 99 98 97 96 95 94 93 90 89 88**; (white) 200
06 **05 04 03 02 01 00 98 96 95**.

CH. HAUT-MARBUZET★★ *St-Estèphe AC, Haut-Médoc, Bordeaux, France*
Impressive ST-ESTEPHE wine worthy of classification with great, rich
mouthfilling blasts of flavour and lots of new oak. Best years: 2007 06 0
04 03 02 01 00 99 98 96 95 94 90 89 88 86.

HAUT-MÉDOC AC *Bordeaux, France* The finest gravelly soil is here in th
southern half of the MEDOC peninsula; this AC covers all the decen
vineyard land not included in the 6 village ACs (MARGAUX, MOULIS, LISTRA
ST-JULIEN, PAUILLAC and ST-ESTÈPHE). Wines vary in quality and style. Bes
producers: d'Agassac★, Belgrave★, Belle-Vue★, Bernadotte★, Cambon
Pelouse★, Camensac, CANTEMERLE★, Charmail★, Cissac★, Citran★, Coufran,
LAGUNE★, Lanessan★, Malescasse★, Maucamps★, Peyrabon★, Sénéjac
SOCIANDO-MALLET★★, la Tour-Carnet★, Tour-du-Haut-Moulin★, Villegeorge
Best years: 2007 06 **05 04 03 02 01 00 99 98 96 95 94 90 89 88 86 85**.

HAUTES-CÔTES DE BEAUNE AC See BOURGOGNE-HAUTES-COTES DE BEAUNE A
HAUTES-CÔTES DE NUITS AC See BOURGOGNE-HAUTES-COTES DE NUITS A

HAWKES BAY *North Island, New Zealand* New Zealand's second largest an
one of its most prestigious wine regions. Plenty of sunshine, moderate
predictable weather during ripening and a complex array of soils make it ide
for a range of wine styles. Traditionally known for Cabernet Sauvignon an
particularly, Merlot, it has recently produced some superb Syrahs. Free
draining Gimblett Gravels is the outstanding area, followed by the Ngatara

Triangle. Best producers: Alpha Domus★, Bilancia★, CHURCH ROAD★, Clearview★, COOPERS CREEK★, CRAGGY RANGE★★, Esk Valley★★, Matariki★, MATUA VALLEY★, MORTON ESTATE★, Newton Forrest★ (Cornerstone★★), NGATARAWA★, Paritua★, C J PASK★, Sacred Hill★, SILENI★, Stonecroft★, Te Awa★, TE MATA★, TRINITY HILL★★, Unison★★, Vidal★★, VILLA MARIA★. Best years: (premium reds) (2008) 07 **04 02 00**.

HEATHCOTE *Central Victoria, Australia*   This wine region's unique feature is the deep russet Cambrian soil, formed more than 600 million years ago, which is found on the best sites and is proving ideal for Shiraz. Jasper Hill★★★, Heathcote Winery★, Red Edge★ and Wild Duck Creek★ are the best of the long-established vineyards, while BROWN BROTHERS and TYRRELL'S (Rufus Stone★★ is outstanding) have extensive new plantings. Heathcote Estate★★ is a brilliant newcomer. Best years: (Shiraz) 2008 06 05 04 03 **02 01 00** 97 96 95 94 91 90.

HECHT & BANNIER *Languedoc, France*   An exciting partnership of two Dijon wine marketing graduates, Gregory Hecht and François Bannier. They are selecting and aging some rich, finely crafted wines from FAUGÈRES★, ST-CHINIAN★, MINERVOIS★ and COTES DU ROUSSILLON-VILLAGES★.

HEDGES *Columbia Valley AVA, Washington State, USA*   Top wines here are Cabernet-Merlot blends using fruit from prime Red Mountain AVA vineyards: Three Vineyards★ is powerful and ageworthy, with bold tannins but plenty of cassis fruit; Red Mountain Reserve★ shows more polish and elegance. Red CMS★ (Cabernet-Merlot-Syrah) and crisp white CMS (Chardonnay-Marsanne-Sauvignon) form the bulk of the production. Best years: (top reds) (2007) 06 05 **04 03 02 01**.

DR HEGER *Ihringen, Baden, Germany*   Joachim Heger specializes in powerful, dry Grauburgunder (Pinot Gris)★★, Weissburgunder (Pinot Blanc)★ and Spätburgunder (Pinot Noir)★, with Riesling a sideline in this warm climate. Winklerberg Grauburgunder★★ is serious stuff, while his ancient Yellow Muscat vines deliver powerful dry wines★ and rare but fabulous TBAs★★. Wines from rented vineyards are sold under the Weinhaus Joachim Heger label. Best years: (white) (2008) 07 **05 04 03 02 01 00**.

CHARLES HEIDSIECK *Champagne AC, Champagne, France*   Charles Heidsieck, owned by Rémy Cointreau, is the most consistently fine of all the major houses, with vintage★★★ Champagne declared only in the very best years. The non-vintage★★, marked with a bottling date (for example, Mis en Cave en 2004), is regularly of vintage quality; these age well for at least 5 years. Best years: 2000 **96 95 90** 89 88 85 82.

HEITZ CELLAR *Napa Valley AVA, California, USA*   Star attraction here is the Martha's Vineyard Cabernet Sauvignon★★. Many believe that early bottlings of Martha's Vineyard are among the best wines ever produced in CALIFORNIA. After 1992, phylloxera forced replanting; although bottling only resumed in 1996, the 1997 vintage was exceptional and set the tone for the modern era. Heitz also produces Trailside Vineyard Cabernet★, Bella Oaks Vineyard Cabernet★ and a NAPA Cabernet★ that takes time to understand but can be good. Grignolino Rosé is an attractive picnic wine. Best years: (Martha's Vineyard) 2004 03 02 **97 96 92 91 86 85** 75 74.

HENRIOT *Champagne AC, Champagne, France*   In 1994 Joseph Henriot bought back the name of his old-established family company. Henriot CHAMPAGNES have a limpid clarity, and no Pinot Meunier is used. The range includes non-vintage Brut Souverain★, Blanc Souverain and Rosé Brut★, vintage Brut★★, Rosé and de luxe Cuvée des Enchanteleurs★★. Best years: 2000 98 96 **95 90** 89 88 85.

HENRIQUES & HENRIQUES *Madeira DOC, Madeira, Portugal* The wines t⊳ look for are the 10-year-old★★ and 15-year-old★★ versions of th⊳ classic varieties. Vibrant Sercial and Verdelho, and rich Malmsey an⊳ Bual are all fine examples of their styles. Henriques & Henriques also ha⊳ vintage Madeiras★★★ of extraordinary quality.

HENRY OF PELHAM *Niagara Peninsula VQA, Ontario, Canada* A pioneer o⊳ *vinifera* wines in this region. Best are Reserve Chardonnay★, Spec⊳ Family Reserve Riesling★, Riesling Icewine★ and a Cabernet-Merlo⊳ blend.

HENSCHKE *Eden Valley, South Australia* Fifth-generation winemaker Stephe⊳ Henschke and his viticulturist wife Prue make some of Australia⊳ grandest reds from old vines: HILL OF GRACE★★★ is stunning. Moun⊳ Edelstone Shiraz★★★, Tappa Pass Shiraz★★, Cyril Henschk⊳ Cabernet★★, Johann's Garden Grenache★, and Shiraz blends Henry⊳ Seven★ and Keyneton Estate★ are also top wines. The whites have lifte⊳ in recent years, led by the seductive, perfumed Julius Riesling★★, toast⊳ yet fruity Louis Semillon★★ and Croft Chardonnay★. **Best years:** (Mour⊳ Edelstone) (2008) (07) 06 05 04 02 **01 99 96 94 92 91 90 88 86**.

HÉRAULT, VIN DE PAYS DE L' *Languedoc, France* A huge region, coverin⊳ the entire Hérault *département*. Red wines predominate, based o⊳ Carignan, Grenache and Cinsaut, and most of the wine is sold in bul⊳ But things are changing. There are lots of hilly vineyards with grea⊳ potential, and MAS DE DAUMAS GASSAC followed by GRANGE DES PERES an⊳ Gérard Depardieu's Référence are making waves internationally. White⊳ are improving, too. The better-known Oc is often used in preference t⊳ Hérault. **Best producers:** Bosc★, Capion★, la Fadèze, GRANGE DES PERES★★, Jan⊳ Limbardié★, Marfée, MAS DE DAUMAS GASSAC★.

HERMITAGE AC *Rhône Valley, France* Great Hermitage, from a steep, ofte⊳ granite, vineyard above the town of Tain l'Hermitage in the norther⊳ RHONE, is revered throughout the world as a rare, rich red wine⊳ expensive, memorable and classic. Not all Hermitage achieves such a⊳ exciting blend of flavours, but the best growers, with mature red Syra⊳ vines, can create superbly original wine, needing 5–10 years' aging eve⊳ in a light year and a minimum of 15 years in a ripe vintage. Whit⊳ Hermitage, from Marsanne and Roussanne, is less famous but the bes⊳ wonderfully rich wines, made by traditionalists, can outlive the red⊳ sometimes lasting as long as 40 years. **Best producers:** A Belle⊳ CHAPOUTIER★★, J-L CHAVE★★★, Y Chave★, Colombier★, COLOMBO★⊳ DELAS★, B Faurie★★, L Fayolle★, Ferraton★, GUIGAL★★, JABOULE⊳ Remizières★, J-M Sorrel★, M Sorrel★★, TAIN co-op★★, Tardieu-Laurent★⊳ les Vins de Vienne★★. **Best years:** (reds) 2007 06 05 04 **03 01 00 99 98 97 9⊳ 95 94 91 90 89 88 85 83 78**.

THE HESS COLLECTION *Mount Veeder AVA, California, USA* Known fo⊳ powerful MOUNT VEEDER Cabernet Sauvignon★ – but after a change i⊳ winemaking direction, recent vintages lack polish and balance; Moun⊳ Veeder Mountain Cuvée★ is better. Hess Estate Cabernet★ is good valu⊳ Chardonnay★ is ripe with tropical fruit and balanced oak. Vineyard⊳ designated NAPA Chardonnay★ and Cabernet★ can be good. Budget labe⊳ Hess Select. **Best years:** (Cabernet) 2003 **01 00 99 98 97 96 95 94 91 90**.

HESSISCHE BERGSTRASSE *Germany* A small (436ha/1070-acre), war⊳ region near Darmstadt. Lovely Eiswein★★ is made by the Staatsweingu⊳ Simon-Bürkle★ is reliable too. Riesling is still the most prized grape.

HEYL ZU HERRNSHEIM *Nierstein, Rheinhessen, Germany* Organic estate whose main strength is substantial dry whites from Riesling, Weissburgunder (Pinot Blanc) and Silvaner. Auslese and higher Prädikat wines are usually of ★★ – and sometimes ★★★ – quality. Only wines from the top sites (Brudersberg, Pettental, Rothenberg) carry the vineyard designation. Quality had slipped, but new owner Detlev Meyer seems keen to restore its reputation. Best years: (2008) 07 06 05 **04 03 02 01 99 98**.

HEYMANN-LÖWENSTEIN *Winningen, Mosel, Germany* A leading estate of the Lower MOSEL. Its dry Rieslings are unusually full-bodied for the region; those from the Röttgen and Uhlen sites often reach ★★. Not all vintages age well. Also powerful Auslese★★. Best years: (2008) 07 06 **05 04 03 02 01**.

HIDALGO *Jerez y Manzanilla DO, Andalucía, Spain* Hidalgo's Manzanilla La Gitana★★ is deservedly one of the best-selling manzanillas in Spain. Hidalgo is family-owned, and only uses grapes from its own vineyards. Brands include Mariscal★, Fino Especial and Miraflores, Amontillado Napoleon★★, Oloroso Viejo★★ and Jerez Cortado★★.

HILL OF GRACE★★★ *Eden Valley, South Australia* A stunning wine with dark, exotic flavours made by HENSCHKE from a single plot of Shiraz. The Hill of Grace vineyard was first planted in the 1860s, and the old vines produce a powerful, structured wine with superb ripe fruit, chocolate, coffee, earth, leather and the rest. Can be cellared for 20 years or more. Best years: (2008) (07) (06) (05) 04 02 01 99 98 **97 96 95 94 93 92 91 90 88 86**.

HILLTOP *Neszmély, Hungary* Under chief winemaker Akos Kamocsay, this winery provides fresh, bright wines, especially white, at friendly prices. Indigenous varieties such as Irsai Olivér and Cserszegi Füszeres line up with Gewürztraminer, Sauvignon Blanc★, Pinot Gris and Chardonnay. Hilltop also produces a good but controversial TOKAJI.

HILLTOPS *New South Wales, Australia* Promising high-altitude cherry-growing region with a small but fast-growing area of vineyards around the town of Young. Good potential for reds from Cabernet Sauvignon and Shiraz. Best producers: Chalkers Crossing, Grove Estate, MCWILLIAM'S/Barwang★, Woodonga Hill.

FRANZ HIRTZBERGER *Wachau, Niederösterreich, Austria* Highly consistent quality for many years. The finest wines are the concentrated, elegant Smaragd Rieslings from Singerriedel★★★ and Hochrain★★. The best Grüner Veltliner comes from Honivogl★★★. Best years: (Riesling Smaragd) (2008) 07 06 **05 04 03 02 01 00 99 98 97**.

HOCHHEIM *Rheingau, Germany* Village best known for having given the English the word 'Hock' for Rhine wine, but with good individual vineyard sites, especially Domdechaney, Hölle (hell!) and Kirchenstück. Best producers: Joachim Flick, Hupfeld, Franz KUNSTLER★★, Werner★. Best years: (2008) 07 06 05 **04 03 02 01 99 98**.

HOLLICK *Coonawarra, South Australia* Ian Hollick makes a broader range of good wines than is usually found in COONAWARRA: irresistible sparkling Merlot★ (yes, Merlot), subtle Chardonnay★, tobaccoey Cabernet-Merlot★ and richer Ravenswood Cabernet Sauvignon★★. Tight, peppery Shiraz from Wrattonbully. Also attractive Sauvignon-Semillon and good limy Riesling★. Best years: (Ravenswood) (2006) 05 02 **01 99 98 96 94 93 91 90 88**.

HORTON VINEYARDS *Virginia, USA* Horton's Viognier★ established VIRGINIA's potential as a wine region and ignited a rush of wineries wanting to make the next CONDRIEU. Innovations include a sparkling

Viognier and varietals such as Tannat and Petit Manseng. The Caberne
Franc★ is consistently among the best red wines of the eastern US.

DOM. DE L'HORTUS *Pic St-Loup, Coteaux du Languedoc AC, Languedoc, Franc*
One of PIC ST-LOUP's pioneering estates. Bergerie de l'Hortus★, a ready-
to-drink unoaked Syrah-Mourvèdre-Grenache blend, has delightfu
flavours of herbs, plums and cherries. Big brother Grande Cuvée★★
needs time for the fruit and oak to come into harmony. The whit
Grande Cuvée★ is a Chardonnay-Viognier-Roussanne blend. Best years
(Grande Cuvée red) (2008) 07 06 05 04 **03 01 00.**

HOSPICES DE BEAUNE *Côte de Beaune, Burgundy, France* Scene of
theatrical auction on the third Sunday in November each year, now
under the auspices of Christie's, the Hospices is an historic foundation
which sells the wine of the new vintage from its holdings in the CÔTE D'O
to finance its charitable works. Pricing reflects charitable status rathe
than common sense, but the auction trend is regarded as an indicator c
which way the market is heading. Much depends on the Hospices
winemaking, which has been variable, as well as on the maturation an
bottling which are in the hands of the purchaser of each lot.

CH. L'HOSPITALET *La Clape, Coteaux du Languedoc AC, Languedoc, Franc*
With his purchase of this domaine, Gérard Bertrand has entered the bi
time in the Languedoc. Best wines are red and white La CLAPE★ and re
and white Vin de Pays d'OC, Cigalus★★. He also has vineyards i
MINERVOIS, CORBIÈRES and LIMOUX. Best years: (2008) 07 06 05 04 **03 01.**

HOUGHTON *Swan District, Western Australia* WESTERN AUSTRALIA's bigges
winery, now owned by Constellation, sources fruit from its ow
outstanding vineyards (unbelievably, many of these are currently for sale
and from growers in premium regions. The budget-priced 'Stripe' rang
includes the flavoursome White Classic★ (formerly White Burgundy, o
HWB in the EU), good Sauvignon Blanc-Semillon★, Chardonnay an
Cabernet. Moondah Brook Cabernet Sauvignon★★ and Shiraz★★ are
leap up in quality and even better value. The regional range has bee
rebadged as Wisdom: a Great Southern Riesling★★; Shiraz★★ fror
Frankland River; a MARGARET RIVER Cabernet★★; and some of the bes
wines yet seen from the emerging PEMBERTON region – sublime funk
Chardonnay★★, pure, taut Sauvignon Blanc★★. Opulent, dense ye
elegant Gladstones Cabernet★★★ from Margaret River and powerfu
lush Jack Mann Cabernet Sauvignon★★★ from Frankland River hav
also contributed to Houghton's burgeoning profile. Best years: (Jack Mann
(2008) (07) (05) 04 **01 99 98 96 95 94.**

HOWARD PARK *Margaret River, Western Australia* Howard Park has i
headquarters, a winery and the Leston vineyard in MARGARET RIVER: in th
GREAT SOUTHERN there is a winery at Denmark
and the 41ha (100-acre) Scotsdale vineyard in
Porongurup planted in 2005 to Chardonnay,
Riesling, Sauvignon Blanc and Pinot Noir.
The classic Cabernet Sauvignon-Merlot★★★
(now known as the Abercrombie) has leapt up
a notch in recent vintages. Also impressive are
the occasional Best Barrels Merlot★★,
intense, floral Riesling★★ and supremely
classy Chardonnay★★. Highlights of the
regional range are the exciting Scotsdale
Shiraz★★ and elegant Leston Cabernet★★,

which are among the best examples of these varieties produced in Western Australia. The more affordable MadFish label is good for Riesling★, Shiraz★, Sauvignon-Semillon★ and unwooded Chardonnay★. Exquisite Chardonnay and Pinot Noir under the super-premium Marchand & Burch label. Best years: (Cabernet) (2007) 05 04 **03 02** 01 99 96 94 92 91 90 88 86; (Riesling) 2008 **06 05** 04 03 02 01 97 95 92 91 89 86.

HOWELL MOUNTAIN AVA *Napa Valley, California, USA* NAPA's north-eastern corner is noted for powerhouse Cabernet Sauvignon and Zinfandel as well as exotic, full-flavoured Merlot. Best producers: BERINGER (Merlot★★), DUNN★★★, La Jota★★, Ladera★★, Liparita★, PINE RIDGE (Cabernet Sauvignon★), Viader★★, White Cottage★★. Best years: (reds) 2005 03 **02** 01 00 **99** 98 97 96 95 94 91 90.

HUADONG WINERY *Shandong Province, China* The first producer of varietal and vintage wines in China, Huadong has received massive foreign investment as well as state support. Money, however, can't change the climate, and excessive moisture from the summer rainy season causes problems. Even so, Riesling and Chardonnay (under the Tsingtao label) are not at all bad and Cabernet Sauvignon and Chardonnay in special 'feng shui' bottles are pretty tasty.

HUET *Vouvray AC, Loire Valley, France* Complex, traditional VOUVRAY that can age for decades. Biodynamic methods are bringing into even sharper focus the individual traits of its three excellent sites – le Haut-Lieu, Clos du Bourg and le Mont. These yield dry★★, medium-dry★★★ or sweet★★★ wines, depending on the vintage – in 2006, 2007 and 2008 the emphasis is on drier wines, including base wines for its very good Vouvray Mousseux★★. Best years: (sec, demi-sec) 2008 07 **06**; (moelleux) 2005 04 **03** 02 **01 00 99 98 97 96 95 90 89.**

HUGEL *Alsace AC, Alsace, France* Best wines are sweet ALSACE Vendange Tardive★★ and Sélection de Grains Nobles★★★. Big-volume Tradition wines can be dull, but Jubilee wines are often ★★. Best years: (Vendange Tardive Riesling) (2008) 07 05 03 01 00 98 97 96 95 90 89 88.

HUNTER VALLEY *New South Wales, Australia* NEW SOUTH WALES' oldest wine zone overcomes a tricky climate to make fascinating, ageworthy Semillon and rich, buttery Chardonnay. Shiraz is the mainstay for reds, aging well but often developing a leathery overtone; Cabernet is occasionally successful. Premium region is the Lower Hunter Valley; the Upper Hunter has few wineries but extensive vineyards. Best producers: Allandale★, Audrey Wilkinson, BROKENWOOD★★, Capercaillie, De Iuliis★, Hope★, Lake's Folly★, Margan Family, Mount Pleasant★★/MCWILLIAM'S, Meerea Park★, Oakvale, THOMAS★★, TOWER★, Tulloch, Keith Tulloch★, TYRRELL'S★★★. Best years: (Shiraz) 2007 06 04 03 02 **00 99 98 97 96 94** 91.

HUNTER'S *Marlborough, South Island, New Zealand* One of MARLBOROUGH's stars, with fine, if austere, Sauvignon★, savoury Burgundian Chardonnay★, vibrant Riesling★ and sophisticated Pinot Noir★. Also attractive Miru Miru fizz★. Best years: (Chardonnay) **2007 06 05 03.**

CH. DU HUREAU *Saumur-Champigny AC, Loire Valley, France* The Vatan family produces exemplary silky SAUMUR-CHAMPIGNY reds. The basic red★ is deliciously bright and fruity. Special cuvées Lisagathe★★ and Fevettes★★ need a bit of time. Jasmine-scented white SAUMUR★ is exceptional in top years. Decent fizz and occasional sweet Coteaux de Saumur, too. Best years: (top reds) (2008) 07 06 **05 04 03 02 99 97 96.**

INNISKILLIN *Niagara Peninsula VQA, Ontario, Canada* One of Canada's leading wineries, with good Pinot Noir★ and Cabernet Franc, well-rounded Chardonnay★ and rich Vidal Icewine★★, Cabernet Franc Icewine★, Riesling Icewine★ and Sparkling Vidal Icewine★. Another Inniskillin winery is in the OKANAGAN VALLEY in British Columbia. Best years: (Vidal Icewine) 2007 05 **04 03 02 00 99**.

IPHOFEN *Franken, Germany* Important wine town in FRANKEN for dry Riesling and Silvaner. Both are powerful, with a pronounced earthiness. Best producers: JULIUSSPITAL★, Johann Ruck★, Hans Wirsching★, Zehntkeller★. Best years: (2008) 07 06 **05 04 03 02 01 00 99**.

IRANCY AC *Burgundy, France* This northern outpost of vineyards, just south-west of CHABLIS, is an unlikely champion of the clear, pure flavour of the Pinot Noir grape. But red Irancy can be delicate and lightly touched by the ripeness of plums and strawberries, and can age well. Best producers: Bienvenu, J-M BROCARD, Cantin, A & J-P Colinot★, Delaloge, Patrice Fort★. Best years: (2008) 07 **06 05 03**.

IRON HORSE VINEYARDS *Sonoma County, California, USA* A pioneer of the Green Valley AVA, part of the RUSSIAN RIVER VALLEY. Outstanding sparkling wines, with vintage Brut★★ and Blanc de Blancs★★ delicious on release but highly suitable for aging. The Brut LD★★★ (Late Disgorged) is a heavenly mouthful – yeasty and complex. Wedding Cuvée★ blanc de noirs and Brut Rosé★ have been joined by Ultra Brut★ and Joy!★★, which is aged for 10–15 years before release.. Still wines include a lovely Pinot Noir★★, a stunningly fresh, crisp Chardonnay★★, a seductive Viognier★★ and a sensational Pinot Noir Rosé★.

IROULÉGUY AC *South-West France* The only Basque wines made in France. Tannat, usually blended with Cabernet Franc, gives fascinating, robust reds that are softer than MADIRAN. Whites are mainly from Petit Courbu. Best producers: Ameztia★, ARRETXEA★★, Brana★, Etxegaray, Ilarria★, Irouléguy co-op (Mignaberry★), Mourguy. Best years: (reds) (2008) 06 **04 02 01**.

ISOLE E OLENA *Chianti Classico DOCG, Tuscany, Italy* Paolo De Marchi has long been one of the pacesetters in CHIANTI CLASSICO. His Chianti Classico★★, characterized by clean, elegant and spicily perfumed fruit, excels in every vintage. The powerful SUPER-TUSCAN Cepparello★★★, made from 100% Sangiovese, is the top wine. Excellent Syrah★★, Cabernet Sauvignon★★★, Chardonnay★★ and VIN SANTO★★★. Best years: (Cepparello) (2008) (07) 06 **04 03 01 99 98 97 95 90 88**.

CH. D'ISSAN★ *Margaux AC, 3ème Cru Classé, Haut-Médoc, Bordeaux, France* This lovely moated property disappointed me far too often in the distant past, but pulled its socks up in the 1990s. When successful, the wine can be one of the most delicate and scented in the MARGAUX AC. Best years: 2007 06 05 **04 03 02 01** 00 **99 98 96 95 90 89**.

PAUL JABOULET AÎNÉ *Rhône Valley, France* During the 1970s, Jaboulet led the way in raising the world's awareness of the great quality of RHÔNE wines. Although many of the wines are still good, they are no longer the star in any appellation. Best wines are top red HERMITAGE La Chapelle (this was a ★★★ wine in its heyday) and whites La Chapelle★★ and Chevalier de Stérimberg★. CROZES-HERMITAGE Thalabert is of regular quality. Attractive CÔRNAS Dom. St-Pierre★, also CÔTES DU RHÔNE VILLAGES, reliable CÔTES DU RHONE Parallèle 45, good-value VENTOUX★ and sweet, perfumed MUSCAT DE BEAUMES-DE-VENISE★★. In January 2006 Jaboulet was bought by Swiss financier Jean-Jacques Frey, owner of

Ch. la LAGUNE. Best years: (La Chapelle) 2007 06 05 **04 03 01 99 98 97 96 95 94 91 90 89 88 78**.

ACKSON ESTATE *Marlborough, South Island, New Zealand* An established grapegrower with vineyards in MARLBOROUGH's most prestigious district. Sauvignon Blanc has regrettably changed from tangy to sweaty since 2007 (please go back to the old style), but barrel-fermented Grey Ghost Sauvignon Blanc★★ can improve with a little age; restrained Chardonnay and Pinot Noir. Best years: (Pinot Noir) **2007 06 05 04 03**.

ACKSON-TRIGGS *Okanagan Valley VQA, British Columbia, Canada* Top-flight reds (Cabernet Sauvignon-Shiraz★★, Shiraz★) and Riesling Icewine★ in the Grand Reserve range. Also the single-vineyard Sun Rock Shiraz★. There's another Jackson-Triggs estate in NIAGARA PENINSULA. Osoyoos Larose★★ is an excellent BORDEAUX blend made at the Jackson-Triggs facility for a joint-venture partnership between Canadian giant Vincor and French group Taillan.

ACOB'S CREEK *Barossa Valley, South Australia* Australia's leading export brand, selling more than 7 million cases a year, is owned by Pernod Ricard. The company is taking advantage of the strength of the Jacob's Creek name to rebrand wines formerly sold under the Orlando label, hence Jacob's Creek Steingarten Riesling★★ from Eden Valley, Jacob's Creek St Hugo Cabernet Sauvignon★ from COONAWARRA and rich Jacob's Creek Centenary Hill Shiraz★★ from the BAROSSA. Flagship reds remain Orlando Jacaranda Ridge Cabernet★ from Coonawarra and Orlando Lawson's Shiraz★★ from PADTHAWAY. Watch for new super-premium Jacob's Creek Johann Shiraz-Cabernet and Reeves Point Chardonnay. Jacob's Creek Reserve and Limited Release★★ wines are very good. Basic Jacob's Creek Cabernet and Semillon-Chardonnay seem stretched, but Riesling★ and Grenache-Shiraz are fine. Best years: (St Hugo) (2008) 05 **04 03 02 01 00 99 98 96 94 91 90 88 86**.

ACQUESSON *Champagne AC, Champagne, France* Top-class small producer of classic vintage Brut★★. Its non-vintage is an austerely-styled one-off that changes each year to produce the best possible blend. Cuvée No. 733★★ (the sixth version made), based on the 2005 harvest, was released in 2008. Superb single-vineyard, single-cru and single grape variety Champagnes from Avize Champ Caïn (Chardonnay)★★, Ay Vauzelle Terme (Pinot Noir)★★ and Dizy Corne Bautray (Chardonnay)★★ and a saignée pink fizz, Dizy Terres Rouges Rosé★★. Best years: (2002) 00 **97 96 95 93 90 89 88 85**.

OUIS JADOT *Beaune, Côte de Beaune, Burgundy, France* Ambitious merchant which has been expanding southward, especially in MOULIN-À-VENT (Ch. des Jacques★) and POUILLY-FUISSÉ (Jeandeau, Ferret★★). Top domaine whites from the CÔTE D'OR include PULIGNY-MONTRACHET Folatières★★ and CHEVALIER-MONTRACHET les Demoiselles★★★, while the reds range from attractive BEAUNE premiers crus★★ through to sumptuous GEVREY-CHAMBERTIN Clos St. Jacques★★ and CLOS ST-DENIS★★. Best years: (top reds) (2008) 07 06 05 03 **02 99 90**; (whites) (2008) 07 **06** 05 **04** 02.

AMET★★★ *Côte-Rôtie AC, Rhône Valley, France* Jean-Paul and Jean-Luc Jamet are two of the most talented growers of CÔTE-ROTIE, one of France's most famous red wine appellations. The full-bodied wines, from excellent vineyards on vertiginous slopes above the Rhône, led by the marvellous Côte Brune★★★, age well for a decade or more. Good, long-lived Syrah vin de pays★★ too. Best years: 2007 **06 05 04 03 01 00 99 98 97 96 95 91 90 89 88**.

JEREZ Y MANZANILLA DO/SHERRY

Andalucía, Spain

The Spanish now own the name outright. At least in th EU, and soon in Australia, South Africa and Californ following the signing of new treaties, the only wines th can be sold as sherry come from the triangle of vineyar land between the Andalusian towns of Jerez de Frontera (inland), and Sanlúcar de Barrameda and Puerto de San María (by the sea).

The best sherries can be spectacular. Three main factors contribute the high-quality potential of wines from this region: the chalky-spong albariza soil where the best vines grow, the Palomino Fino grape unexciting for table wines but potentially great once transformed by th sherry-making processes – and a natural yeast called flor. All sherry mu be a minimum of 3 years old, but fine sherries age in barrel for muc longer. Sherries must be blended through a solera system. About a thir of the wine from the oldest barrels is bottled, and the barrels topped with slightly younger wine from another set of barrels and so on, for minimum of 3 sets of barrels. The idea is that the younger wine takes the character of older wine, as well as keeping the blend refreshed.

MAIN SHERRY STYLES

Fino and manzanilla Fino sherries derive their extraordinary, tang pungent flavours from flor. Young, newly fermented wines destined f these styles of sherry are deliberately fortified very sparingly to ju 15–15.5% alcohol before being put in barrels for their minimum of years' maturation. The thin, soft, oatmeal-coloured mush of flor grow on the surface of the wines, protecting them from the air (and there keeping them pale) and giving them a characteristic sharp, pungent tan The addition of younger wine each year feeds the flor, maintaining even layer. Manzanillas are fino-style wines that have matured in th cooler seaside conditions of Sanlúcar de Barrameda, where the flor grow thickest and the fine, salty tang is most accentuated.

Amontillado True amontillados are fino sherries that have continued age after the flor has died (after about 5 years) and so finish their agi period in contact with air. These should all be bone dry. Medium-swe amontillados are concoctions in which the dry sherry is sweetened wi mistela, a blend of grape juice and alcohol.

Oloroso This type of sherry is strongly fortified after fermentation deter the growth of flor. Olorosos therefore mature in barrel in conta with the air, which gradually darkens them while they remain dry, b develop rich, intense, nutty and raisiny flavours.

Other styles Manzanilla pasada is aged manzanilla, with greater dep and nuttiness. Palo cortado is an unusual, deliciously nutty, dry sty somewhere in between amontillado and oloroso. Sweet oloroso crea and pale creams are almost without exception enriched solely for t export market. Sweet varietal wines are made from sun-dried Ped Ximénez or Moscatel.

See also individual producers.

BEST PRODUCERS AND WINES

Argüeso (Manzanilla San León, Manzanilla Fina Las Medallas).

BARBADILLO (Manzanilla Eva, Manzanilla En Rama, Manzanilla Solear, Amontillado Príncipe, Amontillado de Sanlúcar, Oloroso Seco Cuco, Palo Cortado Obispo Gascón).

Delgado Zuleta (Manzanilla Pasada La Goya).

Díez Mérito (Imperial Fino, Don Zoilo Imperial Amontillado, Victoria Regina Oloroso).

DOMECQ (Fino La Ina, Amontillado 51-1A, Sibarita Palo Cortado, Venerable Pedro Ximénez).

El Maestro Sierra.

Equipo Navazos (La Bota de…)

Garvey (Palo Cortado, Amontillado Tio Guillermo, Pedro Ximénez Gran Orden).

GONZALEZ BYASS (Tio Pepe Fino, Amontillado del Duque, Matusalem Oloroso Muy Viejo, Apóstoles Oloroso Viejo, Noé Pedro Ximénez, Oloroso Viejo de Añado).

HIDALGO (Manzanilla La Gitana, Manzanilla Pasada, Jerez Cortado, Amontillado Napoleon, Oloroso Viejo).

LUSTAU (Almacenista single-producer wines, East India Solera, Puerto Fino).

OSBORNE (Amontillado Coquinero, Fino Quinta, Oloroso Bailén, Oloroso Solera India, Pedro Ximénez).

Rey Fernando de Castilla.

Sánchez Romate (Pedro Ximénez Cardenal Cisneros).

Tradición.

VALDESPINO (Amontillado Coliseo, Amontillado Tio Diego, Amontillado Don Tomás, Palo Cortado Cardenal, Fino Inocente, Oloroso Don Gonzalo, Pedro Ximénez Niños).

Williams & Humbert (Pando Fino, Alegría Manzanilla).

JANUIK *Columbia Valley AVA, Washington State, USA* Before starting his own winery, Mike Januik oversaw operations at CHATEAU STE MICHELLE. His experience and knowledge of Washington's vineyards allow him to source fruit from exceptional sites. His Chardonnays (Elerding★ and Cold Creek★★) are among the top in the state. Lewis Vineyard Syrah★★ is rich, earthy and bold, and Cabernet Sauvignons (Champoux Vineyard★★ and Ciel du Cheval★★) are chocolaty, complex and ageworthy. Best years: (reds) (2007) 06 05 **04 03 02**.

JARDIN See JORDAN, South Africa.

JASNIÈRES AC *Loire Valley, France* Tiny AC north of Tours. Reputation for long-lived, bone-dry whites from Chenin Blanc, though new movers and shakers here and in neighbouring appellation Coteaux du Loir (which additionally makes delicate Pineau d'Aunis and Gamay reds) are picking Chenin riper. Sweet wine may be made in good years. Best producers: Bellivière★★, Le Briseau★, J Gigou★★, Les Maisons Rouges, J P Robinot★. Best years: (2008) 07 **05 04 03 02 01 99 97 96**.

JEREZ Y MANZANILLA DO/SHERRY See pages 178–9.

JERMANN *Friuli-Venezia Giulia, Italy* Silvio Jermann produces non-DOC Chardonnay★, Sauvignon Blanc★, Pinot Bianco★ and Pinot Grigio★. Deep, long-lived Vintage Tunina★★ is based on Sauvignon Chardonnay with Ribolla, Malvasia and Picolit. Barrel-fermented Chardonnay★★ is labelled, rather ungrammatically, 'Were dreams, now it is just wine'. Vinnae★ is based on Ribolla; Capo Martino★ is also a blend of local varieties. The wines are plump but pricey.

JOHANNISBERG *Rheingau, Germany* Probably the best known of all the Rhine wine villages, with 10 vineyard sites, including the famous Schloss Johannisberg. Best producers: Prinz von Hessen★, Johannishof★★, Schloss Johannisberg★, Trenz. Best years: (2008) 07 06 **05 04 03 02 01 99**.

KARL H JOHNER *Bischoffingen, Baden, Germany* Johner specializes in new oak-aged wines. The vividly fruity Pinot Noir★ and Pinot Blanc★ are excellent, the Chardonnay SJ★★ is one of Germany's best Chardonnays and the rich, silky Pinot Noir SJ★★ can be one of Germany's finest reds. Best years: (Pinot Noir SJ) (2008) 07 06 05 **04 03 02 01**.

JORDAN *Alexander Valley AVA, Sonoma County, California, USA* Ripe, fruity Cabernet Sauvignon★ with a cedar character rare in California. The winery has recently moved toward greater use of mountain-grown Cabernet. Chardonnay★ from RUSSIAN RIVER VALLEY fruit is nicely balanced. J★ fizz is an attractive mouthful, now made independently by Judy Jordan's J Wine Co.; J also makes top-notch Russian River Pinot Noir★. Best years: (Cabernet) 2005 04 03 02 **01 00 97 96 95 94 91 86**.

JORDAN *Stellenbosch WO, South Africa* Meticulously groomed hillside vineyards, with a variety of aspects and soils. Chardonnays (regular★★ with creamy/limy complexity; Nine Yards★★, dense, nutty, but balanced) and delicious peppery Chenin★ head a strong white range. Syrah★★, Cabernet Sauvignon★, Merlot★ and BORDEAUX-blend Cobblers Hill★★ are understated but beautifully balanced for aging. Sophia★ is a rich Bordeaux-blend red. Sold under the Jardin label in the USA. Best years: (Chardonnay) 2008 07 **06 05 04 03 02 01**; (Cobblers Hill) 2006 **05 04 03 02 01 00**.

TONI JOST *Bacharach, Mittelrhein, Germany* Peter Jost has put the MITTELRHEIN on the map. From the Bacharacher Hahn site come some delicious, racy Rieslings★; Auslese★★ adds creaminess without losing that pine-needly scent. Best years: (2008) 07 06 **05 04 03 02 01 99**.

JULIÉNAS AC *Beaujolais, Burgundy, France* One of the more northerly BEAUJOLAIS Crus, Juliénas is attractive, 'serious' Beaujolais which can be big and tannic enough to develop in bottle. Best producers: Coquard★, DUBOEUF (Château des Capitans★), D Desvignes★, Ch. de Juliénas★, J-P Margerand★, Pelletier★, B Santé★, M Tête★. Best years: **2008 07 06**.

JULIUSSPITAL *Würzburg, Franken, Germany* A 16th-century charitable foundation, with 170ha (420 acres) of vineyards, known for its dry wines – especially from IPHOFEN and WÜRZBURG. Look out for the Würzburger Stein wines, sappy Müller-Thurgau, grapefruity Silvaners★★ and petrolly Rieslings★★. Best years: (2008) 07 06 **05 04 03 02 01**.

JUMILLA DO *Murcia and Castilla-La Mancha, Spain* Jumilla's reputation is for brutal alcoholic reds, but dense, serious reds from Monastrell (Mourvèdre) show the region's potential. Very few whites. Best producers: Casa Castillo★★, Casa de la Ermita, Hijos de Juan Gil★, Luzón★, El Nido★★, Agapito Rico. Best years: (2007) 06 05 **04 03 01 00 99 98 96**.

JURA See ARBOIS, CHÂTEAU-CHALON, CÔTES DU JURA, CREMANT DU JURA, l'ETOILE.

JURANÇON AC *South-West France* The sweet white wine made from late-harvested and occasionally botrytized grapes can be heavenly, with floral, spicy, apricot-quince flavours. The lemony dry wine, Jurançon Sec, can be ageworthy. Best producers: Bellegarde★, Bordenave★, Bru-Baché★, Castera★, CAUHAPE★★, Clos Guirouilh★, Clos Lapeyre★★, Clos Thou★, CLOS UROULAT★★, Larrédya★, Souch★★. Best years: (sweet) (2007) **05 04 01 00 99 98 97**.

KAISERSTUHL *Baden, Germany* A 4000ha (10,000-acre) volcanic stump rising to 600m (2000ft) and overlooking the Rhine plain. Pinot varieties excel. Best producers: BERCHER★★, Dr HEGER★★, Karl H JOHNER★★, Franz Keller★, Königsschaffhausen co-op, Salwey★, Schneider★★. Best years: (dry whites) (2008) 07 **05 04 02 01 99**.

KAMPTAL *Niederösterreich, Austria* 3870ha (9560-acre) wine region centred on the town of Langenlois, making some impressive dry Riesling and Grüner Veltliner. Best producers: BRUNDLMAYER★★★, Ehn★★, Eichinger★, Hiedler★, Hirsch★, Jurtschitsch★, Fred Loimer★★, Schloss Gobelsburg★★, Topf. Best years: (2008) 07 06 **05 04 03 02 01 99**.

KANONKOP *Stellenbosch WO, South Africa* Winemaker Abrie Beeslaar is confidently creating traditional, long-lived red wines – now, thanks to virus-free vine material, often with brighter fruit. Muscular, savoury BORDEAUX-blend Paul Sauer★★ really does mature for 10 years or more. A straight Cabernet Sauvignon★ adds to this enviable red wine reputation: Pinotage★★, from 50-year-old vines, is indelibly associated with the estate. Best years: (Paul Sauer) 2005 04 **03 02 01 00 99 98 97 95 94 91**.

KARTHÄUSERHOF *Trier, Mosel-Saar-Ruwer, Germany* Top Ruwer estate which has gone from strength to strength under Christoph Tyrell and winemaker Ludwig Breiling. Rieslings combine aromatic extravagance with racy brilliance. Most wines are now ★★, some Auslese and Eiswein ★★★. Best years: (2008) 07 06 **05 04 03 02 01 99 97 94**.

KATNOOK ESTATE *Coonawarra, South Australia* Chardonnay★★ has consistently been the best of the fairly expensive whites, though Riesling★ and Sauvignon★★ are pretty tasty, too. Well-structured Cabernet Sauvignon★ and treacly Shiraz★ lead the reds, with Odyssey Cabernet Sauvignon★★ and Prodigy Shiraz★★ reaching a higher level. Best years: (Odyssey) (2008) (06) (05) 04 03 02 **01 00 99 98 97 96 94 92 91**.

KÉKFRANKOS See BLAUFRANKISCH.

KELLER *Flörsheim-Dalsheim, Rheinhessen, Germany* Klaus Keller and son Klaus-Peter are the leading winemakers in the hill country of RHEINHESSEN, away from the Rhine riverbank. They produce a range of varietal dry wines and naturally sweet Rieslings, as well as extra-special dry Rieslings★★ from the Dalsheimer Hubacker site. Astonishing TBA★★★ from Riesling and Rieslaner. Best years: (2008) 07 06 **05 04 03 02 01 99**.

KENDALL-JACKSON *Sonoma County, California, USA* Jess Jackson founded KJ in bucolic Lake County in 1982 after buying a vineyard there; now based in SONOMA COUNTY, with operations throughout the state, and producing about 4 million cases. Since the 2004 vintage, KJ's volume leader, the Vintner's Reserve Chardonnay (2 million cases) is made entirely from estate-grown fruit. Higher levels of quality are found in the Grand Reserve reds and whites, the vineyard-based Highland Estates★ series and the top-of-the-range Stature★★ (red meritage).

KENWOOD *Sonoma Valley AVA, California, USA* This winery has always represented very good quality at reasonable prices. The Sauvignon Blanc★ has floral and melon flavours with a slightly earthy finish. Long-lived Artist Series Cabernet Sauvignon★★ is the flagship, Jack London Zinfandel★★ is impressive, and RUSSIAN RIVER VALLEY Pinot Noir★ is superb value. Best years: (Zinfandel) 2005 04 **03 02 01 00 99 98 97 96 95 94**.

VON KESSELSTATT *Trier, Mosel, Germany* Good traditional Rieslings (★ to ★★) from some top sites at GRAACH (Josephshöfer) and PIESPORT in the MOSEL, Scharzhofberg in the Saar and Kasel in the Ruwer. Best years: (2008) 07 06 **05 04 03 02 01**.

KIEDRICH *Rheingau, Germany* Top vineyard here is the Gräfenberg, giving long-lived, mineral Rieslings. Other good sites are Sandgrub and Wasseros. Best producers: Prinz von Hessen, Knyphausen★, WEIL★★. Best years: (2008) 07 06 05 04 **02 01 99 98 97**.

KING ESTATE *Oregon USA* Over 400ha (1000 acres) are certified organic at the King Estate vineyard in Lorane, far south of the more popular WILLAMETTE VALLEY. A tremendous amount of time and money has been invested in this property, and the results are beginning to pay off. The Pinot Gris★ is first-rate. The Pinot Noirs have taken time to perfect but today The Signature Collection Pinot Noir★ is a powerful currant- and cassis-flavoured wine, and the Domaine Collection★ is a fine example of Oregon Pinot Noir. Best years: (reds) (2008) 07 06 **05 04**.

CH. KIRWAN★ *Margaux AC, 3ème Cru Classé, Haut-Médoc, Bordeaux, France* This MARGAUX estate has shown considerable improvement since the mid 1990s. Investment in the cellars, more attention to the vineyards and the advice of consultant Michel Rolland (until 2007) have produced wines of greater depth and power but less perfume. Second wine: Les Charmes de Kirwan. Best years: 2007 06 05 **04 03 01 00 99 98 96 95**.

KISTLER *Sonoma Valley AVA, California, USA* One of California's hottest Chardonnay producers, with wines from individual vineyards: Kistler Vineyard, Durell Vineyard and Dutton Ranch can be ★★★; McCrea Vineyard and ultra-cool-climate Camp Meeting Ridge Vineyard ★★. All possess great complexity and good aging potential. Also a number of single-vineyard Pinot Noirs★★ that go from good to very good. Best years: (Kistler Vineyard Chardonnay) 2006 **05 04 03 02 01 00 99 98 97**.

LEIN CONSTANTIA *Constantia WO, South Africa* Showpiece estate fast regaining deserved stature. The area's aptitude for white wines is reflected in crisp, nicely weighted Sauvignon Blanc★ (expressive, vibrant Perdeblokke★★ from a higher vineyard), good Chardonnay, excellent barrel-fermented white blend Madame Marlbrook★★, attractive and now much drier Riesling and Vin de Constance★★ (recent vintages ★★★), a thrilling Muscat dessert wine based on the 18th-century Constantia. In reds, Marlbrook, a Cabernet-led Bordeaux-style blend, is showing the benefit of clean, brighter fruit. Best years: (Vin de Constance) 2005 **04 02 01 00 99 98 97 96 95 94 93 92 91.**

NAPPSTEIN *Clare Valley, South Australia* Justin Langworthy, from the winemaking team at WYNNS, has taken over at Knappstein, revitalized under Lion Nathan's ownership. There are three outstanding single-vineyard wines from mature vines: Ackland Riesling★★★, Enterprise Cabernet★★ and Yertabulti Shiraz★★. The regular Riesling★★ is reliably good and Three★ intriguingly combines Gewürztraminer with Riesling and Pinot Gris. The Enterprise Brewery★ (established 1878) has been re-opened with refreshing results and will give Langworthy a chance to try his home-brewing skills in the commercial world. Best years: (Enterprise Cabernet Sauvignon) (2008) (06) 05 04 03 02 **01** 00 99 98.

NAPPSTEIN LENSWOOD VINEYARDS See RIPOSTE.

MMERICH KNOLL *Unterloiben, Wachau, Niederösterreich, Austria* Since the late 1970s, some of the greatest Austrian dry white wines. His rich, complex Riesling and Grüner Veltliner are packed with fruit and invariably ★★ quality, with versions from both the Loibenberg and Schütt sites ★★★. They repay keeping for 5 years or more. Best years: (Riesling Smaragd) (2008) 07 06 **05 04 03 02** 01 00 99 98 97 96.

OEHLER-RUPRECHT *Kallstadt, Pfalz, Germany* Bernd Philippi makes powerful, very concentrated dry Rieslings★★★ from the Kallstadter Saumagen site, oak-aged botrytized Elysium★ and Burgundian-style Spätburgunder (Pinot Noir)★. Best years: (Saumagen Riesling) (2008) 07 06 05 **04 03 02 01** 00 99 98.

LOOYONG *Mornington Peninsula, Victoria, Australia* Owned by the Gjergja family, who also have nearby Port Phillip Estate, and driven by the winemaking talents of Sandro Mosele. From 1995, 30ha (74 acres) at Kooyong were planted to Pinot Noir (the Haven★★★, Ferrous★★ and Meres★ Vineyards) and Chardonnay (the Faultline★★ and Farrago★★ Vineyards). Entry-level Clonale Chardonnay★ and Massale Pinot Noir★ show varietal character at bargain prices, while the Kooyong Estate Chardonnay★★ is structured, complex and restrained and the Estate Pinot Noir★★ needs time to show its seductive best.

LOIS KRACHER *Illmitz, Burgenland, Austria* Unquestionably Austria's greatest sweet winemaker until his untimely death in 2007. Son Gerhard is following in his footsteps. Nouvelle Vague wines are aged in new barriques while Zwischen den Seen wines are aged in large casks. The Grande Cuvée and TBAs from Scheurebe, Welschriesling and Chardonnay-Welschriesling are all ★★★. Best years: (whites) (2008) 07 **06** 05 04 **02** 01 00 99 96 95.

REMSTAL *Niederösterreich, Austria* 2170ha (5365-acre) wine region around Krems, producing some of Austria's best whites. From 2007 the DAC appellation can be used for dry Riesling and Grüner Veltliner. Best producers: Malat★★, Mantlerhof★, NIGL★★, NIKOLAIHOF★★, Franz Proidl★, Salomon★★, Sepp, Stadt Krems★. Best years: (2008) 07 06 **05 04 03 02** 01 99.

KRUG *Champagne AC, Champagne, France* Serious CHAMPAGNE house, making seriously expensive wines. The non-vintage Grande Cuvée★★ used to knock spots off most other de luxe brands in its rich, rather over-the-top traditional style. Under new owners LVMH the style seems to have changed dramatically: it's fresher, leaner, more modern – good, but that's not why I buy Krug. Also an impressive vintage★★, a rosé★★ and ethereal, outrageously expensive, single-vineyard Clos du Mesnil★★★ Blanc de Blancs. Single-vineyard Clos d'Ambonnay is for millionaires only. Best years: (1998) 96 95 **90 89 88 85 82 81 79**.

KRUTZLER *Deutsch-Schützen, Südburgenland, Austria* Perwolff★★, one of Austria's finest red wines, is a generously oaked blend of Blaufränkisch and Cabernet Sauvignon. The Blaufränkisch Reserve★ is almost as fine. Best years: 2007 06 **05 04 03 02 01 00 99**.

PETER JAKOB KÜHN *Oestrich, Rheingau, Germany* A brilliant grower and winemaker, Kühn frequently makes headlines with his substantial dry Rieslings and full, juicy Auslese. These wines are usually ★★. Best years: (2008) 07 06 **05 04 03 02 01 99**.

KUMEU/HUAPAI *Auckland, North Island, New Zealand* A small but significant viticultural area north-west of Auckland. The 11 wineries profit from their proximity to New Zealand's largest city, but most make little or no wine from grapes grown in their home region. Best producers: COOPERS CREEK★, KUMEU RIVER★★, MATUA VALLEY★, West Brook. Best years: (reds) **2007 05 04 02 00**.

KUMEU RIVER *Kumeu, Auckland, North Island, New Zealand* This family winery has been transformed by New Zealand's first Master of Wine, Michael Brajkovich, with adventurous, high-quality wines: a big, complex Chardonnay★★★ and three single-vineyard Chardonnays – Maté's★★★ Coddington★★ and Hunting Hill★★ – complex oak-aged Pinot Gris, and a MARLBOROUGH Sauvignon Blanc. Only Pinot Noir disappoints so far. Best years: (Chardonnay) **2007 06 05**.

KUNDE ESTATE *Sonoma Valley, California, USA* The Kunde family have grown wine grapes in SONOMA COUNTY for more than 100 years; in 1990 they started producing wines, with spectacular results. The Chardonnays are all impressive – Kinneybrook★★, Wildwood★★ and the powerful buttery Reserve★★. The Century Vines Zinfandel★★ gets rave reviews as do the peppery Syrah★★, the zesty Sauvignon Blanc★★ and the explosively fruity Viognier★★. Best years: (Zinfandel) 2005 **02 01 00 99 97 96 94**.

FRANZ KÜNSTLER *Hochheim, Rheingau, Germany* Gunter Künstler makes some of the best dry Rieslings in the RHEINGAU – powerful, mineral wines★★, with the Hölle wines often ★★★. Sweet wine quality has been erratic lately, but the best are fantastic. Powerful, earthy and pricey Pinot Noir. Best years: (2008) 07 06 **05 04 03 02 01 98**.

KWV *Paarl WO, South Africa* This industry giant producing a huge range of South African spirits as well as wine, has now appointed an Australian winemaker, Richard Rowe, ex-Group Chief Winemaker at Evans & Tate, to get it back on course. Neil ELLIS and Ian McKenzie (ex Southcorp) are still consulting. The flagship Cathedral Cellar range features bright-fruited, well-oaked Triptych★ (Cabernet-Merlot Shiraz), rich bold Cabernet Sauvignon★ and modern-style Pinotage. Among whites, barrel-fermented Chardonnay shows pleasing fruit/oak balance, and Sauvignon★ is tangy. Produced in best years only, and in very limited quantities, single-vineyard Perold is an ultra-ripe international-style Shiraz lavishly adorned with new American oak. PORT-style and Muscadel fortifieds remain superb value.

LA ROSA *Cachapoal, Rapel, Chile* Recently rejuvenated old family operation. The La Palma unoaked Chardonnay and La Palma Merlot are good easy drinkers. The La Capitana★ and Don Reca★ labels are a step up in quality and always terrific value. New 'icon' Ossa Sixth Generation★★ proves La Rosa can also produce world-class reds.

CH. LABÉGORCE-ZÉDÉ★ *Margaux AC, Haut-Médoc, Bordeaux, France* Cherished and improved by Luc Thienpont of POMEROL until 2005, this property is now owned by neighbouring Ch. Labégorce. The wine isn't that perfumed, but is well poised between concentration and finesse. Age for 5 years or more. Second wine: Domaine Zédé. Best years: 2007 06 05 **04 03 01 00 99 98 96 95 90 89**.

LADOIX AC *Côte de Beaune, Burgundy, France* Most northerly village in the CÔTE DE BEAUNE. The village includes some of the Grand Cru CORTON, and the lesser vineyards may be sold as Ladoix-Côte de Beaune or CÔTE DE BEAUNE-VILLAGES. Reasonably priced reds, quite light in colour and a little lean in style, from several good growers. Best producers: (reds) Cachat-Occquidant★, Chevalier★, E Cornu★, M Mallard★; (whites) R & R Jacob★, S Loichet★. Best years: (reds) (2008) 07 05 **03 02 99**.

MICHEL LAFARGE *Volnay, Côte de Beaune, Burgundy, France* The doyen of VOLNAY; son Frédéric is now in charge. Some outstanding red wines, notably Volnay Clos des Chênes★★★, Volnay Clos du Château des Ducs★★★ (a monopole) and less fashionable BEAUNE Grèves★★. BOURGOGNE Rouge★ is good value. Top wines may seem a little lean at first, but will blossom after 10 years' or more aging. Best years: (top reds) (2008) 07 06 05 03 02 99 **98 97 96 95 93 91 90**.

CH. LAFAURIE-PEYRAGUEY★★ *Sauternes AC, 1er Cru Classé, Bordeaux, France* One of the most improved SAUTERNES properties of the 1980s and now frequently one of the best Sauternes of all, sumptuous and rich when young, and marvellously deep and satisfying with age. Best years: 2007 06 05 **04 03 02 01 99 98 97 96 95 90 89 88 86 85 83**.

CH. LAFITE-ROTHSCHILD★★★ *Pauillac AC, 1er Cru Classé, Haut-Médoc, Bordeaux, France* Already famous in the early 19th century, this property was bought by the Rothschild banking family in 1868 and they still own it today. This PAUILLAC First Growth is frequently cited as the epitome of elegance, indulgence and expense. Since the late 1990s vintages have been superb, with added depth and body to match the wine's traditional finesse. Second wine: les Carruades de Lafite-Rothschild. Best years: 2007 06 05 04 03 **02 01 00 99 98 97 96 95 94 90 89 88 86 85 82**.

CH. LAFLEUR★★★ *Pomerol AC, Bordeaux, France* Using some of POMEROL's most traditional winemaking, this tiny estate can seriously rival the great PETRUS for texture, flavour and aroma. But a high percentage (50%) of Cabernet Franc makes this a more elegant wine. Second wine: Pensées de Lafleur. Best years: 2007 06 05 04 **03 02 01 00 99 98 96 95 90 89 88**.

LAFON *Meursault, Côte de Beaune, Burgundy, France* One of Burgundy's current superstars, with prices to match. Early exponent of biodynamics for brilliant MEURSAULT including Clos de la Barre★★, Charmes★★★, Perrières★★★, le MONTRACHET★★★ and exciting long-lived reds from VOLNAY (Santenots-du-Milieu★★★). Since 1999, also MÂCON★ (Clos du Four★, Clos de la Crochette★). Best years: (whites) (2008) 07 06 05 04 03 **02 00**; (reds) (2008) 07 06 05 03 02 99 **98 96 95 90**.

CH. LAFON-ROCHET★ *St-Estèphe AC, 4ème Cru Classé, Haut-Médoc, Bordeaux, France* Good-value, affordable Classed Growth claret. Recent vintages have seen an increase of Merlot in the blend, making the wine less austere. Delicious and blackcurranty after 10 years. Best years: 2006 05 04 03 02 01 00 99 98 96 95 94 90 89 88.

ALOIS LAGEDER *Alto Adige DOC, Trentino-Alto Adige, Italy* Leading producer in ALTO ADIGE, making good, medium-priced varietals and pricey estate and single-vineyard wines such as Löwengang Cabernet★ and Chardonnay★★, Sauvignon Lehenhof★★, Cabernet Cor Römigberg★★, Pinot Noir Krafuss★, Pinot Bianco Haberlehof★ and Pinot Grigio Benefizium Porer★. Also owns the historic Casòn Hirschprunn estate, source of excellent Alto Adige blends. White Contest★★ is based on Pinot Grigio and Chardonnay, with small amounts of Marsanne and Roussanne. The red equivalent, Casòn★★, is Merlot-Cabernet based; a second red, Corolle★, and white Etelle★ show similar style.

CH. LAGRANGE★★ *St-Julien AC, 3ème Cru Classé, Haut-Médoc, Bordeaux, France* Since the Japanese company SUNTORY purchased this large estate in 1983 it has become a single-minded wine of good fruit, meticulous winemaking and fine quality, an occasional surfeit of tannin being the only cautionary note. Dry white les Arums de Lagrange since 1997. Second wine: les Fiefs de Lagrange. Best years: 2006 05 04 03 02 01 00 99 98 96 95 90 89 88.

LAGREIN Black grape of ALTO ADIGE, producing deep-coloured, brambly chocolaty reds called Lagrein Dunkel or Scuro, and full-bodied, attractively scented rosé (known as Kretzer). Best producers: Colterenzio co-op (Cornell★), Graziano Fontana★, Franz Gojer★, Gries co-op★, Hofstätter★, LAGEDER★, Laimburg★, Muri-Gries★, J Niedermayr★, I Niedrist★, Plattner-Waldgries★, Hans Rottensteiner★, Santa Maddalena co-op★, Simoncelli★, Terlano co-op★★, Thurnhof★★, TIEFENBRUNNER★★, Zemmer★.

CH. LA LAGUNE★ *Haut-Médoc AC, 3ème Cru Classé, Haut-Médoc, Bordeaux, France* The closest MEDOC Classed Growth to Bordeaux city. The soils are sandy-gravel and the wines round and elegant in style. Took a dip in the late 1990s but new investment from 2000, and quality has improved. Second wine: Moulin de la Lagune. Best years: 2005 04 03 02 00 98 96 95 90 89.

LALANDE-DE-POMEROL AC *Bordeaux, France* To the north of its more famous neighbour POMEROL, this AC produces ripe, plummy wines with an unmistakable mineral edge that are very attractive to drink at 3–5 years old, but age reasonably well too. Even though they lack the concentration of top Pomerols, the wines are not particularly cheap. Best producers: Annereaux★, Bertineau St-Vincent★, La Croix des Moines★, La Croix-St-André★, les Cruzelles★, la Fleur de Boüard★★, Garraud★, Grand Ormeau★, Haut-Chaigneau, les Hauts Conseillants, Jean de Gué★, Laborderie-Mondésir★, Perron (La Fleur★), Sergant, la Sergue★, Siaurac★, Tournefeuille★, Viaud. Best years: 2007 06 05 04 03 02 00 98 96 95 90 89.

LAMBRUSCO *Emilia-Romagna, Italy* 'Lambrusco' refers to a family of black grape varieties, grown in 3 DOC zones on the plains of Emilia and around Mantova in LOMBARDY, but it is the screwcap bottles of non-DOC Lambrusco that made the name famous, even though some contain no wine from Lambrusco grapes at all. Proper Lambrusco is a dry or semi-sweet fizzy red with high acidity to partner the rich local foods, such as rich, buttery cheese sauces and salami, and is worth trying (especially Lambrusco di Sorbara and Grasparossa di Castelvetro). Best producers: Barbieri, Barbolini, F Bellei★, Casali, Cavicchioli★, Chiarli, Vittorio Graziano★, Oreste Lini, Stefano Spezia, Venturini Baldini.

AMOREAUX LANDING *Finger Lakes AVA, New York State, USA* One of the most versatile and consistently good wineries in the FINGER LAKES. Its Chardonnay Reserve★ is a consistent medal winner, and the Pinot Noir★ is arguably the region's best. Merlot★ and Cabernet Franc★ are also attractive, as are Dry Riesling★ and good, quaffable fizz.

ANDMARK *Sonoma County, California, USA* This producer concentrates on Chardonnay and Pinot Noir. Chardonnays include Overlook★★ and the oakier Damaris Reserve★★ and Lorenzo★★. Tropical-fruited Courtyard Chardonnay★ is lower-priced. Pinot Noir from Kastania Vineyard★★ (SONOMA COAST) is beautifully focused.

ANGHE DOC *Piedmont, Italy* Important DOC covering blends (Rosso, Bianco) and varietals from the Langhe hills around Alba, the 'varietals' crucially allowing 15% grapes other than that announced on the label. The varietals – such as Chardonnay, Barbera, Nebbiolo – embrace many former vino da tavola blends of the highest order, as well as most of what Angelo GAJA used to sell as Barbaresco and Barolo. Best producers: (reds) ALTARE★★, Boglietti (Buio★★), Bongiovanni (Falletto★★), CERETTO★★, CHIARLO★★, Cigliuti★★, CLERICO★★, Aldo CONTERNO★★, Conterno-Fantino (Monprà★★), Luigi Einaudi★★, GAJA★★★, A Ghisolfi★★, Marchesi di Gresy (Virtus★★), F Nada (Seifile★★), Parusso (Bricco Rovella★★), Rocche dei Manzoni (Quatr Nas★), Vajra★, Gianni Voerzio (Serrapiu★★), Roberto VOERZIO★★. Best years: (reds) (2008) (07) 06 **04 03 01 00 99**.

H. LANGOA-BARTON★★ *St-Julien AC, 3ème Cru Classé, Haut-Médoc, Bordeaux, France* Owned by the Barton family since 1821, Langoa-Barton is usually less scented and elegant, though often richer than its ST-JULIEN stablemate LEOVILLE-BARTON, but it is still extremely impressive and excellent value. Drink after 7 or 8 years, although it may keep for 15. Second wine: Réserve de Léoville-Barton (a blend from the young vines of both Barton properties). Best years: 2007 06 05 04 **03** 02 **01 00 99 98 96 95 90 89 88 86 85**.

ANGUEDOC-ROUSSILLON *France* This vast area of southern France, nning from Nîmes to the Spanish border and covering the *départements* of e GARD, HERAULT, Aude and Pyrénées-Orientales, is still a source of distinguished cheap wine, but is also one of France's most exciting wine gions. The transformation is the result of better grape varieties, modern nemaking and ambitious producers, from the heights of GRANGE DES PÈRES to ry good local co-ops. The best wines are the reds, particularly those from ORBIÈRES, MINERVOIS, COTEAUX DU LANGUEDOC and PIC ST-LOUP, and some new-ave Cabernets, Merlots and Syrahs, as well as the more traditional *vins doux turels*, such as BANYULS, MAURY and MUSCAT DE RIVESALTES; but we are now eing exciting whites as well, particularly as new plantings of Chardonnay, arsanne, Roussanne, Viognier, Vermentino (Rolle) and Sauvignon Blanc ature. An all-embracing appellation, called simply Languedoc AC, was reed in 2007 and includes all of Coteaux du Languedoc, Corbières, inervois and the ROUSSILLON appellations. Producers can opt into this new pellation or stick to the old areas. See also CABARDES, COLLIOURE, COSTIÈRES DE

NÎMES, CÔTES DU ROUSSILLON, CÔTES DE THONGUE, FAUGERES, FITOU, LIMOUX, MUSCA
DE FRONTIGNAN, MUSCAT DE ST-JEAN-DE-MINERVOIS, OC, RIVESALTES, ST-CHINIAN.

LANSON *Champagne AC, Champagne, France* Non-vintage Lanson Blac
Label★ is reliably tasty and, like the rosé★ and vintage★★ wines
especially de luxe Noble Cuvée★★, improves greatly with aging. In 200€
Lanson (and associated brands Besserat de Bellefon, Gauthier, Mass
and Alfred Rothschild) was bought by Boizel Chanoine Champagne
where Bruno PAILLARD is the majority shareholder. Best years: (1999) 98 9
96 **95 93 90** 89 88 85 83 82.

DOM. LAROCHE *Chablis, Burgundy, France* Dynamic CHABLIS producer, wit
good St-Martin★ and impressive Grand Cru Les Clos★★★. One of th
first Burgundians to use screwtop closures. Also owns MAS LA CHEVALIÈRE i
the Languedoc and L'AVENIR in Stellenbosch, South Africa. Best year
(Chablis) (2008) 07 **06 05 02 00.**

CH. LASCOMBES★ *Margaux AC, 2ème Cru Classé, Haut-Médoc, Bordeaux, Franc*
One of the great underachievers in the MARGAUX AC and little wort
drinking in the 1980s and 90s, but new American ownership and inves
ment and the advice of consultant enologist Michel Rolland have begu
to make a difference – and the 2004 is the best effort for a generatio
Just about worthy of ★ now. Best years: 2007 06 05 **04 03 01 00 96 95.**

CH. LATOUR★★★ *Pauillac AC, 1er Cru Classé, Haut-Médoc, Bordeaux, Franc*
Latour's reputation is based on powerful, long-lasting classic wine
Strangely, in the early 1980s there was an attempt to make lighter, mo
fashionable wines, with mixed results. The late 80s saw a return to class
Latour, much to my relief. Its reputation for making fine wine in le
successful vintages is well deserved. After 30 years in British hands
returned to French ownership in 1993. Spanking new cellars from 200
Second wine: les Forts de Latour. Best years: 2007 06 05 04 03 **02 01 00 9
98 97 96 95 94 93 90 89 88 86.**

LOUIS LATOUR *Beaune, Burgundy, France* Merchant almost as well know
for his COTEAUX DE L'ARDÈCHE Chardonnays as for his Burgundies. Latou
white Burgundies are much better than the reds, although the re
CORTON-Grancey★★ can be very good. Latour's oaky CORTON
CHARLEMAGNE★★, from his own vineyard, is his top wine, but there is al
good CHEVALIER-MONTRACHET★★, BÂTARD-MONTRACHET★★ and
MONTRACHET★★. Even so, as these are the greatest white vineyards
Burgundy, there really should be more top performances. Best years: (t
whites) (2008) 07 **06 05 02 00.**

CH. LATOUR-MARTILLAC *Pessac-Léognan AC, Cru Classé de Graves, Bordeau
France* The vineyard here is strictly organic, and has many ancient vine
The deep, dark, well-structured reds★ improved considerably in th
1990s. Whites★ are thoroughly modern and of good quality. Good valu
as well. Best years: (reds) 2007 06 05 **04 03 02 01 00 98 96 95 90;** (white
2007 06 05 04 02 01 00 99 98 96.

CH. LATOUR-À-POMEROL★ *Pomerol AC, Bordeaux, France* Directed
Christian MOUEIX of PETRUS fame, this property makes luscious wines wi
loads of gorgeous fruit and enough tannin to age well. Best years: 2007
05 **04 03 02 01 00 99 98 95 90 89 88.**

LATRICIÈRES-CHAMBERTIN AC See CHAMBERTIN AC.

LAUREL GLEN *Sonoma Mountain AVA, California, USA* Owner/winemak
Patrick Campbell makes only Cabernet at his mountaintop winery. T
top wine, Laurel Glen★★, is rich with deep fruit flavours, aging aft

6–10 years to a perfumed, complex BORDEAUX style. Counterpoint is a label for wine that does not make it into the top-level Cabernet. Terra Rosa (Malbec) is from established vineyards in MENDOZA, Argentina. Zinfandel-based Reds, from Lodi-grown fruit, is great value. Best years: (2005) **02 01 99 98 97 96 95 94 91 90**.

AURENT-PERRIER *Champagne AC, Champagne, France* Large, family-owned CHAMPAGNE house, offering flavour and quality at reasonable prices. Non-vintage★ is light and savoury; the vintage★★ is delicious, and the top wine, Grand Siècle★★★, is among the finest Champagnes of all. Non-vintage rosé★ is good and vintage Alexandra Rosé★★★ is excellent. Best years: (2000) **99 97 96 95 90 88 85 82**.

'AVENIR *Stellenbosch WO, South Africa* Chenin Blanc and Pinotage remain the focus under new owner Chablis merchant Michel LAROCHE. Three Pinotages, from cheerfully fruity, via well-oaked★ to ageworthy Grand Vin Pinotage★★, are echoed by a stylish pair of Chenin Blancs (Platinum range★). Promising Chardonnay★, Cabernet★ and BORDEAUX-blend Stellenbosch Classic★. Best years: (Pinotage) 2007 **06 05 04 03 02 01 00 99**.

:H. LAVILLE-HAUT-BRION★★★ *Pessac-Léognan AC, Cru Classé de Graves, Bordeaux, France* One of the finest white PESSAC-LEOGNANs, with a price tag to match. Fermented in barrel, it needs 10 years or more to reach its savoury but luscious peak. Best years: 2007 06 **05** 04 03 02 01 00 98 96 95 94 93 90 89.

OMAINE COSTA LAZARIDI *Drama, Greece* State-of-the-art, Bordeaux-inspired winery making good use of indigenous and international varieties. Fresh gooseberry Amethystos white★ (Sauvignon Blanc, Sémillon and Assyrtiko); a fascinatingly intense Viognier★ with a stunning, oily, peach kernel finish; tasty Château Julia Chardonnay★; and fine Amethystos Cava★, an oak-aged Cabernet from very low yields.

AZIO *Italy* Region best known for FRASCATI, Rome's white glugger. There e also various bland whites from Trebbiano and Malvasia, such as EST! EST!! T!!! DI MONTEFIASCONE. The region's most interesting wines are reds based on abernet, Merlot and Sangiovese; the local Cesanese can also do well. Best 'oducers: Casale del Giglio★, Castel de Paolis (Quattro Mori★★), Cerveteri co-op 'ertium★), FALESCO (Montiano★), Paolo di Mauro (Vigna del Vassallo★★), Pietra nta★, Trappolini★.

EASINGHAM *Clare Valley, South Australia* A satellite of Constellation, Leasingham is one of CLARE VALLEY's largest wineries and is well respected, with quality under Simon Osicka at an all-time high. However, it is in doubt whether this will continue given Constellation's decision to sell off the winery and some prize vineyards. Riesling★★ can be among Clare's best, and Sparkling Shiraz★★ is excellent. Bin 56 Cabernet-Malbec★ and Bin 61 Shiraz★ are powerful, mid-price reds, while Classic Clare Shiraz★★ and Cabernet★ which were high-alcohol, heavily oaked, heavily priced blockbusters, have become more restrained, even elegant. The budget-priced Magnus range represents good value.

ECOLE No 41 *Walla Walla Valley AVA, Washington State, USA* Velvety and deeply flavoured Seven Hills Vineyard Merlot★, good Cabernet Sauvignon★ and lush Syrah★★; a BORDEAUX blend called Apogee★★ from the Pepper Bridge vineyard in WALLA WALLA is dark and challenging. The best wines are the barrel-fermented Semillons: a nutty COLUMBIA

VALLEY★★ version and exciting single-vineyard Fries Vineyard★★ an
Seven Hills Vineyard★★. The Chardonnay★ is pleasant and mineral!
Best years: (top reds) (2007) 06 05 **04 03 02 01**.

LEEUWIN ESTATE *Margaret River, Western Australia* MARGARET RIVER's hig
flier, with pricey Art Series Chardonnay ★★★ that gets Burgundy love
drooling. Art Series Cabernet Sauvignon★★ (sometimes ★★★) h
improved dramatically since 1998 and exhibits superb blackcurrant an
cedar balance. Art Series Riesling★★ is complex and fine, and look o
for exceptional Shiraz★★. New labels Prelude (Chardonnay★) an
Siblings (Sauvignon Blanc-Semillon) give Leeuwin pleasure at low
prices. Best years: (Art Series Chardonnay) (2008) (07) 06 05 **04 02 01 00 9**
98 97 96 95.

DOM. LEFLAIVE *Puligny-Montrachet, Côte de Beaune, Burgundy, France* Famou
white Burgundy producer with extensive holdings in some of the greate
vineyards of PULIGNY-MONTRACHET, including les Pucelles★★★, Chevalie
MONTRACHET★★★, BÂTARD-MONTRACHET★★★ and a tiny slice of
MONTRACHET★★★. Anne-Claude Leflaive has taken the family domai
right back to the top using biodynamic methods. These extraordinari
fine wines can age for 20 years and are understandably expensive. Mo
reasonably priced Mâcon-Verzé was launched in 2004. Best years: (200
07 06 05 **03 02 01 00** 99.

OLIVIER LEFLAIVE *Puligny-Montrachet, Côte de Beaune, Burgundy, Fran*
Négociant Olivier Leflaive specializes in crisp, modern white wines fro
the CÔTE D'OR and the CÔTE CHALONNAISE, mostly for early drinking. Less
ACs – ST-ROMAIN★, MONTAGNY★, ST-AUBIN★, RULLY★ – offer good valu
but the rich, oaky BÂTARD-MONTRACHET★★★ is the star turn. Best yea
(top whites) (2008) 07 **06 05 04**.

PETER LEHMANN *Barossa Valley, South Australia* BAROSSA doyen Lehmar
buys grapes from many local growers and owns the superb Stonew
vineyard, which contributes its fruit and name to his best Shiraz★★
Juicy, old-fashioned, fruit-packed reds include Grenache-Shiraz
Mentor (Cabernet)★★ and Eight Songs Shiraz★★. The talking point
the past few years has been the consistently sublime quality of the t
Peter Lehmann whites: impeccably balanced Wigan Eden Vall
Riesling★★★ and rich, pure, zesty, unwooded Margaret Semillon★★
sourced from rare Barossa Valley old vines. Also lemony Semillon★
and Chenin★, and dry, long-lived Eden Valley Riesling★★. Bought
California-based Donald HESS in 2003. Befuddling array of new budg
lines – but the quality is holding up so far. Best years: (Stonewell Shir
(2008) (06) 05 04 03 02 **01 99 98 96 94 93 90 89**.

JOSEF LEITZ *Rüdesheim, Rheingau, Germany* Some of the RHEINGAU's best d
and off-dry Rieslings come from this RUDESHEIM grower, especially fro
the Berg Rottland★★ and Berg Schlossberg★★ sites, whose rece
vintages have been the best yet. Best years: (2008) 07 06 **05 04 03 02 01 9**

LEIWEN *Mosel, Germany* This unspectacular village has become a hotbe
the MOSEL Riesling revolution. Nowhere else in the region is there suck
concentration of dynamic estates and new ideas. Best producers: GRA
FASSIAN★★, Carl Loewen★★, Josef Rosch★★, St Urbans-Hof★★, He
Schmitt. Best years: (2008) 07 06 **05 04 03 02 01** 99.

LEMBERGER See BLAUFRANKISCH.

LENZ WINERY *Long Island, New York State, USA* A leading LONG ISLAND win
focused on BORDEAUX varietal reds exclusively from estate fruit. T
Estate Merlot★★ is elegant and powerful with soft, balanced tannins;

Gewürztraminer★ is spicy and tasty. Sparkling wines are limited in quantity though not in quality. Chardonnay★ is mostly good. Wines made from the estate's oldest vines (Cabernet Sauvignon, Merlot, Chardonnay) are reserved for subscribers only.

LEONETTI CELLAR *Walla Walla Valley AVA, Washington State, USA* The first winery in WALLA WALLA VALLEY opened in 1977. Today, it produces highly sought-after, rich and velvety Cabernet Sauvignon★★ and Merlot★★ aged in a combination of French and American oak. A dense and powerful Reserve★★★ uses the best barrels. Sangiovese★★ has very fine texture and lots of new wood. The focus is on vineyard management and most of the fruit is now estate grown. Best years: (2007) 06 05 **04 03** 02 01.

CH. LÉOVILLE-BARTON★★★ *St-Julien AC,* *2ème Cru Classé, Haut-Médoc, Bordeaux, France* Made by Anthony Barton, whose family has run this ST-JULIEN property since 1826, this fine claret is a traditionalist's delight. Dark, dry and tannic, and not overly oaked, the wines are often underestimated, but over 10–15 years they achieve a lean yet sensitively proportioned beauty rarely equalled in Bordeaux. Moreover, they are never overpriced. Second wine: Réserve de Léoville-Barton. Best years: 2007 06 05 04 03 **02 01** 00 99 98 96 95 94 93 90 89 88 86 85.

CH. LÉOVILLE-LAS-CASES★★★ *St-Julien AC, 2ème Cru Classé, Haut-Médoc, Bordeaux, France* The largest of the three Léoville properties, making wines of startlingly deep, dark concentration. I now find them so dense and thick in texture that it is difficult to identify them as ST-JULIEN. Second wine: Clos du Marquis. Best years: 2007 06 05 04 03 **02 01** 00 99 98 96 95 94 93 90 89 88 86 85.

CH. LÉOVILLE-POYFERRÉ★★ *St-Julien AC, 2ème Cru Classé, Haut-Médoc, Bordeaux, France* Since the 1986 vintage Didier Cuvelier has gradually increased the richness of the wine without wavering from its austere style. A string of excellent wines in the 90s and 00s frequently show more classic ST-JULIEN style than those of neighbour LEOVILLE-LAS-CASES. Second wine: Moulin-Riche. Best years: 2007 06 05 04 03 **02 01** 00 **99** 98 96 95 94 90 89 86.

DOM. LEROY *Vosne-Romanée, Côte de Nuits, Burgundy, France* In 1988 Lalou Bize-Leroy bought the former Dom. Noëllat in VOSNE-ROMANEE, renaming it Domaine Leroy, which should not be confused with her *négociant* house, Maison Leroy, which contains stocks of great mature vintages, or her personal estate, Dom. d'Auvenay. Here she produces fiendishly expensive, though fabulously concentrated, wines with biodynamic methods and almost ludicrously low yields from top vineyards such as CHAMBERTIN★★★, CLOS DE VOUGEOT★★★, MUSIGNY★★★, RICHEBOURG★★★ and ROMANEE-ST-VIVANT★★★. Best years: (top reds) (2008) 07 06 05 03 02 **01** 00 **99** 98 96 90 89.

LEYDA See SAN ANTONIO.

LIEBFRAUMILCH *Pfalz, Rheinhessen, Nahe and Rheingau, Germany* Sweetish and low in acidity, Liebfraumilch rightly has a downmarket image. It can come from any of the four regions and 70% of the blend must be Müller-Thurgau, Kerner, Riesling and Silvaner, though if you find any decent Riesling therein, you're drinking on a different planet from me.

LIGER-BELAIR *Côte de Nuits, Burgundy, France* Vicomte Louis-Michel Liger
Belair makes stylish, perfumed wines at the family estate in VOSNE-
ROMANEE, including the monopoly of la ROMANEE★★★ itself, while hi
cousin Thibault Liger-Belair makes rich, plump wines from his NUITS-ST-
GEORGES base, including Premier Cru les St-Georges★★ and Grand
Crus RICHEBOURG★★ and CLOS DE VOUGEOT★★. Best years: (Vicomte) (2008)
07 06 05 03 **02 01**; (Thibault) (2008) 07 06 05 **04 03 02**.

LIGURIA *Italy* Thin coastal strip of north-west Italy, running from th
French border at Ventimiglia to the Tuscan border. Best-known wines
though mostly drunk by natives or tourists, are the Cinqueterre, Colli d
Luna, Riviera Ligure di Ponente and Rossese di Dolceacqua DOCs.

LIMARÍ *Chile* Best known in Chile for pisco (the local brandy), during th
past decade this valley – 400km (250 miles) north of Santiago – has show
that its cold ocean influence and its clay and chalky soil can produce world
class wines. Chardonnay and Syrah are the top performers, both expressin
fresh, vibrant flavours and subtle yet clear minerality. Tabalí is the bes
producer so far (Syrah★★) followed by Maycas, but expect more challenges i
the near future. Best producers: DE MARTINO, Maycas/CONCHA Y TORO, Tabalí/SA
PEDRO, Tamaya.

LIMESTONE COAST *South Australia* Zone for south-east of South Australia
including COONAWARRA, PADTHAWAY, Mount Benson and Wrattonbully
Plantings near Mount Gambier, Bordertown and Robe may seek officia
recognition in the future. New vineyards in this far-flung area hav
Coonawarra-like terra rossa soil with great potential. The Foster's Win
Group, YALUMBA, Constellation and Pernod Ricard are all involved.

LIMOUX AC *Languedoc, France* The first AC in the LANGUEDOC to allow
Chardonnay and Chenin Blanc, which must be vinified in oak
Production is dominated by the SIEUR D'ARQUES co-op. Red Limoux AC
(from 2004) is made from Merlot and Cabernet with local varieties. Be
producers: d'ANTUGNAC★, Begude★, Rives-Blanques★, SIEUR D'ARQUES★.

LINDEMANS *Murray Darling, Victoria, Australia* Large, historic – but current
underperforming – company, part of the Foster's Wine Grou
Traditionally strong in COONAWARRA, where the best wines are the miner
St George Cabernet★★, spicy Limestone Ridge Shiraz-Cabernet★★ an
red BORDEAUX-blend Pyrus★★. Decent mass-market wines in the Bi
range and Reserve-label reds from the LIMESTONE COAST. Using th
Lindemans name for non-Australian blends is a worrying developmen
Best years: (Coonawarra reds) 2008 06 05 **04 01** 99 98 96 94 91 90.

LIRAC AC *Rhône Valley, France* Underrated AC between TAVEL an
CHÂTEAUNEUF-DU-PAPE. Reds have the dusty, spicy red fruit of Châteaune
without quite the intensity. They age well but are delicious youn
Refreshing rosé has lovely strawberry fruit, and whites can be good
drink them young before the perfume goes. Best producers: Amidor
Aquéria, Beaumont★, Bouchassy★, Corne-Loup, Devoy Martine, Duseigneu
la Genestière, Joncier★, Lafond-Roc-Épine★★, Lorentine★, Maby★, Mon
Redon★, la Mordorée★★, Pélaquié★, Roger Sabon★★, St-Roch★, Ségriè
Tavel co-op★, Zobel. Best years: **2007 06 05 04 03 01**.

LISTRAC-MÉDOC AC *Haut-Médoc, Bordeaux, France* Set back from th
Gironde and away from the best HAUT-MEDOC gravel ridges, Listrac win
can be good but never thrilling, and are marked by solid fruit, a slight

coarse tannin and an earthy flavour. More Merlot is now being used to soften the style. **Best producers: Cap Léon Veyrin, CLARKE★, Ducluzeau, Fonréaud, Fourcas-Dupré★, Fourcas-Hosten, Fourcas-Loubaney, Grand Listrac co-op, Mayne-Lalande★, Saransot-Dupré. Best years: 2005 03 01 00 96 95 90.**

LOIRE VALLEY *France* The Loire river cuts right through the heart of France. The middle reaches are the home of world-famous SANCERRE and POUILLY-FUMÉ. The region of TOURAINE makes good Sauvignon Blanc and Gamay, while at VOUVRAY and MONTLOUIS the Chenin Blanc makes some pretty good fizz and scintillatingly fresh, minerally still whites, ranging from sweet to very dry. The Loire's best reds are made in SAUMUR-CHAMPIGNY, CHINON, ST-NICOLAS-DE-BOURGUEIL and BOURGUEIL, mainly from Cabernet Franc, with ANJOU-VILLAGES improving fast. Anjou is famous for rosé, but the best wines are white Chenin Blanc, either sweet from the Layon Valley or dry from SAVENNIÈRES and ANJOU where a new generation of producers are making richer, barrel-fermented and aged wines. Near the mouth of the river around Nantes is MUSCADET. See also ANJOU BLANC, ANJOU ROUGE, BONNEZEAUX, CABERNET D'ANJOU, CHEVERNY, CÔTE ROANNAISE, COTEAUX DE L'AUBANCE, COTEAUX DU LAYON, CREMANT DE LOIRE, GROS PLANT DU PAYS NANTAIS, JASNIÈRES, MENETOU-SALON, POUILLY-SUR-LOIRE, QUARTS DE CHAUME, QUINCY, REUILLY, ROSE DE LOIRE, ST-NICOLAS-DE-BOURGUEIL, SAUMUR, SAUMUR MOUSSEUX, VAL DE LOIRE.

LOMBARDY *Italy* Lombardy, whose capital is Milan, is a larger consumer than producer. Many of the best grapes, especially from OLTREPÒ PAVESE, go to provide base wine for Italy's *spumante* industry. However, there are some interesting wines in Oltrepò Pavese, VALTELLINA, LUGANA and high-quality sparkling and still wines in FRANCIACORTA.

LONG ISLAND *New York State, USA* Long Island encompasses 3 AVAs: the Hamptons; North Fork; and the broader Long Island AVA. People have likened growing conditions to BORDEAUX, and the long growing season, combined with a maritime influence, does produce similarities. Certainly Merlot and Cabernet Franc are the best reds, with Chardonnay the best white. **Best producers: BEDELL★★, CHANNING DAUGHTERS★, LENZ★★, Macari, Martha Clara, Palmer★, Paumanok★, Pellegrini★, Pindar, Raphael, Shinn Estate, WÖLFFER★. Best years: (reds) (2008) (07) 06 02 01 00.**

LONG SHADOWS VINTNERS *Columbia Valley AVA, Washington State, USA* This is a series of small partnerships, led by Allen Shoup, encompassing a coterie of wineries in the heart of the COLUMBIA VALLEY AVA. It includes Pedestal★★ with Michel Rolland, Feather★ with Randy DUNN, Poet's Leap★ with Armin Diel of Schlossgut DIEL, Saggi★ with Ambrogio and Giovanni FOLONARI, Sequel★★ with John DUVAL, and Chester-Kidder★ with Allen Shoup and Gilles Nicault, the head winemaker for the group. The arrangement is unique in that each winery is individually owned and managed as a separate partnership. **Best years: (reds) (2007) 06 05 04.**

DR LOOSEN *Bernkastel, Mosel, Germany* Loosen's estate has portions of some of the MOSEL's most famous vineyards: Treppchen and Prälat in ERDEN, Würzgarten in URZIG, Sonnenuhr in WEHLEN, Himmelreich in GRAACH and Lay in BERNKASTEL. Most of the wines achieve ★★, and Spätlese and Auslese from Wehlen, Ürzig and Erden frequently ★★★. His basic Riesling is excellent, year in year out. A joint venture with CHATEAU STE MICHELLE in Washington is proving exciting. **Best years: (2008) 07 06 05 04 03 02 01 99 98 97 96 95.** See also J L WOLF.

LÓPEZ DE HEREDIA *Rioja DOCa, Rioja, Spain* Family-owned RIOJA compar
still aging wines in old oak casks. Younger red wines are called Vi
Cubillo★, and mature wines Viña Tondonia★ and Viña Bosconia
Good, oaky whites, especially Viña Gravonia★. Best years: (Viña Tondon
2000 99 **98 96 95 94 93 91 87 86 85**.

LOUPIAC AC *Bordeaux, France* A sweet wine area across the Garonne riv
from BARSAC. The wines are attractively sweet without being goo
Drink young in general, though the best can age. Best producers: C
Jean★, Cros★, Loupiac-Gaudiet, Mémoires★, Noble★, Ricaud, les Roques
Best years: 2007 **05 03 02 01 99 98 97 96 95 90**.

CH. LA LOUVIÈRE *Pessac-Léognan AC, Bordeaux, France* The star of PESSA
LEOGNAN's non-classified estates, its reputation almost entirely due
owner André Lurton. Well-structured reds★ and fresh, Sauvigno
based whites★★ are excellent value. Best years: (reds) 2007 06 05 **04 02
00 99 98 96 95 90 89**; (whites) **2007** 06 05 04 03 02 01 00 99 98 96 9

LUBÉRON AC *Rhône Valley, France* Production is dominated by the co-c
east of Avignon; their light, easy wines drink young. Domaine wines h
more body. Best producers: Bonnieux co-op, Ch. la Canorgue, la Citadelle
Fontenille★, Ch. de l'Isolette★, la Tour-d'Aigues co-op, Ch. St-Estève de N
Ch. des Tourettes, Val Joanis, la Verrerie★. Best years: **2007 06**.

STEFANO LUBIANA *Tasmania, Australia* One of the new stars of t
Tasmanian wine scene. Vintage★, non-vintage★ and Prestig
(10 years on lees) sparkling wines rank with the best in Austral
Chardonnay★ is restrained and elegant, Sauvignon Blanc sho
greengage and passionfruit characters, while the Pinot Noir★ has weig
concentration and a velvety texture.

LUGANA DOC *Lombardy, Italy* Dry white (occasionally sparkling) from
Trebbiano di Lugana grape grown on the southern shores of La
Garda. Well-structured wines from the better producers can deve
excitingly over a few years. Best producers: Ca' dei Frati★★, Ottella
Provenza★, Visconti★, Zenato★, Zeni.

LUJÁN DE CUYO *Mendoza, Argentina* Argentina's first DOC (in 198
with an average altitude of 1000m (3200ft), Luján de Cuyo's reputati
lies in its magnificent old Malbec vines. Best producers: Luigi BOSCA
CATENA★★, COBOS★, Dominio del Plata★, FABRE MONTMAYOU★, Finca la An
TERRAZAS DE LOS ANDES★★, WEINERT★. Best years: (Malbec) 2006 **05 04**

LUNGAROTTI *Torgiano DOC, Umbria, Italy* Leading, nearly sole, producer
the fine, black-cherry-flavoured Torgiano DOC. The Torgiano Rise
(Vigna Monticchio★★) is DOCG. Also makes red San Giorgi
(Cabernet-Sangiovese) and Chardonnay Palazzi.

LUSSAC-ST-ÉMILION AC *Bordeaux, France* Much of the wine from t
AC, which tastes like a lighter ST-EMILION, is made by the first-rate lo
co-op and should be drunk within 4 years of the vintage; cert
properties are worth seeking out. Best producers: Barbe-Blanche★, Bel-A
Bellevue, Courlat★, la Grenière, Lussac★, Lyonnat★, Mayne Blanc,
Rochers★. Best years: **2005** 03 01 00 98 96 95 90.

EMILIO LUSTAU *Jerez y Manzanilla DO, Andalucía, Spain* Specializes
supplying 'own-label' wines to supermarkets. Quality is generally go
and there are some real stars at the top, especially the Almaceni
range★★: very individual sherries from small, private producers.

CH. LYNCH-BAGES *Pauillac AC, 5ème Cru Classé, Haut-Médoc, Bordeaux, Fra*
I am a great fan of Lynch-Bages red★★★ – with its almost succul
richness, its gentle texture and its starburst of flavours, all but

blackcurrants and mint – and it is now one of PAUILLAC's most popular wines. Sadly, it's no longer underpriced but it's still worth the money. Impressive at 5 years, beautiful at 10 and irresistible at 20. Second wine: Haut-Bages-Averous. Since 1990 there has been a small amount of white wine, Blanc de Lynch-Bages★. Best years: (reds) 2007 06 05 04 03 **02 01 00 99 98 96 95 94 90 89 88 86 85**.

.YNMAR *Russian River Valley AVA, California, USA* Small producer of superb Chardonnay★★ and Pinot Noir★★, using largely estate-grown fruit from its Quail Hill Vineyard. The gracious, supple Pinots age well, and winemaker Hugh Chappelle also makes a peppery, cold-climate Syrah as well as an elegant Pinot Noir rosé.

RÉDÉRIC MABILEAU *St-Nicolas-de-Bourgueil, Loire Valley, France* Although established only in 1991, meticulous attention to detail and a gentle handling regime yield ST-NICOLAS-DE-BOURGUEIL (Les Rouillères★, Les Coutures★★, Éclipse★★) and BOURGUEIL (Racines★) of startling fruit purity and finesse. White SAUMUR★★ (maiden vintage 2007) is ample testament to Frédéric's passion for Chenin Blanc. ANJOU Cabernet Sauvignon also new in 2007. Certified organic with effect from 2009. Best years: (top reds) (2008) **07** 06 05 04 03 02 01 00 99 98 97 96.

E MACCHIOLE *Bolgheri, Tuscany, Italy* Eugenio Campolmi died prematurely in 2002, having established Le Macchiole as one of the leading quality estates of the new Tuscany. Mainstay is Paleo Rosso★★, a pure Cabernet Franc. Best known is the Merlot Messorio★★, while Scrio★★ is one of the best Syrahs in Italy. Best years: (2008) (07) 06 **04 03 01 00 99**.

ÂCON AC *Mâconnais, Burgundy, France* The basic Mâconnais AC, but most whites in the region are labelled under the superior MÂCON-VILLAGES AC. The wines are rarely exciting. Chardonnay-based Mâcon Blanc, especially, is a rather expensive basic quaffer. Drink young. Mâcon Supérieur has sensibly been discontinued. Best producers: Bertillonnes, Bruyère, DUBOEUF, LAFON★.

ÂCON-VILLAGES AC *Mâconnais, Burgundy, France* There is a sea of modestly priced and often modest wines under this appellation, which covers 26 villages. Co-ops still dominate production, but these days a handful of growers make more exciting wines from individually named villages such as Mâcon-Lugny and Mâcon la Roche Vineuse. Co-ops dominate production. Best villages: Bussières, Chaintré, Chardonnay, Charnay, Clessé, Cruzille, Davayé, Igé, Lugny, Prissé, la Roche Vineuse, Uchizy, Verzy. Best producers: D & M Barraud★★, A Bonhomme★★, Bret Brothers★★, Deux Roches★, E Gillet★★, la Greffière★★, Guillot-Broux★★, LAFON★, J-J Litaud★, Jean Manciat★, O Merlin★★, R Michel★, Rijckaert★, Robert-Denogent★★, Saumaize-Michelin★, J Thévenet★★, Valette★, VERGET★★, J-J Vincent★. Best years: (2008) 07 **06** 05. See also VIRE-CLESSE.

ACULAN *Breganze DOC, Veneto, Italy* Fausto Maculan makes an impressive range under the Breganze DOC, led by Cabernet-Merlot blend Fratta★★ and Cabernet Palazzotto★, along with excellent reds★★ and whites★★ from the Ferrata vineyards. Even more impressive are sweet Torcolato★★ and outstanding Acininobili★★★, made mainly from botrytized Vespaiolo grapes.

ADEIRA DOC *Madeira, Portugal* The subtropical holiday island of Madeira seems an unlikely place to find a serious wine. However, Madeiras are very serious wines indeed and the best can survive to a great age. Modern Madeira was shaped by the oïdium epidemic of the 1850s, which wiped out the vineyards, and phylloxera, which struck in the

1870s. Replantation was with hybrid, non-vinifera vines greatly inferio
to the 'noble' and traditional Malvasia (or Malmsey), Boal (or Bual)
Verdelho and Sercial varieties. There are incentives to replant the hybrid
with European varieties, but progress is slow, and most of th
replantations are of the red Tinta Negra. The typically burnt, tang
taste of inexpensive Madeira comes from *estufagem*, heating in huge vats
but modern controls give better flavours than used to be possible. Th
best wines are aged naturally in the subtropical warmth. All except dr
wines are fortified early on and may be sweetened with fortified grap
juice before bottling. Basic 3-year-old Madeira is made mainly fror
Tinta Negra, whereas higher-quality 10-year-old, 15-year-old an
vintage wines (from a single year, aged in cask for at least 20 years) ten
to be made from 1 of the 4 'noble' grapes. Colheita is an early-bottle
vintage Madeira, which can be released after 5 years in wood (7 years fc
Sercial). Best producers: Barbeito, Barros e Souza, H M Borges, HENRIQUES
HENRIQUES, Vinhos Justino Henriques, MADEIRA WINE COMPANY, Pereir
d'Oliveira.

MADEIRA WINE COMPANY *Madeira DOC, Madeira, Portugal* This compan
ships more than half of all Madeira exported in bottle. Among the bran
names are Blandy's, Cossart Gordon, Leacock and Miles. Nov
controlled by the Symington family from the mainland. B
improvements are taking place in 5-, 10- and 15-year-old wine
including a tasty 5-year-old (a blend of Malvasia and Bual) calle
Alvada★. The vintage wines★★★ are superb. Specially blended 'earl
release' colheita wines are surprisingly tasty and complete.

MADIRAN AC *South-West France* The gentle hills of Vic-Bilh, north of Pa
have seen a steady revival of the Madiran AC. Several of the be
producers use new oak and micro-oxygenation, which helps to soften th
rather aggressive wine, based on the tannic Tannat grape – if you'
lucky, you'll taste damsons and bitter chocolate. Best producers: AYDIE★★
Barréjat★★, BERTHOUMIEU★★, Bouscassé★★, Capmartin★★, CHAPEL
LENCLOS★★, du Crampilh★, Labranche-Laffont★★, Laffitte-Teston★
MONTUS★★, Producteurs PLAIMONT, Viella★. Best years: (2005) 04 03 02 **01 0**
98 97 96.

CH. MAGDELAINE★ *St-Émilion Grand Cru AC, 1er Grand Cru Classé, Bordeau
France* Dark, rich, aggressive wines, yet with a load of luscious fruit an
oaky spice. In lighter years the wine has a gushing, easy, tender fruit an
can be enjoyed at 5–10 years. Owned by the quality-conscious compa
of MOUEIX. Best years: 2006 05 **04 03 01 00 99 98 96 95 90 89 88**.

MAIPO *Central Valley, Chile* Historic heart of the Chilean wine industry ar
increasingly encroached upon by Chile's capital, Santiago. Cabernet
king and many premium-priced reds come from here. Good Chardonn
from vineyards close to the Andes. Best producers: ALMAVIVA★★
Antiyal★★, CARMEN★★, CONCHA Y TORO★★, Cousiño Macul★, DE MARTINO★
ERRÁZURIZ (Viñedo Chadwick★★), HARAS DE PIRQUE★★, Pérez Cruz★, QUEBRAC
DE MACUL★★, SANTA RITA★★, Undurraga.

MAJELLA *Coonawarra, South Australia* The Lynn family are long-ter
grapegrowers turned successful winemakers. A trademark lush, swe
vanillin oakiness to the reds is always balanced by dense, opulent fru
The profound Malleea★★★ (Cabernet-Shiraz) is the flagship, while t
Cabernet Sauvignon★★★ (a succulent, fleshy cassis bomb) ar
Shiraz★★ are almost as good and very reasonably priced; t
Musician★★ (Cabernet-Shiraz) is rich but easy drinking.

MÁLAGA DO *Andalucía, Spain*   Málaga is a curious blend of sweet wine, alcohol and juices; production is dwindling. The best are intensely nutty, raisiny and caramelly. A 'sister' appellation, Sierras de Málaga (created in 2001) includes non-fortified wines. **Best producers: Gomara★, López Hermanos★★, Jorge Ordóñez★★, Telmo RODRIGUEZ★, Friedrich Schatz★.**

CH. MALARTIC-LAGRAVIÈRE★ *Pessac-Léognan AC, Cru Classé de Graves, Bordeaux, France*   A change of ownership in 1997 and massive investment in the vineyard and cellars have seen a steady improvement here since the 98 vintage. The tiny amount of white★★ is made from a majority of Sauvignon Blanc and usually softens after 3–4 years into a lovely nutty wine. **Best years: (reds) 2007 06 05 04 03 02 01 00 99 98 96 90 89; (whites) 2007 06 05 04 03 02 01 99.**

MALBEC   A red grape, rich in tannin and flavour, from South-West France. The major ingredient in CAHORS wines, where it is known as Auxerrois, it is also planted in the LOIRE, where it is called Côt. However, it is also successful in Chile and especially in Argentina, where it produces lush-textured, ripe, perfumed, damsony reds. In California and New Zealand it sometimes appears in BORDEAUX-style blends. In South Africa and Australia it is used both in blends and for varietal wines.

CH. MALESCOT ST-EXUPÉRY★ *Margaux AC, 3ème Cru Classé, Haut-Médoc, Bordeaux, France*   Once one of the most scented, exotic reds in Bordeaux, a model of perfumed MARGAUX. In the 1980s Malescot lost its reputation as the wine became pale, dilute and uninspired, but since 1995 it has begun to rediscover that cassis and violet perfume and return to its former glory. Can reach ★★, for example in 2004. **Best years: 2007 06 05 04 03 02 01 00 99 98 96 95 90.**

HERDADE DA MALHADINHA NOVA *Alentejo DOC, Portugal*   2003 arrival on the ALENTEJO wine scene, owned by the Soares family (who also have an Algarve wine-shop chain). Ultra-modern winery and wines, making Monte da Peceguinha red, white and rosé, and top wines, Malhadinha Tinto★★, Malhadinha Branco★ and Marias da Malhadinha★★.

MALVASIA   This grape, probably of Greek origin, is widely planted in Italy and is found in many guises, both white and red. In Friuli, it is known as the Malvasia Istriana and produces light, fragrant wines of great charm, while in TUSCANY, UMBRIA and the rest of central Italy it is used to improve the blend for wines like ORVIETO and FRASCATI. On the islands, Malvasia is used in rich, dry or sweet wines in Bosa and Cagliari (in SARDINIA) and in Lipari off the coast of SICILY to make really tasty, apricotty sweet wines. As a black grape, Malvasia Nera is blended with Negroamaro in PUGLIA and with Sangiovese in CHIANTI. Variants of Malvasia grow in Spain and mainland Portugal. On the island of MADEIRA it produces sweet fortified wine, usually known by its English name, Malmsey.

LA MANCHA DO *Castilla-La Mancha, Spain*   Spain's vast central plateau is Europe's biggest delimited wine area. Since 1995, DO regulations have allowed for irrigation and the planting of new, higher-quality grape varieties, including Macabeo (Viura), Verdejo, Chardonnay, Caberne Sauvignon, Petit Verdot, Merlot and Syrah – and also banned nev plantings of the simple white Airén grape. Whites are rarely (see AIREN exciting but nowadays are often fresh and attractive. Reds can be ligh and fruity, or richer. Best producers: Ayuso, Campos Reales★, Vinícola de Castilla (Castillo de Alhambra, Señorío de Guadianeja), Finca Antigua★ Fontana★, Muñoz (Blas Muñoz★), Rodriguez & Berger (Santa Elena), Torre Filoso (Arboles de Castillejo), Casa de la Viña.

DOM. ALBERT MANN *Alsace AC, Alsace, France* Powerful, flavoursome an ageworthy wines from a range of Grand Cru vineyards, includin intense, mineral Rieslings from Furstentum★★ and Schlossberg★★ an rich Furstentum Gewurztraminer★★. Impressive range of Pinot Gri culminates in some astonishingly concentrated Sélections de Grain Nobles★★★. Basic wines are increasingly stylish. Best years: (Sélection d Grains Nobles Gewurztraminer) (2007) 05 **01 00 98 97 94 89.**

MARANGES AC *Côte de Beaune, Burgundy, France* AC right at the souther tip of the CÔTE DE BEAUNE. Slightly tough red wines of medium dept which are mainly sold as CÔTE DE BEAUNE-VILLAGES. Less than 5% c production is white. Best producers: B Bachelet★, M Charleux★, Conta Grange★, DROUHIN, GIRARDIN★. Best years: (reds) (2008) 07 **05 03 02 99.**

MARCASSIN *Sonoma County, California, USA* Helen Turley focuses on coo climate Chardonnay and Pinot Noir. Incredible depth and restrain power are the hallmarks here. Tiny quantities of single-vineyar Chardonnays (Alexander Mountain Upper Barn, Three Sister Vineyard, Marcassin Vineyard) and Pinot Noirs (Marcassin Vineyar Three Sisters Vineyard, Blue Slide Vineyard) are very difficult to obtai but can rank ★★★ with those who manage to get a mouthful. Best year (2005) 04 03 02 01 **00 99 98.**

MARCHE *Italy* Adriatic region producing increasingly good reds fron Montepulciano and Sangiovese, led by ROSSO CONERO and ROSSO PICENO, als from the curiously aromatic, indigenous Lacrima di Morro d'Alba. Goo international varietals such as Cabernet, Chardonnay and Merlot under th Marche IGT or Esino DOC are becoming more common, as well as blenc with the native grapes. Best of the reds are Boccadigabbia's Akronte★ (Cabernet), Oasi degli Angeli's Kurni★★ (Montepulciano), Monte Schiavo Adeodato★★ (Montepulciano), Umani Ronchi's Pelago★★ (Montepulcianc Cabernet-Merlot), La Monacesca's Camerte★★ (Sangiovese-Merlot) and L Terrazze's Chaos★★ (Montepulciano-Merlot-Syrah). However, the tru original wines here are whites based on VERDICCHIO, from Bucci★★ Colonnara★, Coroncino★★, Garofoli★★, Mancinelli★, La Monacesca★★ Monte Schiavo★★, Sartarelli★, Umani Ronchi★.

MARCILLAC AC *South-West France* Curranty, dry red wines (and a litt rosé), largely made from a local grape, Mansois. The reds are rustic bu full of fruit and should be drunk at 2–5 years old. Best producers: Coste Cros/Philippe Teulier★, Marcillac-Vallon co-op, Jean-Luc Matha★, Mioula★.

MAREMMA *Tuscany, Italy* The name given to the Tuscan Tyrrhenian coas notably the southern part, which was only discovered wine-wise in th early 1970s, thanks to SASSICAIA. DOCs include (south to north Capalbio, Parrina, Bianco di Pitigliano, MORELLINO DI SCANSANC Montecucco, Monteregio di Massa Marittima, Val de Cornia, BOLGHEF And of course there's IGT Maremma Toscana, covering the province

Grosseto. In these climes, compared with inland, Sangiovese comes softer and jammier, the BORDEAUX grapes thrive and vintages count for much less.

ARGARET RIVER *Western Australia* Planted on the advice of agronomist John Gladstones from the late 1960s, this coastal region quickly established its name as a leading area for Cabernet, with marvellously deep, BORDEAUX-like structured reds. Now Chardonnay, concentrated and opulent, vies with Cabernet for top spot, but there is also fine grassy Semillon, often blended with citrus-zest Sauvignon. Increasingly popular Shiraz provides the occasional gem, but there's too much dull stuff. Best producers: Amberley★, Brookland Valley★, CAPE MENTELLE★★, Chapman Grove, Clairault★, CULLEN★★★, Devil's Lair★, Edwards★, Evans & Tate★★, Gralyn★, Hay Shed Hill★, HOWARD PARK★★, Juniper Estate, LEEUWIN ESTATE★★★, Lenton Brae★, McHenry Hohnen★, MOSS WOOD★★, PIERRO★★★, SANDALFORD★★, Stella Bella★★, VASSE FELIX★★, VOYAGER ESTATE★★, Windance, Woodlands★★, Xanadu. Best years: (Cabernet-based reds) 2008 07 05 04 03 01 **00** 99 98 96 95.

ARGAUX AC *Haut-Médoc, Bordeaux, France* AC centred on the village of Margaux. Gravel banks dotted through the vineyards mean the wines are rarely heavy and should have a divine perfume after 7–12 years. Best producers: (Classed Growths) Boyd-Cantenac★, BRANE-CANTENAC★★, Cantenac Brown, Dauzac★, FERRIÈRE★★, Giscours★★, ISSAN★, KIRWAN★, LASCOMBES, MALESCOT ST-EXUPERY★, MARGAUX★★★, PALMER★★, PRIEURE-LICHINE★, RAUZAN-SEGLA★★, Tertre★; (others) ANGLUDET★, Eyrins★, la Gurgue★, LABEGORCE-ZEDE★, Monbrison★, SIRAN★. Best years: 2006 05 **04** 03 02 01 00 99 96 95.

H. MARGAUX★★★ *Margaux AC, 1er Cru Classé, Haut-Médoc, Bordeaux, France* Frequently the greatest wine in the MEDOC. Has produced almost flawless wines since 1978, and inspired winemaker Paul Pontallier continues to produce the best from this great *terroir*. Also some delicious white, Pavillon Blanc★★, from Sauvignon Blanc, but it must be the most expensive BORDEAUX AC wine by a mile. Second wine: Pavillon Rouge★★. Best years: (reds) 2007 06 05 04 03 **02** 01 00 99 98 96 95 94 93 90 89 88 86 85; (whites) 2007 06 05 04 02 01 00 99 98 96 95.

ARIAH *Mendocino Ridge AVA, Mendocino County, California, USA* Boutique winery producing Zinfandel from a vineyard at 600m (2000ft) overlooking the Pacific Ocean. The wines have cherry fruit and naturally high acidity. Mariah Vineyard Zinfandel★★ is the flagship; Poor Ranch★ is lighter but elegant. A tiny amount of fruit-forward Syrah★ is also made. Best years: (Zinfandel) 2005 **02** 01 00 99.

ARLBOROUGH *South Island, New Zealand* This wine region has enjoyed ach spectacular success that it is difficult to imagine that the first commercial nes were planted as recently as 1973. Marlborough is now home to more an half the country's vines. Its 2 main vineyard areas are Wairau Valley and VATERE VALLEY, and its long, cool and relatively dry ripening season, cool ghts and free-draining stony soils are the major assets. Its snappy, aromatic uvignon Blanc first brought the region fame worldwide. Fine-flavoured hardonnay, steely Riesling, elegant CHAMPAGNE-method fizz and luscious trytized wines are other successes. Pinot Noir is now establishing a strong gional identity. Best producers: Cape Campbell★, Clifford Bay★, CLOUDY Y★★, The Crossings★, Dog Point★★, Forrest Estate★★, Foxes Island★, amingham★, FROMM★★, HUNTER'S★, Isabel, JACKSON ESTATE, Lawson's Dry Hills★,

Mansion House★, MONTANA, MORTON ESTATE★, Mount Riley★, Nautilus★, SAIN
CLAIR★★, SERESIN★, Stoneleigh★, VAVASOUR★★, VILLA MARIA★★, WITHER HILLS
Yealands★. Best years: (Chardonnay) **2007 06 05 03**; (Pinot Noir) **2007 06 05 0**
03 01; (Sauvignon Blanc) **2007 06**.

MARQUÉS DE CÁCERES *Rioja DOCa, Rioja, Spain* Go-ahead RIOJA wine:
making crisp, aromatic, modern whites★ and rosés★, and fleshy, frui
reds (Reservas★) with the emphasis on aging in bottle, not barrel. The
is also a luxury red, Gaudium★. Best years: (reds) (2006) 05 **04 03 01 99 9**
96 95 94 92 91 90 89.

MARQUÉS DE GRIÑÓN *Castilla-La Mancha, Spain* From his estate
Malpica, near Toledo, now with its own Dominio de Valdepusa D(
Carlos Falcó (the eponymous Marqués) produces some impressive
super-ripe wines: Dominio de Valdepusa Cabernet Sauvignon★, Pe
Verdot★★, Syrah★ and the top wine, Eméritus★, a blend of the
varieties. A new Graciano★★ vineyard went into production in 200
with stunning results. The joint venture with the Arco/BERBERANA grou
which developed the Marqués de Griñón wines from RIOJA, has bee
phased out. Best years: (Eméritus) 2004 03 **02 01 00 99 98**.

MARQUÉS DE MURRIETA *Rioja DOCa,*
Rioja, Spain This RIOJA bodega
faithfully preserves the traditional
style of long aging, but typical time in
barrel has been reduced by a third.
The ornately labelled Castillo Ygay
Gran Reserva★★ is less forbidding
than in the past. There's a more
international-styled, oaky, upmarket
cuvée, Dalmau★★. Whites are
dauntingly oaky but age brilliantly,
reds are packed with savoury mulberry

fruit. Best years: (reds) (2006) 05 04 **03 01 00 99 96 95 94 92 91 89 87 8**

MARQUÉS DE RISCAL *Rioja DOCa, País Vasco and Rueda DO, Castilla y León, Spa*
A producer which has restored its reputation for classic pungent RIC
reds (Reserva★). Expensive, Cabernet-based Barón de Chirel★★ is ma
only in selected years. Attractively aromatic RUEDA whites
Best years: (Barón de Chirel) **2001 96 95 94**.

MARSALA DOC *Sicily, Italy* Fortified wines, once as esteemed as sherry
Madeira. A taste of an old Vergine (unsweetened) Marsala, fine a
complex, will show why. Today most is sweetened. Purists say this ma
its delicate nuances, but DOC regulations allow for sweetening Fine a
Superiore versions. Best producers: DE BARTOLI★★, Florio (Baglio Florio
Terre Arse★), Pellegrino (Soleras★, Riserva 1962★).

MARSANNAY AC *Côte de Nuits, Burgundy, France* Village almost in Dijo
best known for its pleasant but quite austere rosé. Reds are much bette
light, but frequently one of Burgundy's most fragrant wines. Whit
mostly dull. Best producers: Audoin★, P Charlopin★★, B CLAIR★★, Geant
Pansiot★★, JADOT★, MEO-CAMUZET★, D MORTET★★, Pataille★★, J & J
Trapet★. Best years: (reds) (2008) 07 **06 05 03 02**.

MARSANNE Undervalued white grape yielding rich, nutty, wines in t
northern Rhône (notably HERMITAGE, CROZES-HERMITAGE, ST-JOSEPH and S
PERAY), often with the more lively Roussanne. Generally drink your

except the Hermitage, which can mature for decades. Also used in southern Rhône, PIC ST-LOUP and other LANGUEDOC wines, and performs well in Australia at Mitchelton and TAHBILK. As Ermitage, it produces some good wines in Swiss VALAIS.

MARTINBOROUGH *North Island, New Zealand* A cool, dry climate, free-draining soil and a passion for quality are this region's greatest assets. Mild autumn weather promotes intense flavours balanced by good acidity: top Pinot Noir and complex Chardonnay, intense Cabernet blends, full Sauvignon Blanc and honeyed Riesling. Best producers: ATA RANGI★★★, CRAGGY RANGE★, DRY RIVER★★★, Escarpment★, MARTINBOROUGH VINEYARD★★, Murdoch James★, Nga Waka★, PALLISER ESTATE★★. Best years: (Pinot Noir) (2008) **07 06 03 01 00**.

MARTINBOROUGH VINEYARD *Martinborough, North Island, New Zealand* Famous for Pinot Noir★★ but also makes impressive Chardonnay★, spicy Riesling★, creamy Pinot Gris★ and luscious botrytized styles★★ when vintage conditions allow. Good vineyard sites and sensitive winemaking have produced a string of very elegant wines. Best years: (Pinot Noir) (2008) 07 **06** 03 01 00.

MARTÍNEZ BUJANDA *Rioja DOCa, País Vasco, Spain* This family-owned firm, known for producing some of the best modern RIOJA, was split in two in 2007: Carlos and Pilar Martínez-Bujanda retain the Finca Valpiedra and Finca Antigua estates and the Cosecheros y Criadores wine company, while Jesús Martínez-Bujanda keeps the Valdemar winery in Rioja. The 2006 vintage saw a commendable modernization of style for Valpiedra; young-vines red Cantos★ is soft and lush, Reserva★★ is scented and refined. Whites and rosés are young and crisp.

MARZEMINO This red grape of northern Italy's TRENTINO province makes deep-coloured, plummy and zesty reds that are best drunk within 3–5 years. Best producers: Battistotti★, La Cadalora★, Cavit★, Concilio Vini★, Isera co-op★, Letrari★, Mezzacorona, Eugenio Rosi★, Simoncelli★, Spagnolli★, De Tarczal★, Vallarom★, Vallis Agri★.

DOM. DU MAS BLANC *Banyuls AC, Roussillon, France* Run by the Parcé family, this estate makes great traditional BANYULS, specializing in the *rimage* (early-bottled vintage) style (La Coume★★). Also Banyuls Hors d'Age from a solera laid down in 1955, plus a range of Jean-Michel Parcé COLLIOURES★★. Best years: 2005 04 03 **01 00** 98.

MAS BRUGUIÈRE *Pic St-Loup, Coteaux du Languedoc AC, Languedoc, France* The basic PIC ST-LOUP red, L' Arbouse★ has rich, spicy Syrah character, while La Grenadière★★ develops buckets of black fruit and spice after 3 years. Super-cuvée Le Septième★★ (seventh generation) is a blend of Mourvèdre with some Syrah. Calcadiz is an easy-drinking red from young vines. Aromatic, fruity and refreshingly crisp Roussanne-based white Les Mûriers★. Best years: (reds) (2008) 07 06 05 **04 03** 01.

MAS LA CHEVALIÈRE *Vin de Pays d'Oc, Languedoc, France* State-of-the-art winery created by Chablis producer Michel LAROCHE in the early 1990s. Innovative wines include La Croix Chevalière★, a blend of Merlot, Syrah and Grenache, and Mas la Chevalière Rouge★, from the estate vineyard. Also new range of inexpensive varietals. Best years: (2008) 07 06 05 **04 03** 01.

MAS DE DAUMAS GASSAC *Vin de Pays de l'Hérault, Languedoc, France* Aimé
Guibert has proved for over 20 years that the HERAULT, normally
associated with cheap table wine, can produce fine, ageworthy reds. The
tannic yet rich Cabernet Sauvignon-based red★, more concentrated
Cuvée Emile Peynaud★★ and the lush, scented white★ (Viognier,
Chardonnay, Petit Manseng and Chenin) are impressive, if expensive.
Sweet Vin de Laurence★★ is a triumph. Best years: (reds) 2007 06 05 **04** 03
02 01 00 99 98.

MAS DOIX *Priorat DOCa, Cataluña, Spain* The Doix and Llagostera families
own some extraordinary old Garnacha and Cariñena vineyards, which
provide the grapes for some equally impressive wines. Doix Vinyes
Velles★★★ is probably the first of the new generation PRIORATS to reach
the heights of the pioneers such as CLOS ERASMUS, CLOS MOGADOR and
Alvaro PALACIOS' L'Ermita. Best years: 2006 05 04 03 **02 01**.

BARTOLO MASCARELLO *Barolo DOCG, Piedmont, Italy* Bartolo Mascarello
died in 2005; his daughter Maria Teresa has run the winery since the
early 1990s. Proudly traditional, the BAROLO★★★ wines have an exquisite
perfume and balance. The Dolcetto★ and Barbera★ can need a little time
to soften. Best years: (Barolo) (2008) (07) (06) 04 **03 01 00 99 98 97 96 95
90 89 88 86 85**.

GIUSEPPE MASCARELLO *Barolo DOCG, Piedmont, Italy* The old house of
Giuseppe Mascarello (now run by grandson Mauro) is renowned for
dense, vibrant Dolcetto d'Alba (Bricco★★) and intense Barbera
(Codana★★), but the pride of the house is BAROLO from the superb
south-west-facing Monprivato★★★ vineyard in Castiglione Falletto. A
little is now produced as a Riserva, Cà d'Morissio★★★, in top years.
Small amounts are also made from the Bricco, Santo Stefano di Perno
and Villero vineyards. Best years: (Monprivato) (2008) (07) (06) 04 03 01 **00
99 98 97 96 95 93 91 90 89 88 85 82 78**.

MASI *Veneto, Italy* Family firm, one of the driving forces in VALPOLICELLA.
Brolo di Campofiorin★ (effectively if not legally a *ripasso* Valpolicella) is
worth looking out for, as is AMARONE (Mazzano★★ and Campolongo di
Torbe★★). Valpolicella's Corvina grape is also used in red blend Toar★;
Osar★ is made from a local grape, Oseleta, rediscovered by Masi. The
wines of Serègo Alighieri★ are also produced by Masi. Best years:
(Amarone) (2008) (07) 06 **04 03 01 00 97**.

MASTROBERARDINO *Campania, Italy* This family firm has long flown the
flag for CAMPANIA in southern Italy, though it has now been joined by
others. Best known for red TAURASI★★ and white Greco di Tufo★ and
Fiano di Avellino★. Best years: (Taurasi Radici) (2008) (07) (06) 05 **04 03 0**
99 97 96 95 90 89 88 85 68.

MATANZAS CREEK *Bennett Valley AVA, Sonoma County, California, USA*
Sauvignon Blanc★★ is taken seriously here, and it shows in a complex
zesty wine; Chardonnay★★ is rich and toasty but not overblown.
Merlot★★ has silky, mouthfilling richness. Journey Chardonnay★★ and
Merlot★★ are opulent but pricey. Much experimentation by French-
trained winemaker François Cordesse, who (among other projects) is
aging a bit of Chardonnay in acacia wood barrels. Owned by Jess Jackson
(of KENDALL-JACKSON). Best years: (Chardonnay) 2006 05 04 **03 02 01 00**
(Merlot) 2005 04 03 02 **01 00 99 97 96 95**.

MATETIC VINEYARDS *San Antonio, Chile* Matetic has been making high-
quality wines from the SAN ANTONIO Valley – especially under the EQ
label – since it burst on to the scene in 2001. Exceptional, concentrated

and scented Syrah★★ is the star, but there's also a fleshy Pinot Noir★, juicy Sauvignon Blanc★ and refreshing new Coastal Sauvignon★.

MATUA VALLEY *Auckland, North Island, New Zealand* In 2001 Matua became part of Beringer-Blass (now Foster's Group), with the consequent introduction of an uninspired budget range. Top wines are still good, with whites more consistent than reds: sensuous, scented Ararimu Chardonnay★★; lush, strongly varietal Gewürztraminer★; tangy MARLBOROUGH Sauvignon Blanc★; fine Merlot★; and Ararimu★, a normally blended red which was 100% Merlot in 2004. Second label: Shingle Peak. Best years: (Ararimu red) (2007) **04 03 02 00**.

CH. MAUCAILLOU★ *Moulis AC, Haut-Médoc, Bordeaux, France* Maucaillou shows that you don't have to be a Classed Growth to make high-quality claret. Expertly made by the Dourthe family, it is soft but classically flavoured. It is accessible early on but ages well for 10–12 years. Best years: 2006 **05 04 03 02 00 98 96 95 90**.

MAULE *Central Valley, Chile* The most southerly sub-region of Chile's CENTRAL VALLEY, with wet winters and a large day/night temperature difference. Nearly 30% of Chile's vines are planted here, with nearly 10,000ha (25,000 acres) of Cabernet Sauvignon. Merlot does well on the cool clay soils, and there is some tasty Carmenère and Syrah. Whites are mostly Chardonnay and Sauvignon Blanc. A new and exciting community of producers has recently been redefining Maule's identity, and there's a feeling that Maule's old 'bulk' mentality must give way to a quality focus if the area's great potential is to be realized. Best producers: J Bouchon, Calina (KENDALL-JACKSON), Casa Donoso, CONCHA Y TORO★, DE MARTINO★★, O Fournier★, Gillmore★★, La Reserva de Caliboro★★, Odfjell★, VALDIVIESO★.

MAURO AC *Castilla y León, Spain* After making a name for himself as VEGA SICILIA's winemaker for 30 years, Mariano García propelled his family's estate to the forefront in Spain and abroad. Wines include Crianza★★, Vendimia Seleccionada★★ and Terreus★★★. Best years: (2007) 06 05 **04 03 02 01 00 99 98 97 96 95 94**.

MAURY AC *Roussillon, France* A *vin doux naturel*, mainly from Grenache Noir. This strong, sweetish wine can be made in either a young, fresh style (vintage) or the locally revered old *rancio* style. Best producers: la Coume du Roy★, Mas Amiel★★, Maury co-op★, Maurydoré★, la Pléiade★.

MAXIMIN GRÜNHAUS *Grünhaus, Mosel-Saar-Ruwer, Germany* One of Germany's great wine estates. Dr Carl von Schubert vinifies separately the wines of his 2 top vineyards, Abtsberg and Herrenberg, both of monastic origin. He makes chiefly dry and medium-dry wines of great subtlety. In good vintages the top wines are certainly ★★★ and are among the most long-lived white wines in the world. Best years: (2008) 07 06 05 **04 03 01 00 99 97 95 94 93 92 90 89**.

MAZIS-CHAMBERTIN AC See CHAMBERTIN AC.

MAZOYÈRES-CHAMBERTIN AC See CHAMBERTIN AC.

McLAREN VALE *South Australia* Sunny maritime region south of Adelaide, producing superb full-bodied wines from Shiraz, Grenache and Cabernet. Its warmth means that the whites rarely impress, though Coriole's Fiano has raised eyebrows. More than 60 small wineries, plus big boys Constellation and the Foster's Wine Group. Best producers: Cascabel, CHAPEL HILL★★, CLARENDON HILLS★★, Coriole★, D'ARENBERG★★, FOX CREEK★★, Gemtree, HARDYS★★, Kangarilla Road, Maxwell★, Geoff MERRILL★, Mitolo★★, Oliver's Taranga★, S C PANNELL★★, Paxton, Penny's Hill,

Pirramimma, PRIMO ESTATE★★, RockBare, Shingleback, Tatachilla★, WIRRA WIRRA★★, Woodstock.

McWILLIAM'S *Riverina, New South Wales, Australia* Large family winery whose Hanwood brand is a joint venture with California's GALLO delivering good flavours at a fair price. Best are the Mount Pleasant wines from the HUNTER VALLEY: classic bottle-aged Semillons (Elizabeth★★★ Lovedale★★★), buttery Chardonnays★ and special-vineyard Shirazes – Old Paddock & Old Hill, Maurice O'Shea (★★ in the best years) and Rosehill★. Classy Liqueur Muscat★★ from RIVERINA, and good table wines from HILLTOPS Barwang★ vineyard. McWilliam's own Lillydale in the YARRA (sublime Chardonnay★★), BRAND'S in COONAWARRA, and in 2008 bought the outstanding Evans & Tate label following the collapse of the MARGARET RIVER-based company. **Best years:** (Elizabeth Semillon) (2008) (06) (05) 04 03 02 01 **00 99 98 97 96 95 94 87 86 84 83**.

MÉDOC AC *Bordeaux, France* The Médoc peninsula north of Bordeaux on the left bank of the Gironde river produces a good fistful of the world's most famous reds. These are all situated in the HAUT-MEDOC, the southern more gravelly half of the area. The Médoc AC, for reds only, covers the northern part. Merlot dominates in these flat clay vineyards and the wines can be attractive in warm years: dry but juicy. Best at 3–5 years old. **Best producers:** Bournac★, Escurac★, les Grands Chênes★, Greysac★ Goulée★, L'Inclassable★, Loudenne, Lousteauneuf★, les Ormes-Sorbet★ Patache d'Aux, POTENSAC★★, Preuillac, Ramafort★, Rollan de By★ (Haut Condissas★), la Tour de By★, la Tour Haut-Caussan★, Tour St-Bonnet★ Vieux-Robin★. **Best years: 2006 05 04 03 01 00 96 95.**

MEERLUST *Stellenbosch WO, South Africa* Elegant, fresh Chardonnay★ was the earliest beneficiary of new cellarmaster Chris Williams's thoughtful informed approach. His maiden vintage of reds show similar attention. Cabernet★★ is supple yet vibrant, Merlot★ plush and finely textured together with Cabernet Franc in Rubicon★, one of the Cape's first BORDEAUX blends, achieving harmony and complexity. A silky Pinot Noir completes the range from this venerable estate. **Best years:** (Rubicon) (2005) 04 03 01 00 99 98 97 95; (Chardonnay) (2008) **07 06 05 04 03 01.**

ALPHONSE MELLOT *Sancerre AC, Loire Valley, France* Biodynamic producer with an equal focus on white and red SANCERRE, made with obsessive attention to detail by Alphonse 'Junior', the 19th generation of the family. Other than unoaked white cuvée La Moussière★, wines come exclusively from shy-bearing old vines and show a fine balance of fruit and oak. New cuvée En Satellite de Sancerre comes from Chavignol vines planted in 1948. White Edmond★★ and red and white Génération XIX★★ are outstanding and reward keeping. Also makes aromatic, fruity Chardonnay and Pinot Noir, Les Pénitents, in neighbouring Vin de Pays des Coteaux Charitois. **Best years:** (Edmond) 2008 07 **06 05 04 03 02 01 00.**

CHARLES MELTON *Barossa Valley, South Australia* One of the leading lights in the renaissance of hand-crafted Shiraz, Grenache and Mourvèdre in the BAROSSA. Fruity Grenache rosé Rose of Virginia★★ is arguably Australia's best; RHÔNE-blend Nine Popes★★ (can be ★★★), heady sumptuous Grenache★★, smoky Shiraz★★ and Sparkling Red★★ have all attained cult status. Cabernet Sauvignon is variable, but ★★ at best. Two new single-site Shiraz: fleshy, blackberry-pastille Grains of Paradise from the Barossa Valley, and fragrant, elegant, brambly Voices of Angels from the Eden Valley. **Best years:** (Nine Popes) (2008) 05 04 **03 02 01 99 98 96 95 94 91 90.**

MENDOCINO COUNTY *California, USA* The northernmost county of the North Coast AVA. It includes cool-climate ANDERSON VALLEY, excellent for sparkling wines and a little Pinot Noir; and the warmer Redwood Valley AVA, with good Zinfandel and Cabernet. Coro is a stylish Zinfandel-based blend made by numerous Mendocino wineries. Best producers: Brutocao★, Claudia Springs★, FETZER, Goldeneye★, HANDLEY★★, Husch, Lazy Creek★, McDowell Valley★, NAVARRO★★★, ROEDERER ESTATE★★, Saracina★, SCHARFFENBERGER CELLARS★. Best years: (reds) 2006 05 04 **03 01 00 99 97 96 95 94 93 91 90**.

MENDOCINO RIDGE AVA *California, USA* One of the most unusual AVAs in California. Mendocino Ridge starts at an altitude of 365m (1200ft) on the timber-covered mountaintops of western MENDOCINO COUNTY. Because of the topography, the AVA is non-contiguous: rising above the fog, the vineyards are commonly referred to as 'islands in the sky'. Currently only 30ha (75 acres) are planted, primarily with Zinfandel. Best producers: Edmeades★, Greenwood Ridge★, MARIAH★, STEELE★★.

MENDOZA *Argentina* The most important wine province in Argentina, accounting for around 80% of the country's wine. Situated in the eastern foothills of the Andes, Mendoza's bone-dry climate produces powerful, high-alcohol reds. Just south of Mendoza city, Maipú and LUJAN DE CUYO are ideal for Malbec, Syrah and Cabernet Sauvignon. High-altitude regions nearer the Andes, such as UCO VALLEY, produce better whites, particularly Chardonnay, but also thrilling reds. Best producers: ACHAVAL-FERRER★★, ALTOS LAS HORMIGAS★, Luigi bosca★, CATENA★★, COBOS★, Doña Paula★, Finca El Retiro★, Finca Sophenia, O FOURNIER★★, Nieto Senetiner (Cadus★★), NORTON★, Pulenta★, Salentein★, TERRAZAS DE LOS ANDES★★, ZUCCARDI★.

MENETOU-SALON AC *Loire Valley, France* Attractive, chalky-clean Sauvignon whites and cherry-fresh Pinot Noir reds and rosés from west of SANCERRE. Best producers: R Champault, Chatenoy★, Chavet★, J-P Gilbert★, P Jacolin, J Mellot, H Pellé★, J-M Roger★, J Teiller★, Tour St-Martin★.

MÉO-CAMUZET *Vosne-Romanée, Côte de Nuits, Burgundy, France* Super-quality estate, run by Jean-Nicolas Méo. New oak barrels and luscious, rich fruit combine in superb wines, which also age well. CLOS DE VOUGEOT★★★, RICHEBOURG★★★ and CORTON★ are the grandest wines, along with the VOSNE-ROMANEE Premiers Crus, aux Brulées★★, Cros Parantoux★★★ and les Chaumes★★. Fine NUITS-ST-GEORGES aux Boudots★★ and aux Murgers★★, and now also some less expensive *négociant* wines. Best years: (2008) 07 06 05 03 02 **01 00 99 96 95 93 90**.

MERCUREY AC *Côte Chalonnaise, Burgundy, France* Most important of the 4 main CÔTE CHALONNAISE villages. The red is usually pleasant and strawberry-flavoured, sometimes rustic, and can take some aging. There is not much white, but I like its buttery, even spicy, taste. Best at 3–4 years old. Best producers: (reds) FAIVELEY★, Hasard★, E Juillot★, M Juillot★, Lorenzon★★, F Raquillet★★, RODET★, de Suremain★★, de Villaine★★; (whites) FAIVELEY (Clos Rochette★), M Juillot★, O LEFLAIVE★, Ch. de Chamirey★/RODET. Best years: (reds) (2008) **07 05 03 02 99**.

MERLOT See pages 206–7.

GEOFF MERRILL *McLaren Vale, South Australia* High-profile winemaker with a long track record. There's a nicely bottle-aged Reserve Cabernet★ in a light, early-picked, slightly eccentric style, Reserve Shiraz★ (Henley Shiraz★★) and Chardonnay★ (Reserve★★). Also a moreish unoaked and ageworthy Bush Vine Grenache★★.

MERLOT

Red wine without tears. That's the reason Merlot has vaulted from being merely Bordeaux's red wine support act, well behind Cabernet Sauvignon in terms of class, to being the red wine drinker's darling, planted like fury all over the world. It i able to claim some seriousness and pedigree, but – crucially - can make wine of a fat, juicy character mercifully low in tannic bitterness which can be glugged with gay abandon almost as soon as the juice ha squirted from the press. Yet this doesn't mean that Merlot is the jell baby of red wine grapes. Far from it.

WINE STYLES

Bordeaux Merlot The great wines of Pomerol and St-Émilion, on the right bank of the Dordogne, are largely based on Merlot and the best o these – for example, Château Pétrus, which is almost 100% Merlot – ca mature for 20–30 years. In fact there is more Merlot than Caberne Sauvignon planted throughout Bordeaux, and I doubt if there is a singl red wine property that does not have some growing, because the variet ripens early, can cope with cool conditions and is able to bear a heav crop of fruit. In a cool, damp area like Bordeaux, Cabernet Sauvigno cannot always ripen, so the soft, mellow character of Merlot is fundamental component of the blend even in the best, Cabernet dominated, Médoc estates, imparting a supple richness an approachability to the wines. Up-and-coming areas like Blaye and Côte de Castillon depend on it.

Other European regions The south of France has briskly adopted th variety, producing easy-drinking, fruit-driven wines, but in the ho Languedoc the grape often ripens too fast to express its full personalit and can seem a little simple, even raw-edged, unless handled well. Ital has long used very high-crop Merlot to produce a simple, light quaffer i the north, particularly in the Veneto, though Friuli and Alto Adige mak fuller styles and there are some very impressive examples from Tuscan and as far south as Sicily. The Swiss canton of Ticino is often unjustl overlooked for its intensely fruity, oak-aged versions. Eastern Europe ha the potential to provide fertile pastures for Merlot and so far the mos convincing, albeit simple, styles have come from Hungary and Bulgaria the younger examples are almost invariably better than the old. Spain ha developed decent Merlot credentials since the mid-1990s, but has fe sites cool enough for the variety.

New World Youth is also important in the New World, nowhere mor so than in Chile. Chilean Merlot, mostly blended with Carmenère, ha leapt to the front of the pack of New World examples with gorgeou garnet-red wines of unbelievable crunchy fruit richness that cry out to b drunk virtually in their infancy. California Merlots often have mor serious pretensions, but the nature of the grape is such that its soft, juic quality still shines through. The cooler conditions in Washington Stat have produced some impressive wines, and the east coast of the US ha good examples from places such as Long Island. With some Frenc input, South Africa is starting to get Merlot right, and in New Zealan the warm, dry conditions of Hawkes Bay and Waiheke Island ar producing classic styles. Only Australia seems to find Merl problematic, but there are some fine exceptions from cooler area including some surprisingly good fizzes – red fizzes, that is!

WOODWARD CANYON

2005

Columbia Valley
Merlot

BEST PRODUCERS

France

Bordeaux (St-Émilion) ANGELUS, AUSONE, BEAU-SEJOUR BECOT, Clos Fourtet, la Mondotte, TERTRE-ROTEBOEUF, TROPLONG-MONDOT, VALANDRAUD; *(Pomerol)* le BON PASTEUR, Certan-de-May, Clinet, la CONSEILLANTE, l'EGLISE-CLINET, l'EVANGILE, la FLEUR-PETRUS, GAZIN, LATOUR-A-POMEROL, PETIT-VILLAGE, PETRUS, le PIN, TROTANOY.

Other European Merlots

Italy (Friuli) Livio FELLUGA; *(Tuscany)* Castello di AMA, AVIGNONESI, Castelgiocondo (Lamaione), Ghizzano, Le MACCHIOLE, ORNELLAIA, Petrolo, San Giusto a Rentennano, TUA RITA; *(Lazio)* FALESCO; *(Sicily)* PLANETA.

Spain (Navarra) Nekeas; *(Penedès)* Can Ràfols dels Caus; *(Somontano)* ENATE; *(Vino de la Tierra de Castilla)* Pago del Ama.

Switzerland Gialdi (Sassi Grossi), Daniel Huber, Stucky, Tamborini, Christian Zündel.

New World Merlots

USA (California) ARROWOOD, BERINGER, CHATEAU ST JEAN, MATANZAS CREEK, MERRYVALE, NEWTON, Pahlmeyer, SHAFER, STERLING; *(Washington)* ANDREW WILL, LEONETTI, LONG SHADOWS (Pedestal), WOODWARD CANYON; *(New York)* BEDELL, LENZ.

Australia BRAND'S, CLARENDON HILLS, COLDSTREAM HILLS, Elderton, Irvine, PARKER COONAWARRA ESTATE, Tatachilla, YALUMBA (Heggies).

New Zealand CRAGGY RANGE, Esk Valley, GOLDWATER, C J PASK, Sacred Hill (Broken Stone), TRINITY HILL, VILLA MARIA.

South Africa STEENBERG, THELEMA, VEENWOUDEN, VERGELEGEN.

Chile CARMEN, CASA LAPOSTOLLE (Cuvée Alexandre), CASABLANCA (Santa Isabel), CONCHA Y TORO, CONO SUR (20 Barrels), Gillmore.

MERRYVALE *Napa Valley AVA, California, USA* A Chardonnay powerhouse (Silhouette★★, CARNEROS★★, Starmont★★), but reds are not far behind, with BORDEAUX-blend Profile★★ and juicy NAPA VALLEY Merlot★★. Best years: (Chardonnay) 2007 06 **05 04 03 02 01 00 99**.

MEURSAULT AC *Côte de Beaune, Burgundy, France* The biggest and most popular white wine village in the CÔTE D'OR. There are no Grands Crus, but a whole cluster of Premiers Crus, of which Perrières, Charmes and Genevrières stand out. The general standard is better than in neighbouring Puligny. The golden wine is lovely to drink young but better aged for 5–8 years. Virtually no Meursault red is now made. Best producers: R Ampeau★★, M BOUZEREAU★★, V Bouzereau★, Boyer-Martenot★★, Coche-Bizouard★★, COCHE-DURY★★★, Deux MONTILLE★, DROUHIN★, A Ente★★★, J-P Fichet★★, Henri Germain★, V GIRARDIN★★, Grux★, JADOT★★, P Javillier★★, François Jobard★★, Rémi Jobard★★, LAFON★★★, Latour-Labille★, Matrot★★, Mikulski★, Pierre Morey★★, G Roulot★★★. Best years: (2008) 07 06 05 **04 02 00 99**.

CH. MEYNEY★ *St-Estèphe AC, Haut-Médoc, Bordeaux, France* One of the most reliable ST-ESTÈPHEs, producing broad-flavoured wine with dark, plummy fruit. Second wine: Prieur de Meyney. Best years: 2006 05 **04 03 02 01 00** 99 98 96 95 94 90 89.

PETER MICHAEL WINERY *Sonoma County, California, USA* British-born Sir Peter Michael has turned a country retreat into an impressive winery known for its small-batch wines. Les Pavots★★ is the estate red BORDEAUX blend, and Mon Plaisir★★ and Cuvée Indigène★ are his top Chardonnays, both noted for their deep, layered flavours. Best years: (Les Pavots) 2006 05 04 03 02 01 **00 99 97 96 95 94 91 90**.

MILLTON *Gisborne, North Island, New Zealand* Organic vineyard using biodynamic methods, whose top wines include the sophisticated Clos de Ste Anne Chardonnay★★, Opou Vineyard Riesling★ and complex barrel-fermented Chenin Blanc★. Chardonnays and Rieslings both age well. Best years: (whites) **2007 05 04**.

MINER FAMILY VINEYARDS *Oakville AVA, California, USA* Dave Miner has 32ha (80 acres) planted on a ranch 300m (1000ft) above the OAKVILLE valley floor. Highlights include yeasty, full-bodied Chardonnay★ (Oakville Ranch★★, Wild Yeast★★) as well as intense Merlot★★ and Cabernet Sauvignon★★ that demand a decade of aging. Also a stylish Viognier★★ and a striking Rosé★ from purchased fruit.

MINERVOIS AC *Languedoc, France* Attractive, mostly red wines from north-east of Carcassonne, made mainly from Syrah, Carignan and Grenache. The local co-ops produce good, juicy, quaffing wine at reasonable prices, but the best wines are made by the estates: full of ripe, red fruit and pine dust perfume, for drinking young. It can age, especially if a little new oak has been used. A village denomination, La Livinière, covering 6 superior communes whose wines can be particularly scented and fine, can be appended to the Minervois label. Best producers: (reds) Aires Hautes★, Ch Bonhomme★, Borie de Maurel★, CLOS CENTEILLES★★, Pierre Cros★, Fabas★, Grave, HECHT & BANNIER★, Maris★, Oupia, Oustal Blanc★, Primo Palatum, Pujol, Rieux, Senat★★, Ste-Eulalie★, TOUR BOISÉE★, Villerambert-Julien★. Best years: (2008) 07 06 05 **04 03 02 01**.

CH. LA MISSION-HAUT-BRION★★★ *Pessac-Léognan AC, Cru Classé de Graves, Bordeaux, France* 2008 was the year I finally accepted the true brilliance of La Mission. In the past I had often found the wine long on power but short on grace, but the owners laid on a vertical tasting reaching way back into the 1920s and the general quality level was majestic, with the vintages since 1990 actually outshining the admittedly beautiful earlier wines. Muscularity and richness combined with depth and fragrance is quite a challenge, but La Mission meets it triumphantly. Best years: 2007 06 05 04 **03** 02 **01** 00 **98 96 95 94 90 89 88 85**.

MISSION HILL *Okanagan Valley VQA, British Columbia, Canada* The winery has expanded its operations and hired consultant Michel Rolland to help Kiwi winemaker John Sims craft some of the most noteworthy wines from the OKANAGAN VALLEY. Excellent Chardonnay★★, Pinot Blanc★ and Sauvignon-Semillon★ are joined by Merlot★, Cabernet Sauvignon, Pinot Noir and Shiraz★, and a red BORDEAUX-style blend, Oculus★★.

MITCHELL *Clare Valley, South Australia* Jane and Andrew Mitchell turn out some of CLARE VALLEY's most ageworthy Watervale Riesling★★ and a classy barrel-fermented Growers Semillon★. Growers Grenache★ is a huge, unwooded, heady fruit bomb. Peppertree Shiraz★★ and Sevenhill Cabernet Sauvignon★ are plump, chocolaty and typical of the region.

MITTELRHEIN *Germany* Small (465ha/1150-acre), northerly wine region. Almost 70% of the wine here is Riesling, but the Mittelrhein vineyards are shrinking as the sites are steep and difficult to work. The best growers (like Toni JOST★, Müller★, Perll★ and Weingart★★), clustered around Bacharach and Boppard, make wines of a striking mineral tang and dry, fruity intensity. Best years: (2008) 07 06 **05 04 02 01**.

MOËT & CHANDON *Champagne AC, Champagne, France* Moët & Chandon dominates the CHAMPAGNE market (more than 25 million bottles a year), and has become a major producer of sparkling wine in California, Argentina, Brazil and Australia too. Non-vintage has started to exhibit distressing unreliability, and some recent releases have really not been acceptable. There has been a change of winemaker and hopefully this will put the vintage release at least back on track. Interestingly, the vintage rosé★★ can show a rare Pinot Noir floral fragrance. Dom Pérignon★★★ is the de luxe cuvée. It can be one of the greatest Champagnes of all, but you've got to age it for a number of years after release or you're wasting your money. Best years: 2003 (02) 00 99 **98 96 95 90 88 86 85 82**.

MARKUS MOLITOR *Bernkastel-Wehlen, Mosel, Germany* Dynamic estate with fine vineyards throughout Middle MOSEL and Saar. Brilliant Riesling Auslesen, often ★★★, and probably the best Spätburgunder (Pinot Noir)★ from the Mosel. Best years: (2008) 07 06 **05 04 03 02 01 99**.

MONBAZILLAC AC *South-West France* BERGERAC's best-known sweet wine. An increasing number of estates are making wines of a richness to rival some SAUTERNES, with the ability to age 10 years and more. Best producers: l'ANCIENNE CURE★★, Bélingard (Blanche de Bosredon★), le Fagé, Grande Maison★★, Haut-Bernasse, Haut-Montlong (Grande Cuvée), les Hauts de Caillevel★, Pécoula, La Rayre, Theulet★, Tirecul-la-Gravière★★, les VERDOTS★★. Best years: (2008) 07 **05** 03 01 99 97 95.

CH. MONBOUSQUET★ *St-Émilion Grand Cru AC, Grand Cru Classé, Bordeaux, France* Gérard Perse, owner of Ch. PAVIE, has transformed this struggling estate into one of ST-EMILION's 'super-crus'. The reward was promotion to Grand Cru Classé in 2006. Rich, voluptuous and very expensive, the wine is drinkable from 3–4 years but will age longer. Also a plush white Monbousquet★ (BORDEAUX AC). Best years: 2006 05 **04 03** 02 **01** 00 99 98 96 95 94.

ROBERT MONDAVI *Napa Valley, California, USA* A Californian institution best known for open and fruity regular Cabernet Sauvignon★ and Reserve Cabernet★★ with enormous depth and power. A regular★ and Reserve★★ Pinot Noir are velvety smooth and supple wines with style, perfume and balance. For many years the Mondavi signature white was Fumé Blanc (Sauvignon Blanc), but in recent years Chardonnay (Reserve★★) has overtaken it. The Robert Mondavi Winery is now part of Constellation's Icon Estates portfolio; Mondavi's lower-priced 'lifestyle' lines, Private Selection and Woodbridge (from Lodi in th CENTRAL VALLEY), are promoted separately. Recent vintages of Cabernet Sauvignon seem to have become far weightier than any that ever appeared under the late Bob Mondavi's stewardship. Best years: (Cabernet Sauvignon Reserve) 2005 04 03 **02 01 00 99 98 97 96 95 94 92 91 87**.

MONSANTO *Chianti Classico DOCG, Tuscany, Italy* Fabrizio Bianchi, with h daughter Laura, makes a range of Sangiovese-based wines topped by th CHIANTI CLASSICO Riserva Il Poggio★★★, a complex and attention demanding single-vineyard cru which until recently would have bee considered too 'traditional' for its discreet austerity and need of bott age. 100% Sangiovese IGT 'Fabrizio Bianchi'★★ is almost as fine. Be years: (2008) (07) 06 04 **01 99 97 88 82 77**.

MONT TAUCH, LES PRODUCTEURS DU *Fitou AC, Languedoc-Roussillo France* A big, quality-conscious co-op producing a large range of wine from good gutsy FITOU★ and CORBIÈRES to rich MUSCAT DE RIVESALTES★ an light but gluggable vin de pays. Top wines: Les Quatre★, Les Douze★ Best years: (Les Douze) (2008) 07 06 **05 03 01 00**.

MONTAGNE-ST-ÉMILION AC *Bordeaux, France* A ST-ÉMILION satelli which can produce rather good red wines. The wines are normally read to drink in 4 years but age quite well in their slightly earthy way. Be producers: Beauséjour★, Calon★, La Couronne, Croix Beauséjour★, Faizeau★ Gachon★, Haut Bonneau, Maison Blanche, Montaiguillon★, Rocher Corbin Roudier, Teyssier, Vieux-Ch.-St-André★. Best years: **2005 03 01 00 98 96 9**

MONTAGNY AC *Côte Chalonnaise, Burgundy, France* Wines from this Cô Chalonnaise village can be rather lean, but are greatly improved now th some producers are aging their wines for a few months in new oa Generally best with 2–5 years' bottle age. Best producers: S Aladame★ BOUCHARD PÈRE ET FILS★, la BUXYNOISE★, Davenay★, FAIVELEY, Louis LATOUR O LEFLAIVE★, A Roy★, J Vachet★. Best years: (2008) **07 06 05**.

MONTALCINO See BRUNELLO DI MONTALCINO DOCG.

MONTANA *Auckland, Gisborne, Hawkes Bay and Marlborough, New Zeala* Owned since 2005 by French giant Pernod Ricard, which produces a estimated 40% of New Zealand's wine. Montana's MARLBOROUG Sauvignon Blanc★ and GISBORNE Chardonnay are in a considerable way thank for putting New Zealand on the international wine map. Esta bottlings of whites, especially in the Terroir series, are also general good. Montana is now one of the world's biggest producers of Pin Noir★, and each vintage the quality improves and the price stays fa Consistent Lindauer fizz and, with the help of the Champagne hou DEUTZ, austere yet full-bodied Deutz Marlborough Cuvée NV Brut★ CHURCH ROAD, in HAWKES BAY, aims to produce premium reds, b Chardonnay★★ is better. As well as Corbans, Pernod Ricard al acquired Stoneleigh, with top-selling Marlborough Sauvignon Blanc and Riesling★ and tasty new Rapaura Series★. Extensive plantings Waipara are now bearing exciting results under the Camshorn label.

MONTECARLO DOC *Tuscany, Italy* Distinctive reds (Sangiovese with Syrah) and whites (Trebbiano with Sémillon and Pinot Grigio). Also non-DOC Cabernet, Merlot, Pinot Bianco, Roussanne and Vermentino. **Best producers: Buonamico★, Carmignani★, Montechiari★, La Torre★, Wandanna★. Best years: (reds) (2008) (07) 06 04 03 01 00.**

MONTEFALCO DOC *Umbria, Italy* Good Sangiovese-based Montefalco Rosso is outclassed by dense, massive Sagrantino di Montefalco DOCG (dry) and glorious sweet red Sagrantino Passito from dried grapes. **Best producers: (Sagrantino) Adanti★, Antonelli★, Caprai★★ (25 Anni★★), Colpetrone★★. Best years: (Sagrantino) (2008) (07) (06) 04 03 01 00 99 98 97.**

MONTEPULCIANO Grape grown mostly in eastern Italy (unconnected with TUSCANY's Sangiovese-based wine VINO NOBILE DI MONTEPULCIANO). Can produce deep-coloured, fleshy, spicy wines with moderate tannin and acidity. Besides MONTEPULCIANO D'ABRUZZO, it is used in ROSSO CONERO and ROSSO PICENO in the MARCHE and also in UMBRIA, Molise and PUGLIA.

MONTEPULCIANO D'ABRUZZO DOC *Abruzzo, Italy* The Montepulciano grape's most important manifestation, dark and deeply brambly when red, bright pink and intensely fruity when rosé (Cerasuolo). Quality varies from insipid or rustic to concentrated and characterful. **Best producers: Barba, Cataldi Madonna★, Contesa★★, Cornacchia★, Filomusi Guelfi★, Illuminati★ (Zanna★★), Marramiero★★, Masciarelli★★, A & E Monti★, Montori★, Nicodemi★, Roxan★, Cantina Tollo★, Umani Ronchi★, La Valentina★, Valentini★★, L Valori★, Ciccio Zaccagnini★. Best years: (2008) (07) 06 04 03 01 00 98 97 95.**

MONTEREY COUNTY *California, USA* Large CENTRAL COAST county south of San Francisco in the Salinas Valley. The most important AVAs are Monterey, Arroyo Seco, Chalone, Carmel Valley and Santa Lucia Highlands. Best grapes are Chardonnay, Riesling and Pinot Blanc, with some good Cabernet Sauvignon and Merlot in Carmel Valley and superb Pinot Noir in the Santa Lucia Highlands in the cool middle of the county. **Best producers: Bernardus★★, Estancia★, Jekel★, Joullian★★, Mer Soleil★★, Morgan★★, TALBOTT★★, Testarossa★★, Ventana★. Best years: (reds) 2006 05 04 03 01 00 99 97 96 95 94 91 90.**

MONTES *Colchagua, Chile* One of Chile's pioneering wineries in the modern era, notable for innovative development of top-quality vineyard land on the steep Apalta slopes of COLCHAGUA and the virgin country of Marchíhüe out toward the Pacific. Sauvignon Blanc★ (Leyda★★) and Chardonnay★  (Alpha★★) are good and fruit-led; all the reds are more austere and need bottle age. Since 2001, top-of-the-line Cabernet-based Montes Alpha M★★ has begun to shine. The most impressive reds, however, are two massive Syrahs, Montes Alpha★★ and Montes Folly★★, and Purple Angel★★, a vibrant, scented Carmenère. New Montes Alpha Pinot Noir shows ripe flavours and extensive use of oak.

MONTEVERTINE *Tuscany, Italy* Based in the heart of CHIANTI CLASSICO, Montevertine is famous for its non-DOC wines, particularly Le Pergole Torte★★★. This was the first of the SUPER-TUSCANS made solely with Sangiovese, and it remains one of the best. A little Canaiolo is included

in the excellent Montevertine Riserva★★. Best years: (Le Pergole Tort◗
(2008) (07) (06) **04 03 01 00 99 97 95 93 90 88 85**.

MONTHELIE AC *Côte de Beaune, Burgundy, France* Attractive, mainly re◗
wine village lying halfway along the CÔTE DE BEAUNE behind MEURSAULT an◗
VOLNAY. The wines generally have a lovely cherry fruit and make pleasa◗
drinking at a good price. Best producers: BOUCHARD PERE ET FILS, COCH◗
DURY★, Darviot-Perrin★, P Garaudet★, R Jobard★, LAFON★★, O LEFLAIVE◗
G Roulot★★, de Suremain★. Best years: (reds) (2008) 07 **06 05 03 02 99**.

MONTILLA-MORILES DO *Andalucía, Spain* Sherry-style wines that used t◗
be sold almost entirely as lower-priced sherry substitutes. However, th◗
wines *can* be superb, particularly the top dry amontillado, oloroso an◗
rich Pedro Ximénez styles. Best producers: Alvear★★, Aragón, Grac◗
Hermanos, Pérez Barquero★★, Toro Albalá★★.

DOM. DE MONTILLE *Côte de Beaune, Burgundy, France* Brought to fame b◗
Mondovino star Hubert de Montille, and now run by son Étienn◗
Consistent producer of stylish reds that demand aging, from VOLN◗
(especially Mitans★★, Champans★★, Taillepieds★★★) and POMMAR◗
(Pezerolles★★, Rugiens★★). Also top PULIGNY Les Caillerets★★★. Ve◗
expensive. From 2005 outstanding VOSNE-ROMANEE Malconsorts★★◗
Étienne and his sister have also started a *négociant* business, De◗
Montille★. Best years: (2008) 07 05 03 **02 99 96 93 88**.

MONTLOUIS-SUR-LOIRE AC *Loire Valley, France* On the opposite bank◗
the Loire to VOUVRAY, Montlouis makes similar styles (dry, mediur◗
sweet and CHAMPAGNE-style fizz) that are typically more accessible wi◗
exuberant fruit. Mousseux, the green, appley fizz, is best drunk youn◗
Still wines need 5–10 years, particularly the sweet Moelleux. Be◗
producers: L Chatenay★, F Chidaine★★, S Cossais★, Delétang★★, Levasseu◗
Alex Mathur★, des Liards/Berger★, F Saumon★, Taille aux Loups★★/BLOT. Be◗
years: (sec) (2008) **07 06**; (moelleux) **2005 04 03 02 01 99 97 96 95**.

MONTRACHET AC *Côte de Beaune, Burgundy, France* This world-famo◗
Grand Cru straddles the boundary between the villages of CHASSAGN◗
MONTRACHET and PULIGNY-MONTRACHET. Wines have a unique combinatio◗
of concentration, finesse and perfume; white Burgundy at its mo◗
sublime. Chevalier-Montrachet, immediately above it on the slop◗
yields slightly leaner wine that is less explosive in its youth, but go◗
examples become ever more fascinating with age. Best produce◗
BOUCHARD★★★, M Colin★★★, DROUHIN (Laguiche)★★★, LAFON★★★, Lo◗
LATOUR★★, Dom. LEFLAIVE★★★, LEROY★★★, RAMONET★★★, Dom. de◗
ROMANEE-CONTI★★★, SAUZET★★, Thénard★★. Best years: (2008) 07 06 05◗
03 02 **00 99 97 95 92 90 89 85**.

MONTRAVEL AC *South-West France* Mostly dry white wines from t◗
western end of the BERGERAC region. Medium-sweet whites from Côtes◗
Montravel AC and ultra-sweet Haut-Montravel AC. Ambitious r◗
Montravel is made from a minimum 50% Merlot, although most re◗
from the area are sold as Bergerac or Côtes de Bergerac. Best produce◗
du Bloy★, Jonc Blanc★, Laulerie, Libarde, Mallevieille, Masburel★, Mou◗
Caresse★, Pique-Sègue, Puy-Servain★, le Raz. Best years: (sweet) 2005 **02**◗
98 96; (red) **2005 03 01**.

CH. MONTROSE★★ *St-Estèphe AC, 2ème Cru Classé, Haut-Médoc, Bordea◗
France* A leading ST-ESTÈPHE property, once famous for its dark, broodi◗
wine that would take around 30 years to reach its prime. In the late 197◗
and early 80s the wines became lighter, but Montrose has now return◗
to a powerful style, though softer than before. Recent vintages have be◗

extremely good. Sold in 2006, so let's see what happens to the style. Second wine: la Dame de Montrose. **Best years:** 2007 06 05 04 03 **01** 00 **99 98 96 95**.

CH. MONTUS *Madiran AC, South-West France* Alain Brumont pioneered MADIRAN's revival, using 100% Tannat, deft public relations and high investment. All the AC wines are aged in new oak. He has 2 properties: Montus (Prestige★★) and Bouscassé (Vieilles Vignes★★). Both also make enjoyable dry PACHERENC DU VIC-BILH★ and fine Moelleux★★ in varying degrees of sweetness. **Best years:** (2008) 06 05 **04 01 00 98 96 94 90**.

MOON MOUNTAIN *Sonoma Valley AVA, California, USA* Formerly known as Carmenet (which is now a brand of the Foster's Group – the wines are not related), Moon Mountain specializes in intensely flavoured reds from mountain vineyards. Full-throttle Cabernet Franc★ and Reserve Cabernet Sauvignon★★ can age for a decade. Reserve Sauvignon Blanc★★ from Edna Valley grapes features plenty of creamy oak. **Best years:** (reds) 2005 04 03 02 **01 00 99** 98 97 96 95 94.

MORELLINO DI SCANSANO DOC *Tuscany, Italy* Morellino is the local name for the Sangiovese grape in the south-west of TUSCANY. The wines can be broad and robust, but the best are delightfully perfumed. **Best producers:** E Banti★, Belguardo★/FONTERUTOLI, Carletti/POLIZIANO (Lohsa★), Cecchi★, Il Macereto★, Mantellassi★, Morellino di Scansano co-op★, Moris Farms★★, Podere 414★, Poggio Argentaria★★, Le Pupille★★. **Best years:** (2008) 07 **06 04 03 01 00 99**.

MOREY-ST-DENIS AC *Côte de Nuits, Burgundy, France* Morey has 5 Grands Crus (CLOS DES LAMBRAYS, CLOS DE LA ROCHE, CLOS ST-DENIS, CLOS DE TART and a share of BONNES-MARES) as well as some very good Premiers Crus. Basic village wine is sometimes unexciting, but from a quality grower the wine has good fruit and acquires an attractive depth as it ages. A tiny amount of startling nutty white wine is also made. **Best producers:** Pierre Amiot★, Arlaud★★, Dom. des Beaumonts★, CLAIR★★, DUJAC★★★, A Jeanniard★★, Dom. des Lambrays★★, H Lignier★★★, Lignier-Michelot★★, H Perrot-Minot★★, Ponsot★★, ROUMIER★★, ROUSSEAU★★, Sérafin★★, Taupenot-Merme★★. **Best years:** (2008) 07 06 05 03 02 **01 00 99 98 96 95 93 90**.

MORGENHOF *Stellenbosch WO, South Africa* A 300-year-old Cape farm grandly restored and run with French flair by owner Anne Cointreau. The range spans Cap Classique sparkling to PORT styles. Best are a well-oaked, muscular Chenin Blanc, structured Merlot★ and the dark-berried, supple The Morgenhof Estate★, a BORDEAUX-style blend.

MORGON AC *Beaujolais, Burgundy, France* The longest-lasting of BEAUJOLAIS Crus, wines that – at their best – have the structure to age and delightful cherry fruit; look out for named sub-zones like Côte de Py and Jarvernières, which are considered to be the source of many of the best Morgons. There are, however, many more Morgons, made in a commercial style for early drinking, which are nothing more than a pleasant, fruity – and pricey – drink. **Best producers:** N Aucoeur★, D Desvignes★, L-C Desvignes★, DUBOEUF (Jean Descombes★), J Foillard★★, M Jonchet★, M Lapierre★★. **Best years:** **2008** 07 06.

MORNINGTON PENINSULA *Victoria, Australia* Exciting cool-climate maritime region dotted with small vineyards. Chardonnay runs the gamut from honeyed to harsh; Pinot Noir can be very stylish in warm years, especially as more vineyards in the mild Moorooduc area mature. **Best producers:** Dexter, Eldridge, Hurley★, KOOYONG★★, Main Ridge★★, Montalto, Moorooduc★★, Paringa Estate★★★, Port Phillip Estate★, Scorpo,

STONIER★★, Ten Minutes by Tractor★, T'Gallant★, Tuck's Ridge, Willo
Creek, Yabby Lake★★. Best years: (Pinot Noir) 2007 06 **05 04 03 02 01 00 9**
98 97 95 94.

MORRIS *Rutherglen, Victoria, Australia* Historic winery with an outstandin
fortified wine portfolio. The proposed sale by Pernod Ricard is off and s
David Morris remains the custodian of a store of aged fortifieds that ha
been with his family since the 19th century. He continues to make o
favourites like Liqueur Muscat★★ and Tokay★★ (Old Premium★★★
'ports', 'sherries' and robust table wines to very high quality levels.

DENIS MORTET *Gevrey-Chambertin, Côte de Nuits, Burgundy, France* Before h
untimely death in 2006, Denis Mortet had built a brilliant reputation f
his GEVREY-CHAMBERTIN (various cuvées, all ★★★) and tiny amounts
CHAMBERTIN★★★. Early vintages are deep coloured and powerful; rece
years show increased finesse, a trend being continued by son Arnau
Best years: (2008) 07 06 05 **03 02 01 00 96 95 93**.

MORTON ESTATE *Marlborough, Hawkes Bay, Bay of Plenty, Auckland, New Zeala*
Founded in 1983 by Morton Brown, who built a distinctive Cape-sty
winery in Katikati. Now owned by John Coney, it is one of the country
larger wineries, making wine from all major regions. Top-of-the-li
Black Label wines can be very good and include a full-bodi
Chardonnay★★ and Merlot-Cabernet★ from HAWKES BAY plus a styli
MARLBOROUGH Sauvignon Blanc★ and a rich, complex vintage-date
sparkling wine. White Label wines offer excellent value, particular
Chardonnay and Pinot Gris★. Best years: (Chardonnay) 2007 06 **04**.

GEORG MOSBACHER *Forst, Pfalz, Germany* This small estate makes d
white and dessert wines in the village of FORST. Best of all are the d
Rieslings★★ from the Forster Ungeheuer site, which are among t
lushest in Germany. Delicious young, but worth cellaring for a few yea
Best years: (2008) 07 06 05 **04 02 01 99 98 97**.

MOSCATO D'ASTI DOCG *Piedmont, Italy*
Utterly beguiling, delicately scented,
gently bubbling wine, made from
Moscato Bianco grapes grown in the
hills above Acqui Terme, Asti and
Alba in north-west Italy. The DOCG is
the same as for ASTI, but only select
grapes go into this wine, which is

frizzante (semi-sparkling) rather than fully sparkling. Drink while they
bubbling with youthful fragrance. Best producers: Araldica/Alasia
ASCHERI★, Bava★, Bera★★, Braida★, Cascina Castlèt★, La Caudrina★
Michele CHIARLO★, Giuseppe Contratto★, Coppo★, Cascina Fonda★, Forte
della Luja★, Icardi★, Marenco★, Beppe Marino★, La Morandina★, Mar
Negri★, Perrone★, Cascina Pian d'Or★, Saracco★★, Scagliola★,
Spinetta★★, I Vignaioli di Santo Stefano★, Gianni Voerzio★.

MOSCATO PASSITO DI PANTELLERIA DOC *Sicily, Italy* Power
dessert wine made from the Muscat of Alexandria, or Zibibbo, gra
Pantelleria is a small island south-west of SICILY, closer to Africa than i
to Italy. The grapes are picked in mid-August and laid out in the hot s
to shrivel for a couple of weeks. They are then crushed and fermented
give an amber-coloured, intensely flavoured sweet Muscat. The wines
best drunk within 5–7 years of the vintage. Best producers: Benant
D'Ancona★, DE BARTOLI★★, Donnafugata (Ben Ryé★), Murana★, Nue
Agricoltura co-op★, Pellegrino.

MOSEL *Germany* A collection of vineyard areas on the Mosel and its tributaries, the Saar and the Ruwer, amounting to 8990ha (22,215 acres). The Mosel river rises in the French Vosges before forming the border between Germany and Luxembourg. In its first German incarnation in the Upper Mosel the light, tart Elbling grape holds sway, but with the Middle Mosel begins a series of villages responsible for some of the world's very best Riesling wines: LEIWEN, TRITTENHEIM, PIESPORT, BRAUNEBERG, BERNKASTEL, GRAACH, WEHLEN, ÜRZIG and ERDEN. The wines have tremendous slatiness and an ability to blend the greenness of citrus leaves and fruits with the golden warmth of honey. Great wines are rarer between Erden and Koblenz, although WINNINGEN is an island of excellence. The Saar can produce wonderful, piercing wines in villages such as Serrig, Ayl, OCKFEN and Wiltingen. Ruwer wines are slightly softer; the estates of MAXIMIN GRUNHAUS and KARTHAUSERHOF are on every list of the best in Germany. Since 2007 only the name 'Mosel' is permitted on labels in place of the region's former name Mosel-Saar-Ruwer.

MOSS WOOD *Margaret River, Western Australia* Seminal MARGARET RIVER winery at the top of its form. Supremely good, scented Cabernet★★★ needing 5 years to blossom, classy Chardonnay★★, pale, fragrant Pinot Noir★ and crisp, fruity but ageworthy Semillon★★. Range is expanding with excellent Ribbon Vale★★ wines and the very good Amy's Cabernet★. Best years: (Cabernet) (2008) 07 05 04 03 **02** 01 **00 99 98 96 95 94 91 90 85**.

P MOUEIX *Bordeaux, France* As well as owning PETRUS, la FLEUR-PETRUS, BELAIR, MAGDELAINE, TROTANOY, Hosanna and other properties, the Moueix family runs a thriving merchant business specializing in the wines of the Right Bank, particularly POMEROL and ST-EMILION. Quality is generally high.

MOULIN-À-VENT AC *Beaujolais, Burgundy, France* Potentially the greatest of the BEAUJOLAIS Crus, taking its name from an ancient (now renovated) windmill that stands above Romanèche-Thorins. The granitic soil yields a majestic wine that with time transforms into a rich Burgundian style more characteristic of the Pinot Noir than the Gamay. Best producers: Champagnon★, DUBOEUF (Tour du Bief★), Ch. des Jacques★/JADOT, P Janin, O Merlin, Richard Rottiers (Climat Champ de Cour★), B Santé★. Best years: **2008 07 06**.

MOULIS AC *Haut-Médoc, Bordeaux, France* Small AC within the HAUT-MEDOC. Much of the wine is excellent – delicious at 5–6 years old, though good examples can age 10–20 years – and not overpriced. Best producers: Anthonic, Biston-Brillette★, Branas-Grand-Poujeaux, Brillette, CHASSE-SPLEEN★, Duplessis, Gressier-Grand-Poujeaux★, MAUCAILLOU★, Moulin-à-Vent, POUJEAUX★. Best years: 2006 **05 03 02 01 00 96 95 90 89**.

MOUNT HORROCKS *Clare Valley, South Australia* Stephanie Toole has transformed this label into one of the CLARE VALLEY's best, with taut, minerally, limy Riesling★★★ from a single vineyard in Watervale; classy, cedary Semillon★; complex, savoury Shiraz★; and one of Australia's most delicious stickies (dessert wine), the Cordon Cut Riesling★★★, which shows varietal character with a satisfying lush texture.

MOUNT LANGI GHIRAN *Grampians, Victoria, Australia* This winery made its reputation with remarkable dark plum, chocolate and pepper Shiraz★★. Delightful Riesling★, honeyed Pinot Gris★ and melony unwooded Chardonnay★. Joanna★★ Cabernet is dark and intriguing. Best years: (Shiraz) 2006 05 04 **03 99 98 97 96 95 94 93**.

MOUNT MARY *Yarra Valley, Victoria, Australia* Founder and YARRA VALLEY pioneer, Dr John Middleton, died in 2006 but this classic property continues to produce controversial cult wines. It uses only estate-grown BORDEAUX grapes, with dry white Triolet★★ blended from Sauvignon, Semillon and Muscadelle, and Quintet★★ (★★★ for keen Francophiles) from Cabernet Sauvignon and Franc, Merlot, Malbec and Petit Verdot that ages beautifully. The Pinot Noir★★ is almost as good. Best years (Quintet) (2007) 06 05 03 02 01 **00 99 98 97 96 95 94 93 92 91 90 88 86 84**

MOUNT VEEDER AVA *Napa Valley, California, USA* Small AVA in south west NAPA, with Cabernet Sauvignon and Zinfandel in an impressive rough-hewn style. **Best producers:** Chateau Potelle★, Robert Craig★★, HESS COLLECTION★, Lokoya★★, Mayacamas Vineyards★, Mount Veeder Winery★

MOURVÈDRE The variety originated in Spain, where it is called Monastrell. It dominates the JUMILLA DO and also Alicante, Bullas and Yecla. It needs lots of sunshine to ripen, which is why it performs well on the Mediterranean coast at BANDOL. It is increasingly important as a source of body and tarry, pine-needle flavour in the wines of CHATEAUNEUF-DU-PAPE and parts of LANGUEDOC-ROUSSILLON. It is beginning to make a reputation in Australia and California, where it is sometimes known as Mataro, and is also starting to make its presence felt in South Africa.

MOUTON-CADET *Bordeaux AC, Bordeaux, France* The most widely sold red BORDEAUX in the world was created by Baron Philippe de Rothschild in the 1930s. Blended from the entire Bordeaux region, the wine is undistinguished – and never cheap. A new label and somewhat fruitier style were introduced in 2004. Also a white, rosé, MEDOC and GRAVES.

CH. MOUTON-ROTHSCHILD★★★ *Pauillac AC, 1er Cru Classé, Haut-Médoc, Bordeaux, France* Baron Philippe de Rothschild died in 1988, having raised Mouton from a run-down Second Growth to its promotion to First Growth in 1973, and a reputation as one of the greatest wines in the world. It can still be the most magnificently opulent of the great MEDOC reds, but inexcusable inconsistency frequently makes me want to downgrade it. Recent vintages seem back on top form. When young, it is rich and indulgent on the palate, aging after 15–20 years to a complex bouquet of blackcurrant and cigar box. There is also a white wine, Aile d'Argent. Second wine: Le Petit-Mouton. **Best years:** (red) 2007 06 05 04 03 **02** 01 00 **99 98 97 96 95 90 89 88 86 85.**

MUDGEE *New South Wales, Australia* Small, long-overlooked region neighbouring HUNTER VALLEY, with a higher altitude and marginally cooler temperatures. Major new plantings are giving it a fresh lease of life and producers are beginning to make the best use of very good fruit. **Best producers:** Abercorn, Farmer's Daughter, Logan, Lowe Family, Miramar, Oatley

MUGA *Rioja DOCa, Rioja, Spain* Traditional family winery making high quality, rich red RIOJA★ (Gran Reserva Prado Enea★★). It is the only bodega in Rioja where every step of red winemaking is still carried out in oak containers. The modern Torre Muga Reserva★ marks a major stylistic change. New top cuvée is Aro★★. Whites and rosés are good too. **Best years:** (Torre Muga Reserva) (2005) 04 **03 01 99 98 96 95.**

J-F MUGNIER *Chambolle-Musigny, Côte de Nuits, Burgundy, France* Since giving up his other career as an airline pilot in 1998, Frédéric Mugnier has produced a series of beautifully crafted, lightly extracted wines at the Château de Chambolle-Musigny, especially from les Amoureuses★★ and Grand Cru le MUSIGNY★★★. In 2004 the 9ha (23-acre) NUITS-ST-GEORGES Clos de la Maréchale★★ vineyard came back under his control; first vintages are very stylish and a small section has been grafted over to white wine production. Best years: (2008) 07 06 05 **04** 02 **01 00** 99 98 96 **93 90 89**.

MULDERBOSCH *Stellenbosch WO, South Africa* Consistency is one of the hallmarks of this white-dominated range. Sleek, gooseberry-infused Sauvignon Blanc★★ is deservedly a cult wine; drink young and fresh. Purity and intensity mark out the Chardonnays (regular★ and barrel-fermented★★) and oak-brushed Chenin Blanc★ (previously labelled Steen op Hout)★. The handful of reds includes Faithful Hound, a Cabernet-Merlot blend, BORDEAUX-like but easy-drinking. Best years: (barrel-fermented Chardonnay) 2007 **06 05 04 03** 02 01.

MÜLLER-CATOIR *Neustadt-Haardt, Pfalz, Germany* This PFALZ producer makes wine of a piercing fruit flavour and powerful structure rarely surpassed in Germany, including Riesling, Scheurebe, Rieslaner, Gewürztraminer, Muskateller and Pinot Noir – all ★★. BA and TBA are invariably ★★★. Best years: (2008) 07 06 **05 04** 03 02 **01** 99 98 97 94.

EGON MÜLLER-SCHARZHOF *Scharzhofberg, Mosel, Germany* Some of the world's greatest – and most expensive – sweet Rieslings are this estate's Auslese, Beerenauslese, Trockenbeerenauslese and Eiswein: all usually rating ★★★. Regular Kabinett and Spätlese wines are pricey but classic. Best years: (2008) 07 06 05 04 **03** 02 **01** 99 97 95 93 90 89 88.

MÜLLER-THURGAU The workhorse grape of Germany, largely responsible for LIEBFRAUMILCH, with almost 14% of the country's vineyards, but diminishing. When yields are low it produces pleasant floral wines, but this is rare since modern clones are all super-productive. It is occasionally better in England – and a few good examples, with a slightly green edge to the grapy flavour, come from Switzerland (here known as Riesling-Sylvaner), Luxembourg (as Rivaner) and Italy's TRENTINO and ALTO ADIGE, which latter boasts one of Europe's highest vineyards in TIEFENBRUNNER's Feldmarschall at 1000m (3280ft). In New Zealand, Müller-Thurgau acreage is in terminal decline.

G H MUMM *Champagne AC, Champagne, France* Mumm's top-selling non-vintage brand, Cordon Rouge, disappointing in the 1990s, improved when Dominique Demarville took over as winemaker in 1998, but he left in 2006 to join VEUVE CLICQUOT. His efforts at improving quality were confirmed by the 2005 release of Mumm Grand Cru★ and elegant new de luxe Cuvée R Lalou★★, launched in 2007 with the 1998 vintage. Improvements seem to have stayed on track under Pernod Ricard's ownership. Best years: 1999 98 96 **95 90 89 88** 85 82.

MUMM NAPA *Napa Valley AVA, California, USA* The California offshoot of Champagne house MUMM has always made good bubbly, and after a slight dip is now back on form. Cuvée Napa Brut Prestige★ is a fair drink; Brut Rosé★ is better than most pink Champagnes. Elegant vintage-dated Blanc de Blancs★★ and flagship DVX★★. Part of Pernod Ricard.

MUSCAT

It's strange, but there's hardly a wine grape in the world which makes wine that actually tastes of the grape itself. Yet there's one variety which is so joyously, exultantly grapy that it more than makes up for all the others – the Muscat, generally thought to be the original wine vine. In fact there seem to be about 200 different branches of the Muscat family worldwide, but the noblest of these and the one that always makes the most exciting wine is called Muscat Blanc à Petits Grains (the Muscat with the small berries). These berries can be crunchily green, golden yellow, pink or even brown – as a result Muscat has a large number of synonyms. The wines they make may be pale and dry, rich and golden, subtly aromatic or as dark and sweet as treacle.

WINE STYLES

France Muscat is grown from the far north-east right down to the Spanish border, yet is rarely accorded great respect in France. This is a pity, because the dry, light, hauntingly grapy Muscats of Alsace are some of France's most delicately beautiful wines. It pops up sporadically in the Rhône Valley, especially in the sparkling wine enclave of Die. Mixed with Clairette, the Clairette de Die Tradition is a fragrant grapy fizz that deserves to be better known. Muscat de Beaumes-de-Venise is a delicious manifestation of the grape, this time fortified, fragrant and sweet. Its success has encouraged the traditional fortified winemakers of Languedoc-Roussillon to make fresher, more perfumed wines as well as unfortified late-harvest wines and, especially around Rivesaltes, dry vins de pays.

Italy Various types of Muscat are grown in Italy. In the north-west, especially Piedmont, Moscato Bianco/Moscato di Canelli makes the fragrantly sweet sparklers called Asti or (less bubbly) Moscato d'Asti; the same grape makes Tuscany's Moscadello di Montalcino. Orange Muscat (Moscato Giallo/Goldmuskateller) is used in the north-east for making passito-style dessert (or occasionally dry) wines, while Muscat of Alexandria prevails in the south, especially in relation to the great passito of Pantelleria. Italy also has red varieties: Moscato Nero for rare sweet wines in Lazio, Lombardy and Piedmont; Moscato Rosa/Rosenmuskateller for delicately sweet wines in Trentino-Alto Adige and Friuli-Venezia Giulia.

Other regions Elsewhere in Europe, Muscat is a component of some Tokajis in Hungary, Crimea has shown how good it can be in the Massandra fortified wines, and the rich golden Muscats of Samos and Patras are among Greece's finest wines. As Muskateller in Austria and Germany it makes primarily dry, subtly aromatic wines. In Spain Moscatel de Valencia is sweet, light and sensational value, Moscatel de Grano Menudo is on the resurgence in Navarra and Castilla-La Mancha and it has also been introduced in Mallorca. Portugal's Moscatel de Setúbal is also wonderfully rich and complex. California grows Muscat, often calling it Muscat Canelli, but South Africa and Australia make better use of it. With darker berries, and called Brown Muscat in Australia and Muscadel in South Africa, it makes some of the world's sweetest and most luscious fortified wines, especially in the north-east Victoria regions of Rutherglen and Glenrowan in Australia.

BEST PRODUCERS

Sparkling Muscat
France (*Clairette de Die*) Achard-Vincent, Clairette de Die co-op, Jean-Claude Raspail.

Italy (*Asti*) G Contratto, Gancia; (*Moscato d'Asti*) Bera, Braida, Caudrina, Saracco, La Spinetta, Gianni Voerzio.

Dry Muscat
Austria (*Muskateller*) Gross, Lackner-Tinnacher, POLZ, TEMENT.

France (*Alsace*) J-M Bernhard, Paul Buecher, Dirler-Cadé, Kientzler, Kuentz-Bas, Ostertag, Rolly Gassmann, SCHOFFIT, Bruno Sorg, TRIMBACH, WEINBACH, ZIND-HUMBRECHT.

Germany (*Muskateller*) BERCHER, Dr HEGER, Huber, MULLER-CATOIR, REBHOLZ.

Spain (*Alicante*) Bocopa co-op; (*Málaga*) Jorge Ordóñez; (*Penedès*) TORRES (Viña Esmeralda).

Italy (*Goldmuskateller*) LAGEDER.

Sweet Muscat
Australia (*Liqueur Muscat*) All Saints, Baileys of Glenrowan, BROWN BROTHERS, Buller, Campbells, CHAMBERS, John Kosovich, MCWILLIAM'S, MORRIS, Seppeltsfield, Stanton & Killeen, Talijancich, YALUMBA.

France (*Alsace*) Ernest Burn, Rolly Gassmann, René MURE, SCHOFFIT; (*Beaumes-de-Venise*) Bernardins, Durban, JABOULET, Pigeade; (*Frontignan*) la Peyrade; (*Lunel*) Lacoste; (*Rivesaltes*) CAZES, Jau.

Greece SAMOS co-op.

Italy (*Goldmuskateller*) Viticoltori Caldaro, Thurnhof; (*Pantelleria*) DE BARTOLI, Murana.

Portugal (*Moscatel de Setúbal*) BACALHÔA, J M da FONSECA.

South Africa KLEIN CONSTANTIA.

Spain (*Navarra*) Camilo Castilla, CHIVITE; (*Valencia*) Gandía; (*Alicante*) Gutiérrez de la Vega, Enrique Mendoza, Primitivo Quiles; (*Jumilla*) Silvano García; (*Sierras de Málaga*) Jorge Ordóñez, Telmo RODRIGUEZ.

RENÉ MURÉ *Alsace AC, Alsace, France* The pride and joy of this domaine's
fine vineyards is the Clos St-Landelin, a parcel within the Grand Cru
Vorbourg. The Clos is the source of lush, concentrated wines, with
particularly fine Riesling★★ and Pinot Gris★★. Since 2005, most Muré
wines have been getting drier, and are all the better for it. The Muscat
Vendange Tardive★★ is rare and remarkable, as is the opulent old-vine
Sylvaner Cuvée Oscar★. The Vendange Tardive★★ and Sélection de
Grains Nobles★★★ wines are among the best in Alsace. Best years: (Clos
St-Landelin Riesling) (2008) 07 06 05 **04 02 01 00 97 96 95**.

ANDREW MURRAY VINEYARDS *Santa Barbara County, California, USA*
Working with RHÔNE varieties, winemaker Andrew Murray has created
an impressive array of wines. Rich, aromatic Viognier★ and
Roussanne★★ as well as several Syrahs, including Roasted Slope★
and Hillside Reserve★★. Espérance★ is a spicy blend patterned after
a serious CÔTES DU RHÔNE. Best years: (Syrah) 2005 **04 03 02 01 00 99
98 97**.

MUSCADET AC *Loire Valley, France* AC for the region around Nantes in
north-west France, best drunk young and fresh as an apéritif or with the
local seafood. Wines from 3 better-quality zones (Muscadet Coteaux de la
Loire, Muscadet Côtes de Grand-Lieu and Muscadet Sèvre-et-Maine)
are typically labelled *sur lie*. They must be matured on the lees for a
maximum of 12 months and show greater depth of flavour and more fruit.
Ironically, ageworthy top cuvées from specific vineyards or soils (granite,
gneiss, schist) are usually aged *sur lie* for well over 12 months so cannot
use this term on the label. Best producers: Bidière, Bonhomme, Bonnet-
Huteau, Chéreau-Carré★, Choblet/Herbauges★, Bruno Cormerais, Michel
David★, Dorices★, Douillard, l'ECU★★, Gadais★, Jacques Guindon★, les Hautes
Noëlles★/Serge Bâtard, l'Hyvernière, Landrons★, Luneau-Papin★, Metaireau★,
RAGOTIERE★, Sauvion★, la Touché★. Best years: (sur lie) **2008 07 05**.

MUSCAT See pages 218–19.

MUSCAT OF ALEXANDRIA This grape rarely shines in its own right but
performs a useful job worldwide, adding perfume and fruit to what would
otherwise be dull, neutral white wines. It is common for sweet and
fortified wines throughout the Mediterranean basin (in Sicily it is called
Zibibbo) and in South Africa (where it is also known as Hanepoot), as
well as being a fruity, perfumed bulk producer there and in Australia
where it is known as Gordo Blanco or Lexia.

MUSCAT DE BEAUMES-DE-VENISE AC *Rhône Valley, France* Delicious
Muscat *vin doux naturel* from the southern Rhône. It has a fruity acidity
and a bright fresh feel, and is best drunk young to get all that lovely grapy
perfume and bright fruit at its peak. Can surprise when aged, though.
Best producers: Beaumalric★, Beaumes-de-Venise co-op, Bernardins★★,
DELAS★, Durban★, Fenouillet★, JABOULET★★, Pigeade★★, Vidal-Fleury★.

MUSCAT BLANC À PETITS GRAINS See MUSCAT, pages 218–19.

MUSCAT DE FRONTIGNAN AC *Languedoc, France* Muscat *vin doux
naturel* on the Mediterranean coast. Quite impressive but can be a bit
cloying. Muscat de Mireval AC, a little further inland, can have a touch
more acid freshness and quite an alcoholic kick. Also Muscat de Lune
further east. Best producers: (Frontignan) Mas Rouge, la Peyrade★, Stony
(Lunel) Mas de Bellevue★; (Mireval) la Capelle★, Mas des Pigeonniers, Moulinas

MUSCAT DE LUNEL, MUSCAT DE MIREVAL See MUSCAT DE FRONTIGNAN.

MUSCAT DE RIVESALTES AC *Roussillon, France* Made from Muscat Blanc à Petits Grains and Muscat of Alexandria, the wine can be very good from go-ahead producers who keep the aromatic skins in the juice for longer periods to gain extra perfume and fruit. Most delicious when young. Best producers: Baixas co-op (Dom. Brial★, Ch. les Pins★), la CASENOVE★, CAZES★★, Chênes★, Corneilla, Fontanel★, Força Réal★, l'Heritier, Jau★, Laporte★, MONT TAUCH★, de Nouvelles★, Piquemal★.

MUSCAT DE ST-JEAN-DE-MINERVOIS AC *Languedoc, France* Small AC in the remote Minervois hills for fortified Muscat. Less cloying, more tangerine and floral than some Muscats from the plains. Best producers: Barroubio, CLOS BAGATELLE, Combebelle, Vignerons de Septimanie.

MUSIGNY AC *Grand Cru, Côte de Nuits, Burgundy, France* One of a handful of truly great Grands Crus, combining power with an exceptional depth of fruit and lacy elegance – an iron fist in a velvet glove. A tiny amount of BOURGOGNE Blanc is currently made from the Musigny vineyard by de VOGÜE★★. Best producers: DROUHIN★★★, JADOT★★★, Dom. LEROY★★★, J-F MUGNIER★★★, J Prieur★★, ROUMIER★★★, VOGÜE★★★, VOUGERAIE★★★. Best years: (2008) 07 06 05 03 02 01 **00 99 98 96 95 93 90 89 88**.

NAHE *Germany* 4200ha (10,375-acre) wine region named after the River Nahe, which rises below Birkenfeld and joins the Rhine by BINGEN, opposite RÜDESHEIM in the RHEINGAU. The Rieslings from this geologically complex region are often among Germany's best. The finest vineyards are those of Niederhausen and SCHLOSSBÖCKELHEIM, situated in the dramatic, rocky Upper Nahe Valley, and at Dorsheim and Münster in the lower Nahe.

CH. NAIRAC★ *Barsac AC, 2ème Cru Classé, Bordeaux, France* An established name in BARSAC which, by dint of enormous effort, produces a sweet wine sometimes on a par with the First Growths. The influence of aging in new oak casks, adding spice and even a little tannin, means this can age for 10–15 years. Best years: 2007 05 **04 03 02 01** 99 98 97 96 95.

NAPA VALLEY AVA *California, USA* An AVA so inclusive that it is almost completely irrelevant. It includes vineyards that are outside the Napa River drainage system – such as Pope Valley and Chiles Valley. A number of sub-AVAs have been and are in the process of being created; a few such as CARNEROS and STAGS LEAP DISTRICT are discernibly different from their neighbours, but the majority are similar in nature, and many fear that these sub-AVAs will simply dilute the magic of Napa's name. See also pages 222–3.

NAVARRA DO *Navarra, Spain* This buzzing region has increasing numbers of vineyards planted to Cabernet Sauvignon, Merlot and Chardonnay in addition to Tempranillo, Garnacha and Moscatel (Muscat). This translates into a wealth of juicy reds, barrel-fermented whites and modern sweet Muscats, but quality is still more haphazard than it should be. Best producers: Artazuri, Camino del Villar★, Camilo Castilla (Capricho de Goya Muscat★★), CHIVITE★ (Señorío de Arínzano estate★★), Iñaki Núñez★, Inurrieta★, Lezaun★, Magaña★, Castillo de Monjardín★, Nekeas co-op★, Ochoa, Palacio de la Vega, Parraldea, Príncipe de Viana, Quaderna Via, Señorío de Otazu, Señorío de Sarria. Best years: (reds) **2006 05** 04 03 01 99 98.

NAVARRO VINEYARDS *Anderson Valley AVA, California, USA* Small, family-owned producer of sensational Gewürztraminer★★★, Pinot Gris★★, Riesling★★, Dry Muscat★★ and late-harvest Riesling★★★, perfectly balanced Pinot Noir★★ and a dozen other stellar wines.

221

NAPA VALLEY

California, USA

 From the earliest days of California wine, and through all its ups and downs, the Napa Valley has been the standard-bearer for the whole industry and the driving force behind quality and progress. The magical Napa name – derived from an Indian word for plenty – applies to the fertile valley itself, the county in which it is found and the AVA for the overall area, but the region is so viticulturally diverse that the appellation is virtually meaningless.

The valley was first settled by immigrants in the 1830s, and by the late 19th century Napa, and in particular the area around the communities of Rutherford and Oakville, had gained a reputation for exciting Cabernet Sauvignon. Despite the long, dark years of Prohibition, this reputation survived and when the US interest in wine revived during the 1970s, Napa was ready to lead the charge.

GRAPE VARIETIES

Most of the classic French grapes are grown and recent replantings have done much to match varieties to the most suitable locations. Cabernet Sauvignon is planted in profusion and Napa's strongest reputation is for varietal Cabernet and Bordeaux-style (or meritage) blends, mostly Cabernet-Merlot. Pinot Noir and Chardonnay, for both still and sparkling wines, do best in the south, from Yountville down to Carneros. Zinfandel is grown mostly at the north end of the valley. Syrah and Sangiovese are relatively new here.

SUB-REGIONS

The most significant vine-growing area is the valley floor running from Calistoga in the north down to Carneros, below which the Napa River flows out into San Pablo Bay. It has been said that there are more soil types in Napa than in the whole of France, but much of the soil in the valley is heavy, clayish, over-fertile, difficult to drain and really not fit to make great wine. Some of the best vineyards are tucked into the mountain slopes at the valley sides or in selected spots at higher altitudes.

There is as much as a 10°C temperature difference between torrid Calistoga and Carneros at the mouth of the valley, cooled by Pacific fog and a benchmark for US Pinot Noir and cool-climate Chardonnay. About 20 major sub-areas have been identified along the valley floor and in the mountains, although there is much debate over how many have a real claim to individuality. Rutherford, Oakville and Yountville in the mid-valley produce Cabernet redolent of dust, dried sage and ultra-ripe blackcurrants. Softer flavours come from Stags Leap to the east. The higher-altitude vineyards of Diamond Mountain, Spring Mountain and Mount Veeder along the Mayacamas mountain range to the west produce deep Cabernets, while Howell Mountain in the north-east has stunning Zinfandel and Merlot.

See also CARNEROS AVA, HOWELL MOUNTAIN AVA, MOUNT VEEDER AVA, NAPA VALLEY AVA, OAKVILLE AVA, RUTHERFORD AVA, STAGS LEAP DISTRICT AVA; and individual producers.

(2008) (07) (06) 05 04 03 **02**
01 00 99 95 94 91 90 87 86

BEST PRODUCERS

Cabernet Sauvignon and meritage blends
Abreu, Altamura, Anderson's Conn Valley, ARAUJO, Barnett (Rattlesnake Hill), BEAULIEU, BERINGER, Bryant Family, Burgess Cellars, Cafaro, Cakebread, CAYMUS, CHATEAU MONTELENA, Chateau Potelle (VGS), CHIMNEY ROCK, Cliff Lede, Clos Pegase, CLOS DU VAL, Colgin, Conn Creek (Anthology), Corison, Cosentino, Robert Craig, DALLA VALLE, Darioush, Del Dotto, DIAMOND CREEK, DOMINUS, DUNN, Elyse, Far Niente, FLORA SPRINGS, Forman, Freemark Abbey, Frog's Leap, Grace Family, Groth, HARLAN ESTATE, HARTWELL, HEITZ, Jarvis, Leo Joseph, Ladera, La Jota, Lewis Cellars, Livingston Moffett, Lokoya, Long Meadow Ranch, Long Vineyards, Markham, Mayacamas Vineyards, MERRYVALE, Peter MICHAEL, MINER, MONDAVI, Monticello, Mount Veeder Winery/FRANCISCAN, NEWTON, OPUS ONE, Pahlmeyer, Paradigm, Robert Pecota, Peju Province (HB Vineyard), PHELPS, PINE RIDGE, Plumpjack, Pride Mountain, Quintessa, Raymond, Rubicon/COPPOLA, Rudd Estate, Saddleback, St Clement, SCREAMING EAGLE, Seavey, SHAFER, SILVER OAK, SILVERADO, SPOTTSWOODE, Staglin Family, STAG'S LEAP WINE CELLARS, STERLING, Swanson, The Terraces, Philip Togni, Turnbull, Viader, Villa Mt Eden (Signature Series), Vine Cliff, Vineyard 29, Von Strasser, Whitehall Lane, ZD.

NEBBIOLO The grape variety responsible for the majestic wines of BAROLO and BARBARESCO, found almost nowhere outside north-west Italy. Its name may derive from the Italian for fog, *nebbia*, because it ripens late when the hills are shrouded in autumn mists. It needs a thick skin to withstand this fog, so often gives very tannic wines that need years to soften. When grown in the limestone soils of the Langhe hills around Alba, Nebbiolo produces wines that are only moderately deep in colour but have a wonderful array of perfumes and an ability to develop great complexity with age. Barolo is usually considered the best and longest-lived of the Nebbiolo wines; the myth that it needs a decade or more to be drinkable has been dispelled by new-style Barolo, and the best Barolo now reach a plateau within 10 years and then subtly mature for decades. Barbaresco also varies widely in style between the traditional and the new. NEBBIOLO D'ALBA and ROERO produce lighter styles. The variety is also used for barrique-aged blends, often with Barbera and/or Cabernet and sold under the LANGHE DOC. Nebbiolo is also the principal grape for red of northern PIEDMONT – Carema, GATTINARA and GHEMME. In LOMBARDY it is known as Chiavennasca and is used in the Valtellina DOC and VALTELLINA SUPERIORE DOCG wines. Outside Italy, rare good examples are made in Australia (S C PANNELL is outstanding), California and South Africa.

NEBBIOLO D'ALBA DOC *Piedmont, Italy* Red wine from Nebbiolo grown around Alba, but excluding the BAROLO and BARBARESCO zones. Vineyards in the LANGHE and ROERO hills are noted for sandy soils that produce a fragrant, fruity style for early drinking, though some growers make wine that improve for 5 years or more. **Best producers:** Alario★, ASCHERI, Bricco Maiolica★★, Bruno, Burlotto★, CERETTO, Cascina Chicco★, Correggia★★, GIACOSA★, Giuseppe MASCARELLO★, Pio Cesare★, PRUNOTTO★, RATTI★, SANDRONE★, Vietti★. **Best years:** (2008) (07) 06 **04 03 01 00 99**.

NELSON *South Island, New Zealand* A range of mountains separates Nelson from MARLBOROUGH at the northern end of South Island. Nelson is made up of a series of small hills and valleys with a wide range of mesoclimates. Pinot Noir, Chardonnay, Riesling and Sauvignon Blanc do well. **Best producers:** Greenhough★, Himmelsfeld, Kina Beach, NEUDORF★★, Rimu Grove★, SEIFRIED★, Spencer Hill. **Best years:** (whites) **2007 06 05 04 03**.

NERO D'AVOLA The name of SICILY's great red grape derives from the town of Avola near Siracusa, although it is now planted all over the island. Its deep colour, high sugars and acidity make it useful for blending, especially with the lower-acid Nerello Mascalese, but also with Cabernet, Merlot and Syrah. On its own, and from the right soils, it can be brilliant with a soft, ripe, spicy black fruit character. Examples range from simple quaffers to many of Sicily's top reds.

NEUCHÂTEL *Switzerland* Swiss canton with high-altitude vineyards, mainly Chasselas whites and Pinot Noir reds and rosé. **Best producers** Ch. d'Auvernier, Chambleau, Châtenay-Bouvier, Montmollin.

NEUDORF *Nelson, South Island, New Zealand* Owners Tim and Judy Finn produce some of New Zealand's most stylish and sought-after wines, including gorgeous, honeyed Chardonnay★★★, rich but scented Pinot Noir★★, Sauvignon Blanc★★, Riesling★★ and Pinot Gris★. **Best years** (Chardonnay) 2007 **06 05 04 03 02**; (Pinot Noir) 2007 **06 05 03 02 01**.

EW SOUTH WALES *Australia* Australia's most populous state is sponsible for about 25% of the country's grape production. The largest ntres of production are the irrigated areas of RIVERINA, and Murray Darling, wan Hill and Perricoota on the Murray River, where better viticultural and inemaking practices and lower yields have led to significant quality nprovements. Smaller premium-quality regions include the old-established UNTER VALLEY, Cowra and higher-altitude MUDGEE, Orange and HILLTOPS. ANBERRA is an area of tiny vineyards at chilly altitudes, as is Tumbarumba at ne base of the Snowy Mountains.

EW YORK STATE *USA* Wine grapes were first planted on Manhattan land in the mid-17th century, but it wasn't until the early 1950s that a rious wine industry began to develop in the state as *vinifera* grapes were anted to replace natives such as *Vitis labrusca*. Weather conditions, articularly in the north, can be challenging, but improved vineyard practices ave made a good vintage possible in most recent years. The most important gion is the FINGER LAKES in the north of the state, which is enjoying a surge of onsumer interest in Riesling. The boom that had LONG ISLAND vintners witter turn of the century seems to have fizzled, though the region's top oducers still make noteworthy, BORDEAUX-styled reds. The Hudson River egion has a couple of good producers and a few upstarts are producing oteworthy wines amid the ocean of plonk along the shores of Lake Erie.

EWTON *Napa Valley AVA, California, USA* Spectacular winery and steep vineyards high above St Helena, owned by French luxury giant LVMH. Cabernet Sauvignon★★, Merlot★★ and Claret★ are some of California's most pleasurable examples. Even better is the single-vineyard Cabernet Sauvignon-based The Puzzle★★★. Newton pioneered the unfiltered Chardonnay★★★ style and this lush mouthful is one of California's best. Age Chardonnays for up to 5 years, reds for 10–15. Best years: (Cabernet Sauvignon) 2005 03 02 01 **00 99 97 96 95 94 91 90**.

GATARAWA *Hawkes Bay, North Island, New Zealand* Viticulture here is organic, with Chardonnay★, botrytized Riesling and Cabernet-Merlot under the premium Alwyn Reserve label. The Glazebrook range includes attractive Chardonnay★ and Cabernet-Merlot★, both of which are best drunk within 5 years. Best years: (reds) (2008) 07 **06 04 02 00**.

IAGARA PENINSULA *Ontario, Canada* Sandwiched between lakes Erie and Ontario, the Niagara Peninsula benefits from regular through-breezes created by the Niagara escarpment. Icewine, from Riesling and Vidal, is the showstopper, with growing international acclaim. Chardonnay leads the dry whites, with Pinot Noir, Merlot and Cabernet Franc showing most promise among the reds. Best producers: Cave Spring★, Chateau des Charmes★, Le CLOS JORDANNE★★, HENRY OF PELHAM★, Hidden Bench★★, INNISKILLIN★, Southbrook★, Stratus★★, Tawse★★, THIRTY BENCH★. Best years: (icewines) 2007 05 04 **03 02 00 99 98**.

IEPOORT *Port DOC and Douro DOC, Douro, Portugal* Remarkable small wine and PORT producer of Dutch origin. Outstanding Vintage ports★★★, old tawnies★★★ and colheitas★★★. Unfiltered LBVs★★ are among the best in their class – intense and complex. The Vintage port second label is called Secundum★★. Niepoort also produces fine red, white and rosé DOURO Redoma★★; red Vertente★★, Batuta★★★ and Charme★★ are already established as three of Portugal's leading reds. Best years: (Vintage) 2005 **03 00 97 94 92 91 87 85 82 80 77 70 66 63**.

225

NIERSTEIN *Rheinhessen, Germany* Confusingly, both a small town and large Bereich which includes the infamous Grosslage Gutes Domta The town boasts 23 vineyard sites and the top ones (Pettenthal, Bruder berg, Hipping, Oelberg and Orbel) are some of the best in the Rhir Valley. Best producers: GUNDERLOCH★★, HEYL ZU HERRNSHEIM★★, Kühlin Gillot★, St Antony★, Schneider★. Best years: (2008) 07 06 **05 04 02 01 9**

NIGL *Senftenberg, Kremstal, Austria* Consistently fine and crystalline Rieslir and Grüner Veltliner from this organic estate. Top vineyard is calle Piri★ but each year Martin Nigl releases his best wines under th Privat★★ label. Best years: (2008) 07 06 **05 04 03 02 01 99**.

NIKOLAIHOF *Wachau, Niederösterreich, Austria* The Saahs family mak some of the best wines in the WACHAU as well as in nearby Krems-Stein i KREMSTAL, including steely, intense Rieslings from the famous Stein Hund vineyard, always ★★. A biodynamic estate. Best years: (2008) 07 (05 **04 02 01 99**.

DOM. DE NIZAS *Languedoc, France* Owned by NAPA-based CLOS DU VA Nizas makes an intense, red Réserve★, a blend of Petit Verdot, Cabern Sauvignon and Syrah; a spicy COTEAUX DU LANGUEDOC (Syrah, Mourvèdr Grenache); and an old-vine Carignan★. Entry-level red Le Mas Cabernet Sauvignon-Merlot-Syrah and white is Sauvignon with a dre of Viognier. Best years: (Réserve) 2007 06 05 **04**.

NOBILO *Kumeu/Huapai, Auckland, North Island, New Zealand* Wines range fro medium-dry White Cloud to premium varietals. Tangy thoug restrained Sauvignon Blanc and a vibrant Chardonnay★ are the te wines from MARLBOROUGH. In 1998 Nobilo bought Selaks, with wineri in AUCKLAND and Marlborough (Drylands); since then they have add the intense Drylands Marlborough Sauvignon Blanc★, Chardonnay and Riesling★ to their list. The Selaks label has the most characte Nobilo is part of Constellation. Best years: (Chardonnay) **2007 06 05**.

NORTON *Mendoza, Argentina* Austrian-owned winery where reds impre more than whites (though Torrontés★ is good), with chocola Sangiovese, soft, rich Merlot★ and good Barbera. Higher up the sca quality has enormously improved in the past few vintages, especially Reserva★ releases; Privada★★ is enjoyable young but ages beautiful New top-end single-vineyard labels.

QUINTA DO NOVAL *Port DOC and Douro DOC, Douro, Portugal* Owned by AXA-Millésimes, this property is the source of extraordinary Quinta do Noval Nacional★★★, made from ungrafted vines – virtually unobtainable except at auction. Other Noval ports (including Quinta do Noval Vintage★★★ and Silval★★) are excellent too. Also fine colheitas★★ and stunning 40-year-old tawnies★★★. Also DOURO re Quinta do Noval Tinto★★. Best years: (Nacional) 2003 00 **97 94 87 85** 66 63 62 60 31; (Vintage) 2004 **03 00 97 95** 94 91 87 85 70 66 63 60 3

NUITS-ST-GEORGES AC *Côte de Nuits, Burgundy, France* This large AC one of the few relatively reliable 'village' names in Burgundy. Althougl has no Grands Crus, many of its Premiers Crus (it has 38!) are extreme good. The red can be rather slow to open out, often needing at leas years, but it ages to a delicious, chocolaty, deep figs-and-prune fru Minuscule amounts of white are made by GOUGES★, l'Arlot, Chevill and RION. Best producers: l'Arlot★★, R Arnoux★★, S CATHIARD, J Chauvenet★★, R Chevillon★★, J-J Confuron★★, FAIVELEY★★, H GOUGES★★, GRIVOT★★, Jayer-Gilles★★, Lechenaut★★, T LIGER-BELAIR★★, MEO-CAMUZET★★, A Michelot★, Mugneret★★, J-F MUGNIER★★, POTEL★★, RION★★. Best years: (reds) (2008) 07 06 05 03 **02 01** 99 98 96 95 93 90.

NYETIMBER *West Sussex, England* England's flagship sparkling wine producer. Two wines are made – Classic Cuvée★★ (Chardonnay-Pinot Noir-Pinot Meunier) and Chardonnay-based Blanc de Blancs★★ – though they also released a 2003 Pinot Meunier Blanc de Noirs. A new winemaking team took over in 2007, although Nyetimber still retains the services of the Champagne-based enologist who has been there from the start. Although some recent bottlings showed quality inconsistencies, the wines continue to exhibit exceptional depth, with delicious toasty flavours and great length. New plantings have taken the area under vine from 16ha (40 acres) to 104ha (257 acres) and a new winery is planned. Since their reputation has been based on well-aged sparklers, let's hope they don't try to expand too fast. Best years: 2003 01 **00** 98.

OAKRIDGE *Yarra Valley, Victoria, Australia* Outstanding boutique winery, admirably showcasing the YARRA's strengths. Run by David Bicknell, one of Australia's most exciting winemaking talents, formerly at the brilliant Evans & Tate in MARGARET RIVER. The 864 range includes complex, restrained Chardonnay★★★, lush, structured Cabernet-Merlot★★ and ultra-concentrated yet seamless Shiraz★★. The medium-priced Oakridge range (especially Chardonnay★ and Pinot Noir) and budget-priced Over the Shoulder range represent excellent value.

OAKVILLE AVA *Napa Valley, California, USA* This region is cooler than RUTHERFORD, which lies immediately to the north. Planted primarily to Cabernet Sauvignon, the area contains some of NAPA's best vineyards, both on the valley floor (MONDAVI, OPUS ONE, SCREAMING EAGLE) and hillsides (HARLAN ESTATE, DALLA VALLE), producing wines that display lush, ripe black fruits and firm tannins. Best years: (Cabernet Sauvignon) 2005 04 03 **02 01** 00 99 97 96 95 94 91 90.

OC, VIN DE PAYS D' *Languedoc-Roussillon, France* Important vin de pays covering LANGUEDOC-ROUSSILLON. Overproduction and consequent underripeness have not helped its reputation, but an increasing number of fine reds and whites show what can be done. Best producers: l'Aigle★, Clovallon (Viognier★), Condamine Bertrand, Croix de St-Jean, J-L DENOIS★, l'HOSPITALET, J & F Lurton★, MAS LA CHEVALIÈRE, Ormesson★, Pech-Céleyran (Viognier★), Quatre Sous★, SKALLI-FORTANT, VAL D'ORBIEU (top reds★).

OCKFEN *Mosel* Village with one famous individual vineyard site, the Bockstein. The wines can be superb in a sunny year, never losing their cold steely streak but packing in delightful full-flavoured fruit as well. Best producers: St Urbans-Hof★★, Dr Heinz Wagner★, ZILLIKEN★★. Best years: (2008) 07 06 05 **04 03 02** 01 99 97.

OKANAGAN VALLEY *British Columbia, Canada* The most important wine-producing region of British Columbia and first home of Canada's rich, honeyed icewine. The Okanagan Lake helps temper the bitterly cold nights but October frosts can be a problem. Chardonnay, Pinot Blanc, Pinot Gris and Pinot Noir are the top performers. South of the lake, Cabernet, Merlot and even Shiraz are now being grown successfully. Best producers: Black Hills Estate★★, Blue Mountain★, Burrowing Owl★, CedarCreek★, INNISKILLIN, JACKSON-TRIGGS★, MISSION HILL★★, Quails' Gate★, Road 13★★, SUMAC RIDGE★. Best years: (reds) 2006 05 04 03 **02 01** 00.

OLTREPÒ PAVESE DOC *Lombardy, Italy* Italy's main source of Pinot Nero used mainly for sparkling wines that may be called Classese when made by the CHAMPAGNE method, though base wines supply *spumante* industries elsewhere. Still reds from Barbera, Bonarda and Pinot Nero and whites from the Pinots, Riesling and Chardonnay can be impressive. Much mediocre Pinot Grigio. Best producers: Cà di Frara★, Le Fracce★, Frecciarossa★, Fugazza, Castello di Luzzano, Mazzolino★, Monsupello★, Montelio★, Vercesi del Castellazzo★, Bruno Verdi★. Best years: (reds) (2008) 07 **06 04 03 0**

WILLI OPITZ *Neusiedlersee, Burgenland, Austria* The eccentric and publicity conscious Willi Opitz produces a remarkable, unusual range of dessert wines from his 12ha (30-acre) vineyard, including red Eiswein. The best are ★★, but dry wines are average.

OPUS ONE★★ *Oakville AVA, California, USA* BORDEAUX-blend wine, a joint venture initially between Robert MONDAVI and Baron Philippe de Rothschild of MOUTON-ROTHSCHILD, now between Constellation and Baroness Philippine de Rothschild. Most Opus bottlings have been in the ★★ range, some achieving ★★★, in a beautifully cedary, minty manner whose balance and elegance can be a delight in modern-day NAPA. Best years: 2005 04 03 02 **01** 99 98 97 96 95 94 93 92 91 90 86 85 84

DOM. DE L'ORATOIRE ST-MARTIN *Côtes du Rhône AC, Rhône Valley, France* Careful fruit selection in a mature, high-slopes vineyard is the secret of Frédéric and François Alary's intense Côtes du Rhône-Villages CAIRANNE reds and whites. Haut-Coustias white★ is ripe with peach and exotic fruit aromas, while the red★★ is a luscious mouthful of raspberries, herbs and spice. Top red Cuvée Prestige★★ is deep and intense with dark, spicy fruit. Best years: (Cuvée Prestige) **2007 06** 05 04 03 01 98.

OREGON *USA* Oregon shot to international stardom in the early 1980, following some perhaps overly generous praise of its Pinot Noir, but it is only with the release of a succession of fine recent vintages (2007 being an unfortunate exception) and some soul-searching by the winemakers about what style they should be pursuing that we can now begin to accept that some of the hype was deserved. Consistency is still a problem, however, with surprisingly warm weather now offering challenges along with the traditional ones of overcast skies and unwelcome rain. Chardonnay can be quite good in an austere, understated style. The rising star is Pinot Gris, which can be delicious, with surprising complexity. Pinot Blanc and Riesling are also gaining momentum. The WILLAMETTE VALLEY is considered the best growing region, although the more BORDEAUX-like climate of the Umpqua and Rogue Valleys can produce good Cabernet Sauvignon and Merlot. Best producers (Rogue, Umpqua) Abacela★, Bridgeview, Foris★, Henry Estate, Valley View. Best years: (reds) (2007) 06 **04** 03 02.

TENUTA DELL'ORNELLAIA *Bolgheri, Tuscany, Italy* This beautiful property was developed by Lodovico ANTINORI, brother of Piero. Now owned by FRESCOBALDI-controlled Tenute di Toscana. Ornellaia★★, a Cabernet/Merlot blend, doesn't quite have the class of neighbouring SASSICAIA, but is more lush. Also top Merlot, Masseto★★, and second wine Le Serre Nuove di Ornellaia★. Best years: (Ornellaia) (2007) (06) (05) 04 03 **01 00 99** 98 97 96 95.

ORTENAU *Baden, Germany* A chain of steep granitic hills between Baden-Baden and Offenburg, which produce the most elegant (generally dry) Rieslings in BADEN, along with fragrant, medium-bodied Spätburgunder

(Pinot Noir) reds. Best producers: Franckenstein★, Laible★★, Nägelsförst★, Schloss Neuweier★, Wolff Metternich★.

ORVIETO DOC *Umbria, Italy* Traditionally a lightly sweet (*abboccato*) white wine made from a blend of grapes including TREBBIANO and Umbria's native Grechetto, Orvieto at the basic level is today usually dry and ordinary. In the superior Classico zone, however, the potential for richer, more complex wines exists, especially in the Superiore category. Not generally a wine for aging. There are also some very good botrytis-affected examples. Best producers: (dry) Barberani-Vallesanta★ (Superiore Castagnolo★★), La Carraia★, Decugnano dei Barbi★, Palazzone★ (Superiore Campo del Guardiano★★), Castello della SALA★, Salviano★, Conte Vaselli★, Le Velette★; (sweet) Barberani-Vallesanta (Calcaia★★), Decugnano dei Barbi★, Palazzone (Muffa Nobilis★★), Castello della SALA★.

OSBORNE *Jerez y Manzanilla DO, Andalucía, Spain* The biggest drinks company in Spain, Osborne does most of its business in brandy and other spirits. Its sherry arm in Puerto de Santa María specializes in the light Fino Quinta★. Amontillado Coquinero★, rich, intense Bailén Oloroso★★ and Solera India Oloroso★★ are very good indeed. It has also created a large red wine estate at Malpica de Tajo in CASTILLA-LA MANCHA.

PAARL WO *South Africa* South Africa's second most densely planted district after Worcester, accounting for 17% of all vineyards. A great diversity of soil and climate favour everything from Cap Classique sparkling wines to sherry styles, but the fact that Paarl was famous for sherry tells you that it's fairly hot, and it is now big reds that are setting the quality pace, especially Shiraz. Its white RHÔNE counterpart, Viognier, solo and in white blends, is also performing well. FRANSCHHOEK, Simonsberg-Paarl, Voor Paardeberg and Wellington are wards within the Paarl district. Best producers: (Paarl) Boschendal, DISTELL (Nederburg), FAIRVIEW★★, VEENWOUDEN★, Vilafonté★; (Simonsberg-Paarl), DISTELL (Plaisir de Merle★), FAIRVIEW★★, GLEN CARLOU★, Rupert & Rothschild★; (Voor Paardeberg) Scali★, Vilafonté★, Welgemeend★; (Wellington) Diemersfontein★, Mont du Toit★. Best years: (premium reds) 2007 06 **05 04 03 02 01 00.**

PACHERENC DU VIC-BILH AC *South-West France* MADIRAN's white wines, ranging from dry to sweet late-harvest styles Best producers: AYDIE★, Barréjat, BERTHOUMIEU★, Brumont (Bouscassé★, MONTUS★), Capmartin★, du Crampilh★, Damiens, Labranche-Laffont★, Laffitte-Teston★, PLAIMONT★. Best years: (sweet) (2008) **07 05 04.**

PACIFIC RIM VINEYARDS *Washington State, USA* Randall Grahm, whose BONNY DOON wines are a Californian legend, headed to WASHINGTON STATE 'to craft the best Riesling in America'. The single-vineyard wines are exceptional examples of New World Riesling: the Wallula Vineyard★ bottlings (one being biodynamic) are both expressive of their *terroir*; the Dauenhauer is from Oregon's WILLAMETTE VALLEY; the Solstice Vineyard★★ is the jewel.

PADTHAWAY *South Australia* This wine region has always been the alter ego of nearby COONAWARRA, growing whites to complement Coonawarra's reds; Chardonnay has been particularly successful. Nowadays there are some excellent reds, especially from Henry's Drive; even GRANGE has included Padthaway grapes. Orlando's premium Lawson's Shiraz★★ is 100% Padthaway, HARDYS' Eileen Hardy Shiraz★★★ usually includes Padthaway fruit. Best producers: Browns of Padthaway, Henry's Drive★★, LINDEMANS★, Orlando/JACOB'S CREEK★, Padthaway Estate, SEPPELT, Stonehaven★.

BRUNO PAILLARD *Champagne AC, Champagne, France*   Bruno Paillard is on
of the very few individuals to have created a new CHAMPAGNE house ove
the past century. Paillard still does the blending himself. Non-vintag
Première Cuvée★ is lemony and crisp; Réserve Privée★ is a blanc d
blancs; vintage Brut★★ is a serious wine. De luxe cuvée Nec Plu
Ultra★★ is a barrel-fermented blend of Grands Crus made in to
vintages. Also owns Philipponnat and the great single-vineyard site, Clo
des Goisses★★★. Best years: 1999 96 **95 90 89 88**.

ALVARO PALACIOS *Priorat DOCa, Cataluña, Spain*   The young Alvar
Palacios was already a veteran with Bordeaux and Napa experience whe
he launched his boutique winery in PRIORAT, in the rough hills of souther
CATALUNA in the late 1980s. He is now one of the driving forces of th
area's rebirth. His red wines (super-expensive, highly concentrate
L'Ermita★★★, Finca Dofí★★ and affordable Les Terrasses★) from ol
Garnacha vines and a dollop of Cabernet Sauvignon, Merlot, Cariñe
and Syrah have won a cult following. Best years: 2006 05 04 03 **01 00 99 9
97 96 95 94**.

PALETTE AC *Provence, France*   Tiny AC just east of Aix-en-Provence. Eve
though the local market pays high prices, I find the reds and rosés rathe
tough and charmless. However, Ch. Simone manages to achieve a whit
wine of some flavour from basic southern French grapes. **Best producer
Crémade, Ch. Simone★.**

PALLISER ESTATE *Martinborough, North Island, New Zealand*   State-of-the-a
winery producing some of New Zealand's best Sauvignon Blanc★
(certainly the best outside MARLBOROUGH) and Riesling★, delightfu
Chardonnay★★ and Pinot Gris★, and impressive, rich-textured Pine
Noir★★. Exciting botrytized dessert wines in favourable vintage
Méthode★ fizz is good, too. Best years: (Pinot Noir) (2008) 07 **06 03 0**

CH. PALMER★★ *Margaux AC, 3ème Cru Classé, Haut-Médoc, Bordeaux, Fran*
This estate was named after a British major-general who fought in th
Napoleonic Wars, and is one of the leading properties in MARGAUX A
The wine is wonderfully perfumed, with irresistible plump fruit (lots
Merlot). The very best vintages can age for 30 years or more. Secor
wine: Alter Ego★ (frequently an excellent, scented red). Best years: 200
06 05 04 **03 02 01 00 99 98 96 95 90 89 88 86 85**.

S C PANNELL *McLaren Vale, South Australia*   Steve Pannell enjoyed corpora
success as BRL HARDYS' chief red winemaker, but he is not new to sma
family vineyards: he grew up on the MOSS WOOD vineyard in its earlie
days. Without vineyards or a winery, S C Pannell is curiously
producing MCLAREN VALE Shiraz and Grenache, and he has had equal
rapid-fire success with ADELAIDE HILLS Sauvignon★. Textural and lavish
concentrated Shiraz-Grenache★★ and complex Shiraz★★ show mo
restraint and elegance than is common in the region, while Nebbiolo★
(from Adelaide Hills) is some of the best you'll find outside BAROLO.

CH. PAPE-CLÉMENT *Pessac-Léognan AC, Cru Classé de Graves, Bordeaux, Fran*
The expensive red wine★★ from this GRAVES Classed Growth has n
always been as consistent as it should be – but things settled down int
high-quality groove during the 1990s. In style it is mid-way between th
refinement of HAUT-BRION and the firmness of la MISSION-HAUT-BRION. Mo
elegance and seduction since 2001. Also produces a small amount of fir
aromatic white wine★★. Second wine: (red) Clémentin. Best years: (re
2007 06 05 04 **03 02 01 00 99 98 96 95 90 89 88**; (white) 2007 06 05 04
02 01 00 99 98.

ARELLADA This Catalan exclusivity is the lightest of the trio of white grapes that go to make CAVA wines in north-eastern Spain. It also makes still wines, light, fresh and gently floral, with good acidity. Drink it as young as possible, while it still has the benefit of freshness.

ARKER COONAWARRA ESTATE *Coonawarra, South Australia* Established by John Parker, who built the estate into one of the region's finest boutiques. Following his death, it was bought by the Rathbone family, who own Yering Station, MOUNT LANGI GHIRAN and Xanadu, and is performing better than ever. The top label, cheekily named First Growth★★ in imitation of illustrious BORDEAUX reds, has enjoyed much critical acclaim. It is released only in better years. Second-label Terra Rossa Cabernet Sauvignon★ is lighter and leafier. The Merlot★★ is among the best in Australia. Best years: (First Growth) (2008) 06 05 04 01 **99 98 96 93 91 90**.

J PASK *Hawkes Bay, North Island, New Zealand* Chris Pask made the first wine in the now-famous Gimblett Gravels area of HAWKES BAY. Flagship Declaration label includes an intense Syrah★, rich Merlot★ and a powerful Cabernet-Merlot-Malbec★ blend. Mid-range wines under the Gimblett Road label. Best years: (reds) (2008) **07** 06 04 02 00.

ASO ROBLES AVA *California, USA* A large AVA at the northern end of SAN LUIS OBISPO COUNTY. Cabernet Sauvignon and Zinfandel perform well in this warm region, and Syrah is gaining an important foothold, but too many producers are chasing OTT alcohol levels. The Perrin family from Ch. de BEAUCASTEL selected this AVA to plant RHÔNE varieties for their California project, Tablas

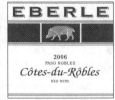

EBERLE

2006
PASO ROBLES
Côtes-du-Rôbles
RED WINE

Creek, whose whites so far outshine their mid-weight reds. Best producers: Adelaida★, Eberle★, Justin★, J Lohr★, Peachy Canyon★, Tablas Creek★, Wild Horse★.

ATAGONIA *Argentina* Located 750km (465 miles) south of MENDOZA, Patagonia used to be called 'the vineyards of the winds'. Those constant winds, along with relentless sunshine and cool nights, allow a super-healthy viticulture where Malbec flavours are fresh and scented and plump, Cabernet and Merlot are juicy and Pinot Noir looks to have great potential. There are two main areas: Río Negro, to the east, is where the first vines were planted in the 19th century. The Neuquén area to the north-west has seen dramatic development during the past 5 years. Best producers: (Río Negro) Humberto Canale, Chacra★★, FABRE MONTMAYOU★★, Noemía★★; (Neuquén) Fin del Mundo, NQN, Familia Schroeder★.

UÍS PATO *Bairrada, Beira Litoral, Portugal* Leading 'modernist' in BAIRRADA, passionately convinced of the Baga grape's ability to make great reds on clay soil. He labels his wines as BEIRAS after arguing with Bairrada's bosses. Wines such as the Vinhas Velhas★, Vinha Barrosa★★, Vinha Pan★★ and the flagship Quinta do Ribeirinho Pé Franco★★ (from ungrafted vines) rank among Portugal's finest modern reds: some can reach ★★★ with age. Good white, Vinha Formal★, is 100% Bical. Also good fizz. Daughter Filipa makes delightful reds and whites under Lokal★★ and Ensaios FP★★ labels. Best years: (reds) (2008) **05 04 03 01 00** 97 96 95 92.

AUILLAC AC *Haut-Médoc, Bordeaux, France* The deep gravel banks around the town of Pauillac in the HAUT-MEDOC are the heartland of Cabernet Sauvignon. For many wine lovers, the king of red wine grapes finds its ultimate expression in the 3 Pauillac First Growths (LATOUR, LAFITE-ROTHSCHILD and MOUTON-ROTHSCHILD). The large AC also contains 1 other Classed Growths. The uniting characteristic of Pauillac wines their intense blackcurrant fruit flavour and heady cedar an pencil-shavings perfume. These are the longest-lived of BORDEAUX great red wines. **Best producers:** Armailhac★, BATAILLEY★, Bellegrave Clerc-Milon★, Duhart-Milon★, Fonbadet, GRAND-PUY-DUCASSE★, GRAND-PUY-LACOSTE★★, HAUT-BAGES-LIBERAL★, HAUT-BATAILLEY★, LAFITE-ROTHSCHILD★ LATOUR★★★, LYNCH-BAGES★★★, Lynch-Moussas, MOUTON-ROTHSCHILD★★★ Pibran★, PICHON-LONGUEVILLE★★★, PICHON-LONGUEVILLE-LALANDE★★ PONTET-CANET★★. **Best years:** 2007 06 05 04 03 **02 01 00** 96 95 90 89 88 8(

CH. PAVIE★★ *St-Émilion Grand Cru AC, 1er Grand Cru Classé, Bordeaux, Franc* The style of the wine may be controversial – dense, rich, succulent – an it has as many enemies as friends, but there's no doubting the progre made at Pavie since Gérard Perse acquired the property in 1998. Th price has also soared. Pavie-Decesse★ and MONBOUSQUET★ are part of th same stable. **Best years:** 2007 06 05 04 **03 02 01** 00 **99 98 90** 89 88 86.

CH. PAVIE-MACQUIN★★ *St-Émilion Grand Cru AC, 1er Grand Cru Class Bordeaux, France* This has become one of the stars of the ST-EMILION GRAN CRU since the 1990s, with promotion to Premier Grand Cru Classé i 2006. Rich, firm and reserved, the wines need 7–8 years and will ag longer. **Best years:** 2007 06 05 04 03 **02 01 00** 99 98 96 95 94 90.

PÉCHARMANT AC *South-West France* Improving red wines from small A north-east of BERGERAC. The wines are full-bodied, deriving their firmne from the iron in the sub-soil. Good vintages easily last 10 years an match a good HAUT-MEDOC. **Best producers:** Chemins d'Orient★, Clos l Côtes★, Costes★, d'Elle, Grand Jaure, Haut-Pécharmant★, Terre Vieilles Tiregand★. **Best years:** (2008) **05 04 01 00 98.**

PEGASUS BAY *Canterbury, South Island, New Zealand* Matthew Donaldso and Lynette Hudson make lush, mouthfilling Chardonnay★★, an almo chewy Pinot Noir★★ and its even richer big sister Prima Donna Pine Noir★★, powerful Sauvignon Blanc-Semillon★★ and very stylis medium Riesling★★. These are some of the most original wines in Ne Zealand, and all will age well. **Best years:** (Pinot Noir) (2008) 07 **06 04 (02 01 00.**

PEMBERTON *Western Australia* Exciting emergent cool-climate regio deep in the Karri forests of the south-west, which has long divide opinion about which varieties will most suit the region. At this stage, th whites have done best, especially taut, tangy Sauvignon Blanc ar thrilling, minerally Chardonnay. There are the occasional super examples of Riesling, Viognier, Semillon and Marsanne as well Western Australia's only distinguished sparkling wine. Best of the re so far is Pinot Noir, with Shiraz rewarding the patient in its best vintage HOUGHTON leads the way – thanks to the outstanding fruit coming fro the vineyard they purchased in 1992 – with their Wisdom rang (sparkling Chardonnay-Pinot Noir★, Sauvignon Blanc Chardonnay★★). **Best producers:** Angelicus, Bellarmine★, Fonty's Poo HOUGHTON★★, Lillian, Merum, Picardy★, Salitage, Smithbrook.

PENEDÈS DO *Cataluña, Spain* The booming CAVA industry is based Penedès, and the majority of the still wines are white, made from th Cava trio of Parellada, Macabeo and Xarel-lo, clean and fresh whe young, but never exciting. Better whites are made from Chardonna The reds are variable, the best made from Cabernet Sauvignon and/

Tempranillo and Merlot. Best producers: Albet i Noya★, Can Feixes★, Can Ràfols dels Caus★★, Cavas Hill, Jean León★, Marques de Monistrol, Masía Bach★, Albert Milá i Mallofré, Puig y Roca★, Sot Lefriec★, TORRES★, Vallformosa, Jané Ventura★.

PENFOLDS *Barossa Valley, South Australia* While it was part of the giant Southcorp group, Penfolds proved that quality can go hand in hand with quantity, but so far its performance as part of the Foster's Wine Group has been uneven, particularly at the lower end. It still makes the country's most famous red wine, GRANGE★★★, and other superb reds such as RWT Shiraz★★★, Magill Estate★★, St Henri★, Bin 707 Cabernet★★, Bin 389 Cabernet-Shiraz★, Bin 28 Kalimna★ and Bin 128 Coonawarra Shiraz. Its Cellar Reserve wines are difficult to find but outstanding, and occasional releases of Special Bin reds are among Australia's best. However, further down the range a dispiriting blandness has entered into previously reliable wines like Koonunga Hill and Rawson's Retreat. Whites are led by expensive but excellent Yattarna Chardonnay★★★; there's also citrus Eden Valley Riesling★ and decent Rawson's Retreat Riesling. Thomas Hyland Cabernet, Shiraz and Chardonnay are pretty good. Best years: (top reds) 2008 06 05 04 **02 98 96 94 91 90**.

PENLEY ESTATE *Coonawarra, South Australia* Kym Tolley, a member of the PENFOLD family, combined the names when he left Southcorp and launched Penley Estate in 1991. From 1997 Cabernet Sauvignon★★★ has been outstanding. Chardonnay and Hyland Shiraz can reach ★★; Gryphon Merlot★ and fizz★ are also worth a try. Best years: (Cabernet Reserve) (2008) (07) 06 05 **04 02 00 99 98 96 94 93 92 91**.

PERNAND-VERGELESSES AC *Côte de Beaune, Burgundy, France* The little-known village of Pernand-Vergelesses contains a decent chunk of the great Corton hill, including much of the best white CORTON-CHARLEMAGNE Grand Cru vineyard. The red wines sold under the village name are very attractive when young, with a nice raspberry pastille fruit and a slight earthiness, and will age for 6–10 years. Best vineyard: Île de Vergelesses. As no one ever links poor old Pernand with the heady heights of Corton-Charlemagne, the whites sold under the village name can be a bargain. The wines can be a bit lean and dry to start with but fatten up beautifully after 2–4 years in bottle. Best producers: (reds) CHANDON DE BRIAILLES★★, C Cornu★, Denis Père et Fils★, Dubreuil-Fontaine★, Laleure-Piot★; (whites) CHANDON DE BRIAILLES★, Dubreuil-Fontaine★, Germain/Ch. de Chorey, A Guyon, JADOT★, J-M Pavelot★, Rapet★, Rollin★. Best years: (reds) (2008) 07 05 03 02 99; (whites) (2008) 07 **06 05 04**.

ANDRÉ PERRET *Condrieu AC, Rhône Valley, France* A top CONDRIEU grower, with 2 standout cuvées: Clos Chanson★★ is direct and full, Chéry★★★, made with some later-picked Viognier, is gloriously musky, floral and rich. Impressive white and red ST-JOSEPH, notably Les Grisières★★ from old Syrah vines. Very good vin de pays Syrah and Marsanne. Best years: (Condrieu) (2008) **07 06 05 04**.

JOSEPH PERRIER *Champagne AC, Champagne, France* The NV Blanc de Blancs★ is classy stuff and the NV Cuvée Royale★ is biscuity and creamy. Prestige Cuvée Josephine★★ has length and complexity, but the much cheaper Cuvée Royale Vintage★★ is the best deal. Best years: **1999 98 96 95 90 89 88 85 82**.

PERRIER-JOUËT *Champagne AC, Champagne, France* Perrier-Jouët has had three owners in the past 10 years (it's now owned by Pernod Ricard). This doesn't help consistency, but Perrier-Jouët had fallen so low during the 1990s that any change would be beneficial. Certainly the NV is now a decent drink once more, the Blason Rosé★ is charming and the de luxe vintage cuvée Belle Époque★ (known as Fleur de Champagne in the US) reasonably classy. So keep up the improvement for this grand old label. Best years: (2002) **99 98 96 95 90 89 85 82**.

PESQUERA *Ribera del Duero DO, Castilla y León, Spain* Tinto Pesquera reds, richly coloured, firm, fragrant and plummy-tobaccoey, have long been among Spain's best. They are 100% Tempranillo and sold as Crianza★ and Reserva★. Gran Reserva★★ and Janus★★★ are made in the best years. The firm founded by Alejandro Fernández in 1972 owns another RIBERA DEL DUERO estate, Condado de Haza★ (Alenza★★), plus ventures in Zamora (Dehesa La Granja★) and La MANCHA (Vínculo). Best years: (Pesquera Crianza) 2006 05 **04 01 99 96 95 94 93 92 91 90 89**.

PESSAC-LÉOGNAN AC *Bordeaux, France* AC created in 1987 for the northern (and best) part of the GRAVES region and including all the Graves Classed Growths. The supremely gravelly soil tends to favour red wines over the rest of the Graves. Now, thanks to cool fermentation and the use of new oak barrels, this is also one of the most exciting areas of France for top-class white wines. Best producers: (reds) Carbonnieux★, les Carmes Haut-Brion★, Dom. de CHEVALIER★★, Couhins-Lurton★★, FIEUZAL★, HAUT-BAILLY★, HAUT-BRION★★★, Larrivet-Haut-Brion★, LATOUR-MARTILLAC★, la LOUVIÈRE★, MALARTIC-LAGRAVIÈRE★, la MISSION-HAUT-BRION★★★, PAPE-CLEMENT★★★, SMITH-HAUT-LAFITTE★★; (whites) Brown★, Carbonnieux★, Dom. de CHEVALIER★★★, Couhins-Lurton★★, FIEUZAL★, HAUT-BRION★★★, LATOUR-MARTILLAC★, LAVILLE-HAUT-BRION★★★, la LOUVIÈRE★★, MALARTIC-LAGRAVIÈRE★★, PAPE-CLEMENT★★, Rochemorin★, SMITH-HAUT-LAFITTE★★. Best years: (reds) 2006 05 04 **02 01 00 99 98 96 95**; (whites) **2007 06 05 04 02 01 00 99 98 96**.

PETALUMA *Adelaide Hills, South Australia* A public company (which includes KNAPPSTEIN, STONIER, Mitchelton in Victoria and Smithbrook in Western Australia) founded by Brian Croser, probably Australia's most influential winemaker. It was taken over by brewer Lion Nathan in 2001 and Croser is no longer involved (see TAPANAPPA). CHAMPAGNE-style Croser★ is stylish but lean. COONAWARRA (Cabernet-Merlot)★★ and Chardonnay★★ are consistently fine and Hanlin Hill Riesling★★★ from the CLARE VALLEY is at the fuller end of the spectrum and matures superbly. Best years: (Coonawarra) (2008) (07) (06) 05 **04 03 02 01 00 99 97 94 91 90 88**.

PETIT VERDOT A rich, tannic variety, grown mainly in Bordeaux's HAUT-MEDOC to add depth, colour and violet fragrance to top wines. Late ripening and erratic yield limit its popularity, but warmer-climate plantings in Australia, California, South Africa, Chile, Argentina, Spain and Italy are giving exciting results.

CH. PETIT-VILLAGE★ *Pomerol AC, Bordeaux, France* This POMEROL used to be rather dry and dense, but has considerably softened up in recent vintages. New cellar and even better quality from 2006. Generally worth aging for 8–10 years. Best years: 2007 06 05 **04 03 01 00 99 98 96 95 90 88**.

PETITE ARVINE A Swiss grape variety from the VALAIS, Petite Arvine has a bouquet of peach and apricot, and develops a spicy, honeyed character. Dry, medium or sweet, the wines have good aging potential – thank goodness: I've still got one from 1969. Best producers: Chappaz★, A Mathier, Maye, Dom. du Mont d'Or★, Rouvinez★, Varone.

PETITE SIRAH Once used primarily as a blending grape in California, this variety is identical to the Rhône blender Durif. Some 275 California wineries now make a varietal Petite Sirah. At its best, it is deep, tannic and long-lived, but can be monstrously huge and unfriendly. Australian, Mexican and Israeli examples are softer though still hefty, and can occasionally develop a floral scent and blackberry fruit. **Best producers:** (California) FETZER, Foppiano, RAVENSWOOD★, Stags' Leap Winery★★, TURLEY★★; (Australia) Rutherglen Estates★, WESTEND★; (Mexico) L A CETTO★.

CH. PÉTRUS★★★ *Pomerol AC, Bordeaux, France* One of the most expensive red wines in the world (alongside other superstars from POMEROL, such as le PIN). The powerful, concentrated wine produced here is the result of the caring genius of Pétrus' owners, the MOUEIX family, who have maximized the potential of the vineyard of almost solid clay, although the impressive average age of the vines has been much reduced by recent replantings. Drinkable for its astonishingly rich, dizzying blend of fruit and spice flavours after a decade, but top years will age for much longer, developing exotic scents of tobacco and chocolate and truffles as they mature. **Best years:** 2007 06 05 04 03 **02** 01 00 **99 98 96 95 90 89 88 86 85**.

DOM. PEYRE ROSE *Coteaux du Languedoc AC, Languedoc, France* Organic viticulture, ultra-low yields, lengthy aging, but total absence of oak are all marks of the individuality of Marlène Soria's wines. Syrah is the dominant grape in both the raisin- and plum-scented Clos des Cistes★ and the dense, velvety Clos Syrah Léone★★. **Best years:** (reds) 03 **02** 98.

CH. DE PEZ★ *St-Estèphe AC, Haut-Médoc, Bordeaux, France* One of ST-ESTÈPHE's leading non-Classed Growths, de Pez makes mouthfilling, satisfying claret with sturdy fruit. Slow to evolve, good vintages often need 10 years or more. Owned by Champagne house ROEDERER. **Best years:** 2007 06 05 04 03 02 01 00 99 98 96 95 90 89.

PFALZ *Germany* This immense wine region, with 23,360ha (57,720 acres), makes a lot of mediocre wine, but the quality estates can match the best that Germany has to offer. The Mittelhaardt can produce profound Riesling, especially round the villages of BAD DURKHEIM, WACHENHEIM, FORST and Deidesheim, though Freinsheim, Kallstadt, Ungstein, Gimmeldingen and Haardt also produce fine Riesling as well as Scheurebe, Rieslaner and Pinot Gris. In the Südliche Weinstrasse the warm climate makes the area an ideal testing ground for Spät-, Weiss- and Grauburgunder (aka Pinots Noir, Blanc and Gris), as well as Gewürztraminer, Scheurebe, Muscat and red Dornfelder, the last often dark and tannic, sometimes with oak influence.

JOSEPH PHELPS *Napa Valley AVA, California, USA* Joseph Phelps' BORDEAUX-blend Insignia★★ is usually one of California's top reds, strongly fruit-driven with a lively spicy background. Phelps' pure Cabernets include Napa Valley★ and huge Backus Vineyard★★, beautifully balanced with solid ripe fruit. The Napa Merlot★ is ripe and elegant, with layers of fruit. Phelps was the first California winery to successfully major on

Rhône varietals, and makes an intense Viognier★ and complex Syrah★. A project at cold FREESTONE near the Sonoma coast is producing superb Chardonnay and Pinot Noir. Best years: (Insignia) 2005 04 03 02 **01 00 99 96 95 94 93 91 85**.

CH. DE PIBARNON *Bandol AC, Provence, France* Blessed with excellently located vineyards, Pibarnon is one of BANDOL's leading properties. The reds★★, extremely attractive when young, develop a truffly, wild herb character with age. Average white and a ripe, strawberryish rosé. Best years: (reds) 2007 06 05 **03 01 00 99 98 96**.

PIC ST-LOUP *Coteaux du Languedoc AC, Languedoc, France* This aspiring Languedoc appellation, north of Montpellier, is one of the coolest growing zones in the Midi and, along with la CLAPE, produces some of the best reds in the Languedoc. Syrah is the dominant variety, along with Grenache and Mourvèdre. Whites from Marsanne, Roussanne and Rolle are showing promise. Best producers: Cazeneuve★, CLOS MARIE★, Ermitage du Pic St-Loup, l'Euzière★, l'HORTUS★, Lancyre★, Lascaux★, Lavabre★, MAS BRUGUIERE★, Mas de Mortiès★. Best years: (reds) 2007 06 05 **04 03 01**.

FRANZ X PICHLER *Wachau, Niederösterreich, Austria* One of Austria's most famous producers of dry wines. Grüner Veltliner and Riesling 'M'★★★ (for monumental) and Riesling Unendlich★★★ (endless) – alcoholically potent but balanced – are amazing. Red Arachon★★ is a joint venture with TEMENT and Szemes in BURGENLAND. A new generation is now taking over. Best years: (Riesling/Grüner Veltliner Smaragd) (2008) 07 06 05 04 03 02 **01 00 99**.

RUDI PICHLER *Wachau, Niederösterreich, Austria* Pichler has progressed from being one of the WACHAU's most reliable producers to a secure place in the top tier. Riesling Achleiten and Grüner Veltliner Kollmütz and Hochrain are regularly ★★. Best years: (2008) 07 06 05 **04 02**.

CH. PICHON-LONGUEVILLE★★★ *Pauillac AC, 2ème Cru Classé, Haut-Médoc Bordeaux, France* Despite its superb vineyards, Pichon-Longueville (called Pichon-Baron until 1988) wines were 'also-rans' for a long time. In 1987 the property was bought by AXA and Jean-Michel Cazes of LYNCH-BAGES took over the management. The improvement was immediate and thrilling. Cazes has now left, but most recent vintages have been of First Growth standard, with firm tannic structure and rich dark fruit. Cellar for at least 10 years, although it is likely to keep for 30. Second wine: les Tourelles de Pichon. Best years: 2007 06 05 04 03 **02 0 00 99 98 96 95 90 89 88 86**.

CH. PICHON-LONGUEVILLE-LALANDE★★★ *Pauillac AC, 2ème Cru Classé Haut-Médoc, Bordeaux, France* The inspirational figure of May de Lencquesaing forged the modern reputation of this property. It's now (since 2007) controlled by Champagne house ROEDERER but with the same winemaking and management team. Divinely scented and lush at 6–7 years, the wines usually stay gorgeous for 20 at least. Recent years have been excellent. Second wine: Réserve de la Comtesse. Best years: 2007 06 05 04 03 **02 01 00 99 98 96 95 90 89 88 86 85**.

PIEDMONT *Italy* The most important Italian region for the tradition of quality wines. In the north, there is Carema, GHEMME and GATTINARA. To the south, in the LANGHE hills, there's BAROLO and BARBARESCO, both masterful examples of the Nebbiolo grape, and other wines from Dolcetto and Barbera grapes. In the Monferrato hills, in the provinces of Asti and Alessandria, the Barbera, Moscato and Cortese grapes hold sway. The broad DOCs of

Langhe and Monferrato and the regionwide Piemonte appellation are designed to classify all wines of quality from a great range of grape varieties. See also ASTI, ERBALUCE DI CALUSO, GAVI, MOSCATO D'ASTI, NEBBIOLO D'ALBA, ROERO.

PIEROPAN *Veneto, Italy* Exceptionally good SOAVE Classico★ and, from 2 single vineyards, Soave Classico crus Calvarino★★ and La Rocca★★. Excellent RECIOTO DI SOAVE Le Colombare★★ and opulent Passito della Rocca★★, a barrique-aged blend of Sauvignon, Riesling Italico (Welschriesling) and Trebbiano di Soave. Single-vineyard Soaves can improve for 5 years or more, as can the Recioto and other sweet styles.

CH. PIERRE-BISE *Coteaux du Layon AC, Loire Valley, France* Claude Papin, a former President of the Technical Institute of the Vine and of Wine, has a professorial grasp of *terroir*. His COTEAUX DU LAYON vineyard is divided into over 20 mini parcels based on factors like soil depth, topography and wind and sun exposure that help him analyse optimum ripeness. And the results are sublime: rich, yet pure-fruited and precise Coteaux du Layon★★★ and QUARTS DE CHAUME★★★ with a mineral undertow. Very good dry ANJOU BLANC★, SAVENNIÈRES★ and ANJOU-VILLAGES★★. Best years: (sweet) 2007 05 03 02 **01 00 97 96 95 90 89**.

PIERRO *Margaret River, Western Australia* Mike Peterkin doesn't make that much Pierro Chardonnay★★★, yet it is a masterpiece of elegance and complexity. The Semillon-Sauvignon LTC★ is full with just a hint of leafiness, while the Pinot Noir★ approaches ★★ as the vines age. Dark, dense Cabernet Sauvignon-Merlot★ is the serious, BORDEAUX-like member of the family. The Fire Gully range is from a vineyard next door to MOSS WOOD and is consistently good. Best years: (Chardonnay) (2008) 07 06 05 04 03 02 01 00.

PIESPORT *Mosel, Germany* Generic Piesporter Michelsberg wines, soft, sweet and forgettable, have nothing to do with the excellent Rieslings from the top Goldtröpfchen site. With their intense peach and blackcurrant aromas they are unique among MOSEL wines. Best producers: GRANS-FASSIAN★★, J Haart★, Reinhold HAART★★, Kurt Hain★, von KESSELSTATT★, Lehnert-Veit, St Urbans-Hof★★. Best years: (2008) 07 06 05 **04 02 01 00 99 98 97**.

CH. LE PIN★★★ *Pomerol AC, Bordeaux, France* Now one of the most expensive wines in the world. The first vintage was 1979 and the wines, which are concentrated but elegant, are produced from 100% Merlot. The tiny 2ha (5-acre) vineyard lies close to those of TROTANOY and VIEUX-CH.-CERTAN. Best years: 2007 06 05 04 **02 01 00** 99 98 96 95 94 90 89 88 86 85.

PINE RIDGE *Stags Leap District AVA, California, USA* Wines come from several NAPA AVAs, but its flagship Cabernet remains the supple, plummy STAGS LEAP DISTRICT★★. Andrus Reserve★★, a BORDEAUX blend, has more richness and power, while the HOWELL MOUNTAIN Cabernet★ offers intense fruit and structure for long aging. CARNEROS Merlot★ is spicy and cherry fruited, and Carneros Chardonnay★ looks good. Best years: (Stags Leap Cabernet) 2005 03 **02 01 00** 99 97 96 95 94 91.

DOMINIO DE PINGUS *Ribera del Duero DO, Castilla y León, Spain* Peter Sisseck's tiny vineyards and winery have attracted worldwide attention since 1995 due to the extraordinary depth and character of the cult wine they produce, Pingus★★★. Second wine Flor de Pingus★★ is also super. Best years: (Pingus) (2006) 05 04 **03 01 00** 99 96 95.

PINOT BIANCO See PINOT BLANC.

237

PINOT NOIR

There's this myth about Pinot Noir that I think I'd better lay to rest. It goes something like this. Pinot Noir is an incredibly tricky grape to grow and an even more difficult grape to vinify; in fact Pinot Noir is such a difficult customer that the only place that regularly achieves magical results is the thin stretch of land known as the Côte d'Or, between Dijon and Chagny in France, where mesoclimate, soil conditions and 2000 years of experience weave an inimitable web of pleasure.

This just isn't so. The thin-skinned, early-ripening Pinot Noir is undoubtedly more difficult to grow than other great varieties like Cabernet or Chardonnay, but that doesn't mean that it's impossible to grow elsewhere – you just have to work at it with more sensitivity and seek out the right growing conditions. And although great red Burgundy is a hauntingly beautiful wine, many Burgundians completely fail to deliver the magic, and the glorious thing about places like New Zealand, California, Oregon, Chile, Australia and Germany is that we are seeing an ever-increasing number of wines that are thrillingly different from anything produced in Burgundy, yet with flavours that are unique to Pinot Noir.

WINE STYLES

France All France's great Pinot Noir wines come from Burgundy's Côte d'Or. Rarely deep in colour, they should nonetheless possess a wonderful fruit quality when young – raspberry, strawberry, cherry or plum – that becomes more scented and exotic with age, the plum turning to figs and pine, and the richness of chocolate mingling perilously with truffles and well-hung game. Strange, challenging, hedonistic. France's other Pinots – in north and south Burgundy, the Loire Valley, Jura, Savoie, Alsace and now occasionally in the south of France – are lighter and milder, and in Champagne its pale, thin wine is used to make sparkling wine.

Other European regions Since the 1990s, helped by good vintages, German winemakers have made considerable efforts to produce serious Pinot Noir (generally called Spätburgunder). Switzerland, where it is called Blauburgunder, and Italy (as Pinot Nero) both have fair success with the variety, especially in Alto Adige. Austria and Spain have produced a couple of good examples, and Romania, the Czech Republic and Hungary produce significant amounts of Pinot Noir, though of generally low quality.

New World Light, fragrant wines have bestowed upon Oregon the reputation for being 'another Burgundy'; but I get more excited about the sensual wines of the cool, fog-affected areas of California: the ripe, stylish Russian River Valley examples; the exotically scented wines of Carneros, Anderson Valley and Sonoma Coast; the startlingly original offerings from Santa Barbara County (notably Santa Rita Hills) and Santa Lucia Highlands on east-facing slopes of western Monterey County.

New Zealand produces wines of thrilling fruit and individuality, most notably from Martinborough, Canterbury's Waipara district and Central Otago, with its wild thyme-flavoured wines. In the cooler regions of Australia – including Yarra Valley, Adelaide Hills, north-east Victoria and Tasmania – producers are beginning to find their way with the variety. New Burgundian clones bode well for South African Pinot Noir. Chile's Leyda and Bío-Bío areas are beginning to shine.

BEST PRODUCERS

France (Burgundy) d'ANGERVILLE, l'Arlot, Comte Armand, D Bachelet, G Barthod, J-M Boillot, BOUCHARD, CATHIARD, CHANDON DE BRIAILLES, R Chevillon, CLAIR, J-J Confuron, DROUHIN, C Dugat, B Dugat-Py, DUJAC, FAIVELEY, GIRARDIN, GOUGES, GRIVOT, Anne Gros, JADOT, LAFARGE, LAFON, Dom. LEROY, H Lignier, MEO-CAMUZET, de MONTILLE, MORTET, J-F MUGNIER, Ponsot, POTEL, RION, Dom. de la ROMANEE-CONTI, E Rouget, ROUMIER, ROUSSEAU, Sérafin, TOLLOT-BEAUT, de VOGUE; *(Alsace)* J-B ADAM.

Germany BERCHER, FURST, Huber, JOHNER, KELLER, Kesseler, Meyer-Näkel, MOLITOR, REBHOLZ, Stodden.

Switzerland A Fontannaz, GANTENBEIN, Adrian Mathier.

Italy CA' DEL BOSCO, Franz Haas, Haderburg, Hofstätter, Nals-Margreid.

New World Pinot Noirs
USA (California) ACACIA, AU BON CLIMAT, Byron, CALERA, Clos Pepe, DEHLINGER, DE LOACH, DUTTON GOLDFIELD, Merry Edwards, Gary Farrell, FLOWERS, HARTFORD FAMILY, KISTLER, Kosta Browne, La Crema, LANDMARK, Littorai, LYNMAR, MARCASSIN, Morgan, Papapietro Perry, Patz & Hall, RASMUSSEN, ROCHIOLI, SAINTSBURY, SANFORD, Sea Smoke, Siduri, Joseph SWAN, Talley, WILLIAMS SELYEM; *(Oregon)* ARGYLE, BEAUX FRERES, DOMAINE DROUHIN, DOMAINE SERENE, Ken WRIGHT.

Australia Ashton Hills, BANNOCKBURN, Bass Phillip, BAY OF FIRES, Bindi, Bream Creek, Castle Rock, COLDSTREAM HILLS, Curly Flat, Diamond Valley, By FARR, Freycinet, GIACONDA, Giant Steps, Hurley, KOOYONG, Stefano LUBIANA, Moorooduc, OAKRIDGE, Paringa, STONIER, Tamar Ridge, TARRA-WARRA, Tomboy Hill, Yabby Lake.

New Zealand ATA RANGI, Carrick, CRAGGY RANGE, DRY RIVER, Escarpment, FELTON ROAD, Foxes Island, FROMM, Greenhough (Hope Vineyard), MARTINBOROUGH VINEYARD, NEUDORF, PALLISER ESTATE, PEGASUS BAY, Peregrine, Quartz Reef, VAVASOUR, WITHER HILLS.

South Africa BOUCHARD FINLAYSON, CAPE CHAMONIX, HAMILTON RUSSELL.

Chile CONO SUR (20 Barrels, Ocio), Viña Leyda, Porta, Villard.

239

PINOT BLANC Wines have a clear, yeasty, appley taste, and good examples can age to a delicious honeyed fullness. In ALSACE it is taking over the 'workhorse' role from Sylvaner and Chasselas and is the mainstay of most CREMANT D'ALSACE. Important in northern Italy as Pinot Bianco and especially in ALTO ADIGE where it reaches elevated levels of purity, complexity and longevity. Taken seriously in southern Germany and Austria (as Weissburgunder), producing imposing wines with ripe pear and peach fruit and a distinct nutty character. Also successful in Hungary, Slovakia, Slovenia and the Czech Republic and promising in California (notably from Robert Sinskey), Oregon's WILLAMETTE VALLEY and British Columbia, Canada.

PINOT GRIGIO See PINOT GRIS.

PINOT GRIS At its finest in ALSACE; with lowish acidity and a deep colour the grape produces fat, rich dry wines that somehow mature wonderfully. It is very occasionally used in BURGUNDY (as Pinot Beurot) to add fatness to a wine. Italian Pinot Grigio, often boring, occasionally delicious, is currently so popular worldwide that New World producers are tending to use the Italian name in preference to the French version. Also successful in Austria and Germany as Ruländer or Grauburgunder, and as Malvoisie in the Swiss VALAIS. There are good Romanian and Czech examples, as well as spirited ones in Hungary (as Szürkebarát). In a crisp style, it can be successful in Oregon and is showing promise in California, Virginia and OKANAGAN VALLEY in Canada. Now very fashionable in New Zealand and cooler regions of Australia.

PINOT MEUNIER An important ingredient in CHAMPAGNE, along with Pinot Noir and Chardonnay – though it is the least well known of the three. Occasionally found in the LOIRE, and also grown in Germany under the name of Schwarzriesling.

PINOT NERO See PINOT NOIR.
PINOT NOIR See pages 238–9.

PINOTAGE A Pinot Noir x Cinsaut cross, conceived in South Africa in 1925 and covering 6% of the country's vineyards. Highly versatile; classic versions are full-bodied and well-oaked with ripe plum, spice and maybe some mineral, banana or marshmallow flavours. New Zealand and California have interesting examples. **Best producers:** (South Africa) Ashbourne★, Graham BECK★, BEYERSKLOOF★★, Clos Malverne★ DeWaal★ (Top of the Hill★★), Diemersfontein★, FAIRVIEW★ (Primo★★), GRANGEHURST★, Kaapzicht★, KANONKOP★★, Laibach★, L'AVENIR★★ SIMONSIG★ (Redhill★★), Stony Brook★, Tukulu; (New Zealand) Muddy Water★, Te Awa★.

PIPER-HEIDSIECK *Champagne AC, Champagne, France* They've put a big effort into restoring Piper's reputation and the work has paid off. Non-vintage★ is now gentle and biscuity, and the vintage★★ is showing real class. They've also launched a plethora of new cuvées: Sublime (demi-sec), Divin (blanc de blancs), Rosé Sauvage and Rare★★, a de luxe blend available in 1999, 98, 88 and 79 vintages. **Best years:** 2000 96 95 9 89 85 82.

ISANO *Canelones, Uruguay* Family-owned winery with some of Uruguay's truest expressions of the Tannat grape: RPF is a good example and pure, dense Axis Mundi is from old vines. The more sophisticated Arretxea★ blends Tannat with Cabernet and Merlot. Best years: (reds) **2005 04 02**.

OBERT PLAGEOLES *Gaillac AC, South-West France* Both traditionalists and modernizers, Robert and Bernard Plageoles have revived 14 ancient Gaillac grape varieties, including Prunelard, Verdanel and the rare Ondenc, which goes into their lusciously sweet Vin d'Autan★★★. Dry wines include Mauzac★, Ondenc★ and bone-dry Mauzac Nature★ fizz.

RODUCTEURS PLAIMONT *Madiran AC, Côtes de St-Mont VDQS and Vin de Pays des Côtes de Gascogne, South-West France* This Gascon grouping is the largest, most reliable and most go-ahead co-op in the South-West. The whites, full of crisp fruit, are reasonably priced and are best drunk young. The reds, especially Ch. de Sabazan★, are very good too. Also good MADIRAN and sweet PACHERENC DU VIC-BILH★.

LANETA *Sicily, Italy* Rapidly expanding, dynamic estate. Chardonnay★★ is one of the best in southern Italy; Cabernet Sauvignon Burdese★★ and Merlot★★ are among Italy's most impressive; and rich, peppery Santa Cecilia★★ (Nero d'Avola) has star quality. The white Cometa★★ is a fascinating Sicilian version of FIANO. Gluggable Cerasuolo di Vittoria★ and La Segreta red★ and white★ blends are marvellously fruity.

LANTAGENET *Great Southern, Western Australia* Influential winery in the GREAT SOUTHERN region with former CAPE MENTELLE whizz, John Durham, enjoying a new challenge. The spicy Shiraz★★ is among the best produced in the West; limy Riesling★★ and classy Cabernet Sauvignon★ also impress. Omrah is the second label, made from bought-in grapes: Sauvignon Blanc★, Chardonnay★ and Pinot Noir★ stand out. Best years: (Shiraz) (2008) 07 05 04 03 **02 01 99 98 97 95 93**.

ENUTA IL POGGIONE *Brunello di Montalcino DOCG, Tuscany, Italy* Extensive property (more than 100ha/250 acres of vineyard) which sets the standard for traditional-style BRUNELLO DI MONTALCINO★★ (Riserva★★★) at a reasonable price. Also fine ROSSO DI MONTALCINO★ and SUPER-TUSCAN Cabernet-Sangiovese blend San Leopoldo★. Best years: (2008) (07) (06) 04 **03 01 99 98 97 95 90 88 85**.

OL ROGER *Champagne AC, Champagne, France* Non-vintage Brut Réserve★ (formerly known as White Foil) is biscuity and dependable rather than thrilling. The new ultra-dry wine is called Pure. Pol Roger also produces a vintage★★, a vintage rosé★★ and a vintage Chardonnay★★. Its top Champagne, the Pinot-dominated Cuvée Sir Winston Churchill★★, is a deliciously refined drink. All vintage wines will improve with at least 5 years' keeping. Best years: (2000) **99 98 96 95 90 89 88 85 82**.

OLIZIANO *Vino Nobile di Montepulciano DOCG, Tuscany, Italy* A leading light in Montepulciano. VINO NOBILE★★ is smoother if more international than average, especially the Riserva Vigna Asinone★★. SUPER-TUSCAN Le Stanze★★ (Cabernet Sauvignon-Merlot) has been outstanding in recent vintages – the fruit in part coming from owner Federico Carletti's other estate, Lohsa, in MORELLINO DI SCANSANO. Best years: (Vino Nobile) (2008) (07) 06 **04 03 01 99 98 97**.

OLZ *Steiermark, Austria* Consistent producer of aromatic dry white wines: few wines fail to reach ★, and Weissburgunder (Pinot Blanc), Morillon (Chardonnay), Muskateller and Sauvignon Blanc frequently deserve ★★ for their combination of intensity and elegance. Steierische Klassik indicates wines vinified without oak. Best years: (2008) 07 06 **05 04 03 02**.

PORT DOC

Douro, Portugal

The Douro region in northern Portugal, where th grapes for port are grown, is wild and beautiful, and no classified as a World Heritage Site. Steep hills covered i vineyard terraces plunge dramatically down to the Dou river. Grapes are one of the few crops that will grow i the inhospitable climate, which gets progressively drier the further inlan you travel. But not all the Douro's grapes qualify to be made into port. quota is established every year, and the rest are made into increasing good unfortified Douro wines.

Red port grapes include Touriga Franca, Tinta Roriz, Tourig Nacional, Tinta Barroca, Tinta Cão and Tinta Amarela. Grapes fo white port include Côdega, Gouveio, Malvasia Fina, Rabigato an Viosinho. Grapes for both are partially fermented, and then *aguarden* (grape spirit) is added – fortifying the wine, stopping the fermentatio and leaving sweet, unfermented grape sugar in the finished port.

PORT STYLES

Vintage Finest of the ports matured in bottle, made from grapes fro the best vineyards. Vintage port is not 'declared' every year (usually the are 3 or 4 declarations per decade), and only during the second calend year in cask if the shipper thinks the standard is high enough. It is bottle after 2 years, and may be consumed soon afterwards, as is not uncommo in the USA; at this stage it packs quite a punch. The British custom aging for 20 years or more can yield exceptional mellowness. Vintag port throws a thick sediment, so requires decanting.

Single quinta (Vintage) A true single-quinta wine comes from individual estate; however, many shippers sell their vintage port under quinta name in years which are not declared as a vintage, even though may be sourced from 2 or 3 different vineyards. It is quite possible fe these 'off vintage' ports to equal or even surpass the vintage wines fro the same house.

Aged tawny Matured in cask for 10, 20, 30 or even 40 years befo bottling, older tawnies have delicious nut and fig flavours.

Colheita Tawny from a single vintage, matured in cask for at lea 7 years – potentially the finest of the aged tawnies.

Late Bottled (Vintage) (LBV) Port matured for 4–6 years in vat, the usually filtered to avoid sediment forming in the bottle. Tradition unfiltered LBV has much more flavour and requires decanting; it ca generally be aged for another 5 years or more.

Crusted Making a comeback, this is a blend of good ports from 2-vintages, bottled without filtration after 3–4 years in cask. A depos (crust) forms in the bottle and the wine should be decanted. A gentle junior type of 'vintage' flavour.

Reserve (most can be categorized as Premium Ruby) has an average 3–5 years' age. A handful represent good value.

Ruby The youngest red port with only 1–3 years' age. Ruby port shou be bursting with young, almost peppery, fruit, and there has been improvement in quality of late, except at the cheapest level.

Tawny Cheap tawny is either an emaciated ruby, or a blend of ruby ar white port, and is both dilute and raw.

White Only the best taste dry and nutty from wood-aging; most a coarse and alcoholic, best with tonic water and a slice of lemon.

BEST YEARS

2007 05 **03 00 97 94 92 91
87 85 83 80 77 70 66 63 60
55 48 47 45 35 34 31 27 12
08 04 1900**

BEST PRODUCERS

Vintage BURMESTER, CHURCHILL, COCKBURN, CROFT, Delaforce, DOW, FERREIRA, FONSECA, GRAHAM, NIEPOORT, Quinta do NOVAL, Portal, RAMOS PINTO, SMITH WOODHOUSE, TAYLOR, WARRE.

Single quinta (Vintage) CHURCHILL (Quinta da Gricha), COCKBURN (Quinta dos Canais), Quinta do CRASTO, CROFT (Quinta da Roêda), DOW (Quinta do Bomfim, Quinta Senhora da Ribeira), FONSECA (Guimaraens), GRAHAM (Malvedos), NOVAL (Silval), Quinta do Passadouro, Pintas, Quinta de la ROSA, TAYLOR (Quinta de Terra Feita, Quinta de Vargellas), Quinta do Vale Dona Maria, Quinta do Vale Meão, Quinta do Vallado, Quinta do VESUVIO, WARRE (Quinta da Cavadinha).

Aged tawny Barros, BURMESTER, COCKBURN, DOW, FERREIRA, FONSECA, GRAHAM, Krohn, NIEPOORT, NOVAL, RAMOS PINTO, SANDEMAN, TAYLOR, WARRE.

Colheita Andresen, Barros, BURMESTER, Cálem, Feist, Kopke, Krohn, Messias, NIEPOORT, NOVAL.

Traditional Late Bottled Vintage Andresen, CHURCHILL, Quinta do CRASTO, FONSECA, Quinta do Infantado, NIEPOORT, NOVAL, Poças, RAMOS PINTO, Quinta de la ROSA, SMITH WOODHOUSE, WARRE.

Crusted CHURCHILL, DOW, FONSECA, GRAHAM.

Ruby COCKBURN, FERREIRA, FONSECA, GRAHAM, Quinta de la ROSA, SANDEMAN, SMITH WOODHOUSE, TAYLOR, WARRE.

White CHURCHILL, NIEPOORT.

POMEROL AC *Bordeaux, France* This AC includes some of the world's mos
sought-after red wines. Pomerol's unique quality lies in its deep clay
(though gravel also plays a part in some vineyards) in which the Merlo
grape flourishes. The result is seductively rich, almost creamy wine wit
wonderful mouthfilling fruit flavours: often plummy, but wit
blackcurrants, raisins and chocolate, too, and mint to freshen it up. Bes
producers: Beauregard★, Bonalgue, le BON PASTEUR★★, Certan-de-May★
Clinet★★, Clos l'Église★★, Clos René, la CONSEILLANTE★★, l'EGLISE-CLINET★★
l'EVANGILE★★, Feytit-Clinet★, la FLEUR-PETRUS★★, GAZIN★★, Hosanna★
LAFLEUR★★★, LATOUR-A-POMEROL★, Montviel, Nénin★, PETIT-VILLAGE★
PETRUS★★★, Le PIN★★★, Rouget, TROTANOY★★, VIEUX-CHATEAU-CERTAN★
Best years: 2007 06 05 **04 01 00 98 96 95 94 90 89 88 86 85**.

POMINO DOC See CHIANTI RUFINA.

POMMARD AC *Côte de Beaune, Burgundy, France* The first village south o
Beaune. At their best, the wines should have full, round, bee
flavours. Can age well, often for 10 years or more. There are no Gran
Crus but les Rugiens Bas and les Épenots (both Premiers Crus) occup
the best sites. Best producers: Aleth-Girardin★, Comte Armand★★
J-M Boillot★★, Courcel★★, Dancer★, M Gaunoux★, V GIRARDIN★
Huber-Verdereau★★, LAFARGE★★, Lejeune★, de MONTILLE★★, J & A Parent★
Ch. de Pommard★, Pothier-Rieusset★. Best years: (2008) 07 06 05 03 02 99 9
96 **95 90**.

POMMERY *Champagne AC, Champagne, France* High-quality CHAMPAGNE hous
now owned by Vranken, who have maintained the traditional Pomme
style but in recent years have launched 9 – yes 9 – non-vintage cuvées!
can't keep up. Along with Brut Royal and Apanage★, the range no
includes Summertime blanc de blancs, Wintertime blanc de noirs an
Springtime, a Pinot Noir-dominated rosé. Austere vintage Brut★
delicious with maturity, and the prestige cuvée Louise, both white★
and rosé★★, can be the epitome of discreet, perfumed elegance. Be
years: (2000) (99) 98 96 **95 92 90 89 88 85 82**.

PONDALOWIE *Bendigo, Victoria, Australia* Dominic and Krystina Morris ar
dynamic producers making a name for their red wines, including som
absolutely ripper Shiraz★, Shiraz-Viognier★ and dramatic, opule
Tempranillo★★.

CH. PONTET-CANET★★ *Pauillac AC, 5ème Cru Classé, Haut-Médoc, Bordea*
France This property's vineyards are located close to those of MOUTON
ROTHSCHILD and are run organically. Since 1975, when the Tesserons o
LAFON-ROCHET bought the property, there has been a gradual return to th
typical PAUILLAC style of big, chewy, intense claret that develops a beautif
blackcurrant fruit, and since 2000 the property has been on fine form. I
one of the wines of the vintage in 2004 and 2005 – and that's sayin
something. One of the best value of the Classed Growths. Best year
2007 06 05 04 03 **02 01 00 99 98 96 95 94 90 89 86 85**.

PONZI VINEYARDS *Willamette Valley AVA, Oregon, USA* The dream becam
reality in 1974, when Dick and Nancy Ponzi sold their first wine from
vineyard they bought in the late 1960s. The pioneering Ponzi family no
has a second generation, who are taking the business to new height
Winemaker Luisa Ponzi is crafting exceptionally fine Pinot Gris★
Pinot Blanc★ and Chardonnay★ – juicy whites for early drinking. Th
Pinot Noirs★ are developing in complexity and profile. Best years: (red
(2008) 07 06 **04**.

PORT See pages 242–3.

NICOLAS POTEL *Burgundy, France* Energetic *négociant* owned by Cottin brothers of Labouré-Roi, producing consistently fine wines at attractive prices. Particularly strong in their native VOLNAY★★, VOSNE-ROMANEE and in NUITS-ST-GEORGES★★. Now increasing white wine production. Nicolas set up his own eco-friendly domaine in Beaune from the 2007 vintage. Best years: (2008) 07 06 05 **03 02 99**.

CH. POTENSAC★★ *Médoc AC, Bordeaux, France* Owned and run by the Delon family, of LEOVILLE-LAS-CASES, Potensac's fabulous success is based on quality, consistency and value for money. The wine can be drunk at 4–5 years, but fine vintages will improve for at least 10 years. Best years: 2007 06 05 **04 03 02 01 00 99 98 96 95**.

POUILLY-FUISSÉ AC *Mâconnais, Burgundy, France* The sexiest name in the MÂCONNAIS sometimes lives up to its billing for heady white Burgundy. But there is quite a difference in style from producers who vinify their wines simply in stainless steel to those who age them for 18 months or more in oak. The AC covers 5 villages in all: the richest wines come from Fuissé, the most mineral from Vergisson. Best producers: D & M Barraud★★, Bret Brothers★★, Cordier★★, Corsin★★, C & T Drouin★, J-A Ferret★★, Ch. Fuissé★★, Guffens-Heynen (VERGET)★★, R Lassarat★★, R Luquet★, O Merlin★★, Robert-Denogent★★, Ch. des Rontets★★, Saumaize-Michelin★★, Valette★★. Best years: (2008) 07 **06 05 04 02 00 99**.

POUILLY-FUMÉ AC *Loire Valley, France* Fumé means 'smoked' in French and a good Pouilly-Fumé has a pungent smell often likened to gunflint – as if you'd know. The grape is Sauvignon Blanc, and the extra smokiness comes from a flinty soil called silex. Despite the efforts of a few producers, this is a disappointingly underperforming and overpriced AC. Best producers: F Blanchet★, Henri BOURGEOIS★, A & E Figeat, J-C Chatelain★, Didier DAGUENEAU★★, Serge Dagueneau★, A & E Figeat, Fouassière★, Ladoucette★, Landrat-Guyollot★, Masson-Blondelet★, M Redde★, H Seguin, Thibault/André Dezat, Tinel-Blondelet★, Ch. de Tracy★. Best years: 2008 07 **06 05 02 00**.

POUILLY-LOCHÉ AC See POUILLY-VINZELLES AC.

POUILLY-SUR-LOIRE AC *Loire Valley, France* Light appley wines from the Chasselas grape from vineyards around Pouilly-sur-Loire, the town which gave its name to POUILLY-FUME. Drink as young as possible. Best producers: Serge Dagueneau★, Landrat-Guyollot★.

POUILLY-VINZELLES AC *Mâconnais, Burgundy, France* Small AC which, with its neighbour Pouilly-Loché, lies somewhat in the shadow of POUILLY-FUISSE. Most wines come through the co-operative, but there are some good domaines. Best producers: Cave des Grands Crus Blancs, la Soufrandière★★, Tripoz★, Valette★. Best years: (2008) 07 **06 05**.

CH. POUJEAUX★ *Moulis AC, Haut-Médoc, Bordeaux, France* Frequently Poujeaux is the epitome of MOULIS – beautifully balanced, gentle ripe fruit jostled by stony dryness – but just lacking that something extra to propel it to a higher plane. Attractive at 5–6 years old, good vintages can easily last for 10–20 years. Since 2007 same ownership as Clos Fourtet in ST-EMILION. Best years: 2006 05 **04 03 02 01 00 99 98 96 95 90 86**.

PRAGER *Wachau, Niederösterreich, Austria* Toni Bodenstein is one of the pioneers of the WACHAU, producing top dry Rieslings from the Achleiten and Klaus vineyards★★★ and excellent Grüner Veltliners from Achleiten★★. Best years: (Riesling/Grüner Veltliner Smaragd) (2008) 07 06 05 **03 02 01 00 99 98 97**.

245

PREMIÈRES CÔTES DE BLAYE AC *Bordeaux, France* A much improve
AC on the right bank of the Gironde. The fresh, Merlot-based reds ar
ready at 2–3 years but will age for more. Top red wines can be labelle
under the quality-driven Blaye AC from 2000. Part of new Côtes d
Bordeaux AC from 2008. Best producers: (reds) Bel-Air la Royère★
Confiance★, Gigault (Cuvée Viva★), les Grands Maréchaux, Haut-Bertinerie★
Haut-Colombier★, Haut-Grelot, Haut-Sociando, les Jonqueyres★, Mondési
Gazin★, Montfollet★, Roland la Garde★, Segonzac★, Tourtes★; (whites) Hau
Bertinerie★, Charron (Acacia★), Cave des Hauts de Gironde (Chapelle c
Tutiac★), Tourtes (Prestige★). Best years: 2005 04 03 01 00 98 96 95.

PREMIÈRES CÔTES DE BORDEAUX AC *Bordeaux, France* Hilly regio
overlooking GRAVES and SAUTERNES across the Garonne. For a long time th
AC was best known for its sweet wines, particularly from CADILLAC
LOUPIAC and STE-CROIX-DU-MONT, but the juicy reds and rosés have no
forged ahead. Usually delicious at 2–3 years old, but should last for 5–
years. Part of new Côtes de Bordeaux AC from 2008. Best producer
(reds) Bauduc★, Carignan★, Chelivette, Clos Ste-Anne, Grand-Mouëys★
Lamothe-de-Haux, Lezongars★, Mont-Pérat★, Plaisance★, Puy-Bardens★
REYNON★, Ste-Marie (Alios★), Suau★. Best years: (reds) 2005 00 98 96 95.

CH. PRIEURÉ-LICHINE★ *Margaux AC, 4ème Cru Classé, Haut-Médoc, Bordeau
France* Underachieving property that saw several false dawns befor
being sold in 1999. Right Bank specialist Stéphane Derenoncourt (PAVI
MACQUIN★, CANON-LA-GAFFELIERE★★) is now the consultant winemake
and the wines have more fruit, finesse and perfume, especially the 200
Best years: 2007 06 05 04 03 02 01 00 99 98 96 95 90 89.

PRIEURÉ DE ST-JEAN DE BÉBIAN★ *Coteaux du Languedoc AC, Languedoc, Fran
One of the pioneering estates in the Midi, producing an intense, spic
generous red★★, second wine La Chapelle de Bébian and a barre
fermented white★. Best years: (reds) 2007 06 05 04 02 01 00.

PRIMITIVO DI MANDURIA DOC *Puglia, Italy* The most importar
appellation for PUGLIA's Primitivo grape, which has been enjoying
renaissance of interest since it was found to be almost identical t
California's Zinfandel. The best wines combine outstanding ripeness an
concentration with a knockout alcohol level. Good Primitivo is also sol
as IGT Primitivo del Tarantino and as Gioia del Colle DOC. Be
producers: Felline★★, Pervini★★, Giovanni Soloperto. Best years: (2008) 07 0
05 04 03 01.

PRIMO ESTATE *McLaren Vale, South Australia* Joe Grilli continues to be or
of Australia's most thoughtful and innovative winemakers. For h
premium label, Joseph, Grilli adapts the Italian AMARONE method f
Moda Cabernet-Merlot★★ (★★★ with 10 years' age!) and makes
dense, eye-popping, complex Joseph Red fizz★★. He also does
sensuous Botrytis Riesling La Magia★★, fabulous honeyed fortifie
Fronti★★★, surprising dry white La Biondina Colombard★, cherry-ri
Il Briccone★ (Shiraz-Sangiovese), bright, velvety Merlesco (Merlo
fine, powerful Nebbiolo★ – and superb olive oils. Best years: (Mo
Cabernet-Merlot) (2007) 06 05 04 02 01 00 99 98 97 96 95 94 93 91 90.

PRIORAT DOCa *Cataluña, Spain* A hilly, isolated district with very lov
yielding vineyards planted on precipitous slopes of deep slate soil. Ol
style fortified *rancio* wines used to attract little attention. Then in th
1980s a group of young winemakers revolutionized the area, bringing
state-of-the-art winemaking methods and grape varieties such
Cabernet Sauvignon to back up the native Garnacha and Cariñer

Their rare, expensive wines have taken the world by storm. Ready at 5 years old, the best will last much, much longer. **Best producers:** Bodegas B G (Gueta-Lupía★), Burgos Porta, Capafons-Ossó★, Cims de Porrera★★, CLOS ERASMUS★★★, CLOS MOGADOR★★★, Combier-Fischer-Gérin★★ (Trio Infernal 2/3★★★), La Conreria d'Scala Dei★, Costers del Siurana (Clos de l'Obac★), J M Fuentes (Gran Clos★★), Ithaca★, Mas La Alta★★, MAS DOIX★★★, Mas

d'en Gil (Clos Fontà★), Mas Martinet (Clos Martinet★), Merum, Alvaro PALACIOS★★★, Pasanau Germans (Finca la Planeta★), Rotllan Torra★, Scala Dei★, Terroir al Limit/SADIE FAMILY (Dits del Terra★★), TORRES★, VALL-LLACH★★. **Best years:** (reds) 2005 **04 03 01 00 99 98 96 95 94 93**.

PROSECCO DI CONEGLIANO-VALDOBBIADENE DOC *Veneto, Italy*
The Prosecco grape gives soft, scented wine made sparkling by a second fermentation in tank, though Prosecco can also be still, or *tranquillo*. Generally, however, it is a spumante or frizzante for drinking young. The Cartizze sub-zone near Valdobbiadene supposedly produces the most refined, certainly the most expensive, wines. **Best producers:** Adami★, Bernardi★, Bisol★, Carpenè Malvolti★, Le Colture, Col Vetoraz★, Nino Franco★, La Riva dei Frati★, Ruggeri★, Tanorè★, Zardetto★.

PROVENCE *France* Provence is home to France's oldest vineyards but the region has been better known for its beaches and arts festivals than for its vines. However, it seems even Provence is caught up in the revolution sweeping through the vineyards of southern France. The area has 5 small ACs BANDOL, les BAUX-DE-PROVENCE, BELLET, CASSIS and PALETTE), but most of the wine comes from the much larger areas of the CÔTES DE PROVENCE (and three new sub-appellations: Ste-Victoire, La Londe and Fréjus), COTEAUX VAROIS, Coteaux de Pierrevert and COTEAUX D'AIX-EN-PROVENCE. Vin de Pays des BOUCHES-DU-RHÔNE and Vin des Pays des Alpilles are also becoming increasingly important. Reds can be good but are often too lean, rosés are getting fresher, though not less expensive. Whites have a way to go but top producers are making good wines from Rolle.

J J PRÜM *Bernkastel, Mosel, Germany* Estate making some of Germany's best Riesling in sites like the Sonnenuhr★★★ in WEHLEN, Himmelreich★★ in GRAACH and Lay★★ and Badstube★★ in BERNKASTEL. Slow to develop but they all have great aging potential. **Best years:** (2008) 07 06 05 04 03 02 01 99 **98 97 96 95 94 93 90 88**.

S A PRÜM *Wehlen, Mosel, Germany* There are a confusing number of Prüms in the MOSEL – the best known is J J PRÜM, but S A Prüm comes a decent second. The estate's most interesting wines are Riesling from WEHLENER Sonnenuhr, especially Auslese★★, but it also makes good wine from sites in BERNKASTEL★ and GRAACH★. **Best years:** (2008) 07 06 05 **04 03** 02 01 99 97.

PRUNOTTO *Barolo DOCG, Piedmont, Italy* One of the great BAROLO producers, now ably run by Albiera, Piero ANTINORI's eldest daughter. Highlights include Barolo Bussia★★★ and Cannubi★★, BARBERA D'ALBA Pian Romualdo★★, BARBERA D'ASTI Costamiòle★★, BARBARESCO Bric Turot★★ and NEBBIOLO D'ALBA Occhetti★. Also good MOSCATO D'ASTI★, Barbera d'Asti Fiulot★ and ROERO Arneis★. **Best years:** (Barolo) (2008) (07) (06) 04 **03 01 00 99 98 97 95 90 89 88 85**.

PUGLIA *Italy* This southern region is a prolific source of blending wines but exciting progress has been made with native varieties: red Uva di Troia in CASTEL DEL MONTE; white Greco for characterful Gravina, revived by Botromagno; and Verdeca and Bianco d'Alessano for Locorotondo. The red Primitivo, led by examples from producers under the RACEMI umbrella, make a big impact (whether under the PRIMITIVO DI MANDURIA DOC or more general IGTs). But it is the Negroamaro grape grown on traditional bush-trained or *alberello* vines in the Salento peninsula that provides the best wines, whether red or rosé. Outstanding examples include Vallone's Graticciaia★★, Candido's Duca d'Aragona★★, Masseria Monaci's le Braci★★ and Taurino' Patriglione★★. Brindisi and SALICE SALENTINO are good-value, reliable DOCs

PUISSEGUIN-ST-ÉMILION AC *Bordeaux, France* Small ST-ÉMILION satellite
The wines are generally fairly solid but with an attractive chunky frui and usually make good drinking at 3–5 years. Best producers: Bel-Air Branda, Durand-Laplagne★, Fongaban, Guibeau-la-Fourvieille, Laurets, Mauriane★, Producteurs Réunis, Soleil★. Best years: **2005 03 01 00 98 96 95**

PULIGNY-MONTRACHET AC *Côte de Beaune, Burgundy, France* Puligny i
one of the finest white wine villages in the world and adds the name of its greatest Grand Cru, le MONTRACHET, to its own. There are 3 other Grand Crus (BÂTARD-MONTRACHET, Bienvenues-bâTARD-MONTRACHET an Chevalier-MONTRACHET) and 11 Premiers Crus. The flatter vineyards are the Puligny-Montrachet AC. Good vintages really need 5 years' aging while Premiers Crus and Grands Crus may need 10 years and can las for 20 or more. A few barrels of red wine are made. Best producer J-M Boillot★★, CARILLON★★★, Chavy★, Deux MONTILLE★, DROUHIN★★ A Ente★★, B Ente★, FAIVELEY★★, JADOT★★, Larue★★, LATOUR★ Dom. LEFLAIVE★★★, O LEFLAIVE★, P Pernot★★, Ch. de Puligny-Montrachet★★ RAMONET★★, SAUZET★★. Best years: (2008) 07 **06** 05 **04** 02 00 99.

PYRENEES See GRAMPIANS AND PYRENEES.

QUARTS DE CHAUME AC *Loire Valley, France* The Chenin Blanc grap
finds one of its most rewarding mesoclimates here. Quarts de Chaume i a 40ha (100-acre) AC within the larger COTEAUX DU LAYON AC overlookin the Loire; steep, sheltered, schistous slopes favour optimal ripening an noble rot. The result is intense, sweet wines with a mineral backbone which can last for longer than almost any in the world – although man can be drunk after 5 years. Best producers: BAUMARD★★★, Bellerive★★ Bergerie★★, Laffourcade★, PIERRE-BISE★★★, Plaisance★, Joseph Renou★★ Suronde★★, la Varière★. Best years: 2007 06 05 **03** 02 **01 99 97 96 95 90 89**

QUEBRADA DE MACUL *Maipo, Chile* East of Santiago, at the foot of th
Andes, this garage winery was created by winemaker Ignacio Recabarre to produce superbly idiosyncratic Cabernet Sauvignon-based Domu Aurea★★, a red packed with MAIPO character. Bordelais Jean-Pasc Lacaze is now in charge. Best years: (Domus Aurea) (2006) 04 **03** 02 01.

QUEENSLAND *Australia* The Queensland wine industry – closely linked t tourism – is expanding fast. About 60 wineries perch on rocky hills in th main region, the Granite Belt, near the NEW SOUTH WALES border. New area South Burnett (north-west of Brisbane), Darling Downs (around the town Toowoomba) and Mount Tamborine in the Gold Coast hinterland ar showing promise. Best producers: Barambah, BOIREANN★★, Robert Channon★ Clovely Estate, Heritage, Jimbour Station, Lucas Estate, Preston Peak★, Pyrami Road, Robinsons Family, Sirromet, Summit Estate, Witches Falls.

QUERCIABELLA *Chianti Classico DOCG, Tuscany, Italy* Modern Chianti producer with a gorgeously scented, rich-fruited CHIANTI CLASSICO★★. But it has made an even greater splash with its 3 SUPER-TUSCANS: Burgundy-like white Batàr★★ (Pinot Bianco-Chardonnay); tobaccoey, spicy Camartina★★★ (Sangiovese-Cabernet); and Palafreno★ (Sangiovese-Merlot). Best years: (Camartina) (2008) (07) 06 **04 03 01 99 97 95 90 88**.

QUILCEDA CREEK *Washington State, USA* One of America's top Cabernet Sauvignons★★★, a wine with intense concentration and exceptional character. It benefits from cellaring for 7–10 years. Supple, rich Merlot★★★ is produced in small quantities. A less expensive Columbia Valley Red★★ offers a tantalizing glimpse of the winemaking style. Best years: (2007) 06 05 04 03 **02 01 99 97**.

QUINCY AC *Loire Valley, France* Appealingly aggressive gooseberry-flavoured, dry white wine from Sauvignon Blanc vineyards west of Bourges. Can age for a year or two. Best producers: Ballandors★, H BOURGEOIS★, Mardon★, J Rouzé, Silices de Quincy★, Tremblay, Trotereau★.

QUINTARELLI *Valpolicella DOC, Veneto, Italy* Giuseppe Quintarelli is the great traditional winemaker of VALPOLICELLA. His philosophy is one of growing the very best grapes and letting nature do the rest. His Classico Superiore★★ is left in cask for about 4 years and his famed AMARONE★★★ and RECIOTO★★ for up to 7 years before release. Alzero★★ is a spectacular Amarone-style wine made from Cabernets Franc and Sauvignon. Best years: (Amarone) (2008) (07) (06) 04 **03 01 99 97 95 93 90 88 85 83**.

QUPÉ *Santa Maria Valley AVA, California, USA* Owner/winemaker Bob Lindquist makes a savoury, tasty Bien Nacido Syrah★. His Reserve Chardonnay★★ and Bien Nacido Cuvée★★ (a Chardonnay-Viognier blend) have sublime appley fruit and perfume. A leading exponent of red and white RHÔNE-style wines, including Viognier★ and Marsanne★. Best years: (Syrah) 2006 05 04 03 **02 01 00 99 98 97 96 95 94 91 90**.

RACEMI *Puglia, Italy* Premium venture run by Gregory Perrucci, scion of a long-established family of bulk shippers of basic Puglian wines. Modern-style reds, mainly from Primitivo and Negroamaro, under various producers' names: Felline (Vigna del Feudo★★), Pervini (PRIMITIVO DI MANDURIA Archidamo★★), Masseria Pepe (Dunico★★). Best years: (reds) (2008) 07 06 **05 04 03 01**.

CH. DE LA RAGOTIÈRE *Muscadet Sèvre-et-Maine, Loire Valley, France* The Couillaud brothers claim to have salvaged the reputation of Muscadet in US restaurants with M★★, an old-vines wine matured *sur lie* for almost 3 years. The standard Muscadet★ is elegant and built to last, too; lighter ones come from the Couillauds' other property, Ch. la Morinière. Vin de pays Chardonnay★ is a speciality and experimental varieties appear under the Collection Privée label, including Sauvignon Gris★, Viognier and late-harvest Petit Manseng. Best years: (M) (2006) **01 99 97**.

RAÏMAT *Costers del Segre DO, Cataluña, Spain* Owned by CODORNÍU, this large, irrigated estate makes pleasant and refreshingly balanced wines from Tempranillo, Cabernet Sauvignon (Mas Castell vineyard★) and Chardonnay. Lively 100% Chardonnay CAVA and upscale red blend 4 Varietales. Best years: (reds) **2006 05 04 03 01 00 99 98**.

DOM. DE LA RAMAYE *Gaillac AC, South-West France* High-quality wines: whites, mostly from Mauzac, include Les Cavaillés Bas★★, sweeter Sous-Bois de Rayssac★★ and, in great years, Quintessence★★★. Reds include La Combe d'Avès★★, a Duras-Braucol blend, and Prunelard-based Le Grand Tertre★★. Best years: (2008) **05 04 02 01 98 95**.

RAMONET *Chassagne-Montrachet, Côte de Beaune, Burgundy, France* The Ramonets (Noël and Claude) produce some of the most complex of all white Burgundies from 3 Grands Crus (BÂTARD-MONTRACHET★★★, Bienvenues-BÂTARD-MONTRACHET★★★ and le MONTRACHET★★★) and Premiers Crus including Ruchottes★★★, Caillerets★★★, Boudriotte★★, Vergers★★, Morgeot★★ and Chaumées★★★. If you want to spare your wallet try the ST-AUBIN★★ or the CHASSAGNE-MONTRACHET white★★ or red★★. Best years: (whites) (2008) 07 06 05 **04 02 00 99 92 90 89**.

JOÃO PORTUGAL RAMOS *Alentejo, Portugal* João Portugal Ramos is one of Portugal's foremost winemakers. Smoky, peppery Trincadeira★★, spicy Aragonês (Tempranillo)★, powerful Syrah★ and intensely dark-fruited red blend Vila Santa★★. Good Marquês de Borba★ reds and whites, and a brilliant red Reserva★★. Tagus Creek is setting new standards in juicy, affordable styles. Best years: (2008) **05 04 01 00 99 97**.

RAMOS PINTO *Douro DOC and Port DOC, Douro, Portugal* Innovative PORT company owned by ROEDERER, making complex, full-bodied Late Bottled Vintage★ and aged tawnies (10-year-old Quinta de Ervamoira★★ and 20-year-old Quinta do Bom Retiro★★). Vintage ports★★ are rich and early maturing. DOURO reds Duas Quintas (Reserva★, Reserva Especial★★) and Bons Ares★ are reliable. Best years: (Vintage) 2004 **03 00 97 95 94 83**.

CASTELLO DEI RAMPOLLA *Chianti Classico DOCG, Tuscany, Italy* Outstanding if French-influenced CHIANTI CLASSICO★★. SUPER-TUSCAN Sammarco, sometimes ★★★, is mostly Cabernet with some Sangiovese; Vigna d'Alceo★★★ adds Petit Verdot to Cabernet Sauvignon. Best years: (Sammarco) (2008) (07) (06) 04 **03 01 00 99 98 97 95**; (Vigna d'Alceo) (2008) (07) (06) 04 **03 01 00 99 98 97**.

RANDERSACKER *Franken, Germany* Important wine village just outside the city of WÜRZBURG, producing excellent dry Rieslings, dry Silvaners, spicy Traminer and piercingly intense Rieslaner. Best producers: Bürgerspital, JULIUSSPITAL★, Schmitt's Kinder★, Störrlein★, Trockene Schmitts. Best years: (2008) 07 06 **05 04 03 02 01**.

RAPEL *Central Valley, Chile* One of Chile's most exciting red wine regions, the cradle of Chilean Carmenère, Rapel covers both the Cachapoal Valley in the north and the COLCHAGUA Valley in the south. Best producers: Altaïr★★/SAN PEDRO, Anakena★, CASA LAPOSTOLLE★★, CONCHA Y TORO★★, CONO SUR★, EMILIANA ORGÁNICO★★, Gracia★, LA ROSA★, Misiones de Rengo★, MONTES★, MontGras, Neyen★★, Ventisquero★, Viu Manent★.

KENT RASMUSSEN *Carneros AVA, California, USA* Burgundian-style Chardonnay★★ capable of considerable aging and a fascinating juicy Pinot Noir★★ are made by ultra-traditional methods. Ramsay is the second label, for Pinot Noir★, Cabernet Sauvignon and Merlot. Best years: (Pinot Noir) 2006 05 **02 01 00 99 98 95 94 91 90**.

RASTEAU *Rhône Valley, France* The single-village AC is for fortified Grenache red or white wine and a reviving *rancio* version which is left in barrel for 2 or more years. However, much of the best wine from Rasteau is big, robust, dry red, which comes under the CÔTES DU RHÔNE-VILLAGES AC. Best producers: E Balme, Beaurenard★, Cave des Vignerons, Gourt de Mautens★★, Perrin★, Rabasse-Charavin, ST-GAYAN, Santa Duc★, la Soumade★, du Trapadis★.

RENATO RATTI *Barolo DOCG, Piedmont, Italy* The late Renato Ratti was a leading modernist in the Alba area with BAROLO and BARBARESCO of better balance, colour and richness and softer in tannins than the traditional models. Today his son Pietro and nephew Massimo Martinelli produce sound Barolo Marcenasco★ and crus Conca★★ and Rocche★★ from the Marcenasco vineyards at La Morra, as well as good BARBERA D'ALBA Torriglione★, Dolcetto d'Alba Colombè★, NEBBIOLO D'ALBA Ochetti★ and Monferrato DOC Villa Pattono★, a Barbera-Cabernet-Merlot blend.

RAUENTHAL *Rheingau, Germany* Only a few producers live up to the reputation earned by this RHEINGAU village's great Rieslings. Best producers: Georg BREUER★★, Eser, Langwerth von Simmern★, Staatsweingut. Best years: (2008) 07 06 05 **04 03 02 01 99**.

CH. RAUZAN-SÉGLA★★ *Margaux AC, 2ème Cru Classé, Haut-Médoc, Bordeaux, France* A dynamic change in winemaking in 1982 and the purchase of the property by Chanel in 1994 propelled Rauzan-Ségla up the quality ladder. Now the wines have a rich blackcurrant fruit, round, mellow texture, powerful woody spice and good concentration. Second wine: Ségla. Best years: 2007 06 05 04 **03 02 01 00 99 98 96 95 94 90 89 88 86 85**.

JEAN-MARIE RAVENEAU *Chablis, Burgundy, France* Beautifully nuanced CHABLIS from 3 Grands Crus (Blanchot★★★, les Clos★★★, Valmur★★★) and 4 Premiers Crus (Montée de Tonnerre★★★, Vaillons★★, Butteaux★★★, Chapelot★★), using a combination of old oak and stainless-steel fermentation. The wines can age for a decade or more. Best years: (top crus) (2008) 07 06 05 **02 00 99 95 92 90**.

RAVENSWOOD *Sonoma Valley AVA, California, USA* Zinfandel expert Joel Peterson established Ravenswood in 1976. During the lean years, when most Zin was pink and sweet, he added an intense Chardonnay, a sometimes very good Cabernet Sauvignon★ and several tasty Merlots (Sangiacomo★★). But Zinfandel remains the trump card. Early 21st-century offerings were disappointing – especially large-volume Vintners Blend – but this has now picked up, and Amador★ and Lodi★ wines are tasty and characterful, and sometimes outperform the Sonoma versions (single-vineyard wines can be ★★). New super-premium blend Icon★★ is Syrah-based. Constellation bought the winery in 2001, but Peterson remains in charge. Best years: (Zins) **2002 01 00 99 97 96 95 94 91 90**.

CH. RAYAS *Châteauneuf-du-Pape, Rhône Valley, France* Emmanuel Reynaud, nephew of the eccentric Jacques Reynaud, runs this estate in his uncle's inimitable rule-breaking style, producing exotically fragrant rich reds★★★ and whites★★ that also age well. Prices are high, but recent vintages are on top form – at its best Rayas is

thrilling. The red is made entirely from low-yielding Grenache vines, while the white is a blend of Clairette, Grenache Blanc and (so rumour has it) Chardonnay. Second-label Pignan can also be impressive. CÔTES DU RHÔNE Ch. de Fonsalette★★ is usually wonderful. Also VACQUEYRAS Ch. des Tours★. Best years: (Châteauneuf-du-Pape) 2007 06 05 04 03 **01 99 98 96 95 94 91 90 89 88 86**; (whites) 2007 06 05 **04 03 01 00 99 98 97 96 95 94 91 90 89**.

REBHOLZ *Siebeldingen, Pfalz, Germany* This estate in the southern PFALZ produces crystalline Riesling★★, Weissburgunder★★ (Pinot Blanc) and Grauburgunder★ (Pinot Gris), with vibrant fruit aromas. Top of the range are intensely mineral dry Riesling★★★ from the Kastanienbusch and Sonnenschein vineyards, powerful dry Gewürztraminer★★ and extravagantly aromatic dry Muskateller★★. The sparkling wine★★, from barrel-fermented Pinot varieties, is among Germany's most elegant. Also Germany's finest Chardonnay★★ and serious Spätburgunder★★ (Pinot Noir) reds. Best years: (whites) (2008) 07 06 05 **04 03 02 01 99**; (reds) (2008) 07 06 **05 04 03 02 01**.

RECIOTO DELLA VALPOLICELLA DOC *Veneto, Italy* The great sweet wine of VALPOLICELLA, made from grapes picked earlier than usual and left to dry on straw mats until February or even March. The wines are deep in colour, with a rich, bitter-sweet cherryish fruit. Top wines age well for 10 years, but most are best drunk young. As with Valpolicella, the Classico tag is important, if not essential. Best producers: Accordini★, ALLEGRINI★★, Bolla (Spumante★★), Brigaldara★, BUSSOLA★★★, Michele Castellani★★, DAL FORNO★★★, MASI★, QUINTARELLI★★, Le Ragose★, Le Salette★, Serègo Alighieri★★, Speri★, Tedeschi★, Tommasi★, Villa Monteleone★★, VIVIANI★★. Best years: (2008) 06 **05 04 03 01 00**.

RECIOTO DI SOAVE DOCG *Veneto, Italy* Sweet white wine made in the SOAVE zone from dried grapes, like RECIOTO DELLA VALPOLICELLA. Garganega grapes give wonderfully delicate yet intense wines that age well for up to a decade. One of the best, ANSELMI's I Capitelli, is now sold as IGT Veneto. Best producers: ANSELMI★★, La Cappuccina★★, Cà Rugate★, Coffele★★, Gini★★, PIEROPAN★★, Bruno Sartori★, Tamellini★★. Best years: (2008) 06 **04 03 01 00 98 97**.

RÉGNIÉ AC *Beaujolais, Burgundy, France* In good years this BEAUJOLAIS Cru is light, aromatic and enjoyable along the style of CHIROUBLES, but can be thin in lesser years. Best producers: J-M Burgaud★, DUBOEUF (des Buyats★), Maison des Bulliats★, Gilles Roux/de la Plaigne★. Best years: **2008 07**.

DOM. LA RÉMÉJEANNE *Côtes du Rhône AC, Rhône Valley, France* First-class property making a range of strikingly individual, sometimes heady wines. CÔTES DU RHÔNE-VILLAGES les Genèvriers★★ has the weight and texture of good CHÂTEAUNEUF-DU-PAPE, while CÔTES DU RHÔNE Syrah les Eglantiers★★ is superb. Both need at least 3–5 years' aging. Also good Côtes du Rhône les Chèvrefeuilles★ and les Arbousiers★ (red and white). Best years: (les Eglantiers) **2007 06 05 04 03**.

REMELLURI *Rioja DOCa, País Vasco, Spain* Organic RIOJA estate producing red wines with far more fruit than usual and good concentration for aging – the best are ★★. There is also a delicate, barrel-fermented white blend★★. Best years: (Reserva) 2005 04 **03 02 01 99 98 96 95 94 91 89**.

RETSINA *Greece* Resinated white (and rosé) wine common all over Greece, although both production and sales are falling. Poor Retsina is diabolical but the best are deliciously oily and piny. Drink young – and cold.

REUILLY AC *Loire Valley, France* Extremely dry but attractive Sauvignon from west of SANCERRE. Some pale Pinot Noir red and Pinot Gris rosé. Best producers: H Beurdin★, G Bigonneau, D Jamain, C Lafond, A Mabillot, J-M Sorbe, J Vincent.

CH. REYNON *Premières Côtes de Bordeaux AC, Bordeaux, France* Property of enology professor Denis Dubourdieu. The dry whites, particularly the fruity, minerally Sauvignon Blanc★, are delightful and the red★ has come on tremendously since 1997. In the same stable is the lovely GRAVES Clos Floridène★★, which is vinified at Reynon. Best years: (reds) 2007 06 **05 04 03 01 00**; (whites) **2007 06 05 04 02 01 00 99**.

RHEINGAU *Germany* 3106ha (7675-acre) wine region on a south-facing stretch of the Rhine flanking the city of Wiesbaden, planted mostly with Riesling and some Spätburgunder (Pinot Noir). At their best, the Rieslings are racy and slow-maturing. Famous names are no longer a guarantee of top quality, as a new generation of winemakers is producing many of the best wines. See also ELTVILLE, ERBACH, GEISENHEIM, HATTENHEIM, HOCHHEIM, JOHANNISBERG, KIEDRICH, RAUENTHAL, RUDESHEIM, WINKEL. Best years: (2008) 07 06 05 **04 03 02 01 99**.

RHEINHESSEN *Germany* 26,330ha (65,060-acre) wine region with a number of famous top-quality estates, especially at Bodenheim, Nackenheim, NIERSTEIN and Oppenheim. BINGEN, to the north-west, also has a fine vineyard area along the left bank of the Rhine. Further away from the river a handful of growers, such as KELLER and WITTMANN, also make superlative wines. Riesling accounts for only 10% of the vineyard area; Weissburgunder (Pinot Blanc) is the rising star. Best years: (2008) 07 05 **04 03 02 01 99**.

RHÔNE VALLEY *France* The Rhône starts out as a river in Switzerland, rambling through Lake Geneva before hurtling westward into France. In the area south of Lyon, between Vienne and Avignon, the valley becomes one of France's great wine regions. In the northern part vertigo-inducing slopes overhang the river and the small amount of wine produced is of remarkable individuality. The Syrah grape reigns here in CÔTE-RÔTIE and on the great hill of HERMITAGE. ST-JOSEPH, CROZES-HERMITAGE and CORNAS also make excellent reds, while the white Viognier grape yields perfumed, musky wine at CONDRIEU and the tiny CHÂTEAU-GRILLET. In the southern part the steep slopes give way to hot, wide plains, with hills both in the west and east. Most of these vineyards are either CÔTES DU RHONE or CÔTES DU RHÔNE-VILLAGES, reds, whites and rosés, but there are also specific ACs, the best known being CHÂTEAUNEUF-DU-PAPE, GIGONDAS and the luscious, golden dessert wine, MUSCAT DE BEAUMES-DE-VENISE. See also BEAUMES-DE-VENISE, CAIRANNE, CLAIRETTE DE DIE, COSTIÈRES DE NÎMES, COTEAUX DE L'ARDÈCHE, COTEAUX DU TRICASTIN, LIRAC, LUBERON, RASTEAU, ST-PERAY, TAVEL, VACQUEYRAS, VENTOUX, VINSOBRES.

RÍAS BAIXAS DO *Galicia, Spain* The best of GALICIA's DOs, Rías Baixas is making some of Spain's best whites. The magic ingredient is the Albariño grape, making dry, fruity whites with a glorious fragrance and citrus tang. Drink young or with short aging. Best producers: Agro de Bazán★★, Castro Martín, Martín Códax★, Condes de Albarei★, Quinta de Couselo, Fillaboa★, Adegas Galegas★, Lagar de Besada★, Lagar de Fornelos★, Lusco do Miño★★, Gerardo Méndez (Do Ferreiro Cepas Vellas★★), Viña Nora★, Pablo Padín, Palacio de Fefiñanes★★, Pazo de Barrantes★, Pazo de Señorans★★, Santiago Ruiz★, Terras Gauda★★, La Val★, Valmiñor★.

RIBATEJO *Portugal* Portugal's second-largest wine region straddles the river Tagus (Tejo). Hotter and drier than ESTREMADURA to the west, vineyards in the fertile flood plain are being uprooted in favour of less vigorous soils away from the river, though D F J VINHOS still believes in the quality of the original alluvial sites. The Ribatejo DOC includes 6 sub-regions. Vinho Regional wines are labelled Ribatejano. Best producers: (reds) Quinta da Alorna, Quinta do Alqueve, Casa Cadaval★, Quinta do Casal Branco (Falcoaria★), D F J VINHOS★, Caves Dom Teodosio, Quinta do Falcão, Falua (Reserva★), Fiúza-BRIGHT, Quinta da Lagoalva da Cima★, Companhia das Lezírias, Quinta da Ribeirinha Vale de Lobos).

RIBERA DEL DUERO DO *Castilla y León, Spain* The dark, mouthfilling reds in this DO, from Tinto Fino (Tempranillo), sometimes with a little Cabernet Sauvignon and more rarely Merlot, are generally naturally richer and more concentrated than those of RIOJA. But excessive expansion of vineyards, increase in yields and excessive use of oak may threaten the region's supremacy. Best producers: AALTO★★, Alión★★, Arroyo, Arzuaga★, Astrales★, Dominio de Atauta★★, Balbás, Hijos de Antonio Barceló, Briego, Felix Callejo, Cillar de Silos★, Convento San Francisco★, Hermanos Cuadrado García, O FOURNIER★, Hacienda Monasterio★★, Matarromera★, Montecastro★★, Emilio Moro★★, Pago de los Capellanes★★, Pago de Carraovejas★★, Parxet, Pedrosa, Hermanos Pérez Pascuas, PESQUERA★★, PINGUS★★★, Protos★, Rodero★, Telmo RODRIGUEZ★, Hermanos Sastre★★, Tarsus★, Valdubón, Valduero★, Valtravieso, VEGA SICILIA★★★, Alonso del Yerro★★. Best years: 2005 **04 03 01 00 99 96 95 94 91 90 89 86 85**.

BARONE RICASOLI *Chianti Classico DOCG, Tuscany, Italy* The estate where modern CHIANTI was perfected by Baron Bettino Ricasoli in the mid-19th century. The flagship is Chianti Classico Castello di Brolio★★. Riserva Guicciarda★ is good value. SUPER-TUSCAN Casalferro★★ is a Sangiovese-Merlot blend. Best years: (Casalferro) (2008) (07) 06 **04 03 01 00 99 97**.

DOM. RICHEAUME *Côtes de Provence AC, Provence, France* German-owned property, run on organic principles and producing impressively deep-coloured reds★; Les Terrasses★★ is from Syrah aged in new wood. Best years: (Terrasses) 2007 06 05 04 **03**.

RICHEBOURG AC *Grand Cru, Côte de Nuits, Burgundy, France* Rich, fleshy wine from the northern end of VOSNE-ROMANÉE. Most domaine-bottlings are exceptional. Best producers: GRIVOT★★★, Anne GROS★★★, A-F GROS★★★, Hudelot-Noëllat★★, Dom. LEROY★★★, T LIGER-BELAIR★★ MEO-CAMUZET★★★, Dom. de la ROMANÉE-CONTI★★★. Best years: (2008) 07 06 05 03 02 **01 00 99 98 97 96 95 93 91 90**.

DOM. RICHOU *Loire Valley, France* One of the most consistent and good-value domaines in the LOIRE. Best are the ANJOU-VILLAGES Brissac Vieille Vignes★★ and sweet COTEAUX DE L'AUBANCE les Trois Demoiselles★★. Les Rogeries★ is a good example of modern dry ANJOU BLANC. Best years: (les Trois Demoiselles) 2005 **04 03 02 01 99 97 96 95 90 89**.

MAX FERD RICHTER *Mülheim, Mosel, Germany* Racy Rieslings from some of the best sites in the MOSEL, including WEHLENer Sonnenuhr★★ BRAUNEBERGer Juffer★★ and GRAACHer Domprobst★. Richter's Mülheimer Helenenkloster vineyard produces a magical Eiswein★★★ virtually every year unless wild boar eat the crop. Best years: (2008) 07 06 **05 04 03 02 0 99 98 97 96**.

RIDGE VINEYARDS *Santa Cruz Mountains AVA, California, USA* Paul Draper Zinfandels★★★, made with grapes from various sources, have great intensity and long life. Other reds, led by Cabernet-based Monte Bello★★★, show impressive personality. Geyserville★★ is a fascinating blend of Zinfandel with old-vine Carignan, Syrah and Petite Sirah. There's fine Chardonnay★★, too. Best years: (Monte Bello) 2005 03 02 0 **00 99 98 97 95 94 93 92 91 90 87 85 84**.

RIDGEVIEW *West Sussex, England* Specialist sparkling wine producer using classic CHAMPAGNE varieties to make an excellent – and improving – range of wines. Cavendish★★ and Bloomsbury★★ are traditional 3-variety blends; Knightsbridge★ is a blanc de noirs; Fitzrovia★ is a Chardonnay Pinot Noir rosé. New vineyards coming onstream in the next couple of years will add considerable capacity. Best years: **2006 05 03**.

RIECINE *Chianti Classico DOCG, Tuscany, Italy* Small estate in Gaiole making exquisite wines. Yields are low, so there is a great intensity of fruit and a superb definition of spiced cherry flavours. English winemaker Sean O'Callaghan continues to fashion ever better CHIANTI CLASSICO★★, Riserva★★★ and barrique-aged La Gioia★★★. Best years: (La Gioia) (2008) (07) 06 **04 03 01** 99 98 97 95.

RIESLANER One of the few German grape crossings of real merit, Rieslaner resembles Riesling, but with greater breadth and even higher acidity. This makes it an ideal sweet wine grape, as MULLER-CATOIR (Pfalz), KELLER (Rheinhessen) and some Franken growers have demonstrated.

RIESLING See pages 256–7.

RIESLING ITALICO See WELSCHRIESLING.

CH. RIEUSSEC★★★ *Sauternes AC, 1er Cru Classé, Bordeaux, France* Apart from the peerless Ch. d'YQUEM, Rieussec is often the richest, most succulent wine of SAUTERNES. Cellar for at least 10 years. Dry white 'R' is nothing special. Second wine: Carmes de Rieussec. Owned by LAFITE-ROTHSCHILD. Best years: 2007 06 05 04 **03 02** 01 99 98 97 96 95 90 89 88.

RIOJA DOCa *Rioja, Navarra, País Vasco and Castilla y León, Spain* Rioja, in northern Spain, is not all oaky, creamy white wines and elegant, barrel-aged reds, combining oak flavours with wild strawberry and prune fruit. Over half Rioja's red wine is sold young, never having seen the inside of a barrel and as such is one of Spain's best glugging reds, and most of the white is fairly anonymous. Wine quality, as could be expected from such a large region with more than 400 producers, is inconsistent but a growing gang of ambitious new producers is taking quality seriously. Best producers: (reds) ALLENDE★★, Altanza, Altos de Lanzaga★/Telmo RODRIGUEZ, ARTADI★★★, Baron de Ley★, Bodegas Bilbaínas, CAMPILLO★, CAMPO VIEJO, CONTINO★★, CVNE★, FAUSTINO, Viña Ijalba, Lan (Culmen★), LÓPEZ DE HEREDIA★, MARQUES DE CÁCERES★, MARQUES DE MURRIETA★★, MARQUES DE RISCAL★, Marqués de Vargas★★, MARTÍNEZ BUJANDA★, Abel Mendoza★★, Montecillo★, MUGA★, Ostatu, Viñedos de Páganos★★, Palacios Remondo★, REMELLURI★★, Fernando Remírez de Ganuza★★, La RIOJA ALTA★★, RIOJANAS★, Roda★★, ROMEO★★, Sierra Cantabria★★, Señorío de San Vicente★★, Tobía, Valdemar★, Valpiedra★, Ysios; (whites) ALLENDE★★, CAMPO VIEJO, CONTINO★, CVNE★, LÓPEZ DE HEREDIA★★, MARQUES DE CÁCERES★, MARQUES DE MURRIETA, REMELLURI★★, RIOJANAS★, Valdemar★. Best years: (reds) 2005 **04 01 00** 96 95 94 91 89 87 85.

LA RIOJA ALTA *Rioja DOCa, Rioja, Spain* One of the best of the older RIOJA producers, making mainly Reservas and Gran Reservas. Its only Crianza, Viña Alberdi, fulfils the minimum age requirements for a Reserva anyway. Viña Arana★ and Viña Ardanza★★ Reservas age splendidly, and Gran Reservas 904★★ and 890★★ (made only in exceptional years) are among the very best of traditional Rioja wines. Baron de Oña★ and Áster★ are high-quality, modern, single-estate wines. Best years: (Gran Reserva 890) **1995 94 89** 87 85 82 81 78.

BODEGAS RIOJANAS *Rioja DOCa, Rioja, Spain* Quality winery producing Reservas and Gran Reservas in 2 styles – elegant Viña Albina★ and richer Monte Real★ – plus refined Gran Albina★ and now a more modern Monte Real Crianza. White Monte Real Blanco Crianza★ is one of RIOJA's best. The whites and Reservas can be kept for 5 years after release, Gran Reservas for 10 or more. Best years: (Monte Real Gran Reserva) **1998 96 95 94** 91 89 87 85.

RIESLING

If you have tasted wines with names like Laski Riesling, Olasz Riesling, Welschriesling, Gray Riesling, Riesling Italico, Cape Riesling and the like and found them bland or unappetizing – do not blame the Riesling grape. These wines have filched Riesling's name, but have nothing whatsoever to do with the great grape itself.

Riesling is Germany's finest contribution to the world of wine – and herein lies the second problem. German wines fell to such a low level of general esteem through the proliferation of wines like Liebfraumilch during the 1980s that Riesling was dragged down with them.

So what is true Riesling? It is a very ancient German grape, probably the descendant of wild vines growing in the Rhine Valley. It certainly performs best in the cool vineyard regions of Germany's Rhine, Nahe and Mosel Valleys, and in Alsace and Austria. It also does well in Canada, New Zealand and both warm and cool parts of Australia. Ironically, the Riesling revival is being led more by Australia than Germany. It is widely planted in Washington State, less so in northern Italy, and there's a tiny amount in South Africa and in Chile.

Young Rieslings often show a delightful floral perfume, sometimes blended with the crispness of green apples, often lime, peach, nectarine or apricot, sometimes even raisin, honey or spice depending upon the ripeness of the grapes. As the wines age, the lime often intensifies, and a flavour perhaps of slate, perhaps of petrol/kerosene intrudes. In general Rieslings may be drunk young, but top dry wines can improve for many years, and the truly sweet German styles can age for generations.

WINE STYLES

Germany These wines have a marvellous perfume and an ability to hold on to a piercing acidity, even at high ripeness levels, so long as the ripening period has been warm and gradual rather than broiling and rushed. German Rieslings can be bone dry, through to medium and even lusciously sweet. Styles range from crisp elegant Mosels to riper, fuller wines from the Rheingau and Nahe, with rounder, fatter examples from the Pfalz and Baden regions in the south. The very sweet Trockenbeerenauslese (TBA) Rieslings are made from grapes affected by noble rot; for Eiswein (icewine), also intensely sweet, the grapes are picked and pressed while frozen.

Other regions In the valleys of the Danube in Austria, Riesling gives stunning dry wines that combine richness with elegance, but the most fragrant wines, apart from German examples, come from France's Alsace. The mountain vineyards of northern Italy and the cool vineyards of the Czech Republic, Slovakia and Switzerland can show a floral sharp style. Australia is the southern hemisphere's world-class producer, with cool areas of South Australia, Victoria and Western Australia all offering superb – and different – examples typified by a citrus, mineral scent, and often challenging austerity. New Zealand's style is floral, fresh and frequently attractively off-dry, but with enough acidity to age. South Africa's best examples are sweet, but some dry versions are appearing. Chile is growing some light, fragrant examples. The USA has fragrant dry Rieslings from New York, mostly off-dry from the Pacific Northwest and sweet styles from California; Michigan and Ohio also have excellent potential. Canada produces bone-dry to ultra-sweet icewine.

BEST PRODUCERS

Germany
Dry BASSERMANN-JORDAN, Georg BREUER, BURKLIN-WOLF, Christmann, HEYMANN-LOWENSTEIN, KELLER, KOEHLER-RUPRECHT, KUNSTLER, J LEITZ, REBHOLZ, SAUER, WITTMANN.

Non-dry DIEL, DONNHOFF, GUNDERLOCH, HAAG, HAART, HEYMANN-LOWENSTEIN, KARTHAUSERHOF, von KESSELSTATT, KUHN, KUNSTLER, Carl Loewen, Dr LOOSEN, MAXIMIN GRUNHAUS, MOLITOR, MULLER-CATOIR, Egon MULLER-SCHARZHOF, J J PRUM, St Urbans-Hof, Willi SCHAEFER, SELBACH-OSTER, WEIL, ZILLIKEN.

Austria
Dry Alzinger, BRUNDLMAYER, Hiedler, HIRTZBERGER, J Högl, KNOLL, Loimer, NIGL, NIKOLAIHOF, F X PICHLER, Rudi PICHLER, PRAGER, Schloss Gobelsburg, Schmelz.

France
(Alsace) Dry J-B ADAM, P BLANCK, A Boxler, DEISS, Dirler-Cadé, HUGEL, Josmeyer, Kientzler, Kreydenweiss, A MANN, MURE, Ostertag, SCHOFFIT, TRIMBACH, WEINBACH, ZIND-HUMBRECHT.

Non-dry Léon Beyer, DEISS, HUGEL, Ostertag, TRIMBACH, WEINBACH, ZIND-HUMBRECHT.

Australia
Tim ADAMS, Leo Buring (Leonay), Eden Valley, Frankland Estate, Freycinet, GROSSET, HENSCHKE, HOUGHTON, HOWARD PARK, JACOB'S CREEK (Steingarten), KNAPPSTEIN, Peter LEHMANN, Mesh, MOUNT HORROCKS, O'Leary Walker, PETALUMA (Hanlin Hill), Pewsey Vale (Contours), Pipers Brook, SEPPELT (Drumborg), SKILLOGALEE.

New Zealand
CLOUDY BAY, DRY RIVER, FELTON ROAD, Foxes Island, FROMM, MILLTON, Mt Difficulty, Mount Edward, NEUDORF, PEGASUS BAY, VILLA MARIA.

South Africa
Sweet CLUVER, Fleur du Cap, Neethlingshof.

USA
(Washington) CHATEAU STE MICHELLE (Eroica), LONG SHADOWS (Poet's Leap); *(New York)* FOX RUN, Dr Konstantin FRANK, Hermann J WIEMER.

RION *Nuits-St-Georges, Côte de Nuits, Burgundy, France* Patrice Rion was wine maker at Dom. Daniel Rion from 1979 to 2000, making consistently fin but often austere reds such as VOSNE-ROMANEE les Beauxmonts and le Chaumes, ECHEZEAUX and CLOS DE VOUGEOT. His own label brings rich concentrated BOURGOGNE Rouge★★, CHAMBOLLE-MUSIGNY les Cras★★ an NUITS-ST-GEORGES Clos des Argillières★★ from his own vines plus a sma' *négociant* range. Best years: (top reds) (2008) 07 06 05 **03 02**.

RIPOSTE *Adelaide Hills, South Australia* Since leaving KNAPPSTEIN to move to th cool ADELAIDE HILLS, Tim Knappstein has run Lenswood Vineyard and Th Wines. In 2003, the Knappsteins sold the Lenswood Vineyard, althoug Tim is still able to access its fruit. He now acts as consultant winemake at Wicks Estate in the Adelaide Hills and has his own brand, Ripost focusing on Sauvignon Blanc★, Gewürztraminer★ and Pinot Noir.

RIVERA *Puglia, Italy* The CASTEL DEL MONTE Riserva Il Falcone★ is a good, full blooded southern red. Also a series of varietals under the Terre al Mont label, best of which are Aglianico★, Pinot Bianco and Sauvignon Blanc

RIVERINA *New South Wales, Australia* Centred on the town of Griffith an irrigated by the waters of the Murrumbidgee River, the Riverina is a important source of reliable quaffing wines. Many of Australia's best known brands, though not mentioning the Riverina on the label, a based on wines from here. There is definite potential for quality, an locally based companies such as DE BORTOLI (Deen, Montage, Sacre Hill), Casella (YELLOWTAIL, Yendah), MCWILLIAM'S (Hanwood, Inheritance Nugan Estate★ (Cookoothama, Talinga Park) and WESTEND★ (Richlane have lifted quality at budget prices. Remarkable sweet wines, led b Noble One Botrytis Semillon★★★ from De Bortoli; others fro Cookoothama★, Lillypilly, McWilliam's, Westend (Golden Mist★).

RIVERLAND *Australia* This important irrigated region, responsible fe about 12% of the national grape crush, lies along the Murray River i SOUTH AUSTRALIA near the border with VICTORIA. A great deal goes to chea quaffers but an increased awareness of quality has seen inferior varieti replaced and yields lowered. Here and there, wines of real character a emerging, including some remarkable reds from the Petit Verdot grap Best producers: Angove, Banrock Station, Kingston Estate, Renmano, YALUMB (Oxford Landing).

RIVESALTES AC *Roussillon, France* *Vin doux naturel* from a large area aroun the town of Rivesaltes. These fortified wines are greatly underrated b some of southern France's best and can be made from an assortment grapes, mainly white Muscat (when it is called MUSCAT DE RIVESALTES) an Grenache Noir, Gris and Blanc. A *rancio* style ages beautifully. Be producers: Baixas co-op, la CASENOVE★, CAZES★★, Chênes★, Fontanel★, For Réal★, GAUBY★, Joliette★, Laporte, Nouvelles★, Rivesaltes co-op, Sard Malet★.

ROBERTSON WO *South Africa* Hot, dry inland area with lime-rich soi' uncommon in the Cape, that are ideal for vines. Chenin Blanc a Colombard remain the major white varieties, though just over a quart of all South Africa's Chardonnay also grows here, for both still a sparkling styles. Sauvignon can also be good. Muscadel (Muscat Blanc Petits Grains) yields a benchmark fortified wine, usually unoaked a released young. A red revolution is under way: Shiraz, Merlot a Cabernet have made an excellent start. Best producers: Graham BECK★, B Courage, De Wetshof, Quando, Robertson Winery, SPRINGFIELD ESTATE★, V Loveren, Weltevrede, Zandvliet.

ROC DE CAMBES★★ *Côtes de Bourg AC, Bordeaux, France* François Mitjaville of TERTRE-ROTEBOEUF has applied diligence and genius to this property since he acquired it in 1988. Full and succulent, with ripe dark fruit, this wine takes the COTES DE BOURG appellation to new heights. Best years: 2007 06 05 **04 03 02 01 00** 99 98 97 96 95.

DOM. DES ROCHES NEUVES *Saumur-Champigny AC, Loire Valley, France* A shift to biodynamic methods and more hands-off winemaking (including less extraction and new oak) has elevated very good wines to a higher level. Fresh, pure and mineral, top cuvées Insolite SAUMUR★★ (Chenin Blanc) and Marginale SAUMUR-CHAMPIGNY★★ (Cabernet Franc) are excellent expressions of fruit and *terroir*; generic Saumur-Champigny and Terres Chaudes★ are good value. New to the line-up are Bulles de Roche, a finely fruity sparkler, and Franc de Pieds, Cabernet Franc from young, ungrafted vines. Best years: (Marginale) **2006** 05 04 03 02 01 00 99 97.

ROCHIOLI *Russian River Valley AVA, California, USA* Well-known grape growers, the Rochioli family are equally good at winemaking, offering silky, black cherry Pinot Noir★★ and a richer, dramatic West Block Reserve Pinot★★. Also fine Sauvignon Blanc and a range of cult Chardonnays★★. Best years: (Pinot Noir) 2007 06 05 04 **03 02 01 00** 99 98 97.

ROCKFORD *Barossa Valley, South Australia* Wonderfully nostalgic wines from Robert O'Callaghan, a great respecter of the old vines so plentiful in the BAROSSA, who delights in using antique machinery to create wines of irresistible drinkability. Masterful Basket Press Shiraz★★, Riesling★★, Moppa Springs★ (Grenache-Shiraz-Mourvèdre), Rifle Range Cabernet★★ and Australia's best sparkling Black Shiraz★★★. Best years: (Basket Press Shiraz) (2008) 06 05 04 03 **02 01** 99 98 96 95 92 91 90.

ANTONIN RODET *Mercurey, Côte Chalonnaise, Burgundy, France* Merchant specializing in CÔTE CHALONNAISE, but with an excellent range throughout Burgundy. Rodet owns or co-owns 5 domaines – Ch. de Rully★, Ch. de Chamirey★, Ch. de Mercey★, Dom. des Perdrix★ and Jacques Prieur★★ – which are the source of the best wines. BOURGOGNE Vieilles Vignes★ is one of the best inexpensive Chardonnays available. Best years: (reds) (2008) 07 06 05 **03 02** 99; (whites) (2008) 07 06 05 04 02.

TELMO RODRÍGUEZ *Spain* The former winemaker for REMELLURI has formed a 'wine company' that is active throughout Spain. With a team of enologists and viticulturists, it forms joint ventures with local growers and manages the winemaking process. The results are often spectacular. Top wines: Molino Real★ (Sierras de MÁLAGA), Matallana★ (RIBERA DEL DUERO), Altos de Lanzaga★ (RIOJA), Dehesa Gago Pago La Jara★★ (TORO), Viña 105 (Cigales), Basa★ (RUEDA).

LOUIS ROEDERER *Champagne AC, Champagne, France* Renowned firm making some of the best, full-flavoured CHAMPAGNE around. As well as the excellent non-vintage★★ and pale vintage rosé★★, it also makes a big, exciting vintage★★, delicious vintage Blanc de Blancs★★ and the famous Roederer Cristal★★★ and Cristal Rosé★★★, de luxe cuvées which are nearly always magnificent. Both the vintage and Cristal can usually be aged for 10 years or more; the non-vintage benefits from a bit of aging, too. Best years: (2004) (03) 02 **00 99 97 96 95 90** 89 88 85.

ROEDERER ESTATE *Anderson Valley AVA, California, USA* Offshoot of Louis ROEDERER. The Brut★★ (sold in the UK as Quartet) is austere but impressive, and it will age beautifully. Lovely rosé★★, and the top bottling, L'Ermitage★★★, is stunning. Best years: (L'Ermitage) 2002 00 99 97 96 **94 92 91.**

ROERO DOCG *Piedmont, Italy* The Roero hills lie across the Tanaro river from the LANGHE hills, home of BAROLO and BARBARESCO. Long noted as a source of supple, fruity Nebbiolo-based red wines to drink in 2–5 years, Roero has recently been turning out Nebbiolos of Barolo-like intensity from producers such as Correggia and Malvirà. **Best producers: (reds)** G Almondo★, Ca' Rossa★, Cascina Chicco★, Correggia★★, Deltetto★★, Funtanin★, F Gallino★, Malvirà★★, Monchiero Carbone★, Angelo Negro★, Porello★. **Best years: (reds)** (2008) (07) (06) **04 03 01 00 99**. See also ARNEIS.

ROMAGNA *Emilia-Romagna, Italy* Romagna's wine production is centred on 4 DOCs and 1 DOCG. The whites are from Trebbiano (ineffably dull), Pagadebit (showing promise as both dry and sweet wine) and Albana (Albana di Romagna DOCG can be dry or sweet). The best of the Sangiovese-based reds can rival good CHIANTI CLASSICO. **Best producers: (Sangiovese)** La Berta★, Castelluccio★★, L Conti★, Drei Donà-La Palazza★★, G Madonia★, San Patrignano co-op/Terre del Cedro★ (Avi★★), Tre Monti★, Zerbina★★.

LA ROMANÉE AC *Grand Cru, Côte de Nuits, Burgundy, France* Tiny Grand Cru★★★ of the very highest quality, owned and now made by Vicomte LIGER-BELAIR; up to 2002 it was distributed by BOUCHARD PÈRE ET FILS. **Best years:** (2008) 07 06 05 03 02 99 **98**.

LA ROMANÉE-CONTI AC *Grand Cru, Côte de Nuits, Burgundy, France* For many extremely wealthy wine lovers this is the pinnacle of red Burgundy★★★. It is an incredibly complex wine with great structure and pure, clearly defined fruit flavour, but you've got to age it 15 years to see what all the fuss is about. The vineyard, wholly owned by Dom. de la ROMANEE-CONTI, covers only 1.8ha (4½ acres). **Best years:** (2008) 07 06 05 03 02 01 00 99 98 97 96 95 93 **90 89 85 78**.

DOM. DE LA ROMANÉE-CONTI *Vosne-Romanée, Côte de Nuits, Burgundy, France* This famous domaine owns a string of Grands Crus in VOSNE-ROMANEE (la TÂCHE★★★, RICHEBOURG★★★, ROMANEE-CONTI★★★, ROMANEE-ST-VIVANT★★★, ECHEZEAUX★★★ and Grands-Échézeaux★★★) as well as a small parcel of le MONTRACHET★★★. The wines are ludicrously expensive but can be sublime – full of fruit when young, but capable of aging for 15 years or more to a marriage made in the heaven and hell of richness and decay. **Best years: (reds)** (2008) 07 06 05 03 02 01 **00** 99 98 97 96 95 93 **90 89 85 78**.

ROMANÉE-ST-VIVANT AC *Grand Cru, Côte de Nuits, Burgundy, France* The largest of VOSNE-ROMANEE's 6 Grands Crus. At 10–15 years old the wine should reveal the keenly balanced brilliance of which the vineyard is capable, but a surly, rough edge sometimes gets in the way. **Best producers:** l'Arlot★★, R Arnoux★★★, S CATHIARD★★★, J-J Confuron★★★, DROUHIN★★★, Hudelot-Noëllat★★, JADOT★★★, Dom. LEROY★★★, Dom. de la ROMANEE-CONTI★★★. **Best years:** (2008) 07 06 05 03 02 **01 00** 9 **98 97 96 95 93 90**.

CH. ROMANIN *Les Baux de Provence AC, Provence, France* Jean-Louis Charmolüe, former owner of Ch. MONTROSE in Bordeaux, now owns this biodynamically run vineyard. Top wine is Le Coeur du Château Romanin★ from Syrah, Mourvèdre, Cabernet Sauvignon and Grenache. Second wine is La Chapelle de Romanin, while Jean le Troubadour is for everyday drinking. **Best years:** (Le Coeur) 2007 06 05 04 **03 01 00**.

BENJAMIN ROMEO *Rioja DOCa, La Rioja, Spain* ARTADI's former winemaker launched his own estate with a collection of tiny old vineyards, and immediately caused a sensation with his superripe, dense, powerful wines, Contador★★, La Viña de Andrés Romeo★★ and La Cueva del Contador★★. Best years: (2006) 05 04 **03 02 01 00**.

QUINTA DOS ROQUES *Dão DOC, Beira Alta, Portugal* One of DAO's finest producers, the wines of 2 estates with quite different characters are made here. Quinta dos Roques red★ is ripe and supple, while Quinta das Maias★ is a smoky, peppery red. The top wines are the Roques Reserva★★, made from old vines and aged in 100% new oak, and Touriga Nacional★★. Both estates also have a decent dry white, especially Roques Encruzado★. Best years: 2008 **05 04 03 01 00 97 96**.

QUINTA DE LA ROSA *Douro DOC and Port DOC, Douro, Portugal* The Bergqvist family have transformed this property into a small but serious producer of both PORT and unfortified DOURO★ (Reserva★★) wines. The Vintage Port★★ is excellent, as is unfiltered LBV★★; Finest Reserve and Tonel No. 2, a 10-year-old tawny★, are also good. Best years: (Vintage) 2005 04 **03 00 97 96 95 94 92 91**.

ROSÉ DE LOIRE AC *Loire Valley, France* Dry rosé from ANJOU, SAUMUR and TOURAINE. It can be a lovely drink, full of red berry fruits, but drink as young as possible, chilled. It's far superior to Rosé d'Anjou AC, which is usually sweetish without much flavour. Best producers: Hautes Ouches, Passavant, St-Arnoud, Trottières.

ROSÉ DES RICEYS AC *Champagne, France* Still, dark pink wine made from Pinot Noir grapes in the southern part of the CHAMPAGNE region. Best producers: Alexandre Bonnet★, Devaux★, Guy de Forez, Morel.

ROSEMOUNT ESTATE *Hunter Valley, New South Wales, Australia* Winery buying and growing grapes in several regions to produce some of Australia's most popular wines, but many seem sweeter and flatter than before and any sense of 'estate' has virtually disappeared. The flagship Roxburgh Chardonnay★ has undergone a dramatic and not entirely successful style change. Best of the other whites is Orange Vineyard Chardonnay★. Top-level Show Reserve reds are a bit stodgy, as is dense Balmoral Syrah, but GSM★ (Grenache-Syrah-Mourvèdre) can be good. Part of the Foster's Wine Group. Best years: (Balmoral Syrah) 2008 06 05 04 02 01 **00 98 97 96 94 92 91 90**.

ROSSO CÒNERO DOC *Marche, Italy* Red wines from the Adriatic coast, made solely or principally from Montepulciano. The best are classed Cònero DOC and have a wonderfully spicy richness. Best producers: Fazi Battaglia★, Garofoli★ (Grosso Agontano★★), Lanari★ (Fibbio★★), Leopardi Dittajuti★, Malacari★, Mecella (Rubelliano★★), Monte Schiavo (Adeodato★★), Moroder★ (Dorico★★), Le Terrazze★ (Sassi Neri★★, Visions of J★★), Umani Ronchi★ (Cúmaro★★). Best years: (2008) (07) 06 **04 03 01 00**.

ROSSO DI MONTALCINO DOC *Tuscany, Italy* The little brother of BRUNELLO DI MONTALCINO spends less time aging in wood, enabling the wines to retain a wonderful exuberance of flavour. In lesser years the best Brunello grapes may cascade here, so off-years (like 2002) can be surprisingly good. Best producers: Agostina Pieri★★, Altesino★, Argiano★, Gianni Brunelli★, Camigliano★, Caparzo★, Casanova di Neri★★, Ciacci Piccolomini d'Aragona★★, Col d'Orcia★, Collemattoni★, COSTANTI★★, Fuligni★, Gorelli-Due Portine★, M Lambardi★, Lisini★, Siro Pacenti★, Poggio Antico★, Poggio Salvi★, il POGGIONE★, Salicutti★★, San Filippo-Fanti★, Talenti★, Valdicava★. Best years: (2008) 07 **06 05 04 03 02 01 00**.

ROSSO DI MONTEPULCIANO DOC *Tuscany, Italy* Some VINO NOBILE producers use this DOC in order to improve selection for the main wine; the best deliver delightfully plummy, chocolaty flavours. **Best producers:** La Braccesca★/ANTINORI, La Ciarliana★, Contucci★, Dei★, Del Cerro★, Il Faggeto★, Fassati★, Nottola★, POLIZIANO★, Salcheto★★, Valdipiatta★, Villa Sant'Anna★. **Best years:** (2008) 07 **06 04 03 01**.

ROSSO PICENO DOC *Marche, Italy* Often considered a poor relative of ROSSO CONERO, but it can be rich and seductive when the full complement (70%) of Montepulciano is used, and also when it comes from the more restricted Superiore zone. **Best producers:** Boccadigabbia★ (Villamagna★★), Le Caniette★, Laurentina★, Monte Schiavo★, Saladini Pilastri★, Velenosi★. **Best years:** (2008) 07 **06 04 03**.

RENÉ ROSTAING *Côte-Rôtie AC, Rhône Valley, France* Modern, slightly oaked, rich wines with deep colour and softly elegant fruit flavours, from some of the best sites in CÔTE-RÔTIE: classic Côte-Rôtie★, Côte Blonde★★★ and la Landonne★★. There's a very good CONDRIEU★★ too. **Best years:** (top crus) 2007 06 05 **04 03 01 00** 99 98 95 94 91 90 88.

DOM. ROTIER *Gaillac AC, South-West France* This estate makes wines using local and more classic grapes. Red Renaissance★, with flavours of wild thyme, blends Duras, Braucol, Syrah and Cabernet Sauvignon. There are both dry and sweet★★ versions of white Renaissance, based on local grape Len de l'El. **Best years:** (2008) **06 05 04 02 00**.

GEORGES ROUMIER *Chambolle-Musigny, Côte de Nuits, Burgundy, France* Christophe Roumier is one of Burgundy's top winemakers, devoting as much attention to his vineyards as to cellar technique, believing in severe pruning, low yields and stringent grape selection. Roumier rarely uses more than one-third new oak. His best wine is often BONNES-MARES★★★; other Grands Crus include MUSIGNY★★★, Ruchottes-Chambertin★★ and CORTON-CHARLEMAGNE★★. Best value are usually the village CHAMBOLLE★★ and an exclusively owned Premier Cru in MOREY-ST-DENIS, Clos de la Bussière★★. **Best years:** (reds) (2008) 07 06 05 03 02 **01 00** 99 **98 96 95 90**.

ROUSSANNE The RHÔNE VALLEY's best white grape, frequently blended with Marsanne. Roussanne is the more aromatic and elegant of the two, less prone to oxidation and with better acidity, but growers usually prefer Marsanne due to its higher yields and greater body. Now being planted in the Midi. There are some examples in SAVOIE (where it is called Bergeron) and Australia. While much of the Roussanne first planted in California has been identified as Viognier, there are a few true plantings that produce fascinating, complex wines.

ARMAND ROUSSEAU *Gevrey-Chambertin, Côte de Nuits, Burgundy, France* Highly respected CHAMBERTIN estate, with vineyards in Chambertin★★★, Clos-de-Bèze★★★, Mazis-Chambertin★★ and Charmes-Chambertin★★ as well as GEVREY-CHAMBERTIN Clos St-Jacques★★★ and CLOS DE LA ROCHE★★★ in MOREY-ST-DENIS. The long-lived wines are outstandingly harmonious, elegant, yet rich. Charles Rousseau has been making great wines since 1959, and his son Eric has rediscovered consistency of late. **Best years:** (2008) 07 06 05 03 02 99 96 **93 91 90 89 88 85**.

ROUSSETTE DE SAVOIE AC *Savoie, France* Separate SAVOIE AC for dry or off-dry, floral and mineral whites made from the Altesse grape variety. **Best producers:** Dupasquier★★, Jacquin★, Lupin★, Prieuré Saint Christophe★★, Saint-Germain. **Best years:** 2007 **06 05 04**.

ROUSSILLON *France*   The snow-covered peaks of the Pyrenees form a spectacular backdrop to the ancient region of Roussillon, now the Pyrénées-Orientales *département*. The vineyards produce a wide range of fairly priced wines, mainly red, from the ripe, raisin-rich *vins doux naturels* to light, fruity-fresh vins de pays. Once dominated by co-operatives, there are now some really exciting wines, both white and red, appellation and vin de pays, being made, especially by individual estates. See also BANYULS, COLLIOURE, CÔTES DU ROUSSILLON, CÔTES DU ROUSSILLON-VILLAGES, MAURY, MUSCAT DE RIVESALTES, RIVESALTES.

RUCHOTTES-CHAMBERTIN AC   See CHAMBERTIN AC.

RÜDESHEIM *Rheingau, Germany*   Village producing silky, aromatic wines from some steep terraced vineyards high above the Rhine (Berg Schlossberg, Berg Rottland, Berg Roseneck and Bischofsberg). Best producers: Georg BREUER★★★, Johannishof★, Kesseler★★, Josef LEITZ★★, Ress, Schloss Schönborn★. Best years: (2008) 07 06 05 **04 03 02 01 99 97**.

RUEDA DO *Castilla y León, Spain*   The RIOJA firm of MARQUES DE RISCAL launched the reputation of this white wine region in the 1970s, first by rescuing the almost extinct Verdejo grape, then by introducing Sauvignon Blanc. Fresh young whites have been joined by barrel-fermented wines aiming for a longer life, particularly at Castilla La Vieja, Ossian and Belondrade y Lurton. Best producers: Alvarez y Diez★, Antaño (Viña Mocén★), Belondrade y Lurton★, Castelo de Medina★, Bodegas de Crianza Castilla La Vieja★, Cerrosol (Doña Beatriz), Dos Victorias (José Pariente★), Hermanos Lurton, MARQUES DE RISCAL★, Viñedos de Nieva★, Ossian★, Palacio de Bornos★, José Pariente★, Javier Sanz★, Vinos Sanz, Viña Sila★ (Naia, Naiades), Sitios de Bodega★, Angel Rodríguez Vidal (Martinsancho★).

RUFFINO *Tuscany, Italy*   Huge operation now partly owned by American giant Constellation Brands; production is still controlled by brothers Marco and Paolo Folonari, and is increasingly orientated toward quality. SUPER-TUSCANS include La Solatia★ (Chardonnay); Modus★ (Sangiovese-Cabernet-Merlot); Nero del Tondo★ (Pinot Noir); and the unique blend of Colorino and Merlot, Romitorio di Santedame★★. Ruffino also owns VINO NOBILE estate Lodola Nuova, BRUNELLO Il Greppone Mazzi and Borgo Conventi in COLLIO. See also FOLONARI.

RUINART *Champagne AC, Champagne, France*   Ruinart has a surprisingly low profile given the quality of its wines. Non-vintage★ is very good, as is Blanc de Blancs★, but the top wines here are the supremely classy Dom Ruinart Blanc de Blancs★★ and the Dom Ruinart Rosé★★. Best years: (2004) 02 00 **98 96 95 90 88 85 83 82**.

RULLY AC *Côte Chalonnaise, Burgundy, France*   Best known for white wines, often oak-aged. Reds are light, with a fleeting strawberry and cherry perfume. Most wines are reasonably priced. Best producers: (whites) d'Allaines★, J-C Brelière★, M Briday★, DROUHIN★, Dureuil-Janthial★, Duvernay, FAIVELEY★, V GIRARDIN★, Hasard★, H & P Jacqueson★★, JADOT★, O LEFLAIVE★, RODET★, Villaine★; (reds) Dureuil-Janthial★, la Folie, H & P Jacqueson★. Best years: (whites) (2008) **07** 06; (reds) (2008) 07 **05**.

RUSSIAN RIVER VALLEY AVA *Sonoma County, California, USA*   Beginning south of Healdsburg this valley cools as it meanders toward the Pacific. Green Valley, a sub-AVA, is home to IRON HORSE, DUTTON GOLDFIELD and Marimar TORRES. It has now superseded CARNEROS as the top spot in North Coast California for Pinot Noir and Chardonnay. Best producers: DE LOACH★, DEHLINGER★★, DUTTON GOLDFIELD★★, Merry Edwards★★, Gary Farrell★★, IRON HORSE★★, Kosta Browne★, LYNMAR★★, Moshin★, Papapietro

263

Perry★, Ramey★★, ROCHIOLI★★, SONOMA-CUTRER★, Rodney Strong★, Joseph SWAN★, Marimar TORRES★★, WILLIAMS SELYEM★★. **Best years:** (Pinot Noir) (2007) 06 05 04 **03 02 01 00 99 97 95.**

RUST EN VREDE *Stellenbosch WO, South Africa* Jean Engelbrecht, son of original owner/winemaker Jannie Engelbrecht, has carried out a thorough springclean since returning to run this red-only property. A return to form for this farm's excellent reds is promised under new winemaker Coenie Snyman. Rust en Vrede★, a Cabernet-Shiraz-Merlot blend, reflects the farm's *terroir*; Shiraz★, Merlot and Cabernet all benefit from young, virus-free vines, showing fine, soft tannins and fresh fruit. **Best years:** (Rust en Vrede estate wine) 2005 **04 03 02 01 00.**

RUSTENBERG *Stellenbosch WO, South Africa* Top-notch wines led by single-vineyard Peter Barlow★★, a big but classically structured Cabernet, and bold Five Soldiers★★ (Chardonnay). There's also a complex, layered BORDEAUX-style blend John X Merriman★★ and lean but scented Roussanne, a first in South Africa. Occasionally produced The Last Straw★★ is a heavenly 'sticky'. A delightful, heady Viognier★★, increasingly complex savoury Shiraz★ and bright-fruited Cabernet★ are the pick of the value Brampton range. **Best years:** (Peter Barlow) (2006) 05 **04 03 01** 99; (Five Soldiers) 2007 **06 05 04 03 02 01 00.**

RUTHERFORD AVA *Napa Valley, California, USA* This viticultural area in mid-NAPA VALLEY has inspired hours of argument over whether it has a distinct identity. The heart of the area, the Rutherford Bench, does seem to be a prime Cabernet Sauvignon zone, and many traditional Napa Cabernets come from here and exhibit the 'Rutherford dust' flavour. **Best producers:** BEAULIEU (Private Reserve★★), Cakebread, CAYMUS★★, FLORA SPRINGS★★, Freemark Abbey★ (Bosché★★), Frog's Leap★★, Hall★, PINE RIDGE★, Quintessa★, Rubicon/COPPOLA★★, Sequoia Grove★, Staglin★★. **Best years:** (Cabernet) 2005 04 03 **02 01 00 99 96 95 94 93 91 90 86.**

RUTHERGLEN *Victoria, Australia* This region in north-east VICTORIA is the home of heroic reds from Shiraz, Cabernet and Durif (Petite Sirah), and luscious, world-beating fortifieds from Muscat and Tokay (Muscadelle). Good sherry- and PORT-style wines. **Best producers:** (fortifieds) All Saints★, Buller★★, Campbells★★, CHAMBERS★★, MORRIS★★, Stanton & Killeen★★.

SAALE-UNSTRUT *Germany* Vines can only flourish in the folds of the river valleys in this bleak expanse of the former East Germany near Leipzig. This far north, it is only just possible to ripen most grape varieties, yet global warming is having an effect, and 80 different varieties are now grown here, 15 of which are of some importance: Riesling, Müller-Thurgau, Silvaner and Weissburgunder (Pinot Blanc) are the current favourites. Only 630ha (1550 acres), mostly on limestone slopes, with a very dry, fragrant style being the most successful. **Best producers:** Gussek, Lützkendorf★, Pawis.

SACHSEN *Germany* 470ha (1160-acre) wine region centred on the cities of Meissen and Dresden along the Elbe Valley. At more than 50°N, grapes don't ripen easily, and as recently as 1996 frosts of -28°C virtually destroyed the year's harvest; global warming is easing conditions, and some lovely, delicate dry Rieslings are beginning to appear, along with good Müller-Thurgau,

Gewürztraminer, Silvaner and Weissburgunder (Pinot Blanc). **Best producers:** Schloss Proschwitz★, Schwartz, Klaus Zimmerling★.

THE SADIE FAMILY *Swartland WO, South Africa* Eben Sadie takes a non-interventionist approach in his vineyards, with biodynamics playing an increasing role. He crafts minute quantities of a red and a white wine: both benefit from aging. Columella★★, Syrah with a little Mourvèdre, combines richness and power and is clearly influenced by Eben's project in Spain, a PRIORAT called Dits del Terra. Palladius★★, a Viognier-based dry white, is a generously textured wine whose flavours evolve endlessly in the glass. Sequillo, a slightly larger Swartland venture, produces a mineral-fresh Syrah-based red★★ and elegant barrel-fermented Chenin-based white★★. **Best years:** (Columella) 2006 05 **04 03 02 01 00**.

ST-AMOUR AC *Beaujolais, Burgundy, France* The most northerly BEAUJOLAIS cru, much in demand through the romantic connotation of its name. The granitic vineyards produce wines with great intensity of colour that may be initially harsh, needing a few months to soften. **Best producers:** des Billards★, DUBOEUF★ (des Sablons★), des Duc★. **Best years: 2008 07 06.**

ST-AUBIN AC *Côte de Beaune, Burgundy, France* These days almost as good a source of white Burgundy (though in a softer style) as its MONTRACHET neighbours, PULIGNY and CHASSAGNE, and much more affordable. En Remilly and Murgers Dents de Chien stand out as vineyards, along with Frionnes for pretty, perfumed Pinot Noir. **Best producers:** J-C BACHELET★, F & D Clair★, M Colin★, Deux MONTILLE★, DROUHIN★, JADOT★, H Lamy★, Lamy-Pillot★, Larue★★, O LEFLAIVE★, B Morey★, RAMONET★★. **Best years:** (reds) (2008) 07 **06 05 03 02**; (whites) (2008) **07 06 05 04 02**.

ST-BRIS AC *Burgundy, France* Appellation near CHABLIS for Sauvignon Blanc; wines are less interesting than a decade ago. Drink young. **Best producer:** J-H Goisot.

ST-CHINIAN AC *Languedoc, France* Large AC of hill villages, covering strong, spicy red wines with more personality and fruit than run-of-the-mill HÉRAULT. **Best producers:** Berloup co-op, BORIE LA VITARÈLE★, CANET-VALETTE★, Cazal-Viel★, CLOS BAGATELLE★, HECHT & BANNIER★, Jougla★, Mas Champart★, Maurel Fonsalade★, Moulin de C’îffre, Moulinier, Navarre, Rimbert★, Roquebrun co-op, Tabatau (Lo Tabataire★). **Best years:** 2007 06 05 **04 03 01 00**.

SAINT CLAIR *Marlborough, South Island, New Zealand* A top performer thanks to some great vineyard sites. Whites are led by the intensely fruity Wairau Reserve Sauvignon Blanc★★ and a variety of single-vineyard wines under the Pioneer Block★★ label made when vintage conditions allow. Excellent Reserve Chardonnay★★, tasty Riesling★ and Gewürztraminer★. Vicar's Choice is impressive entry-level label. Various Pinot Noirs★ (Doctor's Creek★) and serious, chocolaty Rapaura Reserve Merlot★★ lead the reds. **Best years:** (Sauvignon Blanc) **2007 06 04**.

T-ÉMILION AC *Bordeaux, France* The scenic Roman hill town of St-Émilion is the centre of Bordeaux's most historic wine region. The finest vineyards are on the plateau and *côtes*, or steep slopes, around the town, although an area to the west, called the *graves*, contains 2 famous properties, CHEVAL BLANC and FIGEAC. It is a region of smallholdings, with over 1000 properties, and consequently the co-operative plays an important part. The dominant early-ripening Merlot grape gives wines with a 'come hither' softness and sweetness rare in red BORDEAUX. St-Émilion AC is the basic generic AC, with 4 'satellites' (LUSSAC, MONTAGNE, PUISSEGUIN, ST-GEORGES) allowed to annex their name to it. The best producers, including the Classed Growths, are found in the more tightly controlled ST-EMILION GRAND CRU AC category but there are anomalies, e.g. La Mondotte★★. Best years: **2005 03 01 00 98 96 95 90**.

ST-ÉMILION GRAND CRU AC *Bordeaux, France* ST-EMILION's top-quality AC, which includes the estates classified as Grand Cru Classé and Premier Grand Cru Classé (below). The classification is revised approximately every 10 years; the 2006 revision is in doubt due to legal squabbles. There are currently 57 Grands Crus Classés. This AC also includes many of the new wave of limited edition *vins de garage*. Best producers: (Grands Crus Classés) l'ARROSEE★, Balestard-la-Tonnelle★, CANON-LA-GAFFELIÈRE★★, Clos de l'Oratoire★★, la Dominique★, Fleur Cardinale★, Grand Mayne★★, Grand Pontet★, Larcis Ducasse★, Larmande★, MONBOUSQUET★, Pavie-Decesse★, la Tour Figeac★; (others) Bellevue★, Faugères★, Fombrauge★, la Gomerie★, Gracia★, Moulin St-Georges★, Quinault l'Enclos★, Rol Valentin★, TERTRE-RÔTEBOEUF★★, Teyssier, VALANDRAUD★★. Best years: 2005 **03 01 00 98 96 95 90 89 88**.

ST-ÉMILION PREMIER GRAND CRU CLASSÉ *Bordeaux, France* The St-Émilion élite level, divided into 2 categories – 'A' and 'B' – with only the much more expensive CHEVAL BLANC and AUSONE in category 'A'. There are 13 'B' châteaux, with PAVIE-MACQUIN and TROPLONG MONDOT added from the 2006 Classification. Best producers: ANGELUS★★★, AUSONE★★★, BEAU-SEJOUR BECOT★★, Beauséjour★, BELAIR★, CANON★, CHEVAL BLANC★★★, Clos Fourtet★, FIGEAC★★, la Gaffelière★, MAGDELAINE★, PAVIE★★, PAVIE-MACQUIN★★, TROPLONG MONDOT★★, Trottevieille★. Best years: 2007 06 05 04 **03 02 01 00 99 98 96 95 90 89 88**.

ST-ESTÈPHE AC *Haut-Médoc, Bordeaux, France* Large AC north of PAUILLAC with 5 Classed Growths. St-Estèphe wines have high tannin levels, but given time (10–20 years) those sought-after flavours of blackcurrant and cedarwood do peek out. More Merlot has been planted to soften the wines and make them more accessible at an earlier age. As summers get drier and hotter, these wines are coming into their own. Best producers: CALON-SEGUR★★, COS D'ESTOURNEL★★★, Cos Labory, HAUT-MARBUZET★★, LAFON-ROCHET★, Lilian-Ladouys★, Marbuzet★, MEYNEY★, MONTROSE★★, les Ormes-de-Pez★, PEZ★, Phélan Ségur★. Best years: 2006 05 04 **03 02 01 00 96 95 94 90 89 88 86**.

DOM. ST-GAYAN *Gigondas AC, Rhône Valley, France* The Meffre family's holdings include some very old vines, which lend power to the chunky long-lived GIGONDAS★ (★★ in top years). Other reds, such as RASTEAU, are good value. Best years: (Gigondas) 2007 06 05 **04 03 01 00 99 98 97 95 90**.

ST-GEORGES-ST-ÉMILION AC *Bordeaux, France* The smallest satellite of ST-EMILION, with lovely, soft wines that can nevertheless age for 6–10 years. Best producers: Calon, Macquin St-Georges★, St-André Corbin★, Ch. St Georges★, Tour-du-Pas-St-Georges★, Vieux-Montaiguillon★. Best years: 200? **03 01 00 98 96 95 90**.

ST HALLETT *Barossa Valley, South Australia* Following a merger with MCLAREN VALE's Tatachilla, the wineries were snapped up by brewer Lion Nathan. So far, the bargain Gamekeeper's Reserve red, Poacher's Blend white and EDEN VALLEY Riesling★ are performing pretty well, as are venerable Old Block Shiraz★ and the excellent Shiraz siblings Blackwell★ and Faith★. Best years: (Old Block) (2008) (06) 04 **03 02 98 96 94 93 91 90**.

ST-JOSEPH *Rhône Valley, France* Large, mainly red AC, along the opposite bank of the Rhône to HERMITAGE. Made from Syrah, the reds have mouthfilling fruit with irresistible blackcurrant richness. Brilliant a

1–2 years, they can last for up to 10. The white wines are usually pleasant and flowery to drink young, although an increasing number can age. **Best producers:** (reds) Boissonnet, CHAPOUTIER★, J-L CHAVE★★, Chêne★, L Chèze★, Courbis★, COURSODON★★, CUILLERON★, DELAS★, E & J Durand★★, Faury★, Florentin★, P Gaillard★★, Gonon★★, GRAILLOT★★, B Gripa★★, GUIGAL★★, JABOULET, Monier★, Monteillet★★, Paret★, A PERRET★★, C Pichon★, Richard (Nuelles★), St-Désirat co-op, TAIN co-op★, Tardieu-Laurent★★, Vallet★, G Vernay★, F Villard★★; (whites) CHAPOUTIER (Granits★★), Chêne★★, L Chèze★, Courbis★ (Royes★★), CUILLERON★, DELAS, Ferraton★, P Finon, G Flacher, Florentin★, P Gaillard★★, Gonon★★, B Gripa★, GUIGAL, Monteillet★, A PERRET★, Villard★★. **Best years:** (reds) **2007 06 05 03 01 00 99 98 95**; (whites) (2008) **07 06 05 04 03 00 98**.

ST-JULIEN AC *Haut-Médoc, Bordeaux, France*
For many, St-Julien produces perfect claret, with an ideal balance between opulence and austerity and between the brashness of youth and the genius of maturity. It is the smallest of the HAUT-MEDOC ACs but almost all is first-rate vineyard land and quality is high. **Best producers:** BEYCHEVELLE★, BRANAIRE-DUCRU★★, DUCRU-BEAUCAILLOU★★★, GLORIA★, GRUAUD-LAROSE★★, LAGRANGE★★, LANGOA-BARTON★★, LEOVILLE-BARTON★★★, LEOVILLE-LAS-CASES★★★, LEOVILLE-POYFERRE★★, ST-PIERRE★★, TALBOT★. **Best years:** 2007 06 05 04 **03 02 01 00 99 98 96 95 94 90 89 88 86**.

ST-NICOLAS-DE-BOURGUEIL AC *Loire Valley, France* An enclave within the larger BOURGUEIL AC, and similarly producing light wines from vineyards toward the river, sturdier bottles from up the hill. Almost all the wine is red and with the same piercing red fruit flavours of Bourgueil, and much better after 7–10 years, especially in warm vintages. **Best producers:** Y Amirault/Pavillon du Grand Clos★★, T Amirault, Clos des Quarterons★, Dom. de la Cotelleraie/Vallée★, L & M Cognard-Taluau★, F MABILEAU★★, J Taluau★. **Best years:** (2008) 07 **06** 05 **04** 03 02 01 97 96.

ST-PÉRAY AC *Rhône Valley, France* Rather hefty CHAMPAGNE-method fizz from Marsanne and Roussanne grapes. Still white is usually dry, fragrant and mineral on the finish. **Best producers:** S Chaboud★, CHAPOUTIER★, CLAPE★, COLOMBO★, DELAS, Fauterie, B Gripa★★, J Lemenicier★, TAIN co-op★, Tardieu-Laurent★, J-L Thiers★, Tunnel★, Vins de Vienne, A Voge★ (Fleur de Crussol★★). **Best years:** (2008) **07 06 05 04 03 01 00 99**.

CH. ST-PIERRE★★ *St-Julien AC, 4ème Cru Classé, Haut-Médoc, Bordeaux, France* Small ST-JULIEN property making wines that have become a byword for ripe, lush fruit wrapped round with the spice of new oak. Drinkable early, but top vintages can improve for 20 years. **Best years:** 2006 05 04 **03 02 01 00 99 98 96 95 94 90 89 85**.

ST-ROMAIN AC *Côte de Beaune, Burgundy, France* Red wines with a firm, bitter-sweet cherrystone fruit and flinty-dry whites. Usually good value by Burgundian standards, but take a few years to open out. **Best producers:** (whites) Bazenet★, H & G Buisson, Chassorney★★, A Gras★★, O LEFLAIVE★, VERGET★★; (reds) A Gras★. **Best years:** (whites) (2008) 07 **06** 05 **04** 02; (reds) (2008) 07 **05**.

ST-VÉRAN AC *Mâconnais, Burgundy, France* Often thought of as a POUILLY-FUISSE understudy, this is gentle, fairly fruity, normally unoaked Mâconnais Chardonnay. Overall quality is good. Drink young. **Best producers:** D & M Barraud★, Cordier★, Corsin★★, Deux Roches★,

DUBOEUF★, Gerbeaux★, R Lassarat★, O Merlin★, Poncetys★, Saumaize-Michelin★, J C Thévenet★★, VERGET★, J-J Vincent★. Best years: (2008) **07** 06.

STE-CROIX-DU-MONT AC *Bordeaux, France* Best of the 3 sweet wine ACs that gaze jealously at SAUTERNES and BARSAC across the Garonne river (the others are CADILLAC and LOUPIAC). The wine is mildly sweet rather than splendidly rich. Top wines can age for at least a decade. Best producers Crabitan-Bellevue★, Loubens★, Lousteau-Vieil, Mailles, Mont, Pavillon★, la Rame★. Best years: 2007 **05 03 02 01 99 98 97 96 95**.

SAINTSBURY *Carneros AVA, California, USA* Deeply committed CARNEROS winery. Its Pinot Noirs★★ are brilliant examples of the perfume and fruit quality of Carneros; vineyard-designated Pinots, led by the exquisite Brown Ranch★★★, are deeper and oakier, while Garnet★ is a delicious lighter style. The Chardonnays★★ are also impressive, best after 2–3 years. Best years: (Pinot Noir) (2007) 06 05 04 **03 02 01 00 99 98 97 96 95**

CASTELLO DELLA SALA *Orvieto DOC, Umbria, Italy* Belongs to the ANTINORI family, making good ORVIETO★ and outstanding oak-aged Cervaro★★★ (Chardonnay and a little Grechetto). Also Pinot Nero★ and sweet Muffato della Sala★★.

DUCA DI SALAPARUTA *Sicily, Italy* Corvo is the brand name for Sicilian wines made by this firm. Red and white Corvo are pretty basic, but there are superior whites, Colomba Platino★ and Bianca di Valguarnera★, and 2 fine reds, Terre d'Agala★ and Duca Enrico★★.

SALICE SALENTINO DOC *Puglia, Italy* One of the better DOCs in the Salento peninsula, using Negroamaro tempered with a dash of perfumed Malvasia Nera for ripe, chocolaty wines that acquire hints of roast chestnuts and prunes with age. Drink after 3–4 years, although they may last as long again. The DOCs of Alezio, Brindisi, Copertino, Leverano, Squinzano and others, plus various IGTs, are similar and are all scheduled to be subsumed under the DOP Salento according to the new EU wine regime. Best producers: Candido★, Casale Bevagna★, Leone De Castris★, Due Palme★, Taurino★, Vallone★★, Conti Zecca. Best years: (reds) (2008) 06 **04 03 01 00**.

SALTA *Argentina* The vineyards of Salta province, 700km (435 miles) north of MENDOZA, are concentrated along the Calchaquí Valley. The most important location is Cafayate, at about 1750m (5750ft), where all the traditional producers are located, but Colomé is also showing tremendous potential and there are new vineyards as high as 3100m (over 10,000ft) – truly the highest in the world. High altitude, sandy soils and almost no rain produce wines of intense colour and high alcohol content, scented white Torrontés and lush red Malbec. Best producers: (Cafayate) Etchart, Finca Las Nubes, San Pedro de Yacochuya; (Colomé) Colomé.

SAMOS *Greece* The island of Samos has a centuries-old reputation for rich, sweet, Muscat-based wines. The Samos co-op's wines include deep gold honeyed Samos Nectar★★, made from sun-dried grapes; apricotty Palaio★, aged for up to 20 years; and seductively complex Samos Anthemis★, fortified and cask-aged for up to 5 years.

SAN ANTONIO *Chile* A region of many parts, the most prominent of which has so far been Leyda. Closeness to the Pacific Ocean and the icy Humboldt Current decides whether you are best at snappy Sauvignon Blanc and fragrant Pinot Noir (Lo Abarca, Leyda), or scented, juicy laden Syrah (Rosario). There are half a dozen estates, but big companies like CONCHA Y TORO, CONO SUR, MontGras, SANTA RITA and MONTES are also making exciting wine from the region's fruit. Water shortage is problem but expect Leyda in particular to become a new mini-CASABLANCA. Best producers: CASA MARÍN★★, Garcés Silva/Amayna★, Viña Leyda★★, MATETIC★.

SAN LEONARDO *Trentino, Italy* Marchese Carlo Guerrieri Gonzaga, a former winemaker at SASSICAIA, has established his Cabernet-Merlot blend San Leonardo★★★ as the northern equivalent of the famous Tuscan. Recently launched is an almost equally impressive Merlot called Villa Gresti★★. Best years: (2008) (07) (06) **04 03 01 00 99 97 96 95.**

SAN LUIS OBISPO COUNTY *California, USA* CENTRAL COAST county best known for Chardonnay, Pinot Noir, a bit of old-vine Zinfandel, Syrah and Cabernet Sauvignon. There are 5 AVAs: Edna Valley, PASO ROBLES, SANTA MARIA VALLEY (shared with SANTA BARBARA COUNTY), Arroyo Grande Valley and York Mountain. Best producers: ALBAN★★, Claiborne & Churchill★, Eberle★, Edna Valley★★, Justin★, Laetitia, J Lohr (Hilltop Cabernet Sauvignon★★), Meridian★, Norman★, Saucelito Canyon★, Savannah-Chanelle★, Talley★★, Wild Horse★. Best years: (reds) 2005 04 **03 02 01 00 99 98 97 95 94.**

SAN PEDRO TARAPACÁ *Curicó, Chile* The biggest Chilean wine news of 2008/9 was the fusion of two of Chile's largest and longest-running wine groups: San Pedro and Tarapacá. The new group counts 11 wineries among its subsidiaries, including 2 in Argentina (Tamarí and Finca la Celia). Most prominent among the Chilean operations are the quality-focused Viña Leyda in SAN ANTONIO and Tabalí in LIMARÍ. After a shaky start, Cachapoal-based Altaïr★★ found its stride in the excellent 2005 vintage. San Pedro remains the dominant player: its Castillo de Molina Reservas★ are reliable, Cabo de Hornos Cabernet Sauvignon★ is a true Chilean classic and look out for exciting new reds from MAULE and Elqui.

SANCERRE AC *Loire Valley, France* White Sancerre can provide the perfect expression of the bright green tang of the Sauvignon grape, and from a good grower can be deliciously refreshing – as can the rare Pinot Noir rosé – but the very best also age well. Some growers produce a richer style using new oak. Pinot Noir reds from top producers are now a serious proposition. The wines are more consistent than those of neighbouring POUILLY. Prices reflect the appellation's popularity. Best producers: F & J Bailly-Reverdy★, G Boulay★★, H BOURGEOIS★★, H Brochard★, R Champault★, F Cotat★★, F Crochet★, L Crochet★, Delaporte★, Gitton★, P Jolivet★, Serge Laloue★, Dom. Martin★, A MELLOT★★, J Mellot★, P Millérioux★, Mollet-Maudry★, H Natter★, A & F Neveu★, R Neveu★, V Pinard★★, J Reverdy★, P & N Reverdy★, C Riffault★, J-M Roger★, Thomas-Labaille★★, VACHERON★★, André Vatan★. Best years: 2008 **07 06 05 02.**

SANDALFORD *Swan Valley, Western Australia* One of WESTERN AUSTRALIA's original wineries (founded in 1840) and a pioneer of the MARGARET RIVER, where Sandalford planted a large vineyard in 1972. However, it generally underperformed until the arrival of winemaker Paul Boulden in 2001. With the premium wines, Boulden has focused on the Margaret River, and quality has leaped ahead. Whites – Sauvignon Blanc-Semillon, Verdelho★ and Chardonnay★ – are impressive, and reds are even better: dark, classically ripe, fleshy Shiraz★★, Cabernet Sauvignon★★★ and lush Cabernet Prendiville Reserve★★★. Element range offers quality at fair prices. Best years: (Cabernet Sauvignon) (2008) 07 05 04 **03** 02 01 **00** 99.

SANDEMAN *Port DOC, Douro, Portugal, and Jerez y Manzanilla DO, Spain* The PORT operation is now owned by SOGRAPE, but run by George Sandeman (7th-generation descendant of the founder). Excellent aged tawnies:

20-year-old★ and 30-year-old★★. Vintage ports are more patchy. Vau Vintage★ is good second label, for early drinking. In 2004 Sogrape sold its Jerez assets to Garvey, which now makes the Sandeman brands as a sub-contractor. Best years: (Vintage) 2003 00 97 94 66 63 55.

LUCIANO SANDRONE *Barolo DOCG, Piedmont, Italy* Luciano Sandrone ha become one of PIEDMONT's leading wine stylists, renowned for his BAROLC Cannubi Boschis★★★ and Le Vigne★★★, as well as BARBERA D'ALBA★★ and Dolcetto d'Alba★★, which rank with the best.

SANFORD *Santa Rita Hills AVA, California, USA* Richard Sanford planted th great Sanford & Benedict vineyard in the Santa Ynez Valley in 1971 thus establishing SANTA BARBARA as a potentially top-quality vineyar region. An estate vineyard planted west of Highway 101 is in the SANT RITA HILLS, an area that subsequently burst on to the Pinot Noir scene wit some spectacular wines. Sanford now makes sharply focused, dark fruited Pinot Noir★★, Chardonnay★★ and Sauvignon Blanc★. Richar Sanford left the project in 2005 to found high-quality Alma Rosa labe Best years: (Pinot Noir) 2007 06 05 04 03 02 01 00 99 98 97 96 95.

DOM. LE SANG DES CAILLOUX *Vacqueyras AC, Rhône Valley, France* To VACQUEYRAS estate with big, peppery, authentic red wines led by the old vines Grenache-Syrah Cuvée de Lopy★★ that bursts with fruit an vigour over 10 or more years. Doucinello★ and Azalaïs★ reds are mor restrained. Punchy, compelling white. Best years: 2007 06 05 04 03 01 0 99 98.

SANGIOVESE Sangiovese, the most widely planted grape variety in Italy reaches its greatest heights in central TUSCANY, especially in Montalcinc whose BRUNELLO must be 100% varietal. This grape has produced a wid range of sub-varieties, plus a growing number of 'improved' clones which makes generalization difficult. Much care is being taken in th current wave of replanting, whether in CHIANTI CLASSICO, Brunello (Montalcino, VINO NOBILE DI MONTEPULCIANO or elsewhere. Styles rang from pale, lively and cherryish through vivacious, mid-range Chiantis t excellent top Riservas and SUPER-TUSCANS. Some fine examples are als produced in ROMAGNA. California producers including Robert Pepi, Vin Noceto and SEGHESIO are having a go at taming the grape, without muc success. Australia has good examples from King Valley in VICTORIA (Gar Crittenden, Pizzini) and MCLAREN VALE (Coriole), but poor-quality clone have thus far hampered progress. Also grown in Argentina and Chil and both South Africa and NEW YORK are trying it.

SANTA BARBARA COUNTY *California, USA* CENTRAL COAST county, nort west of Los Angeles, known for Chardonnay, Riesling, Pinot Noir an Syrah. The main AVAs are SANTA RITA HILLS, Santa Ynez Valley and mo of SANTA MARIA VALLEY (the remainder is in SAN LUIS OBISPO COUNTY), all to areas for Pinot Noir. Best producers: AU BON CLIMAT★★, Babcoc Beckmen★★, Brander★, Brewer-Clifton★★, Byron★★, Cambria, Fole Foxen★★, Hitching Post★★, Lane Tanner★★, Longoria★, Melville★, Andre MURRAY★★, Ojai★★, Fess Parker★, QUPE★★, SANFORD★★, Zaca Mesa★. Be years: (Pinot Noir) 2007 06 05 04 03 02 01 00 99 98 97 95 94.

SANTA CRUZ MOUNTAINS AVA *California, USA* A sub-region of th CENTRAL COAST AVA. Notable for long-lived Chardonnays and Caberne Sauvignons, including the stunning Monte Bello from RIDGE. Also sma amounts of robust Pinot Noir. Best producers: BONNY DOON★★, Dav

Bruce★★, Clos La Chance★, Thomas Fogarty★, Kathryn Kennedy★★, Mount Eden Vineyards★★, RIDGE★★★, Santa Cruz Mountain Vineyard★.

SANTA MARIA VALLEY AVA *Santa Barbara County and San Luis Obispo County, California, USA* Cool Santa Maria Valley is coming on strong as a producer of Chardonnay, Pinot Noir and Syrah. Look for wines made from grapes grown in Bien Nacido and Sierra Madre vineyards by several small wineries. Best producers: AU BON CLIMAT★★, Byron★★, Cambria, Foxen★★, Lane Tanner (Pinot Noir★★), Longoria★, QUPE★★.

SANTA RITA *Maipo, Chile* Long-established MAIPO giant. Red blends such as superb Triple C★★ (Cabernet Franc-Cabernet Sauvignon-Carmenère) show real flair. Floresta whites (Leyda Sauvignon Blanc★★) and reds (Apalta Cabernet Sauvignon★★) are tremendous. Cabernet-based Casa Real★ is expensive and old fashioned, but some people love it.

SANTA RITA HILLS AVA *Santa Barbara County, California, USA* This small AVA lies at the western edge of the Santa Ynez Hills in SANTA BARBARA COUNTY. Fog and wind from the Pacific keep temperatures cool. Pinot Noir is the primary grape (along with small amounts of Syrah and Chardonnay) and the wines have deeper colour, greater varietal intensity and

higher acidity than others in the region but are still very ripe and dense. Best producers: Babcock, Brewer-Clifton★★, Clos Pepe★★, Fiddlehead★★, Foley★★, Lafond★, Melville★, SANFORD★★, Sea Smoke★★.

SANTENAY AC *Côte de Beaune, Burgundy, France* Red Santenay wines often promise good ripe flavour, though they don't always deliver it, but are worth aging for 4–6 years in the hope that the wine will open out. Many of the best wines, both red and white, come from les Gravières Premier Cru on the border with CHASSAGNE-MONTRACHET. Best producers: (reds) R Belland★, F & D Clair★, M Colin★, J Girardin★, V GIRARDIN★★, Monnot★, B Morey★★, L Muzard★★, J-M Vincent★★; (whites) V GIRARDIN★, Jaffelin, René Lequin-Colin★. Best years: (reds) (2008) 07 05 **03** 02 99.

CASA SANTOS LIMA *Alenquer DOC, Estremadura, Portugal* A beautiful estate with a wide range. Light, fruity and tasty Espiga reds and whites, spicy red★ and creamy, perfumed white Palha Canas, and red and white Quinta das Setencostas★. Also Touriz★ (from DOURO varieties), varietal Touriga Nacional★, Touriga Franca★, Trincadeira★ and Tinta Roriz★ and peachy, herby Chardonnay★.

CAVES SÃO JOÃO *Beira Litoral, Portugal* A pioneer of cool-fermented, white BAIRRADA, and makes rich, oaky Cabernet Sauvignon from its own vines. Rich, complex traditional reds and whites include outstanding Reserva★★ and Frei João★ from Bairrada and Porta dos Cavaleiros★★ from DAO – they demand at least 10 years' age to show their quality.

SARDINIA *Italy* Grapes of Spanish origin, like the white Vermentino and Torbato and the red Monica, Cannonau and Carignano, dominate production on this huge, hilly Mediterranean island, but they vie with a Malvasia of Greek origin and natives like Nuragus and Vernaccia. The cooler northern part (Gallura) favours whites, especially Vermentino, while the southern and eastern parts are best suited to reds from Cannonau and Monica, with Carignano dominating in the south-west. The wines used to be powerful, alcoholic monsters, but the current trend is for a lighter, modern, more international style. Foremost among those in pursuit of quality are ARGIOLAS, SELLA & MOSCA and the Santadi co-op. See also CARIGNANO DEL SULCIS.

SASSICAIA DOC★★★ *Tuscany, Italy* Legendary Cabernet Sauvignon-Cabernet Franc blend. Vines were planted in 1944 to satisfy the Marchese Incisa della Rocchetta's thirst for fine red Bordeaux, which was in short supply during the war. The wine remained purely for family consumption until nephew Piero ANTINORI and winemaker Giacomo Tachis persuaded the Marchese to refine production practices and to release several thousand bottles from the 1968 vintage. Since then, Sassicaia has proved itself to be one of the world's great Cabernets, combining a blackcurrant power of blistering intensity with a heavenly scent of cigars. Since 1995 it has its own DOC within the BOLGHERI appellation. Best years: (2008) (07) 06 04 **03 01 99** 98 97 95 90 88 85 68.

HORST SAUER *Escherndorf, Franken, Germany* Horst Sauer shot to stardom in the late 1990s. His dry Rieslings★★ and Silvaners★ are unusually juicy and fresh for a region renowned for blunt, earthy wines. His late-harvest wines are unchallenged in the region and frequently ★★★; they will easily live a decade, sometimes much more. Best years: (dry Riesling, Silvaner) (2008) 07 06 **05 04 03 02 01**.

SAUMUR AC *Loire Valley, France* Dry white wines, mainly from Chenin Blanc, with up to 20% Chardonnay; the best combine bright fruit with a mineral seam. The reds are lighter than those of SAUMUR-CHAMPIGNY and Saumur Puy-Notre-Dame, which was recently awarded its own AC. Also dry to off-dry Cabernet rosé, and sweet Coteaux de Saumur in good years. Best producers: Château-Gaillard★, Clos Rougeard★★, Collier★, Filliatreau★, Fosse-Seche, HUREAU★, Langlois-Château★, R-N Legrand★, F MABILEAU★★, la Paleine★, ROCHES NEUVES★★, St-Just★, Saumur co-op, Tour Grise, VILLENEUVE★, Yvonne★★. Best years: (whites) 2008 **07 06 05 04 03 02**.

SAUMUR-CHAMPIGNY AC *Loire Valley, France* Saumur's best red wine. Cabernet Franc is the main grape, and in hot years the wine can be superb, with a piercing scent of blackcurrants and raspberries easily overpowering the earthy finish. Delicious young, it can age for 6–10 years. Best producers: Clos Cristal★, Clos Rougeard★★, de la Cune, Dubois★, Filliatreau★, HUREAU★★, R-N Legrand★, Nerleux★, la Perruche★, Retiveau-Rétif★, ROCHES NEUVES★★, A Sanzay★, St-Vincent★/Patrick Vadé★, VILLENEUVE★★, Yvonne★. Best years: (2008) **06** 05 04 03 02 01 96.

SAUMUR MOUSSEUX AC *Loire Valley, France* Reasonable CHAMPAGNE method sparkling wines, mainly from Chenin Blanc. Adding Chardonnay and Cabernet Franc makes the wine softer and more interesting. Usually non-vintage. Small quantities of rosé are also made. Best producers: Bouvet-Ladubay★, Gratien & Meyer★, Grenelle★, la Paleine★, la Perruche★, St-Cyr-en-Bourg co-op★, Veuve Amiot.

SAUTERNES AC *Bordeaux, France* The name Sauternes is synonymous with the best sweet wines in the world. Sauternes and BARSAC both lie on the banks of the little river Ciron and are 2 of the very few areas in France where noble rot occurs naturally. Production of these intense, sweet, luscious wines from botrytized grapes is a risk-laden and extremely expensive affair, and the wines are never going to be cheap. From good producers the wines are worth their high price – as well as 14% alcohol they have a richness full of flavours of pineapples, peaches, syrup and spice. Good vintages should be aged for 5–10 years and often last twice as long. Best producers: Bastor-Lamontagne★, Clos Haut-Peyraguey★★, Cr

Barréjats★, DOISY-DAENE★★, DOISY-VEDRINES★★, FARGUES★★, GILETTE★★, GUIRAUD★★, Haut-Bergeron★, les Justices★, LAFAURIE-PEYRAGUEY★★, Lamothe-Guignard★, Malle★, Rabaud-Promis★, Raymond-Lafon★★, Rayne-Vigneau★, RIEUSSEC★★★, Sigalas Rabaud★★, SUDUIRAUT★★, la TOUR BLANCHE★★, YQUEM★★★. Best years: 2007 05 **03 02 01** 99 98 97 96 95 90 89 88 86 83.

SAUVIGNON BLANC See pages 274–5.

SAUZET *Puligny-Montrachet, Côte de Beaune, Burgundy, France* A producer with a reputation for classic, rich, full-flavoured white Burgundies, made in an opulent, fat style, but recently showing more classical restraint. Prime sites in PULIGNY-MONTRACHET★ and CHASSAGNE-MONTRACHET★ (Premiers Crus usually ★★), as well as small parcels of BÂTARD-MONTRACHET★★★ and Bienvenues-BÂTARD-MONTRACHET★★★. Best years: (2008) **07 06 05 04 02**.

SAVENNIÈRES AC *Loire Valley, France* Wines from Chenin Blanc, produced on steep vineyards south of Anjou. Usually steely and dry, although some richer wines are being produced by a new generation using new oak and malolactic fermentation. The top wines usually need at least 8 years to mature, and can age for longer. Two very good vineyards have their own ACs: la Coulée-de-Serrant and la Roche-aux-Moines. Best producers: BAUMARD★★, Bergerie, CLOS DE LA COULEE-DE-SERRANT★★, Closel★★, Épiré★★, Dom. F L★, Damien Laureau, aux Moines★, Eric Morgat★, PIERRE-BISE★, Taillandier★. Best years: (2007) 06 05 **04 03** 02 **01** 99 97 96 95 90.

SAVIGNY-LÈS-BEAUNE AC *Côte de Beaune, Burgundy, France* Large village with reds dominating; usually dry and lean, they need 4–6 years to open out. The top Premiers Crus, such as Lavières, Peuillets and La Dominode, are more substantial. The white wines show a bit of dry, nutty class after 2–3 years. The wines are generally reasonably priced. Best producers: S Bize★, Camus-Bruchon★★, Champy★, CHANDON DE BRIAILLES★, B Clair★★, M Écard★★, J J Girard★, Guyon★, L Jacob★★, Dom. LEROY★★, C Maréchal★, J-M Pavelot★★, TOLLOT-BEAUT★★. Best years: (reds) (2008) 07 05 **03 02 99**.

SAVOIE *France* Savoie's high Alpine vineyards produce fresh, snappy white wines from the local Jacquère grape (to drink young), Chasselas and the more interesting Altesse (see ROUSSETTE DE SAVOIE) and Bergeron grapes (aka Roussanne, grown only in Chignin). There are attractive light reds and rosés, too from Gamay or Pinot, and, in hot years, some positively Rhône-like reds from the Mondeuse grape. From 2008 the main AC is simply Savoie AC and the 17 best villages can add their own name to the label; these include Apremont, Abymes, Chignin and Arbin, near Chambéry, and Jongieux near Aix-les-Bains. Two further small ACs are Seyssel for sparkling and dry whites, and Crépy for whites from the Chasselas grape. Between Lyon and Savoie are the vineyards of the Vin du Bugey VDQS, with light, easy-drinking reds and whites. Best producers: Belluard★, Berlioz★, Berthollier★, Dupasquier★, l'Idylle, E Jacquin★, Magnin★, J Masson, Prieuré Saint Christophe★★, & M Quenard★★, J-P & J-F Quenard★, P & A Quénard★, Ch. de Ripaille★, Saint-Germain, Trosset★; (Bugey) Angelot, Charlin, Monin.

SAXENBURG *Stellenbosch WO, South Africa* In-demand red wines, led by dense, burly Private Collection Shiraz★★ and an even richer, bigger Shiraz Select★★, plus excellent Cabernet★★ and Merlot★. Private Collection Sauvignon Blanc★★ and Chardonnay★ head the white range. Drink whites young; reds will improve for 5–8 years. Best years: (premium reds) 2006 05 **04 03 02 01 00** 99 98.

SAUVIGNON BLANC

Of all the world's grapes, the Sauvignon Blanc is leader of the 'love it or loathe it' pack. It veers from being wildly fashionable to totally out of favour depending upon where it is grown and which country's wine writers are talking, but you, the consumers, love it – and so do I. Sauvignon is always at its best when full rein is allowed to its very particular talents, because this grape does give intense, sometimes shocking flavours, and doesn't take kindly to being put into a straitjacket. Periodically, producers lose confidence in its fantastic, brash, tangy personality and try to calm it down. Don't do it. Let it run free – it's that lip-smacking, in-yer-face nettles and lime zest and passionfruit attack that drinkers love. There's no more thirst-quenching wine than a snappy, crunchy young Sauvignon Blanc. Let's celebrate it.

WINE STYLES

Sancerre-style Sauvignon Although it had long been used as a blending grape in Bordeaux, where its characteristic green tang injected a bit of life into the blander, waxier Sémillon, Sauvignon first became trendy as the grape used for Sancerre, a bone-dry Loire white whose green gooseberry fruit and slightly smoky perfume inspired the winemakers of other countries to try to emulate, then often surpass, the original model.

The range of styles Sauvignon produces is as wide as, if less subtly nuanced than, those of Chardonnay. It is highly successful when picked slightly underripe, fermented cool in stainless steel, and bottled early. This is the New Zealand model and they in turn adapted and improved upon the Sancerre model from France. New Zealand is now regarded as the top Sauvignon country, and many new producers in places like Australia, South Africa, southern France, Hungary, Spain and Chile are emulating this powerful mix of passionfruit, gooseberry and lime. South African and Chilean examples, from the coolest coastal regions, with tangy fruit and mineral depth, are beginning to challenge New Zealand for quality.

Using oak Sauvignon also lends itself to fermentation in barrel and aging in new oak, though less happily than does Chardonnay. This is the model of the Graves region of Bordeaux, although generally here Sémillon would be blended in with Sauvignon to good effect.

New Zealand again excels at this style, and there are good examples from California, Australia and northern Italy. The mix, usually led by Sémillon, is becoming a classy speciality of South Africa's coastal regions. In Austria, producers in southern Styria (Steiermark) make powerful, aromatic versions, sometimes with a touch of oak. In all these regions, the acidity that is Sauvignon's great strength should remain with a nectarine fruit and a spicy, biscuity softness from the oak. These oaky styles are best drunk either within about a year, or after aging for years or so, and can produce remarkable, strongly individual flavours that you'll either love or loathe.

Sweet wines Sauvignon is also a crucial ingredient in the great sweet wines of Sauternes and Barsac from Bordeaux, though it is less susceptible than its partner Sémillon to the sweetness-enhancing 'noble rot' fungus, botrytis.

Sweet wines from the USA, South Africa, Australia and New Zealand range from the interesting to the outstanding – but the characteristic green tang of the Sauvignon should be found even at ultra-sweet levels.

FLORESTA
LEYDA

SAUVIGNON BLANC 2007
80 VALLE DE LEYDA - CHILE

Santa Rita

BEST PRODUCERS

France
Pouilly-Fumé J-C Chatelain, Didier DAGUENEAU, Ladoucette, Masson-Blondelet, de Tracy; *Sancerre* H BOURGEOIS, F Cotat, L Crochet, A MELLOT, V Pinard, J-M Roger, VACHERON; *Pessac-Léognan* Dom. de CHEVALIER, Couhins-Lurton, FIEUZAL, HAUT-BRION, MALARTIC-LAGRAVIERE, SMITH-HAUT-LAFITTE.

Other European Sauvignons
Austria Gross, Lackner-Tinnacher, POLZ, E Sabathi, Sattlerhof, TEMENT.

Italy Colterenzio co-op, Peter Dipoli, GRAVNER, Edi Kante, LAGEDER, Castello di Montepò/Jacopo BIONDI-SANTI, SCHIOPETTO, Vie di Romans, Villa Russiz.

Spain (*Rueda*) Alvarez y Diez (Mantel Blanco), Castelo de Medina, MARQUES DE RISCAL, Palacio de Bornos, Javier Sanz, Sitios de Bodega; (*Penedès*) TORRES (Fransola).

New Zealand
ASTROLABE, Cape Campbell, Clifford Bay, CLOUDY BAY, Crossings, Forrest Estate, JACKSON ESTATE, Lawson's Dry Hills, NEUDORF, PALLISER, PEGASUS BAY, SAINT CLAIR, SERESIN, VAVASOUR, VILLA MARIA.

Australia
BANNOCKBURN, Bird in Hand, Brookland Valley, DE BORTOLI (YARRA VALLEY), Edwards, HANGING ROCK, HOUGHTON (Wisdom), KATNOOK ESTATE, Lenton Brae, Nepenthe, S C PANNELL, SHAW & SMITH, Stella Bella, Tamar Ridge, Geoff WEAVER.

USA
California Abreu, ARAUJO, Brander, DRY CREEK (DCV3), FLORA SPRINGS (Soliloquy), Honig, KENWOOD, KUNDE, Mason, MATANZAS CREEK, Murphy-Goode, Quivira, Saracina, SPOTTSWOODE, St. Supery, Voss.

Chile
CASA MARÍN (Cipreses), CASAS DEL BOSQUE, CONCHA Y TORO, CONO SUR (20 Barrels), Viña Leyda, MONTES (Leyda), SANTA RITA (Floresta), Ventolera.

South Africa
CAPE POINT VINEYARDS, Neil ELLIS, Flagstone, Fryer's Cove, MULDERBOSCH, Oak Valley, SPRINGFIELD ESTATE, STEENBERG, THELEMA, VERGELEGEN.

WILLI SCHAEFER *Graach, Mosel, Germany* Classic MOSEL wines: Riesling Spätlese and Auslese from the GRAACHer Domprobst vineyard have a balance of piercing acidity and lavish fruit that is every bit as dramatic as Domprobst's precipitous slope. Extremely long-lived, they're frequently ★★★, as is the sensational Beerenauslese Schaefer produces in good vintages. Even his QbA wines are ★. Best years: (Riesling Spätlese, Auslese) (2008) 07 06 05 **04 03 02 01 99 98 97 95 94**.

SCHÄFER-FRÖHLICH *Bockenau, Nahe, Germany* From vineyards in SCHLOSSBOCKELHEIM and the more obscure Bockenau, Tim Fröhlich has since 2003 been producing racy dry Rieslings★★ and sumptuous nobly sweet wines★★★. Best years: (2008) 07 06 **05 04 03 02**.

SCHARFFENBERGER CELLARS *Anderson Valley AVA, California, USA* The quality trailblazer in the chilly ANDERSON VALLEY, now owned by top-performing neighbour ROEDERER. Non-vintage Brut★★, with lovely toasty depth, exuberant Rosé★★ and excellent vintage Blanc de Blancs★★.

SCHEUREBE Silvaner x Riesling crossing found in Germany's PFALZ and RHEINHESSEN. In Austria it is sometimes labelled Sämling 88. At its best in Trockenbeerenauslese and Eiswein. When ripe, it has a marvellous flavour of honey, exotic fruits and the pinkest of pink grapefruit.

SCHILCHER Rosé and sparkling wine from the Blauer Wildbacher grape, a speciality of the West STEIERMARK in Austria. Its very high acidity means you either love it or detest it. Best producer: Strohmeier.

SCHIOPETTO *Friuli-Venezia Giulia, Italy* The late Mario Schiopetto pioneered the development of scented varietals and high-quality, intensely concentrated white wines from COLLIO. Outstanding are (Tocai) Friulano★★, Pinot Bianco★★ and Sauvignon★★, which open out with age to display fascinating flavours. New COLLI ORIENTALI vineyards Poder dei Blumeri can only add further prestige.

SCHLOSS LIESER *Lieser, Mosel, Germany* Since Thomas Haag (son of Wilhelm, of the Fritz HAAG estate) took over the winemaking in 1992 (and then bought the property in 97), this small estate has shot to the top. MOSEL Rieslings★★ marry richness with great elegance. Best years: (2008) 07 06 **05 04 03 02 01 99**.

SCHLOSS REINHARTSHAUSEN *Erbach, Rheingau, Germany* Estate formerly owned by the Hohenzollern family, rulers of Prussia. Top sites include the great ERBACHer Marcobrunn. Much improved under new management since 2003. Good Rieslings (Auslese, Beerenauslese, TBA ★★) and Sekt★. Best years: (2008) 07 06 **05 04 03 02 01 99 97**.

SCHLOSS SAARSTEIN *Serrig, Mosel, Germany* Fine Saar estate with austere Riesling Trocken; Kabinett★, Spätlese★ and Auslese★★ are better balanced, keeping the startling acidity but coating it with fruit, often with the aromas of slightly unripe white peaches. Occasional spectacular Eiswein★★★. Best years: (2008) 07 06 05 **04 03 02 01 99 97**.

SCHLOSS VOLLRADS *Oestrich-Winkel, Rheingau, Germany* Quality at this historic estate has improved greatly this century, with some brilliant Eiswein★★ and TBA★★. Best years: (2008) 07 06 **05 04 02 01**.

SCHLOSSBÖCKELHEIM *Nahe, Germany* This village's top sites are the Felsenberg and Kupfergrube, but good wines also come from Mühlberg and Königsfels. Best producers: Dr Crusius★, DONNHOFF★★★ Gutsverwaltung Niederhausen-Schlossböckelheim★, SCHAFER-FROHLICH★★. Best years: (2008) 07 06 **05 04 03 02 01 99**.

SCHNAITMANN *Württemberg, Germany* A rising star, with varietal red and white wines of equal excitement. Rainer Schnaitmann trained in New Zealand, and his Sauvignon Blanc★ is one of Germany's best. Fine Spätburgunder★ too. Best years: (2008) 07 06 **05** 04 03.

DOM. SCHOFFIT *Alsace AC, Alsace, France* One of the two main owners of the outstanding Rangen Grand Cru vineyard, also making a range of deliciously fruity non-cru wines. Top-of-the-tree Clos St-Théobald wines from Rangen are often ★★★ and will improve for at least 5–6 years after release, Rieslings for even longer. The Cuvée Alexandre range is essentially declassified ALSACE Vendange Tardive. Best years: (Clos St-Théobald Riesling) (2008) 07 05 **04** 02 01 00 99 98 97 96 95.

SCHRAMSBERG *Napa Valley AVA, California, USA* The first California winery to make really excellent CHAMPAGNE-style sparklers from the classic grapes. Though all releases do not achieve the same heights, these wines can be among California's best, and as good as most Champagne. The Crémant★ is an attractive slightly sweetish sparkler, the Blanc de Noirs★★ and the Blanc de Blancs★★ are more classic. Bold, powerful J Schram★★ is rich and flavoursome and increasingly good. Top of the line is the Reserve Brut★★. Vintage-dated wines can be drunk with up to 10 years' age and can achieve ★★★ quality. 2005 saw the debut of the winery's first red, a 2002 J Davies Cabernet Sauvignon★★ from Diamond Mountain, in honour of the late founder, Jack Davies.

SCREAMING EAGLE *Oakville AVA, California, USA* Real estate agent Jean Phillips first produced a Cabernet Sauvignon from her OAKVILLE valley floor vineyard in 1992. Made in very limited quantities, Screaming Eagle★★★ is one of California's most sought-after Cabernets each vintage, a huge, brooding wine that displays all the lush fruit of Oakville. Sold in 2006; the new owners propose to change as little as possible.

SEGHESIO *Sonoma County, California, USA* Having grown grapes in SONOMA COUNTY for a century, the Seghesio family is today known for its own Zinfandel. All bottlings, from Sonoma County★★ to the single-vineyard San Lorenzo★★ and Cortina★★, display textbook black fruit and peppery spice. Sangiovese★ from 1910 vines is one of the best in the state. Also look for fascinating Aglianico★ and crisp Italian whites such as Pinot Grigio★ and Arneis★.

SEIFRIED *Nelson, South Island, New Zealand* Estate founded in 1974 by Austrian Hermann Seifried and his New Zealand wife Agnes. The best wines include Sauvignon Blanc★, Gewürztraminer★ and botrytized Riesling★★. Best years: (whites) **2007** 06 05 04 03.

SELBACH-OSTER *Zeltingen, Mosel, Germany* Johannes Selbach is one of the MOSEL's new generation of star winemakers, producing very pure, elegant Riesling★★ from the Zeltinger Sonnenuhr site. Also fine wine from WEHLEN, GRAACH and BERNKASTEL. Best years: (2008) 07 06 **05** 04 03 02 01 00 99 98 97.

SELLA & MOSCA *Sardinia, Italy* As well as rich, port-like Anghelu Ruju★ made from semi-dried Cannonau grapes, this much-modernized old firm, today part of the Campari group, produces good dry whites, Terre Bianche★ (Torbato) and La Cala★ (Vermentino), and oak-aged reds, Marchese di Villamarina★ (Cabernet) and Tanca Farrà★ (Cannonau-Cabernet). Best years: (Marchese di Villamarina) (2008) (07) 06 05 **04** 01 00 97.

SELVAPIANA *Chianti Rufina DOCG, Tuscany, Italy* This estate has always produced excellent CHIANTI RUFINA. But since 1990 it has vaulted into the top rank of Tuscan estates, particularly with single-vineyard crus Fornace★★

277

and Vigneto Bucerchiale Riserva★★. Very good VIN SANTO★★. Best years (Bucerchiale) (2008) (07) (06) **04 01 99 98 95 93 91 90 88 85**.

SÉMILLON Found mainly in South-West France, especially in the sweet wines of SAUTERNES, BARSAC, MONBAZILLAC and Saussignac, because it is prone to noble rot (*Botrytis cinerea*). Also blended for its waxy texture with Sauvignon Blanc to make dry wine – almost all the great PESSAC-LEOGNAN Classed Growths are based on this blend. Performs well in Australia (aged Semillon from the HUNTER, BAROSSA and CLARE VALLEY can be wonderful) on its own or as a blender with Chardonnay (the accent over the é is dropped on New World labels). Sémillon is also blended with Sauvignon in Australia, New Zealand, California (including St Supery's Virtu★ white Meritage) and Washington State. In cooler regions of South Africa it is producing some outstanding results, often barrel-fermented, and, increasingly, in flagship blends with Sauvignon.

SEÑA★ *Aconcagua, Chile* Seña is one of those trailblazing wines – initially a joint venture with MONDAVI – that was supposed to change the face of Chilean wine, but didn't, because it was too Californian. Now 100% Chilean-owned (by the Chadwick family of ERRÁZURIZ), this ripe, dense Cabernet-based super-blend may indeed blaze a trail because quality has leapt since Errázuriz took total control in 2005.

SEPPELT *Grampians, Victoria, Australia* In one of 2008's most controversial moves, Foster's sold Seppeltsfield (the BAROSSA base of Seppelt and its entire fortified resources) to a group centring on the CLARE VALLEY producer, Kilikanoon. From its GRAMPIANS base, Seppelt continues to excel with its flagship St Peters Shiraz★★, the definitive Show Sparkling Shiraz★★★ and the Original Sparkling Shiraz★. The sparkling whites appear to be suffering from a lack of focus. Drumborg Riesling★ from the super-cool Henty region of southern VICTORIA stands out, and there are some excellent budget-priced table wines in the Victorian range.

SERESIN *Marlborough, South Island, New Zealand* Film producer Michael Seresin's winery has made a big impact on the MARLBOROUGH scene with its range of stylish organic wines. Intense Sauvignon Blanc★ is best within a year or two of the vintage, but creamy Chardonnay★★, succulent Pinot Gris★ and rich, oaky Pinot Noir★ will age for up to 3 years. Best years: (Sauvignon Blanc) **2007 06**.

SETÚBAL DOC *Portugal* Fortified wine from the Setúbal Peninsula south of Lisbon, called 'Moscatel de Setúbal' when made from at least 85% Moscatel, and 'Setúbal' when it's not. Best producers: BACALHÔA VINHOS D PORTUGAL★★, José Maria da FONSECA★★.

SEYVAL BLANC Hybrid grape whose disease resistance and ability to continue ripening in a damp autumn make it a useful variety in England, Canada, NEW YORK STATE and other areas in the eastern US. Gives clean, sappy, grapefruit-edged wines that with age can sometimes give a very passable imitation of bone-dry CHABLIS.

SHAFER *Stags Leap District AVA, California, USA* One of the best NAPA wineries run by the erudite and thoughtful Doug Shafer, and making unusually fruity One Point Five Cabernet★★ and stunning, focused Reserve-style

Hillside Select★★★. Merlot★★ is also exciting. Relentless★ is made from estate-grown Syrah. Red Shoulder Ranch Chardonnay★★★ is classic CARNEROS style. Best years: (Hillside Select) (2005) 04 03 **02 01 00 99 98 97 96 95 94 93 91 90 84**.

SHARPHAM *Devon, England* Beautiful vineyard on a bend in the river Dart with consistent winemaking and a stylish range of still and sparkling wines, including white Bacchus★ and Madeleine Angevine-based Estate Selection, and red Beenleigh (Cabernet Sauvignon-Merlot).

SHAW & SMITH *Adelaide Hills, South Australia* This winery has been influential in determining the styles that other Australian wineries have adopted. Tangy Sauvignon Blanc★★ has been a runaway success since its first vintage in 1989; increasingly brilliant single-vineyard M3 Chardonnay★★★; and an impressive, fleshy, scented, cool-climate Shiraz★★. More recently, there have been small amounts of Riesling and Pinot Noir. Cousins Martin Shaw and Michael Hill Smith are now able to source much of their fruit from their Balhannah vineyard and the wines are showing the benefit. Best years: (M3 Chardonnay) **2008 07 06 05 04 03 02**.

SHERRY See JEREZ Y MANZANILLA DO, pages 178–9.

SHIRAZ See SYRAH, pages 290–1.

SICILY *Italy* Sicily is emerging with a renewed spirit and attitude to wine production. Those who led the way, such as PLANETA, Duca di SALAPARUTA and TASCA D'ALMERITA, have been joined by others, including Donnafugata and the revitalized Spadafora. The huge, 6500ha (16,000-acre) Settesoli estate, headed by Diego Planeta, has transformed itself over the past 10 years: Inycon is its tasty budget label and Mandrarossa (Cartagho★★) the premium range. Other exciting estates include Abbazia Santa Anastasia, especially noted for its Cabernet Sauvignon-Nero d'Avola blend, Litra★★; Cottanera, for excellent varietal Merlot (Grammonte★★), Mondeuse (L'Ardenza★★) and Syrah (Sole di Sesta★★); Cusumano, for 100% Nero d'Avola (Sàgana★) and a Nero d'Avola-Cabernet-Merlot blend (Noà★), as well as deep, lush but balanced Jalé Chardonnay; Morgante, for a pure Nero d'Avola (Don Antonio★★); Palari, for its Nerello Mascalese-Cappuccio blend (Faro Palari★★); and Ceuso, for a Nero d'Avola-Merlot-Cabernet blend (Ceuso Custera★). Firriato, aided by consultant Kym Milne, also makes excellent reds★ (Harmonium Nero d'Avola★★) and whites★. Latest vineyard destination of choice is high on the slopes of Etna, with grapes like Nerello Mascalese (Benanti★) and Carricante. See also MARSALA, MOSCATO PASSITO DI PANTELLERIA.

SIEUR D'ARQUES, LES VIGNERONS DU *Limoux AC, Languedoc, France* This modern co-op makes around 80% of the still and sparkling wines of LIMOUX. The BLANQUETTE DE LIMOUX★ and CREMANT DE LIMOUX★ are reliable, but the real excitement comes with the Toques and Clochers Chardonnays★ (occasionally ★★). The co-op also makes a range of vins de pays and has a joint venture with GALLO in California (Red Bicyclette).

SILENI *Hawkes Bay, North Island, New Zealand* Established by millionaire Graeme Avery, with a view to making nothing but the best, this modern winery brings a touch of the NAPA VALLEY to HAWKES BAY. Refreshing unoaked Chardonnay★, tangy MARLBOROUGH Sauvignon★ and ripe, mouthfilling Semillon★ are all tasty. Pinot Noir★ is good (from Hawkes Bay and Marlborough), as is Merlot (The Triangle★), and Syrah★★ is delicate and scented. Best years: (reds) (2008) 07 **06 04 02 00**.

SILVER OAK CELLARS *Napa Valley, California, USA* Only Cabernet Sauvignon is made here, with bottlings from ALEXANDER VALLEY★★ and NAPA VALLEY★★ grapes. Forward, generous, fruity wines, impossible not to enjoy young, yet with great staying power. Best years: (Napa Valley) (2005) 04 03 **02 01 00 99 97 96 95 94 93 92 91 90 86 85 84**.

SILVERADO VINEYARDS *Stags Leap District AVA, California, USA* The regular Cabernet Sauvignon★ has intense fruit and is drinkable fairly young; Solo★★ and Limited Reserve★★ have more depth and are capable of aging; a STAGS LEAP DISTRICT Cabernet Sauvignon★★ displays the cherry fruit and supple tannins of this AVA. Also a fruity Merlot★, refreshing Sauvignon Blanc★ and Chardonnay★ with soft, inviting fruit and a silky finish. A more restrained Chardonnay, called Vineburg★, is very tasty. Best years: (Limited Reserve) 2005 04 03 02 **01 99 95 94 91 90**.

SIMI *Alexander Valley AVA, California, USA* Historic winery purchased by Constellation in 1999. Currently the ALEXANDER VALLEY Cabernet Sauvignon★, Chardonnay★ (Reserve★★) and Sauvignon Blanc★ attain fair standards. Best years: (reds) **01 99 97 95 94 91 90**.

SIMONSIG *Stellenbosch WO, South Africa* Family-run property with broad range of styles. Most consistent are the reds: regular Shiraz and lavishly oaked Merindol Syrah; a delicious unwooded Pinotage★★ and well-oaked old-vine Redhill Pinotage★★; the svelte BORDEAUX-blend Tiara★; and dense, powerful Frans Malan Reserve★, a Cape blend of Pinotage, Cabernet Sauvignon and Merlot. Whites are sound, if less exciting. Cap Classique sparklers, Kaapse Vonkel and Cuvée Royale, are biscuity and creamy. Best years: (premium reds) (2007) 06 **05 04 03 02 01 00 99**.

CH. SIRAN★ *Margaux AC, Haut-Médoc, Bordeaux, France* Owned by the same family since 1848, this estate produces consistently good claret – increasingly characterful, approachable young, but with enough structure to last for as long as 20 years. Second wine: S de Siran. Best years: 2007 06 05 04 **03 02 01 00 99 98 96 95 90 89 86**.

SKALLI-FORTANT DE FRANCE *Languedoc-Roussillon, France* Robert Skalli was a pioneer of varietal wines in the Midi. Modern winemaking and the planting of international grape varieties were the keys to success. After a dip in quality, now one of the most influential producers in the south of France. The Fortant de France brand includes a range of single-variety Vins de Pays d'OC. Grenache and Chardonnay are among the best, along with Reserve F Merlot and Cabernet Sauvignon. Also estates in CORSICA, CHATEAUNEUF-DU-PAPE and CALIFORNIA.

SKILLOGALEE *Clare Valley, South Australia* Very good range from the cool CLARE VALLEY: a stony Riesling★ typical of the region and an attractive lemony Gewürztraminer★. Reds include lovely full, fresh Shiraz★★ and minty Cabernet Sauvignon★★. Also a rich, raisiny Liqueur Muscat★★

CH. SMITH-HAUT-LAFITTE *Pessac-Léognan AC, Cru Classé de Graves, Bordeaux, France* This property was floundering until a change of ownership in 1990 heralded a decade of hard graft, resulting in massively improved quality. The reds, traditionally lean, now have much more fruit and perfume and can approach ★★. The Sauvignon-dominated white is a shining example of modern white Bordeaux and at best is ★★★. Second wine (red and white): Les Hauts de Smith. Best years: (reds) 2007 06 05 04 **03 02 01 00 99 98 96 95**; (whites) 2007 06 05 04 03 02 01 00 99 98 96 95

SMITH WOODHOUSE *Port DOC, Portugal* Underrated but consistently satisfying PORT from this shipper in the Symington group. Good Vintage★★ and single-quinta Madalena★★. Late Bottled Vintage★★ i the rich and characterful, figgy, unfiltered type. Best years: (Vintage) **2003 00 97 94 92 91 85 83 80 77 70 63**; (Madalena) **2001 99 96 95**.

SOAVE DOC *Veneto, Italy* In the hilly Soave Classico zone near Verona, the Garganega and Trebbiano di Soave grapes can produce ripe, nutty, scented wines. Since 1992, the blend may include 30% Chardonnay, and good examples are definitely on the increase. Soave Superiore has been DOCG for some years, but the top private producers continue to ignore it in protest at the anomalous rules governing the denomination. Best producers: Bertani★, Ca' Rugate★, La Cappuccina★, Coffele★★, Fattori★, Gini★★, Inama★, MASI★, Cecilia Beretta★, PIEROPAN★★, Portinari★, Prà★★, Suavia★★, Tamellini★. See also ANSELMI, RECIOTO DI SOAVE DOCG.

CH. SOCIANDO-MALLET★★ *Haut-Médoc AC, Haut-Médoc, Bordeaux, France* It wasn't classified in 1855, but every single vintage nowadays outshines many properties that were. The wines massively repay 10–20 years' aging, but exhibit classic Bordeaux flavours from as early as 5 years old. Best years: 2007 06 05 04 03 **02 01 00 99 98 96 95 94 90 89 88 86 85**.

SOGRAPE *Portugal* This Portuguese giant revolutionized quality in some of Portugal's most reactionary wine regions. Mateus Rosé is still the company's golden egg, but Sogrape makes good to very good VINHO VERDE (Quinta de Azevedo★★), DOURO (Reserva Tinto★) and ALENTEJO (Vinha do Monte, Herdade do Peso★★). A high-tech winery in DÃO produces Duque de Viseu★ and the Quinta dos Carvalhais range, with promising varietal Encruzado★ (white) and Touriga Nacional (red); Reserva★★ and Único★★★ reds are further steps up. Callabriga★ reds from Douro, Alentejo and Dão are based on Aragonez (Tempranillo), blended with local varieties. Subsidiaries FERREIRA, SANDEMAN and Offley provide top-flight ports. Also owns Finca Flichman in Argentina and Framingham in New Zealand.

SOLAIA★★★ *Tuscany, Italy* One of ANTINORI's SUPER-TUSCANS, sourced, like TIGNANELLO, from the Santa Cristina vineyard. Solaia is a blend of Cabernet Sauvignon, Sangiovese and Cabernet Franc. Intense, with rich fruit and a classic structure, it is not produced in every vintage. Best years: (2008) (07) (06) 04 03 01 **99 98 97 95 94 93 91 90 88 86 85**.

SOMONTANO DO *Aragón, Spain* This region in the foothills of the Pyrenees is encountering some difficulties due to uneven quality, too many indifferent wines and, perhaps, too much success too soon. Reds and rosés from the local grapes (Moristel and Tempranillo) can be light, fresh and flavourful, and international varieties such as Chardonnay and Gewürztraminer can yield promising wines. An interesting development is the rediscovery of the powerful native red grape, Parraleta, and of old-vines Garnacha. Best producers: Otto Bestué, Blecua★★, ENATE★★, Fábregas, Irius★, Lalanne★, Laus★, Pirineos★, VINAS DEL VERO★. Best years: (reds) 2005 **04 03 01 99 98 97 96**.

SONOMA COAST AVA *California, USA* A huge appellation, defined on its western boundary by the Pacific Ocean, that attempts to bring together the coolest regions of SONOMA COUNTY. It encompasses the Sonoma part of CARNEROS and overlaps parts of SONOMA VALLEY and RUSSIAN RIVER. The heart of the appellation are vineyards on the high coastal ridge only a few miles from the Pacific. Intense Chardonnays and Pinot Noirs are the focus. Best producers: DUTTON GOLDFIELD★★, FLOWERS★★, FREESTONE★, HARTFORD FAMILY★★, KISTLER★★, Kosta Browne★, Littorai★★ (Hirsch Pinot Noir★★★), MARCASSIN★★, W H Smith★★, Sonoma Coast Vineyards★★ (Balistreri Vineyard★★★).

SPARKLING WINES OF THE WORLD

Made by the Traditional (Champagne) Method

Although Champagne is still the benchmark for top-class sparkling wines all over the world, the Champagne houses themselves have taken the message to California, Australia and New Zealand via wineries they've established in these regions. However, Champagne-method fizz doesn't necessarily have to feature the traditional Champagne grape varieties (Chardonnay, Pinot Noir and Pinot Meunier), and this allows a host of other places to join the party. Describing a wine as Champagne method is strictly speaking no longer allowed (only original Champagne from France is officially sanctioned to do this), but the use of a phrase like Traditional Method should not distract from the fact that these wines are still painstakingly produced using the complex system of secondary fermentation in the bottle itself.

STYLES OF SPARKLING WINE

France French fizz ranges from the sublime to the near-ridiculous. The best examples have great finesse and include appley Crémant d'Alsace, produced from Pinot Blanc and Pinot Gris, sometimes with a little Chardonnay too; often inexpensive yet eminently drinkable Crémant de Bourgogne, based mainly on Chardonnay; and some stylish examples from the Loire Valley, notably in Saumur and Vouvray. Clairette de Die and Crémant de Limoux in the south confuse the issue by sometimes following their own idiosyncratic method of production, but the result is delicious.

Rest of Europe Franciacorta DOCG is a success story for Italy. Most *metodo classico* sparkling wine is confined to the north, where ripening conditions are closer to those of Champagne, but a few good examples do pop up in unexpected places – Sicily, for instance. Asti, Lambrusco and Prosecco are not Champagne-method wines. In Spain, the Cava wines of Cataluña offer an affordable style for everyday drinking. German Sekt comes in two basic styles: one made from Riesling grapes, the other using Champagne varieties. England is proving naturally suited to growing grapes for sparkling wine.

Australia and New Zealand Australia has a wide range of styles, though there is little overt varietal definition. Blends are still being produced using fruit from many areas, but regional characters are starting to emerge. Chilly Tasmania is the star performer, making some top fizz from local grapes. Red sparklers, notably those made from Shiraz, are an irresistible Australian curiosity with an alcoholic kick. Cool-climate New Zealand is now producing some world-class examples difficult to tell from good Champagne; as in Australia, some have Champagne connections.

USA In California, some magnificent examples are produced – the best ones using grapes from Carneros or the Anderson Valley. Quality has been transformed by the efforts of French Champagne houses. Oregon is also a contender in the sparkling stakes.

South Africa Cap Classique is the local name for the Champagne method. The best are very good and those from the limy soils of Robertson are starting to show particularly well, but too many brands seem to lack the desire to excel. Consistency is a problem; also, high demand means many are released too young.

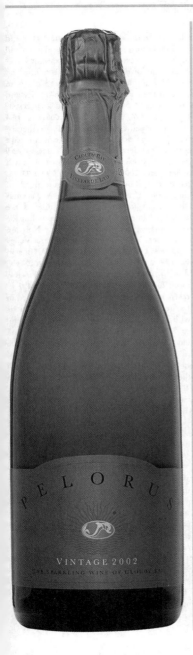

BEST PRODUCERS

Australia *white* BAY OF FIRES (Arras), BROWN BROTHERS, Cope-Williams, DOMAINE CHANDON (Green Point), Freycinet (Radenti), HANGING ROCK, Stefano LUBIANA, PETALUMA (Croser), Pipers Brook (Kreglinger), Taltarni (Clover Hill), Tamar Ridge, YALUMBA (Jansz), Yarrabank, Yellowglen (Perle); *red* Peter LEHMANN (Black Queen), Charles MELTON, PRIMO ESTATE, ROCKFORD, SEPPELT.

Austria BRUNDLMAYER, Schlumberger.

France *Alsace* Ostertag, TURCKHEIM co-op; *Burgundy* Bailly co-op, Louis Bouillot, Lugny co-op, Albert Sounit; *Die* J-C Raspail; *Limoux* SIEUR D'ARQUES; *St-Péray* Chaboud, J-L Thiers; *Saumur* BOUVET-LADUBAY, Gratien & Meyer; *Vouvray* CLOS NAUDIN, HUET.

Germany *Pfalz* Bergdolt, REBHOLZ; *Rheingau* Barth, BREUER, WEGELER; *Rheinhessen* Raumland.

Italy *Franciacorta* BELLAVISTA, CA' DEL BOSCO; *Trento* FERRARI; *Sicily* TASCA D'ALMERITA.

New Zealand CLOUDY BAY (Pelorus), DEUTZ, HUNTER'S, Nautilus, No. 1 Family Estate, PALLISER.

Portugal Caves ALIANCA, Quinta dos Loridos/BACALHÔA, Vértice (Super Reserva).

South Africa Graham BECK, Bob Courage, High Constantia, STEENBERG, Twee Jonge Gezellen, VILLIERA.

Spain *Cava* Can Ràfols dels Caus, CODORNIU, Colet, FREIXENET, Gramona, Parxet, Signat, Agustí Torelló, Dominio de la Vega.

UK BREAKY BOTTOM, CAMEL VALLEY, CHAPEL DOWN, DENBIES, NYETIMBER, RIDGEVIEW.

USA *California* DOMAINE CARNEROS, DOMAINE CHANDON, Gloria Ferrer, HANDLEY, IRON HORSE, J Wine, Laetitia, MUMM NAPA, ROEDERER ESTATE, SCHARFFENBERGER CELLARS, SCHRAMSBERG; *Oregon* ARGYLE.

283

SONOMA COUNTY *California, USA*   Sonoma's vine-growing area is big and sprawling – some 25,500ha (63,000 acres) – with dozens of soil types and mesoclimates, from the fairly warm SONOMA VALLEY and ALEXANDER VALLEY regions to the cool Green Valley and lower RUSSIAN RIVER VALLEY. The best wines are from Chardonnay, Sauvignon Blanc, Cabernet Sauvignon, Pinot Noir and Zinfandel. Often the equal of rival NAPA in quality and originality of flavours. See also CARNEROS, DRY CREEK VALLEY, SONOMA COAST.

SONOMA-CUTRER *Russian River Valley AVA, Sonoma County, USA*   Rich, oaky, popular, but often overhyped Chardonnays. Single-vineyard Les Pierres★★ is the most complex and richest; Cutrer★★ can also have a complexity worth waiting for; Founders Reserve★★ is made in very limited quantities (screwcapped!). Russian River Ranches★ is much improved in recent releases. **Best years:** 2005 04 03 **02 01 00 99 98 97 95**.

SONOMA VALLEY AVA *California, USA*   The oldest wine region north of San Francisco, Sonoma Valley is on the western side of the Mayacamas Mountains, which separate it from NAPA VALLEY. Best varieties are Chardonnay and Zinfandel, with Cabernet and Merlot from hillside sites also good. Some cooler-climate grapes including Pinot Noir are being tried in slightly cooler Bennett Valley, within the Sonoma Valley AVA. **Best producers:** ARROWOOD★★, CHATEAU ST JEAN★, B R Cohn, Fisher★, GUNDLACH-BUNDSCHU★★, KENWOOD★, KUNDE★★, LANDMARK★★, LAUREL GLEN★★, MATANZAS CREEK★★, MOON MOUNTAIN★★, RAVENSWOOD★, St Francis★, Sebastiani★. **Best years:** (Zinfandel) 2005 04 03 **01 00 99 98 97 96 95 94**.

DOM. SORIN *Bandol AC, Provence, France*   Luc Sorin, from CHABLIS, arrived in Provence in 1995. As well as red and rosé BANDOL★, he makes various CÔTES DE PROVENCE wines: white Cuvée Tradition★ is a mouthwatering oak-aged blend of Rolle and Sémillon; Terra Amata★ is crisp pink grapefruit- and cranberry-flavoured rosé. **Best years:** (red Bandol) 2007 06 05 **03 01**.

SOTER VINEYARDS *Willamette Valley AVA, Oregon, USA*   A sage and a scientist, Tony Soter worked in the NAPA VALLEY in the 1980s, and founded Etude Wines in 1982. When he sold the business, he followed his passion for Pinot Noir and moved to Oregon. He planted his first Pinot Noir in 2002. The Mineral Springs Pinot Noir★ is outstanding, with *terroir*-driven flavours showing from a very young site. The Beacon Hill Pinot Noir★ has appealing ripe cherry character. The basic wine is the North Valley Pinot Noir★. Also small amounts of sparkling wine★★. **Best years:** 2008 07 06.

SOUTH AUSTRALIA   Australia's biggest grape-growing state, with some 70,000ha (173,000 acres) of vineyards and almost half the country's total production. Covers many climates and most wine styles, from bulk wines to the very best. Established regions are ADELAIDE HILLS, Adelaide Plains, CLARE, BAROSSA and Eden Valleys, MCLAREN VALE, Langhorne Creek, COONAWARRA, PADTHAWAY and RIVERLAND. Newer regions creating excitement include Mount Benson and Wrattonbully, both in the LIMESTONE COAST zone.

SOUTH-WEST FRANCE   Away from BORDEAUX, South-West France has many lesser-known, less expensive ACs, VDQS and vins de pays, over 10 *départements* from the Massif Central to the Pyrenees. Bordeaux grapes (Cabernet Sauvignon, Merlot and Cabernet Franc for reds; Sauvignon Blanc, Sémillon and Muscadelle for whites) are common, but the further you get from Bordeaux the more interesting are local varieties such as Tannat (in

MADIRAN), Gros and Petit Manseng (in Gascony and JURANCON) and Mauzac (in GAILLAC). See also BERGERAC, BUZET, CAHORS, CÔTES DE DURAS, CÔTES DE GASCOGNE, CÔTES DU MARMANDAIS, FRONTON, IROULEGUY, MONBAZILLAC, MONTRAVEL, PACHERENC DU VIC-BILH, PECHARMANT, TURSAN.

SPÄTBURGUNDER See PINOT NOIR.

SPICE ROUTE WINE COMPANY *Swartland WO, South Africa* Owned by Charles Back of FAIRVIEW. Ripe, well-oaked Flagship Syrah★★ and polished, Shiraz-based Malabar★★ now head the pack. Whites showing promise include rich, barrel-fermented Chenin Blanc★, fresh, flavoursome Viognier and pure yet restrained Sauvignon Blanc★ from Darling. Best years: (premium reds) 2006 **05 04 03 02 01 00.**

SPOTTSWOODE *Napa Valley AVA, California, USA* Replanted in the mid-1990s, this beautifully situated 16ha (40-acre) vineyard west of St Helena has not missed a beat since the winery opened in 1982. Deep, blackberry- and cherry-fruited Cabernet Sauvignon★★★ is wonderful to drink early, but is best at 5–10 years. Sauvignon Blanc★★ (blended with a little Semillon and barrel fermented) is a sophisticated treat. Best years: (Cabernet) 2006 05 **04 03 02 01 00 99 98 97 96 95 94 91.**

SPRINGFIELD ESTATE *Robertson WO, South Africa* Abrie Bruwer's approach is strictly hands-off in his efforts to capture his vineyard's *terroir*. Méthode Ancienne Chardonnay★ is barrel fermented with vineyard yeasts and bottled without any fining or filtration. Not every vintage makes it! Cabernet Sauvignon is also made as Méthode Ancienne★. The unwooded Wild Yeast Chardonnay★ and flinty, lively Life from Stone Sauvignon Blanc★★ are also notably expressive. The Cabernet Franc-Merlot-based Work of Time★ is the farm's first blend. Best years: (Sauvignon Blanc) 2008 **07 06 05.**

STAGS LEAP DISTRICT AVA *Napa County, California, USA* One of California's best-defined appellations. Located in south-eastern NAPA VALLEY, it is cooler than OAKVILLE or RUTHERFORD to the north, and the red wines have a recognizably mellow, balanced character. A little Sauvignon Blanc and Chardonnay are grown, but the true stars are Cabernet Sauvignon and Merlot. Best producers: CHIMNEY ROCK★★, Cliff Lede★, CLOS DU VAL★★, HARTWELL★★, PINE RIDGE★★, SHAFER★★★, SILVERADO★★, Robert Sinskey★★, STAG'S LEAP WINE CELLARS★★, Stags' Leap Winery★.

STAG'S LEAP WINE CELLARS *Stags Leap District AVA, California, USA* The winery rose to fame when its Cabernet Sauvignon came first at the famous Paris tasting of 1976. Cabernet Sauvignon★★ can be stunning, particularly the SLV★★★ from estate vineyards and the Fay★★; the Cask 23 Cabernet Sauvignon★★ can be very good, but is overhyped. After a dip in quality, recent vintages are back on form. A lot of work has gone into the Chardonnay★ (Arcadia Vineyard★★) and the style is one of NAPA's more successful. Sauvignon Blanc★ (Rancho Chimiles★★) is intensely flavoured, with brisk acidity. Founder Warren Winiarski sold the property in 2007 to CHATEAU STE MICHELLE and ANTINORI of Italy. Best years: (Cabernet) 2005 04 03 02 **01 00 99 98 97 96 95 94 91 90 86.**

STANLAKE PARK *Berkshire, England* Formerly known as Valley Vineyards, this 10ha (25-acre) vineyard has, over the past 25 years, produced many stunning wines. The range includes several varietal whites and fragrant Regatta blend; Ruscombe red and occasional barrel-aged Pinot Noir; sparkling Heritage Brut (from Seyval Blanc and other grapes) and Stanlake Park★ (Pinot Noir-Chardonnay).

SUPER-TUSCANS

Tuscany, Italy

The term 'Super-Tuscans', first used by English and American writers, has been adopted by Italians themselves to describe the new-style red wines of Tuscany. The 1970s and 80s were a time when enormous strides were being made in Bordeaux, Australia and California, yet these changes threatened to bypass Italy completely because of its restrictive wine laws. A group of winemakers, led by Piero Antinori – who created the inspirational Tignanello and Solaia from vineyards within the Chianti Classico DOCG – abandoned tradition to put their best efforts and best grapes into creative wines styled for modern tastes.

Old large oak casks were replaced with French barriques, while Cabernet Sauvignon and other trendy varieties, such as Cabernet Franc, Merlot and Syrah, were planted alongside Sangiovese in vineyards that emerged with sudden grandeur as crus. Since the DOC specifically forbade such innovations, producers were forced to label their wines as plain Vino da Tavola. The 'Super-Tuscan' Vino da Tavolas, as they were quickly dubbed, were a phenomenal success: brilliant in flavour with an approachable, upfront style. Some found it hard to believe that table wines with no official credentials could outrank DOCG Chianti. A single mouthful was usually enough to convince them.

However, after 9/11 the market for most of the less established Super-Tuscans collapsed, since when there has been more interest in international markets in established DOC(G)s such as Brunello di Montalcino and Chianti Classico Riserva. The current economic crisis will probably prove equally negative as these wines are often perceived to be overpriced.

WINE STYLES

Sangiovese, the Cabernets and Merlot are the basis for most Super-Tuscans, usually in a blend. All also appear varietally, with Sangiovese forming the largest group of top-quality varietal Super-Tuscans. To some Sangiovese-based wines, a small percentage of other native varieties such as Colorino, Canaiolo or Malvasia Nera may be added. Syrah is of growing importance, mostly varietally, but also in innovative new blends such as Argiano's Solengo, where it features along with Cabernet and Merlot. Super-Tuscan wines also show considerable differences in vinification and aging. Top wines are invariably based on ripe, concentrated grapes from a site with special attributes.

CLASSIFICATIONS

A law passed in 1992 has finally brought the Super-Tuscans into line with official classifications. Sassicaia now has its own DOC under Bolgheri. Chianti Classico's now independent DOCG could cover many a Sangiovese-based Super-Tuscan, but the majority are currently sold under the region-wide IGT Toscana alongside wines made from international varieties. There are also 3 sub-regional IGTs, but only a few producers use these.

See also BOLGHERI, CHIANTI CLASSICO, SASSICAIA, SOLAIA, TIGNANELLO; and individual producers.

BEST YEARS

(2008) (07) **06 04 03 01 00 99 98 97 95**

BEST PRODUCERS

Sangiovese and other Tuscan varieties Badia a Coltibuono (Sangioveto), BOSCARELLI, CASTELLARE (I Sodi di San Niccolò), FELSINA (Fontalloro), FONTODI (Flaccianello della Pieve), ISOLE E OLENA (Cepparello), Lilliano (Anagallis), MONTEVERTINE (Le Pergole Torte), Paneretta (Quattrocentenario, Terrine), Poggio Scalette (Il Carbonaione), Poggiopiano (Rosso di Sera), Querceto (La Corte), RIECINE (La Gioia), San Giusto a Rentennano (Percarlo), VOLPAIA (Coltassala).

Sangiovese-Cabernet and Sangiovese-Merlot blends BANFI (Summus), Colombaio di Cencio (Il Futuro), FONTERUTOLI (Siepi), Gagliole, Montepeloso (Nardo), QUERCIABELLA (Camartina), Castello dei RAMPOLLA (Sammarco), RICASOLI (Casalferro), Sette Ponti (Oreno), TIGNANELLO.

Cabernet Col d'Orcia (Olmaia), Fossi (Sassoforte), ISOLE E OLENA (Collezione), Le MACCHIOLE (Paléo Rosso), Nozzole (Il Pareto), Castello dei RAMPOLLA (Vigna d'Alceo), SOLAIA.

Merlot Castello di AMA (L'Apparita), Le MACCHIOLE (Messorio), ORNELLAIA (Masseto), Petrolo (Galatrona), TUA RITA (Redigaffi).

Cabernet-Merlot blends ANTINORI (Guado al Tasso), Argiano (Solengo), BANFI (Excelsus), Capezzana (Ghiaie della Furba), ORNELLAIA (Ornellaia), Poggio al Sole (Seraselva), POLIZIANO (Le Stanze), Le Pupille (Saffredi), Trinoro, TUA RITA (Giusto di Notri).

STEELE *Lake County, California, USA* Owner/winemaker Jed Steele is a master blender. He sources grapes from all over California and Washington and shapes them into exciting wines, usually featuring vivid fruit with supple mouthfeel. He also offers single-vineyard wines and has, in current release, 4–6 Chardonnays, most ★★. His Zinfandels★★ and Pinot Noirs★★ (CARNEROS, SANTA MARIA VALLEY) are usually very good. Shooting Star label provides remarkable value in a ready-to-drink style.

STEENBERG *Constantia WO, South Africa* The oldest farm in CONSTANTIA produces some of South Africa's best and most consistent Sauvignon Blanc: the smoky, flinty Reserve★★ is brilliantly tangy, but it also ages well; straight Sauvignon★★ is pure upfront fruit. Barrel-fermented Semillon★★ (occasionally pushing ★★★) matches them in quality, while Magna Carta★★, the new Sauvignon Blanc-Semillon blend, will be complex and thrilling after a few years' aging. Reds include minty and nuanced Merlot★★; Catharina★★, a blend featuring Cabernet and Merlot, with Shiraz and an occasional dab of Nebbiolo; and exciting, smoky Shiraz★★. Fast-improving Steenberg 1682 Brut★ Cap Classique fizz is elegant and biscuity. Best years: (whites) 2008 **07 06 05 04 03 02 01**

STEIERMARK *Austria* This 3280ha (8010-acre) region (Styria in English) in south-east Austria is divided into 3 areas: Süd-Oststeiermark, Südsteiermark and Weststeiermark. Technically it is the warmest of the Austrian wine regions, but the best vineyards are in cool, high-altitude sites. The tastiest wines are Morillon (unoaked Chardonnay, though oak is catching on) Sauvignon Blanc and Gelber Muskateller (Muscat). Best producers: Gross★★ Lackner-Tinnacher★, POLZ★★, E Sabathi★, Sattlerhof★, Walter Skoff★, TEMENT★★ Winkler-Hermaden★, Wohlmuth★.

STELLENBOSCH WO *South Africa* This district boasts the greatest concentration of wineries in the Cape, though is only third in vineyard area; the vineyards straddle valley floors and stretch up the many mountain slopes. Climates and soils are as diverse as wine styles; smaller units of origin – wards – are now being demarcated to more accurately reflect this diversity. The renowned reds are matched by some excellent Sauvignon Blanc and Chardonnay, as well as modern Chenin Blanc and Semillon. Best producers: BEYERSKLOOF★, De Toren★, DE TRAFFORD★★ DeWaal★, Dornier★, Neil ELLIS★★, Ernie ELS★, Ken Forrester★, The Foundry★★, GRANGEHURST★★, HARTENBERG★, JORDAN★★, Kaapzicht★ KANONKOP★, Laibach★, L'AVENIR★, Le Riche★, MEERLUST★, Meinert★ MORGENHOF★, Morgenster★, MULDERBOSCH★, Neethlingshof★, Overgaauw★ Quoin Rock★, RUST EN VREDE★, RUSTENBERG★★, SAXENBURG★★, SIMONSIG★ Stellenzicht★, Sterhuis★, THELEMA★★, Tokara★, VERGELEGEN★★, VILLIERA★ WARWICK★, Waterford★★, Waterkloof (Circumstance★).

STERLING VINEYARDS *Napa Valley AVA, California, USA* Merlot is the focus here, led by Three Palms★★ and Reserve★★, both packed with ripe dense fruit. Reserve Cabernet is now ★★. The Winery Lake Chardonnay★ delivers elegant honey and apple fruit. Also Winery Lake Pinot Noir★. Best years: (Merlot) 2005 **02 01 00 99 97 96 94.**

STONIER *Mornington Peninsula, Victoria, Australia* The peninsula's biggest winery and one of its best, though Lion Nathan, via PETALUMA, now has controlling interest. KBS Vineyard★★ and Reserve Chardonnay★★ and Windmill Vineyard★★ and Reserve Pinot Noir★★ are usually outstanding, and there are fine standard bottlings in warm vintages.

STONY HILL *Napa Valley AVA, California USA* Founded by Fred and Eleanor McCrea in 1953, the first winery in NAPA VALLEY after Prohibition, this tiny rock-strewn hillside produces sublime, ageworthy Chardonnays★★, dry Rieslings★ and Gewurztraminers. The McCreas' son Peter and his wife Willinda now operate the property with long-time winemaker Mike Chelini. Followers swear that the Chardonnays improve for decades.

STONYRIDGE *Waiheke Island, Auckland, North Island, New Zealand* The leading winery on WAIHEKE ISLAND, Stonyridge specializes in reds made from Cabernet Sauvignon, Merlot, Petit Verdot, Malbec and Cabernet Franc. The top label, Larose★★★, is a remarkably BORDEAUX-like red of real intensity. Best years: (Larose) 2007 **06 05 04 02 00 99**.

CH. SUDUIRAUT★★ *Sauternes AC, 1er Cru Classé, Bordeaux, France* Together with RIEUSSEC, Suduiraut is regarded as a close runner-up to d'YQUEM. Although the wines are delicious at only a few years old, the richness and excitement increase enormously after a decade or so. Seemed to be under-performing in the 1980s and mid-90s but now owned by AXA (see PICHON-LONGUEVILLE) and back on irresistible song. Best years: 2007 06 05 **04 03 02 01 99 98 97 96 95 90 89 86 82**.

SUMAC RIDGE *Okanagan Valley VQA, British Columbia, Canada* Excellent Sauvignon Blanc★ and Gewürztraminer Reserve★, fine Pinot Blanc and one of Canada's best CHAMPAGNE-method fizzes, Steller's Jay Brut★. Top reds include Cabernet Sauvignon, Cabernet Franc, Merlot, Pinot Noir and Meritage★. Owned by Constellation Brands.

SUNTORY *Japan* Red Tomi and sweet white Noble d'Or (made from botrytized grapes) are top brands for wine made exclusively from grapes grown in Japan. Classic varieties – Cabernets Sauvignon and Franc, Chardonnay, Sémillon and Sauvignon – are also having success.

SUPER-TUSCANS See pages 286–7.

SWAN DISTRICT *Western Australia* The original WESTERN AUSTRALIA wine region, spread along the hot, fertile silty flats of Perth's Swan River. It used to specialize in fortified wines, but SOUTH AUSTRALIA and north-east VICTORIA do them better. New-wave whites and reds are fresh and generous. Best producers: Paul Conti, Faber★, HOUGHTON★, John Kosovich, Lamont★, Oakover, SANDALFORD★, Sittella, Upper Reach.

JOSEPH SWAN VINEYARDS *Russian River Valley AVA, California, USA* The late Joseph Swan made legendary Zinfandel in the 1970s and was one of the first to age Zinfandel★★ in French oak. In the 80s he turned to Pinot Noir★★ which is now probably the winery's best offering. Best years: (Zinfandel) 2005 **02 01 99 98 97 96 95**.

SYRAH See pages 290–1.

LA TÂCHE AC★★★ *Grand Cru, Côte de Nuits, Burgundy, France* Along with la ROMANEE and la ROMANEE-CONTI, the greatest of the great VOSNE-ROMANEE Grands Crus, owned by Dom. de la ROMANEE-CONTI. The wine provides layer on layer of flavours; keep it for 10 years or you'll only experience a fraction of the pleasure you paid big money for. Best years: (2008) 07 06 05 03 02 01 **00 99 98 97 96 95 93 90 89 88 85 78**.

TAHBILK *Goulburn Valley, Central Victoria, Australia* Wonderfully old-fashioned family company making traditionally big, gumleafy/minty reds, matured largely in old wood. 1860 Vines Shiraz★ and the Reserve reds – now Eric Stevens Purbrick Shiraz and Eric Stevens Purbrick Cabernet – are full of character, even if they need years of cellaring. White Marsanne★★ is rich and perfumed, as is a floral-scented Viognier★. Best years: (Eric Stevens Purbrick Shiraz) (2007) (06) (05) 04 03 02 01 **00 99 98 97 96 94**.

SYRAH/SHIRAZ

Syrah's popularity is rising fast and it now produces world-class wines in France, in Australia – where as Shiraz it produces some of the New World's most remarkable reds – and in California and possibly South Africa, Argentina and Chile too. And wherever it appears it trumpets a proud and wilful personality based on loads of flavour and unmistakable originality.

When the late-ripening Syrah grape is grown in the coolest, most marginal areas for full ripening, such as Côte-Rôtie, it is capable of producing very classy, elegant wines. However, producers must ensure low yields if they are to produce high-quality wines. Syrah's heartland - Hermitage and Côte-Rôtie in the northern Rhône Valley – comprises a mere 365ha (900 acres) of steeply terraced, often granite, vineyards producing barely enough wine to spread the word to new drinkers. This may be one reason for its relatively slow uptake by growers in other countries, who simply had no idea as to what kind of flavour the Syrah grape produced, so didn't copy it. But the situation is rapidly changing and Syrah's popularity in both the warm and the reasonably cool wine regions of the world becomes more evident with every vintage.

WINE STYLES

French Syrah The flavours of Syrah are most individual, but with modern vineyard practices and winemaking techniques they are far less daunting than they used to be. Traditional Syrah had a savage, almost coarse, throaty roar of a flavour. And from the very low-yielding Hermitage vineyards, the small grapes often showed a bitter tannic quality. But better selections of clones in the vineyard and improved winemaking have revealed Syrah with a majestic depth of fruit – all blackberry and damson, loganberry and plum – some quite strong tannin, occasionally bacon smoke, but also a warm creamy aftertaste, and promise of chocolate and occasionally a scent of violets. It is these characteristics that have made Syrah popular throughout the south of France as an 'improving' variety for its rather traditional, high-alcohol red wines.

Australian Shiraz Australia's most widely planted red variety has become, in many respects, its premium varietal. Shiraz gives spectacularly good results when taken seriously – especially in the Barossa, Clare, Eden Valley and McLaren Vale regions of South Australia. An increasingly diverse range of high-quality examples is also coming from Victoria's high country vineyards, more traditional examples from New South Wales' Hunter Valley, and exciting, more restrained styles from the Great Southern, Grampians, Pyrenees and Adelaide Hills regions, as well as patches of Canberra and Queensland. Just about everywhere, really. Flavours are rich, intense, thick sweet fruit coated with chocolate, and seasoned with leather, herbs and spice or fragrant, floral and flowing with damson and blackberry fruit.

Other regions In California and Washington State producers are turning out superb Rhône-style blends as well as varietal Syrah modelled closely on Côte-Rôtie or Hermitage. In South Africa Syrah ranks fourth in vineyard area and, as in Chile, more exciting varietal wines and blends appear every vintage. New Zealand's offerings are thrillingly different. Italy (especially Tuscany and Sicily, often in a blend with Nero d'Avola), Spain, Portugal and Argentina are beginning to shine, and even Switzerland and North Africa are having a go.

BEST PRODUCERS

France

Rhône ALLEMAND, F Balthazar, G Barge, A Belle, CHAPOUTIER, CHAVE, Y Chave, Chêne, CLAPE, Clusel-Roch, COLOMBO, Courbis, COURSODON, CUILLERON, E Darnaud, DELAS, Duclaux, E & J Durand, B Faurie, L Fayolle, Gaillard, J-M Gérin, Gonon, GRAILLOT, Gripa, GUIGAL, JAMET, P Jasmin, S Ogier, V Paris, ROSTAING, M Sorrel, Tardieu-Laurent, F Villard; *Languedoc* Jean-Michel ALQUIER, ESTANILLES, GAUBY, PEYRE ROSE.

Other European Syrah

Italy (Piedmont) Bertelli; *(Tuscany)* D'ALESSANDRO, FONTODI, Fossi, ISOLE E OLENA, Le MACCHIOLE, Poggio al Sole; *(Sicily)* Cottanera, PLANETA. *Spain* Albet i Noya, Castaño, Casa Castillo, Finca Sandoval, Enrique Mendoza, Pago del Ama.

New World Syrah/Shiraz

Australia Tim ADAMS, BAROSSA VALLEY ESTATE, Jim BARRY, BEST'S, Rolf BINDER, BROKENWOOD, Grant Burge, CLARENDON HILLS, CLONAKILLA, Craiglee, Dalwhinnie, D'ARENBERG, DE BORTOLI, Dutschke, John DUVAL, FOX CREEK, GLAETZER, HARDYS (Eileen Hardy), Henry's Drive, HENSCHKE, Hewitson, HOWARD PARK (Scotsdale), Jasper Hill, Peter LEHMANN, MAJELLA, Charles MELTON, MOUNT LANGI GHIRAN, S C PANNELL, PENFOLDS, PLANTAGENET, PONDALOWIE, ROCKFORD, SEPPELT (St Peters), SHAW & SMITH, TORBRECK, TURKEY FLAT, TYRRELL'S, WENDOUREE, The Willows, WIRRA WIRRA (RSW), YALUMBA, Yering Station (Reserve), Zema.

New Zealand Bilancia, CRAGGY RANGE, DRY RIVER, Esk Valley, FROMM, Murdoch James, Passage Rock, Stonecroft, Te Awa, TE MATA, TRINITY HILL, Vidal, VILLA MARIA.

South Africa BOEKENHOUTSKLOOF, DE TRAFFORD, FAIRVIEW, The Foundry, HARTENBERG, SADIE FAMILY, SAXENBURG, SPICE ROUTE, STEENBERG, Stellenzicht.

USA (California) ALBAN, ARAUJO, Cline, DEHLINGER, DUTTON GOLDFIELD, Edmunds St John, Havens, Jade Mountain, Lewis, LYNMAR, Andrew MURRAY, Pax, QUPE, Swanson, Sean Thackrey, Truchard.

Chile Falernia, Kingston, Loma Larga, MATETIC, MONTES, Tabalí/SAN PEDRO, Tamaya.

CAVE DE TAIN *Hermitage, Rhône Valley, France* Progressive co-op offering good-value wines from the northern Rhône. Reasonably high quality, despite annual production of 500,000 cases and rather dull basic 'supermarket' cuvées. Impressive CROZES-HERMITAGE les Hauts du Fief★, fine CORNAS★ and both red and white ST-JOSEPH★ and HERMITAGE★★. Topping the range are an old-vine red Hermitage Gambert de Loche★★ and a rich Vin de Paille★★ from Marsanne. Also still and sparkling ST-PERAY★. Best years: (top reds) 2007 **06** 05 **04** 03 01 **00** 99 98 97 95.

TAITTINGER *Champagne AC, Champagne, France* The top wine, Comtes de Champagne Blanc de Blancs★★★, can be memorable for its creamy, foaming pleasures; the Comtes de Champagne rosé★★ is elegant and oozing class. Prélude is an attractive, fuller-bodied non-vintage style made from 4 Grands Crus and aged for 4 years before release. Non-vintage Les Folies de la Marquetterie is from a steeply sloping single vineyard. Best years: (2003) 02 00 **99** 98 96 **95** 90 89 88 85 82.

CH. TALBOT★ *St-Julien AC, 4ème Cru Classé, Haut-Médoc, Bordeaux, France* Chunky, soft-centred but sturdy, capable of aging well for 10–20 years and increasingly good this century. Also a tasty white wine, Caillou Blanc de Talbot★. Second wine: Connétable de Talbot. Best years: 2007 06 05 04 **03** 02 01 **00** 99 98 96 95 90 89 88 86 85.

TALBOTT *Monterey County, California, USA* This estate is known for its Chardonnays from vineyards in the Santa Lucia Highlands in MONTEREY COUNTY. Sleepy Hollow Vineyard★★, Cuvée Cynthia★★ and Diamond T Estate★★ are all packed with ripe tropical fruit and ample oak. Kali Hart Chardonnay★ gives a taste of the style on a budget. Also Chardonnay and Pinot Noir under the Logan label.

TAPANAPPA *Adelaide Hills, South Australia* The partnership of the families of Brian Croser (formerly of PETALUMA), Arnould d'Hautefeuille (BOLLINGER) and Jean-Michel Cazes (LYNCH-BAGES) explores the notion of *terroir* by following Croser's belief in the importance of 'distinguished sites'. Sublime, complex and mouthwatering Chardonnay from the Croser family's Tiers Vineyard★★ in the ADELAIDE HILLS; one of the country's most elegant Cabernet-Shiraz blends from the mature Whalebone Vineyard★★ at Wrattonbully; and Pinot Noir from the Foggy Hill Vineyard★ on the maritime Southern Fleurieu Peninsula.

DOM. DU TARIQUET *Vin de Pays des Côtes de Gascogne, South-West France* On their huge 900ha (2,200-acre) property the Grassa family, innovative CÔTES DE GASCOGNE producers, have transformed Gascony's thin raw whites into some of the snappiest, fruitiest wines in France. Also make oak-aged★ and late-harvest★ styles, and Domaine la Hitaire whites.

TARRAWARRA *Yarra Valley, Victoria, Australia* Founder Marc Besen wanted to make a MONTRACHET, and hang the expense. It's a long haul, but the winemakers are doing well: Chardonnay★★ is deep and multi-faceted. Pinot Noir★★ has almost CÔTE DE NUITS flavour and concentration. Tin Cows is a less pricey brand for both these grapes, plus Shiraz and Merlot. Best years: (Pinot Noir) (2008) 06 05 **04** 03 02 01 **99** 98 97 96 94 92.

TASCA D'ALMERITA *Sicily, Italy* This estate in the highlands of central SICILY makes some of southern Italy's best wines. Native grape varieties give excellent Rosso del Conte★★ (based on Nero d'Avola) and white Nozze d'Oro★ (based on Inzolia), but there are also Chardonnay★★ and Cabernet Sauvignon★★ of extraordinary intensity and elegance. Almerita Brut★ (Chardonnay) is a fine CHAMPAGNE-method sparkler. Relatively simple Regaleali Bianco and Rosato are good value.

TASMANIA *Australia* Tasmania may be a minor state viticulturally, with only 1200ha (2965 acres) of vines, but the island has a diverse range of mesoclimates and sub-regions. The generally cool climate has always attracted seekers of greatness in Pinot Noir and Chardonnay, and good results are becoming more consistent. Riesling, Gewürztraminer and Pinot Gris perform well, but the real star is fabulous premium fizz. Best producers: Apsley Gorge, BAY OF FIRES★★, Bream Creek, Domaine A, Freycinet★★, Frogmore Creek★, Heemskerk★, Stefano LUBIANA★, Moorilla★, Pipers Brook★, Pirie Estate, Pressing Matters, Providence, Stoney Rise, Tamar Ridge★. Best years: (Pinot Noir) 2007 06 05 03 02 01 00 99 98 97 95 94.

TAURASI DOCG *Campania, Italy* MASTROBERARDINO created Taurasi's reputation; now the great potential of the Aglianico grape is being exploited by others, both within this DOCG and elsewhere in CAMPANIA. Drink at 5–10 years. Best producers: A Caggiano★★, Feudi di San Gregorio★★, MASTROBERARDINO★★, S Molettieri★, Struzziero, Terredora di Paolo★. Best years: (2008) 04 **03 01 00 98 97**.

TAVEL AC *Rhône Valley, France* Rosé from north-west of Avignon, in two styles: aromatic-aperitif or chunky and alcoholic. The latter style is best with food, including spiced Asian cuisine. Grenache and Cinsaut are the main grapes. Best producers: Aquéria★, la Forcadière★, Genestière★, GUIGAL, Lafond Roc-Épine★, de Manissy, Montézargues★★, la Mordorée★★, Vignerons de Tavel, Trinquevedel★.

TAYLOR *Port DOC, Douro, Portugal* The aristocrat of the PORT industry, over 300 years old and still going strong. Now part of the Fladgate Partnership, along with FONSECA and CROFT. Its Vintage★★★ (sold as Taylor Fladgate in the USA) is superb; Quinta de Vargellas★★ is an elegant, cedary, single-quinta vintage port made in the best of the 'off-vintages'. Quinta de Terra Feita★★, the other main component of Taylor's Vintage, is also often released as a single-quinta. Taylor's 20-year-old★★ is a very fine aged tawny. First Estate is a successful premium ruby. Best years: (Vintage) **2003 00 97 94 92 85 83 80 77 75 70 66 63 60 55 48 45 27**; (Vargellas) 2005 04 **01 99 98 96 95 91 88 87 86 82 78 67 64 61**.

TE MATA *Hawkes Bay, North Island, New Zealand* HAWKES BAY's glamour winery, best known for its reds, Coleraine★★ and Awatea★★, both based on Cabernet Sauvignon with varying proportions of Merlot and Cabernet Franc. Also delicious toasty Elston Chardonnay★. Exceptional vintages of all 3 wines might be aged for 5–10 years. Also scented, peppery, elegant Bullnose Syrah★★ and trailblazing Woodthorpe Viognier★. Best years: (Coleraine) (2007) 06 **05 04 02 00**.

TEMENT *Südsteiermark, Austria* Austria's best Sauvignon Blanc★★ (single-site Zieregg★★★) and Morillon (Chardonnay)★★. Both varieties are fermented and aged in oak, giving power, depth and subtle oak character. The Gelber Muskatellers are unusually racy – perfect aperitif wines. Red Arachon★★ is a joint venture with FX PICHLER and Szemes in BURGENLAND. Best years: (Morillon, Zieregg) (2008) 07 06 **05 04 03 02**.

TEMPRANILLO Spain's best native red grape can make wonderful wine with wild strawberry and spicy, tobaccoey flavours. It is important in RIOJA, PENEDES (as Ull de Llebre), RIBERA DEL DUERO (as Tinto Fino or Tinta del País), La MANCHA and VALDEPENAS (as Cencibel), TORO (as Tinta de Toro), NAVARRA, SOMONTANO and UTIEL-REQUENA. In Portugal it is found in the ALENTEJO (as Aragonez) and in the DOURO, DAO and ESTREMADURA (as

Tinta Roriz). Wines can be deliciously fruity for drinking young, but Tempranillo also matures well, and its flavours blend happily with oak. It is now being taken more seriously in Argentina, and new plantings have been made in California, Oregon, Washington (CAYUSE), Australia, New Zealand and South Africa.

TEROLDEGO ROTALIANO DOC *Trentino-Alto Adige, Italy* Teroldego is a TRENTINO grape variety, producing mainly deep-coloured, leafy, blackberry-flavoured wine from gravel soils of the Rotaliano plain. Best producers: Barone de Cles★, M Donati★, Dorigati★, Endrizzi★, FORADORI★★, Conti Martini★, Mezzacorona (Riserva★), Cantina Rotaliana★, A & R Zeni★. Best years: (2008) (07) 06 **04 03 01 00 99 97**.

TERRAS DO SADO *Setúbal Peninsula, Portugal* Warm, maritime area south of Lisbon. Vinho Regional with some decent whites and good reds; the best reds are from old Castelão vines, often under the Palmela DOC. SETÚBAL produces sweet fortified wine. Best producers: (reds) Caves ALIANCA (Palmela Particular★), BACALHÔA VINHOS DE PORTUGAL★★, Herdade da Comporta, D F J VINHOS★, Ermelinda Freitas★, José Maria da FONSECA★★, Hero do Castanheiro, Pegões co-op★, Pegos Claros★, Soberanas★. Best years: 2008 07 **05 04 03 01 00 99 97 96 95**.

TERRAZAS DE LOS ANDES *Mendoza, Argentina* Offshoot of the LVMH empire, and a terrific source of reds from high-altitude vineyards around LUJÁN DE CUYO. Top reds are Afincado★, Malbec★★ and Cabernet Sauvignon★★, heading for ★★★. A joint venture with CHEVAL BLANC of ST-EMILION has yielded Cheval des Andes★★★, a stunning Cabernet Sauvignon-Malbec blend.

CASTELLO DEL TERRICCIO *Tuscany, Italy* Estate in the Pisan hills south of Livorno. Changes in philosophy seem to have deprived top red Lupicaia★★ (Cabernet-Merlot) and less pricey Tassinaia★ (Sangiovese-Cabernet-Merlot) of much of their exciting, scented, potentially ★★★ personality. Rondinaia (Chardonnay)★★ and Con Vento (Sauvignon Blanc)★ are the most interesting whites. Capannino is an inexpensive red. Best years: (Lupicaia) (2008) 06 **04 03 01 00 98 97**.

TERTRE-RÔTEBOEUF★★ *St-Émilion Grand Cru AC, Bordeaux, France* ST-EMILION's most exceptional unclassified estate. The richly seductive Merlot-based wines sell at the same price as the Premiers Grands Crus Classés – and so they should. Same ownership as the outstanding ROC DE CAMBES. Best years: 2007 06 05 04 **03 02 01 00 99 98 97 96 95 94 90 89 88**.

TEXAS *USA* Texas has enjoyed the tremendous wine industry growth that has hit the USA this decade, with the number of wineries soaring to 163. The state has 8 AVAs, with the Texas High Plains the most significant. Mediterranean grapes such as Grenache, Tempranillo, Syrah and Sangiovese have risen in favour over the traditional Cabernets and Chardonnay. Thunderstorms are capable of destroying entire crops in minutes. Best producers: Becker, Fall Creek, Flat Creek, Llano Estacado, McPherson, Messina Hof.

THELEMA *Stellenbosch WO, South Africa* This mountainside farm has been among the top Cape wineries for over 20 years: Gyles Webb's meticulous attention to detail results in a consistently good range. A pair of Cabernet Sauvignons – blackcurranty regular★★ and self-descriptive The Mint★★ – ripe fleshy Merlot★ (Reserve★★), spicy, accessible Shiraz★, barrel fermented Chardonnay★★, vibrant Sauvignon Blanc★★ and citrus Riesling★ are among the leaders. Also exciting ELGIN Sauvignon★. Best years: (Cabernet Sauvignon) (2007) 06 05 04 03 **01 00** 99 98 97; (Chardonnay) 2008 07 **06 05 04 03 02 01 00**.

THERMENREGION *Niederösterreich, Austria* Warm, 2330ha (5760-acre) region, south of Vienna, taking its name from the spa towns of Baden and Bad Vöslau. The village of Gumpoldskirchen, near Vienna, has rich and sometimes sweet white wines. The red wine area around Baden produces improving Pinot Noir and Cabernet. Best producers: Alphart, Biegler, Fischer★, Johanneshof★, Schellmann, Stadlmann★, Zierer. Best years: (reds) (2007) 06 **05 04 03 02**.

THIRTY BENCH *Niagara Peninsula VQA, Ontario, Canada* A collaboration of 3 winemakers, Thirty Bench is known for its excellent Rieslings★, very good BORDEAUX-style red blends★ and a fine barrel-fermented Chardonnay★.

THOMAS *Hunter Valley, New South Wales, Australia* Andrew Thomas produces exemplary Semillon and Shiraz. Braemore Vineyard Semillon★★ is a traditional, ageworthy HUNTER white, while the OC Semillon★ is a delicious early-drinking style. Kiss Vineyard Shiraz★★, from old vines, is ripe, powerful, complex and velvety.

THREE CHOIRS *Gloucestershire, England* Martin Fowke makes a large range of wines from 30ha (74 acres) of vines, plus bought-in grapes. Bacchus★ and Sieggerebe★ varietals are fragrant and delightful, reds are some of England's best, plus sparkling Classic Cuvée★ (Seyval Blanc-Pinot Noir). Also occasional Late Harvest dessert wine.

TICINO *Switzerland* Italian-speaking Swiss canton. Eighty per cent of production here is Merlot, usually soft and gluggable, but sometimes more serious with some oak barrel-aging. Best producers: Brivio, Delea★, Gialdi, Huber★, Werner Stucky★, Tamborini, Terreni alla Maggia★, Valsangiacomo, Christian Zündel★. Best years: (2008) 07 06 **05 04 03 02 01**.

TIEFENBRUNNER *Alto Adige DOC, Trentino-Alto Adige, Italy* Herbert Tiefenbrunner began his career at this castle (Schloss Turmhof) as a teenager in 1943. In his 80s, he still helps son Christof in the winery, producing 20-plus wine styles, mostly under the ALTO ADIGE DOC. The focus is on purity of fruit and varietal character, mainly among whites such as Chardonnay Linticlarus★★ and Müller-Thurgau Feldmarschall★★ which, at 1,000m (3280ft), is too high to qualify as DOC under Italy's relentlessly silly laws. Best years: (Feldmarschall) (2008) 07 **06 04 03 01 00 99 98 97**.

TIGNANELLO★★ *Tuscany, Italy* In the early 1970s, Piero ANTINORI employed the almost unheard-of practice of aging in small French oak barrels and used Cabernet Sauvignon (20%) in the blend with Sangiovese. The quality was superb, and Tignanello's success sparked off the SUPER-TUSCAN movement. Top vintages are truly great; lesser years are of decent CHIANTI CLASSICO quality. Best years: (2008) (07) 06 04 **03 01 00 99 98 97 95 93 90 88 85**.

TINTA RORIZ See TEMPRANILLO.

TOCAI FRIULANO Tocai Friulano is a north-east Italian grape producing dry, nutty, oily whites of great character in COLLIO and COLLI ORIENTALI. Friuli producers have now, under pressure from the Hungarians, removed (for the most part) the name Tocai from their labels and call it plain Friulano. Best producers: Borgo del Tiglio★, Livio FELLUGA★, JERMANN★,

Edi Keber★★, Miani★★, Princic★, Ronco del Gelso★★, Russiz Superiore★★ SCHIOPETTO★★, Le Vigne di Zamò★★, Villa Russiz★.

TOKAJI *Hungary* Hungary's classic, liquorous wine of historic reputation, with its unique, sweet-and-sour, sherry-like tang, comes from 28 villages on the Hungarian–Slovak border. Mists from the Bodrog river ensure that noble rot on the Furmint, Hárslevelü and Muscotaly (Muscat Ottonel) grapes is a fairly common occurrence. Degrees of sweetness are measured in *puttonyos*. Discussions continue about traditional oxidized styles versus fresher modern versions. Best producers: Disznókö★★ Château Megyer★★, Oremus★, Château Pajzos★★, Royal Tokaji Wine Co★★ Istvan Szepsy (6 Puttonyos 95★★★, Essencia★★★), Tokaji Kereskedöház★ Best years: **2000 99 97 93**.

TOLLOT-BEAUT *Chorey-lès-Beaune, Burgundy, France* Good reds with lots of fruit and a pronounced new oak character. The village-level CHOREY-LÈS-BEAUNE★★, ALOXE-CORTON★★ and SAVIGNY-LÈS-BEAUNE★★ are all excellent as is the top BEAUNE Premier Cru Clos du Roi★★. Whites are more variable, but at best delicious. Best years: (reds) (2008) 07 06 05 **03 02 99**

TORBRECK *Barossa Valley, South Australia* Dave Powell specializes in opulent well-structured reds from 60–120-year-old Shiraz, Grenache and Mataro (Mourvèdre) vines. Made in minute quantities, the flagship RunRig★★★, single-vineyard Descendant★★ and Factor★★ are all richly concentrated powerful, complex Shiraz. The Steading★ and Juveniles★ are Grenache-Mataro-Shiraz blends (the latter unoaked), while the Woodcutter's Semillon and Shiraz are lightly oaked, mouth-filling quaffers.

TORO DO *Castilla y León, Spain* Mainly red wines, which are robust, full of colour and tannin, and pretty high in alcohol. The main grape, Tinta de Toro, is a variant of Tempranillo, and there is some Garnacha. In the late 1990s, the arrival of some of Spain's top wineries gave the sleepy area a boost, as did the 2008 sale of Numanthia-Termes to France's ritzy LVMH group. Best producers: Viña Bajoz, Fariña★, Frutos Villar (Muruve★), Garanza Matarredonda, Maurodos★★, Monte La Reina, Numanthia-Termes★★ Pintia★★/VEGA SICILIA, Quinta de la Quietud★, Sobreño, Telmo RODRIGUEZ★★ Toresanas/Bodegas de Crianza Castilla la Vieja★, Vega Saúco, Villaester.

TORRES *Penedès DO, Cataluña, Spain* Large family wineries led by visionary Miguel Torres, making good to excellent wines with local grapes and international varieties. Viña Sol★ is a delightful, citrony quaffer, Viña Esmeralda★ (Muscat Blanc à Petits Grains and Gewürztraminer) is grapy and spicy, Fransola★★ (Sauvignon Blanc with some Parellada) is high-quality barrel-fermented yet leafy, and Milmanda★ is a delicate expressive Chardonnay. Successful reds are soft, oaky and blackcurranty Gran Coronas★ (Tempranillo and Cabernet), fine, relatively rich though increasingly international Mas La Plana★★ (Cabernet Sauvignon) floral, perfumed Mas Borràs (Pinot Noir) and raisiny Atrium★ (Merlot) The top reds – Grans Muralles★★, a blend of Catalan grapes, and Reserva Real★★, a BORDEAUX-style blend – are fascinating but expensive and improve with every vintage. The new PRIORAT winery is producing a distinguished red, Perpetual★. Best years: (Mas La Plana) 2005 04 **03 01 00** 99 98 97 96 95 94 91 90 88.

MARIMAR TORRES ESTATE *Sonoma County, California, USA* The sister of Spanish winemaker Miguel TORRES has established her own winery in the cool Green Valley region of RUSSIAN RIVER VALLEY, only a few miles from the Pacific Ocean. She specializes in Chardonnay and Pinot Noir, the best of which are from the Don Miguel Vineyard: the Chardonnay★★ is big and intense, initially quite oaky, but able to age gracefully to fascinating maturity at 10 years old. Recent vintages of full-flavoured Pinot Noir★★ are the best yet. Best years: 2006 05 03 **02 01 00 99 98 97 95 94**.

MIGUEL TORRES *Curicó, Chile* TORRES' Chilean operation is now producing its best ever wines: snappy Sauvignon Blanc★, grassy, fruity Santa Digna rosé★, weighty, blackcurranty Manso de Velasco Cabernet★★, exciting, sonorous old-Carignan-based Cordillera★★ and Conde de Superunda★★, a tremendous, dense blend based on Cabernet and Tempranillo. Best years: (Manso de Velasco) 2006 05 04 **03 02 01 00 99**.

CH. LA TOUR BLANCHE★★ *Sauternes AC, 1er Cru Classé, Bordeaux, France* This estate regained top form in the 1980s with the introduction of new oak barrels for fermentation, lower yields and greater selection. Full-bodied, rich and aromatic, it now ranks with the best of the Classed Growths. Second wine: Les Charmilles de la Tour Blanche. Best years: 2007 06 05 **04 03 02 01** 99 98 97 96 95 90 89 88 86.

CH. TOUR BOISÉE *Minervois AC, Languedoc, France* Top wines here are the red Jardin Secret★, Cuvée Marie-Claude★, aged for 12 months in barrel, the fruity Cuvée Marielle et Frédérique, and the white Cuvée Marie-Claude★, with a hint of Muscat Blanc à Petits Grains for added aroma. Best years: (red) 2007 06 05 **04 03 01**.

CH. TOUR DES GENDRES *Bergerac AC, South-West France* Luc de Conti's BERGERACS are made with as much sophistication as the better Crus Classés of BORDEAUX. Generously fruity Moulin des Dames★ and the more serious la Gloire de Mon Père★★ reds are mostly Cabernet Sauvignon. Full, fruity and elegant Moulin des Dames★★ white is a blend of Sémillon, Sauvignon Blanc and Muscadelle. Best years: (la Gloire de Mon Père) (2008) 06 **05 04 02 01 00**.

TOURAINE AC *Loire Valley, France* General AC in the central LOIRE; largely everyday wines to drink young, though its tradition for wines that could do with more aging is being restored by an ambitious minority, many of whose wines are confusingly  labelled Vin de Pays du VAL DE LOIRE or even Vin de Table. Most reds are from Gamay and, in hot years, can be juicy, rustic-fruited wines. There is a fair amount of red from Cabernets Sauvignon and Franc too, and some good Côt (Malbec). Best whites are Sauvignon Blanc, which can be a good substitute for SANCERRE at half the price, and the rare Romorantin; decent Chenin and Chardonnay. White and rosé sparkling wines are made by the traditional method but rarely have the distinction of the best VOUVRAY and CREMANT DE LOIRE. Best producers: Acacias★, Brulée★, Clos de la Briderie★, La Chapinière★, F Chidaine, Corbillières★, J Delaunay★, Robert Denis★, A Fouassier, David Levin, Marcadet★, H Marionnet/la Charmoise★, J-C Mandard, J-F Merieau★, Michaud★, Octavie★, Pavy★, Pré Baron★, J Preys★, Ricard★, Roche Blanc★, Sauvète. Best years: (reds) (2008) 06 **05 04 03 02**.

TOURIGA NACIONAL High-quality red Portuguese grape, rich in aroma and fruit. It contributes deep colour and tannin in PORT, and is rapidly increasing in importance for table wines throughout the country. Small but important plantings in South Africa enhance some of the impressive port styles emerging across the country.

TOWER ESTATE *Hunter Valley, New South Wales, Australia* This syndicate, founded by the late, great Len Evans, focuses on sourcing top-notch grapes from their ideal regions. So, there is powerful, stylish COONAWARRA Cabernet★★, top-flight BAROSSA Shiraz★★, fine floral CLARE Riesling★★, fruity ADELAIDE HILLS Sauvignon Blanc★ and classic Semillon★★, Shiraz★ and Chardonnay★ from the HUNTER VALLEY.

TRAPICHE *Mendoza, Argentina* The fine wine arm of Peñaflor, Argentina's biggest wine producer, where chief winemaker Daniel Pi has triumphantly turned quality around since taking over in 2002. Medalla Cabernet Sauvignon★★ is dense and satisfying, Malbec-Merlot blend Iscay★ is solid and rich, and single-vineyard Malbecs★★ are sumptuous and individual.

TRÁS-OS-MONTES *Portugal* Impoverished north-eastern province, producing pretty rustic stuff. The Vinho Regional is Transmontano. Best producers: Quinta do Sobreiró de Cima, Casa de Valle Pradinhos.

TREBBIANO The most widely planted white Italian grape variety. As Trebbiano Toscano, it is the base for EST! EST!! EST!!! and any number of other neutral, dry whites, as well as much VIN SANTO. But there are other grapes masquerading under the Trebbiano name that aren't anything like as neutral. The most notable are the Trebbianos from SOAVE, LUGANA and ABRUZZO – grapes capable of full-bodied, fragrant wines. Called Ugni Blanc in France, where it is primarily used for distilling, as it should be.

TRENTINO *Italy* Wines from this northern Italian region rarely have the verve or perfume of ALTO ADIGE examples, but can make up for this with riper, softer flavours, where vineyard yields have been kept in check. The Trentino DOC covers 20 different styles of wine, including whites Pinot Bianco and Grigio, Chardonnay, Moscato Giallo, Müller-Thurgau and Nosiola, and reds Lagrein, Marzemino and Cabernet. Trento Classico is a DOC for CHAMPAGNE-method fizz. Best producers: N Balter★, N Bolognani★, La Cadalora★, Castel Noarna★, Cavit co-op, Cesconi★★, De Tarczal★, Dorigati, FERRARI★★, Graziano Fontana★, FORADORI★★, Letrari★, Longariva★, Conti Martini★, Maso Cantanghel★★, Maso Furli★, Maso Roveri★, Mezzacorona, Pojer & Sandri★, Pravis★, SAN LEONARDO★★★, Simoncelli★, E Spagnolli★, Vallarom★, La Vis co-op. See also TEROLDEGO ROTALIANO.

DOM. DE TRÉVALLON *Provence, France* Iconoclastic Eloi Dürrbach makes brilliant reds★★ (at best ★★★) – a tradition-busting blend of Cabernet Sauvignon and Syrah, mixing herbal wildness with a sweetness of blackberry, blackcurrant and black, black plums – and a tiny quantity of white★★★. Both are labelled Vin de Pays des BOUCHES-DU-RHONE. The reds age well, but are intriguingly drinkable in their youth. Best years: (reds) (2007) (06) 05 04 03 **01 00 99 98 97**.

TRIMBACH *Alsace AC, Alsace, France* An excellent grower/merchant whose trademark is beautifully structured, emphatically dry, subtly perfumed elegance. Top wines are Gewurztraminer Cuvée des Seigneurs de Ribeaupierre★★, Riesling Cuvée Frédéric Émile★★ and Riesling Clos Ste-Hune★★★. Also very good Vendange Tardive★★ and Sélection de Grains Nobles★. Trimbach basics are a bit pricey, but enjoyable in their austere manner. Best years: (Clos Ste-Hune) (2008) 07 05 04 **03 02 01 00 99 98 97 96 95 93 92 90**.

TRINITY HILL *Hawkes Bay, North Island, New Zealand* Talented owner/
winemaker John Hancock produces many top wines from the Gimblett
Gravels area, including flagship Homage Syrah★★★ that's co-fermented
with a small amount of Viognier, a fine peppery Syrah★★, an
impressively proportioned Merlot★★, gutsy long-lived Cabernet
Sauvignon-Merlot★ plus a big and complex Chardonnay★★. Trinity
also makes a good job of less mainstream styles such as Tempranillo★,
Arneis and Viognier★★. Best years: (reds) (2008) 07 **06 04 02 00**.

TRITTENHEIM *Mosel, Germany* Important village with some excellent
vineyard sites, notably the Apotheke (pharmacy) and Leiterchen (little
ladder). The wines are sleek, with crisp acidity and plenty of fruit. Best
producers: Clüsserath-Weiler★, GRANS-FASSIAN★★, Milz-Laurentiushof★, Josef
Rosch★. Best years: (2008) 07 06 05 **04 02 01 99**.

CH. TROPLONG-MONDOT★★ *St-Émilion Grand Cru AC, 1er Grand Cru Classé,*
Bordeaux, France Owner Christine Valette has been producing quality
wines at this property since the mid-1980s. Her reward – elevation to
Premier Grand Cru Classé in 2006. The wines are powerfully structured
and mouthfillingly textured for long aging. Best years: 2007 06 05 **04 03 02**
01 00 99 98 96 95 94 90 89.

CH. TROTANOY★★ *Pomerol AC, Bordeaux, France* Another POMEROL estate
(like PETRUS and LATOUR-A-POMEROL) which has benefited from the brilliant
touch of the MOUEIX family. Back on form after a dip in the mid-80s. Best
years: 2007 06 05 04 03 **02 01 00 99 98 96 95 94 90 89 88**.

TUA RITA *Tuscany, Italy* Since the early 1990s, this estate in the MAREMMA
has established itself at the top of the Italian Merlot tree with
Redigaffi★★★; Cabernet-Merlot blend Giusto di Notri★★ is almost as
renowned. Best years: (2008) 06 **05 04 03 01 00 99 98 97 96 95**.

CAVE VINICOLE DE TURCKHEIM *Alsace AC, Alsace, France* Important co-
op with good basics in all varieties. The Reserve tier of all wines merits
★, while Brand★, Hengst★ and Ollwiller★ bottlings are rich and
concentrated. Reds, rosés and CREMANT D'ALSACE★ are consistent. Best
years: (Grand Cru Gewurztraminer) 2007 **05 04 02 01 00 99 98 97 95**.

TURKEY FLAT *Barossa, South Australia* The Schultz family, BAROSSA growers
with substantial holdings of old-vine Shiraz (planted 1847) and
Grenache, turned to winemaking in 1990. Deeply flavoured, lush
Shiraz★★, delicious Grenache★ and one of Australia's top rosés★.

TURLEY *Napa Valley AVA, California, USA* Larry Turley's ultra-ripe
Zinfandels★★, from a number of old vineyards, are either praised for
their profound power and depth or damned for their tannic, high-
alcohol, PORT-like nature. Petite Sirah★★ is similarly built. Best years:
(Zins) 2005 04 **03 02 01 00 99 98 97 96 95**.

TURSAN VDQS *South-West France* These wines are made on the edge of les
Landes, the sandy coastal area south of Bordeaux. The white is made,
unusually, from the Baroque grape; it is clean, crisp and refreshing. Best
producers: Baron de Bachen★, Dulucq★, Tursan co-op.

TUSCANY *Italy* Tuscany's rolling hills, clad with vines, olive trees and
cypresses, have produced wine since at least Etruscan times. Today, its many
DOC/DOCGs are based on the red Sangiovese grape and are led by CHIANTI
CLASSICO, BRUNELLO DI MONTALCINO and VINO NOBILE DI MONTEPULCIANO, as well as
famous SUPER-TUSCANS like ORNELLAIA and TIGNANELLO. White wines, despite
sweet VIN SANTO, and the occasional excellent Chardonnay and Sauvignon, do
not figure highly. See also BOLGHERI, CARMIGNANO, MAREMMA, MONTECARLO,

MORELLINO DI SCANSANO, ROSSO DI MONTALCINO, ROSSO DI MONTEPULCIANO, SASSICAIA, SOLAIA, VERNACCIA DI SAN GIMIGNANO.

TYRRELL'S *Hunter Valley, New South Wales, Australia* Top-notch family-owned company with prime HUNTER vineyards celebrated its 150th anniversary in 2008. It is expanding into COONAWARRA, MCLAREN VALE and HEATHCOTE, with impressive results. Comprehensive range, from good-value quaffers (Old Winery★, Lost Block★) to excellent Vat 47 Chardonnay★★★ and Vat 9 Shiraz★. Semillon is the speciality, with 4 single-vineyard wines (all ★★) – Lost Block, Stevens, Belford and the rare HVD – and, best of all, the superb Vat 1★★★. Best years: (Vat 1 Semillon) (2007) (05) 04 03 02 **01** 00 **99** 98 97 96 95 94 93 92 91 90 89 87 86 77 76 75; (Vat 47 Chardonnay) (2007) 05 **04 03 02** 01 **00** 99 98 97 96 95.

UCO VALLEY *Mendoza, Argentina* This valley, in the foothills of the Andes, is an old secret of Argentine viticulture, newly rediscovered. Most vineyards are new but there are precious old plantings too. With vineyards at 1000–1500m (3200–4900 ft) above sea level, it's Argentina's best spot for Chardonnays, especially from the Tupungato area. Reds are also showing fascinating flavours – especially Merlot, Malbec, Syrah and Tempranillo. Best producers: ACHAVAL-FERRER★★, Antucura★, CATENA★★, Clos de los Siete★★, Finca Sophenia★, O FOURNIER★★, Salentein★, TERRAZAS DE LOS ANDES★★.

UGNI BLANC See TREBBIANO.

UMATHUM *Frauenkirchen, Neusiedlersee, Burgenland, Austria* Resisting trend in Austria toward heavily oaked blockbuster reds, Josef Umathum emphasizes finesse and sheer drinkability. The single-vineyard Ried Hallebühl★★ is usually his top wine, but the St Laurent Vom Stein★ and the Zweigelt-dominated Haideboden★ sometimes match it in quality. Best years: (reds) 2007 06 05 **04 03** 01 99.

UMBRIA *Italy* Wine production in this region is dominated by ORVIETO, accounting for almost 70% of DOC wines. However, some of the most characterful wines are reds from TORGIANO and MONTEFALCO. Latest interest centres on international-style reds made by the ubiquitous Riccardo Cotarella at estates such as Pieve del Vescovo (Lucciaio★★), La Carraia (Fobiano★★), Lamborghini (Campoleone★★) and La Palazzola (Rubino★★).

ÜRZIG *Mosel, Germany* Middle MOSEL village with the famous red slate Würzgarten (spice garden) vineyard tumbling spectacularly down to the river and producing marvellously spicy Riesling. Drink young or with at least 5 years' age. Best producers: J J Christoffel★★, Erbes, Dr LOOSEN★★★, Mönchhof★★, Peter Nicolay★, Dr Weins-Prüm★. Best years: (2008) 07 06 05 **04 03 02** 01 99 98.

UTIEL-REQUENA DO *Valencia, Spain* Renowned for its rosés, mostly from the Bobal grape. Reds, with Tempranillo often complementing Bobal, are on the up. The groundbreaking Mustiguillo★★ winery now has its own appellation, Vinos de la Tierra Terrerazo. Best producers: Coviñas Gandía, Palmera (L'Angelet★), Schenk, Torre Oria, Dominio de la Vega.

DOM. VACHERON *Sancerre AC, Loire Valley, France* Unusually for a SANCERRE domaine, Vacheron, now biodynamic, is more reputed for its Pinot Noir reds than for its whites, but the whole range is currently on top form. Intense and expensive Belle Dame★★ red and Les Romains★★

white lead the way. The basic Sancerres – a cherryish red★ and a grapefruity white★ – have reserves of complexity that set them above the crowd. Best years: (Belle Dame) (2007) **06 05 04 03 02 01 00 99**.

VACQUEYRAS AC *Rhône Valley, France* Red wines, mainly Grenache, account for 95% of production; they have a warm, spicy bouquet and a rich deep flavour that seems infused with the herbs and pine dust of the south and its plateau vineyards. Lovely to drink at 2–3 years, though good wines will age for 10 years. Best producers: Amouriers★, la Charbonnière★, Clos des Cazaux★★, Couroulu★★, DELAS★, Font de Papier★, la Fourmone★, la Garrigue★, JABOULET★, Alain Jaume, Monardière★★, Montirius★★, Montmirail★, Montvac★, SANG DES CAILLOUX★★, Tardieu-Laurent★★, la Tourade★, Ch. des Tours★, Vacqueyras co-op, Verquière★. Best years: **2007 06 05 04 03 01 00 99 98**.

VAL DE LOIRE, VIN DE PAYS DU *Loire Valley, France* Replaces Vin de Pays du Jardin de la France with effect from the 2007 vintage. It covers all 14 designated wine-producing regions of the LOIRE VALLEY – over 7,300ha (18,000 acres), accounting for around 500,000hl of wine. Key whites are Sauvignon Blanc, Chardonnay and Chenin Blanc, with some Grolleau Gris, Melon de Bourgogne, Folle Blanche and Pinot Blanc. The focus for reds is Gamay, Cabernets Franc and Sauvignon, with some Pinot Noir. It is increasingly a refuge for ambitious producers whose wines punch well above the weight of their appellation, especially in TOURAINE. Best producers: Ampelidae, M Angeli/Sansonnière★★, Brulée★, l'ECU★, Ch. Gaillard, de la Garrelière, L Herbel★, Henry Marionnet★, Alphonse MELLOT★, J-F Merieau★, RAGOTIERE★★, Ricard.

VAL D'ORBIEU, LES VIGNERONS DU *Languedoc-Roussillon, France* One of France's largest wine-exporting companies, selling more than 20 million cases a year. Membership includes several top co-ops (Cucugnan, Cuxac, Montredon, Ribauté) and individual producers (Dom. de Fontsainte, Ch. la VOULTE-GASPARETS). Its upmarket blended wines (Cuvée Chouette★, Chorus★, Elysices★, la Cuvée Mythique★) are a mix of traditional Mediterranean varieties with Cabernet or Merlot.

VALAIS *Switzerland* Swiss canton flanking the Rhône. Between Martigny and Sierre the valley turns north-east, creating an Alpine suntrap, and this short stretch of terraced vineyard land provides many of Switzerland's most individual wines from Fendant, Johannisberger (Silvaner), Pinot Noir and Gamay, and several stunning examples from Syrah, Chardonnay, Ermitage (Marsanne) and Petite Arvine. Best producers: Bonvin★, Cina★, G Clavien★, Cottagnoud★, Dorsaz★, Jean-René Germanier★, Adrian Mathier★, S Maye★, Mercier, Dom. du Mont d'Or★, Provins, Rouvinez★, M Zufferey★.

CH. VALANDRAUD★★ *St-Émilion Grand Cru AC, Bordeaux, France* The precursor of the 'garage wine' sensation in ST-EMILION, a big, rich, extracted wine from low yields, from grapes mainly grown in different parcels around St-Émilion. The core of the wine is a top-quality limestone-based property and we can now see a real, impressive, consistent Valandraud style developing. Best years: 2007 06 05 04 **03 02 01 00 99 98 96 95**.

VALDEPEÑAS DO *Castilla-La Mancha, Spain* Valdepeñas offers some of Spain's best inexpensive oak-aged reds, but there is an increasing number of unoaked, fruit-forward reds as well. In fact, there are more whites than reds, at least some of them modern, fresh and fruity. Best producers: Miguel Calatayud, Los Llanos, Luís Megía, Real, Félix Solís, Casa de la Viña.

VALDESPINO *Jerez y Manzanilla DO, Andalucia, Spain* New owner Grupo
Estévez (Marqués del Real Tesoro, Tio Mateo) is probably the quality
leader in Jerez today, and the exemplary character of Valdespino's
sherries appears unaffected by the change of ownership. Fino
Inocente★★, Palo Cortado Cardenal★★★, Pedro Ximénez Niños★★★
and dry Amontillado Coliseo★★★ are stunning examples of sherry's
different styles.

VALDIVIESO *Curicó, Chile* Important winery, finally getting back on track
after a few lean years. Varietals are attractive and direct, Reserves
from cooler regions a definite step up, and some of the Single
Vineyards are quite impressive (Chardonnay★, Malbec★). Multi-
varietal, multi-vintage blend Caballo Loco★★ (mad horse) is always
fascinating and unpredictable, and Eclat★★, based on old Carignan, is
chewy and rich.

VALENCIA *Spain* The best-known wines from Valencia DO are the
inexpensive, sweet, grapy Moscatels. Simple, fruity whites, reds and rosés are
also good. Alicante DO to the south produces a little-known treasure, the
Fondillón dry or semi-dry fortified wine, as well as a cluster of wines made by
a few quality-conscious modern wineries. Monastrell (Mourvèdre) is the main
red grape variety. **Best producers: (Valencia)** J Belda, Rafael Cambra★, Heretat de
Cesilia★, Cherubino Valsangiacomo (Marqués de Caro), Enguera, Gandía, Los
Pinos★, Celler del Roure★, Schenk; **(Alicante)** Bernabé Navarro★, Bocopa★,
Gutiérrez de la Vega (Casta Diva Muscat★★), Laderas de Pinoso★, Enrique
Mendoza★★, Salvador Poveda★, Primitivo Quiles★. See also UTIEL-REQUENA.

VALL LLACH *Priorat DOCa, Spain* This tiny winery, owned by Catalan folk
singer Lluís Llach, has joined the ranks of the best PRIORAT producers
with its powerful reds★★ dominated by old-vine Cariñena. **Best years:**
(2006) 05 04 03 **01 00 99 98**.

VALLE D'AOSTA *Italy* Tiny Alpine valley sandwiched between PIEDMONT
and the French Alps in northern Italy. The regional DOC covers 19 wine
styles, referring either to a specific grape variety (like Gamay or Pinot Nero)
or to a delimited region like Donnaz, a northern extension of Piedmont'
Carema, producing a light red from the Nebbiolo grape. Perhaps the finest
wine from these steep slopes is the sweet Chambave Moscato. **Best producers:**
R Anselmet★, C Charrère/Les Crêtes★, La Crotta di Vegneron★, Grosjean, Institu
Agricole Regional★, Onze Communes co-op, Ezio Voyat★.

VALPOLICELLA DOC *Veneto, Italy* Styles range from a light, cherryish red
to rich, PORT-like RECIOTO and AMARONE. Most of the better examples are
Valpolicella Classico Superiore from the hills north-west of Verona and
are made predominantly from Corvina and Corvinone grapes. The most
concentrated, ageworthy examples are made either from a particular
vineyard, or by refermenting the wine on the skins and lees of the
Amarone, a style called *ripasso*, or by using a portion of dried grapes. **Best**
producers: Accordini★, ALLEGRINI★★★, Bertani★, Brigaldara★, Brunelli★
BUSSOLA★★★, Michele Castellani★, Valentina Cubi★, DAL FORNO★★★
Guerrieri-Rizzardi★, MASI★, Mazzi★, Cecilia Beretta★, QUINTARELLI★★★, L
Ragose★, Le Salette★, Serègo Alighieri★, Speri★, Tedeschi★, Vill
Monteleone★, VIVIANI★★, Zenato★, Zeni★. **Best years: (Valpolicella Superiore**
(2008) 06 04 03 **01 00 97 95 93 90**.

VALTELLINA SUPERIORE DOCG *Lombardy, Italy*   Red wine produced on
the precipitous slopes of northern LOMBARDY. There is a basic light
Valtellina DOC red, made from at least 70% Nebbiolo (here called
Chiavennasca), but the best wines are made under the Valtellina
Superiore DOCG as Grumello, Inferno, Sassella and Valgella. From top
vintages the wines are attractively perfumed and approachable. Sfursat or
Sforzato is a dense, high-alcohol red (up to 14.5%) made from semi-
dried grapes. **Best producers: La Castellina★, Enologica Valtellinese★, Fay★,
Nino Negri★, Nera★, Rainoldi★, Conti Sertoli Salis★, Triacca★. Best years:
(2008) (07) (06) 04 03 01 99 98 97.**

VAN VOLXEM *Wiltingen, Mosel, Germany*   Roman Niewodniczanski bought
this estate, with its great old vineyards in Scharzhofberg and Wiltinger
Gottesfuss, in 2000. His style, off-dry and opulent, is atypical and
controversial, but often ★★. **Best years: (2008) 07 06 05 04 03.**

CH. VANNIÈRES *Bandol AC, Provence, France*   Leading BANDOL estate, owned
by the Boisseaux family since the 1950s. Under a new winemaker, it has
leapt into the top ranks. Wood has replaced cement tanks, wines are
bottled unfiltered, and the percentage of Mourvèdre has gone from 50 to
95. Besides red Bandol★★, Vannières produces CÔTES DE PROVENCE and
vin de pays. **Best years: 2007 06 05 03 01 00 98 97.**

VASSE FELIX *Margaret River, Western Australia*   MARGARET RIVER's first vineyard
and winery turned 40 in 2007; it is now more focused on the region
under a new winemaking team. The flagship Heytesbury
Chardonnay★★ is tighter, leaner and finer than before, while the
powerful Cabernet-blend red Heytesbury★★ shows greater elegance.
There's a decadently rich, profound Cabernet Sauvignon★ and oak-led
Shiraz★, and the regular Chardonnay★ is pleasurable drinking for a
modest price. **Best years: (Heytesbury red) (2008) 07 05 04 01 99 97 96 95.**

VAUD *Switzerland*   The Vaud's main vineyards border Lake Geneva (Lac
Léman), with 5 sub-regions: la Côte, Lavaux, CHABLAIS, Côtes de l'Orbe-
Bonvillars, Vully. Fresh light white wines are made from Chasselas; at
DEZALEY it gains depth. Reds from Gamay and Pinot Noir. **Best producers:
Henri Badoux, Louis Bovard★, Conne, Dubois, Obrist, J & P Testuz★.**

VAVASOUR *Marlborough, South Island, New Zealand*
First winery in Marlborough's AWATERE
Valley, now enjoying spectacular success.
One of New Zealand's best Chardonnays★★,
a fine, lush Pinot Noir★★ and palate-
tingling, oak-tinged Sauvignon Blanc★★.
Second-label Dashwood is also top stuff,

particularly the tangy Sauvignon Blanc★★. In 2006 Vavasour merged
with high-flying Waiheke winery GOLDWATER. **Best years: (Sauvignon Blanc)
2007 06 04.**

VEENWOUDEN *Paarl WO, South Africa*   Reds based on BORDEAUX varieties
remain the focus of attention: sumptuous, well-oaked Merlot★★ and
firm and silky-fruited Veenwouden Classic★★. Also an expressive yet
well-structured Syrah★. A tiny quantity of fine Chardonnay★ is made.
Best years: (Merlot, Classic) 2005 04 03 02 00 99 98.

VEGA SICILIA *Ribera del Duero DO, Castilla y León, Spain*   Among Spain's most
expensive wines, rich, fragrant, complex and very slow to mature, and by
no means always easy to appreciate. This estate was the first in Spain to
introduce French varieties, and almost a quarter of the vines are now
Cabernet Sauvignon, two-thirds are Tempranillo and the rest Malbec

and Merlot. Vega Sicilia Unico★★★ – the top wine – is aged in wood for 5 or 6 years. Second wine: Valbuena★★. A subsidiary winery produces the more modern Alión★★, and the new Pintia★★ winery makes some of the most distinctive wines in TORO. Best years: (Unico) 1996 **95 94 91 90 89 87 86 85 83 82 81 80 79 76 75 74 70 68**.

VELICH *Neuseidlersee, Burgenland, Austria* Heinz Velich makes Austria's most mineral and sophisticated Chardonnay★★ from old vines in the Tiglat vineyard. Also spectacular ★★ and ★★★ dessert wines. Best years: (Tiglat Chardonnay) (2008) 07 **06 05 04 03 02**; (sweet) (2008) 07 06 05 **04 02 01 99**.

VENETO *Italy* This region takes in the wine zones of SOAVE, VALPOLICELLA, BARDOLINO and Piave in north-east Italy. It is the source of a great deal of inexpensive wine, but the Soave and Valpolicella hills are also capable of producing high-quality wine. Other hilly areas like Colli Berici and Colli Euganei produce large quantities of dull varietal wines, but can offer the odd flash of brilliance. The great dry red of this zone is AMARONE. See also BIANCO DI CUSTOZA, PROSECCO, RECIOTO DELLA VALPOLICELLA, RECIOTO DI SOAVE.

VENTOUX AC *Rhône Valley, France* Vineyards around the southern and western slopes of Mt Ventoux. When well made, the red wines can have a lovely juicy fruit, or in the case of JABOULET and Pesquié, some real stuffing. Best producers: Anges★, Bedoin co-op, Brusset, Cascavel★, Cave Courtoise★, La Croix des Pins★, Fenouillet, Ferme St-Pierre, Font-Sane, Grand Jacquet, JABOULET★, Cave de Lumières★, la Martinelle★, le Murmurium, Pesquié★, Valcombe★, Vidal-Fleury, la Vieille Ferme. Best years: (reds) 2007 06.

VERDICCHIO DEI CASTELLI DI JESI, VERDICCHIO DI MATELICA DOC *Marche, Italy* Verdicchio, grown in the hills near the Adriatic around Jesi and in the Apennine foothills enclave of Matelica, has blossomed into central Italy's most promising white variety. When fresh and fruity it is the ideal wine with fish, but some Verdicchio can age into a white of surprising depth of flavours. A few producers, notably Garofoli with Serra Fiorese★★, age it in oak, but even without wood it can develop an almost Burgundy-like complexity. A little is made sparkling. Best producers: (Jesi) Brunori★, Bucci★★, Colonnara★, Coroncino★★, Fazi Battaglia★, Garofoli★★, Mancinelli★, Monte Schiavo★★, Santa Barbara★, Sartarelli★★, Tavignano★, Terre Cortesi Moncaro★, Umani Ronchi★, Fratelli Zaccagnini★; (Matelica) Belisario★, Bisci★, Mecella★, La Monacesca★★.

VIGNOBLE DES VERDOTS *Bergerac AC and Monbazillac AC, South-West France* David Fourtout's BERGERACs are some of the best, from the everyday, good-value-for-money Clos des Verdots★ range to Château les Tours des Verdots★ (barrique-aged), right to the top of the tree Verdots★★ and Le Vin★★. Outstanding MONBAZILLAC★★, too.

VERGELEGEN *Stellenbosch WO, South Africa* This historic farm's Sauvignon Blancs are considered benchmarks: the regular bottling★★ is aggressive and racy, streaked with sleek tropical fruit: the single-vineyard Reserve★★ is flinty, dry and fascinating. Topping both is barrel-fermented white Vergelegen★★, a Semillon-Sauvignon blend that ages superbly for 3–6 years. There is also a ripe-textured, stylish Chardonnay Reserve★★. Reds are even more attention-grabbing: Vergelegen★★★, a BORDEAUX blend, shows classic mineral intensity, Merlot★★ and Cabernet Sauvignon★★ are often among South Africa's best. Single-vineyard Cabernet Sauvignon-based 'V'★★ (heading toward ★★★) is a striking individual. Best years: (premium reds) 2006 05 **04 03 02 01 00 99**

VERGET *Mâconnais, Burgundy, France Négociant* house run by Jean-Marie Guffens-Heynen, with outstanding Premiers Crus and Grands Crus from the COTE D'OR, notably CHASSAGNE-MONTRACHET★★ and BATARD-MONTRACHET★★. Guffens-Heynen also has his own domaine, with excellent MACON-VILLAGES★★ and POUILLY-FUISSE★★. But beware, the wines are made in a very individualistic style. Best years: (2008) 07 06 05 **04 02**.

VERITAS See Rolf BINDER.

VERMENTINO The best dry white wines of SARDINIA generally come from the Vermentino grape. The best examples – full-bodied and flavoursome – tend to be from the north-east of the island, where the Vermentino di Gallura DOCG zone is located. Vermentino di Sardegna DOC is lighter and less interesting. Vermentino is also grown in coastal areas of LIGURIA and TUSCANY, though here it generally lacks the complexity of Gallura. It is believed to be the same as Rolle, found in many blends in PROVENCE, but increasingly single varietal in the best white wines. Best producers: (Sardinia) ARGIOLAS★, Capichera★★, Cherchi★, Contini★, Gallura co-op★, Giogantinu★, Piero Mancini★, Pedra Majore★, Mura★, Santadi co-op★, SELLA & MOSCA★, Vermentino co-op★; (Provence) Courtade★, Sarrins★.

VERNACCIA DI SAN GIMIGNANO DOCG *Tuscany, Italy* Dry white wines – generally light quaffers – made from the Vernaccia grape grown in the hills around San Gimignano. Up to 10% other grapes, e.g. Chardonnay, are allowed in the blend. There is a San Gimignano DOC for the zone's reds, though the best SUPER-TUSCANS are sold as IGT wines. Best producers: Cà del Vispo★, Le Calcinaie★, Casale-Falchini★, V Cesani★, La Lastra (Riserva★), Melini (Le Grillaie★), Montenidoli★, G Panizzi★, Il Paradiso★, Pietrafitta★, La Rampa di Fugnano★, Guicciardini Strozzi★, Teruzzi & Puthod (Terre di Tufi★★), Casa alle Vacche★, Vagnoni★.

QUINTA DO VESÚVIO★★ *Port DOC, Douro, Portugal* A consistently top vintage PORT from the Symington stable that appears only when the high quality can be maintained. Best with at least 10 years' age. Best years: 2006 05 04 **03 01 00 99 97 96 95 94 92 91 90**.

VEUVE CLICQUOT *Champagne AC, Champagne, France* Owned by the LVMH luxury goods group, these CHAMPAGNES can still live up to the high standards set by the original Widow Clicquot at the beginning of the 19th century, although many are released too young. The non-vintage is full, toasty and satisfyingly weighty, or lean and raw, depending on your luck; the vintage★ used to be reliably impressive, but recent releases have shown none of the traditional Clicquot class. Look out for Veuve Clicquot Rare Vintage★★, recent releases of top older vintages. The de luxe Grande Dame★★★ is both powerful and elegant. Grande Dame Rosé★★★ is exquisite. Best years: 2002 00 99 **98 96 95 90 89 88 85 82**.

VICTORIA *Australia* Despite its relatively small area, Victoria has arguably more land suited to quality grape-growing than any other state in Australia, with climates ranging from hot Murray Darling and Swan Hill on the Murray River to cool MORNINGTON PENINSULA and GIPPSLAND in the south. The range of flavours is similarly wide and exciting. With more than 500 wineries, Victoria leads the boutique winery boom, particularly in Mornington Peninsula. See also BEECHWORTH, BENDIGO, CENTRAL VICTORIA, GEELONG, GRAMPIANS AND PYRENEES, HEATHCOTE, RUTHERGLEN, YARRA VALLEY.

VIEUX-CHÂTEAU-CERTAN★★ *Pomerol AC, Bordeaux, France* Slow-developing, tannic red with up to 30% Cabernet Franc and 10% Cabernet Sauvignon in the blend, which after 15–20 years finally resembles more a fragrant, refined MEDOC than a hedonistic POMEROL. Best years: 2007 06 05 04 **02 01** 00 99 98 96 95 90 89 88 86 85.

DOM. DU VIEUX TÉLÉGRAPHE *Châteauneuf-du-Pape AC, Rhône Valley, France* The vines are some of the oldest in CHATEAUNEUF and the Grenache-based red★★★ is among the best modern-style wines of the RHÔNE VALLEY. There is a small amount of white★★, which is rich and heavenly when very young. Good second wine, Télégramme. Also owns improving la Roquette★ in Châteauneuf and les Pallières★★ in GIGONDAS. Best years (reds) 2007 06 05 **04 03 01** 00 99 98 97 96 95 90 89 88.

VILLA MARIA *Auckland and Marlborough, New Zealand* Founder George Fistonich also owns Esk Valley and Vidal (both in HAWKES BAY). Villa Maria Reserve Merlot-Cabernet★★★, Reserve Merlot★★, Esk Valley The Terraces★★★ and Vidal Merlot-Cabernet★★ are superb. Syrahs are among New Zealand's best: Esk Valley and Villa Maria Reserve both ★★★, Vidal★★. Reserve Chardonnay from Vidal★★ and Villa Maria★★ are power-packed wines. The Villa Maria range includes various MARLBOROUGH Sauvignon Blancs, with Clifford Bay Reserve★★, Wairau Reserve★★ and Taylors Pass★★ outstanding. Also from Marlborough impressive Pinot Noir Reserve★★, Seddon Pinot Gris Reserve★, Reserve Riesling★ and stunning botrytized Noble Riesling★★★. Best years (Hawkes Bay reds) (2008) 07 **06 04 02** 00 98.

CH. DE VILLENEUVE *Saumur-Champigny AC, Loire Valley, France* The secret of this property's success lies in low yields, picked when properly ripe. First-class SAUMUR-CHAMPIGNY★, with concentrated, mineral Vieilles Vignes★★ and le Grand Clos★★. Also good white stainless-steel-fermented SAUMUR★ and barrel-fermented Saumur Les Cormiers★★. Best years (reds) (2008) 06 05 **04 03 02 01** 97 96.

VILLIERA *Stellenbosch WO, South Africa* The speciality is Cap Classique sparklers (Monro Brut★, additive-free Brut Natural Chardonnay★). Still whites include Sauvignon Blanc (Bush Vine★), a consistent Riesling and 2 delicious Chenin Blancs★ with different degrees of oaking. Monro, a structured Merlot-led BORDEAUX blend, is best among the reds. Fired Earth★ is a tasty Late Bottled PORT style. Also 'mentor' to neighbouring M'hudi project (Pinotage★, Sauvignon Blanc★).

VIN SANTO *Tuscany, Italy* The 'holy wine' of TUSCANY can be one of the world's great sweet wines – but the term has been wantonly abused (happily the *liquoroso* version, made by adding alcohol to partially fermented must, is no longer recognized as a legitimate style). Made from grapes either hung from rafters or laid on mats to dry, the wines fermented and aged in small barrels for up to 7–8 years, should be nutty oxidized, full of the flavours of dried apricots and crystallized orange peel concentrated and long. Also made in UMBRIA, and in TRENTINO as Vino Santo using the Nosiola grape. Best producers: Castello di AMA★, AVIGNONESI★★★ Fattoria di Basciano★★, Bindella★★, Cacchiano★, Capezzana★★, Fattoria del Cerro★★, Corzano e Paterno★★, FONTODI★★, ISOLE E OLENA★★★ Romeo★★, San Felice★★, San Gervasio★★, San Giusto a Rentennano★★★ SELVAPIANA★★, Villa Sant'Anna★★, Villa di Vetrice★, VOLPAIA★.

VIÑAS DEL VERO *Somontano DO, Aragón, Spain* Minerally unoaked Chardonnay and its toasty barrel-fermented counterpart★ are joined by more original whites such as Clarión★, a blend of Chardonnay

Gewürztraminer and Macabeo. Top reds are Secastilla★★ (old-vines Garnacha with some Syrah), Gran Vos★ (Merlot-Cabernet-Pinot Noir) and the red blend made by its subsidiary Blecua★★.

VINHO VERDE DOC *Minho and Douro Litoral, Portugal* 'Vinho Verde' can be red or white – 'green' only in the sense of being young. The whites are the most widely seen outside Portugal and range from sulphured and acidic to aromatic, flowery and fruity. One or two that fall outside the DOC regulations are sold as Vinho Regional Minho (Quinta da Covela★, Paço de Teixeiró). Best producers: Afros, Quinta de Alderiz, Quinta do Ameal★, Quinta da Aveleda, Quinta de Azevedo★★/SOGRAPE, Quinta da Baguinha★, Encostas dos Castelos, Moncão co-op (Deu la Deu Alvarinho★, Muralhas de Moncão), Muros de Melgaço★, Quintas de Melgaço, Palácio de Brejoeira, Casa de Sezim★, Quinta de Simães, Quinta de Soalheiro★★, Quinta do Tamariz★.

VINO NOBILE DI MONTEPULCIANO DOCG *Tuscany, Italy* The 'noble wine' from the hills around the town of Montepulciano is made from the Sangiovese grape, known locally as Prugnolo, with the help of a little Canaiolo and Mammolo (and increasingly, today, Merlot and Cabernet). At its best, it combines the power and structure of BRUNELLO DI MONTALCINO with the finesse and complexity found in top CHIANTI. Unfortunately, the best was a rare beast until relatively recently; improvement since the 1990s has been impressive. The introduction of what is essentially a second wine, ROSSO DI MONTEPULCIANO, has certainly helped. Best producers: AVIGNONESI★★, Bindella★, BOSCARELLI★★, La Braccesca★★/ANTINORI, Le Casalte★, La Ciarliana★, Contucci★, Dei★★, Del Cerro★★, Fassati★★, Gracciano★, Il Macchione★, Nottola★★, Palazzo Vecchio★, POLIZIANO★★, Redi★, Romeo★, Salcheto★★, Trerose★ (Simposio★★), Valdipiatta★. Best years: (2008) (07) 06 **04 03 01 00 99 97**.

VINSOBRES AC *Rhône Valley, France* Southern RHONE village whose hallmark is clear fruit; AC for red since 2005. A good area for Syrah, which goes into the blend with Grenache. Best producers: Chaume-Arnaud★, Constant-Duquesnoy, Coriançon★, Deurre★, Gramenon★, Jaume★, Moulin★, Perrin★, la Vinsobraise co-op.

VIOGNIER Traditionally grown only in the northern RHONE, most famously for the rare and expensive wines of CONDRIEU AC, Viognier is a poor yielder, prone to disease and difficult to vinify. The wine can be delicious: pear-fleshy, apricotty with a soft, almost waxy texture, usually a fragrance of spring flowers and sometimes a taste like crème fraîche. New, higher-yielding clones are now being grown in LANGUEDOC-ROUSSILLON, Ardèche and the southern Rhône as well as in Spain, Switzerland, Italy, Austria, the USA, Argentina, Chile, Australia, New Zealand and South Africa. Traditionally used in COTE-ROTIE to co-ferment with Syrah (Shiraz); this practice is now becoming popular in Australia, South Africa, California and South America. It is also increasingly being used as a blender with other, more neutral, white varieties to add perfume, texture and fruit.

VIRÉ-CLESSÉ AC *Mâconnais, Burgundy, France* Appellation created in 1998 out of 2 of the best MACON-VILLAGES. Controversially, the rules outlaw wines with residual sugar, thus excluding Jean Thévenet's extraordinary cuvées. Best producers: A Bonhomme★★, Bret Brothers★, O Merlin★, R Michel★★, Rijckaert★, Cave de Viré★, Ch. de Viré★. Best years: (2008) 07 **06** 05.

VIRGINIA *USA* Virginia has a rapidly growing and improving wine industry, with more than 130 wineries and 6 AVAs. Aromatic Viognier and earthy Cabernet Franc show most promise, and varietal Petit Verdot produces some enticingly aromatic reds. Many growers continue to tinker with other varieties such as Petit Manseng and Tannat. Virginia is also producing some distinguished fizz. Best producers: BARBOURSVILLE★, Chrysalis, HORTON★, Kluge, Linden★, Rockbridge, Valhalla, Veritas, White Hall★.

VIVIANI *Valpolicella DOC, Veneto, Italy* Claudio Viviani's 9ha (22-acre) site is turning out some beautifully balanced VALPOLICELLA. The top AMARONE, Casa dei Bepi★★★, is a model of enlightened modernity, and the Valpolicella Classico Superiore Campo Morar★★ and RECIOTO★★ are of a similar quality. Best years: (2008) 06 **04 03 01 00**.

ROBERTO VOERZIO *Barolo DOCG, Piedmont, Italy* One of the best of the new wave of BAROLO producers. Dolcetto (Priavino★) is successful, as is Vignaserra★★ – barrique-aged Nebbiolo with a little Cabernet – and the outstanding BARBERA D'ALBA Riserva Vigneto Pozzo dell'Annunziata★★★ Barriques are also used for fashioning his Barolo, but such is the quality and concentration of fruit that the oak does not overwhelm. Single-vineyard examples made in the best years include Brunate★★, Cerequio★★★, La Serra★★ and Riserva Capalot★★★. Best years (Barolo) (2008) (07) (06) 04 **03 01 00** 99 98 97 96 95 93 91 90 89 88 85.

COMTE GEORGES DE VOGÜÉ *Chambolle-Musigny, Côte de Nuits, Burgundy France* De Vogüé owns substantial holdings in 2 Grands Crus, BONNES MARES★★★ and MUSIGNY★★★, as well as in Chambolle's top Premier Cru les Amoureuses★★★. It is the sole producer of minute quantities o Musigny Blanc★★, but because of recent replanting the wine is currently being sold as (very expensive) BOURGOGNE Blanc. Best years: (Musigny (2008) 07 06 05 03 00 **99 98 97 96** 93 91 90.

VOLNAY AC *Côte de Beaune, Burgundy, France* Some of the most elegant rec wines of the CÔTE DE BEAUNE; attractive when young, good examples ca age well. The top Premiers Crus are Caillerets, Champans, Clos de Chênes, Santenots and Taillepieds. Best producers: R Ampeau★★ d'ANGERVILLE★★, H Boillot★★, J-M Boillot★★, J-M Bouley★, COCHE-DURY★★★ V GIRARDIN★★, LAFARGE★★, LAFON★★, Matrot★★, MONTILLE★★★ N POTEL★★, J Prieur★★, N Rossignol★★, J Voillot★★. Best years: (2007) 05 0 **02 99 98 97 96 95 93 91** 90.

CASTELLO DI VOLPAIA *Chianti Classico DOCG, Tuscany, Italy* Light perfumed but refined CHIANTI CLASSICO★ (Riserva★★). Two stylish SUPER TUSCANS, Balifico★★ and Coltassala★★, are both predominantl Sangiovese. Sometimes good but not great VIN SANTO★. Riccard Cotarella (FALESCO) is consultant enologist.

VOSNE-ROMANÉE AC *Côte de Nuits, Burgundy, France* The greatest villag in the CÔTE DE NUITS, with 6 Grands Crus and 13 Premiers Crus (notabl les Malconsorts, aux Brûlées and les Suchots) which are often as good a other villages' Grands Crus. The quality of Vosne's village wine is als high. In good years the wines need at least 6 years' aging, but 10–1 would be better. Best producers: R Arnoux★★★, Cacheux-Sirugue★★ S CATHIARD★★★, B CLAIR★★, B Clavelier★★, R Engel★★, GRIVOT★★★, Anr GROS★★★, A-F GROS★★, M GROS★★★, F Lamarche★★, Dom. LEROY★★★ Vicomte LIGER-BELAIR★★★, MEO-CAMUZET★★★, Mugneret-Gibourg★★ RION★★, Dom. de la ROMANEE-CONTI★★★, E Rouget★★★. Best years: (2008 07 06 05 03 02 **01 00** 99 **98 97 96 95 93 91** 90.

VOUGEOT AC *Côte de Nuits, Burgundy, France* Outside the walls of CLOS DE VOUGEOT there are only 11ha (27 acres) of Premier Cru and 5ha (12 acres) of other vines. Look out for Premier Cru Les Cras (red) and the Clos Blanc de Vougeot, first planted with white grapes in 1110. Best producers: Bertagna★, Chopin★★, C Clerget★, VOUGERAIE★★. Best years: (reds) (2008) 07 06 05 03 **02 00 99 98 96**.

DOM. DE LA VOUGERAIE *Côte de Nuits, Burgundy, France* An estate created by Jean-Claude BOISSET in 1999 out of the numerous vineyards – often excellent but under-achieving – that came with Burgundy merchant houses acquired during his rise to prominence since 1964. Wines have been generally outstanding, notably Clos Blanc de VOUGEOT★★★, GEVREY-CHAMBERTIN le MUSIGNY★★★ and Vougeot les Cras★★ reds. Best years: (reds) (2008) 07 06 05 03 **02 01 00 99**.

CH. LA VOULTE-GASPARETS *Corbières AC, Languedoc, France* CORBIERES with flavours of thyme and baked earth from old hillside vines. Cuvée Réservée★ and Romain Pauc★★ can be drunk young, but age well. Also a white Corbières. Best years: (Romain Pauc) 2007 06 05 **04 03 01**.

VOUVRAY AC *Loire Valley, France* Dry, medium-dry, sweet and sparkling wines from Chenin grapes east of Tours. The dry wines acquire beautifully rounded flavours after 6–8 years. Medium-dry wines, when well made from a single domaine, are worth aging for 20 years or more. Spectacular noble-rot-affected sweet wines can be produced when conditions are right. The fizz is some of the LOIRE's best. Best producers: Aubuisières★★, Bourillon-Dorléans★★, Champalou★, F Chidaine, CLOS NAUDIN★★, la Fontainerie★★, Gaudrelle★, Gautier★★, Haute Borne★, HUET★★★, Pichot★★, F Pinon★★, Taille aux Loups★★/BLOT, Vigneau-Chevreau★. Best years: (dry) 2008 **07 06**; (sweet) 2005 **04 03 02 01 99 97 96 95 90 89**.

VOYAGER ESTATE *Margaret River, Western Australia* Originally planted in 1978, owned since 92 by mining magnate Michael Wright and now run by his daughter, Alex. One of the most impressive cellar-door complexes in MARGARET RIVER. Stellar Chardonnay★★★, vibrant Sauvignon Blanc-Semillon★ and grassy Sauvignon Blanc. The Cabernet Sauvignon-Merlot★ and Shiraz have leapt up a notch in recent vintages.

WACHAU *Niederösterreich, Austria* This stunning 1390ha (3400-acre) stretch of the Danube is Austria's top region for dry whites, from Riesling and Grüner Veltliner. Best producers: Alzinger★★, F HIRTZBERGER★★★, Högl★★, Jamek★, KNOLL★★★, NIKOLAIHOF★★, F X PICHLER★★★, Rudi Pichler★★, PRAGER★★★, Schmelz★, Domäne Wachau★. Best years: (2008) 07 06 05 **04 03 02 01 00 99 98 97 95**.

WACHENHEIM *Pfalz, Germany* Wine village made famous by the BÜRKLIN-WOLF estate, its best vineyards can produce rich yet beautifully balanced Rieslings. Best producers: Josef BIFFAR★, BÜRKLIN-WOLF★★, Karl Schaefer★, J L WOLF★★. Best years: (2008) 07 05 **04 03 02 01 99 98**.

WAGRAM *Niederösterreich, Austria* 2730ha (6740-acre) wine region on both banks of the Danube, stretching from just north of Vienna west to St Pölten. Previously known as Donauland – the name changed in 2007 – Wagram is the source of fine Grüner Veltliners. Best producers: J Bauer★, K Fritsch★, Leth★, Bernhard Ott★★, Wimmer-Czerny★.

WAIHEKE ISLAND *North Island, New Zealand* GOLDWATER pioneered wine-making on this island in Auckland harbour in the early 1980s, and this tiny region is now home to over 30 wineries. Hot, dry ripening conditions have made high-quality Cabernet-based reds that sell for high prices. Chardonnay is now appearing, together with experimental plots of Syrah and Viognier. Best producers: GOLDWATER★★, Obsidian, Passage Rock★, STONYRIDGE★★★, Te Whau★. Best years: (reds) 2007 **05 04 02 00**.

WALKER BAY WO *South Africa* This maritime district on the south coast is home to a mix of grape varieties, but the holy grail of the majority is Pinot Noir, with the hub of activity in the Hemel en Aarde (heaven and earth) Valley. Also steely Sauvignon Blanc, minerally Chardonnay and refined Pinotage. Best producers: Ashbourne★, BOUCHARD FINLAYSON★, HAMILTON RUSSELL★★, Hermanuspietersfontein, Newton Johnson★. Best years: (Pinot Noir) 2008 07 **06 05 04 03 02 01 00**.

WALLA WALLA VALLEY AVA *Washington State, USA* Walla Walla has over 100 of WASHINGTON's wineries, but 55 have only been producing wine since 1999. Similarly, vineyard acreage, although only 4% of the state total, has trebled since 99 – and is still growing. If you think there's a gold-rush feel about this clearly exciting area you wouldn't be far wrong. Best producers: CAYUSE VINEYARDS★★, DUNHAM CELLARS★, K Vintners★, L'ECOLE NO. 41★★, LEONETTI CELLAR★★★, LONG SHADOWS VINTNERS★★, Northstar★, Pepper Bridge★, Reininger★, WOODWARD CANYON★★.

WARRE *Port DOC, Douro, Portugal* Part of the Symington group, with top-quality Vintage PORT★★★ and a good 'off-vintage' port from Quinta da Cavadinha★★. LBV★★ is in the traditional, unfiltered style. Warrior★ is a reliable ruby and Otima a solid 10-year-old tawny; Otima★ 20-year-old is much better. Best years: (Vintage) **2003 00 97 94 91 85 83 80 77 70 66 63**; (Cavadinha) 2001 **99 98 96 95 92 90 88 87 86 82 78**.

WARWICK *Stellenbosch WO, South Africa* Warwick produces the complex Trilogy★ BORDEAUX-style blend and a refined, fragrant Cabernet Franc★. The Three Cape Ladies★ red blend includes Pinotage along with Cabernet Sauvignon, Merlot and 'fourth' lady, Shiraz. Whites are represented by an unwooded Sauvignon Blanc and full-bodied, lightly oaked Chardonnay★. Best years: (Trilogy) 2007 06 05 **04 03 02 01 00**.

WASHINGTON STATE *USA* The second-largest premium wine-producing state in the US (after California), with more than 540 wineries. The chief growing areas are in irrigated high desert, east of the Cascade Mountains, where the COLUMBIA VALLEY AVA encompasses the smaller AVAs of YAKIMA VALLEY, WALLA WALLA VALLEY, Wahluke Slope, Horse Heaven Hills, Rattlesnake Hills and Red Mountain. Although the heat is not as intense as in California, long summer days with extra hours of sunshine due to the northern latitude seem to increase the intensity of fruit flavours and result in both red and white wines of great depth. Cabernets Sauvignon and Franc, Merlot, Syrah, Chardonnay, Semillon and Riesling can produce very good wines here.

GEOFF WEAVER *Adelaide Hills, South Australia* Low-yielding vines at Geoff Weaver's Lenswood vineyard produce top-quality fruit, from which he crafts limy Riesling★★, crisply gooseberryish Sauvignon★★ and stylish cool-climate Chardonnay★★. Pinot Noir is promising.

WEGELER *Bernkastel, Mosel; Oestrich-Winkel, Rheingau; Deidesheim, Pfalz, Germany*
The Wegeler family's 3 estates are dedicated primarily to Riesling, and dry wines make up the bulk of production. Whether dry or naturally sweet Auslese, the best merit ★★ and will develop well with 5 or more years of aging. Consistently good 'Geheimrat J' Sekt★★, too. Best years: (Mosel) (2008) 07 06 05 **04 02 01 99 98 97**.

WEHLEN *Mosel, Germany* Village whose steep Sonnenuhr vineyard produces some of the most intense Rieslings in Germany. Best producers: Kerpen, Dr LOOSEN★★★, MOLITOR★★, J J PRUM★★★, S A PRUM★, Max Ferd RICHTER★★, SELBACH-OSTER★★, WEGELER★, Dr Weins-Prüm★. Best years: (2008) 07 06 **04 03 02 01 99 98 97 95**.

ROBERT WEIL *Kiedrich, Rheingau, Germany* Huge investment from Japanese drinks giant SUNTORY, coupled with Wilhelm Weil's devotion to quality, has clearly paid off. Majestic sweet Auslese, Beerenauslese and Trockenbeerenauslese Rieslings★★★ and dry Rieslings★ are crisp and elegant, although the regular wines are less spectacular than the sweet ones. Best years: (2008) 07 06 **05 04 03 02 01 99 98 95**.

WEINBACH *Alsace AC, Alsace, France* This Kaysersberg estate is run by the Faller family. The extensive range (which includes cuvées Théo, Ste-Catherine and Laurence) is complicated, with Théo★★ being the lightest; Laurence wines are from the non-cru Altenbourg; Ste-Catherine★★ bottlings come from the Grand Cru Schlossberg and are late picked, though not technically Vendange Tardive. The top dry wine is the Ste-Catherine Riesling Grand Cru Schlossberg L'Inédit★★★. Quintessence★★★ is an SGN from Pinot Gris or Gewurztraminer. All the wines are exceptionally balanced and, while delightful on release, can age for many years. Best years: (Grand Cru Riesling) (2008) 07 05 **04 02 01 00 99 98 97 96 95 94 93 92 90**.

WEINERT *Mendoza, Argentina* Buying grapes from some of the oldest vineyards in LUJÁN DE CUYO, Weinert has built a reputation for Malbec. Its oxidative approach to winemaking creates complex, long-lived reds such as mocha and black cherry Gran Vino★★. Estrella (Star) Malbec★★ is an eccentric red released decades after the vintage.

WEISSBURGUNDER See PINOT BLANC.

WELSCHRIESLING Unrelated to the great Riesling of the Rhine, this grape makes some of the best sweet wines in Austria, but tends to be rather dull as a dry wine. It is highly esteemed in Hungary as Olasz Rizling. As Riesling Italico it is decreasingly planted in northern Italy, where it can produce decent dry whites.

WENDOUREE *Clare Valley, South Australia* Small winery using old-fashioned methods to make enormous, ageworthy reds★★★ from paltry yields off their own very old Shiraz, Cabernet, Malbec and Mataro (Mourvèdre) vines, plus tiny amounts of sweet Muscat★. Reds can, and do, age beautifully for 30 years or more. Best years: (reds) (2008) 06 (05) 04 03 02 01 **99 98 96 95 94 92 91 90 86 83 82 81 80 78 76 75**.

WESTEND *Riverina, New South Wales, Australia* The Calabria family winery (established in 1945) has dramatically increased production and improved quality in recent years. The 3 Bridges range includes a powerful Durif★ and the lush, honeyed Golden Mist Botrytis Semillon★. Richland is one of Australia's best budget ranges (especially Pinot Grigio and Sauvignon Blanc).

WESTERN AUSTRALIA Only the south-west corner of this state is suited to vines, the SWAN DISTRICT and Perth environs being the oldest and hottest area, with present attention (and more than 260 producers) focused on GREAT SOUTHERN, MARGARET RIVER, Geographe and PEMBERTON. The state produces just over 4% of Australia's grape crush but about 20% of its premium wines.

HERMANN J WIEMER *Finger Lakes AVA, New York State, USA* Wiemer's family has 300 years' experience of winemaking in the MOSEL; it is natural that he would play a role in establishing the FINGER LAKES as a premier region for Riesling. He worked with local pioneer Dr Konstantin FRANK before establishing his own winery in 1979. Wiemer excels in the sweeter style, including an Auslese-style Late Harvest Riesling★. The sparkling wines are not to be missed.

WIEN *Austria* 680ha (1680-acre) wine region within the city limits of Wien (Vienna). The best wines come from south-facing sites in Grinzing, Nussdorf and Weiden, and the Bisamberg hill east of the Danube. The local 'Gemischter Satz' tradition of field-blend vineyards is being revived by many growers. Best producers: Christ, Edlmoser, Mayer, Schilling, WIENINGER★★, Zahel. Best years: (2008) 07 **05 04** 03.

WIENINGER *Stammersdorf, Wien, Austria* Fritz Wieninger has risen above the parochial standards of many Viennese growers to offer a range of elegant, well-crafted wines from Chardonnay and Pinot Noir. The best range is often the Select★★, the pricier Grand Select★ being often over-oaked. Recent additions are brilliant white wines from the renowned Nussberg★★ vineyard. Best years: (2008) 07 **06 05 04** 03.

WILLAMETTE VALLEY AVA *Oregon, USA* Wet winters, generally dry summers, and a so-so chance of long, cool autumn days provide sound growing conditions for cool-climate varieties such as Pinot Noir, Pinot Gris and Chardonnay. Dundee Hills, with its volcanic hillsides, is considered the best sub-region. Best producers: ADELSHEIM★, ARGYLE★ BEAUX FRERES★★, BERGSTROM★★, CRISTOM★, DOMAINE DROUHIN★★, DOMAINE SERENE★★, ELK COVE★, Evesham Wood★, PONZI★, Sineann★, SOTER★, WillaKenzie★, Ken WRIGHT★. Best years: (2007) 06 **04 03** 02 00.

WILLIAMS SELYEM *Russian River Valley AVA, California, USA* The cult following for the Pinot Noirs, especially the J Rochioli Vineyard★★, has diminished somewhat in recent years, but Williams Selyem continues to make exemplary Pinot Noirs from various regions, including SONOMA COAST★ and ANDERSON VALLEY★. Zins are good too. Best years: (Pinot Noir) 2005 04 **03 02** 01 00 99 98 97 96 95 94.

WINKEL *Rheingau, Germany* RHEINGAU village whose best vineyard is the large Hasensprung but the most famous one is Schloss Vollrads – an ancient estate that does not use the village name on its label. Best producers: Hamm, Prinz von Hessen, Johannishof★★, SCHLOSS VOLLRADS★ (since 1999) WEGELER★. Best years: (2007) 06 05 04 **03 02** 01 99 98.

WINNINGEN *Mosel, Germany* A small group of growers has shown that the steep slopes of this little-known village, particularly the Ühlen and Röttgen sites, can produce excellent Rieslings, especially in a rich dry style. Best producers: HEYMANN-LOWENSTEIN★★, Reinhard Knebel★★, Richard Richter★. Best years: (2008) 07 06 05 **04 03** 02 01.

WIRRA WIRRA *McLaren Vale, South Australia* Outstanding producer with fine ADELAIDE HILLS whites – well-balanced and tangy Sauvignon Blanc★ and tight, fine yet creamy Chardonnay★★ – and soft MCLAREN VALE reds led by delicious The Angelus (Dead Ringer outside Australia) Cabernet★★

chocolaty RSW Shiraz★★ and stylish, concentrated Woodhenge Shiraz★. In 2007 purchased outstanding Rayner vineyard in the McLaren Vale. Best years: (RSW Shiraz) 2008 06 05 04 03 **02 01** 98 96 94 91 90.

WITHER HILLS *Marlborough, South Island, New Zealand* Quality-focused winery bought in 2002 by New Zealand brewing group Lion Nathan. Talented founder/winemaker Brent Marris resigned as manager after the 2007 vintage to focus on his label 'The Ned', but long-time winemaker Ben Glover has made sure that quality and styles are maintained. A trio of MARLBOROUGH wines – concentrated, reasonably pungent Sauvignon Blanc★, fruit-focused Chardonnay★ and vibrant Pinot Noir★ – are made in fairly big quantities and though their personality has faded a bit they're still fairly true to the original Wither Hills style. Best years: (Sauvignon Blanc) **2007** 06 04.

WITTMANN *Westhofen, Rheinhessen, Germany* Philipp Wittmann has worked wonders at his family's biodynamic estate, succeeding equally with bold dry Rieslings★★, Chardonnay★★ and voluptuous Trockenbeerenauslese ★★★. Best years: (2007) 06 05 **04 03** 02 01.

J L WOLF *Wachenheim, Pfalz, Germany* Ernst Loosen, of Dr LOOSEN, took over this underperforming estate in 1996. A string of concentrated, mostly dry Rieslings★★ have won it a place among the region's top producers. Best years: (2008) 07 06 **05 03 02** 01.

WÖLFFER ESTATE *Long Island, New York State, USA* One of the few wineries in LONG ISLAND's Hamptons (playground for New York's rich and famous), Wölffer created a sensation in the early 2000s when it released a 'Premier Cru' Merlot priced at a lofty $100. It is good – but overshadowed by the more modestly priced Estate Selection Merlot★, a rich Pinot Gris and a spritely rosé. Wölffer died in a swimming accident in 2008.

WOODWARD CANYON *Walla Walla Valley AVA, Washington State, USA* Big, barrel-fermented Chardonnays (Celilo Vineyard★) were the trademark wines for many years, but today the focus is on reds, led by Artist Series★★ Cabernet Sauvignon and Old Vines★★ Cabernet Sauvignon. Merlot★★ is rich, velvety and deeply perfumed. Red BORDEAUX-style blend is labelled Charbonneau★, the name of the vineyard where the fruit is grown. Best years: (top Cabernet Sauvignon) (2007) 06 05 **04 03** 02.

KEN WRIGHT CELLARS *Willamette Valley AVA, Oregon, USA* Ken Wright produces more than a dozen succulent, single-vineyard Pinot Noirs. Bold and rich with new oak flavour, they range from good to ethereal, led by the Carter★★, Savoya★★, Guadalupe★★, McCrone★★ and Shea★. Fine WASHINGTON Chardonnay from the Celilo Vineyard★★ and a crisp Freedom Hill Vineyard Pinot Blanc★ are made in very small quantities. Best years: (Pinot Noir) (2007) 06 05 **04 03** 02.

WÜRTTEMBERG *Germany* 11,500ha (28,415-acre) region centred on the river Neckar. Two-thirds of the wine made is red, and the best comes from Lemberger (Blaufränkisch) or Spätburgunder (Pinot Noir) grapes. Massive yields are often responsible for pallid wines, especially from the locally popular Trollinger grape. A few of the top steep sites are now producing perfumed reds and racy Riesling. Best years: (reds) (2008) (07) 06 05 **04 03** 02 01.

WÜRZBURG *Franken, Germany* The centre of FRANKEN wines. Some Rieslings can be great, but the real star is Silvaner. Best producers: Bürgerspital★, JULIUSSPITAL★★, Staatlicher Hofkeller, Weingut am Stein★. Best years: (2008) 07 06 05 **04 03 02 01 00 99**.

WYNNS *Coonawarra, South Australia* Wynns' name is synonymous with COONAWARRA. It is now part of the giant Foster's Wine Group, but its personality seems to have suffered less than most of the group's other brands and, even at the top end, prices remain fair. Investment in vineyard rejuvenation is paying off. Wynns is best known for reds, such as good Shiraz★, Black Label Cabernet Sauvignon★★ and Johnson's Block Shiraz-Cabernet★. Top-end John Riddoch Cabernet Sauvignon★★★ and Michael Shiraz★★★ were deep, ripe, oaky styles, but latest releases show more restraint and elegance. Also attractive Chardonnay★ and delightful Riesling★. Best years: (John Riddoch) 2008 06 05 **04 03 99 96 94 91 90 88 86**.

YAKIMA VALLEY AVA *Washington State, USA* Important valley within the much larger COLUMBIA VALLEY AVA. Yakima is planted mostly to Chardonnay, Merlot and Cabernet Sauvignon and has more than 65 wineries. Best producers: Chinook★, DELILLE CELLARS★★, Hogue Cellars, Wineglass Cellars★.

YALUMBA *Barossa Valley, South Australia* Robert Hill Smith has taken his distinguished family firm to the pinnacle of Australian winemaking. There's an increasingly wide range under the Yalumba label, as well as a labyrinthine group under the banner of Hill Smith Family Vineyards. These include Heggies (minerally Riesling★★, plump Merlot★★, opulent Viognier★★), Hill Smith Estate (Sauvignon Blanc★), Pewsey Vale (Contours Riesling★★) and TASMANIA's Jansz★ (vintage★★, non-vintage★). Flagship reds are The Signature Cabernet-Shiraz★★, Octavius Shiraz★★ and The Menzies Cabernet★★, and all age well. Bush Vine Grenache★★, Virgilius Viognier★★ and Shiraz-Viognier★ are good too. High-quality Y Series varietals★ (sometimes ★★) are among Australia's finest quaffers. Budget-priced Redbank , Mawson's, Oxford Landing (Sauvignon★) and Angas Brut are enjoyable. Museum Reserve fortifieds (Muscat★★) are excellent, but rare. Best years: (The Signature) (2008) (07) 06 05 **04** 03 02 **01 00 99 98 97 96 95 93**.

YARRA VALLEY *Victoria, Australia* With its cool climate, the Yarra is asking to be judged as Australia's best Pinot Noir region. Exciting also for Chardonnay and Cabernet-Merlot blends and as a supplier of base wine for fizz. It is not yet clear what effect the disastrous bushfires of February 2009 will have on the vineyards. Best producers: Arthur's Creek★, COLDSTREAM HILLS★★, CARLEI★★, DE BORTOLI★★, Diamond Valley★★, DOMAINE CHANDON/Green Point★, Gembrook Hill, Giant Steps, Métier, MOUNT MARY★★, OAKRIDGE★★, St Huberts, TARRAWARRA★★, Toolangi, Wantirna Estate, Yarrabank★, Yarra Burn★, Yarra Yering★★, Yeringberg★, Yering Station★★.

YATIR *Judean Hills, Israel* Rising star, whose winery is situated in the north-east Negev desert. Rich, full reds from high-altitude vineyards within Israel's largest forest: top red, Yatir Forest★★, has ripe dark fruit backed by Mediterranean herbs; also a silky Cabernet Sauvignon★ and fresh Sauvignon Blanc. Best years: (red) 2005 04 03 **02 01**.

YELLOWTAIL *Riverina, New South Wales, Australia* Yellowtail, Australia's fastest-growing export brand ever, has made the RIVERINA family winery, Casella, a major world player. Artfully crafted but overly sweet wines.

CH. D'YQUEM★★★ *Sauternes AC, 1er Cru Supérieur, Bordeaux, France* Often
rated the most sublime sweet wine in the world, Yquem's total
commitment to quality is unquestionable. Despite a large vineyard
(100ha/250 acres), production is tiny. Only fully noble-rotted grapes are
picked, often berry by berry, and low yield means each vine produces
only a glass of wine! This precious liquid is then fermented in new oak
barrels and left to mature for 3–4 years before bottling. It is one of the
world's most expensive wines, in constant demand because of its
richness and exotic flavours. Quality took a step forward during the
1990s and seems to have gone even further during the 2000s. A dry
white, Ygrec, is made most years. In 1999 LVMH won a takeover battle
with the Lur-Saluces family, owners for 406 years. Best years: 2007 06 05
04 03 **02 01 00** 99 98 97 96 95 94 93 90 89 88 86 83 81 80 79 76 75 71
70 67 62.

ZILLIKEN *Saarburg, Mosel, Germany* Estate specializing in exquisite
Rieslings★★ (Auslese, Eiswein often ★★★) from the Saarburger Rausch.
Best years: (2008) 07 06 05 04 **03 02 01** 99 97 95.

ZIND-HUMBRECHT *Alsace AC, Alsace, France* Olivier Humbrecht is one of
France's outstanding winemakers, with an approach that emphasizes the
individuality of each site and each vintage. Wines from 4 Grand Cru sites
– Rangen, Goldert, Hengst and Brand – are superlative (Riesling★★★,
Gewurztraminer★★★, Pinot Gris★★★ and Muscat★★), the Rangen in
particular producing wines unlike any others in Alsace. Wines from
specific non-Grand Cru vineyards such as Clos Windsbuhl and Clos
Jebsal are also exceptional. Vendange Tardive and Sélection de Grains
Nobles wines are almost invariably of ★★★ quality. Even basic
Sylvaners★ and Pinot Blancs★★ are fine. Wines often have some
residual sugar, but it's all natural. Best years: (Grand Cru Riesling) (2008) 07
05 04 **03 02 01 00** 99 98 97 96 95.

ZINFANDEL CALIFORNIA's versatile red grape can make big, juicy, fruit-
packed wine – often farmed from very old vines – or insipid, sweetish
'blush' labelled as White Zinfandel, or even late-harvest dessert wine.
Some Zinfandel is now made in other countries, with notable examples
in Australia and South Africa. Best producers: (California) Brown★★, Cline
Cellars★★, Dashe★★, DRY CREEK VINEYARD★★, DUTTON GOLDFIELD★★, Gary
Farrell★★, FETZER★, HARTFORD★, MARIAH★, Martinelli★★, Michael-David
(Earthquake), Nalle★★, Preston★, Rafanelli★★, RAVENSWOOD★, RIDGE★★★,
Rosenblum★★, Saddleback★★, St Francis★★, SEGHESIO★★, Trinitas★★,
TURLEY★★; (Australia) CAPE MENTELLE★★, Kangarilla Road, Nepenthe★★,
Smidge, Tscharke. See also PRIMITIVO DI MANDURIA.

FAMILIA ZUCCARDI *Mendoza, Argentina* One of Argentina's great success
stories. Dynamic owner José Zuccardi has created a range of utterly
enjoyable easy-drinking wines, from basic Santa Julia reds★ and Serie
A★ upward. Santa Julia Reservas and Zuccardi 'Q'★ (Tempranillo★★)
wines have improved dramatically with the introduction of up-to-date
equipment. Top-of-the-line Zeta★★, a Malbec-Tempranillo blend, is a
serious yet sensual red. Zuccardi also experiments with more grape
varieties than anyone else in Argentina, including such varieties as
Marselan, Caladoc, Tannat and Touriga Nacional. Son Sebastian is a
whizz-kid with sparklers (red Bonarda★ is ace) and sweeties. He's even
made a sweet botrytized Cabernet! My kind of guy.

GLOSSARY OF WINE TERMS

AC/AOC (APPELLATION D'ORIGINE CONTRÔLÉE)
The top category of French wines, defined by regulations covering vineyard yields, grape varieties, geographical boundaries, alcohol content and production method. Guarantees origin and style of a wine, but not its quality.

ACID/ACIDITY
Naturally present in grapes and essential to wine, providing balance and stability and giving the refreshing tang in white wines and the appetizing grip in reds.

ADEGA
Portuguese for winery.

AGING
An alternative term for maturation.

ALCOHOLIC CONTENT
The alcoholic strength of wine, expressed as a percentage of the total volume of the wine. Typically in the range of 7–15%.

ALCOHOLIC FERMENTATION
The process whereby yeasts, natural or added, convert the grape sugars into alcohol (Ethyl alcohol, or Ethanol) and carbon dioxide.

AMONTILLADO
Traditionally dry style of sherry. See Jerez y Manzanilla in main A–Z.

ANBAUGEBIET
German for growing region; these names will appear on labels of all QbA and QmP wines. There are 13 Anbaugebiete: Ahr, Baden, Franken, Hessische Bergstrasse, Mittelrhein, Mosel-Saar-Ruwer, Nahe, Pfalz, Rheingau, Rheinhessen, Saale-Unstrut, Sachsen and Württemberg.

AUSBRUCH
Austrian Prädikat category used for sweet wines from the town of Rust.

AUSLESE
German and Austrian Prädikat category meaning that the grapes were 'selected' for their higher ripeness.

AVA (AMERICAN VITICULTURAL AREA)
System of appellations of origin for US wines.

AZIENDA AGRICOLA
Italian for estate or farm. It also indicates wine made from grapes grown by the proprietor.

BARREL AGING
Time spent maturing in wood, usually oak, during which wine takes on flavours from the wood.

BARREL FERMENTATION
Oak barrels may be used for fermentation instead of stainless steel to give a rich, oaky flavour to the wine.

BARRIQUE
The *barrique bordelaise* is the traditional Bordeaux oak barrel of 225 litres (50 gallons) capacity.

BAUMÉ
A scale measuring must weight (the amount of sugar in grape juice) to estimate potential alcohol content.

BEERENAUSLESE
German and Austrian Prädikat category applied to wines made from 'individually selected' berries affected by noble rot (*Edelfäule* in German). The wines are rich and sweet. Beerenauslese wines are only produced in the best years in Germany, but in Austria they are a regular occurrence.

BEREICH
German for region or district within a wine region or *Anbaugebiet*. Bereichs tend to be large, and the use of a Bereich name, such as Bereich Bingen, without qualification is seldom an indication of quality – in most cases, quite the reverse.

BIODYNAMIC VITICULTURE
This approach works with the movement of the planets and cosmic forces to achieve health and balance in the soil and in the vine. Vines are treated with infusions of mineral, animal and plant materials, applied in homeopathic quantities. An increasing number of growers are turning to biodynamism, with some

BOTTLE SIZES

CHAMPAGNE

Magnum	1.5 litres	2 bottles
Jeroboam	3 litres	4 bottles
Rehoboam	4.5 litres	6 bottles
Methuselah	6 litres	8 bottles
Salmanazar	9 litres	12 bottles
Balthazar	12 litres	16 bottles
Nebuchadnezzar	15 litres	20 bottles

BORDEAUX

Magnum	1.5 litres	2 bottles
Marie-Jeanne	2.25 litres	3 bottles
Double-magnum	3 litres	4 bottles
Jeroboam	4.5 litres	6 bottles
Imperial	6 litres	8 bottles

astonishing results, but it is labour-intensive and generally confined to smaller estates.

BLANC DE BLANCS
White wine made from one or more white grape varieties. Used especially for sparkling wines; in Champagne, denotes wine made entirely from the Chardonnay grape.

BLANC DE NOIRS
White wine made from black grapes only – the juice is separated from the skins to avoid extracting any colour. Most often seen in Champagne, where it describes wine made from Pinot Noir and/or Pinot Meunier grapes.

BLENDING
The art of mixing together wines of different origin, style or age, often to balance out acidity, weight etc. Winemakers often use the term *assemblage*.

BODEGA
Spanish for winery.

BOTRYTIS
See noble rot.

BRUT
French term for dry sparkling wines, especially Champagne.

CARBONIC MACERATION
Winemaking method used to produce fresh fruity reds for drinking young. Whole (uncrushed) bunches of grapes are fermented in closed containers – a process that extracts lots of fruit and colour, but little tannin.

CHAMPAGNE METHOD
Traditional method used for all of the world's finest sparkling wines. A second fermentation takes place in the bottle, producing carbon dioxide which, kept in solution under pressure, gives the wine its fizz.

CHAPTALIZATION
Legal addition of sugar during fermentation to raise a wine's alcoholic strength. More necessary in cool climates where lack of sun produces insufficient natural sugar in the grape.

CHARMAT
See cuve close.

CHÂTEAU
French for castle: widely used in France to describe any wine estate, large or small.

CHIARETTO
Italian for a rosé wine of very light pink colour from around Lake Garda.

CLARET
English for red Bordeaux wines, from the French *clairet*, which was traditionally used to describe a lighter style of red Bordeaux.

CLARIFICATION
Term covering any wine-making process (such as filtering or fining) that involves the removal of solid matter either from the must or the wine.

CLONE
Strain of grape species. The term is usually taken to mean laboratory-produced, virus-free clones, selected to produce higher or lower quantity, or selected for resistance to frost or disease.

CLOS
French for a walled vineyard – as in Burgundy's Clos de Vougeot – also commonly incorporated into the names of estates (e.g. Clos des Papes), whether they are walled or not.

COLD FERMENTATION
Long, slow fermentation at low temperature to extract maximum freshness from the grapes. Crucial for whites in hot climates.

COLHEITA
Aged tawny port from a single vintage. *See* Port in main A–Z.

COMMUNE
A French village and its surrounding area or parish.

CO-OPERATIVE
In a co-operative cellar, growers who are members bring their grapes for vinification and bottling under a collective label. In terms of quantity, the French wine industry is dominated by co-ops. They often use less workaday titles, such as Caves des Vignerons, Producteurs Réunis, Union des Producteurs or Cellier des Vignerons.

CORKED/CORKY
Wine fault derived from a cork which has become contaminated, usually with Trichloroanisole or TCA. The mouldy, stale smell is unmistakable. Nothing to do with pieces of cork in the wine.

COSECHA
Spanish for vintage.

CÔTE
French word for a slope or hillside, which is where many, but not all, of the country's best vineyards are found.

CRÉMANT
French term for traditional-method sparkling wine from Alsace, Bordeaux, Burgundy, Die, Jura, Limoux, Loire and Luxembourg.

CRIANZA
Spanish term for the youngest official category of oak-matured wine. A red Crianza wine must have had at least 2 years' aging (1 in oak, 1 in bottle) before sale; a white or rosé, 1 year.

CRU
French for growth, meaning a specific plot of

land or particular estate. In Burgundy, growths are divided into Grands (great) and Premiers (first) Crus, and apply solely to the actual land. In Champagne the same terms are used for whole villages. In Bordeaux there are various hierarchical levels of Cru referring to estates rather than their vineyards. In Italy the term is used frequently, in an unofficial way, to indicate a single-vineyard or special-selection wine.

CRU BOURGEOIS
French term for wines from the Médoc that are ranked immediately below the Crus Classés (last revised in 2003). Many are excellent value for money.

CRU CLASSÉ
The Classed Growths are the aristocracy of Bordeaux, ennobled by the Classifications of 1855 (for the Médoc, Barsac and Sauternes), 1955, 1969, 1986, 1996 and 2006 (for St-Émilion) and 1953 and 1959 (for Graves). Curiously, Pomerol has never been classified. The modern classifications are more reliable than the 1855 version, which was based solely on the price of the wines at the time of the Great Exhibition in Paris, but in terms of prestige the 1855 Classification remains the most important. With the exception of a single alteration in 1973, when Ch. Mouton-Rothschild was elevated to First Growth status, the list has not changed since 1855. It certainly needs revising.

CUVE CLOSE
A bulk process used to produce inexpensive sparkling wines. The second fermentation, which produces the bubbles, takes place in tank rather than in the bottle (as in the superior Traditional Method). Also called Charmat.

CUVÉE
French for the contents of a single vat or tank, but usually indicates a wine blended from either different grape varieties or the best barrels of wine.

DEGORGEMENT
Stage in the production of Champagne-method wines when the sediment, collected in the neck of the bottle during *remuage*, is removed.

DEMI-SEC
French for medium-dry.

DO (DENOMINACIÓN DE ORIGEN)
Spain's equivalent of the French AC quality category, regulating origin and production methods.

DOC (DENOMINAÇÃO DE ORIGEM CONTROLADA)
Portugal's top regional classification for wines.

DOCA (DENOMINACIÓN DE ORIGEN CALIFICADA)
Spanish quality wine category, intended to be one step up from DO. So far only Rioja and Priorat qualify.

DOC (DENOMINAZIONE DI ORIGINE CONTROLLATA)
Italian quality wine category, regulating origin, grape varieties, yield and production methods.

DOCG (DENOMINAZIONE DI ORIGINE CONTROLLATA E GARANTITA)
The top tier of the Italian classification system.

DOMAINE
French term for wine estate.

DOSAGE
A sugar and wine mixture added to sparkling wine after *dégorgement* which affects how sweet or dry it will be.

EDELZWICKER
Blended wine from Alsace, usually bland.

EINZELLAGE
German for an individual vineyard site which is generally farmed by several growers. The name is preceded on the label by that of the village; for example, the Wehlener Sonnenuhr is the Sonnenuhr vineyard in Wehlen. The mention of a particular site should signify a superior wine. Sadly, this is not necessarily so.

EISWEIN
Rare, chiefly German and Austrian, late-harvested wine made by picking the grapes and pressing them while frozen. This concentrates the sweetness of the grape as most of the liquid is removed as ice. *See also* Icewine.

ESCOLHA
Portuguese for selection.

FEINHERB
Disliking the unsatisfactory term Halbtrocken, some producers prefer the term Feinherb. It lacks legal definition but usually applies to wines with 9–25g per litre of residual sugar.

FILTERING
Removal of yeasts, solids and any impurities from a wine before bottling.

FINING
Method of clarifying wine by adding a coagulant (e.g. egg whites, isinglass, bentonite) to remove soluble particles such as proteins and excessive tannins.

FINO
The lightest, freshest style of sherry. *See* Jerez y Manzanilla in main A–Z.

FLOR
A film of yeast which forms on the surface of fino sherries (and some other wines) in the barrel, preventing oxidation and imparting a tangy, dry flavour.

FLYING WINEMAKER
Term coined in the late 1980s to describe enologists, many Australian-trained, brought in to improve the quality of wines in many underperforming wine regions.

FORTIFIED WINE
Wine which has high-alcohol grape spirit added, usually before the initial fermentation is completed, thereby preserving sweetness.

FRIZZANTE
Italian for semi-sparkling wine, usually made dry, but sometimes sweet.

GARAGE WINE
See vin de garage.

GARRAFEIRA
Portuguese term for wine from an outstanding vintage, with 0.5% more alcohol than the minimum required, and 2 years' aging in vat or barrel followed by 1 year in bottle for reds, and 6 months of each for whites. Also used by merchants for their best blended and aged wines. Use of the term is in decline as producers opt for the more readily recognized Reserva as an alternative on the label.

GRAN RESERVA
Top category of Spanish wines from a top vintage, with at least 5 years' aging (2 of them in cask) for reds and 4 for whites.

GRAND CRU
French for great growth. Supposedly the best vineyard sites in Alsace, Burgundy, Champagne and parts of Bordeaux –

and should produce the most exciting wines.

GROSSLAGE
German term for a grouping of vineyards. Some are not too big, and have the advantage of allowing small amounts of higher QmP wines to be made from the grapes from several vineyards. But sometimes the use of vast Grosslage names (e.g. Niersteiner Gutes Domtal) deceives consumers into believing they are buying something special. Top estates have agreed not to use Gross-lage names on their labels.

HALBTROCKEN
German for medium dry. In Germany and Austria medium-dry wine has 9–18g per litre of residual sugar, though sparkling wine is allowed up to 50g per litre. See Feinherb.

ICEWINE
A speciality of Canada, produced from juice squeezed from ripe grapes that have frozen on the vine. See also Eiswein.

IGT (INDICAZIONE GEOGRAFICA TIPICA)
The Italian equivalent of the French vin de pays. As in the Midi, both premium and everyday wines may share the same appellation. Many of the Super-Tuscan vini da tavola are now sold under a regional IGT.

IPR (INDICAÇÃO DE PROVENIÊNCIA REGULAMENTADA)
The second tier in the Portuguese wine classifications, for regions awaiting approval for DOC. See page 37.

KABINETT
Term used for the lowest level of QmP wines in Germany.

LANDWEIN
German or Austrian 'country' wine; the

equivalent of French vin de pays. The wine must have a territorial definition and may be chaptalized to give it more alcohol.

LATE HARVEST
See Vendange Tardive.

LAYING DOWN
The storing of wine which will improve with age.

LEES
Sediment – dead yeast cells, grape pips (seeds), pulp and tartrates – thrown by wine during fermentation and left behind after racking. Some wines are left on the fine lees for as long as possible to take on extra flavour.

MACERATION
Important winemaking process for red wines whereby colour, flavour and/or tannin are extracted from grape skins before, during or after fermentation. The period lasts from a few days to several weeks.

MALOLACTIC FERMENTATION
Secondary fermentation whereby harsh malic acid is converted into mild lactic acid and carbon dioxide. Normal in red wines but often prevented in whites to preserve a fresh, fruity taste.

MANZANILLA
The tangiest style of sherry, similar to fino. See Jerez y Manzanilla in main A–Z.

MATURATION
Term for the beneficial aging of wine.

MERITAGE
American term for red or white wines made from a blend of Bordeaux grape varieties.

MESOCLIMATE
The climate of a specific geographical area, be it a vineyard or simply a hillside or valley.

MIDI

A loose geographical term, virtually synonymous with Languedoc-Roussillon, covering the vast, sunbaked area of southern France between the Pyrenees and the Rhône Valley.

MOELLEUX

French for soft or mellow, used to describe sweet or medium-sweet wines, particularly in the Loire.

MOUSSEUX

French for sparkling wine.

MUST

The mixture of grape juice, skins, pips and pulp produced after crushing (but prior to completion of fermentation), which will eventually become wine.

MUST WEIGHT

An indicator of the sugar content of juice – and therefore the ripeness of grapes.

NÉGOCIANT

French term for a merchant who buys and sells wine. A *négociant-éléveur* is a merchant who buys, makes, ages and sells wine.

NEW WORLD

When used as a geographical term, New World includes the Americas, South Africa, Australia and New Zealand. By extension, it is also a term used to describe the clean, fruity, upfront style now in evidence all over the world, but pioneered in the USA and Australia.

NOBLE ROT

(*Botrytis cinerea*) Fungus which, when it attacks ripe white grapes, shrivels the fruit and intensifies their sugar while adding a distinctive flavour. A vital factor in creating many of the world's finest sweet wines, such as Sauternes and Trockenbeerenauslese.

OAK

The wood used almost exclusively to make barrels for fermenting and aging fine wines. It adds flavours such as vanilla, and tannins; the newer the wood, the greater the impact.

OECHSLE

German scale measuring must weight (sugar content).

OLOROSO

The darkest, most heavily fortified style of sherry. *See* Jerez y Manzanilla in main A–Z.

OXIDATION

Over-exposure of wine to air, causing loss of fruit and flavour. Slight oxidation, such as occurs through the wood of a barrel or during racking, is part of the aging process and, in wines of sufficient structure, enhances flavour and complexity.

PASSITO

Italian term for wine made from dried grapes. The result is usually a sweet wine with a raisiny intensity of fruit. The drying process is called *appassimento*. *See also* Moscato Passito di Pantelleria, Recioto della Valpolicella, Recioto di Soave and Vin Santo in main A–Z.

PERLWEIN

German for a lightly sparkling wine.

PÉTILLANT

French for a lightly sparkling wine.

PHYLLOXERA

The vine aphid *Phylloxera vastatrix* attacks vine roots. It devastated vineyards around the world in the late 1800s soon after it arrived from America. Since then, the vulnerable *Vitis vinifera* has generally been grafted on to vinously inferior, but phylloxera-resistant, American rootstocks.

PRÄDIKAT

Grades defining quality wines in Germany and Austria. These are (in ascending order) Kabinett (not considered as Prädikat in Austria), Spätlese, Auslese, Beerenauslese, the Austrian-only category Ausbruch, and Trockenbeerenauslese. Strohwein and Eiswein are also Prädikat wines. Some Spätleses and even a few Ausleses are now made as dry wines.

PRÄDIKATSWEIN

The new term for QmP.

PREMIER CRU

First Growth; the top quality classification in parts of Bordeaux, but second to Grand Cru in Burgundy. Used in Champagne to designate vineyards just below Grand Cru.

PRIMEUR

French term for a young wine, often released for sale within a few weeks of the harvest. Beaujolais Nouveau is the best-known example.

QBA (QUALITÄTSWEIN BESTIMMTER ANBAUGEBIETE)

German for quality wine from designated regions. Sugar can be added to increase the alcohol content. Usually pretty ordinary, but from top estates this category offers excellent value. In Austria *Qualitätswein* is equivalent to German QbA.

QMP (QUALITÄTSWEIN MIT PRÄDIKAT)

German for quality wine with distinction. A higher category than QbA, with controlled yields and no sugar addition. QmP covers 6 levels based on the ripeness of the grapes: *see* Prädikat. The term will be replaced by Prädikats-wein from August 2007.

QUINTA
Portuguese for farm or estate.

RACKING
Gradual clarification of wine; the wine is transferred from one barrel or container to another, leaving the lees behind.

RANCIO
Fortified wine deliberately exposed to the effects of oxidation, found mainly in Languedoc-Roussillon and parts of Spain.

REMUAGE
Process in Champagne-making whereby the bottles, stored on their sides and at a progressively steeper angle in *pupitres*, are twisted, or riddled, each day so that the sediment moves down the sides and collects in the neck of the bottle on the cap, ready for *dégorgement*.

RESERVA
Spanish wines that have fulfilled certain aging requirements: reds must have at least 3 years' aging before sale, of which one must be in oak barrels; whites and rosés must have at least 2 years' age, of which 6 months must be in oak.

RÉSERVE
French for what is, in theory at least, a winemaker's finest wine. The word has no legal definition in France.

RIPASSO
A method used in Valpolicella to make wines with extra depth. Wine is passed over the lees of Recioto or Amarone della Valpolicella, adding extra alcohol and flavour, though also extra tannin and a risk of higher acidity and oxidation.

RISERVA
An Italian term, recognized in many DOCs and DOCGs, for a special selection of wine that has been aged longer

before release. It is only a promise of a more pleasurable drink if the wine had enough fruit and structure in the first place.

SAIGNÉE
Rosé wine takes its colour from the skins of red grapes: the juice is bled off (*saignée*) after a short period of contact with the skins.

SEC
French for dry. When applied to Champagne, it means medium-dry.

'SECOND' WINES
A second selection from a designated vineyard, usually lighter and quicker-maturing than the main wine.

SEDIMENT
Usually refers to residue thrown by a wine, particularly red, as it ages in bottle.

SEKT
German for sparkling wine. The best wines are made by the traditional Champagne method, from 100% Riesling or 100% Weissburgunder (Pinot Blanc).

SÉLECTION DE GRAINS NOBLES
A superripe category for sweet Alsace wines, now also being used by some producers of Coteaux du Layon in the Loire Valley. *See also* Vendange Tardive.

SMARAGD
The top of the three categories of wine from the Wachau in Austria, the lower two being Federspiel and Steinfeder. Made from very ripe and usually late-harvested grapes, the wines have a minimum of 12% alcohol, often 13–14%.

SOLERA
Traditional Spanish system of blending fortified wines, especially sherry and Montilla-Moriles.

SPÄTLESE
German for late-picked (riper) grapes. Often moderately sweet, though there are dry versions.

SPUMANTE
Italian for sparkling. Bottle-fermented wines are often referred to as *metodo classico* or *metodo tradizionale*.

SUPÉRIEUR
French for a wine with a slightly higher alcohol content than the basic AC.

SUPERIORE
Italian DOC wines with higher alcohol or more aging potential.

SUR LIE
French for on the lees, meaning wine bottled direct from the cask/fermentation vat to gain extra flavour from the lees. Common with quality Muscadet, white Burgundy, similar barrel-aged whites and, increasingly, commercial bulk whites.

TAFELWEIN
German for table wine.

TANNIN
Harsh, bitter, mouth-puckering element in red wine, derived from grape skins and stems, and from oak barrels. Tannins soften with age and are essential for long-term development in red wines.

TERROIR
A French term used to denote the combination of soil, climate and exposure to the sun – that is, the natural physical environment of the vine.

TRADITIONAL METHOD
See Champagne method.

TROCKEN
German for dry. In most parts of Germany and Austria Trocken matches the EU definition of dryness – less than 9g per litre residual sugar.

TROCKENBEEREN-AUSLESE (TBA)
German for 'dry berry selected', denoting grapes affected by noble rot (*Edelfäule* in German) – the wines will be lusciously sweet although low in alcohol.

VARIETAL
Wine made from, and named after, a single or dominant grape variety.

VDP
German organization recognizable on the label by a Prussian eagle bearing grapes. The quality of estates included is usually – but not always – high.

VDQS (VIN DÉLIMITÉ DE QUALITÉ SUPÉRIEURE)
The second-highest classification for French wines, behind AC. Being phased out after the 2010 vintage.

VELHO
Portuguese for old. Legally applied only to wines with at least 3 years' aging for reds and 2 years for whites.

VENDANGE TARDIVE
French for late harvest. Grapes are left on the vines beyond the normal harvest time to concentrate flavours and sugars. The term is traditional in Alsace. The Italian term is *vendemmia tardiva*.

VIEILLES VIGNES
French term for a wine made from vines at least 20 years old. Should have greater concentration than wine from younger vines.

VIÑA
Spanish for vineyard.

VIN DE GARAGE
Wines made on so small a scale they could be made in one's garage. Such wines may be made from vineyards of a couple of hectares or less, and are often of extreme concentration.

VIN DE PAILLE
Sweet wine found mainly in the Jura region of France. Traditionally, the grapes are left for 2–3 months on straw (*paille*) mats before fermentation to dehydrate, thus concentrating the sugars. The wines are sweet but slightly nutty.

VIN DE PAYS
The term gives a regional identity to wine from the country districts of France. It is a particularly useful category for adventurous winemakers who want to use good-quality grapes not allowed under the frequently restrictive AC regulations. Many are labelled with the grape variety.

VIN DE TABLE
French for table wine, the lowest quality level.

VIN DOUX NATUREL (VDN)
French for a fortified wine, where fermentation has been stopped by the addition of alcohol, leaving the wine 'naturally' sweet, although you could argue that stopping fermentation with a slug of powerful spirit is distinctly unnatural.

VIN JAUNE
A speciality of the Jura region in France, made from the Savagnin grape. In Château-Chalon it is the only permitted style. Made in a similar way to fino sherry but not fortified and aged for 6 years in oak. Unlike fino, *vin jaune* ages well.

VINIFICATION
The process of turning grapes into wine.

VINO DA TAVOLA
The Italian term for table wine, officially Italy's lowest level of production, is a catch-all that until recently applied to more than 80% of the nation's wine, with virtually no regulations controlling quality. Yet this category also provided the arena in the 1970s for the biggest revolution in quality that Italy has ever seen, with the creation of innovative, DOC-busting Super-Tuscans. *See* Super-Tuscans in main A–Z.

VINTAGE
The year's grape harvest, also used to describe wines of a single year. 'Off-vintage' is a year not generally declared as vintage. *See* Port in main A–Z.

VITICULTURE
Vine-growing and vineyard management.

VITIS VINIFERA
Vine species, native to Europe and Central Asia, from which almost all the world's quality wine is made.

VQA (VINTNERS QUALITY ALLIANCE)
Canadian equivalent of France's AC system, defining quality standards and designated viticultural areas.

WEISSHERBST
German rosé wine, a speciality of Baden.

WO (WINE OF ORIGIN)
South African system of appellations which certifies area of origin, grape variety and vintage.

YIELD
The amount of fruit, and ultimately wine, produced from a vineyard. Measured in hectolitres per hectare (hl/ha) in most of Europe and in the New World as tons per acre or tonnes per hectare. Yield may vary from year to year, and depends on grape variety, age and density of the vines, and viticultural practices.

WHO OWNS WHAT

The world's major drinks companies are getting bigger and, frankly, I'm worried. As these vast wine conglomerates stride across continents, it seems highly likely that local traditions will – for purely business reasons – be pared away, along with individuality of flavour. It's not all bad news: in some cases wineries have benefited from the huge resources that come with corporate ownership, but I can't help feeling nervous knowing that the fate of a winery rests in the hands of distant institutional investors. Below, I have listed some of the names that crop up again and again – and will no doubt continue to do so, as they aggressively pursue their grasp of market share.

Other wine companies – which bottle wines under their own names and feature in the main A–Z – are spreading their nets. GALLO has agreements with SIEUR D'ARQUES in southern France, Leonardo Da Vinci winery in Tuscany, MCWILLIAM'S of Australia and Whitehaven of New Zealand. The HESS COLLECTION in California owns Peter LEHMANN in Australia, GLEN CARLOU in South Africa and Colomé in Argentina. As well as Ch. MOUTON-ROTHSCHILD, the Rothschild family have other interests in France, co-own OPUS ONE and, in partnership with CONCHA Y TORO, produce ALMAVIVA in Chile.

The never-ending whirl of joint ventures, mergers and takeovers shows no signs of slowing down: the following can only be a snapshot at the time of going to press.

AXA-MILLESIMES

The French insurance giant AXA's subsidiary owns Bordeaux châteaux PETIT-VILLAGE, PICHON-LONGUEVILLE, Pibran and SUDUIRAUT, plus Dom. de l'Arlot in Burgundy, Mas Belles Eaux in the Languedoc, TOKAJI producer Disznókö and PORT producer Quinta DO NOVAL.

CONSTELLATION BRANDS

The world's largest wine company is a major producer not only in the USA, but also in Australia, New Zealand and Canada. The US-based company merged with Australia's BRL Hardy in 2003 and its portfolio now includes Amberley, Banrock Station, BAROSSA VALLEY ESTATE, BAY OF FIRES, Brookland Valley, Goundrey, HARDYS, HOUGHTON, LEASINGHAM, Moondah Brook, Chateau Reynella, Starvedog Lane, Stonehaven and Yarra Burn. BRL Hardy had already acquired New Zealand's NOBILO (Selaks, Drylands). In 2004 Constellation bought the prestigious Robert MONDAVI Winery and all its entities, including OPUS ONE (a joint venture with the Rothschild family of Ch. MOUTON-ROTHSCHILD) – although it later surrendered Italian premium wines Luce della Vite and ORNELLAIA to FRESCOBALDI. Robert Mondavi Winery is now part of Constellation's Icon Estates division, along with FRANCISCAN Oakville Estate, Estancia, Mount Veeder Winery and SIMI in California. Constellation acquired Canadian drinks giant Vincor in 2006; the deal included Le CLOS JORDANNE, INNISKILLIN, JACKSON-TRIGGS, SUMAC RIDGE in Canada, as well as Kim Crawford in New Zealand, Kumala in South Africa, Toasted Head in California and Hogue Cellars in Washington State. Other US brands include Blackstone and RAVENSWOOD in California. In South Africa, Flagstone, and its joint venture partner Ses'fikile, are also part of Constellation. In December 2007 the company acquired Beam Wine Estates (part of Fortune Brands), with a portfolio that included California's CLOS DU BOIS; six months later it sold on most of the brands it had purchased, retaining Clos du Bois, as well as Wild Horse in PASO ROBLES. One of the UK's top-selling brands, Stowells, is part of Constellation, which also has a 40% stake in Italy's RUFFINO.

FOSTER'S GROUP

The wine division of Foster's, the Australian brewing giant, was founded on the twin pillars of Australia's Wolf BLASS and BERINGER in California. In May 2005 Foster's won control of Southcorp, Australia's biggest wine conglomerate. It currently controls around 60 different brands and producers. In California it owns, among others, Carmenet, CHATEAU ST JEAN, Etude, Meridian, Souverain, St Clement and Stags' Leap Winery. Australian brands include Annie's Lane, Baileys of Glenrowan, Leo Buring, COLDSTREAM HILLS, Devil's Lair, Heemskerk, Jamiesons Run, LINDEMANS, Metala, Mildara, Greg Norman, PENFOLDS, ROSEMOUNT ESTATE, Rothbury Estate, Rouge Homme, St Huberts, Saltram (Mamre Brook), Seaview, SEPPELT, T'Gallant, Tollana, WYNNS, Yarra Ridge and Yellowglen. Foster's also owns MATUA VALLEY and Secret Stone in New Zealand, and Castello di Gabbiano in Tuscany.

FREIXENET

This famous CAVA producer remains a family-owned business, with winery estates and interests around the world. In Spain, the portfolio includes Castellblanch, Segura Viudas, René Barbier, Morlanda and Valdubón. Further afield it includes the Champagne house of Henri Abelé, Bordeaux *négociant* and producer Yvon Mau, Gloria Ferrer in California, Viento Sur in Argentina and Australia's Wingara group (Deakin Estate, KATNOOK ESTATE).

JACKSON FAMILY WINES

With his wife, Barbara Banke, Jess Jackson, founder of California's KENDALL-JACKSON, owns numerous prestigious properties in California and further afield, including: Atalon, Cardinale, Chateau Potelle, Freemark Abbey, La Jota, Lokoya and Robert Pecota in NAPA VALLEY; ARROWOOD, La Crema, HARTFORD FAMILY, MATANZAS CREEK and Murphy-Goode in SONOMA COUNTY; Edmeades on the North Coast; Byron and Cambria in SANTA BARBARA COUNTY. The Jackson Family Wines portfolio also includes Calina (Chile), Yangarra Estate (Australia), Château Lassègue (ST-EMILION) and Arceno (Tuscany).

LVMH

French luxury goods group Louis Vuitton-Moët Hennessy owns Champagne houses MOËT & CHANDON (including Dom Pérignon), KRUG, Mercier, RUINART and VEUVE CLICQUOT, and has established DOMAINE CHANDON sparkling wine companies in California, Australia and Argentina. It also owns Ch. d'YQUEM, CAPE MENTELLE in Australia, CLOUDY BAY in New Zealand, NEWTON in California, and TERRAZAS DE LOS ANDES in Argentina. In 2008 LVMH acquired the prestigious Bodega Numanthia-Termes in TORO, Spain.

PERNOD RICARD

The French spirits giant owns Australia's all-conquering JACOB'S CREEK brand along with Wyndham Estate and the Orlando, Gramp's, Poet's Corner and Richmond Grove labels. Pernod Ricard's empire also encompasses New Zealand's mighty MONTANA (CHURCH ROAD, Corbans, Lindauer, Stoneleigh), Champagne producers G H MUMM and PERRIER-JOUËT, Californian fizz MUMM NAPA, Long Mountain in South Africa and a number of Argentinian producers, including Balbi, Etchart and Graffigna. In Spain Pernod Ricard controls CAMPO VIEJO, Palacio de la Vega, Marqués de Arienzo Siglo and Tarsus, among others, and in Georgia it has a 75% stake in Georgian Wines & Spirits.

INDEX OF PRODUCERS

Numbers in **bold** refer to main entries.

335

OLDER VINTAGE CHARTS *(top wines only)*

FRANCE										
Alsace	98	97	96	95	90	89	88	86	85	82
(vendanges tardives)	9◇	8♦	8♦	9◇	10♦	9◇	8♦	8♦	9◇	10♦
Champagne (vintage)	98	97	96	95	90	89	88	86	85	82
	7◇	6♦	9◇	8♦	9♦	8♦	8♦	7◇	8♦	9♦
Bordeaux	98	97	96	95	94	90	89	88	86	85
Margaux	7♦	6◇	8♦	8♦	6◇	9♦	8♦	7♦	8♦	8♦
St.-Jul., Pauillac, St-Est.	7♦	6◇	9♦	8♦	7◇	9♦	9♦	8♦	9♦	8♦
Graves/Pessac-L. (red)	8♦	6◇	8♦	8♦	6◇	8♦	8♦	8♦	6◇	8♦
St-Émilion, Pomerol	9♦	6◇	7♦	9♦	6◇	9♦	9♦	8♦	7◇	9♦
Bordeaux (cont.)	83	82	81	75	70	66	61	59	55	53
Margaux (cont.)	9◇	8◇	7◇	6◇	8◇	7◇	10◇	8◇	6◇	8◇
St.-Jul. etc. (cont.)	7◇	10♦	7◇	8◇	8◇	8◇	10◇	9◇	8◇	9◇
Graves etc. (R) (cont.)	8◇	9◇	7◇	6◇	8◇	8◇	10◇	9◇	8◇	8◇
St-Émilion etc. (cont.)	7◇	9◇	7◇	8◇	8◇	6◇	10◇	7◇	7◇	8◇
Sauternes	98	97	96	95	90	89	88	86	83	80
	7♦	9♦	9♦	7♦	10♦	9♦	9♦	9♦	9♦	7◇
Sauternes (cont.)	76	75	71	67	62	59	55	53	49	47
	8◇	8◇	8◇	9◇	8◇	9◇	8◇	8◇	10◇	10◇
Burgundy										
Chablis	98	97	96	95	92	90				
	7◇	7◇	8♦	8♦	7◇	9◇				
Côte de Beaune (wh.)	98	97	96	95	93	92	90	89		
	5◇	7◇	6♦	8♦	7◇	8◇	7◇	9◇		
Côte de Nuits (red)	98	97	96	95	93	90	89	88	85	78
	7♦	8♦	9◇	7♦	8♦	9♦	7◇	8◇	9◇	10◇